Theories and Origins of the Modern Police

The History of Policing

Series Editor: Clive Emsley

Titles in the Series:

Theories and Origins of the Modern Police
Clive Emsley

The New Police in the Nineteenth Century
Paul Lawrence

Globalising British Policing
Georgina Sinclair

Police and Policing in the Twentieth Century
Chris A. Williams

Theories and Origins of the Modern Police

Edited by

Clive Emsley
The Open University

ASHGATE

Wherever possible, these reprints are made from a copy of the original printing, but these can themselves be of very variable quality. Whilst the publisher has made every effort to ensure the quality of the reprint, some variability may inevitably remain.

Published by
Ashgate Publishing Limited
Wey Court East
Union Road
Farnham
Surrey GU9 7PT
England

Ashgate Publishing Company
Suite 420
101 Cherry Street
Burlington
VT 05401-4405
USA

www.ashgate.com

British Library Cataloguing in Publication Data
Theories and origins of the modern police. – (The history of policing)
    1. Police–Europe–History.
    I. Series II. Emsley, Clive.
    363.2'094–dc22

Library of Congress Control Number: 2010931199

ISBN 9780754629498

MIX
Paper from responsible sources
FSC
www.fsc.org   FSC® C013056

Printed and bound in Great Britain by
TJ International Ltd, Padstow, Cornwall.

Contents

PART IV POLICING EIGHTEENTH-CENTURY ENGLAND

Acknowledgements

The editor and publishers wish to thank the following for permission to use copyright material.

Cambridge University Press for the essay: John Styles (1983), 'Sir John Fielding and the Problem of Criminal Investigation in Eighteenth-Century England', *Transactions of the Royal Historical Society*, 5th series, **33**, pp. 127–49. Copyright © 1983 The Royal Historical Society.

Emerald Group Publishing for the essay: Cyril D. Robinson (1979), 'Ideology as History: A Look at the Way Some English Police Historians Look at the Police', *Police Studies*, **2**, pp. 35–49.

Clive Emsley (1983), 'The Military and Popular Disorder in England 1790–1801', *Journal of the Society for Army Historical Research*, **61**, pp. 10–21, 96–112. Copyright © 1983 Clive Emsley.

Copyright Clearance Center & George Mason University for the essay: Steven Hughes (1987), 'Fear and Loathing in Bologna and Rome: The Papal Police in Perspective', *Journal of Social History*, **21**, pp. 97–116. Copyright © 1987 Journal of Social History.

John Wiley & Sons, Inc. for the essay: Allan Silver (1967), 'The Demand for Order in Civil Society: A Review of Some Themes in the History of Urban Crime, Police, and Riot', in D.J. Bordua (ed.), *The Police: Six Essays*, New York: Wiley, pp. 1–24.

Northwestern University School of Law for the essay: Charles Reith (1943), 'Preventive Principle of Police', *Journal of Criminal Law and Criminology*, **34**, pp. 206–209. Copyright © 1943 Northwestern University School of Law.

Oxford University Press for the essays: Roland Axtmann (1992), '"Police" and the Formation of the Modern State. Legal and Ideological Assumptions on State Capacity in the Austrian Lands of the Habsburg Empire, 1500–1800', *German History*, **10**, pp. 39–61. Copyright © 1992 German History Society; Mark Neocleous (2000), 'Social Police and the Mechanisms of Prevention: Patrick Colquhoun and the Condition of Poverty', *British Journal of Criminology*, **40**, pp. 710–26. Copyright © 2000 Centre for Crime & Justice Studies (ISTD); David Philips (1989), 'Good Men to Associate and Bad Men to Conspire: Associations for the Prosecution of Felons in England 1760–1860', in Douglas Hay and Francis Snyder (eds), *Prosecution and Punishment in Britain 1750–1850*, Oxford, Clarendon Press, pp. 113–70. Copyright © 1989 David Philips; Randall McGowen (2005), 'The Bank of England and the Policing of Forgery 1797–1821', *Past and Present*, No. 186, pp. 81–116. Copyright © 2005 Past & Present Society.

Princeton University Press for the essay: David H. Bayley (1975), 'The Police and Political Development in Europe', in Charles Tilly (ed.), *The Formation of the National States in Western Europe*, Princeton, NJ: Princeton University Press, pp. 328–79. Copyright © 1975 Charles Tilly.

Sage Publications for the essay: Iain A. Cameron (1977), 'The Police of Eighteenth-Century France', *European Studies Review*, **7**, pp. 47–75.

Taylor & Francis Limited for the essays: Franz-Ludwig Knemeyer (1980), 'Polizei', *Economy and Society*, **9**, pp. 172–96. Copyright © 1980 RKP; Francis M. Dodsworth (2004), '"Civic" Police and the Condition of Liberty: The Rationality of Governance in Eighteenth-Century England', *Social History*, **29**, pp. 199–216. Copyright © 2004 Taylor & Francis Ltd, http:// www.informaworld.com.

University of Chicago Press for the essay: Joan Kent (1981), 'The English Village Constable, 1580–1642: The Nature and Dilemmas of the Office', *Journal of British Studies*, **20**, pp. 26–49.

Vathek Publishing for the essay: A.M.P. (1981), 'The Old-Time Constable as Portrayed by the Dramatists', *Police Journal*, **2**, pp. 656–73.

Series Preface

In modern society it is scarcely possible to read a newspaper, to enter a bookshop, to watch television or to visit a cinema without rapidly finding a story concerning the police. The police, according to the popular image, fight crime, and are there to protect 'us' – ordinary, law abiding folk - from the criminal 'other' – often some international gang or a vicious, sexual predator-cum-serial killer. When pressed, many ordinary observers will probably admit that this is escapism and that the reality is much more mundane. It is left largely to scholars and academics to probe that reality and, by so doing, to provide a coherent analysis of how the police institution developed and functioned and, through a better overall understanding, to encourage policy-makers and practitioners in reforms and reassessments.

Until the last third of the twentieth century the history of police and policing was rarely undertaken by anyone other than former police officers or people closely connected with the police service. Their research could be extensive and detailed, but their narratives were generally congratulatory. The cultural and intellectual climate of the 1960s, however, prompted a generation of young scholars to reassess the origins and development of police institutions. These scholars came from a variety of discipline areas. They looked back at the origins of the word 'police' and traced how a concept of governance became a bureaucratic institution. They challenged the common-sense assumptions that the police were created to fight crime and to preserve law and order and they probed the conceptualisations of 'crime', 'law' and 'order'.

The volumes in this series note the traditional narrative of police history, but really commence with the significant reappraisals published in the late twentieth century and then continue with the reassessments and debates that followed. The volumes are organised in a broadly chronological manner. The first begins with significant analyses of the concept of 'police' and policing structures under the old regime; subsequent volumes move through the development of policing in the nineteenth century, consolidation in the twentieth and the manner in which models have been structured with a view to export into the twenty-first century. The essays and articles in each volume have been selected by a historian with personal expertise in the area and each volume commences with an editor's introduction reviewing the literature, the shifting perspectives of research and debate, and the lacunae. The result is an accessible, organised and authoritative collection of the key articles on the history of police and policing that will prove an invaluable tool for both research and teaching.

CLIVE EMSLEY
Series Editor
The Open University

Introduction

It is difficult to conceive of a society in the past that did not have ways of enforcing its norms whether or not they were written and labelled as law. The institution most commonly associated with enforcing the laws of contemporary society is the police, and most countries now have institutions with some variant of the word 'police' in them. But the use of the word or a variant of the word 'police' to denote such institutions did not emerge until the late eighteenth and early nineteenth centuries. Moreover in spite of the ubiquity of the policing role and the centrality of institutions called 'police' in contemporary societies, it was not until the last quarter of the twentieth century that any serious analysis of the development of such institutions was undertaken by academic historians.

This volume is the first of four providing some of the most significant, English-language essays on the historical development of the police institution. The essays included in this particular volume introduce some of the theoretical outlines proposed for the origins of police institutions and explore the systems of enforcement, and the criticisms of them, that had emerged on the eve of the revolutionary upheavals that convulsed Europe and inflicted a terminal blow to the *ancien régime* at the close of the eighteenth century. The decision to reproduce essays in their original format obviates the opportunity for including translations of some of the key essays in, for example, French and German that would provide a clearer picture of developments on continental Europe; and there is also the issue of space. Nevertheless, care has been taken to ensure that what follows is not entirely Anglo-centric. Similarly the essays that follow should dispel some of the assumptions about continental policing that have long been based on Anglo-Saxon prejudice rather than on any proper awareness and understanding of what went on in continental Europe.

Theorising Police

Once upon a time it all seemed so simple. Until the early 1970s the history of policing remained the preserve of enthusiasts who were often former police officers or who had cordial connections with the police. The result was that while the research was often prolific and the detail extensive, the history tended to be congratulatory. More serious, however, was the way in which the arguments of late eighteenth- and early nineteenth-century reformers were taken at their face value.

The first historians of police, particularly those working on the British experience, never acknowledged any theoretical position. This was not a deliberate attempt at obfuscation. They took it as read that the police were necessary to society; implicitly they bought into Edmund Burke's assumption that the constitutional structure of Britain was organic, that it had been developed through the wisdom of ancestors and that it provided a model for less fortunate people. Essentially their perception of British history was what Herbert Butterfield defined as Whig. The Whig historian, Butterfield argued, 'busies himself with dividing the world into the friends and enemies of progress' (1931, p. 5); reform generally came about because far-sighted reformers had identified problems correctly and set the appropriate changes in motion. Whig history was a form of presentism by which the historian looked back from the contemporary world and saw movement to his or her present largely in terms of progress. Butterfield did not discuss the interpretation of police history in his book but, extrapolating from his arguments, it is apparent that while the police system in the present of the Whig police historian might not have been perfect, it was broadly fit for the purposes required and it was developing in the appropriate fashion. It was essentially the system that the far-sighted reformers had envisaged when they established the police institution; abuses had been few; such abuses as there were, together with other problems, had been and continued to be ironed out by properly selected commanders abiding by the proper rules and regulations.

There was a further, central element to this Whig theory of police development, namely that British society was based on consensus; and in consequence of this, the Whig argument went, the police were rapidly accepted by the majority of the population. The police in Britain were, as Charles Reith (1952, p. 20) the most prolific and in many ways the most influential of Whig police historians put it, 'kin' police as opposed to the police across continental Europe that were imposed on the citizenry from above by the directing powers of the state.[1] The police in Britain, according to the Whigs, were established because of an awareness of rising crime and increasing public disorder. The reasons for the greater incidence of crime and disorder were never precisely explained; the assertions that these problems were becoming worse were never probed. Indeed, the arguments of those advocating improvements in policing were taken at face value and, in consequence, the London magistrates Henry and Sir John Fielding and Patrick Colquhoun, who made changes or who wrote urging changes, and the Home Secretary Robert Peel, who established the Metropolitan Police in 1829, acquired heroic status. Their critics and opponents, in turn, were dismissed as short-sighted and foolish, or worse. For the Whigs the institution of the police was the rational response of public-minded reformers to real problems of crime and public order, problems with which the old system could not cope. The brief essay by Reith that opens this volume (Chapter 1), written in the patriotic fervour of the Second World War, encapsulates much of this but without openly espousing any theoretical perspective.

The Whig interpretation of police history began to be unpicked and to come under fire from the early 1970s. Chapter 2, by Cyril D. Robinson, was one of the earliest, and most sharply focused of such critiques, stressing the way in which a consensual understanding of social relations in England had shaped the thinking of the best known of the historians of the English police up to that period. Subsequently a succession of books and essays, several of which are included in later volumes of this collection, have further undermined the old certainties.

Historians, however, are often eclectic in their use of theory. As a body they are generally less inclined to develop the broad-brush interpretations and theories of development commonly constructed and deployed by other social scientists. Significantly the earliest, wide-ranging

---

[1]   Reith produced another five books on police history: *The Police Idea* (1938); *Police Principles and the Problem of War* (1940); *British Police and the Democratic Ideal* (1943); *A Short History of the Police* (1948); and *A New Study of Police History* (1956). Reith himself was neither a former police officer nor an academic. He studied medicine at Aberdeen, but never graduated, worked as a tea and rubber planter in Ceylon (now Sri Lanka), served as an officer in the Indian Army and then, returning to London, worked again in the tea and rubber business. See Hjellemo (1977).

arguments about the historical development of the police were presented by Allan Silver and David H. Bayley, neither of whom would probably acknowledge history as their principal academic home. Equally significant, these essays appeared not in academic journals, but in sociological essay collections exploring policing practice and the development of the nation-state respectively.

Silver admits that his essay (Chapter 3) was shaped partly in response to the growing concerns that a new 'dangerous class' was emerging in the USA during the 1960s. His aim in the essay was to examine the historical interrelationships between police reform and the burgeoning research into both the culture of riotous protest and the changing demands for order in eighteenth- and early nineteenth-century England. His perception of the new police in England was shaped by his need to rely largely on the work of the Whig historians and their assumptions about the consensual nature of English society. His understanding of the eighteenth-century English crowd, however, drew on the often unashamedly Marxist research of historians such as George Rudé and Eric Hobsbawm, and his work was one of the prompts to the new generation of police historians such as Wilbur Miller and Robert Storch (see Miller, 1999; Storch, 1975, 1976).

David H. Bayley's aim in Chapter 4 was to explore the interrelationship between the political structures of the emerging nation-states in Europe during the eighteenth, nineteenth and early twentieth centuries and their respective police systems. Like Silver his assessment had to depend on the published work available at the time that he was writing, and much of this followed a Whiggish line. What Bayley brings out clearly, however, is the range of police tasks, the variations in police forms and the sheer complexity of police development. Seeking to assign a single cause to the creation and pattern of police systems is a fruitless enterprise, nevertheless a range of common factors can be identified, but with varying degrees of significance, coming into play at different moments and with different chronologies. Perhaps the most challenging conclusion to the essay is the lack of importance that crime and economic, urban and population change appear to have played in police development – a direct challenge to the Whig argument.

Silver makes the point that in the policed society 'the central power exercises potentially violent supervision over the population by bureaucratic means' (p. 30). Bayley agrees: 'A police force is an organization authorized by a collectivity to regulate social relations within itself by utilizing, if need be, physical force' (p. 47). Elsewhere he has emphasised that the police is the only state institution allowed to use force in its daily dealings with the public and that this 'concentration on the application of force' (Bayley, 1985, pp. 12–13) is a defining characteristic of the police institution – again not something that would fit well with the perspective of the Whig historians.

Shifting Meanings of Police

The institutions that, today, are gathered under the title of 'police' are essentially creations of the bureaucratic nineteenth-century state. The old British Whig historiography of police could conveniently point to the foundation of London's Metropolitan Police in 1829 as the 'first' modern police – though some of their Scots equivalents jealously pointed to the creation of the police of Glasgow in 1800, and of Edinburgh a few years later, both a good twenty years before that for London.[2] Yet, as stressed at the beginning of this introduction, it is difficult to conceive of a society that did not seek to enforce its norms in some way or other.

The word 'police' has its origins in the Classical Greek πολιτεία (*politeia*) which referred to all matters relating to the survival and well-being of the *polis*, the city state. *Politia* had a similar meaning in ancient Rome, and the sense of 'police' meaning 'government', particularly in the sense of good government that maintained a sense of order and well-being within the community, continued through into early modern Europe. The broad sense in which 'police' in its various spellings – *Policey, Pollizey, Pullucey* and so on – was understood in the empires, principalities and city states of, particularly, the German-speaking parts of Europe is addressed in detail in Chapters 5 and 6, by Franz-Ludwig Knemeyer and Roland Axtmann respectively. Knemeyer traces the shifts in meaning over a very long timeframe, beginning in the early modern period and continuing through to the aftermath of the Second World War. Axtmann focuses in detail on the early modern period in the German lands. He describes princes using the term 'police' when seeking ways to maximise the resources and potential of their states. Eighteenth-century German professors gave lectures and wrote treatises on what was called *Polizeiwiβenschaft* (which might be translated as 'police science' or simply 'policy science'). And throughout Europe during the Enlightenment intellectuals used the term 'police' when debating the role of the law and the rights of individuals within the state. Police institutions gradually emerged to enforce the various policies that were formulated.

Marc Raeff (1983) explored this ground in an important monograph focusing on the police ordinances passed in the German lands and in Russia during the seventeenth and eighteenth centuries. The ordinances sought to establish the procedures by which a peaceful and orderly existence could be secured for the population. Simultaneously they had the joint aim of increasing the wealth and happiness of the population at the same time as advancing the power and wealth of the state and its rulers. In his book, and in an article that predated it, Raeff (1983, p. 124) drew attention to Nicolas Delamare's *Traité de Police* (1707), the first serious treatise on police in the seventeenth- and eighteenth-century sense. Delamare was an officer of the Châtelet, the busiest royal court in Paris, and while his work came after many of the German ordinances, Delamare's Paris had a police institution far greater than anything then in existence in the German lands.

In France during the seventeenth and eighteenth centuries, the word 'police' became more firmly tied to the regulation of a town or city, rather than of a state in the broader sense. In 1606 Jean Nicot, in his *Thresor de la langue françoise*, defined police as the regulation of 'supplies, clothing, commerce and other things affecting the good of all'. A century later, in *Nouveau Dictionnaire françoise* (1719), Pierre Richelet considered that 'police consists in making various regulations for the well-being of a city, and these diverse regulations ought to concern themselves with supplies, occupations, streets and roads' (quoted in Williams, 1979, p. 12). Delamare himself divided the duties of police into eleven categories: religion; manners and morals; public health; food and the necessaries of life; highways, including the freedom and safety of movement along them; security and the maintenance of the public peace; sciences and the liberal arts; commerce; manufacturing and the mechanical arts; workers, labourers and domestic servants; the poor. These categories were accepted as the responsibility of the police

---

[2]   A useful introduction to the historiography of Scottish policing can be found in Barrie (2008b, ch. 1).

until the Revolution and beyond, notably, for example, in *L'Encyclopédie* of D'Alembert and Diderot (Emsley, 2007, pp. 63–64). The *lieutenant général de police de Paris*, first appointed by Louis XIV in 1667, was given broad authority for supervision in each of these areas.

In theory the other *lieutenants généaux de police* created by royal ordinance for the principal towns of France in 1699 had similar authority. But there were other local jurisdictions in the towns jealous of their powers and determined to resist, or to absorb, the new *lieutenants*. Moreover Louis XIV's motivation in creating the posts appears to have been primarily to raise money for his wars through the sale of the new appointments. The position of *lieutenant de police*, like other appointments under the *ancien régime*, was venal.

'Police' during the Enlightenment was a concept discussed and debated by a range of thinkers concerned with classifying, controlling and regulating populations. There were those who, following the German notion of *Polizei*, were concerned with theorising the preservation and extension of the state upon which depended all public happiness and security. Adam Smith, in contrast, expected a major reduction in crime with the growing independence of individual workers since this ought to relegate the need for 'police' to the margins of society. For Smith, the close regulation of the workforce impeded prosperity and he considered that the cities that possessed the most rigorous police enjoyed the least security. An acquaintance of Smith, Patrick Colquhoun, who was active in trans-Atlantic trade as well as serving as Lord Provost of Glasgow, appears to have bought in to these ideas. But Colquhoun also regarded a new system of police as essential for enabling the wheels of commerce to prosper and, after moving to London where he became one of the first stipendiary magistrates, he became convinced that there were many who preferred idleness and pillaging the great entrepôt of empire to engaging in honest labour. Colquhoun's *Treatise on the Police of the Metropolis*, which was first published in 1796 and which went through seven editions in ten years, situates him at the significant moment of the change in Britain of understanding police as a specific set of tasks and as an institution of supervision and control.[3] Mark Neocleous (Chapter 14) prefers to see him as writing in the broad European context of *Polizei* than as a simple advocate of the police system that was established for the metropolis in 1829 (see also Barrie, 2008a). And long after the beginning of the nineteenth century 'police' was often (and indeed it continues to be) a descriptive term added to another noun – *agent de police* in France, police constable in Britain.

Constables and Watchmen

The word 'constable' appears to have been brought to England by the Normans: the *comes-stabuli* was originally a post in the feudal lord's stable. But before the Norman Conquest of England there had been a structure for maintaining order in small communities based on the system of locally appointed tythingmen. The English constables, as they developed during the Middle Ages, were officers of the parish, chosen in a variety of ways to serve their community, often for one year at a time. They presented before local courts those that transgressed local regulations and those that committed criminal offences; as an early thirteenth-century authority explained it:

---

[3]   Rigakos *et al.* (2009) is a reader containing significant extracts from German and British thinkers (but sadly nothing from a French source) on policing during the long eighteenth century.

It is the duty of the constable to enrol everything in order, for he has record to the things he sees; but he cannot judge, because ... the third element of a judicial proceeding is lacking, namely a judge and jurisdiction. He has record as to matters of fact, not matters of judgement and law. (quoted in Guth, 1994, pp. 5–6)

Similar kinds of local official were to be found across medieval and early modern Europe. It was the same with watchmen. Town watches had been formed in the Middle Ages; initially they depended on local householders patrolling the streets of their neighbourhood after dark and by rotation. Often the watch was only required to patrol during a time of particular concern about food shortages, with the concomitant potential for riot, or a panic over crime. In the eighteenth century towns and cities sometimes had a permanent, paid watch; but sometimes the watch was confined only to the parishes capable of funding such or where a particular problem had been identified; and, in a few instances, watches continued to be formed only on an ad hoc basis to deal with emergencies or momentary panics.

Many of the traditional histories of English policing, or of the maintenance of law and order, began with references to Shakespeare's comic watchmen and constables, Dogberry and Verges in *Much Ado About Nothing* and Elbow in *Measure for Measure* (see, for example, Keeton, 1975, pp. 14–15; Ascoli, 1979, p. 21). The implication here is that Shakespeare was writing a social critique of the system of policing and that this system essentially continued, without reform, from the late sixteenth century to the early nineteenth. When Oliver Cromwell declared that he understood his position as Lord Protector to be like that of 'a good Constable set to keep the peace of the parish' (Emsley, 2009, p. 14) he clearly did not have Shakespeare's comic characters in mind; and the traditional histories were either ignorant of Cromwell's example, or simply ignored it as it did not fit with their account. The great virtue of A.M.P.'s short, little-known essay (Chapter 10) is that it shows that Elizabethan and Stuart dramatists as a group portrayed a much wider range of constables and watchmen than the two or three usually singled out from Shakespeare by the Whig historians. More recent research, typified by Chapter 11 by Joan Kent, has suggested that parish officials, such as the constables, were not all uneducated, incompetent and ineffectual bumblers. During the sixteenth and seventeenth centuries they appear to have been drawn from the local parish elite. They were men of some substance and social standing, and as such were likely to have had the respect of members of their community (see also Kent, 1986; Herrup, 1987). In Chapter 12 Keith Wrightson's discussion of the differing concepts of order over this period, while recognising that some local officials probably did leave much to be desired, reveals the complexities of resolving nuisances and torts in small communities, not least given the ways in which social divisions were evolving. It seems possible that during the eighteenth century the social standing of the parish constable declined. But it is also the case that some constables became increasingly professional and served for longer periods than the traditional year-long appointment. These semi-professionals offered, for a fee, to serve in place of the householder selected and they worked as the local constable for the fees that various tasks generated. Watchmen too became more professional. Work that has been done on London, for example, reveals parishes carefully selecting fit men, often former soldiers, and kitting them out with overcoats (sometimes emblazoned with the parish name and an individual number), lanterns and various forms of weaponry (Reynolds, 1988).[4] Much more research might usefully be conducted into constables and watchmen during the eighteenth century, and particularly those outside London.[5]

Sbirri, Soldiers and Spies

In continental Europe village headmen seem to have played policing roles similar to those in England who acted as constables, but this is a subject that also needs more research. Similarly, it would be useful to know more of what passed for policing in the widest sense in the towns and cities.

Sbirri (or the singular *sbirro*) is a term of abuse used against policemen in contemporary Italy. From the late medieval period *sbirri* were responsible for many policing roles in Italian towns; they also carried out many punishments, regarded as necessary but 'vile' by respectable citizens. The activities of, and the popular attitudes towards the *sbirri* in the papal cities of Bologna and Rome are discussed in Chapter 7 by Steven Hughes. Similar bodies were to be found elsewhere in the Italian states. Goethe described a run-in with a group in Umbria during the mid-1780s; he got off with offering a gratuity which, in turn, led to an invitation to return to Assisi for the Festival of St Francis and the promise of an introduction to a beautiful and respectable woman (Emsley, 1999, p. 149).

The *sbirri* provided an example of dubious practice that may well have been present beyond the Italian peninsula. The Germans provided extensive theorising about the value and significance of *Polizei* to the emerging state. But, as in so much else, for many, probably most, of the princes of Enlightenment Europe the French provided the best example of police institutions to emulate.

By the middle of the eighteenth century the *lieutenant général de police de Paris* commanded around 3,000 men for a city of about half a million.[6] The *lieutenant*'s men fulfilled a variety of roles in keeping with the broad definition of police. About half of them were uniformed watchmen manning police posts and mounting patrols through the streets. Another 450 or so acted as refuse collectors and fire-fighters; but the *lieutenant*'s principal subordinates were the 48 *commissaires de police* who each had responsibility for the supervision of a separate district and the twenty *inspecteurs* who had separate, city-wide responsibilities. The police were sometimes praised and used by Parisians for their benefit, but they were also disliked and feared for their role in maintaining the regime and prying into people's affairs. *Lieutenant général* Antoine de Sartine allegedly boasted that when three people met in the streets of Paris, one of them would be his informant. The number of spies (*mouches* or *mouchards* as they were known) probably never reached more than 340, but the fear of police ubiquity

---

[4]   There are two important studies of policing developments in the square mile of the City of London during the eighteenth century: Beattie (2001) and Harris (2004).

[5]   But see the comments on Essex, particularly, in King (2000, pp. 65–75) and, more generally, in Emsley (2009, pp. 26–29).

[6]   Other than Williams (1979) there is little in English on the police of eighteenth-century Paris. Darnton (1970) provides a valuable introduction to the memoirs of one of the lieutenants, but four-fifths of the essay (an edited section of the memoirs) remains in French. Some excellent work has been done recently by, among others, Vincent Milliot; see, for example, Milliot (2005a, 2005b, 2006).

suited those seeking to maintain the regime, and to suppress criticism and the potential for disorder (Williams, 1979, pp. 104, 111).[7]

The main roads of eighteenth-century France were patrolled by another police institution, the *maréchaussée*. This was a military body, literally the men of the marshals of France, formally established in the sixteenth century to protect the king's subjects from depredations by the king's soldiers. Under Louis XIV it had been given a number of civilian duties; its role and its effectiveness are the subject of Chapter 8 by Iain A. Cameron, which concentrates particularly on two companies, that of the Auvergne in the centre of France, and that of the western province of the Guyenne. The *maréchaussée*, which was expanded, improved and transformed by the Revolution and Napoleon into the *Gendarmerie nationale*, was essentially an instrument of the state. Yet in eighteenth-century France it was dwarfed by a much larger police institution which was not linked directly to the monarchy. Taxation under the *ancien régime* was literally farmed out to wealthy financiers who organised collection for the monarch at a profit. The tax farmers established their own police largely recruited from the same reservoir as *cavaliers* of the *maréchaussée* but its men no longer had the direct link with the army and the state (see Chapter 9 by Earl Robisheaux). On the ground there could be considerable rivalry and hostility between men of the two forces.

Changes in Eighteenth-Century English Policing

Britain/England and France were rivals throughout the eighteenth century.[8] The rivalry was not just economic and military, but also constitutional. While the French monarchy provided a model for most monarchs and princes, the British constitutional structure was a model for many of those intellectuals seeking to set limits on royal power. The English in particular looked back to the constitutional struggles of the seventeenth century as giving them unique freedoms from absolutist monarchs and also from the Catholic Church, which they perceived as the oppressive kin of such monarchs. The freeborn Englishman, in the popular understanding of the term, enjoyed the liberty of not having his politics and his private life investigated by an absolutist's agents, and not being held in check by the threat of an absolutist's standing army. Such beliefs contributed to the ways in which the freeborn Englishman regarded the police institutions of continental Europe, and those of France particularly.

During the early 1750s Sir William Mildmay lived in Paris and, believing that there was much less robbery and violence there than in London, he set out to assess why this might be the case. Publication of his book, *The Police of France*, was held up because of the Seven

---

    [7]   *Mouche* is the French word for fly, and the idea of the spy, permanently on the wall listening and observing, is apposite. But another story has it that the terms *mouche* and *mouchard* originated from a celebrated sixteenth-century spy named Mouchy.

    [8]   There is a problem of nomenclature here. It was common to speak of the British government, though much of the constitutional structure, especially that 'separation of powers' identified by Montesquieu and various other *philosophes*, was essentially that to be found in England. Wales had been united with England finally under the Tudors. Scotland had been united with England by a common monarchy in 1603, and by the Act of Union in 1707; it maintained its own independent legal system. Ireland was ruled by the British monarch, but had its own parliament until the Act of Union of 1801.

Years' War; it eventually appeared in 1763. Mildmay was full of praise for the police of Paris and for the *maréchaussée* that appeared to exist

> in a kind of war, not against a foreign enemy, but against such of the native subjects as disturb the peace and violate the laws of their country; and who, as such, must be deemed common enemies to all society. Happy therefore is it for the honest part of mankind, to find so formidable a force, ready to fight their quarrels, and protect their properties. (1763, pp. 31–32)

The problem was, however, that both the *maréchaussée* and the Parisian watch were 'military establishments, and consequently cannot as such be imitated by our administration, under a free and civil constitution of government' (Mildmay, 1763, p. vi). It is interesting to note how this attitude in many ways prefigures the Reithian-Whig assumption about the later English/British police and their continental neighbours.

Anglophobes mocked London and, more generally, England for the lack of a police system and the lack of a word for 'police' in the English language. But there were other continental visitors, including the leading *philosophe* Baron Montesquieu, who saw relatively effective policing, though they did not go into any details about the practices of magistrates, constables and watchmen or about the detection, pursuit and surveillance of criminal offenders (Emsley, 2007, p. 63). Nor did they pick up on the fact that, in spite of the boasts of the unique qualities of English liberties regarding a standing army, when it came to dealing with significant outbreaks of public disorder, the military was the last line, and often the only line of defence for both local and central government.

Reith maintains, in Chapter 1, that during the eighteenth and early nineteenth centuries the British were 'the most disorderly people in Europe' (p. 3). While the Gordon Riots, which shook the metropolis for a week in the summer of 1780, were extremely serious, and while foreign visitors often noted that the freeborn Englishman showed a marked lack of deference for his social superiors and his king, this might be difficult to prove. Other European cities had serious riots, and few more so than Paris during the 1790s. The problem for English magistrates was how to deal with disorder. Parish constables were thin on the ground; it was possible to swear in special constables, though this could take time, and there was no certainty that untrained special constables would stand against a crowd, especially a crowd that contained their neighbours. In spite of the general dislike of the army, and particularly the deployment of the army on British soil, magistrates invariably felt more comfortable with military backing when faced with a potential riot. Legally, a rioter was a felon and there should have been no problem about the death of a rioter in a military action to suppress a riot, but this was not how many contemporaries saw the situation. The prosecution of a magistrate and soldiers for firing on a crowd in 1768 left a lasting impression and, as Emsley shows in Chapter 18, led to a lengthy discussion involving the Crown law officers a generation later. This essay also describes similar concerns when a police action involving soldiers or naval personnel was directed against smugglers, and exposes how, in the nervous days of the French Revolution, in spite of its own espousal of English freedom, the British government was prepared to build barracks as, to all intents and purposes, police stations.

Magistrates, unlike *lieutenants*, *commissaires* and *inspecteurs*, did not purchase their posts and thus have a financial interest in them. They were recruited from well-to-do gentlemen; a few of them, particularly those who acted in busy urban centres, took fees. In Chapter 13 Francis Dodsworth sets out to situate the intellectual thinking that underpinned governance, including the system of policing, in eighteenth-century England. Civic duty, carried out voluntarily, was the ideal. Some of the individuals entered onto the Commission of the Peace did very little and a few did not even go to the trouble of swearing the *Dedimus* which enabled them to act as a magistrate. Others went to considerable effort and even expense in undertaking their duties and, in instances of crime, in pursuing offenders. John Hewitt, who was both a county magistrate and an alderman of Coventry, provides one notable example of a magistrate who went to great lengths to track down a particular gang of offenders (Morgan and Rushton, 2004, pp. 87–89). In passing John Styles describes the activities of another, Samuel Lister of Little Horton in the West Riding, in his essay on Sir John Fielding (Chapter 16). But it was also possible to find magistrates who, whatever the perceived seriousness of the situation, were not prepared to spend their own money on something that was not personal to them (Emsley, 1981).

The novelist Henry Fielding and his half brother Sir John Fielding were lionised by the Whig historians for the way in which they sought, from the magistrate's office that they worked from in Bow Street, to develop policing in London through the creation of street patrols and the small detective force of constables popularly known as the Bow Street Runners. Bow Street and its police had acquired a formidable reputation by the end of the eighteenth century. A few of its officers succumbed to the corruption that entrepreneurial policing fostered and appear to have fitted up individuals as earlier thief-takers had done for the sake of the rewards paid by the government for highway robbers and burglars. But at Old Bailey trials the fearsome confrontational barrister William Garrow tended to treat the Bow Street detectives with rather more respect than he did other thief-takers (Beattie, 2006, 2007).

The Bow Street Police Office became the model for the new police offices established by act of parliament in 1792. The reputation of the Runners spread and they were hired to detect crime and pursue offenders elsewhere in the country (Cox, 2010). Sir John Fielding aspired to improving the police system across the country; he and his brother had recognised the importance of the spread of information about crimes and offenders, and with his General Preventive Plan of 1772 he sought to establish an effective nation-wide system (see Chapter 16 by Styles). Clearly, as Randall McGowen shows in Chapter 19, it was possible to develop effective links across the country even with the old system of entrepreneurial police. The key point here was that the Bank of England could afford to make it worth the while of those that they employed in the provinces to track down forgers.

As has been noted above, there remain significant gaps in our knowledge about the policing outside the metropolis, though one area has been studied in some detail. Associations for the Prosecution of Felons are the subject of David Philips's lengthy essay (Chapter 15). A subscription to such an association meant that a victim could call upon its funds for the pursuit and prosecution of an offender; and in some instances the associations provided their own police patrols. These groups, as Philips explains, built on the long tradition of voluntary societies in English history. But Philips challenges the idea that they were, necessarily, a manifestation of a general dissatisfaction with the existing criminal justice system and that their development must be considered as similarly motivated to the calls for change made by the Fieldings, Colquhoun and others.

Perhaps, as Mark Neocleous maintains in Chapter 14, even those historians generally critical of the old Whig line have been too keen to make a link between Colquhoun's arguments for a preventive police and the form of preventive policing created for London in 1829. But Ruth

Paley, who in Chapter 17 gives a good outline of the policing structure in London before the creation of the Metropolitan Police, goes so far as to challenge Colquhoun's role as an influential reformer. She notes, for example, that, in preference to Colquhoun, the central government generally relied on the practical abilities of others among the body of stipendiary magistrates established in 1792. Colquhoun was a self-publicist; and probably there were those within the late eighteenth- and early nineteenth-century Home Office whose hearts sank on the arrival of one of Colquhoun's long, detailed letters in tiny spidery handwriting. In his unpicking of the ideology of governance Dodsworth (Chapter 13) shifts the argument in a novel direction. Rather than emphasise fears about rising crime and disorder and the desire to establish a new threshold of order for urban society – both of which have been central to many of the arguments about why the institution of the New Police was created – he points to concerns about those within the system who ignored the civic ideal. The problem he identifies was how contemporaries felt they should deal with 'obnoxious persons' (p. 304) who worked in the system for their own, rather than the public interest. The answer for many reformers was the development of bureaucratic and disciplinary practices that led, ultimately, to the New Police of 1829.

Further Reading, Further Research

There has been an enormous amount of research and publication since the 1970s on the systems and effectiveness of policing during the *ancien régime*. But much (indeed probably most) of the important theoretical work and empirical work on police and policing structures in Enlightenment Europe remains accessible only in French, in German or in other continental languages. Part One of Clive Emsley's *Crime, Police and Penal Policy* (2007) provides an overview of some of this work and compares the different policing structures of different states. George S. Rigakos *et al.*'s *A General Police System* (2009) provides a useful introduction to some of the theorising about police in Germany and England during the eighteenth century.

As far as policing before the police in Britain is concerned, there has been a concentration on the situation in London, both the square mile of the City proper and the wider metropolis. No one interested in the topic can afford to ignore the work of John Beattie (2001), Andrew Harris (2004) and Elaine Reynolds (1998). Stanley Palmer (1998) compares the development of policing in England and Ireland, but for the eighteenth century his attention on the English side of St George's Channel is largely confined to London. David Barrie's work on urban Scotland (2008b) is important, not merely for being the first serious academic study of the subject, but also for the way in which it demonstrates how, north of the border, policing developments appear to have been much less concerned with crime and disorder, and much more with the older, European perceptions of police.

The old-style thief-takers are addressed in Gerald Howson's book on Jonathan Wild (1970) and in Ruth Paley's essay on the McDaniel Gang (1989). But much remains to be done on, for example, the professionalisation of officers in the cities, even in London: indeed, the availability of fully searchable records of the Old Bailey online should facilitate the study of how watchmen and constables perceived of themselves and their job, and how such perceptions changed, from the late seventeenth century to the formation of the Metropolitan Police. Above all there is the need to explore in more detail how policing functioned outside of the principal cities and especially in the smaller towns and in village communities. Peter King touches on this in *Crime, Justice and Discretion in England* (2000) as do Gwenda Morgan and Peter Rushton (1998, 2004), and there have been several magistrate's journals published that provide the occasional insight into constables' activities (see, for example, Paley, 1991; Morgan and Rushton, 2000), but we still await a serious, extended analysis of eighteenth-century parish constables and non-metropolitan watchmen.

There is also the question of the use of the military. Tony Hayter (1978) has provided a valuable account of the deployment of troops against crowds and the kinds of tactics that the military began to develop. But there has been very little work on the use of the army, and the navy for that matter, as an aid to revenue men along the coasts. The free-born Englishman might have been wary of a standing army, and the ruling elite went along with such ideas. But this did not prevent the use of soldiers and sailors in emergencies, with magistrates and other figures in authority fully aware of potential problems and often acting with great reluctance.

It is easy to challenge the Whig view of eighteenth-century society falling into disorder replaced by a policed society based on consensus. It is equally easy to think in terms of a ruling elite prepared to coerce the majority with its forces of order and to seek to structure a workforce compliant to its needs. But as E.P. Thompson pointed out a generation ago in a paragraph that has particular resonance for the study of the development of police and policing:

> The rhetoric and the rules of a society are something a great deal more than a sham. In the same moment they may modify, in profound ways, the behaviour of the powerful, and mystify the powerless. They may disguise the true realities of power, but, at the same time, they may curb that power and check its intrusions. (1975, p. 265)

References

Ascoli, David (1979), *The Queen's Peace: The Origins and Development of the Metropolitan Police, 1829–1979*, London: Hamish Hamilton.

Barrie, David G. (2008a), 'Patrick Colquhoun, the Scottish Enlightenment and Police Reform in Glasgow in the Late Eighteenth Century', *Crime, histoire et sociétés/Crime, history and societies*, **12**, 2, pp. 59–79.

Barrie, David G. (2008b), *Police in the Age of Improvement: Police Development and the Civic Tradition in Scotland, 1775–1865*, Cullompton: Willan.

Bayley, David H. (1985), *Patterns of Policing: A Comparative International Analysis*, New Brunswick, NJ: Rutgers University Press.

Beattie, J.M. (2001), *Policing and Punishment in London 1660–1750: Urban Crime and the Limits of Terror*, Oxford: Oxford University Press.

Beattie, J.M. (2006), 'Early Detection: The Bow Street Runners in Late Eighteenth-Century London', in Clive Emsley and Haia Shpayer-Makov (eds), *Police Detectives in History, 1750–1950*, Aldershot: Ashgate.

Beattie, J.M. (2007), 'Garrow and the Detectives: Lawyers and Policemen at the Old Bailey in the Late Eighteenth Century', *Crime, histoire et sociétés/Crime, history and societies*, **11**, 2, pp. 5–23.

Butterfield, Herbert (1931), *The Whig Interpretation of History*, London: G. Bell & Sons.

Cox, David J. (2010), *'A Certain Share of Low Cunning': A History of the Bow Street Runners, 1792–1839*, Cullompton: Willan.

Darnton, Robert (1970), 'The Memoirs of Lenoir, Lieutenant de Police of Paris, 1774–1785', *English Historical Review*, **85**, pp. 532–59.

Emsley, Clive (1981), 'An Aspect of Pitt's "Terror": Prosecutions for Sedition during the 1790s', *Social History*, **6**, 2, pp. 155–84.

Emsley, Clive (1999), *Gendarmes and the State in Nineteenth-Century Europe*, Oxford: Oxford University Press.

Emsley, Clive (2007), *Crime, Police and Penal Policy: European Experiences 1750–1940*, Oxford: Oxford University Press.

Emsley, Clive (2009), *The Great British Bobby: A History of British Policing from 1829 to the Present*, London: Quercus.

Guth, DeLloyd J. (1994), 'The Traditional Common Law Constable, 1235–1829: From Bracton to the Fieldings to Canada', in R.C. Macleod and David Schneiderman (eds), *Police Powers in Canada: The Evolution and Practice of Authority*, Toronto: University of Toronto Press, pp. 3–23.

Harris, Andrew T. (2004), *Policing the City: Crime and Legal Authority in London, 1780–1840*, Columbus: Ohio State University Press.

Hayter, Tony (1978), *The Army and the Crowd in Mid-Georgian England*, London: Macmillan.

Herrup, Cynthia B. (1987), *The Common Peace: Participation and the Criminal Law in Seventeenth-Century England*, Cambridge: Cambridge University Press.

Hjellemo, E.O. (1977), 'A Tribute to an Unusual Historian of Police: Charles Edward Williams Reith (1886–1957)', *Police College Magazine*, **14**, 2 (1977), pp. 5–8.

Howson, Gerald (1970), *Thief-Taker General: The Rise and Fall of Jonathan Wild*, London: Hutchinson.

Keeton, G.W. (1975), *Keeping the Peace*, Chichester: Rose.

Kent, Joan R. (1986), *The English Village Constable, 1580–1642: A Social and Administrative Study*, Oxford: Clarendon Press.

King, Peter (2000), *Crime, Justice and Discretion in England, 1740–1820*, Oxford: Oxford University Press.

Mildmay, Sir William (1763), *The Police of France: or, an Account of the Laws and Regulations established in that Kingdom for the Preservation of the Peace, and the Preventing of Robberies. To which is added, a particular Description of the Police and Government of the City of Paris*, London.

Miller, Wilbur R. (1999), *Cops and Bobbies: Police Authority in New York and London, 1830–1870* (2nd edn), Columbus: Ohio State University Press; first published 1973.

Milliot, Vincent (2005a), 'Le metier du commissaire: bon juge et "mauvais" policier?', in Claire Dolan (ed.), *Entre justice et justiciables: les auxiliaries de la justice du Moyen Age au XXe siècle*, Quebec: Presses Universitaires de Laval, pp. 121–36.

Milliot, Vincent (2005b), 'Une ville malade de son espace? Paris et le lieutenant général de police Lenoir (1775–1785)', in Yannick Marec (ed.), *Villes en crise? Les politiques municipals face aux pathologies urbaines (fin XVIIIe–fin XXe siècle)*, Paris: Créaphis, pp. 32–41.

Milliot, Vincent (2006), 'Réformer les polices urbaines au siècle des Lumières: le révélateur de la mobilité', *Crime, histoire et sociétés/Crime, history and societies*, **10**, 1, pp. 25–50.

Morgan, Gwenda and Rushton, Peter (1998), *Rogues, Thieves and the Rule of Law: The Problem of Law Enforcement in North-East England, 1718–1800*, London: UCL Press.

Morgan, Gwenda and Rushton, Peter (eds) (2000), *The Justicing Notebook of Edmund Tew, Rector of Bolden*, Woodbridge: The Surtees Society.

Morgan, Gwenda and Rushton, Peter (2004), *Eighteenth-Century Criminal Transportation: The Formation of a Criminal Atlantic*, Basingstoke: Palgrave.

Paley, Ruth (1989), 'Thief-takers in London in the Age of the McDaniel Gang, c. 1745–1754', in Douglas Hay and Francis Snyder (eds), *Policing and Prosecution in Britain 1750–1850*, Oxford: Clarendon Press.

Paley, Ruth (ed.) (1991), *Justice in Eighteenth-Century Hackney: The Justicing Notebook of Henry Norris and the Hackney Petty Sessions*, London: London Record Society.

Palmer, Stanley H. (1988), *Police and Protest in England and Ireland 1750–1850*, Cambridge: Cambridge University Press.

Raeff, Marc (1983), *The Well-Ordered Police State: Social and Institutional Change through the Law in the Germanies and Russia, 1600–1800*, New Haven: Yale University Press.

Raeff, Marc (1975), 'The Well-Ordered Police State and the Development of Modernity in Seventeenth- and Eighteenth-Century Europe: An Attempt at a Comparative Approach', *American Historical Review*, **80**, 5, pp. 1221–43.

Reith, Charles (1938), *The Police Idea*, Oxford: Oxford University Press.

Reith, Charles (1940), *Police Principles and the Problem of War*, Oxford: Oxford University Press.

Reith, Charles (1943), *British Police and the Democratic Ideal*, Oxford: Oxford University Press.

Reith, Charles (1948), *A Short History of the Police*, Oxford: Oxford University Press.

Reith, Charles (1952), *The Blind Eye of History*, London: Faber and Faber.

Reith, Charles (1956), *A New Study of Police History*, London: Oliver and Boyd.

Reynolds, Elaine A. (1998), *Before the Bobbies: The Night Watch and Police Reform in Metropolitan London, 1720–1830*, Basingstoke: Macmillan.

Rigakos, George S., McMullan, John L., Johnson, Joshua and Ozcan, Gulden (eds) (2009), *A General Police System: Political Economy and Security in the Age of Enlightenment*, Ottawa: Red Quill Books.

Storch, Robert D. (1975), 'The Plague of Blue Locusts: Police Reform and Popular Resistance in Northern England 1840–1857', *International Review of Social History*, **20**, pp. 61–90.

Storch, Robert D. (1976), 'The Policeman as Domestic Missionary', *Journal of Social History*, **9**, 4 (Summer), pp. 481–509.

Thompson, E.P. (1975), *Whigs and Hunters: The Origin of the Black Act*, London: Allen Lane.

Williams, Alan (1979), *The Police of Paris, 1718–1789*, Baton Rouge: Louisiana State University Press.

Part I
Theory

[1]

PREVENTIVE PRINCIPLE OF POLICE*

Charles Reith

Britain is accustomed to hearing the phrase "Your police are wonderful!" from overseas visitors, and people usually greet it with a smile.

They are willing to agree that their police deserve praise, but they are so used to them that they do not see anything particularly "wonderful" in the fact that Britain's high standard of public order and public insistence on law observance is maintained by unarmed policemen who are regarded and treated as friends by men, women, and especially, children of all classes; and whose behavior towards the public is consistently kindly and readily good-humored and helpful at all times in solving personal difficulties and facing dangers, whether the peace-time dangers of the streets or the wartime menace of aerial bombardment.

Foreign visitors often conclude that what they find wonderful and astonishing in Britain's system of police can be accounted for by the highly-developed sense of orderliness and love of public order inherent in the character of the people. It is assumed that these traits make the task of the police easy, and insure for them ready and willing obedience which makes it unnecessary for them to carry arms.

History proves that this reasoning is fallacious. It is true that the people of Britain show how innate faith in Law and respect for it, but during the eighteenth and early decades of the nineteenth centuries they were the most disorderly people in Europe.

They never experienced the *gendarmerie* police-system which had maintained a degree of public order in European countries by military repressive methods. Britain's police-system had been that of the conscript parish-constable, working in conjunction with the local Justices of the Peace, but it was effective only as long as the country was an agricultural community.

With the Industrial Revolution of the eighteenth century, and the accumulations of population in towns, the parish-constable and Justice system broke down completely, at first in London, and later in all other industrial centers throughout the country. There was no *gendarmerie* system to take its place, and Britain embarked on a period in which the helplessness of Law and authority and the sufferings which ensued from the absence of public order are outstanding features.

*This article constitutes a portion of the book "British Police and the Democratic Idea" by Charles Reith, which is soon to be published by the Oxford University Press, England.

The appearance of orderliness and love of public order is coincident with the adoption of the system of Preventive Police inaugurated throughout the country during the middle years of the nineteenth century.

In 1750, Henry Fielding, the novelist, a magistrate in London during the last four years of his life, proposed the formation of a body of men who would go into the streets to frustrate and prevent the activities of potential criminals. Successive governments in the latter part of the century tried to develop the idea by creating a Police Force for London, but the plans were defeated by powerful, gangster-elements among the City Merchants who profited by the inability of the authorities to enforce observance of Law.

Patrick Colquhoun, a Scots magistrate in London, developed the police idea in books and pamphlets, and coined the phrases, "The Preventive Principle of Police" and "The New Science of Preventive Police," but he, also was defeated. Not until 1829, when the helplessness of authority and Law had created an intolerable situation, was the idea of a Preventive Police Force made practicable. Peel succeeded that year in putting through Parliament an Act which created the "New Police," a small Force which tried out the preventive principle in a defined area of London.

The new Police found, as soon as they appeared in the streets, that their creation had united against them, in a demand for their immediate disbandment, all parties, classes, and factions in the state. Even the Tories were their enemies, on account of Peel's own unpopularity with his Party. The Whig Government which succeeded the Tories in 1830 disliked the Police because they were a Tory invention.

Through the medium of the Parish Vestries, whom Peel had deprived of their constables, the opponents of the Police succeeded, by skillful propaganda, in stirring up the hostility of the middle and working-classes, largely on the plea that the New Police were modeled on the Secret Police of France, which was palpably untrue. The criminal classes required no stimulus for their animosity. Every man's hand was against the Police, and their sufferings amounted in many instances to martyrdom. They were attacked in the streets, maltreated, and thrown into the Thames.

Some remarkable consequences followed. The Police, under the able leadership of the first Commissioners, Charles Rowan and Richard Mayne, discovered that they were completely unable to fulfill their task unless they could secure public approval of their existence. By the exercise of a skillful combination of courage and firmness, patience, tact, and modesty of manner, they succeeded in less than a decade.

In the process they made the following additional discoveries. To gain the approval of the public it was necessary to offer unstinted personal service and sacrifice, and to treat all people alike, without distinction of wealth or social standing. It was necessary to avoid carefully behavior that could be construed as pandering to any form of sectional public opinion, and to demonstrate perfect impartiality of service, in complete independence of government policy and Party or class politics, and in complete disregard of the nature of the laws which had to be enforced and the justice or injustice of their substance.

When the motives and the ideals of the Police were at last clearly understood, from the evidence of their daily behavior and accomplishments, the public began not only to approve of their existence, but to respect and like them. These feelings found expression in willingly-offered public co-operation and, in increasing volume, public insistence on law observance without the aid of the Police.

The Police had discovered their fundamental dependence on public approval and co-operation, and had learned that these were an infinitely more powerful force for compelling observance of laws than physical compulsion. They used only the minimum degree of physical force which the occasion made necessary.

Co-operation between the Police and the public produced a new and hitherto-unimagined standard of public order, and people quickly realized the personal and communal benefits which could be derived from it. This sense of order is largely the basis of the national unity which, in 1940, enabled the people of Britain to rally round effective leadership and face, alone, the menace of German aggression after the fall of France.

Another important rule which the Police discovered as the result of their successful application of the preventive principle was the need of keeping completely separate Police and judicial functions.

They realized early the need of consistently refraining from even an appearance of usurping judicial functions such as judgment of guilt or ignorance, and punishment of the guilty.

The Commissioners were active and successful in securing improved legislative definition of Police functions in 1839. By this time the little London Force had become famous. Its organization and the principles on which it was based were being rapidly copied and applied in all parts of the country and throughout the Commonwealth; a process which was complete less than thirty years after the first appearance of the "New Police" in the streets of London.

Today military force is never used either in Britain or in the Commonwealth for the purpose of maintaining internal order, except in support of Police functioning in accordance with the preventive and other principles, who are temporarily unable to secure a Police objective by their own efforts.

Britain's preventive and other principles of Police are among her most valuable contributions to civilization. Their evolution is still in its infancy. Their possibilities in the task of the future reconstructon of the world, and the part they can play in making Democracy secure, are great.

Democracy's strength lies in the methods which it provides for insuring that laws have the approval of the people. Its weakness is the difficulty, inherent in the system, of finding means for securing efficient observance of laws without undue and unjust interference with individual liberties.

In all human communities it is essential to provide authority with force for the purpose of securing observance of laws. Britain's system of a preventive Police Force is one answer to the problem. It is a fully-effective alternative to the use of repressive military force, and to Police who depend for their power on their ability to terrorize the people.

[2]

Ideology as History: A Look at the Way Some English Police Historians Look at the Police

Cyril D. Robinson *California State University, Long Beach, U.S.A.*

This article compares four English police historians whose writings are principally concerned with the founding of the centralized English police in 1829. A comparative study of this kind is able to reveal common ideological strains running through their writing which individual examination might overlook. Moreover, their work has contemporary importance because present rationalizations by American and English police of their relationship to the community being policed is substantially similar to that developed by these writers for the relationship of the English police to the English public.[1]

The rationalizations developed by these authors can be reduced to four themes: (1) that the need for police arises out of the division of society into good and bad citizens; (2) that one result of the growth of police power is to protect the weak against the powerful; (3) that the police is dependent for its effectiveness on public support, and (4) that historically the business of policing has been confided to the people themselves.

The four historians to be discussed are W. Melville Lee, Charles Reith, T.A. Critchley and Leon Radzinowicz. Except for Radzinowicz, who specifically limits his history of the English criminal law "from 1750," these authors begin with an inquiry into the police systems of their Anglo-Saxon forbears. Such a point of departure is in sharp contrast to American police historians who normally begin police history at the end of the eighteenth century.[2] This expansive coverage by these English authors encourages a search for historical themes and for system characteristics purportedly unique to the English people.

There has apparently been no prior attempt to analyze the writings of English police historians apart from contemporary book reviews. Works of police historians have received little notice from British historiographers.[3] Perhaps such lack of attention may be partially explained because, until recently, both English and American police historians generally tended not to be professional historians. Police history has been an avocation directly related to the author's occupation. T.A. Critchley was an Assistant Under-Secretary of State in the Home Office, in charge of a police division. Radzinowicz was Director of the Institute of Criminology at Cambridge University. Writing police history seems to have been Lee's method to prepare himself for a hoped for post of chief constable. As a "political journalist" in the 1930s "with a special concern with the international scene," Reith apparently turned to the police as a means of bringing order to what he conceived to be a world of disorder.[4]

Of the authors, only Radinowicz was attached to a university. This is not surprising if we take into consideration the relative lack of academic interest in police history until recently and the further fact that historians were not generally considered a profession nor were they connected with universities until the latter part of the nineteenth century.[5]

In surveying the works of each author I will organize my analysis around the following five questions:

1. Did the author approach his work with some organizing factor or theory of historical interpretation?
2. How does the author treat the four themes I have set forth above?
3. What developments, in his view, led to or inhibited the formation of the New Police of 1829?
4. How did the author conceive of the police

English Police Historians

function?

5. What has been the author's contribution to police history?

In determining whether these authors employ an accepted theory of historical interpretation, I will use classifications suggested by a standard text, the *Harvard Guide to American History:*

(1) interpretations assuming a plurality of separate civilizations and dealing with the reasons for their cyclical rise and decline, such as those of Toynbee and Spengler; (2) interpretations setting forth, in systematic rules, the general principles of continuous social change applicable to all civilizations, such as those of Hegel and Marx; (3) interpretations, such as F.J. Turner's frontier thesis, which emphasize neglected factors in the historical development of a civilization, without claiming that those factors explain its whole development; (4) interpretations which deny the need for interpretation, asserting that objectivity is an attainable ideal, that the facts "speak for themselves," and that history is ultimately "scientific" . . .; (5) interpretations . . . which assert that objectivity is an unattainable ideal and rest on the frank belief that all history is contemporary history; (6) interpretations which concede that perfect objectivity is unattainable but remain hostile to rigid or dogmatic historical theories.[6]

Our first author, William Lauriston Melville Lee (1865-1955), who in 1901 published *A History of Police in England,* "came from an old distinguished family." He attended the Royal Military Academy and reached the rank of captain during his army service. Aspiring to a position of chief constable, he studied police history to prepare himself for a position that he was finally prevented from attaining by a subsequent injury. Lee calls his book "unpretentious," and he makes no claim that his is scholarly work (Lee, xxi).*

"References have been but sparingly given throughout, and in answer to those critics who may possibly object that the array of authorities quoted is too meagre, the author can only plead in extenuation that opportunities for taking full advantage of good reference libraries are often denied to dwellers in camps and barracks" (xxi).

*Citations to the works of the four Englishmen discussed in this article will be cited in brackets to avoid copious footnoting. The full citations of the writings of these authors will be found at the end of the article under References.

Lee would, I think, have denied that he was approaching the police with any theoretical framework or that the police themselves can be so explained. Like the common law, the police institution, he might have said, does not lend itself to systematic analysis for the police represents an empirical adaptation to changing conditions.

"However numerous and outrageous may be the theoretical imperfections of our method for maintaining the peace, its practical superior has yet to be discovered . . .

"English police, however, is not the creation of any theorist nor the product of any speculative school, it is the child of centuries of conflict and experiment (xxx-xxxi).

The third historical approach, that which emphasizes "neglected factors in the historical development of a civilization," would seem therefore to approximate most closely Lee's method.

Lee writes this book because "on the institution of police, we have not a single work, except perhaps the matter-of-fact publication of the late Dr. Colquhoun."

Lee will

"attempt . . . to approach this strangely neglected subject, not indeed by the avenue that a scientist would use, but simply to trace in outline the story of English police, keeping in view the underlying principles that have directed, as well as those political and other considerations that have controlled, its evolution; . . . amongst all our institutions it would be hard to find one so eminently characteristic of our race, both in its origin and in its development, or one so little modified by foreign influences . . ." (xxv-xxvi).

There are a series of themes that run through his book, common enough so that we will find all or most in the work of the other authors. Unifying all of these "themes" is the conception that England is a democracy and that the police, like her other institutions, either is identical with or is representative of her people. But if this is true, how explain the fact that the police pursue, arrest and imprison some of those people? Lee deals with this apparent paradox by citing the first of the four themes I have suggested above:

"[A]ll but a small minority of the king's subjects were . . . good citizens—and personally interested in keeping the king's peace inviolate; and that they might therefore safely be trusted to do everything in their power to preserve it, without any necessity arising for the use of coercion. Had all men been equally trustworthy in this respect no police measures would have been required and none devised; but there existed on the fringe of Anglo-Saxon society, *as will occur with all societies,* a certain number of delinquents perpetually on the look-out for opportunities of preying on their fellows . . . " (9,328. Emphasis added.)[7]

A second theme found in Lee's writing is that law and order is tied to growth of the royal power [the state] and that the general and final effect of the growth of police power is to protect the weak against the powerful. It is the constabulary which is "the primary constitutional force for the protection of individuals in the enjoyment of their legal rights [citing the Report of the Police Commissioners, 1839], designed to stand between the powerful and the weak, to prevent oppression, danger and crime . . ." (xxix-xxx)[8]

A third theme is embodied in the idea that the police in England has deep historical roots, that it is unique to the English people and dependent on them for its support, and without that support, police effectiveness, even its existence, would be in doubt.

Lee expresses this theme as follows:

"Our English police system . . . rests on foundations designed with the full approval of the people, we know not how many hundreds of years before the Norman conquest, and has been slowly moulded by the careful hand of experience, developing as a rule along the line of least resistance, now in advance of the general intelligence of the country, now lagging far behind, but always in the long run adjusting itself to the popular temper, always consistent with local self-government, and even at its worst, always, English" (xxvii, 329).

Consistent with his belief in this democratic nature of the English police, Lee fairly bristles at the notion that the police might be utilized to stop a popular rebellion:

"It has been said that if anything like an adequate police force had been available in 1381, Wat Tyler's movement [lower-class protest against a poll tax to support wars in France and Scotland] might have been arrested . . . Such may, or may not, be true of this particular rising; but happily for English liberty there has never existed in this country any police force at the disposal of the central government, powerful enough to coerce the nation at large. Our national police has always been of the people and for the people, and obviously at no time could long be used to oppress those from whom its strength was derived, provided only that one and the same sentiment pervaded a majority of the oppressed . . .

The constitution of the general police [is] of such a nature that it was powerless to enforce any universally unpopular measure . . ." (Lee, 61-62).

The fourth theme is taken up by Lee from an earlier treatment by John Wade, published the same year, 1829, that the Metropolitan Police was organized. Wade wrote that "in England the business of police is chiefly confided to the people themselves."[9] Lee derives this principle from his "Anglo-Saxon conception of police functions."

"[T]he internal peace of the country was held by them to be of the first importance, and every free man had to bear his part in maintaining it; theoretically all men were policemen, and it was only for the sake of convenience that the headborough . . . answered for those of his neighbours . . . ."[9]

Lee's discussion of the reasons that led to the formation of the New Police are not particularly enlightening. He recounts in a clear, coherent fashion, but without systematic analysis, the development of the decline of the parish-constable system, the inefficiency of the constables, the dishonesty of the magistrates, the fear of a continental system of police, the inability of soldiers to suppress riots, and so forth. At the end of the century, considering the currents let loose by the French Revolution, he finds "the attitude assumed by the Government . . . altogether incomprehensible" in its apparent unconcern for the need of police to better maintain the peace (Lee, 174).

Lee attributes the creation of the New Police to the work and foresight of Sir Robert Peel, observing that perhaps it was fortunate that there was such a long wait "for when the inevitable change was brought about, we got a better article than we should have done if an earlier model had been adopted . . ." 230).

Lee sees the function of the police "as necessary to the welfare of society as are self-imposed moral and physical restraints to the health of the individual" (xxxix).

Police are seen to have a dual function. "[T]he object of police is not only to enforce compliance with the definite law of the land, but also to encourage a general recognition of the unwritten code of manners which makes for social progress and good citizenship" (xxviii-xxiv).

The police are "not servants of any individual, of any particular class or sect, but servants of the whole community—excepting only that part of it which in setting the law at defiance, has thereby become a public enemy"[10] (328)

Perhaps, most revealingly, Lee quotes the following statement from the *Edinburgh Review* to indicate public reaction to the New Police soon after their appearance:

"The arrangements are so good, the security so general, and the complex machinery works so quietly, that the real danger which must always exist where the wealth and luxury of a nation are brought into juxtaposition with its poverty and crime, is too much forgotten: and *the people*[11] begin to think it quite a matter of course, or one of the operations of providence, that they sleep and wake in safety in the midst of hordes of starving plunderers" (Lee, 229. Emphasis added).

The sum of Lee's thoughts present a belief framework with surface coherence but with clear internal contradictions. At the same time that Lee sees the police as the protector of the *good* part of the population, he likewise sees the relationship between crime, disorder and poverty. For example, Lee perceives with acuity the economic base to transportation of prisoners[12] and sees the "prison-houses and convict establishments" as "universities of crime," (215-16) a metaphor which he may or may not have originated, but one that has endured with the conditions that provoked it.

Though Lee was obviously an extremely perceptive observer of economic injustice, he was unable to mold his individual observations into an overall theory to aid in analyzing the events about which he wrote.[13]

Nevertheless, Lee's contribution to police history is important. He has been called "the father of English police history," and his book, "the pioneer classic in the field" (Introduction by P. J. Stead, Lee x-xvi). Charles Reith is said to have found in Lee's book the "great principle which distinguished English policing—responsibility of the local community as opposed to that of the nation-state" (viii-ix). Lee can still be profitably read as a clear, concise history of the relevant economic, legal and administrative events in the development of the English police from the Anglo-Saxon period to the end of the nineteenth century.

Our next writer, Charles Reith, authored six books on police history spanning a period from 1938 to 1956. Reith worked as a tea and rubber planter in Ceylon, served as an officer in the Indian Army during the First World War, published a novel on army life, worked as a foreign correspondent and edited his own monthly publication of foreign news before writing his books on the police.[14]

Reith writes with such dedicated passion of the cause of the police and with such recurring themes throughout all his books that it is relatively easy to categorize his historical approach. He clearly falls into the first category of historical theory which conceives of the police in terms of the cyclical rise and decline of civilizations.

Reith's most comprehensive attempt to set forth a universal "history of human communities" is in his book, *Police Principles and the Problem of War.* Impressed as he was by the on-coming Second World War, he saw the application of "the preventive principles of police [as] solving the problem of recurring war among the nations" (Reith, 1940 viii).

Reith concludes that there are "certain simple and significant facts of community evolution . . . which are the common experience of all communities since the world began . . . It cannot be too strongly emphasized that a framework of rules and force in adjustment is a fundamental necessity of all community existence" (Reith, 1940:1-2). Reith thereafter attempts to show the universality of his theory to various civilizations throughout history,[15] and concludes:

"The part played by war, disease, and other similar calamities, in the disintegration of communities, is in providing circumstances in which force ceases to act in securing or compelling observance of law . . . The real cause of failure and final disintegration are inability or disinclination to repair it" (2-3).

Can we find the same themes in the work of Reith as in that of Lee? Our first theme involved the idea that the need to use force arose because of the supposed division of society into good and bad citizens. In *The Blind Eye of History*, Reith asserts that in the growth of a community

"there comes, always and inevitably, discovery or recognition of the facts that some members of the community will not keep some or all of the rules; that by their behavior in this respect they weaken and endanger the welfare and lives of other members and the existence of the community as a whole; and that to ensure its continuing welfare and survival, means must be found for compelling observance of rules" (14).

Reith also adheres to the second theme, namely that one result of the growth of police power is to protect the weak against the powerful. Reith makes this theme apparent in various forms, particularly in his oft-repeated notion that "the police have replaced the military as the use of armed force against the people . . ." (Reith, 1943:9). He points to "the sufferings endured by the working classes as the consequence of absence of police . . ." (Reith, 1956:203), and that thief-takers were of some benefit to the wealthy who could bargain back for their goods but of no benefit to the poor (Reith, 1956:204).

At numerous places in his books Reith makes the point that the police are dependent for their support and effectiveness on the people. In *A New Study of Police History,* he states:

"The power of our police is almost entirely derived from cooperation given them by the public. If this, for one reason or another is withdrawn, our police are helpless, and must cease to function"[16] (265).

That the police and the people are one Reith finds embodied in the Seventh Principle adopted by the English police soon after their organization in 1829:
"To maintain at all times a relationship with the public that gives reality to the historic tradition that the police are the public and that the public are the police; the police being only members of the public who are paid to give full-time attention to duties which are incumbent on every citizen, in the interests of community welfare and existence" (Reith, 1952:163).

Reith has a rather elaborate analysis of how the Police Bill became law. In the early part of the nineteenth century there was economic dislocation due to the Napoleonic Wars, fighting between troops and "hunger-driven rioters," shock among the "educated" classes from the Peterloo Massacre, the threat of mutiny in the Guards, and increasing crime. From the standpoint of the likely success of the Police Bill in Parliament, Reith balances the foregoing threats against "growth and

hostility to the idea of establishing police: which spread to men of good-will in all classes." Reith does not, however, indicate the relative importance of these forces in the final result. Instead, he concentrates on the parliamentary skills of Peel, appointed Home Secretary in 1822. Between 1823 and 1828 Peel secured the passage of a number of criminal law reforms which "were expected to ease court and other difficulties" for the police. When Peel believed he had control of both Houses of Parliament he appointed a committee which reported back as planned, favorably recommending a Metropolitan police. According to Reith, Peel was able to secure the acquiescence of the opposing Whig Party and their allies, the City of London, by first including the City in the coverage of the Police bill and then by "compromise," dropping the City from the Bill (Reith, 1956:122, 124).

For Reith, civilization, or at least democratic civilization, literally *depends* on the establishment of the police.
". . . I submit that all means of enforcing laws comprise physical, or military, force, moral and police force, used separately or together, and that military force and moral force alone or together always fail to secure sustained observance of laws in a community unless they are provided with police force, as a medium through which they can function" (Reith, 1952:10).

If laws "are not observed, the most perfect laws which the wit of man can devise are useless, and rulers and governments are impotent" (Reith, 1952:13). Reith begins his book, *British Police and the Democratic Ideal,* with the vision of an Englishman patiently waiting in line in order to pay his taxes, picturing "the smooth and orderly collection of Income Tax in Britain" as "one of the wonders of the world." Looking to the cause of this docility, Reith sees it in the omniscient presence of the English policeman.

"It is true that individual resistance to taxation will lead, quickly and inevitably, to the appearance of a policeman, and to the setting in motion, against the individual, of the smooth-functioning and overwhelming machinery by which the most wonderful police institution in the world unobtrusively enforces the observance of order" (Reith, 1943:1).

But at this point in time, it is not only this show of force that makes him submit. It is, rather, that his "awareness of the consequences has become subconscious," and that "the British mind is more alive to the value of individual contribution to public orderliness than that of any other race on earth" (Reith, 1943:1).

"It is an unquestionable historical fact that the appearance of public orderliness in Britain [after its disappearance for centuries], and of individual willingness to co-operate in securing and maintaining it coincides with the successful establishment of the police institution . . . in 1829 . ." (Reith, 1943:3).

He concludes, therefore, that "British Police Principles may be briefly defined as the process of transmuting crude physical force . . . into the force of public insistence on law observance; and of activating this force by inducing, unobtrusively, public recognition and appreciation of the personal and communal benefits of the maintenance of public order" (Reith, 1943:4).

To Reith it follows that the function of the police is to be found in the maintenance of this finely balanced system, of the interplay between the police and the public, in which the policeman is in the role of teacher of nonviolent conduct in the school of public affairs.

This vision of the police system at work is not inconsistent with Reith's sympathy for the working class. It is, after all, they who had suffered by the violence of the earlier period. A violence might then have been occasionally necessary in order to win the political rights that now allow them to participate in democratic government; they now benefit, at least as much as the rest of the public, from a police that prevents violence and permits democratic processes to take place in a non-Wilkesian, peaceful environment, so thought Reith.

In all Reith's books he continually pounds away at the same idea: that the central task of a civilized nation is to find the means of providing "authority with force which will enable it to compel respect for its laws," concluding that the means to attain that end is the police. A reader of any of Reith's six books finds a familiar echo resounding through all of his works and leaves Reith open to the charge that he has written but one extended book. The failure to take his work more seriously can probably be attributed to his over zealous and repetitious advocacy of the police as the literal answer to all worldly problems.

In reviewing Lee's book in 1951 for the *Police Review*, Reith really describes what he

believes to be the important facets of the police institution:

"[Lee's book] describes the prolonged inability of authority to enforce laws; its helplessness and the people's sufferings in face of the consequences; the Police remedy which was suggested; and the fierce opposition which this encountered, causing long delay in its adoption. . . . It is a basic study of police principles and duties of which it can be truly said that, without it, no subsequently published book on the history of the Police could ever have been written" (Lee, x).

Reith's review reveals his own proclivity to excessively broad statements as well as his generosity to another author to whom he genuinely felt a debt of gratitude.

J.J. Tobias, a contemporary police historian, regards Reith as "an invaluable if somewhat naive and uncritical historian of the Metropolitan Police . . . "[17] I believe this statement to be a just evaluation of Reith. Critchley credits Reith as the source of some of his material.[18] My view is that Reith's most significant contribution to police history is the very thing for which he has been criticized, his attempt to set forth a theory of the police. Naive and incomplete as it is, it is important to have this perspective before us.

T.A. Critchley wrote three books about the police between 1967 and 1971. The two that principally concern us are *A History of Police in England and Wales, 900-1966*, and *The Conquest of Violence, Order and Liberty in Britain*, the latter being of special interest as a comparison of the way Reith and Critchley treat the "taming" of violence. Critchley's other book, *The Maul and the Pear Tree*, coauthored with P.D. James, is a study of early nineteenth century London police organization. This task is accomplished by vividly describing the police investigation of a brutal murder of two London families. The obvious incompetence of the magistrates and the police to adequately investigate the crime (a matter heavily covered by the press of the day), provoked agitation in England for police reform.

In writing his *History of Police*, Critchley sees the historical process of police development in a remarkably similar way to that of Lee—if one disregards the professional cynicism of the long-term public servant to accepted police mythology.

"A central purpose of this book is to attempt to trace the way in which this unique and valuable system has been fashioned by the needs and fears of society as they have been expressed from time to time in political currents. No grand design emerges, and there is no evidence of adherence to lofty constitutional principles. The empirical process about to be described gives little support to the common view that policing in England owes much of its excellence to attachment to the ideal of local responsibility for law and order, or to a mystical fusion between the policeman and the ordinary citizen. The system has never been a tidy one or logical one. It was built up with little regard to principle, but much concern, at the center, for the political expediencies of the day, and the need for popular support for the police and a measure of technical competence" (xiv).

Critchley's hostility to "rigid or dogmatic historical theories" seems to place him in the sixth category of historical interpretation.[19] This is not to say that Critchley took an unsophisticated simplistic view of police history. On the contrary, his disclaimer of a "grand design" seems to be in marked and perhaps intended contrast to the expansive approach taken by Reith.

Critchley's more critical method deprives us, however, of our theme of the division of the population into good and bad. Instead, Critchley recognizes that the confrontations he describes are between the "rulers and the ruled" (1971:201). It is this realization that ultimately the police system has a class base that leads him to reject the "mystical fusion between the policeman and the ordinary citizen." Consistent with this consciousness of class dynamics, he observes a certain identity between the unpaid working constable of Tudor times and the vagabond he was called on to ship out of town (1967:12). Nevertheless, Critchley is agreeable to the next theme, that the poor are better off for having the organized police. He notes:

"The desperate and starving mobs that characterized the latter part of the [eighteenth] century, were left to police themselves . . . After twelve hours in factory or mine, they ought, for all the law cared, to serve in rotation as night-watchmen . . .

"Meanwhile, the wealthy paid game-keepers to protect their property, slept with arms near to hand, and the middle-class tradesmen formed voluntary protection societies. The poor simply managed as best as they could until the reform of rural police was at last put in hand" (1967:24-28).

Critchley is all fours with Lee and Reith in agreeing that the English police is dependent on the public for its effectiveness. "The police," says Critchley, "represent the collective interests of the community . . ." The police "sustains our civilization; and, at the same time, promotes the freedom under a rule of law without which civilization is worthless . . . " (1967:xiii, xiv).

"The device which is most characteristically English has been to arm the police with prestige rather than power, thus obliging them to rely on popular support. Associated with this is the principle that every policeman is personally responsible to the courts for any wrongful act. These arrangements . . . are only likely to continue to work smoothly if the laws which the police enforce are themselves acceptable to public opinion" (1967:xiv, 52, 319-320).

While Critchley has pointedly rejected the "mystical fusion between the policeman and the ordinary citizen," he nevertheless substantially accepts the idea that there is a historical relationship between the police and the people. "By involving everyone in the business of keeping the peace it taught English people from early times to accept that everyone had a stake in it" (1971: 28-29, 199).

His description of the causes of the delay in the enactment of the Metropolitan Police Act and the reasons for its enactment are similar to those of Reith. He gives a good deal of credit to the strategy conceived by Peel; and he attributes more credit to the propagation of ideas on "influential public opinion" than does Reith; but with the same incredulity felt by Reith, Critchley sees the bill's passage as "one of the most remarkable facts about the history of police in England that, after three-quarters of a century of wrangling, suspicion, and hostility toward the whole idea of professional police," the Act "was passed without opposition and with scarcely any debate" (1967:50). Critchley suggests, however, that the reason that "the English upper and middle classes successfully resisted the idea of professional police for three-quarters of a century after Fielding had pointed the way . . . was because some feared the loss of liberty and most objected to the expense" (1967:320). He does not suggest, however, what might have occurred in 1829 to remove these concerns.

On the surface, Critchley's notion of the police function is quite different, if not the

41

exact opposite, from that of Reith. While Reith believes that the "orderliness" of the English people is due to the police, Critchley states that the "gentility" of the police issues from the historical roots of the English people. The source of violence in society is the working class. Although Critchley is sympathetic to that class, it is against them that the police must be used. It is, after all "from the working classes from whom [sic] most criminals" come (quoting a Parliamentary Commission Report, Critchley, 1967:73), and while demonstrations may by peaceful, "evil" may work "its way to the fore" (1967:77). After centuries in which the British were "long habituated to violence [they were "constrained"] by a native self discipline which was rooted in antiquity, and which flowered . . . during part of the twentieth century."[20] This period of relative peace was due to a number of factors, of which the police were but one: the demands of the working-class Chartist movement were met; religious differences disappeared as a motive force in English politics and racial prejudice was absent in Britain.

"The forces of law and order were belatedly strengthened with the spread of professional police forces throughout the country; the unique character of our police (as a force of unarmed civilians, in contrast to the soldiers who had in earlier times provoked as much violence as they repressed) enabled a rapport to be established between police and troublemakers that has been of incalculable value . . . [In addition there was] the growth of trade unions and the use of strike action as a means of protest . . . finally, the spread of the franchise, together with growing literacy and the Penny Press, gave increasing numbers of men and women a sense of involvement in their own destinies that earlier generations lacked. Thus the prime causes of public violence in Britain had, by the year 1900, been largely . . . eliminated . . . (Critchley, 1971:25).

By the General Strike of 1926, "both sides in the encounter 'played the game' according to unwritten rules, as though the standards of Arnold's public schoolboys had permeated all classes" (1971:202). "The police," he says, "are used for different purposes from one generation to another."

"In the nineteenth century the main problems were poaching, vagrancy, and petty crime; during the first three decades of the twentieth, public order constituted a major

problem; now the challenge is from crime of all kinds, and road traffic" (1967:320).

Though Critchley does not discuss which segment of society wrote the rules and delineated the problem, he writes with verve and intellectual pique. His writings are full of literary allusions, catches of song and limerick.

One reviewer of his *History* forecasts that it will be "the main historical manual for a long time," and notes that "the sources to which Mr. Critchley has had special access [as Assistant Secretary in the police department of the Home Office and as secretary of the last Royal Commission on the Police] have enabled him to trace with authority the key development of modern times, which is the bringing of the uneven and assorted police forces of the country into the standardized police service of today."[21] But it should be noted that in order to carry out his plan Critchley relegated 800 years of history to a single chapter so as to concentrate on the "next 200 years" which, he writes, "help illuminate or explain the working and problems of the police service of modern times . . ." (1967:xiv).

This is indeed an understandable decision, but in making it, Critchley obscures the crucial development of change in police function from pre- to post-state transition. Once the state has evolved, some would argue, the function of the police undergoes a qualitative change.

Of like importance is Critchley's treatment of violence in *Conquest of Violence*. In both books Critchley writes from a conservative bent, to be expected from an official of the Home Office writing about mob action. Both books involve Critchley's view of the slow elimination of mob violence (and thereby the elimination of government restriction on its policies in fear of potential violent response) through the action over the years of a series of public servants such as Critchley himself. Critchley gains his perspective on violence by examining "the causes of violence . . . and not[ing] how authority . . . responded to its threat" (1971:2).[22]

Given that mob violence has subsided, the question arises, has the working class gained or lost bargaining power as a result of giving up the "right" to shake the duke's carriage on his way to Parliament? What has been the worth of *political* gains where there is limited *economic* ability to assert these gains? These are questions historians may wish to consider when evaluating Critchley's analysis.

Sir Leon Radzinowicz, Wolfson Professor of

Criminology and Director of the Institute of Criminology at Cambridge, is the author of four volumes of *A History of English Criminal Law and its Administration from 1750*, published over a 20-year period from 1948 to 1968. Radzinowicz's series is certainly the most scholarly and detailed work[23] of the four authors considered.

The magnitude of the labor performed is described in the introduction to the first volume:

"For his chosen period from the middle of the eighteenth century down to the present day he tells us that he had to consult some 1,250 Reports of Commissions and Committees of Inquiry, 3,000 Accounts and Papers, 800 Annual Reports and 1,100 volumes of Parliamentary debates,: British as well as foreign authors, criminological, popular and historical literature so as to produce 'a full and comprehensive study of the phenomena of a great social evolution' . . ." (Radzinowicz, I:v).

Although no theory of analysis is explicitly set forth, it seems evident that Radzinowicz, both from his arrangement of material and from his own sparse comments, is heavily influenced by economic considerations. Of particular interest is his overview of his findings:

"From a study of documents—proclamations, advertisements, offers of reward, Home Office correspondence—there emerges a system by which men hoped that the public peace might be preserved and offenders brought to justice, a system which was as ingenious as it was perplexing. It was largely inspired by the creed of *laissez-faire* and to an appreciable extent was worked by private initiative, principles which were so natural to the Englishman's way of life and thought" (Radzinowicz, II:vii).

What Radzinowicz implies is that the system of criminal justice of the period is a reflection of the economic organization of the rest of the society of which it is a part, in this case, a society in the grips of a rising capitalist class struggling with a declining landed aristocracy.

Of the theories of historical interpretation, Radzinowicz seems to rely principally on the second category, "general principles of continuous historical change." It would be inconceivable for a man of Radzinowicz's erudition and European background to be unfamiliar with the writings of Hegel and Marx, the main exponents of this theory, or that he would undertake a work of this scope without a clear conceptual plan for dividing the relevant from the irrelevant.[24]

Radzinowicz seems considerably concerned with the interplay between events and ideas in the manner of Hegel. As Handlin sums up Hegel's conception of history, and social change,

"the discrepancy between ideas and social conditions reacts upon social conditions: and as ideas bring conditions up to their level, new ideas arise, and out of the ideas new conditions—until history reaches its ultimate fulfillment."[25]

Radzinowicz seems to apply this conception to the subject-matter of the criminal law:

"Child of the Common Law, nourished and moulded by Statute, the criminal law of England has always been sensitive to the needs and aspirations of the English people, and it has continuously changed under the impact of the predominant opinion of the day. Yet while it has never been static, its rate of growth has been uneven, and the main features which it presents today were built up from the movement for reform which began in the middle of the eighteenth century. To that development the forces of morality, of philosophical thought and of social consciousness all made their contribution" (I:ix).

It would not be inaccurate, therefore, to characterize the work of Radzinowicz as a social with a heavy component of intellectual history of the criminal justice system for the period covered. Therefore, in the case of Radzinowicz, in setting out themes, we will usually be setting forth his synthesis of the ideas of others rather than conceptions which purport to be his own.

We cannot, therefore, expect a statement from this author as we did from Lee and Reith, that society can be divided into good and evil men. But we do find that in Radzinowicz's description of the political affairs of the time that a belief in such a division actuated public policy. What for Lee and Reith was division of society into good and bad citizens is for the more sophisticated Radzinowicz clearly a class division. Volume III, *Reform of the Police*, begins with the following statement:

"Severe laws were held to be essential for the internal safety of the nation. Often, as in the case of the Riot Act, they were also a much needed weapon in the hand of the Justice of the Peace who alone with the soldier barred the way of the riotous mob: for 'to those two it is entirely owing that they [the mob] have not long since rooted all the other orders out of the commonwealth'. The diligent and impartial execution of these laws was the honourable mission of the English police ... ".[1]

The ruling class understands this threat only too well. A constant threat of violent mob action runs through the work of Reith and Critchley. They teach that to the police belongs the credit for the taming of the mob.

Although one finds in Radzinowicz an occasional comment concerning the law's protection of the weak from the powerful (as in the quotation from the *Quarterly Review* that because of the current wave of thefts, "The small proprietor ... could hardly be called the owner of what he enjoys, but for the strong hand of the law" Radzinowicz, I:30), such statements are rare. Much more common is the expressed fear of the power of the mob, of the burden of the poor on the rich, or the criminality of the poor.

Radzinowicz is concerned to a greater degree with the actual arrangements made by the government to protect certain of its citizenry than in vague concepts concerning the dependence of the police on the public. In the first place, he shows in considerable detail that the pre-1829 police were totally ineffective in controlling crime. Secondly, as we will hereafter discuss in more detail, it was a time when societal organization promoted "private interest," a concept inconsistent with the notion of collective security. Thus, far from the picture of an historic idyllic continuity that our earlier writers have posited between the "people" and the police, Radzinowicz notes that:

"[W]ith the advent of the eighteenth century, this method [collective security] of stimulating local inhabitants to make better provision for the preservation of the peace ceased to be of any practical importance. Hopes were centred instead on the positive system of incentives. . . , of earning a reward . . . , of sharing in a fine" (Radzinowicz, II:167).

In fact, by the early 1800s, there was strong hostility to the proposed establishment of a new police system for the very reason that the police were regarded by some as having already departed "from those principles by which they had ... been guided ... " (Radzinowicz, III:335).

As to the theme that the business of policing had been confided to the people themselves, with the transformation of the constable and watchman from ordinary citizens who took their turns at service to paid substitutes from the lowest class of society, that idea lost all coherence.

Radzinowicz suggests a more complex path to the enactment of the New Police Act than that described by the other authors. There was, during the time from 1750 to the passage of the act, a series of riots, disturbances, a perceived increasing poor population and mounting crime. Yet,

"During this long period ... there was no section of public opinion, no group in Parliament or outside, no leading newspaper or periodical which would advocate a reform in the traditional machinery for keeping the peace" (Radzinowicz, III:374).

Radzinowicz, like our other authors, is able to explain the opposition to the proposal but not its final successful passage. Until 1732 the word "police" was not even a part of the English vocabulary; it was only slowly that the concept entered public consciousness. The inefficiency of the contemporary system became apparent and was accepted; a further step was taken when it was realized that "arrangements for the maintenance of peace, as distinct from laws relating to offences against the peace, were a fit subject for a parliamentary enquiry . . . " (III:2, 63, 64). Over this whole period there were incremental changes, the effect of which was to broaden laws covering powers of arrest, and various offenses of public order and theft. Inhibiting the acceptance of such a law were the vested interests of the City of London, sheriffs, magistrates, and various other groups that either derived benefits from the old system or foresaw problems with the new (Radzinowicz, IV:167).

In addition, there was the belief among a good part of the members of Parliament and almost all reformers that a centralized police would represent a formidable threat to liberty. An important, though not the sole factor in the successful passage of the Metropolitan Police Act, was Peel's commitment to a scheme of reform of the whole criminal justice system, including earlier reforms of the criminal law. By the time, therefore, that the police bill was presented to Parliament it may no longer have seemed threatening but merely the next incremental step (Radzinowicz, I:567-589).

Radzinowicz does not himself discuss his

concept of the police function but he does re-count that of Colquhoun "whose views on crime, poverty and police made so deep an impression on the public around the turn of the [eighteenth] century . . . " (Radzinowicz, IV:36).

To Colquhoun, "the labouring class represented the productive force of the country" but "inevitably" that class carried within it certain "noxious" elements. Thus the police would perform an important societal task in controlling this class.

"It was inevitable that its members should live in some degree of poverty, and that they might even on occasion sink into indigence or pauperism. The 'indigent and noxious classes', however, were hardly distinguishable from the elements 'supported by criminal delinquency'. Indigence 'is one of the greatest calamities which can afflict civil society, since . . . it generates every thing that is noxious, criminal and vicious in the body politic." (Radzinowicz, III:233).

Colquhoun believed that "it is a state of *indigence*, fostered by idleness, which produces a disposition to moral and criminal offenses, and they are so linked together that it will be found impracticable to ameliorate the condition of the poor without taking more effectual measures at the same time for the prevention of criminal offences" (Emphasis in original Radzinowicz, III:233).

Colquhoun would have the police "promote the moral improvement of the labouring classes by the exercise of supervision and restraint. It would remove temptations and strengthen the moral fiber as well as the social sense of those lower orders which at present filled the ranks of the army of crime, vagrancy, dissipation and insubordination" (Radzinowicz, III:234-235).

Radzinowicz's materials argue for a more straight-forward economic analysis to better explain the conflict over the establishment of the police, the form it took and its function.

Summary and Conclusions

This article began with the statement that the relationship of the police to the community, as developed by the four English police historians discussed, could be reduced to four themes. The themes were united, it was said, by the conception that England is a democracy and that the police, being one of her institutions, is a democratic institution, either identical with or representative of her people. It was found

that these themes ran through the work of the four English police historians in amazingly similar concepts and language, leading to the conclusion that, in varying degree, we are here dealing not merely with history but with ideology serving as history.

Each of these historians accepts a consensual conception of government. For them, as Critchley put it, the English people, as a whole, have a "sense of involvement in their own destinies." The alleged "fusion" of the police and the community is part of this historical "sense." Such a view sees the police as having a historical role in the absorption of the former threatening "mob" into the political process.

It is apparent that these writers have relied heavily on the thinking of John Locke. The themes of the division of society into good and evil men, and the supposed function of the police to protect the innocent from powerful evil-doers are found in Locke's assertion that some men engage in a "state of war" against other men in an otherwise idyllic state of nature. That act of war gives a right, on the part of the man attacked, "to destroy a man who makes war upon him."[26]

Locke further argues that such a right by the injured party to use individual force may be necessary while a society is in the state of nature. But once man enters into the social contract there is a "common superior on earth to appeal to for relief." Then, says Locke, "the state of war ceases . . . because then there lies open the remedy of appeal for the past injury and to prevent future harm." A major reason "of men's putting themselves into society and quitting the state of nature" is that in society, "there is an authority, a power on earth from which relief can be had by appeal . . . "[27]

From Locke too comes the notion that the police are the public and the public are the police. Locke suggests that "every man has a power to punish the crime to prevent its being committed again, by the right he has of preserving all mankind and doing all reasonable things he can in order to that end . . . ."[28]

Even more important is his underlying philosophy of the social contract between free, independent persons to form their own government. Our historians, therefore, like Locke himself, were largely relying on a mythical state of nature out of which issued the "authority to decide between contenders"— the notion of a neutral nation-state dear to the heart of consensualists.[29] The concept of the "neutral" state is itself confused and contradictory for it is this very state, through its police, that supports one part of society against the other—the "good" against the "evil." All of our authors accept this implicit challenge to the consensus theory and apparently resolve it, in the manner of Locke, by placing evil people outside society itself.[30] Thus, the *public* identified with the police, has been purified of its evil segment. It is only in this segmental sense that the people are the police and the police the people.

Yet, each of the writers, being themselves perceptive of the social relations about which they write, cite numerous instances in which this societal division cannot be so easily disposed of, and in which the police cannot so easily be utilized as enforcer of good laws against bad men. In a particularly trenchant comment on the historical role of the police officer, Critchley states:

"The dissolution of the monasteries created a huge army of vagrants whose only alternative to starvation was plunder, and under the barbaric laws of the Tudors the parish constable was the principal agent in maiming, burning with hot irons and other refinements of torture, before whipping the vagabond, until his or her body be bloody, out of the village or town. It is surely fair to suppose that many men refused to have anything to do with such practices (1967:12).

Our authors (Lee, Reith, Critchley and Radzinowicz, quoting Colquhoun), while purportedly discussing good and evil persons, or "authority" and the "mob," were describing class and class conflict under a mystique that divided the population into those who keep and those who wilfully refuse to keep the rules. Even though each of these authors devoted a substantial part of their histories to working-class "mob" action directed against the ruling landed aristocracy and rising bourgeoisie, class was never seen as a relevant "historical question."

As a possible explanation of "patterns in men's relationships, their ideas and their institutions,"[31] class was ignored. Without such an understanding of the ongoing class struggle between the back-sliding land-owning class and the emerging bourgeoisie in the period just before the creation of the centralized police, Lee, Reith and Critchley could be only incredulous (as they were) at the prospect of "authority" refusing to adopt the remedy that seemed to them to be most obvious and efficient—the organized police.

But to the competing classes, replacing an "inefficient" system with an "efficient" police weapon, did not appear to be such an obvious benefit to either class until it was clear at which class this weapon might ultimately be pointed. Neither class could know that the class in power at any moment might not use the weapon against the other. Only when it became clear to leaders of both classes that the police represented a threat to neither but on the contrary could be a means of controlling the threat to both—the working class—could the centralized police become a reality.[32]

In a quotation cited earlier in this article, Critchley describes in detail how a combination of "the forces of law and order" together with a number of liberalizing political concessions by "authority" resulted in working-class "troublemakers" adhering to rules—rules, of course, made by and for the ruling class. This role of the police as teacher-carrier of good behavior from the upper class to the working population has been observed by Reith, Critchley, Colquhoun, as well as contemporary authors, Banton and Silver.[33]

These critical comments do not in any way reduce the extremely important contribution all of these authors have made to police history. It would have been extraordinary, particularly at the time at which they wrote, if they had approached their subject differently. But now it is time to ask, what should be the criteria for a proper *social* history of the police?

Rusche and Kirchheimer, in their history of the penal system, suggest one comprehensive historical approach: "It is thus necessary to investigate the origin and fate of penal systems, the use or avoidance of specific punishments, and the intensity of penal practices as they are determined by social forces, above all by economic and then fiscal forces."[34]

Marxian analysis, which Rusche and Kirchheimer employ, concerns itself with productive forces as they historically affect the configuration of most significant societal institutions.[35] With this perspective in view appropriate questions to be pursued by a social history of the police that do not seem to have been adequately examined by previous writers, English or American, include:

1. What is the origin of the police function? At what point in evolutionary development did the police function begin to appear and in what form?

2. To what extent is the development of the

police function related to changes in the nature of the community, and to resulting changes in social relations?

3. How is the incidence of the police function related to the development of a state society as compared to a stateless society, or to a class society as compared to a classless society.[36]

4. What is the historical development of the ideology necessary to support a police function? What was the process by which an élite was able to obtain and maintain police loyalty?[37]

5. How is the origin and development of the police function related to the mode of production of any particular epoch of history?

6. How do the police fit within the total system of social control?

A comment by Radzinowicz makes a fitting introduction to such an historical effort. In summing up the result of 32 years of English police history, he stated:

"By 1861 the country was covered by a network of professional police charged with the prevention of crime, the detection of offenders and the maintenance of order. Systematic enforcement of the law had replaced suspended terror as the accepted basis of control . . . Tradition, inertia, local jealousies, class distrust, fear of expense and fear of tyranny all contributed to evasions and delays. Yet the poor might engulf the country in a tide of disorder and crime, so the search continued for more acceptable expedients. Charity and relief could be used not merely to placate but to coerce the poor . . . . Of all such expedients the most far-reaching was transportation . . . . What does emerge is that its existence made it easier to relinquish reliance on the death penalty and its withdrawal clinched the argument for a general system of police.

"The nation had to live with its criminals, in or out of confinement. It could no longer eliminate them. It had arranged to police them" (Radzinowicz, IV:v).

Footnotes

1. Typical sentiments found in most American police-community relations texts may be summarized as follows: The police are agents of the people they police; the laws that the police enforce are those of a democratic society in which the people being policed participate and consent; the police do not favor one segment of society over another; all are treated fairly and equally. See L.A. Radelet, *The Police and the Community* (Beverly Hills: Glencoe Press, 1973) pp. vii-viii; *National Advisory Commission on Criminal Justice and Goals* (Washington: GPO, 1973), p. 9; D.W. McCroy, *The Police and Their Public* (Metuchen: N.J.: The Scarecrow Press, 1976), p. 29; R.M. Momboisse, *Community Relations and Riot Prevention*

(Springfield, Ill.: Charles C. Thomas, 1967), p. 4; M. Symonds, "Policeman and Psychodynamic Understanding" in A. Niederhoffer and A.S. Blumberg (eds.), *The Ambivalent Force: Perspectives on the Police* (Hinsdale, Ill.: Dryden Press, 1976), pp. 72-73; W.J. Bopp, *Police Rebellion: A Quest for Blue Power* (Springfield, Ill.: Charles C. Thomas, 1971), p. 47.

2. J. F. Richardson, *Urban Police in the United States* (New York: Kennikat Press, 1974) briefly mentions a few events of the late 17th century for the purpose of showing the "English background of the American police." The doctoral dissertation of S.D. Bacon, *The Early Development of American Municipal Police* (Ann Arbor: University Microfilms, 1966 reprint of 1939 dissertation), traces American policing from the 17th century in five American cities.

3. Police historians go unmentioned in H.J. Ausubel et al., *Some Modern Historians of Britain: Essays in Honor of R.L. Schuyler* (New York: Dryden Press, 1951). In R.W. Prouty, "England and Wales, 1820-1870 Recent Historiography: Selective Bibliography," in E.C. Furber (ed.), *Changing Views on British History, Essays on Historical Writing since 1939* (Cambridge: Harvard University Press, 1966). L. Radzinowicz are mentioned. Among Reith's six books, only *British Police and the Democratic Ideal* is noted.

4. P.J. Stead, Introduction to C. Reith, *The Blind Eye of History* (1975 reprint of 1952 ed.), p. vi.

5. In England, it was 1871 before the Oxford "School of Modern History" permitted undergraduates "to study history, and history alone, for the first time, and Cambridge followed suit" in 1873. The *English Historical Review*, founded in 1886, was the first British periodical devoted to scholarly historical studies. J.R. Hale (ed.), *The Evolution of British Historiography from Bacon to Namier* (Cleveland: World Publishing Co., 1964), p. 56. The same is true for the United States, the study of history until the last decades of the 19th century being "the avocation of gentlemanly scholars and literateurs . . ." Handlin et al., *Harvard Guide to American History* (Cambridge: Harvard University Press, 1955), p. 5.

6. *Id.* at 15-16.

7. It is clear that Lee is much influenced in his argument by the thinking of John Locke. At an early point in his discussion of the origin of the police he says: "When a people emerges from the savage state its first care is the institution of some form of civil government." W.M. Lee, *A History of Police in England* (Montclair, N.J.: Patterson Smith, 1971 repr. of 1901 ed.), p. xx-vii. This point is elaborated hereafter.

8. Lee was not so naive as to think that there was no oppression of weak by the powerful, nor that the police always acted as a benefactor to the weak. But he believed that the overall effect was for the state to protect the weak against the strong. See page 22, where oppression of the poor is attributed to a weak king; and page 149, for his comments on police brutality; the extent of crime at the beginning of the nineteenth century and the relationship of the police thereto is treated at pp. 196-216.

9. The full quotation reads:
   "In despotic countries people are accustomed to the exertions of authority in its most repulsive forms, and the police may be armed with all the powers required to the prompt and efficient discharge of its duties; but in countries aspiring to free institutions, where the persons, property, habitations, and even amusements of the people are guarded by so many barriers, which no one with impunity can violate without legal and adequate occasion, a much more scrupulous and circuitous process is required. Consequently, in England the business of police is chiefly confided to the people themselves . . ."
   J. Wade, *A Treatise on the Police and Crimes of the Metropolis* (Montclair, N.J.: Patterson Smith, 1972 reprint of 1829 ed.) pp. 2-3.

10. Note that this quote updates Lee's earlier statement about those who exist on the "fringe of Anglo-Saxon society."

11. The words, "people," or "society," in these quotations, can be translated to mean the middle and upper classes. Such usage is, of course, not limited to these authors but is pervasive in political science, sociological and criminal justice literature.

12. Lee notes that high prisoner mortality on ships used for transportation continued until payment to the shipowner was

based on each man landed alive rather than on each man embarked (209-210).

13. Lee also observes that the "large majority" of parish constables were from the "poorer classes," were unpaid for their services, were "struggling men, who have to work hard to provide for themselves, and for their families" and therefore, he comments, it is not surprising that they are "incompetent," and the duties performed in a "purely perfunctory manner" (181). But he carries this observation no further. See C. Robinson, "The Deradicalization of the Policeman: A Historical Analysis," *Crime and Delinquency*, 1978, Volume 24 (Number 2), pp 129-151.

14. Almost nothing has been published on the life of Reith. Therefore, it will be useful to provide a biographical footnote. This information was contained in a letter to the author, dated April 6, 1976, frm Patricia Plank, Librarian of New Scotland Yard. The matter was researched by J.B. Rapkin, a former Metropolitan Police Officer. An edited version of the letter follows:

"Charles Edward Williams REITH was born on November 22, 1886 in Aberdeen. His father, a doctor, sent him to schools in Stonehaven and Bridge of Allan, Scotland.

"When he left school, Reith became a tea and rubber planter in Ceylon. With the outbreak of war in 1914 he was commissioned in the Indian Army, served with the 3rd Brahmins and later became a General's A.D.C. in Mesopotamia and Palestine. After the war he went to London and worked in the rubber trades. In 1924 he married Marguerite Hannah Ellen Gordon. In 1925 his first book, a novel, was published entitled 'An Ensign of the 19th Foot'. Three years later he went to Italy but returned to London in 1933 and for a time edited his own monthly magazine. He also wrote for 'Time and Tide' magazine. It was about this time that he developed his keen interest in police matters.

"On the outbreak of the second world war in 1939 Charles Reith went to live in Cornwall, but returned to London after two years. He was asked to lecture Polish Officers in the United Kingdom on the British constitution and way of life and this he did throughout the remainder of the war. The Polish authorities in London awarded him The Cross of Merit. He also lectured on police principles to various law societies and at Cambridge and Durham Universities.

"In 1945 Charles Reith returned to Scotland, firstly to Stonehaven, Kincardineshire, and then, in 1950 to Edinburgh. On several occasions he lectured to students at the Scottish Police College, Tulliallan Castle, Kincardine, Alloa, Clackmannanshire. When he died on February 7, 1957, he left instructions that his books which he had used for his studies of police subjects should be given to the College. They are now recorded at Tulliallan Castle as the 'Charles Reith Bequest.'"

15. One may find many other such notions in Reith. See, for instance, *The Police Idea*, where he states:

"The fundamental problem which confronts the nations of the world today . . . is the finding of means of providing authority with force which will enable it to compel respect for its laws and without which, as all history shows, it must inevitably and repeatedly fail to function" (vi).

16. Like statements will be found in Reith's *British Police and the Democratic Ideal* at pp. 5 and 10.

17. J.J. Tobias, "Police and Public in the United Kingdom," *Journal of Contemporary History* 1972, volume 7, 201-219.

18. In a footnote to a chapter entitled, "New Police of London, 1750-1830," in his book, *A History of Police in England and Wales*, Critchley cites Reith's *British Police and the Democratic Ideal* and *A New Study of Police History*, stating: "Mr. Reith has made valuable accounts of Home Office papers in the Public Record office and the commissioner's papers in the library of New Scotland Yard" (1967:326).

19. Although Critchley states that he has "tried to include everything . . . germane to the development of a theory about the nature and purpose of policing," he actually develops a series of observations about the "origins of the police system," the "emergence of the office of Constable," the "legal obscurity of the Constable's office," and the like. His method then is one of frequent looking back and summing up. While his insights are valuable they do not add up to a "theory." The importance

that he gives to the use of ideas ar̨uably would place him in category two with Radzinowicz, whom he frequently quotes. This approach accentuates the interplay between ideas of the time and other social forces. The role of ideas as advocated by certain social reformers is given a particularly important role by Critchley in the enactment of the Metropolitan Police Act. See pp. 45-50.

20. Critchley admits that such an explanation "begs more questions than it answers" (1971:25).

21. *Times Literary Supplement*, Volume 617, Sept. 28, 1967, p. 921.

22. Compare this rather simple view of violence with R.P. Wolff, "Violence and the Law," in R.P. Wolff *The Rule of Law* (New York: Simon and Schuster ed. 1971), and G. Rudé, *Paris and London In The Eighteenth Century: Studies in Popular Protest* (New York: Viking Press, 1973) and G. Rudé, *Wilkes and Liberty: A Social Study of 1763 to 1774* (London, Oxford University Press, 1962).

23. Volume I, *The Movement for Reform*, undertakes to display the gradual

"growth of public opinion which has led to the reforms brought about by modern criminal legislation . . . [H]e has been able to exhibit in the most vivid form the process of law in the making" (v).

Volume II, *The Clash Between Private Initiative and Public Interest in the Enforcement of the Law*, concerns "the enforcement of the criminal law, as distinct from the reform of its substance, during the eighteenth and early nineteenth centuries" (vii).

In Vol. III, *Cross-Currents in the Movement for the Reform of the Police*,

"the movement for reform is traced through the labyrinth of trial and error, advances and regressions, theoretical anticipations, curious alternative strategems, and alarms which created a momentary readiness for change, only to give way suddenly to apathy and even hostility" (vii).

Volume IV, *Grappling for Control*,

"follows through to their culminating points two protracted campaigns, on one side for the reform of the capital laws, on the other for the establishment of regular police" (v).

24. Radzinowicz describes his approach as

singling out . . . certain main sub-periods, and the examination of all the criminal problems as they appear in that subperiod . . . . It is far from being an accident that in a certain given period of its development society is confronted with certain specific problems and that it solves them in a certain way or disregards them altogether." L. Radzinowicz, "Some Sources of Modern English Criminal Legislation," *Cambridge Law Journal* 1943, volume 8 pp. 180-194.

Radzinowicz sees the contours of criminal law then within the larger "economic, social and political structure of English political society."

25. O. Handlin et al., *Harvard Guide to American History* (Cambridge: Harvard University Press, 1955) p. 5.

26. ". . . it being reasonable and just I should have a right to destroy that which threatens me with destruction; for, by the fundamental law of nature, man being to be preserved, as much as possible when all cannot be preserved, the safety of the innocent is to be preferred; and one may destroy a man who makes war upon him . . . because such men are not under the ties of the common law of reason, have no other rule but that of force and violence, and so may be treated as beasts of prey, those dangerous and noxious creatures that will be sure to destroy him whenever he falls into their power." J. Locke, *The Second Treatise of Government* (Indianapolis: Bobbs-Merrill Co., 1952), p. 11.

27. *Id.* at pp. 13-14.

28. *Id.* at p. 8.

29. To the extent that this idea is attributable to Locke, it is a misinterpretation of Locke's meaning. While all other rights present in the state of nature are retained, it is precisely this right to enforce the law of nature that is lost by transition to a state form of social organization. *Id.* at p. xv.

30. *Id.* at pp. 6-7; *Cf.* T.H. Marshall, *Class, Citizenship, and Social Development* (New York: Doubleday and Co., 1964) pp. 80-81.

31. E.P. Thompson, *The Making of the English Working Class* (New York: Pantheon, 1964) p. 11.

32. *Id.* at pp. 81-82.
33. P. Colquhoun, *A Treatise on the Police of the Metropolis* (Montclair, N.J.: Patterson Smith, 1969 reprint of 1806 ed.); M. Banton, *The Policeman in the Community* (New York: Basic Books, 1964); A. Silver, "The Demand for Order in Civil Society: A Review of Some Themes in the History of Urban Crime, Police and Riot," in David J. Bordua (ed.), *The Police: Six Sociological Essays* (New York: John Wiley & Sons, 1967).
34. G. Rusche and O. Kirchheimer, *Punishment and Social Structure* (New York: Columbia University Press, 1968 reprint of 1939 ed.).
35. M. Bober, *Karl Marx's Interpretation of History, A Study of the Central Thesis of the Marx-Engels Doctrine of Social Evolution* (New York: W.W. Norton, 1965) pp. 3-4; R. Tucker, *The Marxian Revolutionary Idea* (New York: W.W. Norton, 1969) pp. 61-62.
36. M. Fried, *The Evolution of Political Society* (New York: Random House, 1967). Each writer, with the exception of Radzinowicz, who begins his history in 1750, finds the "origin" of the police system in what Reith calls the "kin" police. But it is clear that at the time of which they write, about 900 A.D., there is already a clear-cut feudal class system, and that the vestigal kin structure is being utilized by a "higher authority" in the maintenance of order. C. Jeffery, "The Development of Crime in Early English Society," *Journal of Criminal Law and Criminology* 1957, volume 47, p. 666.
37. C. Robinson, "The Deradicalization of the Policeman: A Historical Analysis," *Crime and Delinquency* 1978, volume 24 (number 2), pp. 129-151.

References

Critchley, T.A. and P.D. James, *The Maul and the Pear Tree, the Ratcliffe Highway Murders, 1811* (London: Constable, 1971). *The Conquest of Violence, Order and Liberty in Britain.* (New York: Schocken Books, 1970).
Critchley, T.A., *A History of Police in England and Wales, 900-1966* (London: Constable, 1967).
Lee, W. Melville, *A History of Police in England* (Montclair, N.J.: Patterson Smith, 1971. Introduction by P.J. Stead.)
Radzinowicz, Leon, *A History of English Criminal Law and its Administration from 1750.* Vol. I, *The Movement for Reform* (1948); Vol. II, *The Clash Between Private Initiative and Public Interest in the Enforcement of the Law* (1956); Vol. III, *Cross-Currents in the Movement for the Reform of the Police* (1956); Vol. IV, *Grappling For Control.* (London: Stevens & Sons, 1968).
Reith, Charles, *The Police Idea, Its History and Evolution in England in the Eighteenth Century and After* (London: Oxford University Press, 1938). *Police Principles and the Problem of War* (London: Oxford University Press, 1940). *British Police and the Democratic Ideal* (London: Oxford University Press, 1943). *A Short History of the British Police* (London: Oxford University Press, 1948). *The Blind Eye of History* (Montclair, N.J.: Patterson Smith, 1975 reprint of 1952 ed. Introduction by P.J. Stead 1952). *A New Study of Police History* (Oliver and Boyd, London 1956).

[3]

The Demand for Order in Civil Society: A Review of Some Themes in the History of Urban Crime, Police, and Riot*

Allan Silver

CRIMINALS AND THE "DANGEROUS CLASSES"

Crime and violence in the life of city dwellers have long evoked complaints which have a quite contemporary tone. Peaceful and propertied people in eighteenth-century London, for example, confronted a level of daily danger to which they and their spokesmen reacted indignantly. It was in such terms that Daniel Defoe dedicated a pamphlet on crime to the Lord Mayor of London:

> The Whole City, My Lord, is alarm'd and uneasy; Wickedness has got such a Head, and the Robbers and Insolence of the Night are such, that the Citizens are no longer secure within their own Walls, or safe even in passing their Streets, but are robbed, insulted and abused, even at their own Doors. . . . The Citizens . . . are oppressed by Rapin and Violence; Hell seems to have let loose Troops of human D——ls upon them; and such Mischiefs are done within the Bounds of your Government as never were practised here before (at least not to such a degree) and which, if suffered to go on, will call for Armies, not Magistrates, to suppress.[1]

* I want to thank Daniel Bell, Burton Fisher, Robert Fogelson, Morris Janowitz, and Jack Ladinsky for their comments on an earlier version. I am indebted to the Russell Sage Foundation's Program in Law and Sociology at the University of Wisconsin for the leisure and stimulus to consider, among other matters, the issues discussed in this paper.
[1] *An Effectual Scheme for the Immediate Prevention of Street Robberies and Suppressing of all other Disorders of the Night; with a Brief History of the Night-houses and an Appendix Relating to those Sons of Hell call'd Incendiaries* (London, 1730).

In the body of his pamphlet, Defoe describes a situation of pervasive insecurity, stressing the mounting and unprecedented extent of criminal attack. The idea of crime wave is already quite explicit:

> Violence and Plunder is no longer confin'd to the Highways. . . . The Streets of the City are now the Places of Danger; men are knock'd down and robb'd, nay, sometimes murther'd at their own Doors, and in passing and repassing but from House to House, or from Shop to Shop. Stagecoaches are robb'd in High-Holbourn, White-Chappel, Pall-Mall, Soho and at almost all the Avenues of the City. Hackney-Coaches and Gentlemen's Coaches are stopt in Cheapside, St. Paul's Church-yard, the Strand, and other the most crowded streets, and that even while the People in Throngs are passing and repassing . . . 'Tis hard that in a well-govern'd City . . . it should be said that her Inhabitants are not now safe. . . .[2]

We may note in passing that equally contemporary themes richly abound in magazines that urban Americans read six decades ago. To cite but two examples:

> Individual crimes have increased in number and malignity. In addition to this . . . a wave of general criminality has spread over the whole nation. . . . The times are far from hard, and prosperity for several years has been wide-spread in all classes. Large sums are in unaccustomed hands, bar-rooms are swarming, pool-rooms, policy shops and gambling houses are full, the races are played, licentiousness increases, the classes who "roll in wealth" set intoxicating examples of luxury and recklessness, and crime has become rampant.[3]

In that period, it was, of course, commonplace also to ascribe the fundamental causes of mass criminality to large-scale immigration:

> In the poorer quarters of our great cities may be found huddled together the Italian bandit and the bloodthirsty Spaniard, the bad man from Sicily, the Hungarian, the Croatian and the Pole, the Chinaman and the Negro, the cockney Englishman, the Russian and the Jew, with all the centuries of hereditary hate back of them. They continually cross each others' path. It is no wonder that altercations occur and blood is shed. . . .

---

[2] *Ibid.*, pp. 10–11.

[3] James M. Buckley, "The Present Epidemic of Crime," *The Century Magazine*, (November 1903), p. 150.

The Demand for Order in Civil Society　　　**3**

We claim to be a rich and prosperous city and yet we cannot afford to employ enough policemen to keep thieves and burglars out of our houses and thugs and robbers from knocking us on the head as we walk along our own streets. . . . The bald, bare, horrible fact is that the conditions existing in Chicago today are the most criminal and damnable of any large city on the face of the earth.[4]

Thus the current rhetoric of concern about crime and violence draws on established motifs of both older and newer vintage: an indignant sense of pervasive insecurity; a mounting current of crime and violence as a result of both unaccustomed prosperity and prolonged poverty; the bad example of the self-indulgent wealthy; the violent proclivities of immigrants and other newcomers; and the ironic contrast between the greatness of the metropolis and the continued spread of crime.

But at times there was a somewhat different attitude toward urban crime and violence. In the London and Paris of the late eighteenth and the early nineteenth centuries, people often saw themselves as threatened by agglomerations of the criminal, vicious, and violent— the rapidly multiplying poor of cities whose size had no precedent in Western history. It was much more than a question of annoyance, indignation, or personal insecurity; the social order itself was threatened by an entity whose characteristic name reflects the fears of. the time—the "dangerous classes." The phrase occurs repeatedly. Thus, an anonymous essayist of 1844 writes of the situation in urban England, where "destitution, profligacy, sensuality and crime, advance with unheard-of-rapidity in the manufacturing districts, and the dangerous classes there massed together combine every three or four years in some general strike or alarming insurrection which, while it lasts, excites universal terrors. . . . ,"[5] But even where the term is not explicitly invoked, the image persists—one of an unmanageable, volatile, and convulsively criminal class at the base of society.[6]

---

[4] James Edgar Brown, "The Increase of Crime in the United States," *The Independent* (April 11, 1907), pp. 832–33.

[5] "Causes of the Increase of Crime", *Blackwood's Magazine* (July 1844), p. 2. The phrase appears in another work published four years later, *The Communist Manifesto*—where, however, it is instantly interpreted in terms of the "lumpenproletariat" idea.

[6] Honoré Antoine Frégier, *Les Classes Dangereuses de la Population dans les Grandes Villes* (Paris, 1840) is a work often cited by contemporaries. A relevant modern work on Paris is Louis Chevalier's *Classes Laborieuses et Classes Dangereuses à Paris pendant la Première Moitié du XIX Siècle* (Paris, 1958).

4   ALLAN SILVER

This imagery is only in part the product of class antagonisms in
early industrial society; rather, the working classes were included
in an older and continuing concern with criminality.[7] Urban administrators regarded the swelling numbers of the poor as unmanageable.
Indeed, the image of the "dangerous classes," as distinct from that
of pervasive criminality, seems to have flourished especially during
periods of very rapid population growth, reflecting the migration of
the numerous poor, without employment skills or a history of urban
life. During this period, the labor force of the metropolis was still
not primarily industrial.[8] Thus, the events and antagonisms of early
industrialism inflamed but did not create the image of the "dangerous
classes." It referred primarily to the unattached and unemployed.
An advocate of police reform in London, writing in 1821, defined
the problem in these terms:

> The most superficial observer of the external and visible ap-
> pearance of this town, must soon be convinced, that there is
> a large mass of unproductive population living upon it, without
> occupation or ostensible means of subsistence; and, it is notori-
> ous that hundreds and thousands go forth from day to day trust-
> ing alone to charity or rapine; and differing little from the bar-
> barous hordes which traverse an uncivilized land. . . . The
> principle of [their] action is the same; their life is predatory;
> it is equally a war against society, and the object is alike to
> gratify desire by stratagem or force.[9]

In the Paris of that time, he writes, "le proliferation des classes dangereuses
était . . . l'un des faits majeurs de l'existence quotienne de la capitale, l'un des
grands problèmes de l'administration urbaine, l'une des principales préoccupations
des tous, l'une des formes les plus incontestables de l'angoisse sociale." The
city was one "où le crime a une importance et une signification que nous ne
comprenons guère. . ." (pp. iii–iv).

[7] Influential books expressing this concern were Henry Fielding's *Enquiry into
the Causes of the Late Increase of Robbers* (1751) and Patrick Colquhoun's
Treatise on the Police of the Metropolis (1796). According to Chevalier (*op.
cit.*, pp. 451–68), the Parisian bourgeoisie made little distinction between the
"industrious" and the "dangerous" poor.

[8] According to the census, the population of London tripled in the first half
of the nineteenth century. On its occupational composition, see the *Census of
Great Britain in 1851* (London, 1854), p. 182, *passim.*

[9] George Mainwaring, *Observations on the Present State of the Police of the
Metropolis* (London, 1821), pp. 4–5. The anonymous essayist of 1844, quoted
above on the connection between the dangerous classes and the "manufacturing
districts," went on to write: "In examining the classes of society from which
the greater part of the crime comes, it will be found that at least three-fourths,
probably nine-tenths, comes from the very lowest and most destitute. . . . If

The Demand for Order in Civil Society   5

As class tensions involving the threat of riot and revolutionary violence subsided in London, the older concern with diffuse criminality rather than the "dangerous classes" reemerged. Thus, Henry Mayhew's immense reportage on London's criminals, vagabonds, and casually employed, published in 1861, was suffused variously by moralism, indignation, pity, compassion, horror, and mere curiosity—but not by the sense of dread that had earlier afflicted those confronted by the dangerous classes.[10] Indeed, contemporary writing in midcentury London exhibits a sense of relief and victory over the forces of mass violence. Contrasting the present with the past, a writer in 1856 observed that "the only quarter in which any formidable riot could take place would be eastward, in the neighborhood of the docks, where there are at least twelve thousand sailors in the river or on shore, ready for a spree, fearless and powerful, and acting with an undoubted esprit de corps. These, if associated with the seven or eight thousand dock labourers and lightermen, would certainly produce a force difficult to cope with."[11] Such a prospect clearly was judged as a great improvement.

To judge from contemporary accounts, New York did not experience a comparable sense of relief or improvement. Indeed, it appears that by 1872 New York was already being compared unfavorably to London with respect to crime and violence:

. . . If the vice and pauperism of New York are not so steeped in the blood of the populace [as in London and other European

we examine who it is that compose this dismal substratum, this hideous *black band of society*, we shall find that it is not made up of any one class more than another—not of factory workers more than labourers, carters or miners—but it is formed by an aggregate of the most unfortunate or improvident of *all classes*. . . ." *Blackwood's Magazine* (July 1844), p. 12 (italics in original).
[10] This was the fourth and final volume of *London Labour and the London Poor*, separately titled *Those That Will Not Work*.
[11] *London Quarterly Review* (July 1856), p. 94. Many observers, though still concerned with criminality, acknowledge a change for the better at this time. Remarking that accounts of the earlier situation in London "seem like tales of another country," a writer in 1852 went on to detail improvements: "No member of Parliament would now venture to say that it was dangerous to walk in the streets of London by day or night. . . . Bad as the dens of infamy in London still are, they are not to be compared with those older places of hideous profligacy. . . . In the most disorderly part of the town, such as St. Giles, Covent Garden, and Holborn, the streets every Sunday morning exhibited the most outrageous scenes of fighting, drunkenness and depravity. . . . Crimes, too, are greatly diminished in atrocity. The large gangs of desperate robbers, thirteen or fourteen in number, now no longer exist. . . ." *Edinburgh Review* (July 1858), p. 12–3.

cities] they are even more dangerous. . . . They rob a bank, when English thieves pick pockets; they murder, where European prolétaires cudgel or fight with fists; in a riot they begin what seems about to be the sacking of a city, where English rioters merely batter policemen or smash lamps. . . .[12]

For this observer, whose book is largely concerned with relief and other remedial programs among New York's poor, the dangerous classes are very much a part of the city—which, after all, had only a decade earlier suffered the great Draft Riot of 1863:

> There are thousands upon thousands in New York who have no assignable home, and "flit" from attic to attic, and cellar to cellar; there are other thousands more or less connected with criminal enterprises; and still other tens of thousands, poor, hard-pressed. . . . Let but Law lift its hand from them for a season, or let the civilizing influences of American life fail to reach them, and, if the opportunity afforded, we should see an explosion from this class which might leave the city in ashes and blood.[13]

Such rhetoric is not, as we have seen, an inevitable expression of concern with criminality, riot, and violence—even when these were of an order unthinkable in daily urban life today.[14]

What are some of the factors that underlie relationships between urban criminality and disorder and the significance ascribed to them by the peaceful and propertied classes? An adequate answer to this question would need to consider important aspects of economic, political, and urban history, the labor movement, and demography. For our purposes, however, we will focus on two aspects of the situation that until recently have been neglected: the significance of the police and the culture of riotous protest.

THE POLICED SOCIETY

Some modern nations have been police states; all, however, are policed societies. Practical men have never underestimated, though

---

[12] Charles L. Brace, *The Dangerous Classes of New York* (New York, 1872), p. 26.
[13] *Ibid.*, p. 29.
[14] Thus, Defoe saw the intolerable conditions of his time as a result of the arrogance and bad influence of a rapidly increasing group of prostitutes and their "bullies"; and his solution was to disperse them by raids (*op. cit.*, pp. 26–32).

The Demand for Order in Civil Society 7

they have often distorted, the importance of the police. Sociological theory in the "social control" tradition, however, has usually slighted the police in favor of normative or voluntary processes.[15] The significance of the police, for our purposes, can best be understood as they appeared to a generation for whom modern police were an unprecedented innovation—Englishmen in the middle third of the nineteenth century.

The London police, created in 1829, were from the beginning a bureaucratic organization of professionals.[16] One of their tasks was to prevent crime by regularly patrolling beats, operating under strict rules which permitted individual discretion. The police also had a mission against the "dangerous classes" and political agitation in the form of mobs or riots. On all fronts they were so successful that initial and strong objections to them rapidly diminished; from being a considerable novelty, they quickly became a part of "British tradition."

[15] In the book which more than six decades ago named and founded this tradition, E. A. Ross was crisply aware of the expanding role of police: "In the field of physical coercion, there is an increase in the number of lictors, bailiffs, police, and soldiers told off to catch, prod, beat, and hold fast recalcitrants, and they are brought under a stricter discipline. They are more specialized for their work, and an *esprit de corps* is carefully cultivated among them." *Social Control* (New York, 1901), pp. 398–9. Furthermore, Ross was quite tough-minded about the cause of this development: "All this does not happen by simple fiat of the social will. Certain groups of persons—the executive, cabinet, the central government, the party machine, the higher clergy, the educational hierarchy, 'authorities' of every kind in short—are always striving for more power. When the need of a more stringent control makes itself felt, they find the barriers to their self-aggrandizement unexpectedly giving way before them. Formerly they were held in check, while now they find encroachment strangely easy" (*Ibid.*). Neither kind of emphasis survived the subsequent failure of works in social control to treat the characteristics of the policed society in a comprehensive way or to see organized and legitimate coercion as intrinsic to social control. (Representative treatises are L. L. Bernard, *Social Control*, New York, 1939, and Richard T. LaPiere, *A Theory of Social Control*, New York, 1954.) Ross himself distinguished between the normative processes of "public opinion"—uniquely flexible, preventive, and ubiquitous—and the coercive effects of "law"—which were clumsy, retrospective, and remote (*op. cit.*, pp. 89–105). Important and influential as this distinction is, it tends to obscure—as we shall see—some of the distinctive features of policed society. Recent attempts to incorporate civil violence in the framework of social theory are included in *Internal War*, Harry Eckstein, ed. (New York, 1964), especially the essays by Eckstein, Parsons, and Feldman.

[16] Useful accounts of British police history are the writings of Charles Reith, especially *The Police Idea* (1938), *British Police and the Democratic Ideal* (1943), *The Blind Eye of History* (1952), and *A New Study of Police History* (1956). See also F. C. Mather, *Public Order in the Age of the Chartists* (Manchester, 1959). Like most contributors to the English literature on "public order," these writers—especially Reith—work from palpably conservative assumptions.

8   ALLAN SILVER

The policed society is unique in that central power exercises potentially violent supervision over the population by bureaucratic means widely diffused throughout civil society in small and discretionary operations that are capable of rapid concentration. All of these characteristics struck contemporary observers as remarkable. Fear of mob or riot diminished when early police showed that fluid organization can overcome numbers:

> There seems to be no fear a London mob will ever prove a serious thing in the face of our present corps of policemen. A repetition of the Lord George Gorden riots would be an impossibility. Those who shudder at the idea of an outbreak in the metropolis containing two millions and a half of people and at least fifty thousand of the "dangerous classes" forget that the capital is so wide that its different sections are totally unknown to each other. A mob in London is wholly without cohesion, and the individuals composing it have but few feelings, thoughts or pursuits in common. They would immediately break up before the determined attack of a band of well-trained men who know and have confidence in each other.[17]

Another writer put the same point in more impersonal terms:

> As each police constable being alone might easily be overpowered, and as the men of each section, or even division, might be inferior in numbers to some aggregation of roughs or criminals collected in a given spot, it is arranged that . . . reserves of force can be gathered . . . and concentrated upon the disquieted area, and as the commissioners command the whole district, and the force is organized and united, while roughs act in small areas, and have diverse and selfish interests, the peace of London may be held secure against violence.[18]

The peaceful and propertied classes appreciated two other advantages of the modern police: they relieved ordinary respectable citizens of the obligation or necessity to discharge police functions, especially

---

[17] "The Police and the Thieves", *London Quarterly Review* (July 1856), p. 93.
[18] "The Metropolitan Police System", *Westminister Review* (January 1873), p. 16. An early historian of the New York Draft Riot of 1863 was similarly impressed by the decisive contribution of the telegraphic system in linking police stations within the city to each other and to those in Brooklyn. He devoted considerable space to the mob's attacks on the telegraphic system, citing the defense of its equipment and personnel as a key phase in the struggle for control of the streets. See J. T. Headley, *The Great Riots of New York* (New York, 1873).

during emergencies; and they also made less likely a resort to the military for the purposes of internal peace-keeping. Both involved changes in the relationship of these classes to the criminal or disorderly.

In unpoliced society, police functions were often carried out—if at all—by citizens rotating in local offices (sheriffs, constables, magistrates) or acting as members of militia, posses, Yeomanry corps, or watch and ward committees.[19] Not only was this system inefficient but it also directly exposed the propertied classes to attack. Agrarian men of property were frequently willing to undertake these tasks. Thus the Yeomanry, a cavalry force whose characteristic tactic was the sabre charge, was largely composed of small landowners[20] who were especially zealous in police duty against mobs and riots and especially disliked by working people.[21] For these reasons, the Yeomanry were particularly popular among the landowning classes as a means of defense. Praising them in the course of a parliamentary debate in 1817, for example, a member observed that "the people would in many instances be debarred from violence by seeing those arrayed against them to whom they were accustomed to look up to as their masters."[22]

But this machinery exposed the Yeomanry, once an emergency had passed, to direct attack in the course of daily life.[23] It also enabled private persons sometimes to modify police missions to suit their own proclivities and convenience. Thus, during the extensive agricultural uprisings of 1830 in southern England, fifty men of the village of Holt enrolled as special constables and "declared their willingness to turn out to protect all property except threshing machines; they did not wish to show disrespect to their poorer neighbors."[24] Yet threshing machines were the very form of property then under attack.

[19] A good summary is in F. C. Mather, *Public Order in the Age of the Chartists*, pp. 75–95.

[20] John Fortesque, *A History of the British Army* (London, 1923) Vol. XI, p. 43). Since the yeomanry were required to supply their own horses and equipment, their status as agrarian men of property was largely assured. See K. Chorley, *Armies and the Art of Revolution* (London, 1943), p. 167.

[21] J. L. and B. Hammond, *The Town Labourer* (London, 1928), p. 89. Also, F. C. Mather, *op. cit.*, p. 148. Yeomanry, for example, precipitated the "Peterloo" massacre.

[22] Quoted in Reith, *The Police Idea*, p. 191.

[23] For example, many resigned when they received threatening letters after Peterloo. See Ione Leigh, *Castlereagh* (London, 1951), p. 127.

[24] J. R. M. Butler, *The Passing of the Great Reform Bill* (London, 1914), p. 132.

10   ALLAN SILVER

The urban and industrial propertied classes, however, were much
less eager to take up the tasks of self-defense as volunteer or co-opted
police. Landowning military officers attempting to encourage self-defense among commercial or industrial capitalists met with much reluctance. Replying in 1819 to advice from Wellington, the army commander in the newly industrializing north of England replied in exasperated terms:

> I have always fought against the dispersal of my force in
> trivial detachments; it is quite impossible to defeat the
> disaffected if they rise, and at the same time to protect any
> town from plunder; that resistance should be made by the in-
> habitants. . . . But I am sorry to say the general remark from
> the manufacturers is that government is bound to protect them
> and their property.[25]

We are dealing here not merely with the classic confrontation of
an agrarian military tradition and a pacific commercial and industrial
one; what also emerges is a specific demand for the bureaucratization
of police functions. Not only did the manufacturing classes wish to
avoid personal danger and inconvenience while protecting their property, but they also saw that—contrary to the social rationale underlying the yeomanry—the use of social and economic superiors as
police exacerbated rather than mollified class violence.[26] This emerges
clearly in the testimony of one Thomas Ashton, "the owner of considerable property in manufactures, and the employer of about 1500
persons," before the Royal Commission of 1839 concerned with extending the professional police from London to the provinces.[27]
Among other reforms, Ashton favored the use of personnel from outside a locality affected by violence and for a reason other than the
reluctance of local personnel to act against their neighbors:

> On such urgent occasions, I think it extremely desirable that
> a stipendiary magistrate should be sent into the district and
> entrusted with the administration of the law. A great majority

---

[25] Despatch of General Byng quoted in Reith, *The Police Idea*, p. 202.
[26] "Respectable tradesmen cannot, without detriment to themselves, be so engaged as constables . . ." (George Mainwaring, *Observations on the Police* . . . ,
p. 46).
[27] *First Report of the Commissioners Appointed as to the Best Means of Establishing an Efficient Constabulary Force in the Counties of England and Wales* (London, 1839), pp. 158–9.

The Demand for Order in Civil Society   11

of the more serious disturbances originate in disputes between master and servant. The local magistracy is chiefly composed of the resident landowners and manufacturers, and the irritation of the workmen against their employers is greatly increased when they find the person, with whom the disputes have arisen openly supported by, and giving directions to, the military, and subsequently punishing them for breaches of the peace, which would never have been committed unless such disputes had occurred. Ought the employer to be placed in such a situation? Is it likely that animosities would be allayed or peace maintained by it? What safety has the proprietor of machinery?

This reasoning was accepted by the commissioners in their report, which was largely written by the Benthamite reformer Edwin Chadwick:

> In several instances where there was an effective resistance given to the rioters, we have been informed that the animosities created or increased, and rendered permanent by arming master against servant, neighbour against neighbour, by triumph on one side and failure on the other, were even more deplorable than the outrages actually committed. . . . The necessity for such painful and demoralizing conflicts between connected persons should be avoided by providing a trained and independent force for action in such emergencies. . . . The constitutional authority of the supreme executive is then emphatically asserted. In reply to recent inquiries made of local authorities in the manufacturing districts, why they took no steps for the repression of riotous or alleged treasonable proceedings within their districts, why so long a career of criminal incitements was permitted, the prevelant answer has been, that such proceedings were understood to be exclusively within the province of government.[28]

Thus, at a time when the agrarian rich often sought to multiply and reconstruct the traditional means of self-defense against violent uprising and attack, those who sprang from the newer sources of wealth turned toward a bureaucratic police system that insulated them from popular violence, drew attack and animosity upon itself,

[28] *Ibid.*, p. 205.

and seemed to separate the assertion of "constitutional" authority from that of social and economic dominance.[29]

Other means than a bureaucratic police—especially the army itself—were available for this purpose. But although the army played a crucial role during crises or situations with revolutionary potential, it was ill-equipped to meet the enduring needs of a policed society.[30] It was largely officered by an agrarian class which sometimes did not distinguish itself for zeal in protecting the property of manufacturers.[31] More fundamentally, however, it was difficult for the army to act continuously in small dispersed units in civilian society, although it might do so on an emergency basis. More characteristic of the army was an alternation between no intervention and the most drastic procedures—the latter representing a declaration of internal war with lingering consequences of hate and resentment.[32] The police were designed to penetrate civil society in a way impossible for military formations and by doing so to prevent crime and violence and to detect and apprehend criminals.[33] Early descriptions by contemporaries describe both sorts of police action, taken today as routine, as novel and startling.[34]

The police penetration of civil society, however, lay not only in its narrow application to crime and violence. In a broader sense, it represented the penetration and continual presence of central politi-

---

[29] "I hope to get up a troop of Yeomanry at Cheltenham," wrote Lord Ellenborough during the critical year of 1832, "but this requires delicate management. . . . Yeomanry however we must have, or we shall be beaten." A. Aspinall, *Three Early Nineteenth Century Diaries* (London, 1952), p. 275.

[30] See the accounts in F. C. Mather, *Public Order in the Age of the Chartists*, pp. 153–81, and Joseph Hamburger, *James Mill and the Art of Revolution* (New Haven, 1963), pp. 203–14.

[31] See, for example, Frank Darvell, *Popular Disturbances and Public Order in Regency England* (Oxford, 1934), pp. 80–1, 267–8.

[32] All these points of superiority of police over army were explicit among those who advocated or created the early professional police. See for example, the *First Report of The Commissioners . . . , op. cit.*, pp. 159–61; George Mainwaring, *Observations on the Present State of the Police . . .* , p. 69; Charles Reith, *British Police and the Democratic Ideal*, pp. 9–30; and *Edinburgh Review* (July 1852), p. 6.

[33] Great stress was initially laid on the "preventive principle," at the time a new principle in internal peace-keeping. See Reith. *ibid.*, pp. 18–23, and the same author's *A New Study of Police History,*, pp. 221–4. For the view of a contemporary advocate of police, see Mainwaring, *op. cit.*, pp. 9–10.

[34] Note, for example, the obvious astonishment that underlies an account of the tracing of a burglar, who had robbed a house in central London, to an obscure hiding place in the East End ("The Police System of London," *Edinburgh Review*, July 1852, pp. 8–10).

The Demand for Order in Civil Society 13

cal authority throughout daily life. In an important defense of characteristically modern social arrangements, Edward Shils has argued that
close integration of the social and geographic periphery is a unique
achievement of "mass society." In his view

> mass society is not the most peaceful or "orderly" society
> that has ever existed; but it is the most consensual. The main-
> tenance of public peace through apathy and coercion in a
> structure of extremely discontinuous interaction is a rather
> different thing from its maintenance through consensus in a
> structure of more continuous interaction between center and
> periphery. . . .[35]

But in Shils' account the integration of the periphery emerges entirely as a moral or normative process:

> The mass of the population is no longer merely an object
> which the elite takes into account as a reservoir of military
> and labor power or as a possible or actual source of public
> disorder. . . . Most of the population . . . stand in closer moral
> affinity and in a more frequent, even though mediated, interac-
> tion with the center than has ever been the case. . . . The
> greater proximity to the center—to the institutions which consti-
> tute it and the views which are embodied in it. There is, accord-
> ingly, a greater feeling within the mass of being a part of the
> same substance of which one is oneself formed.

That the modern nation represents an unprecedented extension of
the organizational and moral community is undoubted. But the wholly
normative language in which this account is cast risks eliding the
simultaneous extension of the police throughout the "periphery" both
as the agent of legitimate coercion and as a personification of the
values of the "center." Far from being a latter-day consequence of
organizing the police for purely coercive tasks, this was explicit in
early police doctrine and much remarked upon by early observers.
Their accounts stress the capacity of bureaucratic organization to
make the values of the "center" palpable in daily life by means of
detached persons operating on organizationally defined missions.

> Amid the bustle of Piccadilly or the roar of Oxford Street,
> P.C.X. 59 stalks along, an institution rather than a man. We
> seem to have no more hold of his personality than we could

[35] "The Theory of Mass Society," *Diogenes* (1962) pp. 53–4 (for this and suc-
ceeding quotations).

possibly get of his coat buttoned up to the throttling-point.
Go, however, to the section-house . . . and you no longer see
policemen, but men. . . . They are positively laughing with
each other![36]

And they also stress the power of the police over mass disorder,
which stems not only from superior organization and the rational
application of force but also from its presence as the official representative of the moral order in daily life:

> The baton may be a very ineffective weapon of offence, but
> it is backed by the combined power of the Crown, the Govern-
> ment, and the Constituencies. Armed with it alone, the constable
> will usually be found ready, in obediance to orders, to face
> any mob, or brave any danger. The mob quails before the simple
> baton of the police officer, and flies before it, well knowing
> the moral as well as physical force of the Nation whose will,
> as embodied in law, it represents. And take any man from that
> mob, place a baton in his hand and a blue coat on his back, put
> him forward as the representative of the law, and he too will
> be found equally ready to face the mob from which he was
> taken, and exhibit the same steadfastness and courage in defense
> of constituted order.[37]

In this setting, early police doctrine and observers agreed from
the beginning that it was necessary to rely on the moral assent of
the general population; even the earliest policemen were elaborately
instructed in the demeanor and behavior required to evoke, establish,
and sustain that assent.[38] This was more than a mere technical convenience. The replacement of intermittant military intervention in
a largely unpoliced society by continuous professional bureaucratic
policing meant that the benefits of police organization—continual pervasive moral display and lower long-term costs of official coercion
for the state and propertied classes—absolutely required the moral
cooperation of civil society.

Thus, the extension of moral consensus and of the police as an
instrument of legitimate coercion go hand in hand. Along with other
ramifying bureaucratic agencies of the center, the police link daily
life to central authority. The police, however, rely not only on a
technique of graduated, discretionary, and ubiquitous coercion but

---

[36] "The Police and the Thieves," *London Quarterly Review* (July 1856), p. 93.
[37] "The Police of London," *London Quarterly Review* (July 1870), p. 48.
[38] Charles Reith, *A New Study of Police History*, pp. 140–2.

The Demand for Order in Civil Society　　　　　　　　15

also on a new and unprecedentedly extensive form of moral consensus. The center is able to supervise daily life more closely and continuously than ever before; but police organization also requires pervasive moral assent if it is to achieve the goals peculiar to its technique. In earlier times, as we have seen, voluntaristic and nonbureaucratic police permitted the sabotage of official coercion by allowing participating classes to make their services conditional. In a policed society (as distinct from a police state), a hostage is also given to fortune: the fundamental assent, not of the classes who comprise volunteer or nonprofessional quasi-police, but of the general population. Without at least a minimal level of such assent, coercive functions become costly in exactly the ways that those who created the policed society in England sought to avoid. In this sense, then, the extension of the moral community and of the police are aspects of the same historical development.

CULTURES OF RIOTOUS PROTEST

The themes of mass criminality and of political riot and mob protest have long been intertwined. In a notable and recent contribution George Rudé has been especially concerned to refute the classic view—associated with such nineteenth-century conservatives as Burke, Taine, and Le Bon—that political crowds, mobs, and riots are essentially criminal in character.[39] According to Rudé's analysis, demonstrating crowds and mobs in the latter half of the eighteenth an the first half of the nineteenth century were characteristically composed not of pauperized, unemployed and disorganized "rabble" but of locally resident, respectable, and employed people.[40] It is not surprising that privileged classes attempt to define popular protest as criminal—that is, fundamentally and unconditionally illegitimate. But this rhetoric and the very real fears of privileged and propertied people facing recurrent popular agitation in an unpoliced age, must not lead us to overlook the evidence for another aspect of this older relationship between elite and agitational population: riots and mobs, however much they were feared and detested, were also often means of protest that articulately communicated the desires of the population to a responsive, if not sympathetic, elite.[41]

[39] *The Crowd in History, 1730–1848* (New York, 1964), pp. 7–8, 199–204.
[40] *Ibid.*, p. 47–65.
[41] Expressions of this fear are vivid and aboundingly frequent. "At this time," wrote the Tory poet Southey in 1812, "nothing but the Army preserves us from the most dreadful of all calamities, an insurrection of the poor against

16   ALLAN SILVER

This is a major feature of Eric Hobsbawm's analysis of the pre-industrial "city mob."[42] While stressing that such mobs were a "prepolitical phenomenon" and often reacted directly to fluctuations in wages and food prices, Hobsbawm also emphasizes, in effect, the normative character of such riots:

> . . . There was the claim to be considered. The classical mob did not merely riot as a protest, but because it expected to achieve something by its riot. It assumed that the authorities would be sensitive to its movements, and probably also that they would make some immediate concession; for the "mob" was not simply a casual collection of people united for some *ad hoc* purpose, but in a recognized sense, a permanent entity, even though rarely permanently organized as such.[43]

---

the rich, and how long the Army may be depended upon is a question which I scarcely dare ask myself" (Elie Halevy, *A History of the English People*, New York, 1912, Vol. I. p. 292). Seven years later a peer discussing the political situation observed: "We are daily assailed with undisguised menace, and are little removed from the expectation of open violence. . ." (*Substance of the Speech of the Rt. Hon. Lord Grenville in the House of Lords, November 19, 1820*, London, p. 23). A year later in a memorandum to Liverpool, Wellington, then Prime Minister—urging the creation of a police force—wrote: "I feel the greatest anxiety respecting the state of the military in London. . . . Very recently strong symptoms of discontent appeared in one battalion of the guards. . . . There are reports without number in circulation respecting all the Guards. . . . Thus, in one of the most critical moments that ever occurred in this country, we and the public have reason to doubt the fidelity of the troops, the only security we have, not only against revolution but for the lives and property of every individual in this country who has anything to lose. . ." (Quoted in Reith, *The Police Idea*, p. 213). Robert Peel, fearing for his family's safety at their country estate, left London during the crisis of 1831 and asked a friend to send weapons. "I have this day got you fourteen carbines, bayonets, and accoutrements," the friend replied. "How will you have them sent to you? I have only desired a cask of ball cartridges to be put in the case" (Tresham Lever, *The Life and Times of Sir Robert Peel*, New York, 1942, p. 144). A general description of the situation is given in Reith, *Police Principles and the Problem of War*, pp. 46–8. In his revisionist account, *James Mill and the Art of Revolution*, Joseph Hamburger maintains that this standard portrait of elite mentality is exaggerated and that it does not apply to the Whig reformers in the period before 1832, who were more concerned with long-range than with imminent crises (see pp. 33–47).
[42] *Primitive Rebels: Studies in Archaic Forms of Social Movements* (Manchester, 1959).
[43] *Ibid.*, p. 111.

The Demand for Order in Civil Society   **17**

Insisting with Rudé on the essentially noncriminal character of such riotous protests, Hobsbawm summarizes the system as a whole:

> Provided that the ruler did his duty, the populace was prepared to defend him with enthusiasm. But if he did not, it rioted until he did. This mechanism was perfectly understood by both sides, and caused no political problems beyond a little occasional destruction of property. . . . The threat of perennial rioting kept rulers ready to control prices and distribute work or largesses, or indeed to listen to their faithful commons on other matters. Since the riots were not directed against the social system, public order could remain surprisingly lax by modern standards.[44]

We will briefly illustrate the system as described by Hobsbawm and Rudé with an example from rather late in this period—London in 1831.[45] "Illuminations" were occasions on which those favoring a given cause or person placed lights in their windows; and it often happened that demonstrating crowds went from house to house demanding that those within "illuminate" and smashing their windows or sacking their houses if they did not. The residences thus besieged were usually selected with precision—the ruling class in eighteenth- and early nineteenth-century cities was not anonymous, physically inaccessible, or effectively insulated by a professional and preventive police force. Such a crowd, pressing for electoral reform of the Commons, gathered in April 1831. The following is a contemporary account of its doings, clearly written from an unfriendly point of view:

> . . . The reformers of London endeavoured to get up an illumination on Monday, the 25th; but that having been a failure, they prevailed on the Lord Mayor to announce another for the evening of Wednesday the 27th. On that evening, the illumination was pretty general. . . . The mobs did a great deal of mischief. A numerous rabble proceeded along the Strand, destroying all windows that were not lighted. . . . In St. James' Square they broke the windows in the houses of the Bishop of London,

[44] *Ibid.*, p. 116.
[45] See the summary of this theme in *The Crowd in History*, pp. 254–7. See also the interesting article by R. B. Rose, "Eighteenth Century Price Riots and Public Policy in England," *International Review of Social History* (1961), pp. 277–92, and the more general remarks in this connection by Joseph Hamburger, *op. cit.*, pp. 199–202.

the Marquis of Cleveland and Lord Grantham. The Bishop of
Winchester and Mr. W. W. Wynn, seeing the mob approach,
placed candles in their windows, which thus escaped. The mob
then proceeded to St. James' street where they broke the windows of Crockford's, Jordan's, the Guards, and other Club houses.
They next went to the Duke of Wellington's residence in Piccadilly, and discharged a shower of stones which broke several
windows. The Duke's servants fired out of the windows over
their heads to frighten them, but without effect. The policemen
then informed the mob that the corpse of the Duchess of Wellington was on the premises, which arrested further violence
against Apsley House. . . .[46] After the action just described the
mob marched off to attack other residences, including that of
Robert Peel, the political founder of the police.

At every point the normative character of the mob is clear. In
this case their cause was generally popular, and they had the support
of the Lord Mayor and many other worthies favoring reform, whereas
many mob actions, of course, lacked such sanctions. But "antagonistic
cooperation" between the mob and parts of the elite had a long history.[47] Indeed, even prereform electoral politics sometimes required
parts of the elite not only to compete for the favor of the people
but to expose themselves to rough treatment by electors and nonelec-
tors alike. Thus, a French observer of 1819, watching the customary
postelection procession of successful parliamentary candidates, de-

---

[46] *Annual Register*, 1831, p. 68. Quoted by Reith in *British Police and the
Democratic Ideal*, pp. 90–1. Hamburger places this incident squarely in the
"tradition of riot" (see *James Mill.* . . . , pp. 139–42).

[47] It is Hamburger's thesis that in the case of the Reform Crisis of 1830–1832,
proreform leaders manipulated the threat of the mob, rather than wielding a
substantial revolutionary threat. But this sort of manipulation was itself a
tradition—for a case that succeeded before the mob ever took to the streets,
see Thomas Perry, *Public Opinion, Propaganda and Politics in Eighteenth Century
England: a study of the Jew Bill of 1753* (Cambridge, Massachusetts, 1962).
So strong was this tradition that Lady Holland, the wife of the great Whig
aristocrat prominent in the struggle for reform, could remark disapprovingly
on Wellington's reaction to the prospect of mob attack on his house: "Is it
not strange that the Duke of Wellington has boarded with very thick planks
all his windows upstairs to Piccadilly and the Park? . . . The work of *darkness*
began on Coronation Day and is now completed. He says, I hear, that it is
to protect his plate glass windows from the mob, who will assail him on the
Reform Bill! As it cannot be for thrift, it looks like defiance; and the mob
will be irritated when they discover his intentions." Earl of Ilchester, ed.,
Elizabeth, Lady Holland to Her Son, (London, 1946), p. 118. (Italics in
original.)

The Demand for Order in Civil Society 19

scribed a scene which Halevy calls "one long familiar to the English public":

> [They] were immediately pelted with filth, greeted with a shower of black mud. . . . I saw Lord Nugent with one side all black. . . . Lord John Russell attempted with difficulty to wipe off the stinking patches of dirt which continually bespattered his cheeks. . . . Some had their windows broken and their furniture damaged. The houses of Lord Castlereagh and several others met with the same fate. The constables were insufficient to restore order, and the troops had to be called out.[48]

The English elite, then, sometimes lived on rather casual terms with popular volatility so long as the latter did not—as for a time the "dangerous classes" and early working class movements seemed to—challenge the fundamentals of the current system. They did not do so willingly, to be sure, but in a kind of symbiosis in which "consideration" was exchanged for "support." Thus, to see everyday, nonrevolutionary violence or unruliness solely or even largely as an impediment to the emergence of stable democracy is to blur important distinctions between kinds of popular violence and ways in which it may be integrated into a political system. Popular violence which forms part of an articulate system of demands and responses, in which needs and obligations are reasonably clear to each party, may not be at all necessarily "irrational," "criminal," or "pointless"—to use words often applied to riotous protest in contemporary democracies. Indeed, the English case suggests that—granted the many other conditions that lie outside our present scope—such a system may well conduce to the establishment of stable democracy. For although Hobsbawm calls the system "pre-political," it is one in which ordinary people express their will and elites have learned to listen.[49] The exist-

---

[48] Halevy, *op. cit.*, p. 118.

[49] It is suggestive to compare Hobsbawm's perceptive comment on the situation in parts of Europe which did not experience a comparably gradual development of democratic institutions. Speaking of popular riot and enthusiasm in support of the *status quo*, he remarks: "Legitimate monarchs or institutions like churches may not welcome this. The Emperor Francis I of Austria took a poor view of the revolutionary legitism of his people, observing correctly: 'Now they are patriots for me; but one day they may be patriots against me!' From the point of view of the genuinely conservative institution, the ideal is obediance, not enthusiasm, whatever the nature of the enthusiasm. Not for nothing was 'Ruhe ist die Erste Bürgerpflicht' (Tranquility is the first duty of every citizen) the slogan of every German princeling" (*Primitive Rebels* . . . , p. 119).

20   ALLAN SILVER

ence of the normative culture of mob and riot in many places other than England is enough to show—if the disclaimer need be made at all—that the mere existence of normative riot and violence is not a sufficient condition for the emergence of institutionalized democracy.[50] Yet in an age when institutions did not organize, represent, or press the claims of ordinary people, and in which the streets were therefore a political arena, it is important to distinguish between kinds of popular violence, rather than consider it wholly as an anachronism.

THE DEMAND FOR ORDER IN CONTEMPORARY DEMOCRACY

Such a protodemocratic system of riotous demand and elite response, however, is confined to unpoliced, hierarchical, pre-industrial society. It is not found where entrepreneurs or managers, career bureaucrats, or professional politicians have displaced former ruling groups; where popular volatility may disrupt tightly woven political and market ecologies; and where the state makes its presence felt ubiquitously in the form of police. In the latter situation, the demand for "law and order" becomes what it was not before—a constitutional imperative stemming from an unprecedentedly pervasive consensus and personified and enforced by police. Simultaneously, the standards of daily decorum increasingly restrict occasions for normative violence; thus Georg Sorel observed at the start of this century how marked had been the decline of daily and casual violence during the last, and how crucial a role these new standards played in the emerging policy of the liberal democratic state toward both the working and dangerous classes.[51]

With rising standards of public order has come an increasing intolerance of criminality, violence, and riotous protest. Daniel Bell

[50] See Hobsbawm, *passim.* See also the comprehensive discussion by Charles Tilly, "Reflections on the Revolution of Paris," *Social Problems* (Summer 1964), pp. 99–121, which, among other matters, deals with the literature on these themes in the case of France.

[51] See Chapter 6 of *Reflections on Violence.* On the special sensitivity of modern society to public disorder, see Karl Polyani, *The Great Transformation* (New York, 1944), pp. 186–7: "The market system was more allergic to rioting than any other economic system we know. . . . In the nineteenth century breaches of the peace, if committed by armed crowds, were deemed an incipient rebellion and an acute danger to the state; stocks collapsed and there was no bottom to prices. A shooting affray in the streets of the metropolis might destroy a substantial part of the nominal national capital."

The Demand for Order in Civil Society   **21**

has suggested that a breakdown of spatial barriers between the daily round of urban propertied classes and the criminal or unruly poor has made the former more aware of violence in daily life.[52] We may perhaps envisage three stages in such a sequence: one in which the prosperous or respectable often lived in unimagineable closeness to crime and the threat of riot or mob; a second in which these groups succeeded in insulating themselves—spatially, by regroupment in and outside the centers of cities and organizationally, by the police;[53] and a third in which penetrations of these barriers evoke a response which would be considered exorbitant by the standards of earlier years.

The character of the police as a public bureaucracy may also raise expectations about the level of public peace it is possible to attain. As the instrument of public policy they are easily seen in terms of a naive social instrumentalism—as technicians applying efficient means that are in principle capable of fully realizing their ends. Have not public bureaucracies eliminated plague, solved the enduring problems of urban sanitation, and prevented gross impurities in purchased foods? Why cannot the police similarly "clean up" crime and control violence?[54] In short, the historic and strategic success of the police raises expectations and exposes them to pressures engendered by the idea of a uniformly peaceful civil society.[55]

Not only are expectations of public order higher than before, but the arena to which these expectations refer has expanded. It has

---

[52] "The Myth of Crime Waves: the actual decline of crime in the United States," in *The End of Ideology* (New York, 1962), pp. 151–74.

[53] "The beats vary considerably in size; in those parts of the town which are open and inhabited by the wealthier classes, an occasional visit from a policeman is sufficient, and he traverses a wide district. But the limits of the beat are diminished, and of course the frequency of the visits increased, in proportion to the character and the density of the population, the throng and pressure of traffic, and concentration of property, and the intricacy of the streets. . . . Nor must it be supposed that this system places the wealthier localities at a disadvantage, for it is an axiom in police that you guard St. James' by watching St. Giles' " ("The Police System of London," *Edinburgh Review*, July 1852, p. 5). St. Giles was one of the most notorious of London's "rookeries."

[54] It is more than accidental that Edwin Chadwick (see p. 26, above) was also a prime mover in the reform of urban sanitation. See his report, *Sanitary Conditions of the Labouring Population in England, 1842* (London, 1843).

[55] See Bell, *op. cit.*, p. 152 on the relationship between better policing and a "higher" crime rate. The artifactual character of this relationship, sometimes hard for contemporaries for whom the police are taken for granted to grasp, was obvious to an observer witnessing the transition to a policed society. See "Causes of the Increase of Crime," *Blackwood's Magazine* (July 1844), p. 5.

done so not only because of the continuing, though obviously very incomplete, extension of a single moral order throughout the national community—a process which takes territoriality rather than the divisions of class, locality, or group as its ideal boundaries. The arena of expectation widens as smaller formations—regions, states, local communities—find it harder to control or influence the moral climate in which they live. The "nationalization" of civil rights, federal involvement in municipal programs like housing, the erosion of the power of localities to control the content of mass media, pressure from judiciaries on informal and quasilegal police practices—all mean that smaller formations come to see themselves as less able to control or influence their moral destiny.[56] Thinking themselves more vulnerable to incursion from the larger society, they extend moral demand and expectations to a wider environment than in the past was thought relevant to daily life.

These trends mesh with others. The imagery of the "dangerous classes" is being reborn in contemporary America. The nascent demand for a pervasively benign environment arises as the urban poor, disorganized, and unemployed—especially Negroes—bear more heavily upon the awareness and daily life of an urban society in which proportionately more people are "respectable" than ever before.[57] Violence, criminality, and riot become defined not only as undesirable but as threatening the very fabric of social life. Police forces come to be seen as they were in the time of their creation—as a sophisticated and convenient form of garrison force against an internal enemy.[58] Lacking a strong tradition of urban violence as a form of

---

[56] Attempting to account for respectable people's greater awareness of violence in daily life, Bell has also suggested that the emergence of heterogeneous audiences for the mass media, which include groups previously less exposed to violent themes, has heightened awareness of violence even as its occurrence in daily life has declined (*ibid.*, pp. 170–4). Simultaneously, local communities and states are losing their formal powers to control such materials and are relying more often on informal control. (See Richard Randall, *Some Political Theories in Motion Picture Censorship Decisions: Prior Restraint Reconsidered.* Paper delivered at the Midwest Conference of Political Science, Bloomington, Indiana, April 1965.)

[57] Here we follow Shils' argument, *op. cit.*, p. 56.

[58] For the American police this situation may render a chronic problem acute. At the time when the police are more urgently charged than ever before to do society's "dirty work" but also are more stringently supervised by the public, various interest groups and the judiciary, their morale and operating problems are further exacerbated by their failure to embody moral consensus in the eyes of the general community, their "clientele," and themselves as thoroughly as do the British police. For detailed observations about some of these matters,

The Demand for Order in Civil Society 23

articulate protest, it is all the easier to define such events as merely criminal.[59] Such definitions work not only on the respectable but also on the riotous poor. Like American society as a whole, the American poor lack a traditional past: on neither side of the boundaries of class and race do the conditions for "articulate riot" exist in generous measure. "Criminal" acts like looting and violent assault are likely to dominate riotous protest, rather than explicitly political gestures. Similarly, the propertied and respectable are ill-prepared to react in terms other than a confrontation with uncontained and shapeless criminality. Articulate riot, however, requires that both rioters and their target or audience jointly define the meaning of riotous acts. The frequency with which recent riots by Negroes in American cities are interpreted officially as "meaningless"[60] contrasts with the ability of the English elite, especially before it was severely threatened from the late eighteenth century on, to interpret the meaning of riotous behavior.

Current concern over violence and riot, then, involves a problem of the political language in which these events are described and interpreted. The problem is likely to sharpen as the official stance, relying in part upon the rhetoric of diagnostic sociology, becomes strained by the urgent pressure of events. The gap between the official diagnostic style and a cultural response that makes little provision for "normative riot" is likely to widen as the urban situation grows even more aggravated. It therefore remains to be seen whether American elites—creative, professional, and political—can or will sustain a diagnostic posture that seeks and interprets the meaning of these events.

It is not to idealize even the optimal "traditional" political society— that of England—with its brutalities, squalidness, and hardness of soul, to point out that it often provided the unorganized poor with

especially the last, see Michael Banton, *The Policeman in the Community* (London, 1964), a comparative account of Scottish and American police forces.
[59] Obviously, the rural South would require special treatment. See W. J. Cash, *The Mind of the South* (New York, 1941), *passim*, and H. C. Brearly, "The Pattern of Violence", in W. T. Couch, ed., *Culture in the South* (Chapel Hill, 1934). Our focus, however, is on urban situations. Thus, for example, there is a suggestion in that the few food riots of nineteenth-century New York, in 1837 and 1857, were carried out largely by foreign-born, rather than native, poor. See the chapters on these episodes in J. F. Headley, *The Great Riots of New York* (New York, 1873).
[60] I am indebted to Robert Fogelson's analysis (as yet unpublished) of these riots and of the official responses to them—notably the McCone Commission's report on the Watts riot of August 1965.

a language by which, in the absence of representative institutions or the ability to participate in them, they might articulately address the propertied classes through riot and disorder. And it is not to derogate the American adventure in modernity to suggest that, however richly endowed with representative and responsive institutions, it has not provided such a language for those in its cities who have long been outside their compass—a language whose grammar is shared by speaker and listener, rioter and pillaged, violent and frightened.

[4]

THE POLICE AND POLITICAL DEVELOPMENT
IN EUROPE

DAVID H. BAYLEY

THE PURPOSE OF this chapter is to explore the relationship between the police and political development during the growth of modern European nation-states. Great Britain, France, Germany, and Italy have been chosen for comparison. Four questions will be answered in the course of the analysis: (1) What is the character of the police system in each country? (2) When did these contemporary police systems emerge? (3) What factors account for the emergence and rate of development of these systems? and (4) What factors account for the characteristic solutions each country found for its modern police problems?

Specification of the nature of police is not as easy as it might seem. Organizations called police perform different functions in different countries; different organizations in the same country carry out police duties; police units handle nonpolice duties just as police duties are handled by nonpolice personnel. In order to cut through this tangle of divergent and imprecise usage, it is necessary to delineate the central preoccupation of this paper, that is, what I shall consider the core of "police" activity. The focus of this chapter will be upon the mandate to regulate interpersonal relations within a community through the applications of coercive sanctions authorized in the name of the community. A police force is an organization authorized by a collectivity to regulate social relations within itself by utilizing, if need be, physical force. Therefore, when the word police is used it should be understood in terms of a particular function and not in terms of a given body of men. The definition is most important for what it excludes. Social regulation, after all, is accomplished by a host of community agencies, from health departments to taxing authorities. By and large only the police have an explicit mandate to use physical force in order to resolve disputes or to enforce community directives. Similarly, individuals are commonly accorded the right to defend themselves by physical means, but they would hardly be considered as policemen when they do so. An army is publicly

DAVID BAYLEY

constituted to use force, just as police are, but its jurisdiction is external to the collectivity. An army uses force to defend a community from threats outside itself; a police force protects against threats from within.

When one studies the performance of a task comparatively among different countries, what should one study? The key analytic problem in this chapter is to pose questions which are both important and meaningful comparatively. For example, one might begin by trying to determine when a police system was created in each nation. This is not, it turns out, a very helpful start. Policing is ubiquitous in human society. One would be hard-pressed to find a society where interpersonal relations were regulated either wholly privately or without recourse to physical force. In modern Europe police agencies antedate most other institutions. What is more, it is difficult, as we shall see later, to characterize informatively police arrangements that were replaced by contemporary police systems; public vs. private or state vs. nonstate does not get at a meaningful difference. Another way of providing a meaningful comparative perspective would be to stipulate a particular kind of police system and determine whether developments in various nations have converged toward the model. Is there perhaps such a thing as a modern police system? When did each nation develop such a system? Can it be compared with a traditional or a premodern one? This too is not a very helpful formulation. National police systems are constituted in importantly different ways; each one exhibits unique features requiring explanation. By fitting diverse situations into a Procrustean mold, loss of empirical richness is assured.

In order to meet this problem of describing change meaningfully among disparate systems performing a similar function, I propose to use as a baseline for comparison in each country the nature of each police system as it exists today. This procedure avoids having to determine whether, and then when, each of these systems underwent a generic shift in character from a traditional to a modern system, an underdeveloped to a developed system, a preindustrial to an industrial system, or an unstructured to a bureaucratic system. It may be true that major characterological changes have occurred. This approach does not preclude finding them. If there are common patterns of development, they will become apparent. If there are not, change can still be described, but in this case with reference to explaining what exists contemporaneously rather than what exists

THE POLICE AND POLITICAL DEVELOPMENT IN EUROPE

only theoretically. In this way empirical diversity is preserved while a meaningful comparative question is answered, namely, when and how did each nation's police system get to be as it is.

It might be argued against this approach that if the entities to be compared are significantly different today, then analysis is almost bound to find few similarities and only unique national differences. This criticism is overdone. Though it is true that this approach assumes a priori that these national systems have nothing in common except their contemporary existence, it does not preclude determining whether their respective development is on a converging course. Indeed, the converse of this formulation is to assume that they are all similar in some respect, for example, modernity, and then to constrain analysis to find similarity in patterns of development. The question of convergence is logically distinct from the question of how several systems developed. Moreover, analysis can be more responsive to unique patterns of national development by disengaging the question of convergence from that of the nature of historical development.

This procedure would not be useful if any of these countries recently experienced a revolutionary shift in police modality, for the baseline of comparison would be unstable. Longevity is the only warrant for concluding that particular features are characteristic. In fact, none of these systems has undergone a major change in the way policing has been performed in the past generation and indeed —with the exception of Germany—in the past half century. The permanence of institutional police patterns in each of these countries is one of the most important findings of this study.

The Character of Contemporary Police Systems

In the following descriptions of the police systems of Great Britain, France, Germany, and Italy, five points of differentiation will be covered: (1) tasks and responsibilities, (2) structure of the national system, (3) nature of accountability, (4) internal organization, and (5) role behavior and professional image.[1] Since the range of descriptive dimensions is very great, any set is incomplete and its adequacy arguable. One dimension particularly is noteworthy by its absence: there is no measure of the efficiency with which policing is accomplished. Surely the most important characterization to be

---

[1] To facilitate comparison Figure 5–1 (p. 341) summarizes the characteristics of each nation's system.

DAVID BAYLEY

made deals with the extent to which a police system performs its central function well. While this is true, adequate measurement of efficiency is difficult methodologically; moreover, the effort would be misleading. The perceived need for police varies over time. Police in Cromwell's time were required to be preoccupied with prevention of blasphemy and the keeping of the sabbath; police in Edward Heath's time are required to be stern with drug-takers and violators of motor-vehicle regulations. Prussian police in the eighteenth century enforced residence requirements on peasants and artisans, while police in the Bonn Republic must defend the right of employees to organize and strike. An efficient police in one age is an irrelevant police in another. Crime is a function of social values, hence so is police efficiency. Even if one could determine an unchangeable human need in successive generations which always fell within the domain of the police function, such as the defense of life against unprovoked attack, data simply do not exist which would allow a test for efficiency. Crime statistics, for example, are notoriously unstable and they are of fairly recent invention. Furthermore, the relation between crime statistics and police efficiency is complex: more efficient police forces may have higher crime rates precisely because they know of and record more crimes; a crime prevented may be attributable to police activity or to social circumstances over which they had no control. Finally, due to differences in legal codes even in the present day, international comparisons are highly questionable.

The police function in Great Britain is carried out by forty-nine separate police forces (Critchley 1967: 311–312).[2] Though the personnel of each force is bound in their professional actions by statutory regulations and the Common Law, there is no single authority in the country that can command them in their day-to-day activities. They are led, deployed, and disciplined by local officers. The commanding officers, known as Chief Constables everywhere except London, are accountable to local political bodies: in towns to the Watch Committees and in counties to the Standing Joint Committees.[3] Membership on each committee is composed of two-thirds of elected members of

[2] These figures include England and Wales, but not Scotland, as of 1966. The forces ranged in size from 700 to 7,000 policemen. In 1960 there were 125 forces in England and Wales (Royal Commission 1962: Cmnd. 1728, p. 6). The amalgamations were a direct result of the recommendations of the Royal Commission.

[3] The designation "Standing Joint Committee" is no longer generally used. These bodies are now called "Police Committees." This change in nomenclature occurred in the last few years.

THE POLICE AND POLITICAL DEVELOPMENT IN EUROPE

the Town Council and County Council, respectively, and one-third of appointed magistrates.[4] The central government has police authority only in London, where responsibility is in the hands of the Home Secretary who appoints the Commissioner of the London Metropolitan Police. Within any jurisdiction police agency is singular. There is only one police force in each locality and specialization occurs within that organization.

The British system is decentralized in command but unified in its practices. This has been accomplished by statutory direction and through the power of the Home Secretary to inspect local forces and withhold financial support if the force is not judged up to par. Since the central government's grant amounts to half the cost of the force, its bargaining power is considerable.

The extent of police responsibilities is narrow in Great Britain. They are similar to American conceptions of police work, dealing largely with maintenance of law and order, the protection of persons and property, and the prevention of crime. British police officials do not have the power to issue ordinances having the force of law;[5] nor do they undertake regulatory work unrelated to offenses under the criminal law.[6] Their most demanding noncriminal responsibility is the regulation of motor-vehicle traffic.

Day-to-day regulation of political activities by English policemen has been very slight. By and large they respond reactively; initiative is not, and has not been, theirs. Political intelligence is collected by

[4] Until the Police Act, 1964, all members of Watch Committees were elected members of the Town Council. Membership of Standing Joint Committees had been composed half of elected members of the County Council and half of appointed magistrates.

[5] This power does belong to the Commissioner of the London Metropolitan Police by virtue of his having the powers of a magistrate as well.

[6] Royal Commission 1962: 22, summarizes the responsibilities of the police in eight points: "First, the police have a duty to maintain law and order and to protect persons and property. Secondly, they have a duty to prevent crime. Thirdly, they are responsible for the detection of criminals and, in the course of interrogating suspected persons, they have a part to play in the early stages of the judicial process, acting under judicial restraint. Fourthly, the police in England and Wales (but not in Scotland) have the responsibility of deciding whether or not to prosecute persons suspect of criminal offences. Fifthly, in England and Wales (but not in Scotland) the police themselves conduct many prosecutions for the less serious offences. Sixthly, the police have the duty of controlling road traffic and advising local authorities on traffic questions. Seventhly, the police carry out certain duties on behalf of Government Departments—for example, they conduct enquiries into applications made by persons who wish to be granted British nationality. Eighthly, they have by long tradition a duty to befriend anyone who needs their help, and they may at any time be called upon to cope with minor or major emergencies."

DAVID BAYLEY

the police, and fairly systematically. This work is performed by the Special Branch of the Criminal Investigation Division (C.I.D.).

The uniformed personnel of the British police are selected according to a single set of recruitment procedures. Except in London, top command officers are uniformed police personnel. Chief Constables, as they are known, have almost all attained their positions by promotion from Constable. The only exceptions are in some rural counties, though the practice of promoting nonpolice officers as Chief Constable even here is declining. In London the highest uniformed rank is that of Superintendent. Superintendents are in charge of major regions within London. Until recently the Commissioner was chosen from outside the police establishment, as by and large were his Deputies and Assistants.

Recruit training, apart from simple military drill, was not established in Britain until 1907 (Stead 1957: 139). It now amounts to an initial course of thirteen weeks plus two two-week refresher courses later on (Critchley 1967: 245–246). Special training for higher ranks was begun in 1948. It is an object of considerable suspicion among British policemen who fear the development of an elite corps within the force (Critchley 1967: 249). The primary functional division within the police is between crime prevention and crime investigation.[7] Detectives are recruited from the ranks of the regular police.

The most difficult dimension of any police system to characterize is the role behavior of its personnel and its professional image. Yet no other attribute is more important to the man-in-the-street. I shall try to present a general characterization for each country. It is important to recognize, however, that the material has often been gleaned from reading between lines, from asides and innuendo. In very few countries have the reputations of police forces been carefully studied employing modern surveying techniques. Britain is one of the few exceptions. The Royal Commission, 1962, not only undertook a large public opinion survey, it devoted considerable space in its final report to police-public relations. Presenting a stereotype of the policeman for any country immediately suggests that opinion about the police is homogeneous. This is rarely the case. Though I believe it is fair to make comparisons among the police of different nations, there are also crucial differences of opinion within nations,

---

[7] The famed Scotland Yard is the headquarters for the London Metropolitan Police. It is not a national criminal investigation unit, though it often lends assistance to other forces when it is asked.

THE POLICE AND POLITICAL DEVELOPMENT IN EUROPE

among classes, ethnic groups, and regions. Often these are as great as differences between nations.

The British police are generally perceived as being honest, approachable, trustworthy, and helpful. They are viewed with respect and an admixture of affection. Generally they work as individuals, not in groups. They carry no firearms, and are commonly nonauthoritative and nonpunitive.

The French police system provides a sharp contrast to the British in almost all respects. The French system is completely centralized. Not only on regulations and procedures identical throughout the country, but the Ministry of the Interior has authority to direct police operations in every corner of the land. Policing is conceived as a responsibility of national government.

For practical reasons operational control of the police cannot be exercised from the Paris officers of the Ministry of the Interior. It is delegated to the Prefects of France's ninety (Ridley and Blondel 1965: 88) Departments and from them to Mayors or *Commissaires* in Communes.[8] The *Commissaire* is the chief of police of the Commune; he is responsible both to the Prefect and to the Mayor, though the Mayor himself can be held accountable by the Prefect for police work. There are three distinct police forces in France, not just one as in England. First, there is the *Police Nationale*, which is the civil police force of the central government. Policing in all Communes with a population of over 10,000 is carried out by the *Police Nationale*. Second, in Communes with less than 10,000 inhabitants the Mayor and the Communal Council may create their own police force.[9] Finally, there is the *Gendarmerie*, which is responsible for policing in rural areas where mobility may be important and where the Communes are unwilling to provide adequate forces of their own. Personnel of the *Gendarmerie* are recruited and paid by the Ministry of War, though they are directed in their police work by the Prefects and the Ministry of the Interior. Units of the *Gendarmerie* are posted to all Departments as a reserve police force. The *Garde Mobile*, which is an armed force for riot operations, and the *Garde Républicaine*, which is wholly ceremonial and stationed in Paris, are both units of the *Gendarmerie*.

Police in France are directed by a larger civilian bureaucracy

---

[8] There are 38,000 Communes in France. A Commune is roughly equivalent to a township in the United States (Ridley and Blondel 1965).

[9] These are the *Gardes champêtres* of rural areas.

DAVID BAYLEY

than is the case in Great Britain, but they are much farther removed
from supervision by elected legislative bodies. Representative supervision exists only through the national Parliament which can call to
account the Minister of the Interior. The actions of individual French
policemen must be conformable to law. Determination of illegality,
however, is made by administrative courts. The French legal system
is bifurcated, as is the case in Germany and Italy; one set of courts
determines matters of right and privilege between individuals, the
other determines the propriety and legality of matters involving the
state and the citizen.

Just as the police of London bear a special relation to the central
government, so the policing of Paris is constituted somewhat differently than in the rest of the country. In the Department of the Seine,
in which Paris is located, the Prefect has been stripped of his police
powers; they have been entrusted to the Prefect of Police, as it were
a specialized Prefect for police affairs.[10] The Prefect of Police is directly responsible to the Ministry of the Interior; there is no elected
Mayor of Paris, and the Municipal Council can withhold funds from
the Prefect, but it cannot direct him to perform specific actions. Because of its size and importance, the police of Paris have often tried
to become self-regulating, to minimize their links with the Ministry
of the Interior, and to aggrandize their influence outside of Paris.
Conflict between the police of Paris and the Sûreté has been
common.

Police power in France, as well as elsewhere on the continent, is
constitutionally indistinguishable from the authority to govern.
Police Générale refers to the power of government to make binding
regulations in the interests of public order and security. It may involve criminal matters, as they would be defined in the United States
or Great Britain, or it may encompass more general directions, such
as supervision of newspapers and films, control of epidemics, licensing of building construction, control of foreigners, and inspection of
asylums and certain children's institutions (Chapman 1953: 506–507).
Authority to govern in France is all inclusive and centralized. Since
the Prefect is responsible for law and order, as the agent of the central government, many commentators have come to the conclusion
that the work of uniformed police personnel is broader than in Eng-

[10] This post was first created in 1800. Until recently the Prefect of Police was responsible for police in all Communes of the Seine Department. Under the terms of a
recent reorganization, the Prefect of Police has authority only within Paris.

THE POLICE AND POLITICAL DEVELOPMENT IN EUROPE

land and the United States. In the past they were assigned to more
distinct formal tasks than were the police in Great Britain. At the
same time, they have never been encouraged to undertake the informal work of mediation, assistance, and advising that has been a
stock-in-trade of the British or American policeman. Generally the
police today are used in France in much the same formal ways as
they are in Anglo-Saxon countries; specialization of function has resulted in giving off tasks not immediately related to criminal work.
However, there are some administrative tasks performed by police
agents which are uncommon in England, such as granting passports,
surveying dangerous buildings, scrutinizing prices and the quality
of produce, and inspecting factory premises (Stead 1957: 168). The
Prefect and the Mayor do have a larger charter of action than any
Commissioner or Chief Constable; they are central administrative
officials and may issue regulations (*arrêtés*) on a wide variety of
subjects.

The police of France have been heavily engaged in politics since
their creation. Though this activity has probably declined in the
twentieth century—certainly it is less obvious and more restrained—
the police continue to be objects of great suspicion by political
parties of both left and right. The police are known to keep a very
close watch on political opinion and activity. French policemen admit to being able to penetrate most political organizations, regardless of how clandestine these may be. Political intelligence is handled
by the *Renseignements Généraux* and counterespionage by the *Surveillance du Territoire*. The police have been sorely tested in France
in recent years with respect to maintaining public order. Mundane
police dispositions reflect the challenges they face. Paris police lor-
ries are equipped with steel side-panels so that they may be used in
barricading broad avenues. London police have nothing comparable.

Until recently officers of the *Police Nationale*, as well as the *Gendarmerie*, were not promoted from the ranks; rather, they were recruited and trained separately as officers. Officers had to have
university degrees. This was also the case in Germany and Italy.
Now, however, it is possible for lower ranks to take the officer candidate examination, though they must do so before they are thirty-
five years of age. Though historically French officers have had higher academic qualifications than their British counterparts, command
responsibilities of French officers have been more limited in scope.

[336]

DAVID BAYLEY

The highest rank for a French officer is that of *Commissaire*. Such individuals have jurisdiction in Communes, which are fairly small areas. They are subordinate to mayors and prefects. French officers are also more closely supervised by a civilian bureaucracy, while the British officers are more closely involved with representative political bodies.

The primary functional division within the police is between the *Police Administrative* and the *Police Judiciaire*: the former handles crime prevention, i.e., patrolling and routine police work, the latter crime investigation. The Ministry of the Interior since 1945 has had its own paramilitary reserves in the *Compagnies Républicaines de Sécurité* (CRS).

Formal training for police officers and men was established in France in 1883 (Stead 1957: 139).

The French police have a reputation for being efficient, indefatigable, and omniscient. They are considered individually to be brusque and rather unapproachable. They are' armed, feared, and disliked, though they are not considered especially corrupt.

In West Germany policing is the responsibility of the state of the Federal Republic.[11] This represents a return to the practice of the Weimar period and the Second Reich and a renunciation of the experiment with national responsibility which was tried during the Hitler era. The Bonn government can legislate in any field except education and cultural affairs; thus it can establish principles for the regulation of police agencies. For field administration, however, it has few cadres of its own and must rely upon the bureaucracies of the ten states (Jacob 1963: 162–163). Thus, German police are overwhelmingly state police, accountable to legislatures in each state. The central government maintains only a border police force and a reserve riot force for use in emergencies; it also operates certain forensic establishments and has a small criminal investigation staff for exclusively federal offenses.[12] Operational control is exercised through the mayor in towns or the *Landrat* in rural areas. The *Landrat* presides over county-size units, much like an Indian district officer or a French Prefect, though the *Landrat*'s powers are not so

[11] The police of East Germany are centralized, as they have been since 1946. I have made no attempt to study police organization and practices in East Germany. Attention will be given in this paper only to Prussia, the Second Reich, Weimar, and the Bonn Republic.

[12] This is the Federal Criminal Police Bureau (Jacob 1963). See also Finer 1962: 531–532.

THE POLICE AND POLITICAL DEVELOPMENT IN EUROPE

extensive as the Prefect's. The *Landrat* exercises his police authority as an agent of the Ministry of the Interior of his particular state.

The *Landrat* will have at his disposal a state police force and a *Gendarmerie* for use primarily in rural areas. Most states also maintain a heavily armed reserve that receives military training and lives in barracks. The German police make a sharp distinction between officers and men. Recruitment is by competitive examination at different levels of the rank hierarchy. Uniformed command personnel are closely supervised by a civilian bureaucracy, much like their French counterparts.

German policemen are accountable not only to state legislatures, democratically elected after 1949, but to the law. Adjudication of cases against policemen for actions taken in the line-of-duty is handled by administrative courts.

German police authorities have possessed vast rule-making power in the past. Though it is less great than before World War II, it is still substantial. I am unable to provide a precise measure of its extent in comparison with police of other nations. Though the *Landrat*, like the Prefect, presides over all the executive functions of government, the police are given a more specialized set of tasks. They are undoubtedly more extensive than the British and probably more than the French. The state police are divided functionally between criminal police and ordinary police—the one not uniformed, the other uniformed. Within the criminal police division separate offices specialize in particular kinds of crime, such as homicide, burglary, auto theft, and so forth. This pattern is general now among European police forces.

German police were heavily involved in politics in the nineteenth century. This is much less true today. They seem to have adopted the stance of neutral referee, a tradition begun though interrupted during the Weimar period. They undoubtedly collect political intelligence and have a substantial capacity with respect to counterespionage.

German policemen are trusted and honest. They are also formal, rather rigid, and authoritarian in manner. They are not known for approachability. They are armed and do not have a reputation for effective informal mediation.

The police system of Italy is highly centralized; it is also plural, in the sense that there are several forces. The two primary police forces are the *Guardia de Pubblica Sicurezza* (P.S.) and the *Corps de*

DAVID BAYLEY

Carabinieri. Towns are permitted to raise their own police, known as *Vigili Urbani*, which enforce municipal laws and regulate traffic. Police operations are directed by the Ministry of the Interior through the Prefects of Italy's eighty-eight provinces (Fried 1963: 275). The Prefect is assisted by the *Questore*, who is in effect the provincial chief of police. The *Questore*, like the Prefect, is appointed by the Ministry of the Interior. There is no local political accountability; popular control is exercised only through the national Parliament.

Though the P.S. and the *Carabinieri* are both under the direction of the Ministry of the Interior, they are quite distinct and can properly be considered rivals in the field of police operations.[13] The *Carabinieri* are part of the army; they are recruited, trained, and paid by the Ministry of War. When assigned to police duties, they come under the control of the Ministry of the Interior. In theory the P.S. are given responsibility for normal police duties, both criminal investigation and prevention, while the *Carabinieri* are held in reserve for dealing with problems of public order and security. In fact, the *Carabinieri* also do criminal investigation work as well as political surveillance. Both forces are jealous of their prerogatives and like to demonstrate superior ability over the other. The *Carabinieri* is heavily armed, military in bearing and training, and stratified between officers and men. The P.S., too, is very martial in training; its officers are taken from the army, though they are required to have law degrees and to undergo special training (Cramer 1964: 327–331).

Italian police officers are subject to the law, though adjudication is performed by administrative courts.

The Prefect and the *Questore* have ordinance-making authority. The P.S. especially carries out a greater range of tasks than English police. I am unable to differentiate Italian from French or German police in this regard. Italian police in the nineteenth century played a shamelessly political role. Though they are somewhat more subtle today, they find it difficult to remain above politics for long. This is especially true in the industrial areas of the north and in the "Red Belt" north of Rome. Violence and agitation are commonplace; involvement by police officials is mandatory (Fried 1963: 250–252).

Italian police are considered corrupt, punitive, and unscrupulous.

[13] Luigi Barzini (Barzini 1964: 215–216), for example, says that they have been carrying on "a running feud for more than a century." Many Italians, he says, consider their antagonism the best safeguard of the citizen's liberties.

THE POLICE AND POLITICAL DEVELOPMENT IN EUROPE

They are feared and disliked. One would not consider going to them for assistance except in time of great stress. They are armed.

It should be obvious now that the diversity among the police forces of Great Britain, France, Germany, and Italy is substantial. The structure of national systems ranges from marked decentralization and local control to extreme centralization and total absence of local control. In one system political control by elected representatives over uniformed personnel is close and direct; in other systems it is screened through layers of civilian bureaucrats. Three countries stratify police between officers and men; two build the police on military lines; all of them specialize according to function within the police. Uniformed police handle very much the same kind of work in all countries, though on the continent their immediate civilian superiors have considerable ordinance-making authority and may direct police into activities that would be considered exceptional in Britain. Some police forces are heavy-handed and set apart from the people; others are trusted and approachable; others are incorruptible and respected; and some are called upon for informal mediation while others are studiously avoided. Quite clearly vigorous national police systems have developed in importantly different ways; these differences will require explanation (see Figure 5–1).

Emergence of National Police Systems

When did the characteristics of these contemporary police systems emerge in recognizable form and what factors account for the timing as well as the rate of subsequent development? The concern in this section will be exclusively with explaining the timing of development. Analysis of the factors which gave each country its unique police features is a separable matter to be taken up in the following section. The first task now is to pinpoint historically the point at which today's characteristics emerged in each country. The second task is to compare political and social processes in each country at these times in order to determine whether similar factors led to the development of national police systems.

Unfortunately for the facilitation of analysis, each police system did not emerge full-blown at a single moment in time. Some features developed earlier than others. Moreover, single features matured over time, surfacing and submerging, so that it is often difficult to say when exactly a particular feature became confirmed in national life. In France, for example, the structure of today's system may be

DAVID BAYLEY

	Great Britain	France	Germany	Italy
1. Tasks				
a. Formal	Narrow	Extensive	Extensive	Extensive
b. Informal	Extensive	Some	Few	None
c. Political	Very Modest	Modest, Extensive Intelligence	Modest	Extensive
2. National Structure				
a. Nature of Authority Aggregation	Decentralized	Centralized	Decentralized	Centralized
b. Number of Distinct Forces	Singular	Plural	Singular	Plural
3. Nature of Control				
a. Political	Local, Representative	Central, Bureaucratic	Local, Bureaucratic	Central, Bureaucratic
b. Legal	Subject to Unified Legal Code	Subject to Administrative Court System	Subject to Administrative Court System	Subject to Administrative Court System
4. Internal Organization				
a. Rank Organization	Singular	Bifurcated	Bifurcated	Bifurcated
b. Training	Civilian	Civilian	Military	Military
c. Functional Specialization	Considerable	Considerable	Considerable	Considerable
5. Role Behavior and Image				
a. Perceived Character	Trustworthy, Approachable, Respected	Distrusted, Unapproach-able, Efficient	Authoritarian, Unapproach-able, Honest	Feared, Corrupt, Quixotic
b. Mode of Intervention	Individual, Informal	Formal	Formal, in Groups	Punitive, in Groups
c. Armament	None	Armed	Armed	Armed

Figure 5–1. Structure of National Police Systems

discerned in the late seventeenth century. Even its essential bureaucratic organization can be found at that time. Yet the civil constabulary was not uniformed until 1829 and its period of greatest expansion was probably the middle of the nineteenth century. The development of the characteristics of today's systems emerged over a period of about two centuries. As a result, though one can discern first appearances, the timing of the development of police systems cannot be considered an exact science.

The problem can be made somewhat more manageable by focusing upon only a few of the features of today's systems. The features

THE POLICE AND POLITICAL DEVELOPMENT IN EUROPE

which are most central to the concerns of political scientists are (1) the structure of the national system, (2) the nature of primary operational units, and (3) the methods of political control. These are the features I shall focus upon. With respect to some of the features which I will neglect, one or two points might be made briefly. Attributes of contemporary internal organization and specialization tend to emerge later than the more political features. Characteristics dealing with role behavior and professional image are very difficult to chronicle at all. The tasks performed by police forces have undergone a similar pattern of development regardless of country; they have gradually been restricted. During the past century many responsibilities have been assigned to separate agencies, until today the work of policemen in each country is very similar.

When did the structure of the national system, its force units, and institutions of political control emerge in Great Britain, France, Germany, and Italy in recognizable contemporary form?

In Great Britain, establishment of a recognizable contemporary system began with the "New Police" in London in 1829 and became implanted throughout the country in the next half-century. In 1829 the central government placed the weight of its authority against the centuries-old and thoroughly discredited parish-constable system. Parliament, acting through the Home Secretary, assumed the responsibility for policing in London and transferred executive responsibility for the police out of the hands of judicial personnel. Sir Robert Peel's police—the "Bobby"—represented the coalescing of bits and pieces of experimentation from the preceding one hundred years. The London Metropolitan Police constable was a full-time, uniformed officer paid from the public rates. The police were organized into a substantial force with jurisdiction coterminous with an entire municipal area. And the force was provided with full-time executive leadership made responsible to an elected political body.

The London police, against enormous public hostility, soon proved its utility over the moribund parish-constable system. In 1839 all former police agencies—except the police of the City of London—were abolished or merged with the metropolitan force; magistrates were stripped of all police authority; and the boundaries of the force were fixed at a radius of fifteen miles from Charing Cross (Critchley 1967: 56–57; Reith 1948: 92). London, however, was not England, and policing in the rest of the country assumed slowly and begrudgingly the form of the London experiment. In 1835 the Municipal Corpora-

DAVID BAYLEY

tions Act allowed towns with charters to establish municipal councils by popular election, which in turn could set up police forces under the direction of a Watch Committee. The precedent of community police forces greater than parish units was expanded to the counties by the County Police Act, 1839. In this case, control was vested in the magistrates corporately and not in an elected body.

Some towns and counties responded to the enabling legislation of 1835 and 1839; many, however, did not. In order to establish some uniformity in policing standards, the County and Borough Police Act of 1856 required creation of full-time professional police organizations in all towns and counties. The central government was empowered to inspect each force and, if found up to the mark, to support them with a grant amounting to one-fourth their total cost. The structure of today's system was now legally in place throughout the kingdom, though with considerable variation in practical detail and performance.

Local political control exercised through representative bodies was not made universal until 1888. The Local Government Act, the last great landmark in the Age of Reform, established Standing Joint Committees in the Counties to supervise the workings of the police. Even so, popular control was not as complete as in the towns. The Standing Joint Committees were composed half of elected representatives and half of magistrates. As we have already seen, the Police Act of 1964, rather than finally abolishing the participation of magistrates, has turned the clock back, appointing magistrates to town Watch Committees as well, though the proportions are now two-thirds elected membership and one-third magistrates in both towns and counties.

Not only did the structure of the British system and its method of control emerge during the sixty-year period after 1829, so also did the distinctive role behavior of its personnel. The "Bobby" was a new kind of police officer. He was unarmed, depending for his success, indeed for his very life, upon his ability to work cooperatively with the populace. He was given little power and told to build respect (Critchley 1967: xiv). He succeeded mightily, and as a result the implacable hostility shown the police in the eighteenth and early nineteenth centuries was transformed into respect and affection.

In France the essential characteristics of today's police system emerged much earlier, becoming recognizable during the years 1660–1700. The first step was the organization of a unique police com-

THE POLICE AND POLITICAL DEVELOPMENT IN EUROPE

mand in Paris. In 1667 Louis XIV appointed the first Lieutenant-General of Police, superseding the Provost of Paris as chief police officer. The Lieutenant-General was a royal officer, responsible to the king and not to the *Parlement* of Paris (Stead 1957: chap. 1; Arnold 1969: 14–23). Specialization and centralization of police authority succeeded so well that by late 1699 Lieutenants-General of Police had been established in all major cities. During the same period the post of *Commissaire* was created to assist the Lieutenants-General. In the countryside police authority was drawn into the hands of the provincial *Intendants*.[14] The *Intendants* were the predecessors of today's Prefects.[15] Though the office of *Intendant* went into temporary eclipse during the *Fronde*, it was reinvigorated by the reforming Colbert as the primary instrument of central administrative direction.[16] The last region to receive an *Intendant* in regular attendance was Brittany in 1689 (Gruder 1968: 5–10). By 1700 police authority throughout France was held by the Crown acting through *Intendants* in the provinces and Lieutenants-General of Police in cities.

At the disposal of these central police officers were various forces. In the rural areas there was the *Maréchaussée*, a mounted military constabulary. It was abolished during the Revolution, which put in its place in 1791 the national *Gendarmerie*. Though the name was changed, the function and personnel of the two forces were very similar. Both were military units providing police services in rural areas. The cities had a variety of forces during the seventeenth and eighteenth centuries devoted exclusively to policing. In Paris, for example, there were detectives in each quarter and a force of *exempts* whose duty it was to maintain order in all public places. In support of the *exempts* were special bodies of soldiers drawn from the foot guards and dispersed as sentinels throughout the city. Another body of men known as "archers," numbering about one hundred, patrolled the city during the night and for part of the afternoon. Finally, there was a watch-guard, both foot and horse, that

[14] The *Intendants'* full title was "intendants de justice, police, et finances, et commissaires départies dans les généralités du Royaume pour l'exécution des ordres du Roi" (Chapman 1955: 11).

[15] Their jurisdiction was the *généralité*. Thirty-two of them were appointed originally by Richelieu in the reign of Louis XIII.

[16] Robert Fried (Fried 1963: 19) says that police powers had not originally been given to the *Intendants* but continued to be held by Royal Governors. The Governors used their police powers against the Crown during the *Fronde*. As a result, Louis XIV transferred police powers to the *Intendants*, whom he could better control.

DAVID BAYLEY

patrolled the city night and day. This force was drawn from disbanded infantry and dragoons. Each of its parties was heavily armed. If a situation exceeded the capacity of these considerable police forces, the military garrison of the city could be called in (Radzinowicz 1957: vol. 3, 540–541). This happened most commonly when rioting broke out. In 1829 a uniformed civil constabulary was introduced for the first time; these were the *Sergents de Ville*, later renamed *Gardiens de la Paix*. The force initially numbered only one hundred men (Stead 1957: 98–99). By 1848 the municipal force had expanded to six hundred men, including *Inspecteurs, Sergents de Ville*, and office staff (Stead 1957: 107–108).

It is clear that by the late seventeenth century there were full-time police functionaries in France under the direction of the central government. Policing was a specialized function and personnel were recruited separately for it, though the police force drew heavily from men with military training and relied for support on formal military units. Civilian detectives were well established, having been appointed as early as 1645 by Mazarin (Stead 1957: 24). Permanent police posts, the beginning of the modern police station, were set up in Paris by the Marquis d'Argenson, the second Lieutenant-General of Police (1679–1718). The practice was then expanded to the rest of France (Stead 1957: chap. 2). The French police system of the late seventeenth century was to grow in authority, and to be challenged many times, but its essential lines were to persist unchanged to the present day. The Revolution affected the nature of political authority at the center, but it did not change the balance of power between center and localities. While developments after the Revolution finally confirmed the manner in which central control was to be exercised, whether through a specialized Ministry of Police or the Ministry of the Interior, they did not undermine the principle of central sovereignty in police affairs—if anything, control became more efficient.

The development of the police in Germany was more attenuated than in France and Great Britain. It began in the eighteenth century but did not become fixed until just after unification in 1871. In seeking for antecedents to contemporary police forms, attention will be given to Prussia, for Prussia not only dominated the German empire in geographical size and population, its administrative and political forms, symbolized in the Hohenzollern crown, were carried over into the Second Reich. The key police development in the eighteenth

THE POLICE AND POLITICAL DEVELOPMENT IN EUROPE

century was the emergence of the *Landrat* and *Steuerrat* as the authoritative instruments of central police power. The *Landrat*, presiding over territories the size of a township or small county, was a royal officer, responsible to Berlin, though he was chosen from the ranks of the local aristocracy. He was not, at least during most of the eighteenth century, a professional bureaucrat but an aristocratic amateur (Muncy 1944: chap. 5; Rosenberg 1958: 166–167; Jacob 1963: 11–12). The *Steuerrat* was responsible for a town. As the positions developed, these officials became the police superintendent with operational control over the *Gendarmerie*, police magistrates, and mayors. They also issued all prohibitory orders, which took the form of police decrees (Jacob 1963: 55). The police authority of the central government was stoutly disputed by the landed aristocracy until 1872 (Holborn 1969: 401). Titled landed proprietors claimed as a traditional right the power to act as sheriffs within their own properties; this right was not repudiated in Prussia until 1872 (Dawson 1914: chap. 1).[17]

Cities were never a source of competing police authority in Prussia, at least not after the decline of city vitality in the fifteenth and sixteenth centuries (Dawson 1914: chap. 4). Frederick II appointed a royal police officer for Berlin in 1742; the post was renamed Police President in 1809.[18] Though the reforms of Baron vom Stein were designed to reinvigorate municipal life in Prussia after the Peace of Tilsit, 1807, towns were expressly denied the right to regulate their own police. It was stipulated, however, that the state could devolve police powers on local authorities if they wished (Dawson 1914: chap. 1).[19] During the nineteenth century preceding unification several royal police presidents were appointed to large Prussian cities, which indicated the growing need for police in the reviving towns (Holborn 1969: 107).

By the time the German Empire was created, police power was aggregated at two levels, the state and the diffused squirearchy,

---

[17] In 1812, the "Reform Era," a *Gendarmerie-Edict* was promulgated which vested power in the hands of the *Landrat*, on the model of the French sub-Prefect. The Junkers, fearing for their traditional powers, successfully resisted the edict and it was eventually revoked (Rosenberg 1958: 226).

[18] Frederick II sent his officer-designate to Paris to study with Sartine, a famous Lieutenant-General of Police. It is a mark of the prestige of the French system that Maria Theresa of Austria asked Sartine in 1748 to answer sixteen questions about police work, preparatory to her establishment of a Police Commissioner for Vienna in 1751.

[19] One of Stein's most influential young assistants was a Police Director of Konigsberg, J. G. Frey, and a bureaucrat of the central government (Holborn 1966: 401).

DAVID BAYLEY

though the latter was rapidly losing ground. The federal configuration of the Second Reich assured supremacy in police affairs to each member state.

Little information is available about the nature of the police forces created in Prussia during the eighteenth and nineteenth centuries. It is fairly clear that royal officers in the larger cities had full-time, though nonuniformed, police personnel available to them in the eighteenth century. The police of Berlin were not put in uniform until 1848, and it is doubtful that other states showed greater initiative (Fosdick 1915: 109ff.). Military forces were available if needed in the countryside. They were replaced by a *Gendarmerie* on the French model after the defeat of Napoleon (Jacob 1963: 11–12). Thus by the early nineteenth century full-time police existed in the major cities and a *Gendarmerie* in the rural areas.

The police system of modern Italy became recognizable between 1815 and 1870. The political act of unification was a much more important factor in the development of the Italian police than the German. Piedmont did not dominate the Italian peninsula by size or example nearly as much as Prussia did Germany. Moreover, the strict centralization of government in Italy represented a sharp break with the past, while German unification left internal government of the states very much as it had been before. Between 1860 and 1870 a federal system was considered and rejected by the statesmen of the *Risorgimento* (Mack Smith 1968; Fried 1963: chap. 1). A centralized police system in Italy dates from 1870, when Rome and Venice were wrested from foreign domination.

The structure of internal organization and political control of the police built upon practices already tried in Piedmont. Responsibility for law and order had been contested between the Ministries of War and Interior during the first half of the nineteenth century. Preeminence of the Ministry of Interior was fixed by law in 1852 and the instrumentality of the Prefect for police affairs was confirmed in 1858 (Fried 1963: chap. 2). The post of *Questore* was created in 1852 as assistant to the *Intendant-General* of a Division, who became in 1858 the Prefect (Fried 1963: chap. 2).

Italy's two police forces, the *Carabinieri* and the *Guardia de Pubblica Sicurezza*, were created in 1816 and 1852 respectively. Both were Piedmontese innovations. The *Carabinieri* was modeled after the French *Gendarmerie* as a force of armed police maintained by the Ministry of War. The Public Security Guards were created to re-

[347]

THE POLICE AND POLITICAL DEVELOPMENT IN EUROPE

place the *Carabinieri*, as well as the National Guard, in Piedmont's largest cities. The *Carabinieri* were considered too rigid to handle the manifold duties of city policing (Cramer 1964: 327–329).

Summarizing this brief essay in comparative history, one finds that the police systems of Great Britain, France, Germany, and Italy developed recognizable modern features with respect to structure, control, and organizational units during a period bounded by 1660 and 1888. The emergence of these features in each country followed a different plan. In Britain the system developed between 1829 and 1888, spreading out from a dramatic experimemt in the nation's capital. The French system was established much earlier. It was not primarily an urban innovation, though the needs were perceived more clearly there, but involved rural and urban areas equally. The police system of Germany could be discerned in important respects during the middle of the eighteenth century. The sovereignty of Germany's several states in police matters survived the formation of the German Empire, as it did the disaster of the Hitler era. The most persistent threat to this sovereignty came not from a central government or even vigorous organs of local government, but from a diffused class of landowning oligarchs. Italy's police system built upon Piedmontese precedents, and in turn upon French, evolving during the period 1816–1858. These were straws in the wind, however, and were not given national life until the drama of the *Risorgimento*, 1859–1870, determined that the Italian peninsula would have a rigidly centralized system of government and administration.

The arrangements for maintaining internal order that were replaced by these new regimes tended to be decentralized in operation, based upon local communities or traditional ascriptive relationships such as were found on feudal estates. The Parish-Constable had been a feature of English life since the fourteenth century, though the Parish itself did not fully emerge as a unit of government until Tudor times (Critchley 1967: chap. 1). The Justice of the Peace, who had the power to direct the constable and to apply the Common Law, bore prime responsibility since the fourteenth century for maintaining the King's peace (Critchley 1967: 7–9). To some extent this responsibility was shared with the Sheriff and Lord Lieutenant of the county. In France, military officers such as the *Prévôt* had acted in a civil defense capacity for two or three hundred years before the seventeenth century. The *Compagnies d'Ordonnance*, for example, France's first standing army, dating from 1455, were di-

DAVID BAYLEY

rected to clear the roads of highwaymen. At the same time, local authority exercised through *Parlements* for urban and rural areas, dominated by nobles and clergy, assumed responsibility for the maintenance of order, prevention of crime, and application of sanctions against criminal activities. The tradition of local self-help was also to be seen in the *Garde Bourgeoise* of the seventeenth century.[20] Similar to the English yeomanry of a later period, it was a volunteer body composed largely of men of property who banded together to assist in maintaining order. In Prussia, feudal arrangements persisted longer than in either France or England, continuing indeed through the seventeenth and eighteenth centuries, despite the fact that this was the great period of growth in the administrative capacity of Hohenzollern government. From the late fourteenth century through the mid-sixteenth century towns bore autonomous responsibility for policing; in rural areas landed nobles exercised police functions as a prerogative of ownership. The Prussian political settlement, confirmed in the seventeenth century by the Great Elector, ensured both the loss of urban autonomy and the continuation of landed-proprietary privilege.

The point should be underscored that today's police systems, diverse in character, replaced systems of marked longevity that were equally diverse. It would be convenient to be able to say that contemporary police systems reflect a shift from private to public agency, from decentralized to centralized organization, or from feudal to state authority. Beyond noting that the transition to contemporary systems did mark a decline in decentralization, none of these generalizations aptly describe what happened in each country. The Parish-Constable was a public functionary; he was answerable to the Common Law. The French police system had been a composite of central authority, local accountability, and remnants of seigneurial privilege. The transition in Prussia is most clearly from feudal obligations to state responsibility, though even in this case there had been a tradition of vigorous self-government in major trading towns. The problem is that the way in which police functions were carried out can be described in all periods with fair precision, but it is difficult to categorize the operation of police authority in informative developmental terminology. It is quite clear that though the exercise of police functions evolved steadily over the past millennium in Europe, the transition to contemporary systems from pre-existing ones

[20] I am indebted to M. Gabriel Ardant for bringing this point to my attention.

THE POLICE AND POLITICAL DEVELOPMENT IN EUROPE

does not coincide with a shift in forms that transcends the straightforward description of the new organizational patterns.

In pinpointing the emergence of modern police systems, it does not seem adequate to confine attention solely to structural characteristics. A police system may exist in embryo, as it were, for many years before becoming an effective force. Surely one needs to consider the growth in capacities of these systems in order to determine a meaningful date for the emergence of a modern system? The simplest and most precise measure of capacity is numbers of police personnel. This is also an indicator of the resources government is willing to expend on policing. Recognizing the importance of data on police recruitment, I scoured sources in the United States for information on the size of foreign police establishments. The conclusion I have reached is that such data do not exist in the United States. Moreover, I doubt very much whether such data exist in English for any country other than Great Britain. Holdings on European policing affairs are extremely meager in the United States regardless of language. Compilation of tables on the strengths of European police forces for the eighteenth, nineteenth, and twentieth centuries will require bibliographic research on the Continent. It will probably involve archival research. I consider the lack of statistical data on police strength a critical shortcoming of this chapter and a point at which research urgently needs to be directed in the future.

Study of impressionistic evidence, as well as the data at hand, convinces me that there is no serious discrepancy between the dating of the development of existing police systems, as I have done it, and police capabilities. Paris was widely recognized during the *Ancien Régime* as being much better policed than London. The coming of the "new police" in Great Britain is considered to have caused a revolution for the better in the security of life and property. Discipline and order were characteristics of German towns and rural districts in the late eighteenth century; certainly the profligacy and criminality of London were unknown. Size of the police establishment in Italy appears to have grown considerably after 1848 and again after 1860. A strong, effective police force centrally directed was continually justified by reference to the brigandage, unrest, and outright rebellion especially in the south after the *Risorgimento*.

Having found approximately when recognizable contemporary police systems emerged in each country, what factors account for their development at these times? The range of factors that might

[350]

DAVID BAYLEY

influence development are very great. I shall examine seven general hypotheses, each hypothesis dealing with a distinctive set of variables. The sets are: (1) growth of population and its distribution between cities and rural areas; (2) extent of criminality and insecurity; (3) occurrence of a social or economic transformation; (4) occurrence of a political transformation; (5) marked change in general governmental capabilities; (6) an external threat, and (7) an ideological *démarche*.

Can the timing as well as the rate of development of these police systems be explained by reference to the growth of population or the growth of cities? I do not believe so. There is certainly no threshold of population size which seems to compel development of a police system. The population of Paris was approximately 540,000 when that post of Lieutenant-General was established (Mulhall 1903: 446); that of London was about 1,500,000 in 1829 (Mulhall 1903: 446); and that of Berlin somewhere between 50,000 and 100,000 in the middle of the eighteenth century (Emerson 1968: 4; Mulhall 1903: 446). Rates of population growth also do not appear to be significant. France inaugurated its police system before the period of most rapid population expansion: the population grew by about 23 percent in the seventeenth century and by 42 percent in the eighteenth century (Mulhall 1903: 445). The population of Paris, however, appears to have remained almost the same between 1675 and 1800 (Mulhall 1903: 445). Berlin's population tripled during the eighteenth century, from about 55,000 to above 150,000 (Mulhall 1903: 446). London's population grew exponentially before a new police system was created: it grew by one-third during the eighteenth century and almost doubled during the first thirty years of the nineteenth century. The rate of increase declined somewhat in the next thirty years, to about 87 percent; it continued to decline in the subsequent thirty, falling to a rate of about 50 percent (Mulhall 1903: 445). Furthermore, within England there was a wide disparity in population-per-police ratios between London and the rest of England. During the period 1836–1856 municipal forces outside London generally had twice as many people per policeman as did London (Critchley 1967: 67, quoting J. M. Hart).

In short, considering that the rate of population growth rose in all of Western Europe during the period under review, it is no more than a truism to remark that population growth and the foundation of police systems coincide. The more informative point is that there

THE POLICE AND POLITICAL DEVELOPMENT IN EUROPE

is no clear pattern of impingement of population size or change in the rate of increase upon the timing of development of police systems.

There has always been a considerable variation among cities of Western Europe with respect to the number of people per policeman.[21] In 1913 the first year for which comparative statistics on police strength for many European cities have been collected, the number of people per policeman ranged from a low of 207 in Rome and 212 in Lisbon to a high of 660 in Berne and 648 in Stuttgart (Fosdick 1915: 401–402). London had 352, Paris 336, and Berlin 324. Edinburgh and Manchester had ratios respectively of 513 and 528, representing 80 percent more people per policeman than in London. The impact of population growth and aggregation on the size of police establishments is indeterminable, except that the more people there are the more policemen there will be. Police establishments are created by human agency, presumably reacting to certain preceived cues. While population growth may enhance those cues, the reading of them is not straightforward; it varies with individual, country, and time.

Can the emergence of police forces be explained in terms of the incidence of criminality or personal insecurity? Because accurate statistics on crime are unavailable for these historical periods, it is exceedingly difficult to be sure. A comparison of events in London and Paris strongly suggests that insecurity is not sufficient to create a police force. London during the eighteenth century was well known for its criminality, violence, and licentiousness. The writings of Henry Fielding and Patrick Colquhoun bear eloquent testimony to the extent of public insecurity. Serious students of British history, such as Sidney and Beatrice Webb, Max Beloff, Charles Reith, T. A. Critchley, Leon Radzinowicz, and members of the Royal Commission on the Police, 1962, seem amazed at the spectacle of that time.[22] European visitors could not understand why an otherwise civilized people did not follow the example of the French or the Germans whose capital cities were models of order. During the eighteenth century Cabinet Ministers went armed in the streets of London at

---

[21] It would be interesting to determine whether there is a convergence in ratios among European cities. Is the difference among cities with respect to people per policeman getting smaller, remaining the same, or increasing? As I have already indicated, this fascinating question cannot be answered at the present time.

[22] See, respectively, Webb 1913; Beloff 1938: 22–23; Reith 1948: chap. 14; Critchley 1967: 18–24; Radzinowicz 1957: vol. III; Royal Commission 1962: 13–15.

DAVID BAYLEY

high noon protected by gangs of retainers; men of property went to bed with firearms at their sides; on the coasts whole towns turned out to plunder shipwrecks, killing sailors or constables who tried to stop the despoilation; brutality to servants and animals was commonplace; gin-mills flourished; prostitution was rampant; and a vast proportion of the population lived utterly outside the law. According to the Royal Commission, 1962, seventeen Parliamentary Committees investigated the problem of law and order in London during the late eighteenth and early nineteenth centuries.[23] Despite this appalling situation, almost nothing was done: "During this long period of more than three-quarters of a century, from 1750 to 1828, there was no section of public opinion, no group in Parliament or outside, no leading newspaper or periodical which would advocate a reform in the traditional machinery for keeping the peace" (Radzinowicz 1957: vol. 3, 374).

England's attempts at curbing crime in these years relied wholly upon deterrence. In 1819 there were 223 capital offenses in the English criminal law; in France there were 6. Never perhaps has the worth of an ounce of prevention been more apparent. England's criminal law was draconian, prevention of crime through policing nonexistent, and crime flourished. In France the criminal law was comparatively more humane, there was a professional police force that patrolled streets regularly, and its cities were relatively law-abiding.[24]

In short, development of police cannot be understood in terms of crime. The reasons for creation are more complex than that. As two careful students of criminology have argued in the case of criminal punishments, for which we may substitute "police":

> Punishment is neither a simple consequence of crime, nor the reverse side of crime, nor a mere means which is determined by the end achieved. Punishment must be understood as a social

[23] Jenifer Hart (Hart 1951: 27) gives a different figure. She says there were six Parliamentary Committees between 1770 and 1828.

[24] The picture of indiscriminate hangings in England is seriously overdrawn in much of the writing on the period. No doubt hangings were more frequent per capita in the late eighteenth century than in the late nineteenth century. J. L. Parker (Parker 1937: 959ff.) says that there were twice as many in the former period as in the latter, though the population was only one-third as great. At the same time, precisely because the law was so severe, juries and judges hesitated to convict. Furthermore, though the severity of the law increased in terms of capital offenses, the practice diminished. Transportation was increasingly substituted for hanging as punishment for serious crimes and habitual criminals.

THE POLICE AND POLITICAL DEVELOPMENT IN EUROPE

phenomenon freed from both its juristic concept and its social ends. We do not deny that punishment has specific ends, but we do deny that it can be understood from its ends alone. By way of analogy, it might be noted that no one would dream of developing the history of military institutions or a specific army out of the immutable purpose of such institutions (Rusche and Kirchheimer 1968: 5).

Can the emergence of police systems be explained in terms of a major social or economic transformation through which these countries were passing? During the period under review the so-called Industrial Revolution, encompassing the decline of feudalism and the rise of capitalism, shattered and rebuilt European social systems. Though containing the thrust of industrialization in a neat chronology is exceedingly difficult, the periods of most vigorous industrial change, when the economic transformation became confirmed in practice, do not coincide with the rise of today's police systems.

Great Britain is generally considered to have preceded most European nations in this enormous social travail, yet it lagged behind France and Germany in the establishment of its modern national police system. The take-off into industrial growth in France occurred in the early nineteenth century, but its police system had been in place for at least a century. Italy's industrial development was an uneven affair, stronger in the North than in the South. Unification, which established the police system, preceded the most vigorous period of industrial development.

It is also true, however, that economic and social development does impinge on police functions in several pervasive ways. First, it creates new law and order tasks. The forms that crime takes are a reflection of the needs and opportunities confronting individuals. Second, socioeconomic change effects the social basis of community, thus influencing the way in which norms are enforced, rules sanctioned. A feudal society has different control mechanisms than does an urban community composed of autonomous individuals. In modern Germany there are no manors and ascriptive obligations, apart from those of family; policing must be handled, if at all, impersonally. Third, to the extent that economic change thrusts new social strata into politics, government will become increasingly sensitized to a range of enforcement tasks that it may hitherto have neglected. In the United States today, for example, minority groups are con-

DAVID BAYLEY

tinually asking that police meet *their* problems and not be so preoccupied with those of the affluent suburbs.

Economic and social change constitute a vector during this entire
period: in all these countries social and economic forms in the late
nineteenth century are vastly different than in the seventeenth century, and it is possible to characterize this change as being singular.
But the striking point, as with population growth, is not that police
development and social change coincide, but that they exhibit
unique patterns of interrelationship in each country. As Barrington
Moore has argued for the relation between economic change and
political evolution more generally, industrialization impinges differently upon institutions in different countries depending upon the
timing of change, the social interests mediating it, and the distribution of political power (Moore 1966). Just as the results for the political system are diverse, so too are they for police systems.[25]

Can the rise of recognizably contemporary police systems be explained in terms of a political transformation? Let us examine various
kinds of political changes that have occurred in Europe and see
whether they are associated with the establishment of police systems.
It would be reasonable to expect that the consolidation of government in an expanded geographical area—state-building—would be
associated with the creation of a police system. Formation of national governments would be a particularly critical time from the point
of view of social control. This is unambiguously the case in France
and Italy. The *Risorgimento* created a national government where
none had existed before, and with a rigidly centralized police system. Monarchical absolutism began in France in the seventeenth
century. Coincidentally with the consolidation of national power at
the royal court came the rise of a new police system in Paris and
throughout the country. In Germany it is more difficult to make a
case for this linkage. Policing had been in the hands of the landed
nobility before the Great Elector and it continued to be so long af-
terward. Police power in the narrow sense for the *Landrat* and the
Steuerrat did not develop until the middle of the eighteenth century,
during the latter part of the reign of Frederick the Great.[26] Prussian

[25] This analysis is less precise than I would like. It might have been instructive to
compare the expansion of police personnel with changes in levels of educational attainment, per capita gross national product, proportion of work-force in agriculture, and
so forth. However, until data have been assembled on police strength over time, this
analysis will have to be postponed.

[26] It is important to note that police powers in a general sense—the authority to

THE POLICE AND POLITICAL DEVELOPMENT IN EUROPE

bureaucratic absolutism was not built on the back of a state police machine. The preoccupation of Prussian government was with taxation and military affairs; it was content to leave policing to the nobles. The famous Boards of War and Domains were not involved with policing. In Great Britain, finally, there is no relation whatsoever between police development and national consolidation.

Association between dynastic consolidation and a new police system is even weaker. Neither Bourbons, Hohenzollerns, Hanoverians, nor the House of Savoy was threatened by a competing dynasty during the time new police systems emerged. One exception was Cromwell's England, where a novel police system was created to support the Commonwealth. Between 1655 and 1657 Cromwell established a national *Gendarmerie*. England was divided into twelve police districts, each covered by a detachment of mounted military police. The purpose of the system was to repress frivolity in support of the social mores of the Puritan revolution. The army was, as a result, brought into enormous disfavor and the system was abandoned. It could be argued that Napoleon III used the police freely to consolidate his regime in the early 1850s. The police were substantially expanded during this period. Generally, however, though regimes certainly use the police to maintain power, whole systems seem rarely to have been inaugurated or expanded in the process of regime-establishment.

Revolutions too have produced little change in modes of policing. They cannot account for the rise of any of our modern systems, unless the *Risorgimento* is termed a revolution. The English Civil War was the occasion of a police experiment, but it was short-lived and left no lasting mark on the Parish-Constable system that continued in a paralyzed state for another century and a half. The French Revolution, certainly the most dramatic and influential political upheaval of this period, promised to sweep into oblivion the police system of the *Ancien Régime*. It singularly failed to do so. If anything, the system was stronger after the revolution. The prefectoral system of Napoleon I was noticeably more efficient than that of the *Intendants* and it did not differ much in principles of organization and control.

Periods of prolonged political turbulence and social violence are associated to some extent with the rise of modern police systems.

regulate—were certainly created by the Elector. But the expansion of general "police" power from commerce and taxation into policing in the narrow sense occurred not until the second half of the eighteenth century.

DAVID BAYLEY

The *Fronde* convinced Louis XIV and Colbert of the importance of holding central power tightly and of the inadvisability of entrusting police powers to provincial *Parlements* and governors. Tax revolts were a common feature of seventeenth-century French life. Ministers from Mazarin to Colbert were preoccupied with problems of domestic order, as their correspondence with Governors and *Intendants* clearly shows.[27] The fact that the *Intendant* was the primary representative of the central government for taxation and police shows the intimate relationship between resource mobilization and social unrest in France at this time. Napoleon III did expand the police of France considerably during the 1850s when memories of political turbulence in 1848 were still fresh in men's minds. The Prussian Kings, by contrast, were not subject to persistent domestic violence during the eighteenth century and Prussian administration nonetheless gradually developed police functions in the narrow sense. During the nineteenth century the relationship is fairly obvious, for Prussian politics was quite repressive after the interlude with Stein and Hardenberg and this is also the greatest period of police development. The British experience is quite anomalous. Rioting was common throughout the eighteenth century; in fact, it was endemic (Rudé 1964; Beloff 1938; Darvall 1934). The Gordon Riots of 1780 devastated London for five helpless days. The first two decades of the nineteenth century were also a period of great unrest in England. A Prime Minister was killed in the lobby of the House of Commons in 1812; Luddite riots the same year brought more troops to the Midlands than Wellesley had taken to the Peninsula in 1808 (Darvall 1934: 1); and the Peterloo massacre of 1819 showed the bankruptcy of the existing police system. Despite all this, the British hesitated to reform the police. Not until after a period of relative calm was a reformed police force inaugurated. And it was a force that was unarmed and nonpunitive in character. If domestic turmoil did play a role in the formation of the "new police," it did so in a way that must surprise and confound most social historians.

Altogether, there is more evidence of an association between the development of police and political changes than with more subterranean social movements such as population growth, urbanization, industrialization, and criminality. Politics and policing are bound together, though similar political events do not always produce the same police development. What is more, dramatic political changes

[27] I am indebted to M. Gabriel Ardant for this point.

THE POLICE AND POLITICAL DEVELOPMENT IN EUROPE

are sometimes completely unassociated with changes in either mode or efficiency of policing.

Has a change in police systems in the past two or three centuries been associated with an expansion of government capabilities generally? Are police developments part of a general growth in government output-functions? The capabilities of all four governments have expanded dramatically since 1660, so that in a general way there is an association. Once again, analysis is handicapped by the lack of data on police strength. The historical evidence suggests that output capacities of government do not expand across the board at the same time. In France, because so much power was held by *Intendants* and then Prefects, reform of the bureaucracy was automatically reform of police control and supervision. More importantly, one can say that regularized, central police capability in France grew together with improvement in the collection of taxes and major changes in the regulation of the nation's economic life—the policy known as mercantilism. In Germany there is no association of this kind. Frederick, the Great Elector and Frederick the Great both concentrated primarily on building the army and improving collection of taxes. They ignored internal policing. The Boards of War and Domains did not deal with domestic law and order problems. In Britain there was a major expansion of central government administration in the period from Charles II through George I, especially from 1689 to 1715 (Plumb 1934). The Parish-Constable system was unaffected. The second great period of expansion came in the second quarter of the nineteenth century. Here police reform marked the onset of reform. Policing was simply one among several areas in which the policy of private, parish, or borough self-help gave way to a national movement of institutional reform. Demands upon government for a national policy with respect to poor-relief, municipal administration, public health, and economic regulation were growing enormously at the time of the new police experiment. Sometimes, then, police arrangements are expanded as part of a general growth of government capability, but the relation is not constant.

Can the development of new police systems be explained by the presence of an external threat to a country? The "Garrison State" hypothesis of Harold Laswell suggests that when a society is under pressure from outside, social groups tend to draw together in the name of national unity, dissent is less freely tolerated, conformity is insisted upon, and regulative capacities of government are strength-

DAVID BAYLEY

ened (Laswell 1962). If this is true, development of police systems or their expansion might be associated with wars. There is little evidence for this. None of the really great wars of the past three centuries seems to have impelled police reform. France and Prussia were often at war during the latter part of the seventeenth century. The strains engendered by almost continual war during this period undoubtedly placed a premium on more efficient state operation. In the French case, the foundation of today's police system was laid; in Prussia's, policing was unaffected. The crucial difference appears to lie with the reaction of the populace to mobilization for war: the French were unruly, the Prussians were docile. Napoleon's reorganization of the administrative system actually preceded his external adventures. So did Hitler's centralization of the German police in 1936. The British, though locked in what they considered to be a life-and-death struggle with Napoleon, did not expand or reform police operations until almost a generation after Waterloo. It is true, however, that secret police activities, involving political surveillance, were common toward the end of the Napoleonic wars in Great Britain. But Britain's new police did not stem from her reactionary period but rather from her liberal one. The expansion of civil police capacities throughout Europe in the nineteenth century are unassociated with wars. The Crimean War was certainly quite incidental to the expansion of the French police undertaken by Napoleon III in the 1850s. The fact is that wars fought by Britain, France, and Prussia after 1815 were short, nonideological, or colonial. They did not occasion social unrest. Until ideology was revived as a part of internal politics in the twentieth century, police had a small role to play in a war effort. National security was seldom threatened by internal subversion.

External intervention was part of the Italian *Risorgimento*. Italy faced the prospect of war with Austria in the northeast during the 1860s and had to be concerned with French pride and commitment, especially as Italy menaced papal Rome. These alarms of war receded rapidly after 1870. No particular value can be placed on external threats in explaining the rise of the centralized police machine; they were one of many exigencies that placed a premium on efficient national administration. One might argue that the military character of the police was confirmed, not created, by these threats during the 1860s. It was undoubtedly simpler to organize, train, and support a single force for both internal and external security, when both were

THE POLICE AND POLITICAL DEVELOPMENT IN EUROPE

so intimately entwined, than to have an army and a distinct civil constabulary.

Can the development of a police system be explained ideologically, in terms of an intellectual reorientation within a country or across the entire Continent? Considering the wide separation in time of the emergence of these systems, no argument can be sustained that a Continent-wide intellectual movement conditioned formation. Within each nation there is some evidence for this association, especially if absolutism is considered an ideology. Perhaps it was, as much as nationalism became in the nineteenth and twentieth centuries. The practice and philosophy of bureaucratic centralization under an absolute sovereign fertilized police development in France and Prussia, though it seems to have blighted it in Great Britain. Sartine and other Lieutenants-General of Police gave advice freely about municipal policing to foreign powers in the eighteenth century. It can be no accident that the Tsar Peter established an imperial police administration in St. Petersburg in 1718, Frederick II a police director in Berlin in 1742, and Maria Theresa a police commissioner in Vienna in 1751 (Emerson 1968: 4–5). There was a pronounced demonstration effect among absolutist states.

Looking back on the emergence of national police systems in Great Britain, France, Germany, and Italy, one finds a remarkable variety in patterns of development. The essential point is that nations develop characteristic solutions to police problems in response to different factors. Very different things were going on in each country when its police force emerged in recognizably contemporary form. The factors which appear to play the most significant role among all the nations are (1) a transformation in the organization of political power; (2) prolonged violent popular resistance to government; and (3) development of new law and order tasks, as well as the erosion of former bases of community authority, as a result of socioeconomic change. But it must be stressed again that even with respect to these factors, there is not an invariant relation between them and either the reform of an existing system or the marked expansion of a new one.

Evolution of Police Forms

Having discovered that contemporary police systems exhibit considerable variation in form, the next task is to explore the factors which account for the differences. Explanations for characteristic

[360]

DAVID BAYLEY

differences will be formulated with respect to the following attributes of police systems: (1) nature of tasks, (2) structure of the national system, (3) nature of accountability, and (4) professional image and role behavior. Variations with respect to internal organization will not be explained because this would involve details of public administration and I should like to keep the focus on matters of direct political relevance.

One important difference among police systems is the extent to which police tasks include an active role in political life as opposed to preoccupation primarily with prevention of crime and the maintenance of public order. Some police forces are almost exclusively concerned with the security concerns of individual citizens, others are involved with the political security of a regime. The French police, for instance, have played an active role in politics since their inception; the British police have from time to time been thrust into political life, largely as a result of widespread public disorder, but the role has been slight. Among the countries of our sample, persistent intrusion of the police into politics can be explained by two factors.

First, police will play a political role if creation of effective state institutions and formation of the nation are accompanied by serious social violence. Conflict that touches the legitimacy and capacity of the state at the moment of its creation is most likely to constrain police development and to shape it according to political ends. It is also true, however, that prolonged social conflict, once again particularly if it touches the legitimacy or capacity of existing political arrangements, will over time encourage the use of police in political ways.

To speak of state-building is really an enormous oversimplification. If the essence of the process is the establishment of coherent authority throughout a given territory, then it is clear that such a process does not occur across the board simultaneously. Authority may be made coherent first in law, then in adjudication, then in some sorts of tax powers, then in conscription, then in economic regulative activities, and so forth. The surmounting of distributional economic problems—the creation of the "welfare state"—may be looked upon as another stage in "state-building." States, it seems to me, are very diverse entities. To say that two states have been built by a particular point in time suggests that they are similar in penetration by governmental institutions. Yet one "state" may have only a coherent legal and adjudicative system, while another has efficient tax and military

THE POLICE AND POLITICAL DEVELOPMENT IN EUROPE

capabilities. The differences in nature of institutional penetration among states is as interesting and important as searching for the moment when a "state" in any territorial region can be considered to exist.

The point is that there are problems with the concept of state-building. When I refer to "state-building," I should be understood to be pointing to a process of penetration of a territory by a coherent set of institutions along any of several dimensions. There is no assumption that penetration proceeds along all dimensions simultaneously. Returning now to the police in politics: the police will be utilized in politics if this process of penetration, regardless of dimension, is resisted by violence.

The converse of this proposition is that the violence of interpersonal crime or among private groups may be tolerated at comparatively high levels without police being forced into a political posture. If violence is not perceived in political terms it is unlikely to lead to an expanded police role. In Britain, for example, in the eighteenth century there was enormous personal insecurity as well as great destruction due to riots, but the police establishment was not reformed nor were existing police directed according to partisan political ends.

In seventeenth-century France serious and persistent threats to public order had to be overcome. The roots of conflict were various: resentment at centralization of bureaucratic power, tax impositions, and religious rivalry. State-penetration and formation of the nation were both threatened. Great Britain experienced violence as part of national amalgamation in the nineteenth and twentieth centuries. The C.I.D.'s famous Special Branch, responsible for political intelligence and surveillance, was created in 1884 as a direct response to the intractability of the Irish. If the activities of the I.R.A. and Sinn Fein had continued longer, it is an open question whether the British police would still have a reputation for studious political neutrality. Religious conflict is a species of a larger genus, namely, ideological conflict. Nations today may be as fractured by secular ideological strife as nations have been by religious disorder. A country like China may have the one, while India the other, but both situations will encourage political use of the police.

The police role of the Prussian police stems from another sort of conflict. The police power of the noble estate-owners was used throughout the seventeenth and eighteenth centuries in a very diffused way to maintain the feudal settlement. In the nineteenth cen-

DAVID BAYLEY

tury, when the state police force was developed and expanded most markedly, police were used to counter the growing political assertiveness of new social strata. New classes sought to obtain political power commensurate with growing economic strength; this was bitterly resented. As a result the police were used throughout the nineteenth century to repress "Liberal" and then "Social Democratic" elements. In Prussia a political role for the state's police was not confirmed until considerably after the Prussian state had established substantial centralized governmental capacities. It might be argued for Germany as a whole, after 1870, that the price Bismarck paid for a German Empire was the right of local politicians to use the power of the police within each of the individual states to maintain the existing social distribution of political power. As the centralized Prussian state was founded on dispersed police power to be used for political purposes, so the centralized German Empire was founded on dispersed police power, no less politically utilized.

Second, police forces are more apt to play a political role if there is a traditional insistence in the country upon the importance of right-belief. Such a tradition justifies scrutiny of very personal aspects of individual lives. Where the Inquisition was strong, there police forces active in politics are to be found from an early time. This is certainly the case in France; my impression is that it is also true of Spain. The French word for spy—"mouchard"—is taken from Antoine di Mouchi who was a theologian of the University of Paris appointed by Francis I to prosecute Protestants. He was extremely efficient, sending many people to the stake, and he flooded Paris wtih spies and informers (Radzinowicz 1957: vol. 3, 544). In Britain, on the other hand, outward conformity was considered sufficient. Elizabeth I said that she wanted to open no windows into men's souls.[28] In Prussia Protestantism won a fairly quick though bloody victory; its security made it unnecessary for the police to censor religious thought.

Religious heritage in European countries thus appears to have been an important factor in police development: it has encouraged police intrusion into political life if religious conflict challenged formation of a nation and if religious tradition sanctioned surveillance for the purpose of achieving right-belief.

In summary, police forces are more likely to play an active role in politics if social violence accompanies state- or nation-building, if

[28] I am indebted for this reference to Professor S. E. Finer.

THE POLICE AND POLITICAL DEVELOPMENT IN EUROPE

mobilization demands at the time state-penetration is going on occasions popular resistance, if the political system is unable to accommodate without violence demands for increased political participation, and if there is a cultural insistence upon right-belief (see Figure 5–2).[29]

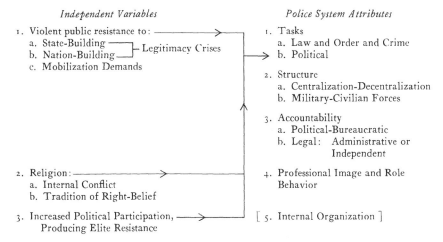

Figure 5–2. Political Involvement of Police

The second aspect of differentiation among national police forces is the structure of the system. Two aspects are important: the extent of centralization and the extent of military participation.

The degree of centralization found in the European examples may be accounted for by four factors.

First, bureaucratic traditions already existing when a new police system is established profoundly influence centralization. Contemporary police systems were not all established at the time state institutions were initially created. In Britain, for instance, state institutions were very much in evidence by the sixteenth and seventeenth centuries; the formation of the contemporary police system was therefore constrained by several centuries of very decentralized bureaucratic tradition. In Prussia, as well, the contemporary system did not begin to grow until almost a century after Frederick the Great Elector. This was a case of an existing centralized bureaucracy becoming involved more and more with a specific new task. It would have been as unthinkable for Prussian administrators to devolve police authority on local government units as it would have been for British

[29] A summary of these relationships is presented schematically in Figure 5–2.

DAVID BAYLEY

statesmen in the nineteenth century to concentrate police authority in the Home Office.

Second, violent public disorder during state- and nation-building encourages police centralization just as it encourages bureaucratic centralization generally. If the legitimacy of new nation-state institutions is jeopardized, resources of the nation-state will be mobilized centrally in their defense.

Third, police systems are more likely to be centralized if mobilization demands are high and stubborn popular resistance is encountered. French kings in the middle and late seventeenth century imposed new taxes and violent resistance was commonplace. The *Intendant* was given power to collect taxes as well as to marshal whatever force was necessary to impose order. These tasks were inextricably mixed. In Prussia, mobilization demands were also great in the late seventeenth century but popular resistance was negligible. As a result, police centralization did not accompany the establishment of the absolutist state. In Great Britain, except for occasional periods such as the Napoleonic wars, mobilization requirements until quite recently have been light and popular violence to state levies has been minimal. In other words, the state could get on financially without coercive instruments in Britain and Prussia but not in France.

Fourth, in all four countries there is a pattern of increased central direction as a result of long-run socioeconomic changes. New law and order tasks have been created in the last hundred years that require national solutions. The boundaries of crime have expanded; crime is increasingly difficult to cope with in small geographical areas. National police agencies, laboratories, training centers, databanks, and communications networks become more and more common.

The argument about centralization can be usefully summarized if the propositions are stated conversely: police systems will be decentralized only if state institutions are created without substantial popular resistance, if mobilization demands are slight or produce little popular resistance, and if bureaucratic traditions derived from state-building are decentralized. The amount of decentralization compatible with efficient policing will decline in the future due to increased intra-national interdependence. This process is already at work.[30]

[30] See Figure 5–3.

THE POLICE AND POLITICAL DEVELOPMENT IN EUROPE

Nations differ considerably with respect to the amount of military involvement in domestic policing. In Italy since unification the military has maintained a separate police establishment—the *Carabinieri*. In Britain there has always been a clear distinction between police constables and military personnel. Though the army was often used from the seventeenth to nineteenth centuries to maintain domestic order, such duty was considered exceptional and was the object of deep public suspicion. Three factors account for the extent of military participation among Great Britain, France, Germany, and Italy: (1) the presence of a large standing-army, (2) the earliness of formation of the standing-army in state experience, and (3) the existence of large-scale and persistent civil strife. It should be noted that the creation of a standing army may itself be explained in terms of geopolitical circumstances, thus the first factor could be reformulated in terms of other variables.

The standing army was a feature of continental state-development. Thus, when order had to be maintained at home, the army was ready-to-hand. In Britain a standing-army did not develop until the seventeenth century and it remained small until the Napoleonic wars. The militia, first created in 1660, was prized by the country politicians precisely because it was an irregular force conceived as a counterpoise to the crown's standing army (Western 1965: part 1). As the army grew during the eighteenth century, it was widely used to maintain order. J. L. and Barbara Hammond say, referring to the latter part of the eighteenth century:

> the north and midlands and the manufacturing region of the south-west came to resemble a country under military occupation. The officers commanding the different districts reported on the temper and circumstances of their districts, just as if they were in a hostile or lately conquered country; soldiers were moved about in accordance with the fluctuations in wages and employment, and the daily life of the large towns was watched anxiously and suspiciously by magistrates and generals (Hammond and Hammond 1967; quoted in Radzinowicz 1957: vol. 4, 121).

Though the standing army grew and was used domestically, a tradition of a separate civilian force had been firmly established in political life. The need for army intervention demonstrated to British

[366]

DAVID BAYLEY

statesmen not that the civil system was expendable but rather that
it needed to be made stronger and more efficient. It is not, therefore,
simply the presence of a standing army but the timing of its growth
in relation to the creation of state political institutions that is
important.

If, however, domestic strife persistently exceeds the capacity of
civilian forces, the military will play a growing role in internal policing. It also seems reasonable to expect that the more internal disorder is associated with a foreign threat, the more likely civilian and
military counterespionage, including political intelligence, will in-
terpenetrate.

The relation between centralization and militarization of police
structures is interesting (see Figure 5–3). Militarization will impel

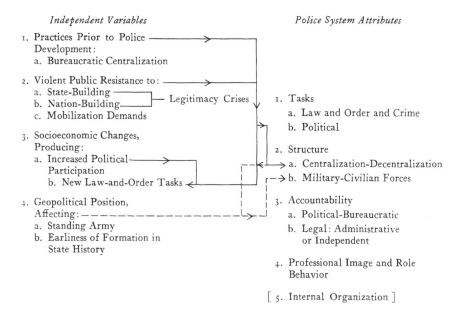

Figure 5–3. Centralization and Military Involvement

centralization, but centralization is irrelevant to militarization. A
central police bureaucracy may defend its domain successfully
against military influence. It might, in fact, be better able to do so
than a decentralized force. A decentralized political elite may welcome military participation in policing. This was the case in Prussia

THE POLICE AND POLITICAL DEVELOPMENT IN EUROPE

during the eighteenth and nineteenth centuries. Military involvement in policing is more a function of political and bureaucratic disposition than organization circumstances.[31]

The third attribute of police systems to be discussed is the manner in which accountability is achieved. Generally, accountability over the police tends to be exercised at that place in the political system where political power is aggregated. There is remarkable coincidence between the structure and control of the police and the organization of police power in any country. If one had no other information about a country except a description in generic terms of the evolution of its police system, it would be possible to identify the country within a very small margin of error. The police are intimately part of the political system. The significance of this discovery lies in what it indicates about the limits for innovation and change in police establishments. It may also provide clues as to future development. For example, in the United States there appears to be a substantial discrepancy between the places at which political power is aggregated and police authority located. I suggest that the pressure on America's 40,000 police forces to amalgamate as well as to accept more state or national government direction will grow in the near future. Increased jurisdiction will probably be given to national police units relative to local ones. In Great Britain the central government has continually extended its supervisory power over local forces, until today it is only a step away from having a national police for all intents and purposes. From 1856 to 1874 the central government made yearly grants to local forces amounting to one-fourth of costs, contingent upon their passing an inspection (Hart 1951: 36). In 1886 the Home Secretary was given the power to make binding regulations upon county forces. The Police Act of 1964, gave supervisory authority to two authorities, the local committees and the Home Secretary. The Home Secretary may make inspections and he may also demand reports. Because he is subject to the will of Parliament, Parliament may now, for the first time, debate matters of law and order anywhere in Great Britain (Critchley 1967: 293–295 and chap. 5).

Conformity between political institutions and police systems was never more clearly demonstrated than in Germany immediately after World War II. In the British, American, and French zones of occupation three separate police systems were established, each of

[31] Ibid.

DAVID BAYLEY

them patterned almost exactly on the model of the occupying power.[32] The Americans created small municipal and communal units of
government, each with elected bodies, and these units served as the basis for police forces. The Americans gave little attention to police
training, believing that radical decentralization and local democracy
were sufficient to ensure a freedom-conserving police force (Jacob
1963: 156–158). The British set up district police commands patterned after British counties. Police committees were established in
each district composed of elected representatives. The state Ministries of Interior were given power to influence police development
through financial grants. The British even tried to create a "highly
professional nonpolitical administration" in these units, including
making the town clerk the chief administrative officer with the may-
or a figurehead. The French, though resisting centralization of police
functions across the Allied occupation zones, placed police forces
under strict control by the state governments, supervised by French
occupation authorities. Police officials were responsible to the
Landrat, little autonomy was given to local officials (Jacob 1963;
Goedhard 1954: especially 109–118 and conclusion). The effect of
these experiments upon German policing was negligible; the structure and control of policing in West Germany today is what it was
in the Weimar Republic and before that in the Second Reich.

The repressiveness of a police regime is not a function of the place
at which political accountability is exercised. Centralized political
regimes are not necessarily more repressive in police policy than decentralized ones. The history of Prussia shows that even extreme
decentralization of police authority is not incompatible with authoritarian regimentation. Similarly in the United States, it would be difficult to convince Blacks in the South that decentralization of police
accountability would augment personal freedom.

Accountability may be obtained through bureaucratic or political
agencies. French police officials report to bureaucrats; British ones
to representative political bodies. Supervision is more likely to be
bureaucratic the greater the scale of police operations and the greater the degree of political centralization. The larger the territorial
scale of police operations, itself a function of political aggregation,
the more likely that the link between police establishment and political authorities, whether representative or oligarchic, will be bureaucratic.

[32] This was also true of the Soviet zone.

THE POLICE AND POLITICAL DEVELOPMENT IN EUROPE

Police accountability can also be achieved through legal mechanisms. The British police, both Parish-Constable and Bobby, have always been as responsible under law as any citizen. Italian police, by contrast, as well as German and French, have special status under law as officials of the state. They are responsible to administrative tribunals and to a corpus of law articulating state interests. One should not jump to the conclusion that a fair measure of justice will not be meted out through an administrative law system; any more than one can conclude that a legal system predicated on individuals as actors is always just. The determination of whether accountability is exercised through administrative or nonadministrative courts is a descriptive, not a normative, exercise. What is more important is the extent to which the legal order—meaning both the body of law and the adjudicating mechanisms—is independent of executive perceptions of interest. Three factors have contributed to independent legal accountability in our four national examples. First, if a state-based legal order predates the creation of a central bureaucracy or a police system, accountability is more likely to be independent of executive requirements. This was the case in Great Britain; it was to some extent the case in France; it was not the case in Prussia or Italy. Second, if the creation of state institutions is uncontested the pressures to centralize law and order administration will be weak and the legal tradition is less likely to be state-centered. Third, if the creation of state institutions does not involve mobilization demands and these in turn do not occasion violent popular resistance, police are more apt to be legally responsible to independent judicial bodies. In short, those factors which encourage utilization of the police for political purposes, especially during the creation of viable state institutions, also erode the opportunity to exercise control over the police through an independent legal order. Those states with police active in politics also have administrative legal systems (see Figure 5–4).

From what has been said, it is clear that police systems fit within a context of political practice and experience. There is a wider lesson as well. Police systems exhibit an enormous inertial strength over time; their forms endure even across the divides of war, violent revolution, and shattering economic and social change. The fact is that people seem to become habituated to certain procedures and organizational patterns; they do not know what else to do even when given the chance. Allied occupation policy in West Germany clearly shows

[370]

DAVID BAYLEY

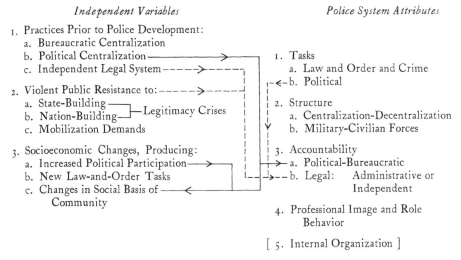

Independent Variables　　　　　　　　　　　*Police System Attributes*

1. Practices Prior to Police Development:
   a. Bureaucratic Centralization
   b. Political Centralization
   c. Independent Legal System

2. Violent Public Resistance to:
   a. State-Building
   b. Nation-Building — Legitimacy Crises
   c. Mobilization Demands

3. Socioeconomic Changes, Producing:
   a. Increased Political Participation
   b. New Law-and-Order Tasks
   c. Changes in Social Basis of
       Community

1. Tasks
   a. Law and Order and Crime
   b. Political

2. Structure
   a. Centralization-Decentralization
   b. Military-Civilian Forces

3. Accountability
   a. Political-Bureaucratic
   b. Legal:　Administrative or
                  Independent

4. Professional Image and Role
   Behavior

[5. Internal Organization]

Figure 5–4. Accountability

the enormous power of hallowed ideas and customary behavior over both occupied and occupier.

Among police systems institutional patterns are very unyielding. Consider the reluctance of the British to abandon the thoroughly dilapidated Parish-Constable system. People were put to enormous danger, inconvenience, and expense for a hundred and fifty years without effective remedial action being taken. They refused to accept a paid, professional force even though it would have been responsible to Parliament. Their reluctance cannot be blamed on the absence of alternatives. The French and the Prussian examples were well known. In London itself there had been successful experiments with full-time paid policemen beginning with Henry and John Fielding in the mid-eighteenth century and Patrick Colquhoun's Thames River Police in 1798. One abortive attempt at establishing a metropolitan police force was made by Pitt in 1785, but it foundered on the obstinacy of the merchants of the City of London. So badly burned was the government of the day by this episode that reform was considered untouchable for almost half a century. How does one explain this muddle-headedness, this inability to use known practices to procure elemental security? The answer is that the notion of a paid, professional police force maintained by non-Parish authorities offended the sense of constitutional propriety of England's po-

THE POLICE AND POLITICAL DEVELOPMENT IN EUROPE

litical elite. It was equated with the destruction of cherished liberties. As Peel put the issue: "I want to teach people that liberty does not consist in having your house robbed by organized gangs of thieves, and in leaving the principal streets of London in nightly possession of drunken women and vagabonds."[33] One can make no greater mistake than to overestimate the ability of circumstances—even quite painful ones—to teach people the value of doing differently. In the British case, the argument against reform was strengthened by international ideological conflict. Professional policing was associated with the tyrannous practices of continental absolutism. Englishmen could not view French or Prussian precedents with an unjaundiced eye. Only after the Jacobin peril receded could the British accept a practice which had continental associations. There may be a lesson in this as well for reform in the United States in our own hardly less ideological age.

The continuity of French administrative practice before and after the revolution is another illustration of the enormous persistence of practice. In the first flush of revolution all the police of the *Ancien Régime* were swept away. But they filtered back, like water rising through sand, both in terms of the forms of administration and the very personnel themselves. As de Tocqueville said, "every time that an attempt is made to do away with absolutism the most that could be done has been to graft the head of liberty onto a servile body" (de Tocqueville 1955: 209). Faced with the requirements of governing, French politicians constructed according to what they knew. Bureaucratic centralism was to persist, constituting a powerful force for stability, continuity, purposeful government, and political socialization.

Even major social dislocations like the Industrial Revolution do not change the course of police history invariably. The structure and control of national police systems continue to display unique features from country to country even though they have felt the effects of what is usually described as a singular economic transformation. Study of the mutations of national police development bears out Dahrendorf's assertion: "Contrary to the beliefs of many, the Industrial Revolution is not the prime mover of the modern world at all. . . . Every country absorbs industrialization into its own traditions; every country assimilates the process in a manner peculiar to it alone;

[33] Critchley 1967: 54, quoting a spoken exchange of Peel with the Duke of Wellington, who led the fight for Peel's reform in the House of Lords.

DAVID BAYLEY

in every country there emerges an amalgamation of cultural traditions and ramifications of industrialization characteristic of it alone" (Dahrendorf 1967: 46–47).

The fourth attribute of contemporary police systems to be explained has to do with professional image and role behavior. Given the general lack of data about this topic and its impressionistic form at best, analysis cannot be as definite as in the preceding discussion. It is possible, however, to link contemporary characteristics with formative historical experiences during the period when these police systems developed.

The London police of 1829 faced enormous public hostility. Peel's system was a revolutionary experiment whose success depended upon persuading people that police did not constitute a threat to cherished liberties. Their behavior was deliberately and dramatically low-key, nonauthoritarian, and informal. They were not allowed to carry weapons. It was not even clear at the time whether it was advisable for them to wear distinctive uniforms. Peel and the first Commissioners, Rowan and Mayne, decided after a great deal of consideration that the police should be uniformed in order to make the constable more visible and hence more responsible. So great was the public dislike of plainclothes policemen that a detective squad was not organized until 1842—and then it numbered only five men—and a formal C.I.D. was not created until 1878. The uniform adopted was dull, completely lacking in military glamor. It consisted of blue tailed coat, blue trousers, and glazed black top hat (Critchley 1967: 51). No suspicion was to be aroused that the police were a state military force in other guise. Police constables were distinguished individually by a number worn prominently on their uniforms. French policemen did not begin to wear numbers until after 1852; German policemen not until after World War II and it may not yet be universal; Italian policemen still do not do so.

British policemen were always imbued with the notion that they were servants, not masters, of the people. Policemen were trained to act individually; rarely did they patrol in groups. They were always accountable to the law. Prevention of crime as well as control of disorder was to be achieved with the least display of force possible. British policemen molded their behavior pragmatically to accomplish very specific ends; being a policeman was not a matter of playing a visible authority-role, though in the end it came to mean that in a peculiarly subtle way.

[373]

THE POLICE AND POLITICAL DEVELOPMENT IN EUROPE

The French police were created to accomplish state purposes. The ethos was not of service to individual citizens but of responsiveness to state direction. Though public opinion was probably not less antagonistic to the plainclothes police officer in France than in Great Britain, detectives, spies, and informers have been a fixture of the French police establishment since its inception. Uniformed police officers have characteristically worked in small groups, rarely alone. They have always been impressively armed. In the seventeenth and eighteenth centuries considerable reliance was placed on army personnel for preventive patrolling. Recruitment from the military to the police has always been heavy at all rank levels. Separation of executive and judicial functions in the exercise of police powers was not confirmed until the nineteenth century. During the eighteenth century, justice had been swift at the hands of the rural *Gendarmerie*, for its officers possessed full judicial powers.

The relatively more authoritarian character of the Prussian and German police is part of the extensive regimentation that has been a feature of this political heritage. The Prussian police, like citizens generally, were taught to emulate the soldier and to serve the state unquestioningly. That the military model was assiduously adopted can be seen in small things. In the middle of the nineteenth century police campaigned for permission to wear the spiked helmet of the Prussian soldier. Over army protests, the favor was granted (Liang 1970: 28). Until Weimar, police officers were invariably retired army officers. After World War I the requirement of military service for recruits was relaxed, but the physical discipline and training of policemen remained very high and was patterned on the army. As a result, only the most robust youths could join. In Berlin during the Weimar period recruits were drawn heavily from rural East Prussia because they were apt to be stronger and more malleable. While they were probably politically more reliable as well, they could not have had much understanding of the human problems of Berlin during those anxious, violent days (Liang 1970: 58–59). Even today in Germany recruits spend several years living a barracks life before being promoted to municipal or state forces.

The Italian police have been dominated by the military since unification. Today the officers of the P.S., supposedly a counterpoise to the *Carabinieri*, are recruited from the military. Circumstances in Italy over the past hundred years have encouraged army discipline, training, and usage. The south of Italy seethed with uprisings, inter-

DAVID BAYLEY

personal violence, and brigandage during the last years of the nine-teenth century. In the burgeoning industrial areas of the north, violence was common. Confrontation continues to be a prime tactic of Italy's labor unions. Italian policemen consider the maintenance of law and order their major responsibility. They are heavily armed and always work in groups.

In sum, the role behavior of policemen in all these countries is a reflection of the purposes for which the force was created and the political culture of the country, especially the way in which authority is manifested by government officials.

The discussion of this section has shown that characteristic solutions to police problems, if one sets aside role behavior and professional image, can be explained in terms of six independent variables. These variables are presented in summary form in Figure 5–5. The

Independent Variables

1. Practices Prior to Police Development:
   a. Bureaucratic Centralization
   b. Political Centralization
   c. Independent Legal System

2. Violent Public Resistance to:
   a. State-Building ⎱
   b. Nation-Building ⎰ Legitimacy Crises
   c. Mobilization Demands

3. Socioeconomic Changes, Producing:
   a. Increased Political Participation
   b. New Law-and-Order Tasks
   c. Changes in Social Basis of Community

4. Geopolitical Position, Affecting:
   a. Standing Army
   b. Earliness of Formation in State History

5. Religion:
   a. Internal Conflict
   b. Tradition of Right-Belief

6. Increased Political Participation, Producing Elite Resistance

Police System Attributes

1. Tasks
   a. Law and Order and Crime
   b. Political

2. Structure
   a. Centralization-Decentralization
   b. Military-Civilian Forces

3. Accountability
   a. Political-Bureaucratic
   b. Legal: Administrative or Independent

4. Professional Image and Role Behavior

[5. Internal Organization]

Figure 5–5. Variables Used in the Analysis of Police Systems

reader should note that there are interrelationships among the independent variables. Of special interest is the fact that increased political participation may generate new law and order problems in two

[375]

THE POLICE AND POLITICAL DEVELOPMENT IN EUROPE

ways. Demand for increased participation may be violent. More interestingly, through representation of new strata, existing but hitherto unperceived law and order tasks may at last be noted. The new law and order needs thus find political voice.

One lesson that has emerged from this study is the impermeability of national police systems over time. This, however, is not the whole story. Systems do change. Moreover, they do so to some extent in converging directions. Areas of convergence in police system development are greatest with respect to internal organization and task-definition. Convergence is least noticeable with respect to national structure, control, and role behavior. Training programs have become longer and more elaborate in all these countries in the past half century. There is also much greater specialization of functions within the forces. The detective-patrolman division has been hardened, with the former being the more prestigious, and functional specialties have developed within each branch. Even in Britain, which recently reaffirmed the practice of selecting top command personnel exclusively by promotion, there is growing recognition that command responsibility requires special talent (Royal Commission 1962: 90–95). So far special training for higher ranks has been the only concession to this requirement, but it may not be long before direct recruitment is permitted or much shortened probationary periods as patrolmen are allowed for highly qualified applicants. In general, those elements of police organization change most readily where a standard of efficiency can be brought to bear. Since efficiency is a function of tasks and environment, if both are similar from country to country, different systems will tend to innovate in convergent ways.

There is evidence of convergence at a few points with respect to structure, control, and role behavior as well. Even in decentralized systems, such as Britain's or Germany's, central training and forensic facilities are common. The Germans and British have made great strides in the twentieth century in the direction of ensuring effective cooperation among forces. The Police Act, 1964, in Great Britain makes local forces responsible to Parliament, through the Home Secretary. Britain has not yet grasped the nettle of full nationalization, but it is much closer to it in practice than it was a century ago. Legal accountability, as well, has shown changes. There is strong support in Great Britain for having the government incur the costs of monetary damages assessed against policemen for actions undertaken in

DAVID BAYLEY

the line of duty. Policemen have always been liable individually for their actions as policemen. Since their ability to pay civil damages was slight, scant recompense was to be had by the aggrieved party. Conversely, on the continent my impression is that administrative courts are more anxious than they used to be to provide relief to citizens against individual policemen. Accordingly, more attention is being given to complaint procedures, to making the police officer identifiable individually to citizens, and to specifying those actions government considers improper in a policeman.

The most difficult area to explore is that of role behavior and professional image. The policemen of each nation still display distinctive traits. At the same time, the importance of good public relations has received much more attention in France, Germany, and Italy in the last decade or so. The British, on the other hand, worried about a decline in respect for policemen, are openly wondering whether they need to provide policemen with firearms.

All in all, there are processes of convergence at work: those which are traceable to conditions of task-performance shift more rapidly than those which involve the organization and control of political power.

Conclusion

This chapter has sought to explain why contemporary police systems have assumed the forms they have. Attributes of contemporary systems have been treated as dependent variables. Analysis has been framed in terms of five attributes of police systems, to which have been linked seven independent variables dealing with historical development. In order to pull together the bits and pieces of this comparative analysis, I shall reprise the major propositions about police development that have been generated:

1. The contemporary police systems of Great Britain, France, Germany, and Italy differ substantially with respect to definition of tasks, structure of the national system, manner in which accountability is achieved, internal organization and practice, and role behavior and professional image.

2. Not only are police systems unique nationally, their distinctive features are relatively impermeable in the face of wars, revolutions, and major social and economic transformations. The distinctive characteristics of these police systems have shown remarkable stability over time.

[377]

THE POLICE AND POLITICAL DEVELOPMENT IN EUROPE

3. The contemporary systems of these nations emerged at different periods of time: Great Britain's between 1829 and 1888; France's in the latter seventeenth century; Germany's (or Prussia's) from the mid-eighteenth century to 1872; and Italy's between 1859 and 1870.

4. The development of today's national police systems cannot be accounted for by population growth, urbanization, incidence of criminality, or industrialization.

5. The development of today's systems can be accounted for in terms of a transformation in the organization of political power, prolonged violent popular resistance to government, and the creation of new law and order tasks as well as the erosion of social bases upon which community authority relations were established.

6. The characteristic forms of police systems can be explained by the interaction among seven variables: practices prior to modern police development having to do with the organization of power, social violence, socioeconomic change, geopolitical position, religion, and elite reactions to demands for increased political participation.

7. Patterns of police system growth are converging very slightly with respect to structure of the national system, nature of force units, and means of exercising accountability. Convergence is most clear in connection with those features involving task-performance where a standard of efficiency may appropriately be applied.

Analysis focusing upon police systems as dependent variables can reveal only half the story about relations between police and their political environment. The other half concerns the effect of police operations and organization upon the encapsulating society. There is a reciprocal relationship between the police and politics. The police are not completely passive; they can play a formative role in determining the character of political life.

The manner and extent to which police have influenced politics in different nations is a complex subject, one that would require extended discussion and considerable further research. Let me only say, at the risk of being provocative without satisfying, that police organizations appear to affect politics in at least five distinguishable ways: (1) by direct impingement of their role activities upon political life; (2) by political socialization of citizens in authoritative contacts; (3) by serving as an avenue for political recruitment and advancement; (4) by socializing policemen to politics; and (5) by be-

DAVID BAYLEY

ing a particular kind of institution, capable of exerting a demonstration effect and creating various kinds of effective demands.

While the characteristics of police systems—tasks, structure, accountability, etc.—can be treated as dependent variables related to conditions of national histories, the political outputs of police systems cannot be treated as dependent variables exclusively related to characteristics of police systems. Another major variable is required to explain political outputs, a variable which is not a function of the police establishment itself. This critical variable is the determination made by a political elite about the use to which it is to be put. Thus, while attributes of police systems do affect their political output, they are not a sufficient cause of the nature of political impingement by the police establishment.

Historical events shape police institutions; police organization and practice affect political life; political life conditions future historical development. This system of interaction feeds back upon itself, though the system is by no means closed. The units of this analysis are presented in Figure 5–6, though the relations among them are too complex for representation in a single chart.

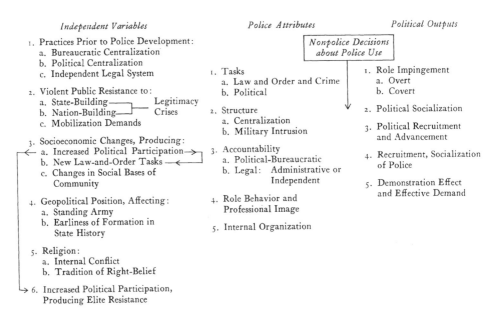

Independent Variables	*Police Attributes*	*Political Outputs*

1. Practices Prior to Police Development:
  a. Bureaucratic Centralization
  b. Political Centralization
  c. Independent Legal System		

	Nonpolice Decisions about Police Use	

	1. Tasks
	  a. Law and Order and Crime
	  b. Political
		1. Role Impingement
		  a. Overt
		  b. Covert

2. Violent Public Resistance to:
  a. State-Building ⎤ Legitimacy
  b. Nation-Building ⎦ Crises
  c. Mobilization Demands
	2. Structure
	  a. Centralization
	  b. Military Intrusion
		2. Political Socialization
		
		3. Political Recruitment and Advancement

3. Socioeconomic Changes, Producing:
← a. Increased Political Participation →
  b. New Law-and-Order Tasks ←
  c. Changes in Social Bases of Community
	3. Accountability
	  a. Political-Bureaucratic
	  b. Legal: Administrative or Independent
		4. Recruitment, Socialization of Police
		
		5. Demonstration Effect and Effective Demand

4. Geopolitical Position, Affecting:
  a. Standing Army
  b. Earliness of Formation in State History
	4. Role Behavior and Professional Image
	
	5. Internal Organization	

5. Religion:
  a. Internal Conflict
  b. Tradition of Right-Belief		

→ 6. Increased Political Participation, Producing Elite Resistance		

Figure 5–6. Police Organization and Political Life

BIBLIOGRAPHY

Arnold, Eric A.

 1969 "Administrative Leadership in a Dictatorship: The Position of Joseph Fouché in the Napoleonic Police, 1800–1810" (unpublished Ph.D. dissertation, Columbia University).

Barzini, Luigi.

 1964 *The Italians* (New York: Atheneum).

Beloff, Max.

 1938 *Public Order and Popular Disturbances, 1660–1714* (London: Oxford University Press).

Chapman, Brian.

 1953 "The Prefecture of Police," *Journal of Criminal Law, Criminology, and Political Science*, 44: 505–521.

Cramer, James.

 1964 *The World's Police* (London: Cassell and Co.).

Critchley, T. A.

 1967 *A History of Police in England and Wales, 900–1066* (London: Constable).

Dahrendorf, Ralf.

 1967 *Society and Democracy in Germany* (New York: Doubleday).

Darvall, Frank O.

 1934 *Popular Disturbances and Public Order in Regency England* (London: Oxford University Press).

Dawson, William H.

 1914 *Municipal Life and Government in Germany* (London: Longmans, Green).

Emerson, Donald E.

 1968 *Metternich and the Political Police* (The Hague: Nijhoff).

Finer, Herman.

 1962 *The Major Governments of Modern Europe* (New York: Harper and Row).

Fosdick, Raymond B.

 1915 *European Police Systems* (New York: The Century Co.).

Fried, Robert C.

 1963 *The Italian Prefects: A Study in Administrative Politics* (New Haven: Yale University Press).

Goedhard, Neil.

 1954 "Organization and Administration of the Police in Western Germany, 1945–1950" (unpublished M.A. Thesis, School of Public Administration, University of Southern California).

BIBLIOGRAPHY

Hammond, J. L., and Hammond, Barbara.

    1967 *The Town Labourer 1760–1832: The New Civilisation* (New York: A. M. Kelley).

Hart, Jenifer M.

    1951 *The British Police* (London: George Allen & Unwin).

Holborn, Hajo.

    1969 *A History of Modern Germany, 1840–1945* (New York: Alfred Knopf).

Jacob, Herbert.

    1963 *German Administration Since Bismarck* (New Haven: Yale University Press).

Laswell, Harold.

    1962 "The Garrison State Hypothesis Today," in Samuel P. Huntington, ed., *Changing Patterns of Military Politics* (Glencoe: Free Press), 51–70.

Liang, Hsi-Huey.

    1970 *The Berlin Police Force in the Weimar Republic* (Berkeley: University of California Press).

Moore, Barrington.

    1966 *Social Origins of Dictatorship and Democracy: Lord and Peasant in the Making of the Modern World* (Boston: Beacon Press).

Mulhall, Michael G.

    1903 *The Dictionary of Statistics* (London: George Routledge).

Muncy, Lysbeth W.

    1944 *The Junker in the Prussian Administration Under William II. 1888–1914* (Providence: Brown University Press).

Parker, J. L.

    1937 "Law and Police," in Edward Eyre, ed., *European Civilisation: Its origins and development—Economic History of Europe since the Reformation* (London: Oxford University Press), 893–993.

Radzinowicz, Leon.

    1957 *A History of English Criminal Law and its Administration from 1750* (New York: Macmillan; 4 vols.).

Reith, Charles.

    1948 *A Short History of the British Police* (London: Oxford University Press).

Ridley, F., and Blondel, J.

    1965 *Public Administration in France* (New York: Barnes and Noble).

Rosenberg, Hans.

    1958 *Bureaucracy, Aristocracy and Autocracy: The Prussian Experience 1660–1815* (Cambridge: Harvard University Press).

Royal Commission on the Police.

    1962 *Final Report* (London: Her Majesty's Stationery Office).

BIBLIOGRAPHY

Rudé, George.

1964 *The Crowd in History: A Study of Popular Disturbances in France and England, 1730–1848* (New York: Wiley).

Rusche, George, and Kirchheimer, Otto.

1968 *Punishment and Social Structure* (New York: Russell and Russell).

Smith, Denis Mack.

1968 *A History of Sicily: Modern Sicily* (London: Chatto and Windus).

1968 *The Making of Italy, 1796–1870* (New York: Walker).

Stead, Philip John.

1957 *The Police of Paris* (London: Staples Press).

de Tocqueville, Alexis.

1955 *The Old Regime and the French Revolution.* Trans. by Stuart Gilbert (Garden City, N.Y.: Doubleday; Anchor Books).

Webb, Sidney, and Webb, Beatrice.

1913 *English Local Government* (London: Longmans, Green).

Western, John R.

1965 *The English Militia in the Eighteenth Century* (London: Routledge & Kegan Paul).

[5]

Polizei

Franz-Ludwig Knemeyer

I. Introduction: Survey of the Term's Development

In the German language the concept 'Polizei' has a history reaching back five hundred years. Deriving from the Greek 'πολιτεία' and adapted as the Latin 'politia' the word 'Polizei' — also written as 'Pollicey', 'Pollicei', 'Policey', 'Policei', 'Pollizey', 'Pollizei' and 'Polluzey' — was adopted into the official language of the German Empire and the language of the estates from the Burgundian Chancellories (Segall, 1914, pp. 13f, 18f.). This foreign term was used first to characterise governmental rule over all those areas of the common good that were not, or only partially, comprehended by the concepts of 'right' and 'peace' (Maier, 1966a p. 121).

Statutes in the years 1464, 1476, 1482, 1488, 1490, 1492, 1495 constitute, so far as can be determined, the first evidence for the use of the word 'Polizei' on the part of German legislators. The statutes of the fifteenth to the seventeenth centuries recognise only two meanings for the term 'Polizei':

a) Polizei = a condition of order in the community;
b) Polizei = Statute aimed at the institution and/or maintenance of order in the community (Knemeyer, 1967, p. 165).

Other writings however, beginning with humanistic and theological literature, display a wider set of definitions. Karolina Zobel has shown in particular the divergence of usage between official and learned writing:

> While the offices cling to the established meaning of 'Polizei' as 'order and government' (*ordenung and regiment*), which represents no extension of the chancellory style, the scholars of the sixteenth and seventeenth centuries make much freer with this terminology only recently introduced from the Burgundian language of administration. Moreover, here direct access to the classical writers of Antiquity through the influence of Humanism plays a part. Scholars, on reading Greek philosophers of the state like Plato and Aristotle, recall the real origin of this term and prepare the way for a significantly extended and deepened conception. (Zobel, 1952, Pt. I p. 10)

For them the concept *Polizei* comprehends Commonality itself. It includes both State and City as well as their constitution (Maier, 1966, p. 122).

The word 'Polizei' eventually took on another meaning in the 'Polizeiwissenschaft' (science of police) of the seventeenth and eighteenth centuries; this can be distinguished from the usage of the statutes by considering the formation and objective of this scientific domain. While the statutes are aimed at the institution and maintenance of order, *Polizeiwissenschaft* is concerned with the *content* of this 'order'. It puts forward theories which are concerned with the detailed conditions for the institution and/or maintenance of order, and in consequence has to grapple with the objective of the State itself and the forms of State activity considered requisite for the establishment of order. Systematic investigations into the content of the laws themselves lead to the demarcation of those State activities comprehended in the concept 'Polizei' from the original task incumbent on the state of preserving peace and legality (the latter in terms of general jurisdiction). 'Polizei' is marked off from the external affairs of the State, from financial and military concerns, and this leads — in a manner which parallels the varied differentiation of authorities in specific territories — to a demarcation from the functions of direction and control on the part of government (Maier, 1966, p. 184ff; Damkowski, 1969, p. 86). The distinction between 'government' and 'Polizei' in the sense of 'internal administration' (*innere Verwaltung*) was however never precisely made. It is significant that even today there is a lack of clear distinction between government (*Regierung*) and administration (*Verwaltung*) in their spheres of responsibility.

Only in the mid-eighteenth century did the three streams of meaning (from statutes, general literature and *Polizeiwissenschaft*) join together and gain some clarity, despite the breadth of material contained in the term 'Polizei'. This is altered of course with the transformation of State objectives (Welfare State, Security State); but this apart, from the second half of the eighteenth century the conceptual development of the concept 'Polizei' is over for the next two hundred years. Only today are there signs that the broad 'practical' concept of 'Polizei' has been suppressed in the attempt to introduce a unified federal police law and legal terminology, leaving the institutional concept — 'polizei' = uniformed police — as a remnant (cf. Knemeyer, 1975, p. 34).[2]

In this institutional conception of 'Polizei' then the term approaches for the first time in its history the generally-understood meaning of 'Polizei'.

This rapid overview has been necessary because the numerous

definitions and explications of the term that can be found, above all in the textbooks of *Polizeirecht* (police law) but also in the dictionaries of the nineteenth and twentieth centuries, frequently confuse the different meanings of the word 'Polizei', or present these in a partial fashion. Textbooks of *Polizeirecht* for instance present almost without exception the definition appropriate to the old *Polizeiwissenschaft*, since naturally enough such scholarly literature is more accessible or at least readable than the sources themselves. Thus it can happen that the dissertation of Hans Harold Scupin which is concerned with the development of the concept 'Polizei' and its usage in the new German laws (and is as such typical for the nineteenth and twentieth centuries) criticises this writer's article on the concept 'Polizei' without taking account of the fact that the passage that he criticises occurs in an article devoted to the concept 'Polizei' between the fifteenth and eighteenth centuries (Scupin, 1970, p. 5; Knemeyer, 1967, p. 153ff).
... In addition to that Scupin's presentation is distorted by his use of the present-day distinction and definition found in legal textbooks between the formal and practical concepts of 'Polizei'. Only in the early eighteenth century does one first meet such a distinction.

II.

1. Concepts of Polizei in Laws and Decrees from the Fifteenth to the Eighteenth Centuries

a) *A Condition of Order in the Community*. 'Polizei existed' when freemen or subjects conducted themselves in an orderly, modest, courteous, and respectable fashion wherever human life was organised communally. A number of Reich and territorial laws promulgated in the period from the fifteenth to the seventeenth centuries (but also into the eighteenth) have this sense. Laws from the second half of the fifteenth century constitute as far as can be ascertained the first instances of the use of the term 'Polizei' by German makers of laws and decrees.

On 26th July 1464 the city of Nuremberg received as an imperial privilege the right to regulate, provide and dispose *pollitzey und regirung*.[3] In a regulation promulgated by Bishop Rudolf von Scherenberg in 1476 in his capacity as *Landesherr* for Würzburg was contained the declaration that 'this town is provided with praiseworthy *polliceien* and good order' (Hoffmann, 1955, p. 182 No. 364).[4] The same Bishop declared in an 'Order of 1490 that he conceived it as his task in "pollicey und wesentlichkeyt (substance)" to make our city of Würzburg of good standing (Hoffmann, 1955,

p. 182 No. 379).'⁵⁻ Two Nuremberg Council Decrees from the years
1482 and 1492, as well as the constitution imposed on the town of
Bingen in 1488 by the Kürfurst Berthold von Henneberg of Mainz,
employ the word 'Polizei' in connection with the word 'Regiment'
(Baader, 1861, pp. 46, 56). Berthold made the freemen swear 'to
be obedient in affairs and orders relating to the *Regiment* and
Polizei of that town' (Segall, 1914, p. 17).⁶ At the end of the
1485 Territorial Regulations of the Baden Markgrafschaft it was
stated that 'regulations had been established and should be followed
for the sake of 'guter policei' and the common good' (Carlebach,
1906, Vol. I. p. 117).⁷ It can also be read in the *Reichspolizeiordnung* of 1530 that while order and *Policey* were necessary, this
had met with no real fulfilment (*Neue und vollständigere* . . .,
1747, Vol. 2 p. 333).⁸ A Cleves law of 1534 was directed against
the 'disorder of *policyen*' (Scotti, 1826, p. 86 No. 39). A Württemberg mandate in the year 1535 directed against the Münster
Anabaptists talked of 'good Christian *Polizei*' (cited in Schmucker,
1958, p. 4).

Laws were promulgated all over Germany in the seventeenth
century as well whose object was the establishment and/or maintenance of good order in the community. Thus for example the
Württemberg Code (*Landrecht*) or 1610 contained regulations
aimed at 'the maintenance of good *Policey*' (Riecke, n.d., 5). A
Saxonian law was promulgated in 1612 'so that good *Policey*,
morals and respectability' could be maintained (Lünig, 1724, Vol. I.
p. 1453).⁹ In 1616 a law of Nassau-Catzenellenbogen declared that
the welfare of the country rested among other things on good
Polizei (von der Nahmer, 1831, Vol. I. p. 115ff.). In a *Kreisabschied*
from Upper Saxony in 1654 it was stated that 'all good order is
gone to ruin, and instead of good *Policey*, morals, and respectability the most disgraceful disorder rules' (Moser, 1747, p. 141).¹⁰
It can be read in a Brandenburg law of 1688 that without the fear
of God a peaceful life could not be led, nor good *Policey* instituted
or maintained (Mylius, 1714, Pt. 3 p. 6).

In all these examples, and in the further cases that can be found
in Zobel and Knemeyer¹¹ the word 'Polizei' has the meaning of a
condition of order in the community — although the word is often
only used once, and then mostly in a preamble (Maier, 1966a,
p. 120).

During the eighteenth century the same thing was in part understood by the term 'Polizei' (Knemeyer, 1967, p. 158). Dithmar,
one of the first *Polizeiwissenschaftler*, defined *'Policei'* as consisting
'in the good order and constitution of the persons and affairs of
a state' (1745, p. 134).¹²

b) *'Polizei' = 'Polizeigesetz' (= duties laid down by authority).* A further, while subsidiary, content for the term exists in a series of sources from the fifteenth to the eighteenth centuries. 'Polizei', without the addition of a second word, partly has the meaning of *Polizeigesetz* i.e. it comprehends a law whose object is the establishment and/or maintenance of good order in the community. In a Bavarian law of 1557 which stated that the previously decreed 'Polizei' had in its execution borne heavily upon the subjects, the term 'Polizei' has the sense of 'Polizeigesetz'. This concerns however only an abbreviation of a term frequently used elsewhere in the same law, 'Polizei-Ordnung'. A regulation issued in 1540 by Markgraf Johann von Cüstrin announced that 'freemen shall comply with this order or any other "Bürgerlichen Policey"' (Mylius, 1740, p. 19).[13] The freemen were thus bidden to comply not only with the law of 1540 within which this expression occurs, but with all other regulations of 'bürgerliche Polizei'.

When in the majority of laws it is stated that 'we have accordingly set up the following order and *Policey*' (Policey Ordnung, 1537, pp. 6, 1, 1751, pp. 39, 44), or when one reads 'citizens must follow this *Policei und Ordnung*', this is devoid of special significance. These are simply expressions that were at the time highly thought of; they comprehend 'Polizeigesetze' as well (Maier, 1966a, p. 120 espec. fn. 26) Thus for example in 1532 the Emperor recalled the *Reformation und Ordnung guter Policey* of 1530 and permitted the estates to improve *Policy und Ordnung* in any instance where they were found to be deficient (*Neue und vollständigere. . .*, 1747, Vol. 2 p. 361). Both meanings — 'community' (*Gemeinwesen*) and 'laws for its maintenance' — were current in the mid-eighteenth century:

> *Policey* or *Polizey*, Lat. *Politia*, is either the community, republic, forms of government (*Regiments-forme*) or also the laws, institutions and regulations given to and prescribed a town or province, which all (*jedermann im Handel und Wandel*) observe so that all affairs proceed in a peaceable and orderly fashion and human society might be maintained. (Zedler, 1741, Vol. 28 p. 1503)

c) *The Content of Polizeigesetze; the earlier 'practical Polizei concept'; specific Polizei matters; Polizei affairs.* In their content the rules of conduct given to subjects by their rulers relate to widely differentiated areas. Since 'disorder, defects and deficiencies' (*Neue und vollständigere,* 1747, Vol. 2 p. 333) arose in diverse spheres of the state-form at different times — in peace and war, times of tumult and famine or of general calm — in a variety of social circumstances, the *Polizeigesetzen* concern themselves with a quite heterogeneous range of matters, since *Polizei* was concerned with the abolition of disorder. The legislator applied himself first to the blurring of differences of estate caused by the wearing of extravagant clothing, and the consequent outflow of money abroad with the import of such luxury items. He also concerned himself with the appropriate behaviour of the citizen or subject when going to church or during festivities, how trades and occupations should be performed, and in particular how servants were to behave towards their superiors and journeymen to their masters.

Paragraph 29 of of 1521 *Reichsabschied* provides for instance an enumeration of the regions that are in a state of disorder. The Paragraph stipulates that a special *Reichsgesetz* should be promulgated to deal with 'extravagant clothing and consumption, . . . blasphemy. . . monopolies, unseemly vendors, duties, weights and measures and similar' (*Römischer . . .*, 1521, Para. 29, p. 207ff.). Even the first two *Reichspolizeiordnungen* in the years of 1530 and 1548 could not finally comprehend all the objects upon which they sought to legislate — which included religious matters (blasphemy), general morality and respectability, drinking, behaviour of servants (*Dienstpersonal*), regulation of weights and measures, usury and extravagance, for the laws allowed 'a superior authority to alter and moderate, but in no way intensify or increase, these our regulations according to the opportunities of each *Land'* (*Neue vollständigere . . .*, 1747, p. 345).[14] The *Landesherren* were thereby empowered to meliorate or even abolish the conditions of the *Reichsrecht* according to their own legal forms, that is, they could decide for themselves what was to be understood by 'matters relating to regulations'. This particular fact led to the varied extent of the earlier 'practical' concept of Polizei.

In one of the first definitions *Polizeisachen* ('police matters') were specified very generally as those matters relating to good order in the community. The Magdeburg *Prozeßordnung* of 1696 stated:

> all become doubtful at times / of what is to be understood by
> *Policey-Sachen* / thus we explain as follows / that all those
> affairs concerned with the maintenance of the community in
> itself which does not augment as a result *interesse singulorem*
> /belong to *Policey-Sachen*. (Mylius, 1714, pt. 2 p. 148; cf.
> Bornhak, 1884, Vol. I p. 380)

A series of *Polizeigesetzen* contained nevertheless conditions related to private law. This concerned in particular the observance of contractual conditions — especially purchase and sale, usury, guardianship and succession—which of course were a central aspect of orderly social existence; and in this way they were incorporated into regulations that had as their object good 'Polizei'. In this way, as Schmelzeisen points out, the regulated duties of *Polizeirecht* were in many laws interwoven with aspects of private law. They were interwoven not only from the point of view of a common domain of responsibility of state administration, but also because of their common objective of realising in this domain an orderly regulation of social affairs. The extent of regulation through *Polizeigesetze* was in large part determined by the functional decline of the estates. The more the distinctions between estates became blurred and the estates were no longer able to fulfil their function of regulation, the more the responsibility for legislation devolved to the *Landesherr*. The assumption of responsibility for regulation on the part of the state — caused by the decline of a society based on estates — is clearly shown by Maier (1966a, pp. 104—5).

d) *On the Restriction of the Earlier 'practical Polizeibegriff'; Separation of the Affairs of Polizei and Justice.* On the presumption of a regular course of the law, the concept of *Polizeisachen* and the associated conception of the legislative duties of the state attains a special significance. In the attempt to extricate *Polizeisachen* as defined above from the control of the courts of law and if necessary admit a form of investigation specific to 'Polizei', its affairs were at the beginning of the eighteenth century separated from those of the judiciary. This involved — to use present-day terminology — the question of jurisdiction over the acts of administration (of. Erichsen, 1971, p. 82ff.). While the law courts at first adjudicated violations of *Polizeigesetze* (*Neue und vollständigere*, 1747, Vol. 3 p. 660), jurisdiction over such matters was later transferred to special authorities. Judicial authorities were then forbidden to involve themselves in matters concerning *Polizei*, as can be seen in the new constitution of the judiciary for Chur- and Mark-Brandenburg for 1709:

> Since in these our residencies. . . disagreements have arisen in *Policey-Sachen*, which require the speediest settlement, such matters shall be referred to the Magistrate and no case brought before our Supreme Court. (Mylius, 1737, p. 382)

The 'improvement in the course of Justice' required that the 'judiciary refrain from involvement in affairs military, *Policey* or economic' (Mylius, 1737, p. 523). A Prussian law of 1735 stated this clearly:

> We wish the *Policey-Wesen* in our lands to be fundamentally revised, and thus for the welfare of our lands we propose to establish and publish regulations (*Verfassungen*) which will reformulate completely the distinction between jurisdiction and court investigation in *Polizeisachen*, thus: that when in the future some one person acts contrary to our *Policey-Verfassungen*, the investigation, punishment and chastisement of such an

offender, whoever it might be, will be the responsibility of the Magistrate and no other; the last being charged to investigate summarily and as rapidly as possible, and this authority then to determine appropriate sentence without appeal, then to fully carry out the aforesaid sentence. We therefore command our institutions of the Judiciary to refrain in the future from the consideration of *Policey-Sachen.* (Mylius, 1740, p. 133ff.)

According to Jablonski's *Lexicon* of 1748 *'Policey* is a means by which subjects might have nourishment and peacefulness. It can be distinguished 'from the concerns of justice, the state and war, in that these are matters of security — while *Policey* on the other hand is a matter of comfort *(bequemlichkeit)'* (1748, Vol. 2 p. 824).

In this manner the principle of legal protection (*Rechtsschutzes*), or more precisely by an exception to customary jurisdiction, led to ·a clear distinction between *Polizeisachen* and *Justizsachen.*[15]

In conclusion it can here be pointed out that this does not involve the detachment of the administration of the law from that of a more comprehensive 'Polizei'; *Justiz* and *Polizei* had always been distinguished from each other (cf. Kneymeyer, 1967, p. 171ff.).

2. 'Polizei' in Theological and Humanistic Scholastic Literature

As has already been indicated in the introduction to this essay, the concept 'Polizei' emerged with a much wider content among scholarly writers than was the case in laws and decrees. The need for a scholarly explication felt among scholarly circles arose, as Hans Maier makes clear (1966a, p. 123), because of the way in which the concept borrowed from Burgundy and 'popularised' in the first *Reichspolizeiordnung* of 1530 related to the Greek 'πολιτεία' and the Latin 'politia'. These last two terms already had a place in the teaching of ethics and politics in Universities, and as a consequence they blended with the modish 'Policei' and added to its meaning: henceforth 'Polizei' signified not only the satis-factory regulation of the community but the community itself — in an exact analogy with the twin meaning the word possessed in Aristotelian ethics and politics.

In addition to the Aristotelian concept 'πολιτεία' another, theologically rooted, concept appeared, which itself closely related to the Christian teaching on estates of the late Middle Ages. Here 'Polizei' was equivalent to 'the order of estates' (*Ständeordnung*). This concept, *a Description of a Christian, good and advantageous Polizei* (Friedlieb, 1614) is most strongly expressed in Reinking's *Biblische Policey* of 1593, which on the basis of a series of Old Testament examples developed the necessary foundations for a well-regulated community. The sub-title of this work clearly demonstrates the content of this usage of 'Polizei':

> *Biblische Policey* is: Holy, Worldly and Domestic Axiomata and Epilogues drawn out of Holy Writings for the Benefit of the Three Principal Estates — Supported with Biblical Proverbs and Instances — to be read with Utility, Service and Grace in all Estates. (1670 ed.)

There is a further set of associations with the concept 'Polizei' that emerges in this literature: 'politeness', 'consideration', 'prudence', 'elegance' and 'beauty'. The 'internal *Polizierung* of Men and States' (1770) derives from the middle Latin *policia* (from *polire, polieren, glätten*) (Grimm, 1889, Vol. 7 p. 981) and can be found in contexts such as: well *policirte* towns; *policiertes* human species; *polizirte* states; *policirtes* people (cf. Zobel, 1952, Pt. I p. 13).

3. 'Polizei' in *Polizeiwissenschaft*

In the extensive writings on *Polizeiwissenschaft* during the seventeenth and eighteenth centuries 'Polizei' gained its most diverse and uncertain meaning. Since 'Polizei' was concerned with communal order, these writings had of necessity to analyse this condition of order (and thereby the purpose of the State itself) as well as the methods and means deployed for the realisation of this condition. Statements on 'Polizei' are therefore dispersed according to the diversity of the many possible views on the question of *Staatszweck* (purpose of the State). Ultimately *Polizeiwissenschaft* had to investigate the legal foundations of the activities, sovereignty and power of *Polizei* contained in the sovereignty of *ius politiae* (cf. Böckenförde, 1958, p. 53ff.). In addition to this it began the systematisation of the variety of 'Polizei' matters (Damkowski, 1969, p. 94ff.; Maier, 1966a, p. 184).

Particularly significant for the concept of 'Polizei' to be found in the writings on *Polizeiwissenschaft* are its descriptions of the nature of order and of 'Polizei' activity — in present-day terms the so-called 'practical' conception of 'Polizei'. The questions of how the ruler could attain a condition of order, and what matters were to be treated under the category of 'Polizei' assumed therefore a central position. This can be clearly seen in one of the first texts on *Polizeiwissenschaft*, Johann Oldendorp's *Advice on the Attainment of Good Politie and Order in Town and Country*,[16] which appeared in Rostock immediately before the promulgation of the first *Reichspolizeiordnung* of 1530. In this text he addresses advice to the Bürgermeister and councillors of his native city of Hamburg advice on the achievement of *gemeiner Policey und wolfart* (public Policey and welfare). Oldendorp is principally concerned to establish the basic principles of regulated social life; and to clarify in particular that only through a correct appreciation of Human Nature is it possible to devise the legal regulations appropriate to the establishment of order (Maier, 1966a, p. 131).

Only a few authors need to be cited here to indicate the breadth of the earlier concept of 'Polizei'. For Melchior von Osse (see Maier, 1966a p. 140) the concerns of 'Polizei' extended far beyond the domain of those objects treated in the *Reichspolizeiordnungen* and included all those areas where state power entered into social life while Seckendorff was the first to introduce some system into these extended regions of state activity in the mid-seventeenth century. In his book entitled *Teutscher Fürsten-Stat* (approximately *The German Sovereign State*) which appeared in Frankfurt in 1656, in addition to the functions of ensuring peace and welfare 'Polizei' is assigned to Church, Education and Cameralism (cf. Maier, 1966b, p. 19ff.). Parallel to the construction of a specialised system of official institutions and the establishment of specific institutions for external affairs — to which the judiciary did not belong — the conception of 'Polizei' in writings on administration became restricted to internal affairs in the modern sense, including cultural administration. Naturally (and this must be emphasised) the statements of the old German discourse on state and administration — *Polizeiwissenschaft* — continually reflect on the one hand the degree of specialisation in the areas of state activities and on the other specific conceptions of the purposes of the State and its regulation; and this in turn creates a similar diversity of 'practical' definitions of 'Polizei' in the learned writings as in the laws themselves.[17] An selection from the descriptions of 'Polizei' activity therefore appears of necessity to be quite arbitrary, but in view of the innumerable definitions and re-descriptions this is in practice unavoidable. A few examples will be sufficient here. Justi for instance in his text *Grundsätze der Policey-Wissenschaft* published in Göttingen in 1756 described the 'ultimate objective of *Policey*' as 'the enlargement of the internal power and strength of the State (1756, p. 337). According to Bergius 'Polizei' cared for the 'order, security and welfare of subjects' (1768, Vol. 2 p. 65). Loen understood by 'Polizei' 'all those institutions and regulations which relate to the public welfare of the State in general and the contribution of each to it' (1750, p. 95). Finally, B. J. C. Majer directly equated the internal affairs of the State with *Staatspolizei* and indicated its business as the 'promotion of public (common) Welfare' (1775, Vol. 1 p. 102); while an anonymous writer opined that good 'Polizei' consisted in the 'arrangement and regulation of all persons and affairs in a State' (1753, cited in Damkowski, 1969, p. 92).

In conclusion, to these few descriptions can be added an enumeration of the domains of 'Polizei' which were generally envisaged. Gosch for example included under 'Polizei' nearly all regions of internal administration, such as agriculture, hunting, fisheries, mining, handicrafts, and arts (1789, p. 22).

The conceptual breadth of the term can be seen most clearly in the contortions individual authors are compelled to perform in the self-imposed task of systematising 'Polizei' activities. Hufeland for example distinguishes between lower and higher 'Polizei' (1798, p. 374); other writers distinguish between a narrow and a broad sense, or introduce like Justi (1760, Vol. 1 p. 6) and Bergius after him (1773, p. 89) a conception divided into three parts.

III. The Modern Concept of 'Polizei' (Polizei' in the Transition to a Modern World)

1. The Initial Situation

If the extent of the concept 'Polizei' at the beginning of the eighteenth century is considered (and at the same time disregarding nuances and the diverse construals of the term) the slogan 'establishment and maintenance of order' can be used, albeit crudely, to characterise the meaning of the term up to that date. 'Good order' here referred both to protection from danger and to concern with matters of welfare. Since these two concerns lie at the heart of domestic administration, a conceptual equivalence emerged between 'Polizei' and 'domestic administration'. This all-embracing conception which had been valid for over three hundred years underwent, however, at the beginning and then principally during the century a shift and restriction in meaning which presages the foundations for the present-day conception. This alteration can be seen at work initially in the introduction of an institutional meaning of 'Polizei'.

2. The Development of an Institutional and Formation of a Formal Concept of 'Polizei'

This imprecise or varying conception of 'Polizei', which, as already mentioned is characteristic for Lexica of the time, achieved for the first time at the beginning of the eighteenth century a specific form in one respect. While those officials and authorities charged with the supervision of 'Polizei' (the relations among citizens and punishment of violations of the same) did not yet possess the

specific name 'Polizei' (this rather relating to the whole activity
of domestic administration), there did emerge during the century
an institutional conception alongside the others. Gradually 'Polizei'
came to mean, as it does today in general, a specific institutional
authority and its members — Police in the sense of an institution.

During the eighteenth century special officials were appointed
with titles such as *Polizeidirektor, Polizeikommissar, Polizei-
inspektor, Polizeiknecht*. The general designation of 'Polizei' was
applied to these officials. This in 1717 the *Commissarius loci* of
Brandenburg-Prussia was called upon to appoint from among the
councillors of the towns in its jurisdiction a *Policey-Inspector* for
each (Knemeyer, 1967, p. 163 n. 44). The 'district outriders'
(Kreisausreitern) appointed in Prussia as organs of the 'Polizei' in
1713 were charged with the furtherance and maintenance of
Polizeiwesen and the related well-being of the town's inhabitants,
but they were not given the name 'Polizei (Mylius, 1740, p. 97f.).
It appears to be significant that these officials were in no respect
concerned with the entirety of domestic administration, but were
simply concerned with the domain of security: 'Polizei' in this
institutional sense was thus only concerned with one part of the
'practical' terrain of 'Polizei'. This is shown clearly in Frederick
the Great's *Einrichtungsreskript* of 20th February 1742 in which
he established for Berlin a state authority for Security, Order and
Communication, dealing in particular with the prevention of
crime; conceived on a French model it was headed by a Royal
Polizeidirektor. These special tasks of security and order were at
the same time removed from the city's Magistrate, since these
authorities, as in the example of Paris, had proved themselves
unequal to the maintenance of security. With the transfer of the
tasks of 'Polizei *in specie*' to a specific state administration or to
individual communal officials who were to treat these as matters
of state, a particular and formal concept of 'Polizei' developed in
the form 'Polizei' = 'the tasks of police authorities or institutions'.
This process led at the same time to a division of the concept
'Polizei': on the one hand the general tasks and competence of
'Polizei' in the sense of the business of domestic administration
remained in force, while on the other the formation of a formal
conception of 'Polizei' detached the 'direct' task of security and
transferred it to special institutions. Accordingly 'Policei *in specie*'
'were placed under the direct control and made reponsible to a
Polizeichef (head of police) for the purpose of greater speed and
effectivity . . . while the remaining domestic administration,
particularly those sections concerned with welfare, charitable
foundations, finance and economy (i.e. the objects of so-called
Cameralism) were collegiately administered from the Magistrate,

although through different offices' (Scupin, 1970. p. 9; also Schilling, 1894, pp. 474, 482; Knemeyer, 1967, p. 163).

The tangible conclusion of the formation of an institutional concept of 'Polizei' is to be found in Paragraph 231, II, 15 of the Prussian Code of 1794 (*Allgemeine Landrecht*, henceforth ALR) which refers to a *Landespolizei-Instanz*. This institutional concept is also clear in Paragraphs 12 and 14 of the ALR, where by 'Polizei' a specific authority is meant. As a result of this ordinary administrative authorities who in certain sections discharged police duties were also known as 'Polizei' authorities. This is clear in the regulations concerning government as a channel of the state of administration. Paragraph 3 of the regulations improving the organisation of provincial police and financial authorities of 26th December 1808 thus runs:

> In their capacity as 'Polizei' authorities of the land the governments (*Regierungen*) are charged with the care and well-being of our loyal subjects, in positive as well as negative aspects. They are hereby permitted and bound not only to prevent and as such remove all that can bring danger or disadvantage to the state and its citizens, consequently the concern of the necessary institutions for the maintenance of public peace, security and order, but also to ensure that the common good is promoted and improved and that each citizen of the state has the opportunity to increase his capabilities and powers from both moral and physical points of view, and to do this in the most advantageous fashion within the boundaries of the law. Governments therefore have supervisory powers in matters of public improvement, education and culture. (Preuß. G. Slg. 1806–1810, 465)

Magistrates were also referred to as 'Polizei' insofar as they performed tasks appropriate to 'Polizei' in its 'practical' aspect.

This connection of institutional, formal and practical instances of 'Polizei' — later designated as 'administrative *Polizei*' survives in some of the German Länder today (Scupin, 1970, p. 33). Here it must be emphasised that the later introduction of a series of 'special *Polizeien*' — health, veterinary, construction, water-control and forest — involved duties that went beyond the restriction of 'Polizei' to questions of dangers and concerned other tasks of administration. Other services, for example the Fire Service, were concerned with purely 'practical' 'Polizei' affairs, without formally bearing the name.

This running together of diverse concepts of 'Polizei' introduced a further lack of clarity, since the matters that were regarded as appropriate tasks for 'Polizei' did not permit of a clear and certain definition even in abstract terms. Only with the distribution of duties and powers within a *Rechtsstaat* [state founded upon law] did the areas of activity appropriate to 'Polizei' gain the necessary clarity.

3. The Practical Concept of 'Polizei'

With the development of an institutional and the formation of a formal concept of 'Polizei' the term gained a certain precision, alongside which a more restricted 'practical' conception emerged. The passage from this conception to the narrow association of 'Polizei' = protection from danger lasted however over a hundred years.

    a) *The Elimination of Welfare as an Objective*. Discussions on the concept 'Polizei' (or rather, the role of the State in the domain in which *staatlich-polizeilich* measures operated) reached their peak in the second half of the eighteenth century as the exercise of state administration was reduced through the exclusion of the Eudæmonian domain. Naturally if placed in a wider context this shift in meaning of 'Polizei' can be seen to be connected with other cultural changes taking place at the same time. All spheres of learning in Germany were until the mid-eighteenth century heavily influenced by the Enlightenment in which practical philosophy, in particular those aspects concerned with the state and law, was closely associated with notions of welfare. From the mid-eighteenth century a new conception of the state developed which was to be embodied in the Kantian philosophy of the state (Vorländer, 1967, p. 86; Maier, 1966a, p. 230f.). Kant's critique led to a complete suppression of the previously-ruling Aristotelian metaphysics; the postulate of freedom made possible the treatment of the rights and freedom of the citizen in the framework of a state founded upon law (Mayer, 1958, p. 127). Fichte then developed this idea and assigned to 'Polizei' two central spheres, first the protection from danger and the function of security, second the supervision and upholding of the laws (1970, pp. 85, 91). In terms of the history of ideas then this principle of Eudæmonism was finally eliminated (Wolzendorff, 1906, p. 24; Mayer, 1958, p. 127).

    This can be seen from the text published by Pütter in 1770 entitled *Institutiones juris publici Germanici*. In a famous revision of Paragraph 331 which appeared in 1792 the tasks of 'Polizei' are described as follows:

    'The task of promoting the public good is not strictly that of police, save to the extent to which the end in view is the improvement of a situation directly contrary to the evil that is feared, or unless by chance the close relation to a certain object necessitates assigning both objectives to police'.[18]

Scupin has thoroughly analysed the significance of this statement in separating questions of public security from those of welfare. It must here be noted however that this statement by Pütter is and has been overrated in the literature, since a complete distinction of welfare from public security does not appear in this Paragraph. It would be more exact to say that Pütter includes those elements of welfare-promotion in his definition of 'Polizei' in terms of the sphere of responsibility for the protection of the public from danger. The struggle over the function of the police and the restriction of their activities, the exclusion of police spies, the attempt to introduce legal boundaries to police powers, in sum the attempt to eliminate or limit what would later be called the methods of a police state (Maier, 1966a, p. 301) — all these find their expression in Pütter's paragraphs. Sonnenfels in his *Grundsätzen der Policey* made the clearest limitation when he stated: '*Policeywissenschaft* is the science which treats of the foundation and operation of security in a state' (1787, Vol. I, p. 51). It is however historically significant that Sonnenfels stated himself that in defining *Polizeiwissenschaft* in this way he was deviating from the usage of most other authors, who continued to associate the term with the entire region of domestic administration. Only in the course of the nineteenth century did meaning change in such a way as to in part approach the contemporary usage. In these learned discussions stretching over a century a whole epoch of *Polizeiwissenschaft* in the sense of 'German discourse on the state and administration' gradually comes to an end (cf. Maier, 1966a). Henceforth this sphere would be dealt with in terms of *Verwaltungsrecht* instead of *Polizeirecht*, and National Economy as an element of *Staatswissenschaft* ceased to have any connection with 'Polizei'.

It would however be a mistake to place the elimination of welfare as an objective too early in this development — as for example is the case during the nineteenth century with Otto Mayer's teleological conception of a process of development from *Polizeistaat* to *Rechtstaat* — or on the other hand to see this process as one which only gradually took place in the course of a century. For example, only a few Universities offered lectures on *Polizeiwissenschaft* by the 1870s (Maier, 1966a, p. 244).

b) *The Phase of Transition between ALR and the Kreuzberg Judgement.* The literary treatment of 'Polizei' experienced its legal defeat in the Prussian Code of 1794. Thus Paragraph 10, 11, 17 of the ALR finally and clearly expressed the modern conception of 'Polizei':

> It is the task of the police to maintain public peace, security and order with the appropriate institutions, and prevent the endangering of the public or its members.

However this provision is judged, either in terms of empowering a particular institution, confirmation of a given condition or norm for specific tasks, it does not involve a transition to the 'modern state' and its associated conception of police. This section of the ALR would indeed be suitable as a foundation for the conception of police associated with the *Rechstaat*, as the reference back to this by the Upper Administrative Court in the Kreuzberg judgement of 1882 shows.[19] But what it does in effect do is establish a definite closure that is however more or less ignored in the following century.[20] Thus the ALR is not characteristic of a breakthrough to the modern conception of police. The Decree concerning the improvement of provincial 'Polizei' and financial authorities of 26th December 1808 (already mentioned above) can be used here as an example of the continuing breadth of the usage of 'Polizei' despite the ALR. It must be emphasised that, apart from the question whether this represents an extension of the concept of 'Polizei' beyond that of the ALR — Scupin shows quite rightly that it is in fact simply a decree on organisation (1970, p. 21; cf. Mayer 1958, p. 129; Wolzendorff, 1906, p. 27) — the concept of 'Polizei' is here retained to designate the most important activities of administration. This is shown particularly clearly in the way that the rules of conduct issued at the same time to the governments relate to the question of welfare. Here Paragraph 50 runs:

> The effectivity of the governments in the exercise of police powers should not confine itself to the prevention of danger and disadvantages and the maintenance of the present order, but should also extend to the extension and promotion of general welfare. (Preuß. Gslg. 1808, 494; Mayer, 1958, p. 129; Scupin, 1970, p. 25ff.)

This broad usage can be also seen above all in the new Royal Prussian 'Decree on the Improved Organisation of Provincial Authorities' of 30th April, 1815. Insofar as this bears on the distribution of official business, and not on the competences and limitations with respect to the judiciary, the concept 'Polizei' is significantly extended. Paragraph 13 states:

> The provincial polizei administers: the *Polizei* of general security, of provisions and other matters; charities, protection against general injuries, the houses of improvement, *milden Stiftungen* and similar public bodies; the supervision of communes and corporations which have no commercial objective. (Schücking, 1906, p. 61 No. 15.)

While it can be seen that security here has priority, a special role is reserved for the function of supervision, in particular the supervision of communes and corporations. If then security is in the foreground — in terms of public peace, security and order — 'Polizei' does then however include a number of tasks appropriate to internal administration. In those spheres in which the tasks of 'Polizei' are performed by authorities not named as 'Police' the execution of responsibility for protection of the public and furtherance of well-being become especially confused. Since this does not merely concern the delineation of spheres of competence for the disposition of legal measures, it must be emphasised that in the first half of the nineteenth century it was not in practice possible to separate 'Polizei' from the rest of the business of internal administration. Most administrations, as Pütter showed, wove together the business of security, order and welfare. Attempts to separate them remained for a long time simply legal academic exercises without practical implications. As Scupin clearly states:

> If 'Polizei' is understood as the upholding of security and order
> as a general aspect of internal administration, then virtually all
> administration becomes *Polizei* administration insofar as it
> independently assumes responsibility for the protection of its
> objects of administration. (1970, p. 71.)

It must on the other hand be emphasised that the distinction between the promotion of welfare and the maintenance of order served in the final analysis to limit the police powers of the state through the invocation of legal regulation.

This tendency was represented by liberals after 1815. The widely-read *Staatsrecht der constitutionellen Monarchie* of 1839 argued that:

> No governmental power is more dangerous to freedom than that
> of *Polizei* — not simply the so-called superior or secret police,
> but the so-called welfare 'Polizei' above all. The prime function
> of the state *should be solely* to secure the domination of Law.
> According to basic constitutional principles *there is only one
> possible* place for *Polizei*, and that is the responsibility for
> security and order in the state; What is known as welfare
> 'Polizei' (especially surveillance and welfare 'Polizei') is nothing
> but open interference with the freedom of the citizen. (von
> Aretin / von Rotteck, 1839, Vol. 2 p. 165).

This typifies the attitude of liberals to welfare 'Polizei'. Aretin's appreciation of 'higher' or 'secret' police is representative of all liberal-bourgeois writing before 1848; the concept and form of the secret State police had been copied from the French example during the Napoleonic period. It is quite understandable that the representatives of 'constitutional state rights' should strongly challenge this form on account of the way in which it detached itself from the responsibility of the 'public' police. Klüber characterised it scornfully as 'an ill-judged attempt to achieve total knowledge' (822, Para. 301).[21] With the approach of the 1848 revolution the association *Polizeistaat* became more and more used in a deprecatory manner (cf. Ladendorf, 1906, p. 247), whether referring to the 'superior', 'secret' or tutelary 'welfare' *Polizei*.

> 'Polizeistaat' is used to characterise censoriously a state in which the operations of the police are so extensive that they interfere in all the activities of the citizen and everywhere have the upper hand. (Manz, 1848, p. 331).

Meyer's *Lexikon* (Fourth Edition) clearly shows the extent and disunity of the concept — taking this source at random — when dealing in 1889 (that is after the Kreuzberg judgement) with the term:

> *Polizei* in the broadest sense is the totality of state activities directed internally to assuring the security and welfare of the state and its members, i.e. the internal administration of the state excluding the administration of justice. . . . The term is often restricted in its definition, although there is no general agreement on this form of restriction. Some place in the foreground compulsion by the state and thence conceive 'Polizei' as the forcible furtherance of public security and welfare. Others wish to confine the term to the activity of protection against transgressions of the law (security police), von Mohl for instance referring to the police in terms of 'preventative judiciary'. Those who on the other hand wish to retain the wider usage distinguish security- from welfare-police. Yet others, for example Bluntschli, would only partially admit this last sphere of government, since they place alongside 'Polizei' separate administration of culture and economy. An overextension of welfare-police leads to over-government, to a system of police tutelage which is dubbed a *Polizestaat*. Constrasted to this is the attempt to establish a *Rechtstaat*, which is certainly pushed too far when all activities of the state and its organs are merely confined to the protection of the law, but which is justifiable insofar as law provides the foundation of the state and all its affairs are conducted according to legal principles. (Meyer, 1889, Vol. 13 p. 185.)

This blending together of diverse usages of 'Polizei', which can be traced to the ALR of 1794, lasted until the Kreuzberg judgement of 1882, and can only be explained in terms of the *Zeitgeist* of the early nineteenth century. With the expiry of Kantean and Fichtean theory Germany became strongly influenced by Hegel. Of course Hegel no longer recognised the natural law theory of felicity, though he did assign to 'Polizei' the task of caring for the 'special well-being' of the citizen (1928, p. 311, Para. 230). In this the major difference between Hegel and the theory is, as Wolzendorff says, solely that Hegel states himself more briefly (1906, p. 24).

The real closure of this process of development, stimulated by the Kreuzberg judgement, appeared with the Prussian Law on Police Administration of 1st July 1931, Paragraph 14:

> The police authorities are charged, within the framework of current law, to take according to their discretion the necessary measures for the suppression of general or isolated dangers which threaten public security or order. (Preuß G. Slg. 1931, 79).

This decision, which relates to both general and particular 'Polizei' authorities and is directly related to Paragraph 10, II, 17 of the ALR, fixed the usage of 'Polizei' in northern Germany until the Second World War.[22]

c) *Bavaria: 'Polizei' = Administration in Possession of Compulsory Powers*; The discussion of the development of the practical meaning for 'Polizei' during the eighteenth and nineteenth centuries has up until this point involved for the most part Prussia and its sphere of influence. In Bavaria however there can be found in the middle of the nineteenth century a clear distinction of 'Polizei' from general administration. Whereas in Prussia the 'material' conceptions of 'Polizei' were determined according to specified objectives (defence against danger, promotion of welfare), in Bavaria it was the question of compulsion which marked out the domain of 'Polizei'. The means through which this was realised was thereby excluded. Pözl thus described 'Polizei' *Grundriß zu Vorlesungen über Polizei* as:

> that state activity called into being to secure, with authoritative powers of coercion, the established order from danger and injury, and also the welfare of the state, insofar as this appears to be an indispensable condition for the security of the established order. (1866, p. 1).

This definition summarises the prevalent conception of 'Polizei' in mid-nineteenth century Bavaria as one which treats protection from danger as the objective, and in the association of welfare with functions of security recalls the description provided by Pütter. The specificity consists in the exclusion of the question of means for the realisation of this objective and consequently marks 'Polizei' off from administration. Henceforth 'Polizei' is simply

that region of administration endowed with coercive powers
(Mayer, 1958, p. 80ff.; Schiedermaier, 1961, p. 37ff.).[23]

IV. *Prospect: The So-Called 'De-Policing' after the Second World War*

The Allies·agreed at the Yalta Conference in February 1945 to
dissolve the existing police powers in Germany after its defeat, to
rebuild and reorganise the police on a new and restricted basis.
The objectives of these measures were the 'denazification',
'democratisation' and 'demilitarisation' of German Police bodies.
While up to this the general category of 'Polizei' related to the
affairs of public administration concerned with the preservation
of public security and order and accordingly demarcated from
other regions of administration by its regulation through police-
law, as far as the Allies were concerned 'Polizei' should refer only
to the function of public security, conceived in terms restricted
to executive duties. Corresponding to these ideas the general
duties of internal security were separated from the police in the
majority of the *Länder.*

Thus the seven Länder of the one-time British and American
Occupied Zones (Bavaria, Berlin, Hamburg, Hesse, Lower Saxony,
North-Rhine Wesfalia and Schleswig-Holstein) distinguish following
'de-policing' (*Entpolizeilichung*) police authorities from authorities
concerned with security and order who assume responsibility for
internal defence. In contrast to this Baden-Württemberg, Rheinland-
Pfalz, the Saar and Bremen have either retained broad-based police
administration, or re-introduced it. This formation of two categories
of 'police' has however more an external character than organisa-
tional effects, since the previous areas of jurisdiction of the
authorities charged with general internal administration and also
some special authorities were retained (although the characterisa-
tion of these authorities as 'Polizei' was avoided). In any case under
the rubric of 'de-policing' two large branches of administration
arose to deal with 'police business', 'Polizei' in the institutional
sense and the authorities concerned with security and/or order.

Bavaria has made a break with the previous police organisation,
in that the Bavarian executive police (*Vollzugspolizei*) were
separated from the security apparatus of the earlier internal
administration. In the local authorities (*Gemeinden*) a distinction
has been made between 'police' and general administration,
avoiding the subordination directly of the police to the authorities
of general internal administration. These authorities can however
refer matters to the police, and in this way the legal situation in

other *Länder* is approached (Mayer, 1958, p. 205ff.; Berner, 1952, pp. 49, 65; Berner, 1957, pp. 810–6; Bachof, 1955, p. 105).

The relation to state power which was destroyed through totalitarian misuse did not disappear for long; commensurate with Dürig's demand that the police laws of a *Rechtstaat* not be abandoned on account of the experience of a shocking and unusual decade, the practical police laws have in the main been retained.

With the division of protection against dangers between the sphere of the regular police and that of the authorities concerned with internal public order, it was necessary to alter at the same time the terminology of specific administrative tasks covered up until then by the general term 'Polizei'. Thus for example the North Rhine-Westfalian Law Regulating Public Authorities of November 6th 1956 Paragraph 55 clearly states:

> The designations will be altered as follows: instead of *Baupolizei*, Building Inspectorate; instead of *Bergpolizei*, Mine Inspectorate, Mine Regulations instead of *Bergpolizeiverordnung* or *Polizeiverordnung*, so far as it concerns the area of Mining Regulations; Dike Inspectorate instead of *Deichpolizei*; Field and Forest Inspectorate instead of *Feld- und Forstpolizei*; Health Inspectorate instead of *Gesundheitpolizei*; Business Supervision instead of *Gewerbepolizei*; Market Control instead of *Marktpolizei*; Municipal Cleansing instead of *Polizei-gemäßige Reinigung*.[24]

These alterations show at once the immense breadth of the term 'Polizei' in its practical use and also the effective identity of 'police' with internal administration.

Service Police (*Vollzugspolizei*) finally became assistants to the normal internal administrative authorities and gained their own special competences in extreme circumstances. In this way the united concept of 'police' fell out of use in the majority of the German *Länder*. The second element associated with the responsibility for defence against danger was separated completely from 'Polizei' through the redesignation of these tasks under laws and administration relating to security and public safety.

This process can finally be summarised in the words of the one-time Chief of the Police Department in the Bavarian Ministry of the Interior, Ministerial Director A. Mayer:

> The new conception of *Polizei* which is restricted to Service

Police (*Vollzugspolizei*) has finally brought a convergence about with popular usage of 'police', which from the point of view of an administration responsible to the public can only be seen as a good thing. The new conception has the advantage of being

freed of the previous associations, carried over from the era of
the police state, with a police power serving to uphold public
security and order through administrative activity. Since this
concern for public security and order is immanent in virtually
all the work of public administration it was in the past difficult
to distinguish 'police' from 'non-police' activities on the part of
the authorities in a manner appropriate to a constitutional state.
It can therefore be seen as nothing but a clarification if it is
finally decided to ditch the term 'Polizei' for the administrative
authorities insofar as they are concerned with the region of
so-called 'defence against danger'. (Mayer, 1952, p. 166).

This has since then taken place in most of the German *Länder*.
'Police' means simply the police authorities and administrators
engaged in public service. The conception of 'Polizei' as a form of
activity or responsibility undertaken by specific authorities, as
could be found in the Prussian Law Concerning Police Administration, is today obsolete usage and can be only found in the old
police textbooks (Götz, 1973, p. 18).

How far it will be possible to unify the existing federal police
laws through the use of the present 'Model Outline' is at the
moment not clear. If there is success in creating a unified federal
body of law relating to the police through the introduction of
parallel legislation, then the conception of 'Polizei' will naturally
also assume an unambiguous form.

Translated by Keith Tribe

Notes

1. This article first appeared in O. Brunner et. al. (eds.) *Geschichtliche
Grundbegriffe* Vol. 4 (Ernst Klett Verlag, Stuttgart 1978) pp. 875–97.
2. This refers to the federal structure of the Bundesrepublik and is taken up
later in the article (Trans.).
3. 'pollitzey und regirung . . . in allen Sachen ordnen, setzen, und fürnemen.'
Original STA Nuremberg: D-Laden-Urk.Nr.491. See also Chmel, 1838, p. 415
(no. 4097), although somewhat inexact.
4. 'dise stat mit vil loblichen polliceien und guten ordnunge verseiien'.
5. 'Gebot der gemeynen verlewmutten frawen der kleydung und ander
gezird halben'; 'uff pollicey und wesentlichkeyt unser stat Wurtzpurg ein
vleissigs aufsehen zu haben.'
6. 'in Sachen und Geboten derselben Stadt Regiment und Polizei berührende
gehorsam zu sein'.
7. 'ordnungen . . . ufgericht, gehandthabt und den nachgevolgt werde, wie
sich zu guter policei und gemeinem nutze . . . gebüret und not ist'.

8. 'daß wiewohl von gutem Ordnungen und Policey ... berathschlagt, so hat doch solche Ordnung zu keiner würklichen Vollziehung gereicht'.
9. 'Damit nun ... gute Policey, Sitten und Erbarkeit erhalten'.
10. 'daß alle wohlgefaßte Ordnungen zerrütet und allenthalben gute Policey, Sitten und Erbarkeit hintangesetzt (seien), dagegen aber schändliche Unordnung ...'.
11. Zobel has in her very detailed work (1952) chiefly drawn on Bavarian sources for the period 1500–1700.
12. 'in guter Ordnung und Verfassung der Personen und Sachen eines Staats'.
13. 'an dieser Ordnung oder anderer Bürgerlichen Policey wollen die (die Bürger) sich ... richten'.
14. 'Doch einer jeden Oberkeit ... unbenommen, diese unser Ordnung, nach eines jeden Lands Gelegenheit, einzuziehen, zu ringern und zu mabigen, aber in keinem Weg zu erhöhen oder zu mehren'.
15. For a differentiation according to the disputed legal relations, see Rüfner (1962) pp. 26, 86; such in Bavaria as well as Prussia, cf. F. Mayer (1958) p. 36.
16. 'Van radtslagende, wo men gude Politie und ordenunge, ynn Steden und landen erholden möhge'.
17. For the varying breadth see the short summary in Damkowski (1969) p. 96. cf. Scheidemantel (1795) Vol. 4 p. 159: 'There is hardly any expression in the whole sphere of *Staatswissenschaften* that has as variable a meaning as the word *"Policey"*. ... Of all the numerous scholars who use the term there are perhaps two who use the term in the exact and similar sense'. Also Krünitz (1810) Vol. 114 p. 178 for many example from the literature.
18. 'Promovendae salutis cura proprie non est politiae, nisi quatenus ea mente agitur, ut tanto lautior sit status isti malo, quod metuebatur, directe oppositus, aut forte connexitas obiecti efficit, ut unum cum altero iunctim politiae committatur' [translation supplied by Pasquale Pasquino].
19. Entscheidungen (1883) Vol. 9 p. 353. The Kreuzberg judgement found its first legislative recognition in the Prussian *Polizeiverwaltungsgesetz* in 1931.
20. Only here and there for example Gönner and Leist, who interestingly were members of the Pütter school — was the concept derivable from the ALR maintained. Gönner stated for instance 'there is no special science or particular part of law dealing with *Polizei* ... *Polizei* has always been concerned with security, furtherance of welfare lies outside its direct objectives', (1805, pt. 2 p. 85 and note z, Para. 328).
21. cf. in addition Brockhaus (1817, Vol. 7 p. 744); Pierer (1844, Vol. 2 p. 244); Mans (1848, Vol. 8 p. 330); Brockhaus, 1854, Vol. 12 p. 243).
22. cf. the revision of the Prussian *Polizeiverwaltungsgesetzin* terms of the sphere of operation in North Rhine Westfalia, 27 November 1953.
23. For the developments in the other German states which effectively correspond to the Prussian and Bavarian systems, see Wolzendorff (1906) p. 41.

References

Anon. (1735) *Verhältnis der Polizei zur Religion.*
von Aretin, J. C. A. M. and von Rotteck, C. (1839) *Staatsrecht der constitutionellen Monarchie* Vol. 2, second ed. Leipzig.
Baader, J. (ed.) (1861) *Nürnberger Polizeiverordnungen aus dem 13–15 Jahrhundert*, Stuttgart.

Bachof, O. (1955) 'Ein neues Polizeigesetz in Bayern', *Die öffentliche Verwaltung* Vol. 8.
Bergius, J. H. L. (1768) 'Cammersachen', *Policey- und Cameral-Magazin* Vol. 2, Frankfurt.
Bergius, J. H. L. (1773) 'Polizey', *Policey- und Cameral-Magazin* Vol. 7, Frankfurt.

Berner, G. (1952) 'Zur Neuordnung der Polizeiorganisation in Bayern', *Die Neue Polizei* Vol. 6 Nos. 4 and 5.

Berner, G. (1957) 'Wandlungen des Polizeibegriffs seit 1945', *Deutsche Verwaltungsblätter* Vol. 72.

Böckenförde, E.-W. (1958) *Gesetz und gesetzgebende Gewalt*, Berlin.

Bornhak, C. (1884) *Geschichte des preußischen Verwaltungsrechts* Vol. 1, Berlin.

Brockhaus (1817) *Conversations-Lexicon für die gebildete Stände* Vol. 7, fourth edition.

Brockhaus (1854) *Conversations-Lexicon* (new series) Vol. 12, tenth edition.

Carlebach, R. (1906) *Badische Rechtsgeschichte* Vol. 1, Heidelberg.

Chmel, J. (1838) *Regesta chronologica-diplomatica Friderice IV. Romanorum regis (imperatoris III.), Auszug aus den Registraturbüchern zu Wien, Pt. 1*, Vienna.

Damkowski, W. (1969) *Die Entstehung des Verwaltungsbegriffes. Eine Wortstudie*, Cologne.

Dithmar, J. C. (1745) *Einleitung in die oeconomische Policei- und Cameral-Wissenschaften*, Frankfurt a.O.

Entscheidungen des königlichen Oberverwaltungsgerichts Vol. 9 (1883) Berlin.

Erichsen, H.-U. (1971) *Verfassungs- und verwaltungsgeschichtliche Grundlagen der Lehre vom fehlerhaften belastenden Verwaltungsakt und seine Aufhebung im Prozeß*, Frankfurt.

Fichte (1970) *Grundlage des Naturrechts nach Principien der Wissenschaftslehre (1797), Gesamtausgabe* Vol. 4.

Friedliebe, C. W. (1614) *Prudentia politica Christiana*, Goslar.

Gönner, N. T. (1805) *Deutsches Staatsrecht* Pt. 2, Augsburg.

Gosch, J. L. (1789) *Philosophische Aphorismen über Staatswirtschaft*, Copenhagen.

Götz, V. (1973) *Allgemeines Polizei- und Ordnungsrecht*, second edition, Göttingen.

Grimm, J. and W. (1889) *Deutsches Wörterbuch* Vol. 7.

Hegel (1928) *Rechtsphilosophie*, Sämtliche Werke Vol. 7.

Hoffman, H. (ed.) (1955) *Würzburger Polizeisätze, Gebote und Verordnungen des Mittelalters 1125—1495*, Würzburg.

Hufeland, G. (1798) *Institutionen des gesammten positiven Rechts oder systematische Encyklopäedie der sämmtlichen allgemeine Begriffe und unstreitigen Grundsätze aller in Deutschland geltenden Rechte*, Jena.

Jablonski, J. T. (1748) *Allgemeines Lexicon der Künste und Wissenschaften*, Vol. 2, second edition.

von Justi, J. H. G. (1756) *Grundsätze der Polizey-Wissenschaft in einem vernünftigen, auf den Endzweck der Polizey gegründeten, Zusammhange und zum Gebrauch Academischer Vorlesungen abgefasset*, Göttingen.

von Justi, J. H. G. (1760) *Die Grundfeste*

zu der Macht und Glückseligkeit der Staaten, Vol. 1, Königsberg.

Klüber, J. L. (1822) *Öffentliches Recht des Teutschen Bundes und der Bundestaaten* second edition, Frankfurt.

Knemeyer, F.-L. (1967) 'Polizeibegriffe in den Gesetzen des 15, bis 18. Jahrhunderts. Kritische Benerkungen zur Literatur über die Entwicklung des Polizeibegriffes' *Archiv des öffentlichen Rechts* Vol. 92.

Knemeyer, F.-L. (1975) 'Deutsches Polizeirecht', *Die öffentliche Verwaltung* Vol. 28.

Krünitz, J. G. (1810) *Oeconomische Encyclopädie oder allgemeines System der Land-, Haus- und Staatswirthschaft* Vol. 114.

Ladendorf, O. (1906) *Historisches Schlagwörterbuch*, Straßburg.

Lieberich, H. (1969) 'Die Anfänge der Polizeigesetzgebung des Herzogtums Baiern', in D. Albrecht et al. *Festschrift Max Spindler*, Munich.

von Loen, J. M. (1750) *Entwurf einer Staatskunst, worinnen die natürlichste Mittel entdeckt werden, ein Land mächtig reich und glücklich zu machen*, Leipzig.

Lünig, J. C. (ed.) (1724) *Codex Augustaeus oder Neuvermehrtes corpus juris Saxonici* Vol. 1, Leipzig.

Maier, M. (1966a) *Die ältere deutsche Staats-und Verwalhngslehre*, Neuwied.

Maier, H. (1966b) *Ältere deutsche Staatslehre und wesentliche politische Tradition*, Tübingen.

Majer, B. J. C. (1775) *Teutsches weltliches Staatsrecht* Vol. 1, Leipzig.

Manz (publ.) (1848) *Allgemeine Realencyclopädie oder Conversations-Lexicon für das katholische Deutschland* Vol. 8.

Maunz, T., Dürig, G., Herzog, R. (1959f) *Grundgesetz, Kommentar.*

Mayer, A. (1952) 'Die Polizeiliche Generalklausel als Problem der kommenden Polizeigestzgebung in Bayern', *Die neue Polizei* Vol. 6 No. 11.

Mayer, F. (1958) *Die Eigenständigkeit des bayerischen Verwaltungsrechts, dargestellt an Bayerns Polizeirecht*, Munich.

Meyer, H. J. (1889) *Neues Konversations-Lexicon für alle Stände* Vol. 13, fourth edition.

Moser, J. J. (1747) *Teutsches Staats-Recht* Pt. 32, Leipzig.

Mylius, C. O. (1714) *Corpus constitutionum Magdeburgicarum novissimarum* Pt. 3, Magdeburg.

Mylius, C.O. (1740) *Corpus constitutionum marchicarum*, Berlin.

von der Nahmer, W. (1831) *Handbuch des Rheinischen Rechts* Vol. 1, Frankfurt.

Neue und vollständigere Sammlung der Reichs-Abschiede (1747), Frankfurt.

Pierer, A. H. (1844) *Encyclopädisches Wörterbuch des Wissenschaften, Künste und Gewerbe* Vol. 2, second edition.

Policey-Ordnung im Lande Sternberg (1537) (1751).

Pözl, J. (1866) *Grundriß zu Vorlesungen über Polizei*, Munich.

Pütter, J. S. (1792) *Institutiones juris publici Germanici*, fifth edition, Göttingen.

Reinking, D. (1670) *Biblische Policey*, Frankfurt.

Riecke, C. H. (n.d.) *Deß Herzogthumbs Würtemberg Erneuer gemein Land-Recht*, Stuttgart.

Römischer Kayserlicher Majestät Abschied auf dem Reichs-Tag zu Wormbs, (1521).

Rüfner, W. (1962) *Verwaltungsrechtsschutz in Preußen von 1749 bis 1842*, Bonn.

Scheidemantel, H. G. (1795) *Repertorium des teutschen Staats- und Lehnsrechts* Vol. 4.

Schiedermair, R. (1961) *Einführung in das bayerische Polizeirecht*, Munich.

Schilling (1894) *'Beiträge des Polizeibegriffs nach Preußischem Recht'*, *Verwaltungsarchiv* Vol. 2.

Schmelzeisen, G. V. (1955) *Polizeiordnungen und Privatrecht*, Cologne.

Schmucker, H. (1958) 'Das Polizeiwesen im Herzogtum Württemburg nach seiner geschichtlichen Entwicklung dargestellt', unpublished dissertation, Tübingen.

Schücking, W. (ed.) (1916) *Quellensammlung zum preußischen Staatsrecht*, Leipzig.

Scotti, J. J. (1826) *Sammlungen der Gesetze und Verordnungen Cleve und Mark*, Düsseldorf.

Scupin, H.-H. (1970) 'Die Entwicklung des Polizeibegriffs und seine Verwendung in den neuen deutschen Polizeigesetzen', unpublished dissertation, Marburg.

Segall, J. (1914) *Geschichte und Strafrecht der Reichspolizeiordnungen von 1530, 1548 und 1577*, Breslau.

von Sonnenfels, J. (1787) *Grundsätze der Polizey, Handlung und Finanz* Vol. 1, fifth edition, Vienna

Vorländer, K. (1967) *Philosophie der Neuzeit*, Hamburg.

Wolzendorff, K. (1906) *Die Grenzen der Polizeigewalt Tl. 2: Die Entwicklung des Polizeibegriffs im 19. Jahrhundert*, Marburg.

Zedler, J. H. (1741) *Großes vollständiges Universallexicon aller Wissenschaften und Künste* Vol. 28.

Zobel, K. (1952) " 'Polizei'. Geschichte und Bedeutungswandel des Wortes und seine Zusammensetzung", unpublished dissertation, Munich.

Part II
Policing Continental Europe

[6]

'Police' and the Formation of the Modern State. Legal and Ideological Assumptions on State Capacity in the Austrian Lands of the Habsburg Empire, 1500–1800

Roland Axtmann (*University of Aberdeen*)

Since the late fifteenth century in German-speaking territories, rulers claimed a general competence in the combating of all social disorder for which existing law and custom did not provide a remedy. The concept of 'police' denoted these state activities. Focusing on developments in Lower Austria and Vienna between 1500 and 1800, I discuss the transition from the practice that regarded policing as the *administration* of the affairs of the state to the practice of 'high policing' which saw the police as a *preventative force* functioning as a means to defend the state against internal enemies. I argue that this transformation was closely bound up with the growing concern of the state since the middle of the seventeenth century with the surveillance of its population.

I

In German-speaking Europe the term 'police' (*Policey*) was first found in the towns and, subsequently, in the principalities; in Würzburg in 1476, in Nuremberg in ordinances of the town council (*Regiment und Pollicei*) of 1482 and 1485, in the Electorate of Mainz (*Regiment und Pollucy*) in 1488. From the early sixteenth century, the combination 'police and good order' or 'good police and order' is used in the sources. In the imperial and the territorial police ordinances (*Polizeiordnungen*) of the sixteenth century the word 'police' was used in a very distinct and specific way. Though the spelling of the word 'Policey' was not fixed—one can find 'Policy(ei)', 'Pollicey(ei)', 'Pollizey(ei)', 'Politzey', 'Polluc(e)y', and 'Pullucey'—its meaning remained invariable: it meant the condition of good order in the public realm and in the common weal. The aim of 'police' was to establish a well ordered civic or territorial community. 'Good police' (*gute Polizei*) meant the redressing and correcting of disorder. Furthermore, the word 'policey' was also used to refer to the

I would like to thank Professor Philip Corrigan, University of Exeter, and Dr Michael Dyer, University of Aberdeen, for comments on an earlier version of this article.

instructions and activities which were considered necessary for the maintenance or reformation of 'good order', thus being identical with 'police ordinance'. In the course of the sixteenth century the term was used in an increasingly extended form to indicate one of the major tasks of government: the ruling authorities claimed a general competence in the combating of all social disorders for which existing law and custom did not provide a remedy.[1]

In so far as the police ordinances were dissociated from custom and traditional law, they constituted a new departure in the history of the formation of the modern state. The police ordinances created *new* law. The ordinances were deliberate acts of will and reason. These new laws stood, in principle, in stark contrast to the old law (*gutes altes Recht*) which had not been *created* and *enacted* by a secular sovereign legislator but was thought of as representing and expressing perennial norms contained in tradition, ethical values, and religious prescriptions. 'Old' law was not enacted but 'found'; changes in the law were thought of, not as a purposeful creation, but as a 'reformation' of still binding traditional norms. The task of the ruler, which emerged from this notion, was to provide *pax et iustitia*. For the medieval ruler to govern meant to sit in judgement; to 'find', ascertain, and confirm law was the ruler's main political responsibility.

The rulers performed this task within two main constraints. The dominant ideology contained the idea that the rulers had received their authority from God, *Dei gratia*. As deputies of Christ, *vicarii Christi*, their office, as *ministerium*, obliged them to perform their duties in a devout and just way. But in so far as the rulers' 'legislative' power was subordinated to their judicial power (or, rather, was by and large comprised by it), they did not only rule under God but also under the law. This constraint of the ruler's authority, which was rooted in religious ideology, was complemented by a political constraint. The power structure of medieval society, which was characterized by a plurality of autonomous, if not autogenous, authorities with economic and military resources of their own, prevented the ruler from imposing law without the consensus of the *meliorum et maiorum terrae*. Herein lies the fundamental tension of the medieval polity: as a consequence of the feudal contract, the vassals were obliged to give aid and counsel, *consilium et auxilium*, to their feudal lord; but given the fragmented power structure, this duty to give advice could be transformed into a right to be consulted and even the right of approval. Likewise, the duty to come to the support of the lord could be interpreted as legitimating the participation in the administration of

---

[1] G. Oestreich, *Neostoicism and the Early Modern State* (Cambridge, 1982), p. 156; H. Maier, *Die ältere deutsche Staats- und Verwaltungslehre* (Munich, 1980), pp. 92–8; F.-L. Knemeyer, 'Polizeibegriffe in Gesetzen des 15. bis 18. Jahrhunderts. Kritische Bemerkungen zur Literatur über die Entwicklung des Polizeibegriffs', *Archiv für öffentliches Recht*, 92 (1967), 155–62; P. Preu, *Polizeibegriff und Staatszwecklehre. Die Entwicklung des Polizeibegriffs durch die Rechts- und Staatswissenschaften des 18. Jahrhunderts* (Göttingen, 1983), pp. 33–5; R. W. Scribner, 'Police and the Territorial State in 16th Century Württemberg', in E. J. Kouri and T. Scott (eds.), *Politics and Society in Reformation Europe* (London, 1987), p. 104.

Police and the Formation of the Modern State 41

the realm. While the nobility was thus providing power resources for the ruler, at the same time it also restricted his use of these resources. In the course of this negotiated confrontation, the nobility acquired (and reaffirmed) legal rights which further bound the ruler. These *iura quaesita* were, in principle, unimpeachable by the ruler. This led to a situation in which particularistic law or individual rights held predominance over general or universal law.[2]

Keeping the peace and providing justice were the two main responsibilities and justifications of royal authority. The task of preserving the peace, however, gave the rulers the opportunity to formulate and create new law in the Imperial and territorial peace statutes (*Landfrieden*). Between 1103 and 1235 eighteen Imperial peace statutes were issued; and between 1093 and 1235 ten territorial peace statutes were published. It was this legislation which turned a ruler increasingly into a *legum conditor*. The peace statutes of the twelve and thirteenth centuries were mainly concerned with preventing violence, blood feuds, and duels, but also with preserving public order more generally, which led to the inclusion of matters of an economic and administrative nature into the statutes. To achieve these goals the existing legal order was systematized and reformed and rulers demanded of all people within their jurisdiction to obey these new laws. This legislation remained firmly rooted in the legal thinking of the time in that it emanated from the rulers' duty to maintain *pax et iustitia*. In the late middle ages the regulative force of these statutes waned and aristocratic self-help to redress perceived wrong came to the fore again. It was only in 1495 that a new Imperial Peace Statute was issued at the imperial diet at Worms forbidding feud and violent self-help. But the '*Ewiger Landfrieden*' ('Eternal Peace of the Land') of 1495 was not an expression of the authority of the Emperor, rather the contrary: the Imperial Estates acquired the right to determine the composition of the Imperial Court (*Reichskammergericht*) which was designed to guarantee the peace by allowing and securing due legal process. The Imperial Peace Statute of 1495 thus restricted, not augmented, the legislative power of the Emperor.[3]

Since the notion of the ruler as legislator was familiar through the tradition of the peace statutes, the police ordinances of the sixteenth century, as *enacted* law, did not break completely with legal tradition. Furthermore, though police

[2] O. Brunner, *Land und Herrschaft. Grundfragen der territorialen Verfassungsgeschichte Oesterreichs im Mittelalter* (Darmstadt; 5th edn. 1973), pp. 133–46; H. Boldt, *Deutsche Verfassungsgeschichte*, vol. 1: *Von den Anfängen bis zum Ende des älteren deutschen Reiches 1806* (Munich, 1984), pp. 48–50, 54–9; H. J. Berman, *Law and Revolution. The Formation of the Western Legal Tradition* (Cambridge, Mass., 1983), pp. 292–4, 482–6; Maier, *Staats- und Verwaltungslehre*, pp. 50–3; M. Raeff, *The Well-Ordered Police State: Social and Institutional Change Through Law in the Germanies and Russia 1600—1800* (New Haven, 1983), p. 53; W. Merk, 'Der Gedanke des gemeinen Besten in der deutschen Staats- und Rechtsentwicklung', in W. Merk (ed.), *Festschrift für Alfred Schultze* (Weimar, 1934), pp. 481–99.

[3] Boldt, *Verfassungsgeschichte*, pp. 56–7, 123–4, 256; Berman, *Law and Revolution*, pp. 493–510; J. Gernhuber, *Die Landfriedensbewegung in Deutschland bis zum Mainzer Reichslandfrieden von 1235* (Mainz, 1952).

legislation was the prerogative of the ruler, co-operation between him and the Estates was by no means ruled out. Thus the police ordinance of Lower Austria of 1552/68 stated that it had been issued with the knowledge and consent of the Estates. It was a kind of emergency legislation, dictated by dire need (*der notturft nach*), and passed in the interest of the common weal (*gemeiner Nutzen*).[4] Well into the seventeenth century, police ordinances were typically drawn up on the instigation of the Estates and with their active participation.[5] The decline in the power position of the Estates in the wake of the Thirty Years War found one of its expressions in their diminished role as participants in police legislation.

The Imperial Police Ordinances of 1530, 1548, and 1577 allow us to gain an understanding of the notion of the 'good order' which informed police ordinances until the middle of the seventeenth century. The Imperial Police Ordinances regulated a wide variety of activities and circumstances. Dress regulations and sumptuary laws were enacted to prevent the blurring of status distinctions. Disregard of these laws was punished either by the confiscation of the luxury item or by the imposition of a high fine. These sumptuary laws also covered excessive expense at christenings, weddings and funerals. Blasphemy and cursing were made punishable, as were adultery, concubinage, and procuration of women. Provisions prohibiting the formation of economic monopolies as well as the practice of selling and buying goods under avoidance of market transactions (*Fürkauf*) were among the most important regulations concerning economic matters. Profiteering, usury, and embezzlement were considered criminal offences and so was breach of trust, particularly in cases of wardship. Slander and libel became punishable; adulterators of wine and of foodstuffs faced severe penalties. Such was the range of the provisions and prohibitions in the Imperial Police Ordinances that increasingly all Imperial criminal law was concentrated in these ordinances.[6] Since the Imperial Peace Statute of 1495 had already outlawed feud or private warfare as a legitimate means of redressing private grievances, issues of 'public order' in the narrow sense of public tranquillity and the absence of illegitimate violence in social relations were marginalized in these ordinances.[7]

By and large the police ordinances of the principalities within the Empire resembled the Imperial Police Ordinances. The Police Ordinance of Lower Austria in 1542, for example, maintained that vice, frivolity, and wrongdoings of the populace had incurred the wrath of God. God's wrath was evident in the threat to the well-being of the population posed by the Turks and by inflation. The reformation of good police (*Reformation guter Pollicey*) was

---

[4] *Codex Austriacus*, ii. 147 (hereafter: *Cod. Aust.*)

[5] R. Schulze, *Policey und Gesetzgebungslehre im 18. Jahrhundert* (Berlin, 1982), p. 39.

[6] J. Segall, *Geschichte und Strafrecht der Reichspolizeiordnungen von 1530, 1548 und 1577* (Breslau, 1914), p. 101.

[7] For an edition of the Imperial Police Ordinances see E. A. Koch (ed.), *Neue und vollständige Sammlung der Reichs-Abschiede* . . . (Frankfurt, 1747), ii. 332–45 (for 1530), 587–606 (for 1548), iii. 379–98 (for 1577).

Police and the Formation of the Modern State 43

therefore necessary.[8] The Police Ordinance of Lower Austria in 1568 reiter-
ated the concerns and objectives of the 1542 ordinance. Vice and frivolity,
annoying bad habits and extravagance, expressed by gluttony and unseemly
and immoderate attire, had brought the wrath of God in the guise of the
Turks upon the populace. Re-establishing a common order and good police
(*eine gemeine Ordnung und Reformation guter Politžey*) made it incumbent
upon the ruler to implant (*Pflantzung*) virtue, propriety, discipline, decency,
and piety in his Christian subjects.[9]

In these as in other territorial police ordinances of the sixteenth century,
'good order' was related to concerns about morality and comprised primarily
the conduct of a virtuous and religious life. Religion, both as a body of beliefs
and as a pattern of behaviour, was the primary concern. Good order was
thought to exist only if the subjects led a modest, orderly *Christian* life: as
apostasy of religious faith was considered to be the root of all social evil and
disorder, the list of regulations in the police ordinances of the sixteenth
century frequently commenced with prohibitions concerning blasphemy and
cursing.[10]

As long as the Estates had not yet been deprived of their power, the notion
of the *bonum commune*, which the ruler had the duty to guarantee, was
entwined in the notion of *pax et iustitia*; the legislative authority of the ruler,
as expressed in the police ordinances, was considered to emanate from his
judicial power. The common weal or welfare was seen as the result of justice
as represented and exercised by the ruler and of the condition of peace to
which this justice gave rise. But this consensual understanding of the legal
and political order was undermined by the development of absolutism. The
definition of the common weal now became the domain of the ruler and his
staff; it was used for legitimating the ruler's attempt to accrue powers to
himself which so far he had had to share with the Estates.[11]

By the ruler's appellation of the common weal, 'policey' could be constituted
as *ius inspectionis* and as *ius reformandi politicum*, i.e., police legislation could
claim to express the ruler's right and duty, not only to oversee the social and
political consequences of the *iura quaesita* as they materialized in 'private'
legal orders, but to redress any resulting harm to the *salus publica*. And even
if this common weal was defined in a traditional way as the maintenance of
the old status order, in a time of fundamental social and economic change the

---

[8] *Polizeiordnung Niederösterreichs von 1542* (Vienna: Hanns Singrüner, n.d.).

[9] *Cod. Aust.* ii. 147–51; on ordinance of 1552: Wilhelm Brauneder, 'Der soziale und rechtliche
Gehalt der österreichischen Polizeiordnungen des 16. Jahrhunderts', *Zeitschrift für historische
Forschung*, 3 (1976), 205–19; on dress regulations: G. Hampel-Kallbrunner, *Beiträge zur Geschichte der Kleiderordnungen mit besonderer Berücksichtigung Oesterreichs* (Vienna, 1962), pp.
45–9.

[10] Raeff, *The Well-Ordered Police State*, pp. 167–8.

[11] Maier, *Staats- und Verwaltungslehre*, pp. 157–9; Merk, 'Der Gedanke des gemeinen Besten',
pp. 503–9.

ever more far-reaching police regulations in defence of the old order could not but strengthen the state as legislator and thus contribute to its rise above the old powers.[12]

Since the late seventeenth century, natural law theorists contributed to a new conceptualization of 'police'. 'Police' was now thought to be concerned with promoting the public good, the happiness, or even bliss (*Glückseligkeit*) of the population: since the mid-seventeenth century the purpose of the state was seen, both by the rulers themselves and by the majority of the natural law theorists, as going beyond the confines of preserving *pax et iustitia* and comprising the task of actively promoting the secular and material welfare of the state and the population. *Salus publica* and *felicitas/beatitudo civitatis* replaced *pax et iustitia* as the primary definition of the 'state-objective' (*Staatszweck*). Not the 'reformation' of a destabilized 'good old order', but the creation and formation of a *new* order based on reason and rationality were now thought to be the ruler's task.[13]

In Christian Wolff's rationalistic natural law theory, *societas civilis*, which was thought to have been established through a social contract and to be identical with the 'state', was 'a means to promote the common weal [*gemeine Wohlfahrt*]'. The contractual relationship between sovereign authority and its subjects comprised the promise by the ruler 'to muster all his powers and diligence to devise those means beneficial to the promotion of the common weal and security and to make all necessary preparations for their deployment'. The subjects, on the other hand, promised 'to consent and accede to any given instructions which are considered by the ruler to be beneficial to them'.[14]

This theory established a particularly strong teleological conceptualization of the 'state'. The state was now conceptualized as a rationally created means to achieve an end which was conceived as prior to the state. This meant, in effect, that political rule could not any longer be derived from, and legitimated by, its origins, for example as being *dei gratia*. Rather, political legitimation was now seen to derive from the purposive and rational pursuit of common welfare as the contractual end.[15] In Wolff's philosophy, every activity was regarded as lawful which conformed to reason. The state as the sole and only

---

[12] Preu, *Polizeibegriff*, pp. 47–51; D. Willoweit, 'Struktur und Funktion intermediärer Gewalten im Ancien Regime', *Der Staat*, supplement 2 (1978), 20; R. Grawert, 'Historische Entwicklungslinien des neuzeitlichen Gesetzesrechts', *Der Staat*, 11 (1972), 11–14.

[13] U. Scheuner, 'Die Staatszwecke und die Entwicklung der Verwaltung im deutschen Staat des 18. Jahrhunderts', in G. Kleinheuer and P. Mikat (eds.), *Beiträge zur Rechtsgeschichte. Gedächtnisschrift für Hermann Conrad*, (Paderborn, 1979), pp. 477–82; H. Wessel, *Zweckmäßigkeit als Handlungsprinzip in der deutschen Regierungs- und Verwaltungslehre der frühen Neuzeit* (Berlin, 1978), pp. 135–50.

[14] Chr. Wolff, *Vernünfftige Gedanken von dem wissenschaftlichen Leben der Menschen und insonderheit dem gemeinen Wesen zur Beförderung der Glückseeligkeit des menschlichen Geschlechtes* . . . (Halle, 1756), §§ 4, 223, 230, 433.

[15] G. Niedhardt, 'Aufgeklärter Absolutismus oder Rationalisierung der Herrschaft?', *Zeitschrift für historische Forschung*, 6 (1979), 201.

Police and the Formation of the Modern State 45

guardian of the common weal was not only entitled but, indeed, obliged to subject to its direct control all facts of social life.[16]

In this theory, as in all the other natural-law theories before the middle of the eighteenth century, the *common good* was not defined by taking the welfare and well-being of individuals as the starting-point. Rather, there was the assumption of a coalescence of the interests of the state and those of the individual subjects (organized in patriarchal families). Should a conflict between these interests arise, then private interests should be curbed in favour of public/state interests. Thus, on the one hand, the state-objective of common welfare confined domination by formulating a 'social' goal the pursuit of which was considered the only legitimate activity of the state. On the other hand, however, it was left to the ruler's discretion to determine the means which would best serve the common weal; to destroy those political or social forces thought to prevent its promotion; and to decide on the degree of 'civil' liberties permissible from the point of view of the common welfare. This ambivalence was particularly manifest in the writings of Justi and Sonnenfels who, in the second half of the eighteenth century, were influential in forming political thinking in the Habsburg monarchy.[17]

Johann Heinrich Gottlob von Justi, who, in the early 1750s, had taught in Vienna, adhered to Wolff's teleological conceptualization of the state. The creation of 'the common blissful happiness [*gemeinschaftliche Glückseligkeit*] of ruler and subjects' was the purpose of the state; it was the duty of the ruler 'to maintain and increase the fortune and assets of the state and make his subjects happy'.[18] Justi conceived the relationship between ruler and subjects as one of mutual obligations: the ruler's responsibility with regard to the promotion of happiness was matched by the subjects' duty to obey.[19] But not only did the state become a means to an end in this theory; the subjects, too, became instrumentalized as a means of the state: it was their duty 'to promote with all their powers the welfare of the state'.[20] This idea was derived from the quintessentially cameralistic notion that the welfare of the individual subject was a necessary precondition for the ruler's financial wealth. Thus, whereas rational natural law served as the springboard for the definition of

---

[16] H. E. Strakosch, *State Absolutism and the Rule of Law. The Struggle for the Codification of Civil Law in Austria, 1753–1811* (Sydney, 1967), p. 120; on Wolff cf. L. Krieger, *The German Idea of Freedom. History of a Political Tradition*, (Boston, 1957), pp. 66–71; on Pufendorf, Wolff, and the influence of natural-law theories on the policies of 'enlightened' absolutism cf. H. von Voltelini, 'Die naturrechtlichen Lehren und die Reformen des 18. Jahrhunderts', *Historische Zeitschrift*, 105 (1910), 65–104.

[17] K. Tribe, *Governing Economy. The Reformation of German Economic Discourse 1750–1840* (Cambridge, 1988), ch. 4.

[18] J. H. G. v. Justi, *Staatswirthschaft oder Systematische Abhandlung aller ökonomischen und Cameral-wissenschaften, die zur Regierung eines Landes erfordert werden* (Leipzig, 1755), vol. ii: § 15; vol: i: § 21.

[19] Ibid.

[20] J. H. G. v. Justi, *Natur und Wesen der Staaten als die Quelle aller Regierungswissenschaften und Gesetze . . .* (Aalen, 1969, reprint of 1771 edn.), § 136.

the state-objective, cameralistic theories informed the thinking about the practical policies and, at the same time, served as their justification.[21]

Justi defined *policey* as the 'science to organize the internal constitution of the state in such a way that the welfare of individual families should constantly be in a precise connection with the common good [*dem allgemeinen Besten*]'.[22] Police was thought of as an activity aimed at mediating between the happiness of the individual (family) and that of the state. Justi thus rejected the idea of a coalescence of private and public interests. The recognition of private interests led to the idea of a sphere of civil liberties which remained outside the reach of the state. Justi argued that 'as long as the citizens are obliged to obey only those laws that had been enacted for the common happiness, they are in fact free. This is the essential characteristic of the civil liberty [*bürgerliche Freyheit*].'[23]

But this assertion of the *libertas civilis* remained restricted in several ways: first, happiness as the purpose of the state remained the determinant of liberty; second, neither ruler nor 'state' were said to be equally bound by enacted law; third, there were no legally fixed guarantees of those liberties. If the common weal was both linked to private welfare and dependent on the balance of individual happiness and the happiness of the state, then the activity of the state had to be concerned, of necessity, with both private and public happiness at the same time. The pursuit of private interests could not be left to the discretion of the individual (family), but had to become an area of intervention within the purview of the state. Furthermore, according to Justi, the overall aim of the state had to be to curb the power and influence of all social groups and the political estates in order to remove any possibility of them challenging the authority of the state and, as a result of their struggles between themselves, destabilizing the community. Neither was thought to be beneficial to the common welfare.[24]

For Justi 'police' comprised all activities concerned with the promotion of the common weal. 'State-objective' and 'police-objective' were identical: the furtherance and maintenance of the *salus publica*. Joseph von Sonnenfels, who took up a professorship in Vienna in 1763 and was to be an influential member of the political classes in the Habsburg monarchy over the following decades, however, departed from the tradition of equating police with welfare. For him 'police is a science to establish and manage the internal security of

---

[21] B. Stollberg-Rilinger, *Der Staat als Maschine. Zur politischen Methaphorik des absoluten Fürstenstaates* (Berlin, 1986), pp. 104–5, 109–10.

[22] J. H. G. v. Justi, *Die Grundfeste zu der Macht und Glückseeligkeit der Staaten . . .* (Königsberg, 1760), vol. i: § 3.

[23] Justi, *Natur und Wesen*, § 235.

[24] Justi, *Staatswirthschaft*, vol. i: § 76; D. Klippel, *Politische Freiheit und Freiheitsrechte im deutschen Naturrecht des 18. Jahrhunderts* (Paderborn, 1976), pp. 63–6; H. Klueting, *Die Lehre von der Macht der Staaten* (Berlin, 1986), pp. 87–114; U. Engelhardt, 'Zum Begriff der Glückseligkeit in der kameralistischen Staatslehre des 18. Jahrhunderts (J. H. G. v. Justi)', *Zeitschrift für historische Forschung*, 8 (1981), 37–79.

the state'.[25] The sphere of internal security, as the area of police intervention, comprised two distinct dimensions: 'public security' as the condition where the state had nothing to fear from its citizens, and 'private security' as the condition where the citizens were protected from illegal encroachments by the state on their civil liberty as well as from attacks on their life, property, and honour.[26] The concern for both 'public security' and the citizen's protection against criminal assault led to Sonnenfels's involvement in the formation of police *forces* under the control of the state.

There are two aspects in Sonnenfels's arguments which are of some importance to our discussion. First, Sonnenfels did not consider activities aimed at promoting (economic) welfare to fall outside the purview of the state now that police was conceptually restricted to establishing and managing internal security. Rather, he accepted that economic changes had brought a certain degree of autonomy for private economic activities. A distinct economic discipline, the *Handlungswissenschaft*, was to analyse these new developments.[27] Freed from economic considerations, the 'security' police (forces) could now be used more efficiently to deal with the disruptive effects of the strengthening of private forces which resulted from the economic changes. The police (forces) were construed as a coercive instrument which intervened to 'keep the private forces in a position of subordination to the forces of the state'.[28] In so far as the control over the police (forces) should reside with the territorial prince, this new definition of police extended the power of the ruler to the detriment of the Estates and local power-holders.[29]

This description of the task of the police as a guarantor of 'public security' sheds ample light on its importance for maintaining 'private security'. For Sonnenfels 'civil liberty' consisted in the 'freedom to act in so far as this act did not violate public welfare [*öffentliche Wohlfahrt*]'.[30] This understanding of civil liberty remained in line with the position already taken by Justi. However, Sonnenfels supported attempts to codify criminal, public, and civil law. For him, such codification was an important step towards establishing 'private security'. He maintained that a certain degree of coherence and predictability of the law should be achieved by formulating legal principles as the cornerstones of codified law.[31]

[25] J. v. Sonnenfels, *Grundsätze der Polizey, Handlung und Finanzwissenschaft: Erster Theil* (Vienna, 2nd edn. 1768), vol. i: § 29.

[26] Ibid., § 31ff; K.-H. Osterloh, *Joseph von Sonnenfels und die österreichische Reformbewegung im Zeitalter des aufgeklärten Absolutismus* (Lübeck, 1970), pp. 49–79 for a summary of Sonnenfels's 'Polizeywissenschaft'.

[27] Osterloh, *Sonnenfels*, pp. 79–104.

[28] J. v. Sonnenfels, *Ueber öffentliche Sicherheit, oder von der Sorgfalt, die Privatkräfte gegen die Kraft des Staats in einem untergeordneten Verhältnisse zu erhalten. Ein Nachlaß* (Vienna, 1817).

[29] Schulze, *Policey*, pp. 102–9; Preu, *Polizeibegriff*, pp. 157–64.

[30] Sonnenfels, *Grundsätze*, vol. i: § 76.

[31] Strakosch, *State Absolutism*, passim.

But in his argumentation, Sonnenfels did not transcend the confines of monarchical absolutism. On the one hand, he was adamant that legislation should bind the ruler as well as the ruled and be limited to those enactments which pertained to the common weal. On the other hand, however, Sonnenfels left it to the monarch's discretion to determine whether any particular law did or did not contribute to the *salus publica*.[32] This bias in favour of the monarch was also reflected in Sonnenfels's notion of 'police'. As the police was charged with controlling social groups in order to prevent any of them gaining a pre-eminence which would threaten not only social harmony and happiness but also the very existence of the state, Sonnenfels understood the police as an instrument used by the absolutist state as a means of securing its own existence.[33]

A second aspect of Sonnenfels's discussion of the police deserves attention. Standing in a legal and theoretical tradition which went back to the late fifteenth century, Justi had conceived police essentially as '*cura promovendi salutem publicam*'. But by removing 'concern for the promotion of public welfare' from the field of activity of the police, Sonnenfels defined the task of police as much narrower than the overarching 'state-objective'. Pütter in 1770 epitomized the new departure in the thinking about police when he conceived police as '*cura avertendi mala futura*'. Not the promotion of the common good, but 'the concern for averting the ills to come' would increasingly define the task of the police. It was this redefinition of police which shifted the meaning of police as the synonym of good government and public order to a conceptualization of the police as an organizational force charged with maintaining public order and safety and with preventing and investigating unlawful activities.[34] I shall return to this point in the third part of this article.

II

In the previous section I have suggested that, until the late Middle Ages, the task of the rulers was seen as providing and maintaining *pax et iustitia*. Their legal role was largely passive: they 'found' and confirmed the old law; they did not create new law. Since the late fifteenth century, however, rulers increasingly assumed the task of reforming and reconstituting a destabilized 'good order' through enacting police ordinances. They claimed a general competence in the combatting of all social disorder for which existing law and custom did not provide a remedy. Since the middle of the seventeenth century police legislation went beyond these restitutive concerns and aimed to bring

[32] Sonnenfels, *Grundsätze*, vol. i: § 76; W. Ogris, 'Joseph von Sonnenfels als Rechtsreformer', in H. Reinalter (ed.), *Joseph von Sonnenfels* (Vienna, 1988), pp. 35, 42–51.

[33] Osterloh, *Sonnenfels*, p. 51.

[34] J. St. Pütter, *Institutiones Iuris Publici Germanici* (Göttingen, 1770), § 321; cf. P. Pasquino, 'Theatrum politicum. The Genealogy of Capital—Police and the State of Prosperity', *Ideology and Consciousness* 4 (1978), pp. 45–7; Preu, *Polizeibegriff*, pp. 167–92.

Police and the Formation of the Modern State 49

about and enhance the secular and material welfare of the state and its population. This state-objective was characteristic of 'enlightened' absolutism, though 'police' was gradually redefined during that period. Though still related to the notion of 'welfare', 'police' came to signify that body of state agents which was charged with maintaining internal, 'public' security.

The police ordinances of the sixteenth and early seventeenth centuries constituted the response by the state to the social and economic transformation of society. The pull of the towns in the fifteenth and sixteenth centuries as well as the expansion of the money economy through trade and industry and the commercialization of agriculture undermined traditional social relations. The religious conflicts since the Reformation added to the social and economic uncertainties. As the stipulations regarding morality or the sumptuary laws demonstrate for Austria, a major goal was the preservation of the established status order by securing the means of subsistence for each established 'estate' and social group according to its respective ranking, standing, and tradition.[35] More generally speaking, the police ordinances aimed to restore the 'good old order' which had been destabilized by urbanization, monetarization, and religious controversy.

In the period of reconstruction after the breakdown of political, economic, and religious order during the Thirty Years War, however, the state's aim of achieving financial strength through economic growth gained priority in economic policy over the maintenance of the old order. It now became the aim of the economic policy of the state to manipulate and mobilize all sections of society in order to increase, and make use of, the economic potential of the country. This new goal was reflected in the new police ordinances.[36] The mobilization of material resources was a geopolitical imperative.[37] The formation of standing armies in the wake of the Peace of Westphalia vastly increased the rulers' fiscal needs for maintaining an efficient, combative military force. In order to achieve or retain 'Great Power' status, rulers had to create economic growth which could then be channelled into the build-up of military forces and the conduct of military campaigns. In order to create economic growth, the state strove to 'police' its population. The monitoring and surveillance of the population as well as the support for the commercialization of the economy through mercantilism formed part of this effort to increase the economic wealth of the state.

This economic policy found its theoretical justification in the writings of the Austrian cameralists such as Johann Joachim Becher and Philip Wilhelm von

[35] F. Hartung, *Deutsche Verfassungsgeschichte. Vom 15. Jahrhundert bis zur Gegenwart* (Stuttgart, 1950), pp. 76–7.

[36] Preu, *Polizeibegriff*, p. 17.

[37] On the importance of geopolitics for state formation and political development in general cf. Ch. Tilly, *Coercion, Capital, and European States, A.D. 900–1990* (Oxford, 1990). See also my reading of Max Weber's political sociology: R. Axtmann, 'The Formation of the Modern State. A Reconstruction of Max Weber's Arguments', *History of Political Thought*, 11 (1990), 295–311.

Hörnigk. They did not only espouse theories about population growth, the creation of a national economy, and the development of trade. They were also convinced that a core element of any economic policy was the creation of a disciplined work force. All available labour power had to be harnessed for the common good; idleness and work-shy behaviour had therefore to be eradicated.[38] It was this concern with disciplining the work force which figured prominently in the new ordinances, though it was by no means a new concern of the state.

The state's attempts to monitor and deploy the country's population in general, and the labour force in particular, manifested very clearly the public and civil law dimensions of police legislation.[39] Numerous pieces of police legislation between the sixteenth and the eighteenth century attempted to secure a continuous supply of the work force and to shape the conditions of work. The fundamental principle, underlying police regulations on work, was simple: idleness is the parent of vice, and, in particular, of begging and vagrancy. Already in 1563, an ordinance for Vienna had laid down that all unemployed people should be expelled from the city. To prevent them from finding accommodation, the police ordinance in 1597 threatened all inn-keepers with severe punishment should they give board and lodging to the unemployed (as well as to vagrants and criminals).[40] Idle persons were not tolerated: an ordinance of 1679 promulgated that, if admonition or imprisonment did not convince idle persons of the social undesirability of their behaviour, they should be ordered to leave the territory.[41] Such was the concern of the authorities with detecting the unemployed that in the early eighteenth century special district commissioners were set up to trace the whereabouts of unemployed individuals. In 1721 these commissioners were placed under a special municipal commission for security.[42]

Closely connected with the question of work and idleness was the problem of the poor and beggars. How best to deal with them had been a major political issue since the Middle Ages. One recurrent trait of the attempts to come to grips with this problem was the distinction between 'deserving' and 'undeserving' poor. In Vienna in 1443 an ordinance regulated the tasks of the city officials (*Sterzenmeister*) who had the penal authority over local and

[38] J. J. Becher, *Politischer Diskurs* (1668); Ph. W. von Hörnigk, *Oesterreich über alles, wann es nur will* (1684); cf. L. Bauer and H. Matis, *Geburt der Neuzeit. Vom Feudalsystem zur Marktgesellschaft* (Munich, 1988), p. 280.

[39] G. K. Schmelzeisen, *Polizeiordnungen und Privatrecht* (Munster, 1955); for an edition of German police ordinances and territorial statutes see *Polizei- und Landesordnungen* (=Quellen zur Neueren Privatrechtsgeschichte Deutschlands, ii, part 1 and 2), ed. G. K. Schmelzeisen (Cologne, 1968/1969)).

[40] E. H. Zimmermann (ed.), *Geschichte der Stadt Wien* (Vienna, n.d.), v, part 2, 133–5.

[41] See e.g. *Cod. Aust.* i. 205 (Jan. 1679) where penalties are listed for 'work-shy vagrants' ranging from expulsion and incarceration to capital punishment 'in order to set a warning example'.

[42] *Geschichte Wien*, p. 135.

foreign beggars.[43] They had to prove to him that circumstances beyond their control had compelled them to take up begging. If he was convinced of the truth of their claim, he could issue a certificate allowing them to beg, provided, however, that they could prove knowledge of the common Christian prayers and that they had gone to confession during the previous year and received the sacraments.[44]

The police ordinance of 1552 made it incumbent upon the parish authorities to provide for their poor. Apart from giving alms to their poor, local authorities discharged their duty by issuing certificates to their 'deserving' poor which allowed their holders to beg within the locality.[45] The financially less well-off parishes, however, were legally entitled to issue certificates granting the right to beg outside the locality. For holders of such a licence, Vienna seemed to be the most rewarding place. But with an increasing number of certified as well as unlicensed beggars and vagrants, particularly during the 'crisis of the seventeenth century', there arose the need for controlling this category of people more stringently.[46]

The local authorities were reminded by the government that they had an obligation to look after their 'deserving' poor; should they not comply with this rule they would face severe penalties. But the reissuing of such admonitions indicates that the local authorities did not heed them.[47] The county courts (*Landgerichte*), which were under the authority of local aristocratic landlords, were urged to co-operate in order to improve the combat of vagrancy.[48] But since the state was rather powerless to coerce the local authorities and power-holders into determined action, it took it upon itself to persecute the beggars and vagrants. In the eighteenth century, 'police' raids across the country to apprehend suspicious individuals were made fairly frequently.[49] In 1721 in one of these raids, the government of Lower Austria deployed more than 1,000 cavalry and four-hundred infantry in addition to the forces provided by the local authorities.[50] Those able-bodied, unlicensed vagrants, caught either in these raids or in the course of normal policing, could be compulsorily

---

[43] A. Luschin von Ebengreuth, *Geschichte des älteren Gerichtswesens in Oesterreich ob und unter der Enns* (Weimar, 1879), p. 233.

[44] K. Weiß, *Geschichte der Stadt Wien* (Vienna, 1882/3), i. 361.

[45] H. Feigl, *Die niederösterreichische Grundherrschaft vom ausgehenden Mittelalter bis zu den theresianisch-josefinischen Reformen* (Vienna, 1964), pp. 128–30.

[46] Alfred Hoffmann states that in 1727 about 8 to 10% of the population of Upper Austria, i.e. almost 26,000 people, were considered by the government to be in need and deserving of support; see A. Hoffmann, *Wirtschaftsgeschichte des Landes Oberösterreich*, vol i: *Werden-Wachsen-Reifen von der Frühzeit bis zum Jahre 1848* (Salzburg, 1952), pp. 246–8.

[47] *Cod. Aust.* ii. 76–7 (for ordinance of 1662 and its reissue in 1682); *Cod. Aust.* i. 207–9 (for ordinance of 1695).

[48] Ibid. 727, 730 (for Ferdinand III's county court regulation of 1656).

[49] See 'Land-Visitations-Ordnung' of June 1727, in *Cod. Aust.* iv. 433; also the 'Visitations-Ordnung' of 1752 for Upper Austria, in *Sammlung aller k.k. Verordnungen und Gesetze vom Jahre 1740 bis 1780, die unter der Regierung des Kaisers Joseph des II. theils noch ganz bestehen, theils zum Theile abgeändert sind* (Vienna, 1787), i, 376–83.

[50] K. Gutkas, *Geschichte des Landes Niederösterreich* (St. Pölten, 1973), pp. 297–8.

conscripted into the army.[51] But while the army thus contributed to the endeavours of the state to police vagrants and beggars, it also contributed to the problem of vagrancy. Discharged soldiers frequently roamed the country begging for money and sustenance but also extorting money by force.[52] Crippled and disabled soldiers who could not find employment added to the problem. The period of war between 1672 and 1714 aggravated the situation and it was in response to deteriorating conditions that the state embarked on a policy of devising state-subsidized invalidity provisions for disabled soldiers. This policy was the starting-point for a comparatively wide-ranging system of state provisions such as pension schemes for civil servants in the course of the eighteenth century.[53]

Yet another way of dealing with the 'undeserving' poor or beggars was to put them into workhouses.[54] There they had to work for the food and shelter they received. The first of these houses was founded in 1671 in Vienna (Leopoldstadt) and over the next hundred years or so eleven more of them were established throughout the Habsburg monarchy.[55] Beginning in the 1720s, mercantilistic ideas penetrated this mechanism of social control. Charles VI envisaged a network of such houses across the country engaged in manufacturing. For small wages the inmates, hitherto 'idle persons', would produce goods out of domestic raw material so cheaply that expensive imports would be unnecessary. This was meant to prevent, 'for the common good', money being taken out of the country.[56] The workhouses thus acquired a double task. First, they should 'socialize' the inmates so that they would become obedient subjects; second, they should instil a strict work discipline in the inmates without which an efficient work process would not be possible.[57]

The 'policing' of economic activities was also manifested in rules forbidding workers to go into service with more than one employer or to change the place of work (or, for employers, to take someone into employment) at times other than stipulated in the ordinances.[58] This provision was meant to contain competition amongst employers for workers in times of scarcity but also to restrain workers from achieving an advantageous wage-bargaining position.[59] With regard to the level of wages, ordinances frequently set an upper limit to

---

[51] *Cod. Aust.* i. 206–7 (Mar. 1693), 210 (May 1697), 216 (Feb. 1698); *Sammlung*, iii. 222 (Aug. 1755), v. 60–1 (June 1766), viii. 492–6 (Dec. 1767).

[52] *Cod. Aust.* i. 4–5 (1606/1609/1611).

[53] B. Wunder, 'Die Institutionalisierung der Invaliden-, Alters- und Hinterbliebenenversorgung der Staatsbediensteten in Oesterreich (1748–1790)', *Mitteilungen des Instituts für österreichische Geschichtsforschung*, 92 (1984), 341–406.

[54] *Cod. Aust.* ii. 545–7 (July 1671), i. 205 (Jan. 1679), 209–19 (May 1697); cf. E. Bruckmüller, *Sozialgeschichte Oesterreichs* (Vienna, 1985), pp. 269–70 on J. J. Becher's report of 1671 on idleness, work-shy behaviour, and the need for disciplining the workforce.

[55] H. Stekl, *Oesterreichs Zucht- und Arbeitshäuser, 1671–1920: Institutionen zwischen Fürsorge und Strafvollzug* (Vienna, 1978), pp. 62–73, 181.

[56] *Cod. Aust.* iv. 160 (Jan. 1724).

[57] Stekl, *Zucht- und Arbeitshäuser*, p. 91.

[58] Schmelzeisen, *Polizeiordnungen*, pp. 328–38.

[59] See 'Dienstbotenordnung' of Sept. 1688 in *Cod. Aust.* i. 281–2.

Police and the Formation of the Modern State   53

prevent workers from taking advantage of the scarcity of labour and demanding higher wages.[60] These regulations harked back to economic measures taken by the territorial rulers and the manorial lords since the second half of the fourteenth century. After the Black Deaths in the middle of the fourteenth century a policy of regulating wages and working-conditions had been pursued to combat the strengthened position of peasants and day-labourers which had resulted from the decline in population. As early as 1352, for example, wage scales for labourers in vineyards had been fixed in response to labour shortages.[61] Ordinances explicitly forbade people to demand, concede, or agree on wages higher than the officially fixed rates. These attempts to coerce workers into compliance were underpinned by outlawing workers' combinations.[62]

Police ordinances also legislated on the conditions of taking up a profession or entering a trade. The 'policing' of the guilds may serve as a prominent example. Typically, craftsmen could only pursue their occupation as members of a guild. But in their policy against monopolies, territorial rulers would sometimes threaten to license outsiders should the guilds not perform the duties which they were considered to have vis-à-vis the public. It could also happen that guilds suffered attacks at the hand of the rulers who tried to suppress them out of opposition to any sort of semi-private associations. The Tyrol Ordinance of 1602, for example, forbade blacksmiths and carpenters to form a corporation or guild.[63] In the second half of the eighteenth century, the guild system in Austria came under sustained political attack. An important step towards curbing their power was the division of industrial enterprises into those producing for the local market ('police' industries) and those producing for a distant market, either domestic or foreign ('commercial' industries) in 1754. These 'commercial' industries were placed outside the guild restrictions. As a consequence, the number of masters working for distant markets was no longer determined by the guilds but by market forces. This policy not only established the state's supervisory control over the guilds, it also allowed the instrumentalization of the guilds for a state policy that aimed at stepping up economic production and increasing the population and thus the economic and political power of the state.[64]

[60] Schmelzeisen, *Polizeiordnungen*, pp. 350–9; on wages for day labourers see *Cod. Aust.* i. 480 (ordinance for woodcutters in 1689); ii. 425–32 (ordinance for labourers in vineyards in 1666).
[61] F. Lütge, 'Das 14./15. Jahrhundert in der Sozial- und Wirtschaftsgeschichte', *Jahrbücher für Nationalökonomie und Statistik*, 162 (1950), 193–8; H. Hon-Firnberg, *Lohnarbeiter und Lohnarbeit im Mittelalter und zu Beginn der Neuzeit* (Baden/Vienna, 1935), pp. 55–112.
[62] *Cod. Aust.* i. 278–81, § 10 (Tyrol Police Ordinance of 1573); Schmelzeisen, *Polizeiordnungen*, pp. 367–8 (Austrian Ordinance for Domestic Servants of 1688).
[63] Ibid., 305 n. 82.
[64] On 'police' industries: J. Slokar, *Geschichte der österreichischen Industrie und ihrer Förderung unter Kaiser Franz I.* (Vienna, 1914), pp. 132–42; K. Pribram, *Geschichte der österreichischen Gewerbepolitik von 1740 bis 1869*, vol. 1: *1740–1798* (Leipzig, 1907), pp. 38, 104, 268; on the guilds: J. Komlos, 'Institutional Change under Pressure: Enlightened Government Policy in the 18th Century Habsburg Monarchy', *Journal of European Economic History*, 15 (1986), 442–8; Hoffmann, *Wirtschaftsgeschichte*, pp. 399–415.

54   Roland Axtmann

The centrality of the state's economic interests in police legislation was not confined to attempts to discipline the work force and to shape the production process. It also informed the new sumptuary and luxury laws. The police ordinance which Leopold I issued in 1671 did indeed impose new sumptuary laws restricting, in particular, the wearing of luxurious dresses.[65] In one respect, this ordinance remained within the traditional form: it asserted the importance of maintaining social distinction and distance between the status groups in society.[66] Conspicuous consumption was accepted as an affirmation of status; attempts of certain sections of society to live outside their station by emulating their social betters were deplored. While the highest three ranks of society were exempted from the regulations concerning the wearing of dresses, the rest of society had to conform to the newly laid-down rules. But in two other respects, this police ordinance expressed the realities of a new age. To start with, the traditional religious motivation for issuing an ordinance had receded. The ordinance was formulated, not in order to redress religious or moral wrong-doings, but to prevent the purchase of expensive foreign goods which led to 'an extremely large sum of money' being taken abroad. Furthermore, the classes which were established by the ordinance were constructed with reference to the sovereign's court; the closer in their political, social, and administrative functions individuals were to the centre of courtly life, the less they were restricted by the provisions concerning the wearing of particular types of clothes. The sovereign became the focal point in the ordinance.

This trend was reinforced in the police ordinance of 1686.[67] Whereas in the ordinance of 1671 the three highest ranks of the status order had been exempted from the provisions concerning 'conspicuous consumption', they, too, were now subjected to the new rules. Their inclusion indicates the increasing incorporation of even the top status groups into a system of domination which centred on the ruler residing at his or her court. Further-more, the ordinance of 1686 put the ruler's officials in charge of executing the new regulations. The responsibility of the state for maintaining good order was thus firmly extended to include not only legislative duties but also executive tasks. This could not but mean a subordination, at least in theory, of the local aristocracy under the supervision by the state.[68] In 1697, finally, the sumptuary laws became a means of enhancing the revenue of the ruler who faced financial difficulties due to the Turkish wars. The ordinance stated that the financial burden of the wars made it necessary for a fine to be imposed

---

[65] *Cod. Aust.* ii. 153–9.

[66] K. Plodek, 'Zur sozialgeschichtlichen Bedeutung der absolutistischen Polizei- und Landesordnungen', *Zeitschrift für bayerische Landesgeschichte*, 39 (1976), 100–1.

[67] *Cod. Aust.* ii. 159–61.

[68] On the police ordinances of 1671 and 1686 cf. Bruckmüller, *Sozialgeschichte*, pp. 276–8; Hampel-Kallbrunner, *Beiträge*, pp. 50–63.

Police and the Formation of the Modern State 55

for the wearing of dresses embroidered with silver or gold, or, alternatively, for licences to be sold which exempted their holders from these provisions.[69] By the end of the seventeenth century, then, the ruler's interests and concerns had firmly taken the central place in the territorial police ordinances.

When in August 1749, during the great reforms of the state under Maria Theresa, the subject-matter of 'police' was raised, the discussion and understanding of 'police' was informed by the developments since the second half of the seventeenth century. For Count Haugwitz, Maria Theresa's chief reforming minister, the main goal of a well-organized police was to ensure that money was not to leave the country in exchange for luxury goods from abroad. In line with mercantilistic thinking and the disciplining thrust of the intensifying absolutist state, the officials in the *Directorium in publicis et cameralibus* were agreed that squanderers had to be compelled to show moderation.[70] It was this reasoning which led 'logically' to an ordinance on luxuries in September 1749. This ordinance did not prohibit the purchase of luxury articles. Rather, it set out to prevent the *import* of luxury goods and articles. It was informed by mercantilistic ideas and a consideration for the status concerns of the aristocracy. But it also reflected the adverse economic impact of sumptuary laws on the domestic industry as well as the administrative difficulties in effectively enforcing them.[71]

It thus retained the main thrust of the luxury 'Patent' of 1732.[72] There, for the first time, it had been explicitly stated that the domestic industry which produced luxury items should be protected against foreign competition. The state's policy concerning luxury had thus taken a decisive turn. Up to the middle of the seventeenth century, sumptuary laws in general, and luxury decrees in particular, were motivated by attempts to stabilize and maintain the traditional religious order and the status distinctions between the ranks of society. After the end of the Thirty Years War these motivations receded in importance and rational considerations commensurate with mercantilistic policies came to inform state policies on luxuries. The ruler's interest in economic protectionism went hand in hand with the realization that economic and social developments had transformed society to such a degree that the traditional status order could not possibly be re-established by passing traditional sumptuary laws.[73]

---

[69] *Cod. Aust.* ii. 165–6.

[70] F. Walter, *Geschichte der österreichischen Zentralverwaltung in der Zeit Maria Theresias* (1740–1780) (=Veröffentlichungen der Kommission für Neuere Geschichte Oesterreichs, vol. 32) (Vienna, 1938), pp. 242–3; I. Mayer, 'Polizeiwesen in Wien und Niederösterreich im 18. Jahrhundert: Reform und Kompetenzverteilung', *Unsere Heimat*, 57 (1986), 77.

[71] *Die Zeit des Directoriums in publicis et cameralibus. Aktenstücke* (=Veröffentlichungen der Kommission für Neuere Geschichte Oesterreichs, vol. 18) (Vienna, 1925), pp. 391ff.

[72] *Cod. Aust.* iv. 770.

[73] M. Stolleis, *Pecunia Nervus Rerum. Zur Staatsfinanzierung in der frühen Neuzeit* (Frankfurt, 1983), pp. 35–50.

56   Roland Axtmann

III

In the previous section I have shown how the state attempted to regulate vagrancy and begging and to manage the problem of the poor. I have argued that the monitoring and disciplining of the population, and the work force in particular, had been a main objective of the police ordinances since the second half of the seventeenth century. Surveillance came to dominate considerations of 'policing'. I want to suggest in this section that this focus on surveillance contributed to the transition from a practice that regarded policing as the *administration* of the affairs of the state to a practice of 'high policing' with the police as a *preventative force* functioning as a means to defend the state against internal enemies.

Attempts to enforce a system of compulsory registration were a major concern in the 'policing' of Vienna. The Vienna Police Ordinance of 1597 stipulated that anyone who did not register guests or visitors with the authorities would lose his status and rights as a citizen.[74] New rules concerning the registration of the people in Vienna which were promulgated in 1696 demonstrated the state's incessant concern with monitoring the population.[75] In July 1746 and June 1751 compulsory registration was justified in two decrees as an important measure against vagrancy.[76] Yet another decree concerning compulsory registration in May 1757 was followed by two further decrees in April 1765.[77] The owners and caretakers of houses were again reminded that they had a duty to register all those individuals living in their house who had not yet had abode in Vienna for at least ten years. Information about these individuals concerning name, religion, nationality, marital status, occupation, and date of arrival and/or (expected) departure had to be forwarded to the authorities.[78]

The second decree in April 1765 stipulated that 'house inspectors' (*Hausvisitationskommissionäre*) had to visit the houses assigned to them for surveillance once a month to enforce compliance with compulsory registration. Eighty years earlier this task of inspecting the houses in Vienna had been assigned to two of the city's three police forces, the City Guards (*Stadtguardi*) and the *Rumorwache*.[79] This task had then been transferred to special officials when the office of *Hausnachseher* was introduced in the early 1750s. They had been put in charge of keeping a close watch over the inhabitants and visitors of Vienna, conducting secret inquiries, if need be, to ascertain whether

---

[74] *Geschichte Wien*, p. 133.

[75] *Cod. Aust.* i. 468–9.

[76] *Sammlung*, i. 32–3, 295–7.

[77] Ibid. iii. 350; iv. 376–81.

[78] Cf. also the stipulations concerning compulsory registration in the new police order for Vienna in 1776, in *Sammlung*, viii. 618–20.

[79] *Cod. Aust.* ii. 273–4; from their inception in 1569, the City Guards had been charged with enforcing registration: Mayer, *Polizeiwesen*, pp. 68–72. An instruction of 1733 for the third police force, the *Sicherheitswache*, defined its task as that of catching beggars: H. Oberhummer, *Die Wiener Polizei* (Vienna, 1938), ii. 216–26.

Police and the Formation of the Modern State 57

they abided by the regulations concerning compulsory registration.[80] In order to improve this system of surveillance, the office of 'special constable' (*Unterkommissar*) was established in 1754. Citizens of Vienna were appointed as special constable by the government of Lower Austria on the suggestion of the city council. They did not receive any pay, but were given certain tax exemptions. In all, 188 special constables were installed in order to improve the enforcement of compulsory registration. But already in 1756, this office was abolished because of drunkenness and lack of diligent performance of duties amongst these special constables.[81]

Thus, such was the concern of the state with surveillance that specialized policemen were employed in Vienna. However, the tasks of the city police forces were more comprehensive than enforcing compulsory registration. The instruction of the *Rumorwache* in 1646 may serve as an example. The *Rumorwache* had to apprehend a wide range of perpetrators: blasphemers, be they drunk or sober; workmen and traders who went about their business on Sundays and public holidays during the time of church services and mass; beggars without permits and those beggars of Catholic faith who could not prove that they went to confession regularly; Jews without permits to stay in Vienna on Sundays and public holidays; magicians, sorcerers and fortune-tellers; prostitutes, adulterers and adultresses; rapists and those who had committed incest; usurers and profiteers, be they Christians or Jews; drunk and disorderly people; those who stayed on in pubs after licensing hours; all persons bearing arms, except soldiers; people involved in routs and riots; gamblers and thieves, burglars and murderers; those people who, as bearers of a contagious disease, had returned to Vienna before their days in quarantine outside the city had lapsed.[82] The Vienna market regulation of 1647 put the *Rumormeister* also in charge of the market police;[83] and the instruction of 1706, which reaffirmed the tasks of the *Rumorwache*, added as new important duties street-lighting and fire-fighting.[84] The *Rumorwache* was thus charged with acting as public health officers, maintaining public order, upholding public morality, and providing internal security. And when in 1776 the Military Police Guard replaced the Security Day and Night Watch, the instructions of this new force were, in effect, an extended version of those issued for the *Rumorwache* in 1706.[85]

Thus, even in the late 1770s, police forces were still given the task of ensuring both 'welfare' and 'security'. In effect, 'police' was still conceptualized in very broad terms. The definition of 'police' by the government of Lower

---

[80] V. Bibl. *Die Wiener Polizei. Eine kulturhistorische Studie* (Leipzig. 1927). p. 204.

[81] *Sammlung*, ii. 357–60 for the instruction to the special constables; Bibl. *Wiener Polizei*, p. 205; Oberhummer, *Wiener Polizei*, i. 23–4.

[82] Oberhummer, *Wiener Polizei*, ii. 203–6.

[83] A. Gigl. 'Geschichte der Wiener Marktordnungen vom sechzehnten Jahrhundert bis zum Ende des achtzehnten', *Archiv für österreichische Geschichte*, 35 (1865). 153–5.

[84] Oberhummer, *Wiener Polizei*, ii. 206.

[85] *Sammlung*, viii. 630–4; Oberhummer, *Wiener Polizei*, ii. 229–55.

58   Roland Axtmann

Austria was still in force. In a draft paper presented to Maria Theresa, the
government had argued—reminiscent of Justi—that police was nothing but
the promotion of the well-being of the individual families in order to bring
about the welfare of the state as a whole.[86] Starting from this premiss, nine
areas of police activities were distinguished: population policy, health, religion
and propriety, supply of victuals, supervision of the quality of foodstuffs and
other vital goods and their price, industry (which included education, soil
cultivation, matters concerning trade, commerce, crafts, and industry proper),
poor relief as well as unemployment relief, building police, and, finally,
'administration', i.e., the execution of police regulations.[87] All these areas
were claimed to fall firmly within the policing duties of the state.

The new departure in Joseph II's reign was not that these state objectives
would have been rescinded. Rather, these activities were no longer contained
in the concept of 'police'. State reforms concerning police can be summarized
under three headings: functional differentiation, structural differentiation,
and specialization.[88] The reorganization of the police in Vienna in April 1782
reflected the processes of differentiation: policing was separated into three
distinct activities and each activity was to be overseen by a distinct body. The
municipal authorities were put in charge of all matters concerning trade,
street-cleaning, street-paving, and street-lighting, but also of the market
police; the town court was made responsible for all aspects concerning security,
in particular for arresting perpetrators and for the compulsory conveyancing
of beggars and other unwanted individuals; finally, the newly created director
of police, who was directly subordinated to the president of the government
of Lower Austria, was put in charge of the secret police and the remaining
matters of police.[89] 'Welfare' functions and 'security' functions were thus
clearly separated. Whatever the changes in policing over the next decade or
so, this functional differentiation remained in force. When the policing system
of Vienna was extended to other parts of the monarchy, the controversy this
raised was not to do with the separation of welfare and security functions, but
with the question which executive body should be put in charge of which
aspect of policing. What exactly was the responsibility regarding policing
of the local directors of police, the municipal authorities, the provincial
governments, the police directorate in Vienna, the president of the government of Lower Austria (Count Pergen) and the Court Chancery? As is well
known, these organizational power struggles were solved with the establishment of an Imperial ministry (*Hofstelle*) for police in the monarchy in 1789
and the appointment of Count Pergen as its head.[90]

[86] Bibl, *Wiener Polizei*, p. 211.
[87] F. Walter, 'Die Organisierung der staatlichen Polizei unter Kaiser Joseph II.', *Mitteilungen
des Vereins für Geschichte der Stadt Wien*, 7 (1927), 22–3; Bibl, *Wiener Polizei*. pp. 211–13.
[88] Cf. Walter, '*Organisierung*', as general overview.
[89] Ibid. 29–30.
[90] Ibid. 37–9.

Police and the Formation of the Modern State 59

It was Count Pergen who argued successfully for the 'specialization' of the state police forces. Throughout his career he maintained that police should concentrate on public security and should not get involved in matters concerning public welfare (*politico-publica*).[91] In 1793, in a time of internal political turmoil and external threat, Pergen, as minister of police, impressed on his subordinates the need to enforce the system of compulsory registration and to pay close attention to the 'subversive machinations' of those political clubs and organizations up and down the country which, inspired by developments in revolutionary France, were trying to arouse the population with 'freedom humbug' (*Freiheitsschwindel*).[92]

Pergen's conviction that the state police forces had the task of maintaining public order/tranquillity and security had found an institutionalized expression in the formation of a secret police in 1786. With regard to maintaining public order and avoiding any threats to the state, the secret police agents were urged to inquire thoroughly into the opinion among the population about the monarch and governmental policies; in particular, they were admonished to monitor the activities of likely 'rabble-rousers' (*Aufwickler des leichtgläubigen Pöbels*). For this purpose, they were also to monitor the movements of suspicious individuals and, particularly, of foreigners. They were advised to ensure the efficiency of the local systems of compulsory registration. But they were also charged with spying on other state officials and the military to ascertain their loyalty to the regime.[93]

Since Joseph II's reign, then, police was seen as a means to defend the state against internal enemies. Rather than to regard policing as the administration of the affairs of the state, it was now seen as denoting a state agency operating as a preventative force. I have argued in this section that this development was intrinsic to the emphasis on surveillance. But I have already pointed out in the first part of this article that Sonnenfels's arguments regarding the dissociation of an all-encompassing notion of *bonum commune* and the narrower concept of internal security could provide the ideological support for these changes.

But Sonnenfels's arguments were also logically open to theoretical developments critical of absolutist government. A re-evaluation of the notion of *salus publica* would lead to yet another, completely different, definition of police. In the last two decades of the eighteenth century, German idealist philosophy set out to destroy the natural law theories regarding the 'objective'

---

[91] Cf. Pergen's instruction to the local directors of police in 1785, in Oberhummer, *Wiener Polizei*, ii. 146, 149.

[92] Cf. A. H. Benna, *Die Polizeihofstelle. Ein Beitrag zur Geschichte der österreichischen Zentralverwaltung* (Vienna, 1942) (= unpublished Ph.D thesis, University of Vienna), pp. 127–45 for Pergen's instructions to his subordinates.

[93] Cf. instruction concerning secret police in Oberhummer, *Wiener Polizei*, ii. 168–76; the spying on other state officials was due to the fact that Joseph II's reversal of 'enlightened' policies in the second half of the 1780s had led to an increasing disenchantment of reform-minded bureaucrats and their gradual move into active political opposition to the regime.

of the state. The concept of *salus publica* was, rightly, interpreted as enabling the state to interfere with the self-determination of the individual. In clear contradistinction it was maintained that it was a *human right* of each individual to embark on 'the pursuit of happiness' unencumbered by the 'police' state.[94]

In this theory, the scope of state activity was limited to guaranteeing a legal framework which would allow each individual to participate in society on the basis of individual property/properties. For Kant, *salus publica* was exactly that legal constitution which guaranteed every man his freedom within the law. Kant maintained that, within such a legal context, every man would retain the right to pursue his own happiness by whatever means, so long as he did not impair the general lawful freedom and thus the rights of his fellow subjects at large.[95] This perspective led to the conceptualization of police, not as a preventative and interventionist force operating under only a few legal restraints, but as an executive body *operating firmly within the law*. This 'liberal' police force was charged with ensuring that all hindrances and threats to the security and welfare of the *citizen*, not the state, were averted, thus enabling his self-determined individual pursuit of happiness.[96]

Towards the end of the eighteenth century in Austria, there was not yet an economic and social basis for a 'bourgeois' society which could have transformed this theory into practice. There, in the last decade of the eighteenth century, the reality was a restorative state. Nevertheless, the policies of social engineering by the absolutist Habsburg monarchy had contributed to the gradual emergence of distinct 'bourgeois' groups such as intellectuals and civil servants who were demanding ever more radical political reforms to establish their right of full political participation and social equality.[97] These demands gradually undermined the material and ideological foundations of the absolutist monarchy. At the same time, the policies of the absolutist state, propelled by (geo-)political requirements since the loss of Silesia in 1740 and legitimated by rationalistic theories of domination, had whittled away the power of the traditional bearers of authority, the aristocracy and the clergy. Their attempt to regain lost ground in the period of the Turkish War and the wars with France contributed to the formation of an authoritarian régime in the 1790s. This restorative state used its police forces to stifle and suppress political and

---

[94] Cf. H. Dippel, *Germany and the American Revolution 1770–1800. A Socio-Historical Investigation of Late Eighteenth-Century Political Thinking* (Wiesbaden, 1978) on the impact of the American Revolution on German political thought.

[95] I. Kant, 'Ueber den Gemeinspruch: Das mag in der Theorie richtig sein, taugt aber nicht in der Praxis (1793)', in E. Cassirer (ed.), *Immanuel Kants Werke* (Berlin, 1914), vi. 355–98; Krieger, *The German Idea of Freedom*, pp. 86–125; Preu, *Polizeibegriff*, pp. 193–273; Klippel, *Politische Freiheit*, pp. 131–4.

[96] G. H. von Berg, *Handbuch des Teutschen Policeyrechts* (Hanover, 1799–1809), 7 vols.; F. X. Funk, 'Die Auffassung des Begriffes Polizei im vorigen Jahrhundert', *Zeitschrift für die gesamte Staatswissenschaft*, 19 (1863), 513–15; Maier, *Staats- und Verwaltungslehre*, pp. 200–7.

[97] On the Austrian 'Jacobins' cf. E. Wangermann, *From Joseph II to the Jacobin Trials* (Oxford, 1959); H. Reinalter, *Aufgeklärter Absolutismus und Revolution* (Vienna, 1980).

Police and the Formation of the Modern State 61

social discontent. It was in the last decade of the eighteenth century that 'police' became now firmly established, and deployed, as the repressive arm of the state.

[7]

FEAR AND LOATHING IN BOLOGNA AND ROME
THE PAPAL POLICE IN PERSPECTIVE

Steven Hughes

"And yet fortune ranked him with policemen, gravediggers, and potty cleaners."
Although hardly an elegant opening, this late fifteenth century literary lament,
from the *Commedia dell'Arte*, brilliantly sums up the status of the police in early
modern Italy.[1] Few travellers, legislators, or literati could refrain from denigrating
the Italian police, or *sbirri*,[2] as vile, rude, and corrupt creatures, worthy only
of censure and contempt. Even though the sbirri served as the executors of the
courts, they shared none of the prestige of the judiciary, inspiring instead a host
of laws, exhortations, and warnings designed specifically to control their ignoble
instincts. Yet, this loathesome image was no accident of recruitment. Italian
administrators often agreed that, by definition, the functions of the police were
best assigned to folk of little faith or character, one step removed from the criminals
they captured. The most visible representatives of the state were thus also the
most odious, incapable of contributing prestige or goodwill to the system they
served. This seeming paradox of authority and repugnance particularly applied
to the sbirri of the Papal States, and they will provide the focus of subsequent
discussion.

Perusing the appropriate archives of Bologna and Rome,[3] one perceives an
underlying logic to the sbirri and their lamentable reputation: A logic based on
the nature of early modern policing, and on the honor, economics, and justice
intrinsic to the development of the Papal States, a country rife with aristocratic
pretensions, semi-autonomous institutions, and special privileges. In short, the
supposed depravity of the central administration's agents enhanced the power
and immunity of competing hierarchies, especially the nobility and the College
of Cardinals. Consequently, serious attempts to change the sbirri and their image
only came with "enlightened" reforms at the end of the eighteenth century, reforms
which were swept away, along with their intended targets, by the intervention
of the French on the peninsula. With the Restoration, the sbirri fell out of step
with the prevailing pattern of government, based on a unified, centralized,
bureaucracy, clearly responsible for the actions of its enforcers. The sbirri could
thus no longer be allowed to reflect shame on the Pope's justice. Discipline,
consistency, and probity (in sum, professionalization) became the order of the
day and the rough and tumble manners of the sbirri could no longer pass muster.
In 1816, they were replaced by a uniformed corps of *Carabinieri* patterned on
the French *Gendarmerie*. What follows is a portrait of these interesting characters
of pre-industrial policing, with some hypotheses explaining their role and their
longevity in the general context of early modern justice and European state
making.

To call the sbirri police is slightly misleading if it conjures up an image of
uniformed patrolmen serving a centralized organization of social control, crime
prevention, and law enforcement. They more closely resembled the sheriffs and

deputies of the old west, their only identification being a badge, backed up by an intimidating array of weapons.[4] Anything but elegant, the sbirri were often quite shabby, dressed in proportion to their notoriously low salaries.[5] A similar lack of uniformity also marked their organization, serving as they did a variety of overlapping and occasionally competing authorities. This confusion arose from the dependence of the sbirri on the courts and the many officials imbued with juridical powers.[6] No clear-cut "police" institution existed before the nineteenth century in the Papal States, and the sbirri's primary function consisted of executing the dictates and warrants of the judiciary.[7] Thus each of Rome's courts had its own *bargello* or captain, who in turn was responsible for the recruitment, payment, and comportment of a specific number of sbirri.

No central authority coordinated or accounted for these different groups, and consequently historical reconstruction of their organization is fraught with difficulties, especially across the many centuries of their existence. Our clearest snapshot of the sbirri as a whole comes from a study completed in 1790 by the papal treasury as part of its attempt to rationalize the state's finances.[8] Certainly the document is not applicable in all of its details to the entire early modern period; but given the notorious institutional inertia of the Roman government, it provides an important clue to the general structure of the sbirri over time and suggests their place within the papal bureaucracy as a whole.

As indicated in Table I, Rome in 1790 had a total of 163 sbirri under 8 bargelli serving seven different courts. Of these, the sbirri of the Governor of Rome formed the largest group, emphasizing his predominant, although not exclusive, control over civil and criminal justice within the city.[9] Serving the criminal tribunal, the Governor's sbirri were popularly known as the *Corte*, but they also provided many functions such as crowd control, preventive patrol, and clandestine surveillance that would fit under the modern rubric of policing.[10] About a third of his sbirri were mounted and spent much of their time in the countryside pursuing banditi, brigands, and similar fugitives from justice.[11] Yet despite the importance of the Governor's sbirri, the jurisdictional picture was often muddled by the conflicting authority of the other courts' police who acted independently, and thus contributed to the public's image of capricious and undisciplined policing.[12]

TABLE I

Bargelli and Sbirri Serving the Courts of Rome in 1790*

Court or Tribunal	Number of Bargelli	Number of Sbirri	Number of Scribes	Total
Court of the Governor of Rome: City	1	94	1	96
Court of the Governor of Rome: Province	2	48	0	50
Court of the Cardinal Camerlengo	1	2	0	3
Court of the Cardinal Vicar	1	2	0	3
Court of Monsignor Auditor Camerae	1	6	0	7
Court of Monsignor Treasurer General	1	5	0	6
Court of the Campidoglio and Conservators	1	6	0	7
Total	8	163	1	172

FEAR AND LOATHING   **99**

*Source: ASR, Camerale II, Birri I, Fascicolo 30, "Stato antico, medio, ed attuale delle Paghe, e numero dei Bargelli, e Birri della Città di Roma Formato nell'Anno 1806," p. 11. In the original table, the Court of Monsignor Treasurer General was listed, but not included in the totals because his court was financially independent of the central administration. Also in the original table, a computing error was made in the final total, substituting 168 for 166. The correct total should have been 166 to which I have added the 6 men serving the Monsignor Treasurer General, resulting in a total of 172.

Outside of Rome, the picture was even more confused, and the 1790 survey revealed a hodgepodge of bargelli and sbirri whose structure and number differed from town to town and region to region, a reflection of the fragmented and incomplete process that had led to the country's formation. Although all of these officials served the regime's courts through the resident governors and mayors, the local communities, as illustrated in Table II, often paid their salaries. Thus in Umbria and Spoleto sixteen communities paid for their own sbirri, twelve relied on the central coffers, and three enjoyed both forms of financing.[13]

TABLE II

Bargelli and Sbirri Operating in the Province of Umbria
and the Duchy of Spoleto Under the Ancien Regime*

Community	Bargelli and Sbirri paid by the central regime	Bargelli and Sbirri paid by the local community
Amelia	3	1
Arquata	0	2
Assisi	0	8
Bevagna	0	3
Bettona	3	0
Cannara	3	0
Cascia	0	8
Cerreto	0	2
Collescipoli	0	2
Cesi	3	0
Citerna	3	0
Città di Castello	0	13
Città della Pieve	4	0
Fuligno	11	0
Gualdo	3	0
Monte Falco	0	3
Marsciano	0	3
Noccia	0	5
Norcia	0	13
Narni	5	2
Otricoli	0	2
Perugia	27	0
S. Gemine	0	3
Spoleto	13	0
Spello	3	0
Stroncone	0	3
Sassoferrato	2	2
Trevi	0	3
Terni	7	0
Tochi	6	0
Visso	0	3
Total	96	81

*Source: ASR, Camerale II, Birri I, Fascicolo 25, "Dimostrazione dello Stato Antico, e Presente del Numero dei Bargelli, e Birri mantenuti negli inscritti luoghi. . . ." Although undated, the document probably refers to the year 1790.

Built on exception rather than rule, the system's complexity often left the central government ignorant of how many police were operating within the realm. Efforts to determine a precise number were hampered by the bargelli, who, it was feared, would pad the roles with bogus sbirri.[14] When for the sake of economy, the treasury attempted such an accounting in 1804, one administrator affirmed that the only reliable method would be to send spies out into the provinces, thereby circumventing the rapaciousness and mendacity of the police themselves.[15] When the sbirri were finally disbanded in 1816, the Secretary of State calculated their number at 1400, but even this figure soon proved erroneous, since it failed to include some fifty sbirri serving the city of Bologna.[16]

In contrast to the doubt surrounding the number and organization of the sbirri, there is no mistaking their image in the eyes of their contemporaries. According to the seventeenth century legal commentator, Giovanni Rainaldo, people generally considered the papal sbirri ". . . ignorant, vile, haughty, voracious, miserly, pushy, insolent, lying, greedy, and fraudulent. . . ."[17] Numerous travellers to the Papal States commented on the disdain with which the populace regarded the police, and did not hesitate to add their own unfavorable judgements.[18] Giuseppe Gorani, in the latter part of the eighteenth century, found the sbirri of Bologna "almost all infamous and corrupt men," while Charles Dupaty suggested that Rome's police were only privileged brigands paid to chase their less fortunate brethren.[19]

Although the police have seldom been particularly popular in any society,[20] one is struck by the intense and universal revulsion inspired by the sbirri across both time and class.[21] Their infamy so pervaded Italian culture that the term *birresco* became a common adjective in the language, implying cruelty and corruption.[22] The papal courts even had to acknowledge that their own executors were ". . . indiscreet and naturally disposed to hurting others, as well as greedy for gain in their functions. . . ."[23] Only the lowest and most vile characters supposedly stooped to such a dishonorable position.[24] Nothing, according to the French Prefect in Rome, Tournon, could compare to the degradation of becoming a sbirro, and hence most were recruited from the criminal classes.[25]

The only people possibly excused for joining the *sbirraglia*, as they were called, were the children of sbirri. So claimed a seventeenth century critic, Giuseppe Retti, who thus forgave such ill-starred offspring because their infamy flowed:

> . . . from a turbid and affected source, the result of a natural defect rather than moral perversity, just as one born a Jew or a Muslim is worthy of greater compassion in his error than a Catholic who embraces heresy.[26]

Whatever their breeding, however, the sbirri were disparaged from all sides. Thus, one bargello, Nicola Manzotti, who wrote a training manual for his office in 1771, spent much time and ink disassociating his fellow bargelli from their vile and despicable subordinates.[27] Bereft of allies, the sbirri faced internal ostracism, cut off from the society they supposedly protected. In Bologna, they may even have been forced to live apart on a remote street that had supposedly been marked by the plague.[28]

Did the sbirri deserve such treatment? Were these champions of justice really as violent and corrupt as their reputation made them out? Certainly there is no evidence that across the centuries every sbirro was dishonest or cruel; but the barrage of legislation leveled against them between 1600 and 1800 clearly suggests that corruption and brutality were always endemic, and sometimes epidemic, problems among the papal police. Year after year, the *Bandi*, or public broadsides, threatened the sbirri with dire penalties should they misuse their authority or seek to defraud the state.[29] In like fashion, the public was alerted to the tricks of the sbirri and of the recourse available against them. More striking than the abundance of such Bandi, were their specificity and constant revision, indicating a response to actual abuses, rather than the rote repetition of previous law.[30]

Among the abuses mentioned in such legislation, extorsion, in a variety of forms, predominated.[31] Tips, gifts, and honorariums often disguised pressure and threats aimed at merchants and travellers by the sbirri, obviously anxious to supplement their low incomes.[32] One favorite ruse was to extort money, under the guise of an admission fee, from foreigners at the city gates.[33] Even easier victims could be found among those unfortunates for whom the sbirri had arrest warrants. An appropriate "present" could reduce the cuffs and kicks usually associated with arrests, while a debtor's lawful right to a last conciliation with his lender often depended on a tip to the sbirro.[34] In 1787, the sbirri of Bologna were discovered to be unjustly confiscating the property of all people arrested, and retaining it for their own purposes.[35] This venality, of course, worked to the advantage of those capable of buying their way out of even the most compromising situations, as many reportedly did.[36]

The countryside, however, offered the sbirri their easiest pickings. Periodically, squads from the provincial capitals would ride into the hinterland in search of fugitives or to transport captives. Free of urban constraints, the sbirri often demanded food and lodging from local peasants, and, just as often, neglected to pay for it.[37] Religion apparently pulled little weight with the sbirri, or at least those of Bologna, who commonly selected the holdings of the San Michele, San Domenico, and Olivetan monasteries for such unofficial exactions.[38] Similarly, the sbirri expected free goods and services from boatmen, innkeepers, and hostelers during their rural expeditions.[39] So common were such abuses in the early seventeenth century that the Legate, on two occasions, called for all victims of the sbirri to come forth and denounce their oppressors, with the promise of summary justice.[40] Eventually, in Bologna the government levied two new taxes on the entire *contado* which were specifically designed to support the sbirri on such excursions and thus relieve the pressure on the local populace.[41]

Just as the Bandi indicate venality, so too they suggest cruelty and licentiousness. The sbirri apparently liked to harass the wives and daughters of their captives,[42] and, in Rome, their exploitation and mistreatment of the prostitutes was commonly acknowledged.[43] Neither did they much restrain themselves in the apprehension of criminals. Dogs used to track fugitives were occasionally allowed to chew upon their prey, with what effects one can imagine.[44] Likewise, the sbirri were not above burning houses in order to flush out suspects, although this practice was eventually placed under the direct control of the court.[45] Despite instructions to the contrary,[46] even simple arrests could entail maltreatment of one kind or another, as was discovered by a certain Don Tonarini, an unlucky priest, suspected by the Archbishop's court of carrying illegal weapons. According to a modern reconstruction:

> . . .one of the sbirri approached the priest and, having only ascertained his identity, struck him hard in the stomach without another word; meanwhile, another grabbed him by the hair and a third delivered a punch right to his face; thus gasping and with bloody visage, they dragged him away.[47]

Resistance of any kind could prove fatal. In 1719, the bargello of Bologna shot and killed Count Girolamo Grassi during a minor altercation over the placement of a carriage at the annual horse race. In the ensuing melee, the bargello and one of his sbirri managed to kill a footman of the Pepoli family and an innocent woman bystander, while wounding a certain Doctor Zecchini in the leg. Count Bianchetti, who had sought to intercede for his friends, survived the encounter thanks only to the sbirro's apparent lack of target practice.[48]

Extreme as it was, the Bologna incident fit into a general pattern of violence and recklessness on the part of the sbirri. For instance, crowd control consisted of kicking and beating people into the desired formation, a technique that occasionally created more disorder than it prevented.[49] In 1688, an indiscriminate blow to a soldier, during a public execution, not only started a riot, but provoked part of Rome's garrison to seek satisfaction from the sbirraglia as a whole.[50] Violence was narrowly averted on that occasion, but similar affronts in 1786 and 1793 led to full fledged revolts by the Pope's militia against the sbirri, who, in the latter case, had to flee Rome in order to avoid a massacre.[51] Despised as a group, the sbirri were to be feared as a group. When finally disbanded in 1816, they were released from duty only a few at a time so as to prevent their combined resurrection as brigands on the other side of the law.[52] That such precautions were necessary was evidenced by the sbirri of Faenza. After the Restoration, in 1814, they took over the entire town and terrorized its citizens for a number of days.[53]

Copious legislation and dramatic examples, however, only provide a limited view of the sbirri's true nature. Horror stories abound throughout the history of police forces, and statutes always seek to curtail the extremes of action. Still, the only available roster of sbirri containing biographical information certainly reaffirms the unflattering portrait painted by popular ssentiment, specific legislation, and sensational vignette. In December, 1814, the acting Prefect of Bologna compiled a detailed list of former sbirri, in hopes of retaining their services during the Restoration. His findings do them little credit. Of thirty-six "candidates," seventeen sported criminal records that swept the spectrum from petty larceny to murder. Pietro Ferri, already accepted as interim commander of the squad, had been accused of calumny in 1798 and armed assault in 1802. In 1807, he had faced five unspecified charges of which one resulted in imprisonment and the other in eventual exile.[54]

FEAR AND LOATHING 103

Ferri's record, however, paled in comparison with that of Giuseppe Vitale, recently reinstated as a police guard. In 1792, Vitale had been arrested for wounding an innocent man, but the victim's absolution had brought his release. The next year, he went to jail for robbery, but got off for lack of evidence. A paucity of proof also saved him from a charge of assault with a deadly weapon in 1796. Two years later, he was accused and acquitted of sexual harassment, but in 1799 his luck ran out. In April of that year, he was accused of threats with a deadly weapon and in October imprisoned for theft. He regained his freedom in February of 1800 only under a *precetto di rigore*, an early form of probation. July 1801 found him back in prison on suspicion of robbery, but he was released in time to be arrested for theft in November of 1802. Natale again found freedom under a precetto in February of 1803 and managed to stay out of the courts until June of the same year, when he was once again accused of molesting a member of the opposite sex. Amazingly, his current conduct was described as "passable" and he was retained in office.[55]

Reviewing the list of candidates the prefect complained ". . . it is difficult in such a profession to find people even partially honorable and honest," and his lament echoed the previous two centuries of legislation aimed at the natural depravity of the sbirri.[56] The obvious question then is why this should have been the case. Why should the servants of papal justice have been, by definition, vile and corrupt, barely distinguishable from the criminals they chased? Moreover, why was there so little attempt to reform the group as a whole, rather than promulgate a patchwork of punishments and threats designed to control people already considered corrupt by their willingness to take the job?

*   *   *

For one thing, the very nature of early modern policing prompted the employment of such folk. Except for the night watch and a few day patrols, preventive policing in the modern sense was virtually unknown. Indeed, the sbirri's pay structure, made up in part by prizes and fees, operated against crime prevention. As one bargello pointed out, why should the sbirri patrol the streets properly, if their income depended on the arrest of criminals after the fact?[57] In general, crime prevention still rested on the vengeful and terrifying retribution of the courts, marked by relatively infrequent, but highly dramatic, punishments. Thus apprehension predominated over prevention, and close contacts with the underworld counted more for the police than personal probity. According to Tournon, the sbirri had no qualms about bartering with brigands for the capture or assassination of one of their cohorts.[58] Recruited from outcasts, the sbirri had useful and informative sources, easily exploited in the name of justice.[59] Such was the opinion of one papal official in 1801 after an eight year experiment using the military for some police functions: "Experience has demonstrated that for the discovery and capture of criminals in all of Italy the soldier will never be as successful as the sbirro."[60] The sbirri knew the dark side of society; and Gorani pointed out that in eighteenth century Bologna, the bargello was indispensable to any public administrator as a source of otherwise unobtainable information.[61] In the context of pre-industrial criminal justice, the sbirri came off as relatively efficient because of, rather than in spite of, their lowly status.

104   journal of social history

Another factor favoring the sbirri was the "vile" nature of some of their functions in the eyes of the populace. For reasons that remain unclear, papal society found the searching, binding, and transportation of captives utterly despicable, degrading not only to the supposed criminal, but to the official involved as well. Shackles and chains were the stigma of the sbirri; and Nicola Manzotti, in his 1771 instruction manual, discouraged his fellow bargelli from carrying such rude paraphernalia.[62] Moreover, he warned that a proper bargello should never deign to assist his subordinates in securing a prisoner.[63] One might attend an arrest for the sake of discipline, but participation would destroy the men's respect for their leader. He further provided details on matching the method of binding to the status of the captive. A bargello should never allow the sbirri to tie a nobleman by both wrists; this would be too great an affront. People of birth should be led, with only one wrist secured, through the least public streets.[64]

Popular prejudice against these now standard police practices automatically limited any attempt at reform, since no one but sbirri could be expected to perform them. When the government shifted some police duties to the military in 1793, it stressed that the material act of arrest be executed by "a birro or some other vile person."[65] Even in 1814, Bologna's leaders felt it imperative to hire a squad of sbirri to aid the military police bequeathed by the French:

> to carry out those most odious tasks which it is not right to assign to the troops such as personal and domiciliar searches, the binding of prisoners and similar acts.[66]

The state thus publicly acknowledged the intrinsic depravity of its own agents and obligations.

The necessity of hiring "vile" people to do the government's dirty work points up an interesting ambiguity in the evolution of the papal regime. The modern "morality" of the state had clearly not yet supplanted older Christian sentiments which attached dishonor to the use of strongarm tactics against those unable to defend themselves. A similar moral mechanism helped account for the surprising survival of sanctuary for churches and monasteries well into the nineteenth century in the Papal States. As for the sbirri, the ferocity and cruelty that they exhibited in the execution of their duties had probably come to taint those duties themselves. Also, policing in the Papal States had not yet been totally extricated from punishment. The sbirri often administered minor, and occasionally major, forms of corporal punishment such as the *corda* and the *cavalletto*,[67] thereby infecting all of their actions with the shame of the *carnefice*.[68] Public antipathy towards executioners had always run deep, and as late as 1827, even the assistant executioner of Bologna was not allowed to eat or drink in public for fear of disorder.[69] The terror that supposedly assured the efficiency of the early modern courts similarly affected its agents, and the sbirri obviously invoked horror rather than respect. Consequently, a vicious circle had probably arisen, in which the belief that only the most base characters would become sbirri had reinforced the recruitment of just such folk, who in turn had become identified with certain tasks in society.

Perceived efficiency and vile functions, however, do not completely explain the paradoxical position of the sbirri in papal society. The antipathy of the lower classes might best be explained in terms of primitive rebellion, by which outlaws, at least of a certain type, were more popular than lawmen, who represented property and authority. But this sheds little light on the denigration of the police by those whose position they supposedly defended and who could have encouraged reform. In order to comprehend upper class hostility, one must consider the sbirri in the context of papal politics, distinguished by the successful efforts of the aristocrats and their religious counterparts, the Cardinals, to remain relatively free of the central regime's control.

*   *   *

With the defeat of the conciliar movement in the fifteenth century, no ruler could claim a more complete absolutism than the Pope, unfettered by parliaments, courts, or statutes.[70] As both spiritual and temporal potentate, his word was incontestable, and lèse-majesté in the Papal States also spelled lèse-divinité. Yet the reality of the Pope's power in no way matched the pretense. Strong centrifugal forces resisted all attempts on the part of the papacy to exercise its sovereignty. Aristocrats, feudatories, and municipalities fought tenaciously to maintain their autonomy in the face of the centralizing tendencies of the state. By the end of the sixteenth century, the Pope could boast many of the trappings of absolute government: a stable border, a prestigious capital, and a nascent bureaucracy, complete with a centralized treasury.[71] Outside of Rome, however, the Pope had had to come to terms with his independently minded opponents. Thus, in many areas, his sovereignty was limited to the control of justice through a variety of Legates, Pro-legates, and Governors, who, in turn, were served by the sbirri.[72]

But just as centralized justice implied sovereignty, so did judicial immunity imply status. Long had members of the nobility considered themselves above the law, free to exact retribution and vengeance as they saw fit. Vendetta was a personal right, as well as an obligation of rank. The many disputes between major families were regarded as affairs of honor, presumably free of the meddling of the courts and their executors.[73] Likewise, laws easily enforced against commoners became problematic when applied to members of the aristocracy.[74] As a result, the chronicles of Bologna and Rome are full of conflicts between sbirri and nobles, with the former usually getting the worst of it. For example, in Bologna in 1699, the sbirri attempted to arrest Count Francesco Ranuzzi at the local theater, but he was quickly liberated by his friends. Six months later, the good Count had one of the sbirri assassinated, presumably for the offense to his honor.[75] In an eighteenth century episode, two unfortunate sbirri stopped a carriage outside of Rome for a routine check of documents. Within, to their dismay, they found the Duke of Sermoneta, who brought their indiscretion to the attention of the Governor of Rome. The two sbirri soon discovered themselves being whipped while riding through the streets of the city atop asses.[76] Back in Bologna, the Marchese Camillo Pepoli, in 1658, went so far as to kill the bargello for trying to arrest a criminal hiding in his palace. Pepoli was eventually pardoned by the papal Legate.[77]

The Marchese's defense of his domicile is well understandable, since individual power could be measured by the immunity that one could provide.[78] In the countryside, nobles occasionally gave sanctuary to bandits and brigands as a symbol of their autonomy. Even in the cities, many noble holdings were off limits to the sbirri, and the palaces of the Cardinals and ambassadors in Rome actually enjoyed the same protected status granted churches and monasteries.[79] According to Charles de Brosses, the sbirri of Rome were obliged to carry a map designating the areas acceptable for pursuit of a criminal.[80] One eighteenth century commentator joked that there were so many sanctuaries in Rome that one had to be asleep, as well as guilty, to fall into the hands of justice.[81]

The obvious counterpart of immunity was protection. Unable or unwilling to count on the forces of the state, many aristocrats preferred personal retainers, who were, more often than not, recruited from the suspect sectors of society. In Bologna, the better families commonly hired gangs of *biricchini*, who always lived on the fringe of legality, but who could provide protection against thefts and muggings.[82] Confrontations between the sbirri and these *bravacci* were not uncommon, since the latter could count on the protective mantle of their patrons.[83] In such a system, the "vileness" of the sbirri clearly worked to the advantage of the nobility and their private forces. Moreover, the privileged classes had little reason to press for reform if they already felt protected by people who worked against, rather than with, the Pope's police.

Given the pretensions of the aristocrats, the Cardinals, and the ambassadors, the agents of the central regime could count on little support from the upper echelons of society. On the contrary, for the purposes of the powerful, the sbirri were best kept vile, wicked, poorly paid, and, of course, easily corruptible. An efficient, disciplined, and respectable corps of armed men would have presented much too dangerous a force, considering the utter absolutism of the papacy, against the relative autonomy of the elite.

The relationship between the elite's judicial pretentions and the sbirri's unfortunate image is evidenced in a negative fashion by the lack of deprecatory description prior to the late fifteenth century; that is, before the period of increased papal pressure on local privileges.[84] Authors such as Rodocanachi, de Bouard, and Partner, do not place the earlier police in a bad light. Indeed, before the mid-fifteenth century, a variety of officials, including *Marescalchi, Bandaresi, Turrieri, Pacieri,* and *Balestieri*, carried out police functions in Rome, apparently without the opprobrium later attached to the sbirri.[85] Tying the image of the sbirri to the growing absolutism of the late Renaissance would also explain the disparity in quality between medieval and early modern executors of justice pointed out by some commentators.[86] Thus, according to the Bolognese historian Bosi:

> Around 1326 the office of Bargello was neither ignominious nor contemptible in the eyes of the Bolognesi, as it has become in more recent times; instead it was held to be a very high honor and of great importance because it did not imply head sbirro, but rather conservator of public tranquillity and protector of the laws against the powerful. Thus, on occasion, the bargello's office was filled by a Magnate, a Noble, or a titled person, who had a distinctive residence and a substantial income and who was followed by members of his family and by officials paid from the public coffers.[87]

FEAR AND LOATHING   107

Such evidence suggests that the degradation of the sbirri and bargello in Bologna began with the final surrender of the province to the papal Legate, and, in Rome, with the establishment of the Governor as the Pope's central enforcer.[88] In addition, these events more or less corresponded with the consolidation of Spanish power on the peninsula and the expansion of the Inquisition, neither of which inspired much popularity for the Pope's regime. The sbirri, therefore, represented the centralizing side of papal absolutism, and in the ensuing struggle for privilege and autonomy, they fared very poorly.

*   *   *

The causes of bad repute, particularly among the elite, also retarded reform of the sbirraglia. An early call for improvement of the police, at the end of the seventeenth century, was most notable in its total lack of recognition or support.[89] Even as late as 1786, the Governor of Rome, Ignazio Busca, failed in an attempted reform because of the hostility of the Cardinals and the nobility.[90] Only in 1793, with the French Revolution fresh in their minds, did the Curia decide on reform. Significantly, no effort or time was expended on upgrading the sbirri per se. Instead, the government simply shifted many of their responsibilities to the army (also in the process of being reformed) and reduced their number accordingly.[91] The sbirri that remained in service were restricted to assisting at executions, as well as searching, binding, and transporting prisoners. Even these "vile" tasks, however, had to be supervised by the military. In an attempt to spruce up the tribunals, *portieri*, or doormen,". . .free in their external appearance and their nature from any idea of infamy or contempt," were to replace the old sbirri guards.[92] The regime's commitment to this revised image of the courts was immediately demonstrated by the Secretary's of State complaint that some unemployed sbirri had slipped in among the portieri, thus subjecting the new office to common discredit and derision.[93]

The 1793 reform endured until 1801 when the government, in the wake of the short-lived Roman Republic, returned some responsibility to the sbirri on account of their newly perceived efficiency.[94] This arrangement proved temporary, since Napoleon took over Rome and her remaining territories in 1809,[95] with significant results for the sbirri. Along with a simplified court system, a unified law code, and a centralized police network, the French introduced the *Gendarmerie*. Uniformed, disciplined, and respected, the Gendarmerie represented a new form of policing, free of the traditions of the sbirraglia, which was abolished. The gendarmes also quickly faded from the scene as Napoleon's empire began to deteriorate, but they provided an example that would endure.

With the Pope's restoration in 1813, the sbirri found a champion for their return in the reactionary Cardinal Rivarola, temporary head of the government during the absence of the more liberal Secretary of State, Cardinal Consalvi, who was attending the Congress of Vienna. Rivarola quickly reestablished the sbirri as part of a general return to the past. Their resurrection, however, was brief at best, for Consalvi, upon taking power in 1815, began to plot a different course for the papal police.

Unlike Rivarola and his fellow *Zelanti*, as they were called, Consalvi accepted and even admired many of the innovations introduced by the French. A consummate politician, he recognized the advantages that the centralized Napoleonic system of administration could offer the newly restored regime in Rome. He further recognized the inherent responsibilities of such centralization, including the proper discipline of the state's agents. Using the unique powers at his disposal, and profiting from the complete disarray of the older order, Consalvi set out to create a police system that complemented his design for a totally absolute and highly centralized government.

In 1816, therefore, he entrusted the country's policing to a special corps of the army, the Carabinieri, carefully modeled on the French Gendarmerie.[96] Well aware of the opposition that the "public force" could inspire through arrogance, extortion, and violence, he carefully fashioned a lengthy set of rules specifying the structure, duties, and discipline for the organization. In a section labeled "Principles to be observed by the Carabinieri," he stressed that success depended on winning public opinion, since popular faith in the corps would remove many obstacles to the efficient fulfillment of an admittedly difficult service. The Carabinieri were to be a "moral force" representing a moral, and all powerful, regime.[97] The execrable functions of binding, searching, etc., that had so sullied the sbirri, were to become honorable tasks, to be carried out according to specific instructions and with military precision.[98] To assure their probity, the Carabinieri were to be carefully selected and paid over normal military scale. So thorough and impressive was Consalvi's outline of the papal Carabinieri that the Austrian government reportedly considered adopting it for the Empire's Italian provinces.[99]

The sbirri fit poorly into Consalvi's scheme, and he treated them accordingly. On the fifth of October, 1816, he abolished the *Corpo dei birri*, and ordered its members to report to the various communes of the country as rural guards.[100] Literally, the sbirri were put out to pasture. He assigned one sbirro to every commune, no matter how small, and he assured that they were posted far from their former places of employment. They were allowed to carry only a carbine for armament, and forbidden to communicate with each other. The plan, according to Consalvi, was to ". . . destroy the very idea of the sbirri," so at odds with the new image of papal power.[101] The sbirri soon justified his concern, for in their new habitats they returned to their old patterns of violence and abuse.[102] By 1824, it was obvious that the government could not trust the remaining sbirri with any form of authority. In October of that year, they were relieved of all duties and promised pensions on the condition that they not leave their assigned areas without permission, nor possess weapons of any kind.[103] In the end, the sbirri became wards of the communes, paid simply to stay out of trouble.

*   *   *

FEAR AND LOATHING   109

In conclusion, the vicissitudes of the sbirri reveal once again the importance of enforcement, as well as the legislation, of criminal justice. Politics and power determined the role of the police of the Papal States at least as much as conceptions of deviance or disorder. Moreover, the modern state, to be truly efficient in its centralization, had to somehow make its representatives palatable to at least part of the populace. As Alfred Soman has suggested for France, at a certain point the consolidation of the nation state converged with a growing sensitization to violence, which increased the use of the king's justice, and gradually led to the domestication of the nobility.[104] All of this worked for a more professionalized police system, and Soman notes the change in the French example: "The cahiers des doléances prepared for the Estates-General of 1789 all demanded increased police protection from the very same police forces that were dreaded in the sixteenth century as the scourge of the countryside."[105] In contrast, the sbirri represented a government that was arrested in its development – a function in part no doubt of the elective nature of the papacy which automatically prohibited direct dynastic succession. Hence, the papal administration served the realm's elite families as much as the Pope, and its agents of enforcement were made the butt of autonomous pretensions. Any real reform could only come with the destruction of the old patterns of privilege, and that only occurred with the arrival of French centralization backed up by Napoleon's bayonets. This was true to some extent throughout the Italian peninsula, but it was particularly apparent in the Papal States.

The sbirri, however, founded a tradition that would die slowly in Italy despite the Napoleonic interlude. During the Risorgimento, critics of the papal regime were quick to identify the Pope's police as the natural heirs of the sbirri. The charge took on considerable veracity when the government, unable to afford enough Carabinieri, turned to irregular forces such as the *Centurioni*, whose tactics and reputation would have suited the sbirri well.[106] On a larger scale, the police of Italy, as a whole, stood in the shadow of the hated sbirraglia. Time and again after unification, Italian administrators bemoaned the public's hatred of the police which endured despite all their attempts at reform; and they inevitably blamed it on the popular memory of the old regime's police.[107] While this excuse handily ignored many of the actual weaknesses and shortcomings of the post-unitary police, the current paper suggests that there was probably some truth in it. Clearly the police in Italy, and especially the Papal States, had a centuries old tradition of unpopularity and infamy that must have made the introduction of a "liberal" police force difficult, and in part helps explain the continued difficulties of the Italian police, even to this day, to win public favor.

Loyola College in Maryland   Steven Hughes
4501 North Charles St.
Baltimore, MD 21210-2699

110   journal of social history

FOOTNOTES

1. The quote is from *La compagnia del Mantellaccio*, an anonymous farce originally, but erroneously, attributed to Lorenzo de Medici. First published in 1489, this version can be found in *Sonetti del Burchihello* (London, 1757), p. 42.

2. The sbirri were also commonly referred to as *sgherri*, *birri*, and *birruarii*. Most authorities agree with Du Cange that the term was derived from the medieval *berrovieri*, used to describe executors of the *Podestà* in thirteenth and fourteenth century law codes, Charles Dufresne Du Cange, *Glossarium Mediae et Infimae Latinitatis*, 10 vols. (Graz, 1954), i, pp. 640-41. As with other foreign words in the present text, the term has only been italicized in its first usage.

3. Specifically, for Bologna I have used the Archivio di Stato di Bologna (ASB), especially the fondi entitled Polizia Pontificia, Buon Governo, and Assunteria del Torrone. Also important for Bologna is the Merlani broadside collection of the Biblioteca Comunale di Bologna which hereafter is simply cited as Merlani. For Rome I have used the Archivio di Stato di Roma (ASR), especially the fondo entitled Camerale II, Birri I.

4. In the late sixteenth century, the sbirri of Rome carried a dagger, a short musket, and two pistols thrust into a large belt. Emilio Rodocanachi, *Les institutions communales de Rome sous la Papauté* (Paris, 1923), p. 340.

5. In 1794 a *sbirro di campagna* received six *scudi* a month. At the same time, the government felt that a horse required a minimum of five scudi a month for proper maintenance. ASR, Camerale II, Birri I, Fascicolo (hereafter referred to as F.), 30, "Stato antico, medio, ed attuale delle paghe e numero dei Bargelli e Birri della città di Roma," p. 3. Outside of Rome salaries apparently decreased, as indicated in a chart contained in the same collection, F. 25, "Dimostrazione dello stato antico, e presente de numero dei Bargelli e Birri mantenuti negli inscritti luoghi. . . ." Dividing the sums provided for salaries by the number of sbirri suggests that many of them made between two and four scudi a month. These salaries could then be supplemented by various fees and rewards for services rendered.

6. On the papal courts see Jader Spizzichino, *Magistrature dello Stato Pontificio* (Lanciano, 1930), pp. 266-386; also Vincenzo Paglia, "*La pietà dei carcerati*," confraternità e società a Roma nei secoli XVI-XVIII (Rome, 1980), pp. 17-19; and Luigi Cajani, "Giustizia e criminalità nella Roma del Settecento," in *Ricerche sulla città del Settecento*, ed. V.E. Giuntella (Rome, 1978), pp. 264-65.

7. In retrospect, the Vice President of Napoleon's Italian Republic claimed, "Dans l'ancien système nous avions l'heureuse absence du besoin de la police. Tout ce qui s'y pouvait rapporter alors était géré par le tribunal criminel et exécuté par les sbires." Francesco Melzi d'Eril, *I carteggi*, 6 vols. (Milan, 1958-61), ii, p. 476.

8. ASR, Camerale II, Birri I, Fascicolo 30.

9. On the Governor of Rome see Nicolò del Re, *Monsignor Governatore di Roma* (Roma, 1972). The number of sbirri indicated for the Governor of Rome in Table I is lower than the figure accepted by other authors, such as Davide Silvagni, *La corte e la società romana nei secoli XVIII e XIX*, 3 vols. (Roma, 1883-85), i, p. 42; Louis Madelin, *La Rome de Napoléon* (Paris, 1906), p. 68; and M. Groshey, *Observations sur l'Italie et sur les Italiens*, 2 vols. (London, 1774), ii, p. 262. The confusion may have stemmed from the use of part-time sbirri; or it may be possible that the Governor's sbirri had declined in number prior to the 1790 accounting. None of these authors, however, cites any archival or administrative sources and may simply have been following popular estimates.

10. A good idea of the various functions of the Governor's sbirri can be gained from reading the extraordinary collection of day books left by the Bargelli of Rome. These contain a summary of each day's events from 1589 to 1743 and promise an exciting resource for future systematic

FEAR AND LOATHING   **111**

study of the sbirri in Rome. See ASR, Governatore di Roma, Tribunale del Governatore, Criminale, Relazioni di Birri, 1589-1743.

11. ASR, Camerale II, Birri I, Fascicolo 30.

12. Besides the seven courts and their sbirri listed in Table I, the jurisdictional confusion was no doubt compounded by the presence of independent military courts. For instance, Andrea da Mosto has pointed out that in 1774 the Commissioner General of the Navy had his own court – complete with sbirri – for crimes committed by his subordinates. Andrea da Mosto, "Milizie dello stato romano (1600-1797)" in *Memorie storiche militari* X (1914): 300.

13. To confuse matters further in the provinces there were also sbirri who worked independently for nobles whose lands were still held in feudatory tenure. By the end of the eighteenth century these were relatively few, but they were still important enough that when Cardinal Consalvi unified the papal administration in 1816 he had to make special exceptions for the judicial powers of the feudal Barons. See Alberto Aquarone "La restaurazione nello Stato Pontificio ed i suoi indirizzi legislativi" in *Archivio della Società romana di storia patria* LXXVIII (1955): 143. Virtually nothing is known about the actual structure and functions of these "feudal" sbirri, but their very presence is a good example of the lack of uniformity in the Papal State's system of law enforcement.

14. For an analysis of the enormous amount of money grafted each year by the bargelli at the beginning of the nineteenth century, see ASR, Camerale II, Birri I, F. 11, "Piano, ossia dimostrazione di una enorme quantità dei furti...nelle materie criminali."

15. *Ibid*, F. 12, "Foglio di osservazioni sulla riforma delle spese di giustizia."

16. ASB, Polizia Pontificia, Riservata, 1816, n. 1579-1825, Lante-Consalvi, Oct. 30, 1816, no. 16050. Also see Consalvi-Lante, Nov. 6, 1816, n.n.

17. Quoted by Giulinano Pisano, "I 'birri' a Roma nel '600 ed un progetto di riforma del loro ordinamento sotto il Pontificato di Innocenzo XI," *Roma* X (1932): 546.

18. M. Groshey, *Observations sur l'Italie*, ii, pp. 362-3. Hatred of the police was commonly remarked throughout Italy, according to R.S. Pine Coffin, *Bibliography of British and American Travel in Italy to 1860* (Florence, 1974), p. 20.

19. Giuseppe Gorani, *Mémoires secrets et critiques des cours, des gouvernements, et des moeurs des principaux états de l'Italie*, 3 vols. (Paris, 1793), ii, p. 462. Dupaty cited by Louis Madelin, *La Rome de Napoléon*, p. 67. Dupaty's description was later echoed by Francis Maceroni, who wrote: "The police called sbirri, mostly pardoned assassins, loaded with grotesque arms and habiliments, compose at once a most ferocious and inefficient band." *Memoirs of the Life and Adventures of Colonel Maceroni*, 2 vols. (London, 1835), i, p. 47.

20. There are some interesting bibliographical comments on police popularity in Eric Monkkonen, *Police in Urban America 1860-1920* (Cambridge, 1981), pp. 211-12. The popularity and image of the English police is well discussed in Barbara Weinberger, "The Police and the Public in Mid-nineteenth-century Warwickshire," in *Policing and Punishment in Nineteenth Century Britain*, ed. Victor Bailey (New Brunswick, 1981), pp. 65-93. On early hostility towards the "new" English police see Robert Storch, "The Plague of Blue Locusts. Police Reform and Popular Resistance in Northern England, 1840-57," *International Review of Social History* XX (1975).

21. According to the police commissioner of Bologna in 1814, "...the sbirri were always poorly viewed in the past." ASB, Buon Governo, Title xii, Rubric 2, Savini-Strasoldo, Sept. 5, 1814, n. 215. Also see Gaetano Moroni, *Dizionario di erudizione storico-ecclesiastica*, 103 vols. (Venice, 1840-1861), v-vi, pp. 248-49; and Davide Silvagni, *La corte e la società romana*, i, p. 54.

22. Salvatore Battaglia, *Grande Dizionario*, 12 vols (Turin, 1961) ii, p. 246. Also see *Dizionario Garzanti della lingua italiana* (Milan, 1965), p. 227. Goldoni was obviously relying on this generally poor opinion of the police in Italy when he wrote the following interchange for two characters: "My parents are not noble. You are not then the son of some sbirro? I'm shocked sir, I was born poor, but of honorable people." This is from *La Bottega del Caffè*, a play originally written in Venetian dialect and then reworked into Tuscan for broader Italian consumption. Goldoni apparently felt that the negative reference to the sbirro would be easily understood throughout the Italian peninsula. This version of the play is from *Tutte le opere di Carlo Goldoni*, 14 vols. (Milan, 1935-56) iii, p. 64.

23. Such was the opinion of the Legate of Bologna in the early seventeenth century. *Bando generale di Cardinale Benedetto Giustiniano* (Bologna, 1608), p. 13.

24. Giuseppe Gorani, *Mémoires secrets*, ii, p. 462.

25. Tournon is quoted in Louis Madelin, *La Rome de Napoléon*, p. 67.

26. Quoted in Giuliano Pisano, "I 'birri' a Roma nel '600'," p. 545.

27. Nicola Manzotti, *Il bargello istruito* (Loreto, 1771), pp. 139-150.

28. Mario Fanti, *Le vie di Bologna* (Bologna, 1974), p. 255.

29. The following Bandi are from the Collezione Merlani of the Biblioteca Comunale di Bologna, hereafter cited as Merlani.

30. Some Bandi, however, were reproduced each year. In particular, the statute preventing imposters from collecting the pay of the sbirri was repeated annually from 1585 to 1648.

31. Although the following examples are mostly from Bologna, extorsion was also considered the most common complaint against the sbirri of Rome. See Vincenzo Paglia, *I carcerati di Roma*, p. 19.

32. E.g. Merlani, Nov. 22, 1679, n. 368, entitled "Sbirri non prendino regalli alle botteghe."

33. *Ibid*, Jan. 12, 1679, n. 352, and Jan. 19, 1663, n. 82. The latter included a provision that a copy of the edict be posted at every gate so that travellers would know that no tip or gratuity was necessary.

34. In the late seventeenth century, Giuseppe Retti complained: "In what other realm can you hear of a poor debtor being maltreated with fists and weapons during an arrest. . . ." Quoted in Giuliano Pisano, "I 'birri' di Roma nel '600'," p. 547. On debt as a crime see Vincenzo Paglia, *I carcerati di Roma*, pp. 61-67.

35. ASB, Assunteria del Torrone, 1780-1794, "Promemoria dei Senatori assunti," July 20, 1787.

36. Cfr. *Bando generale di Cardinale Benedetto Giustiniano*, p. 16.

37. Merlani, Sept. 1594, n. 273, "Sbirri che vanno in contado."

38. *Ibid*, Feb. 6, 1612, n.n., "Commandiamo a te Barigello di campagna." Also see volumes 1761-1764, n. 130, and 1709-1714, n. 36.

39. *Ibid*, Feb. 4, 1671, n. 62, and March 11, 1690, n.n.; also volume 1785-1787, n. 344.

40. *Ibid*, May 22, 1612, n.n.; Sept. 25, 1609, n.n.

FEAR AND LOATHING 113

41. These two taxes are mentioned unfavorably in ASB, Assunteria del Torrone, 1780-1794, note of Giuseppe Gavazzi, Consultore, attached to letter of June 23, 1781.

42. *Bando generale di Cardinale Benedetto Giustiniano*, pp. 13-14. Also "Bando generale di Cardinale Fabrizio Serbelloni" (1756) in *Bollettino delle leggi e regolamenti per il governo della provincia di Bologna*, 3 vols. (Bologna, 1815), iii, p. 450.

43. Giuliano Pisano, "I 'birri' a Roma nel '600,'" p. 546-7, and Davide Silvagni, *La corte e la società romana*, ii, p. 34.

44. Merlani, Feb. 4, 1671, n. 62. This Bando put a halt to the practice, except in extreme cases, since many captives had failed to survive the encounter.

45. *Ibid.*

46. See, for instance, Giovanni Rainaldo, *Syntaxis rerum criminalium* (Rome, 1698), p. 302, and "Bando generale di Cardinale Fabrizio Serbelloni", p. 450.

47. Antonio Simoni and Adolfo Cano, "La pistola a semi-retrocarica, un interessante caso giudiziario," *Armi antiche, Bollettino dell'Accademia di S. Marciano-Torino* ii (1955); p. 87.

48. Ernesto Masi, "Birri e Marchesi nel 1719", *Nuovi studi e ritratti*, 2 vols. (Bologna, 1894), ii, pp. 164-5.

49. Davide Silvagni, *La corte e la società romana*, i, p. 42.

50. *Ibid*, ii, pp. 112-3.

51. ASR, Camerale II, Birri I, F. 20, "Fatti fra sbirri e soldati", letter of March 22, 1786. Also F. 6, letter of May 8, 1793.

52. ASB, Polizia Pontificia, Riservata, 1816, n. 1579-1825, Circular of Oct. 9, 1816.

53. The episode is mentioned in ASB, Buon Governo, 1814, Title xii, Rubric 2, Savini-Strasoldo, Sept. 5, 1814, n. 215.

54. *Ibid*, Rubric 1, Salina-Savini, Dec. 2, 1814, n. 13860, "Elenco delle guardie."

55. *Ibid.* Of the twenty-five members selected for service, eleven had criminal records.

56. Fabrizio Serbelloni, in his aforementioned *Bando generale*, p. 448, stressed the need for strict regulations because of the ". . .temerity, indiscretion, and avarice of these people." His opinion was shared by Giovanni Rainaldo, *Syntaxis rerum criminalium*, p. 305.

57. Nnicola Manzotti, *Il bargello istruito*, pp. 23-24.

58. Quoted in Louis Madelin, *La Rome de Napoléon*, p. 68.

59. The bargello of Bologna was known to often treat with the *Birichini*, or gangs of criminals, for the return of stolen objects or for information. Giuseppe Bosi, *Archivio patrio di antiche e moderne rimembranze felsinee*, 4 vols. (Bologna, 1855-59), i, 157. The police today still rely heavily on such connections for the solution of many cases. Cfr. M.A. Farber, "For Police It's Difficult to Identify Petty Criminals," *New York Times*, Thursday, Nov. 4, 1982, pp. B1-2.

60. ASR, Camerale II, Birri I, F. 9, Tesoriere Generale-Mon. Barbiere March 28, 1801, n.n.

61. Giuseppe Gorani, *Mémoires secrets*, ii, p. 463.

114   journal of social history

62. Nicola Manzotti, *Il bargello istruito*, p. 149.

63. *Ibid*, p. 129.

64. *Ibid*, p. 51.

65. ASR, Camerale II, Birri I, F. 6, decree attached to unaddressed letter of May 8, 1793, n. 88.

66. ASB, Buon Governo, 1814, Title xii, Rubric 2, Savini-Strasoldo, Aug. 30, 1814, n. 94.

67. Cfr. A. Ademollo, *Le annotazioni di Mastro Titta, Carnefice romano* (Città di Castello, 1886), pp. 21-24.

68. Anton Blok has pointed out that in pre-industrial Europe moral integrity was closely bound up with physical integrity. Thus the mutilation and dismemberment of criminals served to cast infamy on their families. The executioner who performed the act no doubt shared heavily in the onus attached to it. Anton Blok, "Theatrical Punishments in Preindustrial Societies, an Example from the Low Countries," a paper prepared for the IAHCCJ conference on law enforcement and social control: University of Maryland, College Park Maryland, Sept. 4-7, 1980, p. 9. The position of Carnefice was so repugnant in the fifteenth century, that the commune of Bologna allowed criminals to expiate their offenses by performing capital punishments. Giuseppe Bosi, *Archivio patrio*, iv, p. 29. For an extremely detailed description and an intriguing interpretation of the infamy of executioners, based on examples from the Netherlands and Germany, see Pieter Spierenberg, *The Spectacle of Suffering* (New York, 1984), pp. 13-42.

69. ASB, Polizia Pontificia, Provvidenze Generali, 1827, Arze-Albani, Jan. 10, 1827, n. 194.

70. Cfr. Paolo Prodi, *Il sovrano pontefice* (Bologna, 1982), pp. 167-89.

71. Paolo Prodi, *Lo sviluppo dell'assolutismo nello Stato Pontificio* (Bologna, 1968), p. 10. On the bureaucracy see Giampiero Carocci, *Lo Stato della Chiesa nella seconda metà del sec. XVI* (Milan, 1961), pp. 55-128.

72. *Ibid*, p. 136. So unimpressive was the Pope's success in gaining control of the provinces, that one noted historian of the sixteenth century, Mario Caravale, has argued that there was no real clear cut policy of centralization on the part of the papacy. Mario Caravale and Alberto Caracciolo, *Lo Stato Pontificio da Martino V a Pio IX* (Turin, 1978), pp. 352-6.

73. Lodovico Frati, *Il Settecento a Bologna* (Bologna, 1922), p. 219, and Nicolò del Re, *Il Governatore di Roma*, pp. 34-5, 44-5. Particularly interesting with regard to vendetta are the comments of John Larner, "Order and Disorder in Romagna 1450-1500," in *Violence and Civil Disorder in Italian Cities*, ed. Lauro Martines (Los Angeles, 1972), pp. 63-9.

74. Ernesto Masi, *La vita, i tempi, e gli amici di Francesco Albergati* (Bologna, 1878), pp. 88-9.

75. Giuseppe Guidicini, *Miscellanea storico-partria bolognese* (Bologna, 1872), pp. 245-6.

76. Davide Silvagni, *La corte e la società romana*, i, p. 184.

77. Giuseppe Guidicini, *Miscellanea*, p. 275.

78. Paolo Prodi, *Lo sviluppo dell'assolutismo*, p. 80; Giampiero Carocci, *Lo Stato della Chiesa*, pp. 147-50. For a contrary view see Mario Caravale, *Lo Stato Pontificio*, pp. 343-6.

79. Gilbert Burnet, *Some Letters Containing an Account of What Seemed Most Remarkable in Travelling through Switzerland, Italy and some parts of Germany* (Rotterdam, 1687), p. 167; Luigi Cajani, "Giustizia e criminalità nella Roma del Settecento," p. 69.

FEAR AND LOATHING 115

80. De Brosses claimed to have this information directly from the Governor of Rome, Buondelmonti. Charles de Brosses, *Lettres familières écrites d'Italie en 1739 et 1740*, 2 vols. (Paris, 1885), ii, p. 200.

81. The commentator, probably Pietro Verri, is quoted in Davide Silvagni, *La corte e la società romana*, ii, p. 320.

82. Lodovico Frati, *Il Settecento a Bologna*, pp. 226-7.

83. Giuseppe Gorani, *Mémoires secrets*, ii, p. 172; Davida Silvagni, *La corte e la società romana*, i, pp. 46-7; Gaetano Moroni, *Dizionario*, v-vi, p. 248.

84. On such papal pressure see Paolo Prodi, *Il sovrano pontefice*, pp. 148-56.

85. Emilio Rodocanachi, *Les institutions communales*, pp. 53, 110, 12, and 129; A. De Bouard, *Le régime politique et les institutions de Rome au Moyenage* (Paris, 1920), pp. 165-170; Peter Partner, *The Papal State under Martin IV* (London, 1958), p. 107.

86. Giovanni Rainaldo, *Syntaxis rerum criminalium*, pp. 305-8. A similar decline in status and authority of law enforcement officials has been pointed out in late sixteenth century Seville by Mary Elizabeth Perry, *Crime and Society in Early Modern Seville* (Hanover, 1980), p. 65.

87. Giuseppe Bosi, *Archivio patrio*, i, 64.

88. I would postulate that the bargello was not even instituted in Rome until the mid-fifteenth century, but this requires archival confirmation. Rodocanachi quotes Francois Deseine as saying that the Pacieri of the Capitoline would have been good for resolving personal conflicts ". . . si le gouverneur de Rome et ses sbires ne lui usurpaient toute l'autorité." *Les institutions communales*, p. 343. The power and repugnance of Rome's bargello also seems tied to the Pope's attempts to prohibit weapons in the city at the beginning of the sixteenth century. See Nicolò del re, *Monsignor Governatore di Roma*, p. 19.

89. Giuliano Pisano, "I 'birri' a Roma nel '600'," pp. 553-4.

90. Giuseppe Gorani, *Mémoires secrets*, ii, pp. 219-220.

91. ASR, Camerale II, Birri I, F. 30, "Stato antico, medio, ed attuale. . . ", p. 11.

92. *Ibid*, F. 6, public notice entitled "Il sistema che in seguito. . . ."

93. *Ibid*, attached letter, Secretary of State-Tesoriere Generale, Jan. 11, 1794.

94. See footnote 60 of the present article.

95. Napoleon had already "liberated" the Legations in 1796.

96. *Collezione di pubbliche disposizioni emanate in seguito del Moto Proprio di N.S. Pio Settimo in data luglio 6, 1816*, 5 vols. (Rome, 1816-1822), iv, pp. 60-68.

97. *Raccolta delle leggi a disposizioni di pubblica amministrazione nello Stato Pontificio*, 7 vols. (1831-33), volume on military, p. 317.

98. Eventually very detailed instructions covering such duties were offered in an appendix to Vincenzo Galassi, *Sentimenti Morali e brevi istruzioni per un Carabiniere* (Rome, n.d.) pp. 77-88.

99. "Dispacci del Nunzio Severoli," Appendix to Massimo Petrocchi, *La restaurazione, il Cardinale Consalvi e la riforma del 1816* (Florence, 1943), p. 222.

100. Giuliano Friz, *Burocrati e soldati dello Stato Pontificio* (Rome, 1974), p. 85.

101. ASB, Polizia Pontificia, Riservata, 1816, n. 1579-1825, "Birri destinati a guardie campestri," Consalvi-Lante, Dec. 26, 1816, n.n.

102. *Ibid*, 1823, dispatch of Sept. 28, 1823, n. 1297.

103. Giuliano Friz, *Burocrati*, p. 85.

104. Alfred Soman, "Deviance and Criminal Justice in Western Europe 1300-1800: An Essay in Structure," *Criminal Justice History* I (1980): 21-22.

105. *Ibid*.

106. The best study to date on such irregulars is in Narciso Nada, *Metternich e le riforme nello Stato Pontificio* (Turin, 1957), pp. 123-59.

107. In particular, see Giorgio Curcio's comments on the police reform law of 1889, quoted in Emilio Saracini, *I crepuscoli della polizia* (Naples, 1922), pp. 39-40. Also Romano Canosa, *La polizia in Italia dal 1945 a oggi*, (Bologna, 1976), pp. 13-15.

[8]

The Police of Eighteenth-Century France

Iain A. Cameron

> La justice n'est pas un fait des lois mais des hommes qui l'appliquent.
> (A judge of Year V)

A century and a half before England or any other European state boasted a nationwide rural police force, France had a body of armed men whose duty it was to carry law and order to the countryside. This force, the maréchaussée,[1] traced its origins to the reign of Philippe Auguste, when companies of 'sergents d'armes' were created to protect the royal person on the Crusades, and to protect royal justice in France during the king's absence. The institution really began to take shape in the fifteenth and sixteenth centuries, when, under the authority of the Grand Prévôt, who exercised military justice on behalf of the Marshals of France, a number of companies of 'maréchaussée' were formed in the provinces to combat pillaging by vagabonds and soldiers lately disbanded from the army. At first ad hoc collections of volunteers, these companies acquired permanence with established posts for officers and men, and increasing powers of jurisdiction over the civilian population. It was a process of growth as haphazard as the growth of royal power itself. The police officers bedecked themselves with a bewildering variety of titles, commanding anything from four to forty men in confused and ill-defined areas of operation. In south-west France companies of maréchaussée established in Montauban, 'Xaintonge', Angoumois and Auch, operated alongside the vice-sénéchaussées of Xaintes, Libourne Sarlat, Périgueux, 'd'Agennais et Condommois', 'des Lannes', 'd'Albret' and 'de Guyenne et Bazadois'.[2] From the little we know about the activities of these early companies, this seems to have been the heroic period of the French police force. The little band of the 'vice-bailli de la Haute-Auvergne', founded by Charles IX on 10 January

1573, fought a grim struggle for the king's party — fifteen to twenty men against the forces of the League, or, in the seventeenth century, the depredations of passing army regiments, local robber barons, gypsies, and hungry, over-taxed peasants.[3] It was not, however, an unsullied heroism. During the period of the Fronde the Haute-Auvergne company hardly set foot outside Aurillac; disturbances elsewhere merely recorded in the policeman's notebook, 'n'ayant osé nous y transporter pour n'estre assez fort pour pousser lesdits rebelles assemblés en armes volans sur les grans chemins et foires. . . .'[4] Police enthusiasm was further dampened by modest wages, irregularly paid; the drafting of the Criminal Code in 1670 inspired a flood of complaints that the provincial maréchaussées were 'plus à craindre que les voleurs mêmes'.[5]

The great reform came in 1720. It was the government of the Regency which found the money and the political will to abolish all these separate provincial companies of police. In place of the jostle of little maréchaussées, a new company of maréchaussée was created in each généralité.* Police boundaries would coincide with the most meaningful unit of local government — for the ancien régime an impressive rationalization which was bound to strengthen the hand of the intendant in so crucial an area of public affairs. This administrative change was accompanied by a transformation in the authorities' conception of the essential functions of the police force. In the sixteenth and seventeenth centuries the various companies of maréchaussée had grouped a number of men together in the chief towns of the different provinces; their role was simply to make periodic forays into the countryside to remind the populace of their existence, and discourage crime by making a sudden, violent purge of evil-doers. After 1720, however, the police brigades were scattered across the country in permanent residence. Each brigade was responsible for patrolling its own district and keeping in touch with brigades round about. In this way the police were to stretch a net over France, to maintain permanent surveillance over the whole country. It was clearly a great step forward in terms of the principle of centralized government. This short study is a preliminary attempt to discover to what extent practice coincided with theory, to answer questions on the range of tasks

---

*Each company was headed by a prévôt-général, who had under his command from two to four lieutenants, and a number of brigades composed of three, four or five constables (*archers*, later known as *cavaliers*), and a brigade commander (the equivalent of a sergeant, with the rank of sous-brigadier, brigadier, or *exempt*).

imposed on the police, on their recruitment, capabilities and efficiency in the period between 1720 and the Revolution.*

After 1720, the central government appeared to place a great deal of confidence in the potential of its police force. Successive waves of penal legislation, aimed for example at the repression and incarceration of beggars and vagrants, depended upon the efficiency of this force. The implementation of the key edicts of 1724, which consigned anyone taken in the act of begging to the *hôpital*, and of 1767, which ordered the imprisonment of persistent beggars and vagrants in *dépôts de mendicité*, was a case in point, and this represented but one aspect of the maréchaussée's work. It was also expected to cope with a desertion rate from the army of 20 to 25 per cent, besides the problem of theft in its manifold forms, routine tasks such as patrolling roads and fairs and markets, supervising *milice* and *corvée* operations, and extra duties enforcing cattle disease regulations, or distributing grain in time of famine. The intendant and his *subdélégués* often took the trouble to attend to the most minute details of these day-to-day operations of the police brigades; the Bordeaux intendant could even speak of the police as his 'children'.[6]

One of the problems faced by policemen in the Guyenne, if not in the Auvergne, was that they had more than one father. They were at the disposal not only of the intendant, but also of the Governor, and enterprising governors like the Maréchal de Richelieu made constant use of the constables in campaigns against the carrying of arms by members of the Third Estate, or even for specifically military operations, like the defence of the coastline against the expected English attack during the Seven Years' War.[7] The police were further obliged to obey the order of Parlements, though the Parlementaires of Bordeaux were usually content to leave the policing of the peasants to institutions accustomed to dealing with such people. In the same cause of religious intolerance, however, they were prepared to call on the maréchaussée and send constables into the homes of Protestants who had refused to baptize their children in the Catholic faith.[8]

It was also in the Guyenne that the maréchaussée, as a national police force, faced the hostility of local municipal governments. Whereas towns in the Auvergne could not see enough of their police

---

*Two provinces – the Auvergne and the Guyenne – have been chosen for study, both for the quality of the documentation, and for the contrasts they might present. It is clear that the police force of the Auvergne, faced with the closed society of mountain villages, operated in an environment totally remote from the more prosperous river valleys of the Guyenne.

brigades, local authorities in the Guyenne, and particularly the *Jurats* of Bordeaux, claimed that it was their right and privilege to police themselves. When the prévot-général Barret de Ferrand, a native of Bordeaux, insisted that his men had duties within city limits, he was denounced as an agent of the despotic central government, 'un homme qui porte journellement atteinte aux droits et privileges de sa propre patrie'.[9] It was the patriotic privilege and duty of every male citizen of the town to turn up for duty in the 'bourgeois militia', and take his turn at patrolling the streets at night. The better-off citizens naturally preferred to pay a substitute, and although the militia was of some use as a financial expedient at the disposal of the very poor, it was respons- ible for more drunken disorders than it ever helped to quell. Eighteenth-century Bordeaux, however, could well afford to pay for an urban police force, and it was companies of the watch* — the 'valets de ville' — who became the bitter rivals of the maréchaussée. Barret de Ferrand's constables were physically harassed if their duties led them on to municipal property; they were subjected by the town council to judicial investigation on specious allegations of corruption or brutality; it was not unknown for a constable to be thrown into the municipal prison for making an arrest inside the city walls.[10] The national police force was effectively prevented from operating in the chief town of the province.

A more general source of conflict to absorb the time and energies of eighteenth-century police officers was the question of their judicial competence. For the prévots and their lieutenants were magistrates as well as policemen, and the prévôtal court was one of the primary penal institutions of the ancien régime. It dealt with 'ces personnes viles et méprisables, indignes de la faveur de l'appel'[11] who formed the ragged edges of society — beggars, vagabonds, and all those with any kind of criminal record. It was also competent to deal with crimes regarded as particularly dangerous to the public welfare or the security of the realm: counterfeiting,** treason and

---

*In mid-century, the Bordeaux *guet* had forty men on foot and thirty on horse- back. Numbers were constantly increased, and the 1780s saw the first appearance of a dozen *commissaires*.

**This was not usually a skilled professional crime in the eighteenth century, but rather another crime of the poor involving the application of a solution to a copper coin to try to persuade a gullible innkeeper or inattentive shopkeeper that it was a silver coin.

lèsemajesté,* highway robbery and burglary,** and until 1731, pre-meditated assault and murder.

What kind of people were the police of eighteenth-century France? How capable were they of coping with the enormous burden of work which lay upon their shoulders, and if they could not cope, where did their priorities lie? Such questions need to be answered before generalizations can be made about the effectiveness of ancien régime government, and before any analysis of crime can be made from the evidence of prévôtal courts.†

Underlying every aspect of the functioning of the eighteenth-century police force was its numerical weakness. While the General Farm employed a force of 23,000 to defend its private interests, the maréchaussée operated for most of the century with no more than three to three and a half thousand men, including eighty officers and men in the Auvergne, and a hundred in the Guyenne. A last minute increase on the eve of the Revolution brought the total up to around five thousand; by 1792 the maréchaussée under its new title of gendarmerie nationale had been pushed to a total of 10,792.[12] Given this numerical weakness of the maréchaussée, economical use had to be made of the policemen, and particular care taken in the stationing of brigades. Priority was given to towns with large centres of population and important fairs and markets, above all to towns which were on a main road so that essential lines of communication could be kept open. Discussing a projected increase in numbers in 1768, the Auvergne intendant noted that 'En général, je me suis attaché à garnir les grandes routes de préférence'[13] and it was only at this late date that the brigade in St Mamet, a village more than half a league from the main road, was transferred to Maurs, 'placé sur une grande route qui est une gîte pour les troupes' and an important market town.[14] One of the Auvergne

* A much less common charge in the eighteenth than in the sixteenth and seventeenth centuries, though so respectable a bourgeois as a Bordeaux merchant found himself before the prévôtal court during the Seven Years War charged with 'complicité de haute trahison contre son prince en faveur des ennemis de l'Etat'. (Archive départementales de la Gironde 11B7 1762 trail of P. Rocaute de Bussac, 1st Lieut. de la Compagnie volontaire de Guyenne, and his brother-in-law and business associates in Geneva.)

** The prévôtal court was concerned only with public security, and could not try cases of domestic theft or 'effraction intérieure', having no interest in '[ce] qui se passe à l'interieur des maisons'. (H.F. d'Aguesseau, Oeuvres [Yverdum, 1772]. VIII, 315.)

† The importance of looking at the police as well as the criminals has tended to be overlooked by a French historiography obsessed by 'la conjuncture' or by the 'vol/violence' thesis originally put forward by Lucien Febvre.

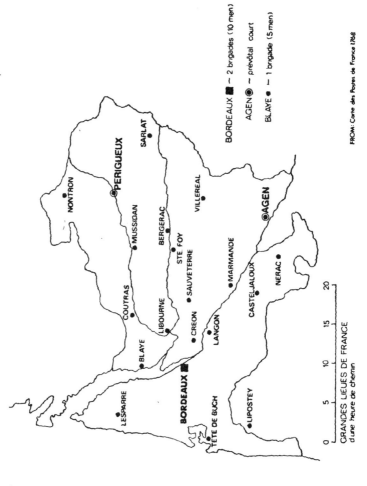

THE MARECHAUSSEE OF BORDEAUX, 1767

BORDEAUX ■ ~ 2 brigades (10 men)

AGEN ◉ ~ prévôtal court

BLAYE ● ~ 1 brigade (5 men)

FROM: Carte des Postes de France 1768

GRANDES LIEUES DE FRANCE
d'une heure de chemin

0   5   10   15   20

THE MARECHAUSSEE OF THE AUVERGNE, 1767

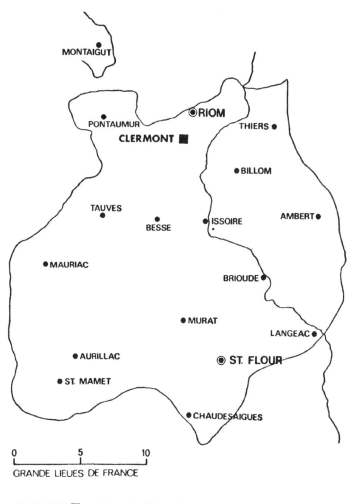

CLERMONT ■ — 2 brigades (10 men)

ST. FLOUR ◉ — prévôtal court

BILLOM ● — 1 brigade (5 men)

brigades was established in Courpières, which had less than 3,000
inhabitants and little through traffic, whereas there was no police
residence in nearby Thiers, one of the biggest towns in the province
with a population of over 18,000 and on the main road from Clermont
to Lyon.[15] The anomaly was not put right till 1734, when a convincing new argument was brought to bear — the need to contain the
mutinous workers at the paper factories.[16] One other possible criterion
had been suggested in 1719 by the War minister Le Blanc: that brigades
should be concentrated where the mountains and the state of the roads
encouraged the natural lawlessness of the inhabitants.[17] This was
obviously difficult to reconcile with other criteria and tended to be
ignored. As the municipality of La Chaise-Dieu complained in 1778,
large tracts of hill country were left to fend for themselves, while on
the plain brigades were no more than three hours journey one from the
other. Having a seigneur (the Cardinal de Rohan) who was above pulling
strings, La Chaise-Dieu was left ignored in its forest-covered mountains
which were the haven of robbers and brigands who would descend on
the town at night like wolves for their plunder.[18]

Virtually no effort seems to have been made to standardize the
amount of work the various brigades were expected to do nor the
area they were supposed to supervise. The two brigades in Bordeaux
covered fifty-two parishes, up to five leagues distant from Bordeaux
with three fairs and sixty-eight fêtes. They were also continually
occupied escorting deserters and prisoners to and from court, carrying
out orders from the prévôt, the intendant or the military commandant
of the province, as well as being on hand at all stages of prévôtal justice
and making arrests for other courts. On the other hand, the brigade in
La Tête de Buch, a fishing village on the Arcachon basin, had only
thirteen fêtes. There were no roads which went anywhere, and with so
much wood and moorland, much of the area was uninhabited.
Compare these happy constables to their colleagues in Périgueux:
apart from their duties at the prévôtal court and routine escort of royal
taxes, they were responsible for 111 parishes which, as the prévôt said,
they could not possibly visit even once every three months. Further
south, in the Agenais, the brigade in Nérac, used by the royal court in
Condom, had no less than 198 parishes to patrol, some as far as
nineteen leagues away, and in the course of a year was expected to keep
public order at 262 fairs, 225 fêtes and 332 markets.[19] It is hardly
surprising that shopkeepers, writing to the maréchaussée to report a
fraud by two merchants, wrote to a brigade commander at some
distance from their town, as they did not know of the existence of their

'local' brigade;[20] or that witnesses to a riot declared to the court that they saw soldiers in blue uniform, without realising they were policemen.[21]

The lack of numbers carried the further implication that the personal qualities of individual policemen were of great importance, for failings of quality could not be masked or compensated for by quantity. This was particularly true of the officers, yet in this area the 1720 reform had been unusually hesitant. Prévôts-généraux and lieutenants continued to buy their posts (for 40,000 and 15,000 livres) until Choiseul's reform of 1768. The government, however, had always imposed an important proviso on the inheritance of these posts. When the Auvergne lieutenant du Jouannet retired in 1742, the appointment of his son was not confirmed on the grounds that he had no military experience, and the lieutenant was told to find another buyer within six months. Meanwhile the intendant was asked to keep a look-out for someone suitable, for

> dans les ventes qui se font de gré à gré, il y a toujours des accomodemens qui sont nuisibles au service et qui écartent les meilleurs sujets.[22]

The government itself was prepared to pay the 15,000 livres for a worthy but improverished candidate.* The formal abolition of venality, and the appointment of prévôts on merit from the ranks of the lieutenants, however, did not mean a dramatic improvement in the quality of police officers, for the competition the reform encouraged 'se porte plus sur les intrigues de protection que sur le mérite personnel'.[23] Both the Auvergne and the Guyenne were relatively fortunate in their senior police officers. There were a few spectacular exceptions — de Robéric, the corrupt prévôt in Bordeaux who was appointed in 1720 and whose nefarious activities were not exposed until the 1730s,[24] or the Riom Lieutenant du Jouannet, who had to stay indoors for a number of years to avoid being arrested for debt, and who was so crippled by gout in his later, more solvent, years that he was unable to mount his horse.[25] Other officers however displayed zeal and intelligence, and tributes to their efforts made by the normally crabby Inspectors at the annual 'Revue'[26] are corroborated by a variety of

---

* Jouannet was finally succeeded by his son-in-law, de la Ribbe-Haute, who had spent six years in the Cavalry, who stood to inherit 10,000 livres and whose wife was to be de Jouannet's heiress. 'Il semble', the Riom subdélégué commented, 'qu'il ne lui manque rien de nécessaire'. (Archives Départementales Puy de Dôme C 6184).

independent testimonials: the high regard in which one intendant of Limoges held one Auvergne prévôt,[27] the municipality of Bergerac's parish for the way the Périgueux lieutenant had handled a serious grain riot, [28] the panegyric by the municipality and nobility of St Flour on the virtues of their lieutenant.[29]

For the ordinary constables and brigade commanders the reform of 1720 had brought the practice of buying posts to a definitive halt. Entrance qualifications however were not very tough: policemen had to have served for four years in the regular army, and be able to provide a certificate of good conduct. Even these tolerant regulations were bent, or waived altogether, for 'enfants du corps', youths whose fathers were already in the force. By 1778 the authorities had become more particular; an ordinance in 1778 stipulated that a would-be constable had to be literate, not less than 5'4" in height, be able to provide 500 livres as the price of his horse and still have enough left to pay for his other equipment. After serving no less than sixteen years in the army, preferably in a cavalry regiment, the prévôt in Bordeaux was one of many who complained about the stringency of these qualifications:

> je n'ai pas le don de fabriquer des hommes de la taille et avec les qualités et les facultés pécuniaires que demandent l'ordonnance .[30]

The inspectors of the maréchaussée themselves argued for a reduction in the service requirement from sixteen to six years. In six years, they argued unavailingly, a soldier acquired as much military discipline as he would need, but

> en seize ans, qu'a-t-il gagne au service? – presque toujours beaucoup de maladies vénériennes, par conséquent un corps usé, maladif, et peu util au service de la maréchaussée.[31]

In the later part of the century the strict application of these regulations operated a natural selection, and a number of posts had to be left unfilled.* Previously, however, more soldiers applied than places were available.

Strings had to be pulled, particularly for posts as brigade commanders. A worthy and impoverished nobleman not only had twenty-five years' distinguished military service, but 'Mme la marquise de Roussille s'intéresse à lui'.[32] M. de St Aubin had trudged through twenty-eight years in the dragoons, only five as a junior officer, and

---

* In the 1780s, the brigade in La Tête de Buch was one constable. (Archives Départementales de la Gironde C4636, correspondence between intendant and prévôt.)

had to his credit 'une figure agréable et une taille avantageuse'; he was however the protégé of the intendant himself, and was appointed to command the Ambert brigade.[33] The inspectors of the police force did not hesitate to complain, in 1779, that the commander of the Sarlat brigade was hopelessly inefficient, having 'parvenu à poste par protection'.[34]

The 1778 ordinance attempted to alleviate this problem by stipulating that posts as brigade commanders would be filled by men who had served for at least five years as constables. This policy had been encouraged in previous decades and its formal adoption had only been delayed by the difficulty officers had had in finding constables worthy of the extra responsibility. For the post of *exempt* in the Auvergne town of Chaudesaigues, the first constable to be proposed was a notorious smuggler who spent the day drinking and the night entertaining a variety of women; he had abandoned his wife and children, who were to be seen every day begging in the street. Two brigadiers were suggested, and rejected, as one did not want to move house, while the other had land near Chaudesaigues, and he would be tempted to spend time looking after it. Another constable, Féfelin, was given the chance of the promotion, but had to be persuaded to refuse it when it was confirmed that he was illiterate. The job finally had to be given to the constable Poisson, who was at least 'un garcon de bonne famille' even if 'un peu indolent'.[35]

It would indeed have been surprising if the eighteenth-century police force had been a well-educated body of men. Most of the constables came from rural parishes or small market towns; all had risen from the lowest ranks of the regular army. The ranks of police constables contained only a handful of noblemen or 'bons bourgeois' reduced to this humble occupation by lack of means or lack of intelligence.* No inspection before 1779 found it worthwhile to raise the question of literacy. In the Auvergne that year, it was still not mentioned for about half the company, and of the remainder twenty-nine could not read or write compared with only fifteen who could.[36] The Guyenne, on the other hand, was a much more civilised province, and the inspectors went to the trouble of distinguishing policemen who could only sign their names from those who could only read a little, from those who could both read and write, and so on. Only one constable was marked out as totally illiterate, and about two-thirds

---

* The 'controles de la maréchaussée' draw particular attention to these representatives of the respectable classes, all categorized either as 'fort pauvre' or as 'peu intelligent'. (Archives de la Guerre Y[b] 858-9).

of the company could read and write. While the élite was a small group of brigade commanders who could 'bien verbaliser', that is to say put words into sentences and so compose a report, it must be said that in most eighteenth-century police reports the writing is childish and unformed, the grammar dubious, and the spelling so fantastic that they must be read aloud to be understood.*

Most of the constables joined in their late twenties or thirties. though there were occasional 'enfants du corps' who joined at twenty-one, or even eighteen, but these youths tended to disappear as service regulations were more strictly enforced. A shift is also evident at the other end of the age scale, as the system of pensions and retirement to the Invalides was better organized and length of service tended to diminish. Earlier in the century many policemen served, literally, until they dropped — ninety of all the constables who served in Clermont between 1720 and 1760 died while still on active service,[37] and constables in their 60s were not uncommon; as late as 1771 the brigade in Casteljaloux had one aged 67 and another 70.[38] The list of retirements in the 1780s, on the other hand, was of men in their fifties, apart from two in their forties.[39]

Health problems were unfortunately not confined to the aged. Some policemen were so stiff that before they went out on patrol each day they had to be helped on to their horses. Annual inspections described in graphic details the afflictions of the humble constable: sciatica, hernia, incontinence, rheumatic pains, war wounds, deafness and in two cases, blindness.[40] But, by far the most common cause of incapacity was drink. The inspectors frequently complained that a policeman was 'trop adonné au vin', and warned that if he did not pull his socks up even a little, he risked expulsion. Drink, along with indebtedness and frequently closely linked with it, was the most common reason for dismissal from the force.**

---

* It is possible to find eighteenth-century police sergeants with literary pretensions. After the St Mamet brigade had been ambushed and beaten up by peasants from the Auvergne parish of Cassaniouze, its commander, Pierre Lasalle, fired off a report distinguished by a whole series of indignant alliterations: the peasants of that parish, he hissed, 'sont sujets à ces sortes de séditions', and so he sent 'le présent procès-verbal pourqu'il y ait des punitions proportionnées aux crimes de ces perturbateurs' (Archives Nationales Z[1c] 351. St Mamet report, 23 April 1755).

**Drunkenness was the most frequently cited complaint in a secret inquiry into the state of the police force held in 1732 by the Auvergne intendant and his staff. Three of the four constables in Montaigut drank, following the example of their sergeant, who was in addition 'paresseuse a monter à cheval, autant qu'il est diligent a aler a la chasse'. The Murat subdélégué did not object to his brigade commander's excessive drinking at home — his wife's wineshop was necessary to feed the family. (Archives Départmentales du Puy de Dôme, C 6177).

Another factor which must seriously have undermined the efficiency of the police was that many could not afford to give their full-time attention to their work. Between 1720 and 1769 a brigade commander earned only 550 to 600 livres a year, a constable 500 livres. To deal with the inflation of half a century, pay was then restructured so that a constable was clothed and his horse fed for him, while his wage packet was reduced to 270 livres a year, or 15 sous a day.

If the basic rate was miserable, opportunities existed for making extra money, since many of his duties — escorting prisoners, supervising *milice*, or giving assistance to court ushers — were not reckoned as part of his routine, and were paid extra as 'service extraordinaire', usually at 3 livres a day. He was paid the same rate for operations which had led to a successful capture, and which had taken the constable too far for him to sleep at home. Although quite large sums of money could be involved — two policemen escorting a deserter from Bordeaux to Flanders would expect to be reimbursed about 450 livres, and a company could earn up to 1,500 livres a year from the royal Domaine alone, while constables were also eligible for payment from the 'extra-ordinaire des guerres', the 'fonds de mendicité' and even for a time from a 'fonds des biens des religionnaires fugitifs' — payment from overtime was far from solving the policemen's financial difficulties. They could never be sure of actually getting the money, and the delay and confusion inherent in the bureaucracy was intensified by the constables' disregard for application formalities. They forgot to sign the claim, or to include necessary details like the time and place an arrest had been made; worst of all, they lumped together on one form operations which were paid by different funds. In the 1760s, the Guyenne police were still demanding payment from the defunct 'fonds des religionnaires' for operations against Protestant assemblies in 1758.[41] The Trésorier des Guerres was so notorious for replying bleakly that he had no money that the brigade in Riom aroused the intendant's ire by refusing to commence militia operations unless paid in advance.[42] Plaintive cries from the Auvergne were echoed from Bordeaux: 'je vois ma trouppe écrasée, hors d'état d'autre service que leurs chevauchées ordinaires'.[43] The Guyenne prévôt had already noted that if finally paid, the money came in a lump sum and was promptly spent at the inn or other, unspecified 'mauvais usages'.[44] In any case, as the brigade commander in Mauriac complained in 1769, inflation had made nonsense of 3 livres a day. It was inevitable that a cavalier got into debt, when escorting the tax collection kept him away from home for three nights, and cost him

at least half a month's pay. The Mauriac brigade had not been paid
a penny for patrols in the specially difficult circumstances of 1763,
six years before. Three of his cavaliers were in debt and to save
money they had to combine the escort of the *recette* with the escort
of prisoners and deserters; since claims for separate horses for the
prisoners, even backed by medical certificates, were being rejected,
the constables had to carry the prisoners on their own horses. What
would happen, he asked rhetorically, if the stage coach were ambushed?
'Le cavalier dont on exige plus qu'il ne peut, se rebute et sert mal
necessairement'.[45]

The eighteenth-century policeman, therefore, lived in poverty. Most
of the constables paid only the minimum assessment of 10 sous as their
côte d'office tax contribution. An Auvergne constable who got into
debt had his possessions valued at 33 livres 10 sous, which was generous
as they included

> une mauvaise couverte de catalogue, une mauvaise paillasse, quatre mauvaise
> chaises de paille et un mauvais tonneau défonceé.[46]

Like the rest of the population, policemen suffered most in years of
general misery and grain shortage. As the Auvergne prévôt pointed out
in 1770, many of his men were married, and found themselves unable
to feed their families. 'Que peut on exiger d'un homme qui meur de
faim?'[47]

The most vivid illustration of the inadequacy of police pay — and
one which had serious consequences for the quality of their service —
is the fact that so many policemen had an additional, part-time job.
Although this was forbidden, the authorities were prepared to turn a
blind eye if it did not interfere too obviously with the constables'
police duties. The Auvergne intendant only stepped in when the
minister himself complained that

> le Sr. Queriau exempt à Clermont ne fait aucun service et s'occupe à des
> fonctions tout à fait oposées à celles ausquelles il est destiné. On cite par
> exemple les ouvrages du pavé de Riom dont il a l'inspection.[48]

The most common alternative source of income was an inn — three of
the four policemen in Montaigut were innkeepers.[49] Other constables
had billiard halls or small businesses — one policeman based in
Mauriac went round the local fairs setting up his stall laden with
cloth. The brigades in Clermont were the most commercially-minded
— there were three grocers and an ironmonger among the constables,
and the brigade commander was a haberdasher. The policemen's

Cameron, *The Police of Eighteenth-Century France* **61**

wives were very much involved in running these shops and inns. If a constable did not have a small business his wife almost certainly had to find unpretentious employment as a seamstress or a hairdresser, or in spinning wool or washing clothes.[50]

In this climate of perpetual penny-pinching and indebtedness eighteenth-century policemen must have been under great temptation to cut corners and pick up a few illicit livres. The constables' petty corruption was consonant with their modest circumstances — thieves or deserters were allowed to go on their way for five or six livres,[51] a hide brought into Aurillac despite disease regulations was sold by the local brigade.[52] Corruption was not always strictly monetary in character. The brigade in Mauriac persisted in failing to arrest two murderers, one of whom was a fellow constable, and the other an old drinking companion.[53] The brigade commander in Ambert failed to capture the accomplice of his daughter-in-law, who was charged with theft.[54] The constables of one maréchaussée in Bordeaux enjoyed the favours of local prostitutes in exchange for the names of criminals for whose arrest warrants had been issued.[55]

Corruption on a grand scale however was the prerogative of the officers, particularly when aided and abetted by their subordinates. The Sieur de Robéric, the Guyenne prévôt-général, organized his protection and extortion rackets in the 1720s and 1730s with the assistance of his private secretary, official police clerks, of constables, and brigade commanders from Agen, Biscarosse, Lipostey, Langon and Bordeaux itself. In both Agen and Bordeaux the police kept all the fines from arms offences, half of which were supposed to be paid to hospitals. Victims of theft were made to pay up before investigations were begun; stolen property was retained to cover police 'expenses'. A charge of murder was dropped, after payment of 500 livres; 'suspects' were thrown into prison and held for months, until they agreed to pay the prévôt substantial sums of money. Robéric also defrauded the government by filling posts with phantom constables, and collecting their pay, and ended by cheating his own men of their overtime pay. While ordinary constables risked imprisonment and destitution for 5 livres, de Robéric expropriated almost 20,000 livres and used the money to buy a cavalry company for his son.[56]

Given the shortage of numbers, the scattered location of the brigades, and the limited hours at their disposal, we should not ask too much of the eighteenth-century police. The policemen themselves were modest in their expectations. They did not hope for a successful arrest if the culprit was not often at home, or did not stay too long in one place.[57] Ten policemen would troop along to arrest one 'suspect'.[58] They would miss a thief by searching his house and forgetting to look in the barn.[59] Lack of knowledge of the area often put them in the hands of guides, and reports would come in assuring the authorities that failure was 'la faute de nos conducteurs et nullement pas la notre'.[60] Matters went better if criminals made it easy for them: escaped prisoners made straight for home;[61] vagabonds were taken asleep behind hedges;[62] most of the deserters were still wearing uniform when arrested. One constable at the barber's made an innocuous remark about an assistant being a likely-looking lad for the army, whereupon the lad blushed and stammered that he was a deserter, unable to contain his guilty secret any longer.[63] The policeman's prey, however, was not always so obliging. The St Mamet brigade pinned down the Bayat brothers in a hut used for drying chestnuts for several hours, until both men, suspected of arson, escaped.[64] Another man, wanted for cutting down trees, almost got away when the whole brigade from Brioude invaded his bedroom and his wife blew the light out.[65] One extremely costly failure was a grand operation involving the setting up by several brigades of an ambush in the château de Duras near Libourne. It was known through an informer that a band of about nine or ten would raid the place between eleven and midnight, so the cavaliers stationed themselves in the hall in total darkness. The robbers arrived on time but when they saw the police they had time to extinguish their lights, fire and flee before a shot was returned. None of the band was captured that night, despite an all-night search; instead one of the constables was shot dead by a peasant who mistook him for a prowling thief.[66]

There were perhaps more success stories in the Guyenne than in the Massif Central — arrests made after a long pursuit through the forests of the Périgord[67] or across the snow and ice of the Landes in winter[68] — not so much because of misdirected effort in the Auvergne as lack of effort. The maréchaussée of the Auvergne was, according to the intendant in 1760 'la plus belle, la mieux montée et al plus paresseuse du royaume'[69] — a qualification he typified by the failure to capture a soldier who stabbed someone in broad daylight in a main street in Clermont, and who was seen in town at least three times later the same day.

The extent of negligence is difficult to gauge, for some of the brigades who rarely left their headquarters sent in false certificates of the fifteen patrols a month that they claimed to have made.[70] Some brigades did not bother to send certificates at all and it is clear from the ones which were sent that the brigades concentrated their legally required minimum effort on keeping order at the home market, patrolling a fixed number of main roads between the larger towns and villages, and leaving the rest of the countryside to fend for itself.[71] Complaints were made of brigadiers who were 'tres difficulteux' when it came to action,[72] or sous-brigadiers 'qui marchent difficilement la nuit'[73]; the Clermont brigade commander was 'un paresseux achevé', and his constables were being heard as witnesses to crimes committed in their presence.[74] The Mauriac brigade failed for several months to catch a murderer who had remained at home 'cedentaire et tranquille'; its 'negligence impardonable' led the subdélégué to reflect

> que cette brigade est bonne pour capturr un homme qu'on luy remettra entre les mains. Elle n'est ny assés rusée ny assés penible pour les fonctions de son état.[75]

The maréchaussée's neglect was blamed too for the unruly behaviour of the young, as in Ambert, where hoodlums were left to throw stones through windows, beat drums in the streets at night and make scandalous rendez-vous in the cemetery.[76] Despite all the regulations, it was usually easy in the Auvergne to get a drink on Sundays or on feast days during the church service, even in inns owned by the police constables themselves.[77] Constables on duty at village fêtes did occasionally try to stop games and dancing during the period of divine service, usually with disastrous results. Two constables from Coutras had spent the day at the fête in St Sulpice, near St Emilion, drinking at the inns, joining in the dancing and giving children rides on horse-back, when they intervened to stop a game of bowls and force the players to go to church. In the resulting riot, one of the policemen escaped with face injuries, the other was dragged from his horse and beaten to death.[78]

On such occasions the weakness in numbers of the maréchaussée was spectacularly obvious and was a particularly crucial factor in this case, for witnesses were to report having heard someone shout in the tense moment of confrontation before the bloodshed: 'Tant de monde que nous sommes bien sots de crindre ces deux B[ougres]. . . '. All the techniques devised by the police had to take this numerical weakness into account. The most obvious palliative was to call in extra help from time to time. The army was on hand when considerable strength was required, to deal with an outbreak of grain disturbances, for example. But regular soldiers were also used in more routine situations: if a police brigade was occupied elsewhere, escorting deserters or tax receipts, the local garrison would sometimes provide a few soldiers to patrol the market.[79] In the Guyenne, co-operation was also possible with local police forces, the bourgeois militia which were useless by themselves but which could be roped in when a responsible officer of the maréchaussée organized a hunt for a band of thieves.[80] It was all the more regrettable that in the incessant climate of mutual vilification there could be no combining of the efforts of the maréchaussée and the Bordeaux Watch, the only effective local police force.

The police relied ultimately on the co-operation of the general public. By comparison with the Auvergne, where mouths were kept shut — and the authorities were never able to decide whether it was through intimidation or bad faith — the Guyenne was a veritable 'pays de délateurs'. The Bordeaux police brigade was led to a deserter who had worked harmlessly for months as a gardener, and who let out his secret one night at the inn.[81] This victim of popular vigilance was a stranger in the province, and the denunciation was atypical only to the extent that the archetypal citizen's arrest in the eighteenth century was the capture of a thief or a suspected thief, or a scruffy stranger who looked at though he might want to make off with someone else's property, who looked, in fact, as though he had no other source of income. Even in the Auvergne it is possible to find the perfect example of the co-operative community effort in defence of property: when the Thiers brigade was too busy escorting the stage coach to deal with an outbreak of thieving, the local peasants organized search parties and located a number of suspicious *colporteurs;* they got a gamekeeper to make an arrest, and the brigade of *gabelous* to escort the suspect to prison.[82] The general public, however, was at its most effective in the arrest of thieves 'en flagrant délit' — pick-pockets at a fair, burglars caught climbing out of a neighbour's window.[83] A series of burglaries in the Garonne valley led the police to make sweeping arrests, but the only suspects to be convicted were those caught by peasants hiding in a barn with a sackful of booty.[84] The police themselves had more success in their search for horse thieves, but the crucial arrest which led to the uncovering of an organization for the disposal of stolen horses was made by peasants, when one of the thieves was foolish enough to try to ride through the village where he had stolen his horse.[85]

The authorities, however, did not conclude from these happy episodes that the best way to solve the problems of the maréchaussée was to encourage intimacy betv---- police and people. It became increasingly rare for a constable, and even more so for a brigade commander, to be stationed in his home town or district. In the course of the eighteenth century policemen were forced into barracks, into which wives were at first admitted, and subsequently excluded. From the 1770s onwards, no married men were admitted into the force; a constable who wished to marry had to ask the minister of war for permission. The holding of part-time jobs was effectively curtailed. The increasing stringency of entrance qualifications made sense in the context of the theory that the more efficiently the police did their duties, the more enemies they were bound to make. The only possible response, therefore, was to face up to vulgar hostility by improving discipline, and emphasizing the military character of the institution.*

While it may have been true that restricted contact with relatives and friends alleviated the problems of slackness and corruption, restricted contact with the civilian population also meant less information about the people the police were supposed to supervise, greater remoteness from the currents of popular feeling. At the simple level of the investigation of prévôtal crimes, it was clear that neither the officers nor the men had much time, nor one would suspect, much flair for detective work. They relied therefore on information, and if it was difficult to tap sources from the general public, they had to employ spies. It seems that in the Guyenne at least, police officers were able to draw on the services of a shady network of informers functioning on a regular basis. The most systematic use of such sources of information was made by the Périgueux lieutenant, Gigounoux de Verdon, who organized campaigns lasting several weeks against bands of robbers, smugglers and escaped convicts, not after complaints from local inhabitants, but on the basis of his secret reports.[86] The policeman's valuable time could be saved when a clear distinction had been established between the role of the informer – to find the criminal – and the role of the policeman himself – to restore public confidence in the available protection against the forces of lawlessness:

> J'ay porté plusieurs de mes mouches dans les environs afin de decouvrir les coupables, et j'y feray de fréquentes chevauchées pour remetre la tranquilité dans cet endroit . . . .[87]

The informer was usually kept anonymous in reports to higher authority. He does emerge into the limelight in the case of the fiasco already mentioned of the ambush in the darkened château. Warning of

---

*The Gendarmerie Nationale is still part of the French Army, and arguably the most respected branch of the contemporary French police.

the raid had come from one Fleuret, a horse dealer who had supplied the brigadier in Bordeaux on previous occasions with names and descriptions of horse thieves. He had numerous contacts in this branch of the underworld, having himself dealt, 'unwittingly', in stolen horses.[88] Contacts with the criminal classes were delicate to manage, and police fingers were easily burnt. A constable in Créon insisted that he had made legitimate use of his contacts to trace stolen horses, one of which he was naive enough to find in the possession of the procureur du roi, and which the procureur was reluctant to return. A short time later, the policeman was arrested and charged with connivance with the band of horse thieves.[89]

While lack of strength made the police brigade dependent on the co-operation of others, it also made them particularly vulnerable to opposition. The eighteenth century did not see the great pitched battles of the popular uprisings which had been so endemic in the previous 'tragic' century; scattering police power over the ground in small, isolated, units was however an open invitation to guerilla warfare, and the constables of the maréchaussée met violent resistance whenever they overstepped the bounds of popular tolerance. They knew they could expect trouble when they tried to confiscate firearms or any of the other weapons commoners were forbidden to carry; they learned the painful cost of interrupting popular festivities by trying to arrest drunken brawlers, or trying to persuade bowlers and dancers that it was time to go to church; even when only providing an escort they fell victim to the popular wrath directed at the *huissiers* who were responsible for seizing property, after failure to pay debts or taxes or tithes or seigneurial dues. From guarding curés against the fury of popular hostility to *monitoires*,* to arresting a fugitive from the *milice*, policemen repeatedly found themselves in situations where they could expect only malevolence, non-co-operation, and conflict.

In situations where the twentieth-century police would have imposed itself with brute force, the eighteenth-century maréchaussée

---

* The *monitoire* was a warning delivered from the pulpit that anyone withholding information from the police on some unsolved crime risked excommunication; according to the peasants of the Périgord, the reading of the *monitoire* meant their crops would be ruined by hail for seven consecutive years. In less controversial circumstances the curé might be able to prevent popular hostility being turned against the constables. The Murat brigade was rescued from the stone-throwing of a crowd of young men by the curé who heard the dispute at his church door half-way through the service and flew to its aid, leaving the pulpit 'en criant à sa paroisse de donner main-forte à la maréchaussée'. (Archives Nationales Z[1c] 352, parish of Valenjol, 1756.)

had to temporize or beat an undignified retreat. Whenever the constables attempted to make an arrest in public they ran the risk of meeting resistance, and the more violent the resistance, the more brutal did the constables appear, and the more likely was the intervention of friends, relatives or the general public. It is therefore rare to find allegations of police violence within the context of an arrest – the few men who met violent deaths at the hands of police constables were usually recognized as victims of circumstances or of their own folly as much as of the police. One constable was given a bonus of 200 livres in lieu of the pay he had lost when suspended for killing a man 'qu'il avait rencontré dans la campagne et qui voulait égorger une femme.'[90] Although local judges did not hesitate to follow up charges of violence that were made against constables of the national police force, with the results of their enquiries subsequently examined by the 'Tribunal de la Connétablie', very few cases of police violence emerged from the provinces to interrupt the parade of 'rébellions à la maréchaussée'.* Constables in the Auvergne were involved in more than twice as many violent incidents as their counterparts in the Guyenne. Only in the Auvergne was there an example of such unprovoked, criminal brutality as the death of Claude Bourgade, a *laboureur* who was insulted in an inn by three constables of the Thiers brigade, dragged outside, robbed of twenty-five louis d'or and 'assassiné à coups de bayonette'.[91] The Guyenne policemen confined many of their physical assaults to their colleagues – a useful safety valve, perhaps, for old soldiers unable to give free rein to their aggressive instincts when dealing with the general public.

In view of all the weaknesses of the eighteenth-century police force, it can be questioned whether the authorities, in spite of sweeping government ordinances, ever conceived of the maréchaussée as the guarantor of public order. The subdélégué in Montaigut frankly acknowledged the impossibility of putting the Declaration of 1724 into effect, and when faced by an influx of 'Moorish' vagrants, had the constables arrest one or two 'qui semblent estre a craindre par leurs figures et discours'.[92] A thief was to be arrested, not as a punishment for his crimes, but 'pour qu'on puisse en faire un exemple'.[93] The police remained the basis and expression of a pre-Beccarian system of justice which believed in the hard but spasmodic example to deter others. Policemen always knew where to find beggars and vagabonds – the best positions for attracting the

---

* In the course of the century, the two companies together managed barely thirty cases, ranging from proven brutality to the flimsiest of allegations.

attention of potential donors, the barns they traditionally slept in –- but action was only taken on the publication of a new law: arrests would rise sharply, only to fall away again a few months later. In 1768, some constables demanded a bonus payment for what they described as 'ce suplément de travail'.[94] When an important theft or series of thefts caused alarm in the neighbourhood, it was again felt necessary for public relations to suspend temporarily the tolerance the police habitually accorded to their clientèle. Brigade commanders would organize the indiscriminate round-up of vagrants, or simply move them on to the district of the next brigade: 'Nous avous fait décamper des métairies tout ce bagage', the Blaye brigade commander reported, 'avec deffance de rester ny d'abiter dans mon distric'.[95] If the eighteenth-century police were at all effective, they were so only in spasms.

Rather than waste their limited time and energy on a futile attempt to keep up with government legislation, the policemen of the eighteenth century preferred to concentrate their efforts to cope with really serious situations. In practice this usually meant the organization of concerted action – the grouping together of several brigades – to repel the incursions of large bands of brigands or smugglers. All the brigades of the Haute-Auvergne got together in the 1730s to intimidate the smugglers who had overrun the province, and the General Farm grudgingly admitted that the smugglers had been dispersed, at least for a time.[96] This method of operating was virtually an admission of the failure of the 1720 system of routine patrols, and a return to the seventeenth-century technique of getting as much strength as possible together, for an impressive foray across the province. In the last decades of the ancien régime it became almost standard procedure in the Guyenne under the initiative of the lieutenants in Agen and Périgueux, and their numerous expeditions against reported bands of thieves or escaped convicts were considered to have been effective as arrests and convictions usually followed. The policemen of the ancien régime *could* cope with an occasional emergency. The Guyenne did *not* become an area of organized bands such as existed in the forests of the Beauce or the mountains of the Forez, though the Guyenne had forests to give refuge to brigands, and important traffic along its roads to offer suitable plunder. It is at least feasible that harassment by the maréchaussée prevented the growth and consolidation of large, dangerous bands.

Unfortunately the sort of effort this problem required, that is, the concentration of a number of brigades in one place, did have the grave inconvenience of leaving most of the province unpoliced. It did not require a Beccaria to persuade the public of the inadequacies of a system of law and order based on so intermittent an imposition of authority. The occasional exemplary punishment and the occasional passage of a patrol were not calculated to bolster the confidence of the public in the protection afforded by the police. Persistent, intimidating beggars, vagrants and thieves would get away with it for years; parishes would put up with their local bully no matter how often he got drunk, beat his wife, threatened the neighbours, and pilfered their property. When the local thug of St Flour was finally arrested, the commander of the police brigade himself was so frightened by menaces of retaliation that the intendant had to reassure him and his constables.[97] In the 1760s the Montaigut area endured for several years the exactions of a convict/deserter with his 'wife' and her brother – 'ses associés qui vivent en paix comme si a l'ombre de sa protection'.[98] The inhabitants of the Guyenne were more prepared to call in the police, but only when a suspicious stranger was involved, and there were of course more strangers around in south-west France than in the remote and inaccessible villages of the Massif Central. Three very respectable Englishmen hardly had time to sit down to dinner in Périgueux before the police were summoned to take them down to the station for questioning.[99] A Prussian sailor who had a fight with his ship's captain in Bordeaux and decided to walk home to Stettin got as far as Mérignac, an hour's walk from the quay-side, before being stopped by peasants.[100] It was hardly a sign of a sense of security that the public should react so nervously to such an individual, or that peace and tranquillity should be so easily shattered by a few thefts. A number of highway robberies in and around Montesquieu's estate at La Brède,* just a few miles south of Bordeaux, caused such panic that local people refused to go to church and travellers formed convoys to cross the area.[101]

The result of the police failure to provide protection was inevitably that men continued to take steps to protect themselves. Threatened with arson, one landowner in the Auvergne never went out without a rifle, and his *métayers* patrolled the property night and day;[102] the Guyenne constable who was killed during the château de Duras operation was shot by a métayer who had been armed by his master

---

* This outbreak of lawlessness took place in 1748, the year Montesquieu's *L'Esprit des Lois* was published.

to protect his property.[103] And it seems that despite all the maréchaussée's attempts to improve discipline and increase its own effectivenss, this feeling of public insecurity tended to grow as the century progressed, particularly when economic conditions began to deteriorate in the 1770s and 1780s. The public was right to feel nervous at a time when more and more were being pushed into the ranks of the destitute, and the incentives for crime and civil disturbance were multiplying. By the late 1770s vigilante patrols were coming into existence to supplement the patrols of the police — even in Royat, a suburb of Clermont itself which had no less than two brigades of maréchaussée.[104]

What is particularly indicative of the state of mind regarding public safety at this time is that so many of the alarms which swept the provinces were false, so many of the panic rumours without foundation. Such was the case, for example, with the report which circulated freely in the Auvergne in the 1780s, that a woman who had told a robber she would be able to identify him had had her eyes gouged out,[105] or the panic caused in the Périgord in the 1770s by rumours that brigands were abducting children in order to eat them.[106] More often the rumours exploited the pathological fear of large numbers. A series of thefts in a given area was always evidence of the existence of an organized band, even if it was too clever to show itself in anything but groups of three.[107] One such band of brigands, chased by a united force of four police brigades and 150 local men turned out to be, as the intendant wryly admitted, a few beggars brought together by their misery.[108]

These forerunners of the Great Fear showed clearly in the years before 1789 that the aims of the 1720 reforms had not been achieved. Laden with duties and starved of funds, the police of the ancien régime had not been able to instil a sense of public security; nor had they been able to establish effective surveillance over the country as a whole. These were tasks to which successive Revolutionary governments addressed themselves with enthusiasm.

Cameron, *The Police of Eighteenth-Century France* **71**

NOTES

1. The history of the French maréchaussée has been curiously neglected, which is the more surprising since the institution is of interest not only to the social historian and the historian of crime, but even to the administrative historian concerned with the functioning of ancien régime government. G. de Chamberet, Précis historique sur la gendarmerie (Paris, 1861); L. Leques, Histoire de la Gendarmerie (Paris, 1874); and H.Delattre, Historique de la gendarmerie française (Paris, 1879), are extremely brief; a more useful, institutional study is G. Larrieu, Histoire de la Gendarmerie (Paris, 1933). The interest of the twentieth-century gendarmerie in its own past has produced a few interesting articles in, Gendarmerie Nationale, Revue d'Etudes d'Informations (notably in 1969, on the maréchaussée of Corsica). Two local studies are J. Plique, Histoire de la maréchaussée du Gevaudan (Mende, 1912) and a 1958 thèse de droit of the University of Aix-en-Provence, M. Grand, La Maréchaussée en Provence 1554-1790 (Archives départementales [hereafter A.D.], Bouches du Rhône, cote VIII, F58). A. Garnier is primarily concerned with the judicial aspects of the institution in his 'Histoire de la maréchaussée de Langres', in Mémoires de la Société pour l'Histoire du Droit et des Institutions des anciens pays bourguignons, comtois et romands, 13 (1951), 211-75, and 14 (1952), 35-129. Some useful pages on the police work of the eighteenth century maréchaussée can be found in: J.P. Gutton, La Société et les Pauvres (Paris, 1971); A. Corvisier, L'Armée française de la fin du XVIIe siècle au ministère de Choiseul: le soldat (Paris, 1964); and O. Hufton, The Poor of Eighteenth-century France, 1750-1789 (Oxford, 1974).

2. A.D. de la Gironde, C3850; Revue of all these various companies in 1680.

3. M. Boudet (ed.), Les Chevauchées des Trois Lacarrière (Riom, 1898) — a severely edited collection of the annual reports drawn up by the commanders of the Haute-Auvergne police between 1587 and 1685.

4. Ibid., 151.

5. President Lamoignon, quoted along with his colleagues by A. Esmein, Histoire de la procédure criminelle en France (Paris, 1882), 219.

6. A.D. Gironde C3460, Letter from intendant Esmangart to Le Noir, vice-chancelier, 6 April 1773.

7. Ibid, C2179: Claim for expenses, 6 December 1760, sent to the war minister Belle-isle, 'les Anglois ayant fait un armement formidable et menassé de faire une descente sur nos cottes . . .'.

8. Ibid. Claim for expenses by the Nérac brigade, December 1764.

9. Ibid., C. 2189. Letter from Barret de Ferrand to intendant, 11 March 1755. 'Comme les Jurats ne sont occupés qu' à tracasser la maréchaussée . . . , d'autant qu'ils me font passer pour un mauvais concitoyen . . . , il est bien disgratieux, Monsieur, de n'agir plus qu'en tremblant, d'être toujours sur les épines . . . .'

10. Two heavy boxes in A.D. Gironde — C2188 and C2189 — contain the

documents relating to the feud between the Jurats and the maréchaussée.

11. D. Jousse, Nouveau commentaire sur l'ordonnance criminelle du mois d'août (Paris, 1763).

12. Archives de la Guerre (hereafter A. de G.) X^F9 Tableau comparatif (of numbers in the police force before and after its change of name).

13. A.D. Puy de Dôme C6188, Letter from intendant de Montyon to Choiseul, 23 January 1768.

14. Ibid., 'Etat des emplacements des nouvelles brigades', 1768.

15. Ibid. C6174, Letter from war minister M. de Breteuil to intendant, 1 October 1724.

16. Ibid., C6182, Letter from intendant Trudaine to war minister d'Angervilliers, 15 September 1734.

17. Ibid., C6173, Le Blanc's memorandum on the 'brigades de maréchaussée à établir'.

18. Ibid. C6120.

19. A.D. Gironde C4636, Tableau.

20. Ibid., 11 B12: Aquiton and Berger, 1752.

21. Ibid., 11 B4: habitants de St Sulpice de Faleyrens, 1754-5.

22. A.D. Puy de Dôme C6184, Minister of War, d'Argenson, to intendant Rossignol (1743).

23. A. de G. X^F4, Mémoire of Devic, Inspecteur-général.

24. Archives Nationales (hereafter A.N.) $Z^{1c}334$.

25. A.D. Puy de Dôme C6174-6176, correspondence between intendant, Riom subdélégué, prévôt and minister of war.

26. A. de G. Y^b 787, 791, 792, 796, 798, 804, and 805 contain all the Revues which survive of the Guyenne and Auvergne companies.

27. A.D. Puy de Dôme C1523, Letter from Limoges intendant to Riom intendant, asking for police assistance in the hunt for de Chaleix, 'homme dangereux', who, 'quoique d'une noblesse asses moderne' was 'bien apparenté et ne paroissoit qu' accompagné de plusieurs gentilhommes pour le défendre en cas d'attaque . . . .' (1732)

28. A. de G. Y^b 796: the Inspector of the Guyenne company reported, in 1773, that 'le corps de ville est venu nous y trouver pour nous témoigner ses obligations et sa reconnaissance . . . .'

29. The testimonial noted his 'assiduité, zèle et ardeur', his operations by night and day, 'son intelligence à commander', etc. Mémoire, A.D. Puy de Dôme C6191.

30. A.D. Gironde C4636, Letter to intendant, 27 September 1787.

31. A. de G. X^F4, 'Mémoire par le Sieur Devic, Inspecteur-général, sur le peu d'inconvénients dans l'ordonnance du 28 avril 1778'.

32. A.D. Puy de Dôme C6185, Letter to intendant from M. de Diene, 16 April 1756.

33. Ibid, C6189 (1769)

34. A. de G. Y^b804.

35. A.D. Puy de Dôme C6179. Correspondence between prévôt, intendant and war minister 1732-3.

36. A. de G. Y^b805.

37. Ibid., Y^b 858.

38. Ibid., Y^b 789.

Cameron, *The Police of Eighteenth-Century France* **73**

39. Ibid., Y^A 59.

40. A.D. Gironde C2181, Controller-general's comments on the 1775 'Etat des Frais'.

41. Ibid., C275.

42. A.D. Puy de Dôme C6177, Letter from Riom subdélégué Urion to intendant Trudaine, 28 December 1730.

43. A.D. Gironde C2178-9. Letters from prévôt Barret de Ferrand to controller-general, 27 June 1759, 22 September 1759, 15 October 1761.

44. Ibid., C4635. Barret de Ferand's memorandum on the 'boete commune'.

45. A.D. Puy de Dôme C6187, Letter to intendant from brigadier Payot, 10 July 1769.

46. Ibid., C6184, List of debts of Belisme, Cavalier in Thiers.

47. ·A. de G. X^F4, Letter from de Deffan to Choiseul. 15 November 1770.

48. A.D. Puy de Dôme C6176, Letter from d'Angervilliers to intendant, July 1729.

49. Ibid., C6186, A confidential inquiry launched by the intendant 31 August 1760 to discover 's'il était vrai que les cavaliers exercent quelque profession particulière ou s'ils faisaient quelque commerce'.

50. Ibid., C6207. Casernes, Ambert, 1755.

51. Ibid., C6182, Letter from Montaigut subdélégué to intendant, 30 June and 5 August 1734.

52. Ibid., C6174, Letter from Aurillac subdélégué to intendant, 21 April 1724.

53. Ibid., C1528, C1529 and C6185. Letters from Mauriac, subdélégué and abbé de la Valette to intendant (1737-8 and 1750).

54. Ibid., C1537. Letters from Ambert subdélégué to intendant (1752).

55. A.D. Gironde C2188, Letter from intendant to ministei d'Armenonville, 14 June 1726.

56. A.N. Z^{1c}334.

57. A.D. Puy de Dôme C1537. Mauriac subdélégué to intendant: 'la maréchaussée a même fait differentes tentatives, mais en vain, par la raison que ces voleurs vaguent d'une paroisse a l'autre, et qu'ils ne sont jamais stables par une part, quoy qu'ils soient trés connûs' (June 1752). Ibid., C1554. 1760 Etat of unpublished crimes, Clermont district, included a thief who had come and gone since 1749, making 'des aparitions si courtes qui ne permettent point de la saisir'. Ibid., C6218, 'Courses . . . de la brigade de Langeac par ordre de l'intendant'; December 1732, brigade noted presence of smugglers, who were unlikely to be captured 'parce qu'ils ne sont presque jamais chez eux'.

58. Ibid., C1537, Memorandum from intendant to Lebey, exempt.

59. Ibid., C1519, Letter from Thiers subdélégué to intendant.

60. Ibid., C1520, Letter from Langeac brigadier to intendant.

61. Ibid., C6256, 1788 List of 'captures, traductions de voleurs . . .'; Pont du Château brigade.

62. Ibid., C1595, Galériens, sentenced 1767 by Aurillac Présidial.

63. A.D. Gironde 11 B12: Frelon (1774).

64. A.D. Puy de Dôme C1546, Letter from Aurillac subdélégué to intendant, July 1766.

65. Ibid., C1536. Letter from Brioude sudélégué to intendant, December 1751.

66. A.D. Gironde 11B 9 (ii), trial of band of 'l'Enfant bleu', 1772/3.

67. Ibid., C2182 procès-verbal by Périgueux brigadier, 6 October 1779.

68. Ibid., C3729, 'Courses extraordinaires', La Tête de Buch brigade, 1789.

69. A.D. Puy de Dôme, C6186, Letter from intendant Ballainvilliers to controller-general, d'ormesson, 20 August 1760.

70. Ibid., C6192, 'Mémoire sur les maréchaussées' (anon, n.d.).

71. Ibid., C6219ff.

72. Ibid., C7686, Letter to intendant from Darinière, *receveur des tailles* at Aurillac, 5 February 1737.

73. Ibid., C1522. Montaigut subdélégué to intendant, 26 December 1759.

74. Ibid., B00384 Mémoire by the Commissaires de police de Clermont (n.d.).

75. Ibid., C1543, Letters from Mauriac subdélégué to intendant 17 August and 23 December 1759.

76. Ibid., Ambert subdélégué to intendant, 17 January 1759.

77. Ibid., C1531 — Correspondence between Granier, Mauriac Inspector of Weights and Measures, and intendant, December 1742-April 1744.

78. A.N. Z^{1C} 351, and A.D. Gironde 11 B4 — trial of *habitants* of St Sulpice de Faleyrens (1754-5).

79. A.D. Puy de Dôme C1529, Aurillac subdélégué to intendant (1737).

80. A.D. Gironde C2186: procès-verbal by Agen lieutenant de Sauveaud, 14 January 1779.

81. Ibid., 11B 12; Luborde (1783).

82. A.D. Puy de Dôme C1548, Thiers subdélégué to intendant, 9 July 1788.

83. E.g. A.D. Gironde 11 B4: Geresme (1775).

84. Ibid., 11B 3 (1736-7).

85. Ibid., 11B 5 (i): Pierre Nogaret, dit Lafon (1755-6).

86? Ibid., C2181: Verdon to intendant, 6 February 1777; andC2186, 28 March 1779 and 16 June 1778.

87. Ibid., C2186, Verdon to intendant, 7 April 1778.

88. Ibid., 11B 9 (ii).

89. Ibid., 11B 10: Mathieu Seret, cavalier; and C4636 (1751).

90. A.D.Puy¹de Dôme C6174: the Sr Cavagnac (1723-4).

91. Ibid., C6184. Jugement de la Connétablie, 15 September 1745, condemning Michel Rougerie, *dit* Clermont and Antoine Renouard *dit* la Jeunesse to be hanged for 'homicide commis volontairement, et sans legitime defense de leur vie'; their colleague Pierre Bard *dit* Lapierre was banished for three years for making false allegations of 'violence excès et insultes' against the peasants of Ecoutoux. Cf. also 'decret de prise de corps', 3 October 1744, A.N. Z^{1C} 341.

92. A.D Puy de Dôme C1523, Correspondence between intendant and Montaigut subdélégué 1732.

93. Ibid., C1528. Intendant to brigadier Fontfreyde, 29 July 1736.

94. Ibid., C1110, Letter from La Ribbe-haute to intendant, 1 June 1708.

95. A.D. Gironde 11B 3, procès-verbal de capture, 12 November 1736.

96. A.D. Puy de Dôme C6182, Correspondence between the intendant and the Farmers General, 1734.

97. Ibid., C1523, Intendant to d'Hervilly, 1734.

98. Ibid., C1566.

99. A.D. Dordogne B698: interrogation of John Weare, 22, of Bristol;

Cameron, *The Police of Eighteenth-Century France*   **75**

Edward Edwards, 36, 'archidiacre de Brechnaud, diocèse de St. David, principauté de Galles en Angleterre'; and James Fisher, 18, 'gentil-homme, étudiant de rétorique à Oxford', 28 September 1768.

    100. A.D. Gironde 11B 12: Johann Christian Dieverik (1787).

    101. Ibid., 11B 11: curé of La Brède to intendant, 30 June 1748.

    102. A.D. Puy de Dôme C1527, Letter from Lafont to intendant (1735).

    103. A.D. Gironde 11B 9: Band of the Enfant bleu.

    104. A.D. Puy de Dôme, C1547: Letter from De l'arbre, curé of Royat to intendant, December 1777.

    105. Ibid., C1548, Letters from prévôt de la Ribbe-haute to intendant, 22 and 26 July 1780.

    106. A.D. Dordogne B629 and B637, passim.

    107. A.D. Puy de Dôme, C1548: de la Ribbe-haute to intendant, 18 July 1780.

    108. Ibid., C1548: Letter from intendant to prévôt du Deffan, 24 May 1777.

[9]

The "Private Army" of the Tax Farms: The Men and their Origins

by Earl ROBISHEAUX *

There is no specialized study of the men who composed the "private army" of the Royal General Tax Farms in 18th century France. We have a good work on the tax farmers themselves,[1] but only modest information about those who did their dirty work for them. Pierre Roux has an outline of their duties;[2] Matthews gives us an idea of their numbers and organization;[3] Lavoisier[4] and Necker[5] describe their deployment. Adrien Delahante's classic work insists that the guards of the Farms were "types of Bohemians scorned and abhorred," and mistakenly believed that they were recruited throughout the kingdom.[6] Who, in fact, were the men in the private army of the Tax Farms? What were the differences between the officers and the men? How did this army function, and how was it organized?

Basically, the "private army" was a paramilitary formation with 23,000 men in 1784, and was divided on paper into 352 divisions scattered throughout the kingdom.[7] The basic operational unit was the brigade composed of from four to twenty men which functioned as an organized unit "to protect the rights of the Farms."[8] There were two types of brigades. Sedentary brigades, by far the most numerous, were stationed at fixed geographical points and seldom went further than a half a day's march from their stations. They were commanded by two officers: a brigadier and a sub-brigadier. Occasionally four officers were attached to the larger units. About a third of the brigades were ambulatory; its men mounted on horseback. Each was led by a captain and a lieutenant with four or more men under their command. All of the brigades were named after small hamlets and villages of the region of lower Normandy where they were stationed, such as "Isigny," "Neuilly," "Bréville," "Deauville," and "Arromanches."

---

* Department of History, University of Oregon.

[1] Yves DURAND, *Les fermiers généraux au XVIIIe siècle* (Paris, 1971).

[2] Pierre ROUX, *La Ferme des impôts sous l'ancien régime* (Paris, 1916), pp. 529-31.

[3] George T. MATTHEWS, *The Royal General Farms in Eighteenth Century France* (New York, 1958), pp. 110-111.

[4] Antoine-Laurent LAVOISIER, *Œuvres* (Paris, 1864-1893), VI, p. 155.

[5] Jacques NECKER, *De l'administration des finances de la France* (n.p., 1784), I, pp. 38, 106; II, p. 34.

[6] Adrien DELAHANTE, *Une Famille de finance au XVIIIe siècle* (Paris, 1881), I, pp. 207-208.

[7] NECKER, *De l'administration*, I, pp. 38, 106.

[8] Authority for the force stems from the periodic leases of the Farms; thus, for instance, from the lease Legendre: "Ledit Legendre pourra établir tel nombre de capitaines, archers, et gardes qu'il sera nécessaire pour la conservation des droits et fermes comprises au présent bail." AN AD^{Ix}429B. The text quotes from AD Calvados 3C 1, reception of new officers at the *grenier à sel*.

The main purpose of the brigades was to supervise the salt trade for the General Farms. The principal duty of the men derived largely from the local regulations concerning its sale and distribution. For administrative reasons, the Farms divided Lower Normandy into two regions, the *pays du quart bouillon,* the larger, and the *pays de grandes gabelles.* The *pays du quart bouillon* comprised most of the *généralités* of Caen and Alençon, 990 parishes in all. Its distinguishing characteristic was that inhabitants of the region were not subject to the *gabelle,* but had the right to procure salt from local salt marches. The Crown claimed a fourth of their procurement (though it was closer to a fifth in actual practice), whence the name "quart bouillon." In this area the local population could obtain salt for less than 1/20 of the going price in the *pays de grandes gabelles.* This latter was the other administrative subdivision of Lower Normandy, and most of the territory around the cities of Caen and Bayeux fell into its jurisdiction. In this region individuals paid the *gabelle* — that is, purchased fixed quantities of salt at high prices. Common to each of these regions was the *sexté* roll, which was a parish register listing the amount of salt that parishioners were required to purchase (in the *pays de grandes gabelles*) or were allowed to procure (in the *quart bouillon*).

The chief responsibility of the employees in the brigades was the verification of the *sexté* register. In the *pays du quart bouillon* they inspected households to insure that the families of the parish took no more than their per-capita allotment of salt. When such was the case, it was a virtually certain indication that the additional quantities were smuggled into the *pays de grandes gabelles* to be sold on the black market. Verifications in the *pays de grandes gabelles* were carried out to insure that all members of the families were listed on the roll and had taken their salt required by the gabelle. Whether in the *pays du quart bouillon* or in the *pays de grandes gabelles,* examinations were carried out in the cities by the sedentary brigades and in the countryside by the mounted.

In addition to their duties with the *sexté,* the brigades of the Farms also performed numerous other functions. They patrolled river crossings and road junctions to prevent the movement of contraband salt and tobacco. They watched over the collectors of the gabelle to insure that they delivered no more than the purchased quantities of salt, and that they deposited the collections in the treasury of the local *grenier à sel* rather than their own pockets. The sedentary brigades supervised retail distributors of salt *(regrattiers)* to discourage them from purchasing on the black market. Before 1778, when the Farms still collected the *aides,* they watched over the movement of cidre, *eaux-de-vie,* and other drinks. After the Crown assumed direct administration of these duties in 1778, the employees were left mostly to the gabelle and tobacco trade. [9]

---

[9] They performed other minor functions involving the customs. "Instructions préliminaires sur toutes les parties des Fermes," AN K 887, no. 7, fos. 28-41 (ms.

Their most difficult task was to combat organized groups out to defraud the Farms. The brigades of the General Tax Farms were organized in the 1680's following the formation of the Company of General Tax Farmers itself. [10] Their paramilitary formation arose from the fact that in the years immediately following their creation, they were often called on to do battle with large bands of outlaws roaming the countryside. Their military organization gave them an advantage of command and control which often proved decisive in their encounters with such gangs.

During the wars of the reign of Louis XIV, the "private army" of the Tax Farms engaged in one of the most extraordinary campaigns in their history. Louis called to the colours an army of immense size, and in the winter when the weather was unfavourable for military operations, the army billeted its troops in the provinces. In Lower Normandy large numbers of men were put into winter quarter in Caen, Bayeux, St. Lô, Mortain, and the small villages and hamlets dotting the region. Invariably these troops began to take advantage of the substantial difference in the price of salt between the *pays de grandes gabelles* and the regions not subject to the *gabelle*. They began to purchase cheap salt in Brittany and in the Cotentin peninsula and to smuggle it into the high-price regions of the *pays de grandes gabelles*. The same quantity of salt purchased in Brittany could usually be sold in the suburbs of Caen or Bayeux for twenty or more times its purchase price. The wars of the reign of Louis XIV brought into being a large force of organized units well placed to make considerable profits from such illicit trade.

They were helped and encouraged by the bad climate and the poor harvests of the period, which made the local population more willing to defraud the Farms. In the region around Bayeux, for example, the wheat harvest, the principle source of nourishment and income, was fair to bad in 1684-1685, 1692-1694, 1697-1701, 1704, 1709-1710, and 1712-1714. [11] The years with good harvests were 1686-1691, 1695-1696, 1702-1703, 1705-1708, 1711, and 1715. Nearly half of the harvests were bad enough to provoke sharp rises in the price of bread. This meant that more money had to be paid for basic foodstuffs and that less was available for other purchases and for paying taxes. In such rigorous conditions, large numbers of individuals, who otherwise would not have purchased or trafficked in smuggled salt, began to do so on a large scale. During his tour of the region in 1707, a year with a good harvest, the intendant Nicolas Foucault noted that

undated); also, DE LA MOTTE, *Le Guide des employés ou instructions pour apprendre à verbaliser* (Amiens, 1751), p. 57, found in AN G¹ 63 dos. 14.

[10] Pierre VIEUVILLE, *Nouveau traité des élections* (Paris, 1739), p. 568 (BN: Lf38/3) traces their origins to similar creations by Charles VII in 1452, François I in 1534, and Henri III, 1581-1583. The Ordinance of the Gabelles of 1680 provided for such a force.

[11] Mohamed EL KORDI, *Bayeux aux XVII* et XVIII* siècles* (Paris, 1970), pp. 284-286; 192-93.

only profits from salt smuggling made it possible for many peasants to pay their taxes and purchase bread.[12]

A necessary source of income even in good years, in the bad the profits from salt running became vital. With the coming of the war, regiments of the royal army in winter quarter were then on the spot to organize much of the provisioning of the black market. The poor harvests of the period combined with the unprecedented size of the French army set the stage for one of the wildest smuggling operations in the history of the General Tax Farms. In Lower Normandy the problem was especially acute, but it occurred throughout the kingdom, notably along the borders of Britanny, the *quart bouillon,* and along the salt marshes of the south and the Midi. Troops in winter quarter moved out for the regions of cheap salt, often bringing in hundreds of horseloads at a time.

When the brigades of the Tax Farms moved into the field to put a stop to the trade, small-scale warfare erupted: in many cases troops abruptly ceased to operate as groups of free-lance soldiers and began to function as military units. Le Riche, Director of the Farms at Caen, wrote that "the troops who are in this *Généralité* and that of Alençon are going to make a frightful disorder and the employees will not know how to remedy it ...."[13] And he was right. By December, 1692, the Company of General Tax Farmers complained to the king that troops "were assembling in such great numbers that it is impossible for the employees and guards of the Farms to stop them."[14] Le Riche complained that, when the troops head out for the frontier with Brittany, "there are officers in front ... and they are marching in battle order."[15]

After 1695 the brigades of the Farms fought a series of desperate actions throughout the countryside with elements of the royal army. In March of that year several brigades fought an action with 20-25 dragoons outside the village of Allemande, winning the day because of their superior position. The battle was fought with pistols, muskets, and even bayonets.[16] All through the late 1690's and early 1700's the situation grew still worse as the brigades clashed with military units running contraband. By 1707 army units were marauding the country with virtual impunity; many took to the offensive, systematically searching out and defeating the brigades in open battle wherever they could catch them. Le Riche wrote:[17]

> Salt smuggling continues with ferocious force, dragoons from Falaise and Argentan are grouping together in bands of 50, 60, and 80, armed to the teeth, our guards are not strong enough to attack them because we can only make detachments of 15 or 20 men .... M. de Marzin [Director of the

---

12 AN G⁷ 217.
13 *Ibid.*
14 AN G⁷1216 letter of 24 December.
15 AN G⁷217 letter of 19 March.
16 AN G⁷214 letter of 25 March from De Marzin.
17 AN G⁷217 letter of 17 March.

Aides at Caen] is now at the head of a large detachment along the frontier with Brittany, and he tells me that there are two numerous bands operating there.... The peasants see that the dragoons can force their way in large numbers, and now are beginning to group themselves together. They are scarcely any worse. In a word, the disorder is great.

The situation was so bad in July 1707 that Foucault ordered the Territorial Police *(Maréchaussée)* to press men into the brigades from wherever they could be found. [18] In November the brigades fought an action with 40-50 cavalry near Villedieu. [19] In the winter of 1709 the infantry regiment Razilly encamped near Bayeux was running a massive trade in salt. [20] Large numbers of troops were in action in 1709, the year of the *"hiver terrible,"* most notably around Caen, Falaise, and Alençon. [21] In January, 1710 De Marzin managed to gather a number of brigades from Caen and Laval. He took them to the field in search of the cavalry regiment St. Aignoy, then running contraband salt from Brittany. On the 15th of January they caught it, and fought a hand-to-hand engagement with 150 troops in open terrain. They captured 49 cavalrymen and 124 horseloads of salt. [22] Several officers of the brigades were killed in the battle. Later in the month De Marzin's group tangled with 180 cavalry near Mortain. [23] Near Laval in June, 1710, the brigades fought a big battle with 200-250 mounted cavalry. [24] Around Falaise in February, 1711, 100-120 troops tried to force their way into the *pays de grandes gabelles* with fifty horseloads of salt. All were armed. They smashed through the defensive ring of brigades separating Brittany from the rest of France, heading into the regions of high-priced salt. A handful of brigades of the Farms together with a large crowd of bounty hunters, some of whom were themselves soldiers, finally arrested their progress after a desperate engagement. [25]

The pressure on the employees of the Farms was so great, for this amounted to small-scale warfare, that many began to fail. Foucault complained in September, 1707, that troops not only picked battles with guards of the Farms, but even set fire to houses refusing their demands. [26] Gangs of smugglers raided jails to free their comrades and openly boasted about their bloody encounters with the brigades. [27] The guards around Dieppe complained bitterly in 1710 that the region was filled with roving bands of troops smuggling salt and openly seeking to do battle with them. [28] Employees around Tours and Poitiers began to balk at the prospect of battling protes-

---

[18] AN G⁷217 letter of 23 July.
[19] AN G⁷217 letter of 24 November.
[20] AN G⁷1235.
[21] AN G⁷1235.
[22] AN G⁷1225.
[23] AN G⁷218 letter of 17 January from La Briffe (intendant).
[24] AN G⁷1225.
[25] AN G⁷1240.
[26] AN G⁷217 letter of 10 September.
[27] AN G⁷217 letter of 22 March 1709 from Foucault de Magny (son of Nicolas Foucault, intendant).
[28] AN G⁷1238.

sional soldiers. [29] The guards of the brigades were usually outnumbered and had inferior training; small wonder they hesitated in the face of such odds.

As the war began to draw to a conclusion and as economic conditions in the countryside improved, these confrontations slowly came to an end. Never again did the brigades have to take on units of the royal army in open battle on such a scale. There were three contributing causes which brought about an end to these actions: first, in the last years of the reign of Louis XIV, most of the French army was demobilized. There remained fewer troops and units to engage in large-scale operations against the brigades in the Tax Farms. Secondly, from 1709/10 the army made a greater effort to stop the excesses of its men. In that year the army sent De Beauveau, Inspector General of Cavalry, into Lower Normandy to discipline the troops. Le Riche, Director of the Farms at Caen, wrote that "he has worked so well that everything is calm for the present." [30] Violent battles still erupted after his mission, but 1710 represents something of a turning point. His most successful method was to pay bounties to troops so they would help to capture rather than participate with other salt smugglers. 1710 was something of a turning point in the cycle of famine as well. In Lower Normandy the harvests of 1710-1712, and 1714 were fair to good, with 1713 the only bad year. [31] Better harvests took some of the burden off the peasants and artisans, who were then less inclined to purchasing smuggled salt, and even

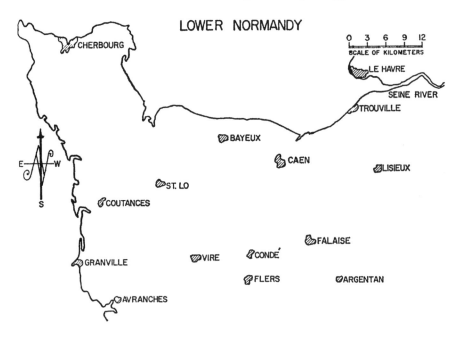

LOWER NORMANDY

---

[29] AN G⁷1237 remonstrance of June, 1710.
[30] AN G⁷1234.
[31] El KORDI, p. 193.

less disposed to trafficking themselves. This third factor, the improvement of the harvests, was probably the most decisive of all. At any rate, by 1715 large engagements between the royal army and the brigades of the Tax Farms had come to an end.

It would be interesting to discover what sort of fellow was attracted to these units of the Tax Farms. To combat regular military units, or to attempt, to root out fraud by house to house inspections, were tasks requiring a particular form of courage. Unfortunately, no significant sources from the earlier years have survived, if indeed the Farms even kept such records. We do know that contemporaries thought little of the men's abilities; that Foucault once complained, "the greater part of those employed there have never served before, and have no courage to face up to salt smugglers." [32] He thought their ranks contained too few ex-soldiers and that a greater effort should be made to recruit more of them. Beyond this one can say little, for the lack of statistical sources. However, we can answer a number of questions concerning the men in the brigades in the late 18th century.

This study is based on 429 officers and men comprising four *capitaineries générales* (a type of administrative subdivision) deployed in Lower Normandy on 1 January 1789. [33] I have selected two *capitaineries générales* from the vicinity of Caen (Sallenelles and Caen), one from the region around Cherbourg, and Grandville. On several charts I have broken the statistics down according to *capitaineries générales* to show how negligible were the differences among the men throughout the region. The resulting homogeneity suggests that a broader statistical base would not substantially alter the conclusions presented here. I have restricted this work to Lower Normandy, however, and the employees in other regions might well have been different from the Normans.

A brief glance at the wages paid to the brigades reveals much about the men in their service. Captains and lieutenants, who commanded the itinerant brigades, annually received 500 and 400-440 *livres* respectively. Officers in the non-mobile brigades, brigadiers and sub-brigadiers, were given 450 and 390 *livres*. Ordinary guards in the ranks earned from 330-400 *livres* a year, with the higher wages going to the men in the itinerant units. The men were paid at the local *grenier à sel,* the local salt magazine. [34]

---

[32] AN G⁷1222 memoir of 1703.

[33] What follows draws on a collection of *cahiers* at the *Archives Nationales* in Paris, AN G¹ 72. They are "*Etats de signalement des employés,*" and are somewhat misleadingly inventoried, "*Mémoires sur la défense des côtes de Normandie.*" Though the carton contains a number of memoirs on the suppression of tax fraud along the Norman coasts, it also has forty-eight *cahiers* which describe the individuals in the paramilitary organization of the General Tax Farms. Farm officials in Lower Normandy compiled these lists from 1770-1789; the *états* treat only employees deployed in the *Direction de Caen.* Similar sources exist for other regions.

[34] AN G¹72 dos. 4, memoir on the organization of the Farms in Normandy.

These were modest wages for the tasks, and the men attracted to them came from modest backgrounds.

Table I indicates the previous occupations of the men employed in the brigades in 1789. Nearly half, 46.8%, were former peasants and soldiers; and the lion's share of these were peasants. The term employed for them is *laboureurs,* which often means a man with more than a few parcels of land, a draught animal, and other modest possessions — the higher echelon of the peasantry, in other words. The "dirty work" of the Farms was thus done largely by organized groups of peasants and soldiers. Tradesmen from the cities counted for a very small portion of the total (9.8%); nor is their representation susbtantially higher in the brigades stationed in or near large cities. In the *capitainerie* of Caen, which contained seven brigades totalling 56 men, tradesmen comprised a mere 8.0%. The *capitainerie* of Cherbourg had 18 brigades totalling 116 men, but only 5.1% (6 men) listed trades as their former profession.

There are three general distinctions which separate the men in the ranks from their officers. The most pronounced and the most important is literacy. Literacy in this case means the ability to write well enough to compose a legal dossier *(procès verbal)* against an individual suspected of defrauding the Tax Farms. The whole system of enforcement of the regulations against smuggling depended on the ability of the employees to deposit formal legal complaints with the local judicial bodies *(élections* and *greniers à sel)* having competence in the matter. Employees who could not do so were severely limited in their usefulness to the Farms. De la Motte wrote, "we do not doubt the activity of some zealous employees, but it happens all too often that those who have this desirable quality are not capable of manifesting it by completing a regular *procès verbal.*" [35] With respect to the men in the ranks, De la Motte was right: only 4.0% of them could write reports (Table II). But among the officers, 64.8% exhibited enough literacy to place themselves in the higher levels of the brigades. The striking thing is the vast gap between the capabilities of the officers and the men. For every man who is literate, there are sixteen such literate officers. Even combining the second level (the ability to write) with the highest, the gulf between them remains wide — 84.3% of the officers were in the two top categories, while only 28.6% of the men. The officers dominate the top literacy levels, the men the lower. 61.4% of the men, almost two-thirds, were capable of no more than writing just a little or signing their own names.

The source of the general superiority of the officers in literacy seems to lie with their former professions. Table I shows that, in the officer corps, no group of former occupation dominates the whole. Numerically, the distribution of former *laboureurs,* sons of former employees, and soldiers,

[35] DE LA MOTTE, p. 1.

is relatively equal. Among the 124 officers for whom information is given, 21.7% were former peasants, 20.1% the sons of former employees, and 25.0% former soldiers. But percentage of numbers is misleading, for in the brigades there are half again as many soldiers as former employees, and more *laboureurs* than either. So another comparison must be used. Table III expresses the ratio between the number of men whose former profession is known, compared to that occupation's representation in the officer corps. Thus of 61 sons of former employees in the brigade as a whole, 25 (40.9%) were officers; 38.8% of all the soldiers in the brigades were officers, but only 20.9% of the *laboureurs*. Thus while these three occupational groups are relatively equal in numbers in the officer corps, they are not equal with respect to the officer-guard ratio within their own group. A man who was the son of a former employee or an ex-soldier had twice the chance to become an officer as the one who was once a peasant. Further still, Table IV shows the literacy patterns within the former occupation groups irrespective of rank. Again, those with the clear advantage are the sons of former employees; 76.8% of them are in the top two literacy categories, compared to 43.8% of the soldiers, and 31.7% of the peasants. The conclusion is that the former occupation made a difference: a son of a former employee or a soldier had a greater opportunity to become an officer than one who was not.

The ability to write reports counted for a lot, but was not everything. The soldiers were the most heavily represented occupational group in the officer corps, this despite the fact that they as a group fall in the lower literacy levels (Table IV). Their proportion is explained largely by their previous military training. Former military men had experience with the royal army, a background which the Farms thought worthy of a command position. One has only to recall Foucault's complaint that there were too few soldiers in the brigades, and the need to recruit more of them. The Farms systematically favoured soldiers who were industrious, such that of the 5 officers in the brigades in Lower Normandy who could do little other than sign their own name, 4 were ex-soldiers. Perhaps these were the diligent types alluded to by De la Motte. If a military man were literate, or at least able to write, then his chances of becoming an officer were virtually certain: he possessed both skills which would enable his brigade to execute its duties most effectively.

The *cahiers* do not provide sufficient data to measure professional mobility of the officers over an extended period of time, though they do indicate the past position each man occupied before assuming his present post. Table V shows that, of the 128 officers for whom information is given, 34 (26.5%) were but simple guards in the ranks before becoming officers. Of the remaining 94, 25 (19.9%) had risen in rank with their last change in position, 61 (47.5%) retained the same rank as before, while 4 (3.0%) fell a notch. In all, 59 officers (46.4%) rose in rank with their last change in position.

The second major distinction between the officers and the men in the ranks was the length of time each tended to serve in the General Tax Farms. The data in Table VI shows that the average officer had been employed in the Farms for 16.09 years, while the average guard could muster only 5.82 years — a ratio between the two of nearly 3:1. The disparity is less marked with respect to the length of time each had served with their present brigades. The men had been with their present unit on the average of 2.59 years, while the officers averaged only 4.32 years. This suggests that the officers entered the Farms at an earlier age and stayed longer. However, this is not the case; there are no substantial differences between the average ages of entry. Average age of entry for officers was 25 years and 26.5 for the men. More than likely the officers, because they were promoted and enjoyed some command responsibility — to say nothing of better pay — tended to remain in the Farms much longer than the men under their command.

Though the difference between the men and their officers is great, even the comparatively short stay of the men (6 years) is long enough to show that the brigades were not filled with floating misfits. Their length of service hints that their superiors might have been pleased with their subordinates. This can be measured statistically, however crudely. Each year the higher officials in the Farms rated the performances of their employees; these evaluations fall into several pro-forma types: *très bon, bon,* or some unsatisfactory remark. There is, of course, no way to determine whether these estimations represent the true inclinations of the superiors, or their effort to justify their own recruiting. For what they are worth, the ratings show (Table VII) that they were satisfied with their men. 29.8% of the employees were considered of superior quality, a number of them receiving the comments of *actif* or *zélé.* Of the rest, 47.2% were good enough to rate a *bon,* while 14.9% of the 429 men surveyed were considered lacking in some manner. Such comments as "stupid," or "dissipated," or *"sans aveux"* are usually cited. For 8.1% of the men, no comment was reported, they having just entered the Farms and lacked the service to provide a basis of judgement.

The third and last major distinction separating the men from their officers is age — the officers were considerably older. Table VIII shows that the men in the ranks were on the average 31.6 years old, their officers 39.2. This difference, we have seen, stems not from the fact that the officers entered the Farms at an earlier age, for they did not, but because they prolonged their service, most likely because of promotion, responsibility, and pay.

A number of factors lead us to believe that some practices of the men in the brigades differed scarcely from the society around them. Marriage is one. The average age of the men in the ranks (31.6 years) is close to the average age of marriage of the parishioners in the region around Bayeux, which

El Kordi had determined to be about 27 years. [36] Unless the men in the brigades stood out from the native population, as Delahante suggests, [37] we would expect about half of them to be married, since the difference between the ages is only about 4 years. The comparison reveals that 52.8% of the men in the brigades were married — almost identical to what El Kordi found. The officers were considerably older (39.6 years) and, hence, 73.4% were married (Table X). The proportion of widowed men and officers is slight, 3.7% and 6.3% respectively. Including these figures with the married men, we see that 58.9% of all employees were married, 4.4% widowed, and 36.7% unmarried. Thus the men in the brigades were mostly family men, not wandering individuals with few attachments.

The greater part of them and their wives came from the local population. 90.9% (Table IX) of the men were born fewer than 25 leagues (100 km) from their present place of work; fewer than 10% came from the more distant regions. Among those who did, one came from Nancy (150 leagues), Houlette en Corse (250), Ancosse (200), and Vernantois en Comté. An even greater portion of their wives came from Lower Normandy. Of the 232 wives for whom information is given, 226 (97.3%) were born within 25 leagues of their current place of residence, while a scant 3% came from the more distant parts of the kingdom. But though the men in the brigades tended to marry local, Norman women, surprisingly few married individuals from their native village. For 253 marriages where the place of birth is recorded for both husband and wife, only 50 (19.7%) came from the same village or hamlet. That the men were Normans is significant: that they married Norman women, more so. It proves that the employees of the Farms had strong local roots, and were not at all "outsiders" enforcing the regulations of distant superiors. When in the summer and fall of 1789 the lower classes struck out against the employees of the Farms, they attacked above all the men in the brigades, who were their neighbours. What set them apart was not their former occupation, or their geographical origins, but what they did, which defined, after all, who they were.

Mostly former peasants and ex-soldiers, half of whom could not write at all or very little: These were the men who went into the brigades of the General Tax Farms. They were not only married, for the most part, but were well on the way to raising families as well. 77.2% of the 272 married men had at least one child, while only 22.8% had none. In all, the 210 men with children had 458 sons and daughters for an average of 2.18 children per family. In this sense too, the employees differed little from the local population from which they were recruited and where they retained strong ties.

The men in the brigades were swept into reorganization by the torrent of 1789. The French Revolution in Lower Normandy began in the spring

---

[36]   EL KORDI, pp. 122-123.
[37]   DELAHANTE, I, p. 208.

and summer of 1787 with the calling of the Provincial Assembly of Lower Normandy; in an instant the new body plunged into an intense struggle with the administrative apparatus of the intendancy and the tax courts, the *élections* and the Cour des Comptes de Normandie at Rouen. The battle raged for control of the system of direct taxes; it was so keen that they collectively destroyed the system in the fall and winter of 1788, generating in the process wild excitement which spilled over into the summer of 1789. In the summer of that year popular uprisings made the first generalized attacks against the brigades of the tax Farms. At Lisieux an administrator wrote, "the general insurrection in the entire kingdom manifested itself in this city last July 10 . . . the employees for the collection of the *aides,* carried away with terror, abandoned their offices and ceased all functions." [38] In September the residents of the bourg of Harcourt demanded to pay their duties directly to the *Comité des Finances* of the National Assembly, and not to the commissaries of the Farms. [39] In November at Bernay, municipal officers complained that the employees consistently over-priced tarifs. [40] An *ancien garde du corps du Roi* in the municipality of Sap, in Lower Normandy, wrote, "salt is selling today in the market place like wheat . . . the *aides* are entirely abolished . . . all the registers are burned . . . the same with tobacco, nobody is paying the old taxes any more, and it is impossible to reestablish the Farms without a horrible effusion of blood." [41]

The popular uprisings contributed to the reorganization of the employees in 1791. The law of 5 November 1790 suspended the internal customs duties and created a national customs union. The decree of 25 April 1791 restructured the employees of the Farms: the guards and their officers were nationalized, formed into 163 *capitaineries générales* comprising 13,284 men. [42] By decrees of 20 March and 31 July 1791 the men in the brigades discharged with more than ten years' service claimed a pension of 50 livres a month until reemployed. The law of 20 March required new appointments in the financial administration to come from former employees of the suppressed services. Thus the National Assembly incorporated the men of the "private army" of the Tax Farms into a national army within the bureaucracy.

---

[38] AN D$^{v'}$24 no. 314. The problem of the guards of the Farms submerged in a sea of popular hostility is treated in F. HINCKER, *Les français devant l'impôt sous l'ancien régime* (Paris, 1971).

[39] AN D$^{v'}$24 no. 315.

[40] *Ibid.,* no. 314.

[41] *Ibid.,* no. 315.

[42] J. F. BOSHER, *The Single Duty Project* (London, 1964), pp. 157-158.

Table I: FORMER OCCUPATIONS

	Men		Officers	
Occupations	*Number*	*%*	*Number*	*%*
Peasants	129	30.0	27	21.7
Soldiers	80	18.6	31	25.0
Sons of former employees	61	14.2	25	20.1
"Chez quelqu'un"	47	11.0	15	11.7
Trades	42	9.8	—	—
Sailors	31	7.2	—	—
Studying	—	—	5	4.0
Miscellaneous	39	9.2	21	17.5
Totals	429	100.0	124	100.0

Table II: LITERACY

	Men		Officers	
Category	*Number*	*%*	*Number*	*%*
Write and verbalize	12	4.0	83	64.8
Write	86	28.6	25	19.5
Write inadequately	85	28.2	14	10.9
Sign only	117	38.8	5	3.9
Not specified	1	0.4	1	0.9
Totals	301	100.0	128	100.0

Table III: FORMER OCCUPATIONS COMPARED

Former Occupations	**% officers**	**% men**
Sons of employees	40.9	59.1
Soldiers	38.8	61.2
Peasants	20.9	79.1

Table IV: LITERACY

Former Occupations	**% write & verbalize**	**write %**	**write in-adequately %**	**sign %**
Sons of employees	29.5	49.1	13.1	8.3
Soldiers	25.0	18.8	25.0	31.2
Sailors	0.0	9.7	16.1	74.2
Peasants	11.6	20.1	27.4	40.9
All employees	22.1	25.8	23.2	28.4

Table V: OFFICERS' CHANGE IN STATUS

Capitainerie gén.	**Rose from Ranks**	**Rose**	**Fell**	**Un-changed**	**Un-specified**	**Totals**
Caen	5	2	0	5	1	13
Grandville	6	8	2	13	2	31
Cherbourg	12	7	0	16	1	36
Sallenelles	11	8	2	27	0	48
Combined	34	25	4	61	4	128
%	26.5	19.9	3.0	47.5	3.0	100.0

Table VI: Length of Service (in years)

Capitainerie générale	Men	Officers	Ratio
Caen	7.24 yrs.	19.11 yrs.	2.6-1
Grandville	6.48	14.98	2.3-1
Cherbourg	5.72	16.88	2.9-1
Sallenelles	4.76	15.41	3.2-1
Average	5.86	16.09	2.7-1

Table VII: Service Evaluation of Men

Capitainerie gén.	Unfavorable	"bon"	"très bon"	Not spec.	Totals
Caen	3	22	21	10	56
Grandville	21	69	22	5	117
Cherbourg	26	47	34	9	116
Sallenelles	14	65	51	10	140
Totals	64	203	128	34	429
	14.9%	47.2%	29.8%	8.1%	100%

Table VIII: Age Average

Capitainerie gén.	Officers	Average	Men	Average
Caen	13	40.0	43	33.3
Grandville	31	37.6	86	31.6
Cherbourg	36	38.2	80	30.6
Sallenelles	48	41.2	92	31.6
Average		39.2		31.6

Table IX: Distances between Parish of Origin and Place of Deployment

Distance	Men	%	Officers	%	Wives	%
Fewer than 25 leagues	272	90.7	102	79.7	246	97.3
26-50 leagues	11	3.7	14	10.9	3	1.2
51 + leagues	16	5.4	8	6.3	3	1.2
Not specified	2	0.2	4	3.1	1	0.3
TOTALS	301	100.0	128	100.0	253	100.0

Table X: Marital Status

Status	Men	%	Officers	%	Combined	%
Married	159	52.8	94	73.4	253	58.9
Single	131	43.5	26	20.3	157	36.7
Widowed	11	3.7	8	6.3	19	4.4
TOTALS	301	100.0	128	100.0	429	100.0

Part III
Constables and Order in
Early Modern England

[10]

The Old-Time Constable

AS PORTRAYED BY THE DRAMATISTS

SERGT. KITE: Pray, who are those honourable gentlemen upon
the bench ?
CONSTABLE : He in the middle is Justice Ballance, he on the
right is Justice Scale, and he on the left is Justice Scruple ;
and I am Mr. Constable : four very honest gentlemen.

The Recruiting Officer (1706).

A STATUTE of King Henry III ordained that in every
village and township there should be appointed a constable
or two, according to the number of the inhabitants ; and the
Statute of Winchester (1285) largely reorganized and regulated
the old institutions for the repression of crime. It issued rules
for the better discovery of robberies and murders : the hue
and cry was to be properly organized ; each district was made
responsible for crimes committed within its bounds ; the gates
of each town were required to be shut at nightfall ; all strangers
were to give an account of themselves to a magistrate. And it
was upon the constable that the duties devolved of preserving
the peace, arresting law-breakers, and carrying out the orders
of the Justices of the Peace. Truly has his office been
described as ' one of the most ancient in the realm for the conservation of peace ' ; indeed, the great Elizabethan lawyer, Sir
Edward Coke, remarked that his office was actually due to the
institutions of King Alfred.

Common law requires that every constable shall be
idoneus homo (a suitable man) ; and he is said in law to be
idoneus if he has three things : viz. honesty, knowledge, and
ability : honesty to execute his office truly, without malice,
affection or partiality ; knowledge to know what he ought duly
to do ; and ability as well in estate as body, ' that he may intend
and execute his office, when need is, diligently, and not for
impotence or poverty neglect it.' If one is elected who is not

idoneus, he may by law be discharged from his office and another who is *idoneus* appointed in his place. He must be an inhabitant of the place for which he is chosen, and he ought not to be the keeper of a public house. So far the Common Law.

By Statute of 31 Geo. 2, cap. 17, sec 13, all men of sixty-three years of age were expressly exempted from serving as constables in the City of Westminster. As nothing therein is stated to the contrary, presumably they became eligible again at sixty-four. Apothecaries practising within seven miles of London were exempt, as were all barber-surgeons ; for these might be called upon at any moment to let blood. If a gentleman of quality be chosen constable, and there are sufficient persons eligible besides, let him be relieved and no more said about it. A woman made a constable by virtue of a custom may procure another to serve for her, and the custom remain good.

I will not weary you with the manner of the constable's appointment ; for that varied in different parts of the realm. For example, in London, in years gone by, he was nominated by the inhabitants of his ward on St. Thomas' Day and sworn in before the aldermen on the Monday next after the Feast of the Epiphany, his oath being long and peculiar. Instead, I will pass on to his duties.

'The Constable,' saith an ancient jurist, 'hath as good authority in his place as the Chief Justice of England hath in his.' Yea, verily he hath. If he see one making affray or assaulting another, or breaking the peace, or hear any one threaten to kill, wound, or maim, he may take him and set him in the stocks. If a felon resists or flies, whether after arrest or before, and cannot be taken, the constable may kill him— though it be imprudent nowadays so to do. If he see any man riding about on a horse in a warlike manner he may arrest him, if he can. If a felon fly, the constable should enter his (the felon's) house and seize all his goods and hold them for the King's use. He can cause all able persons to mow and reap in time of harvest, and if they refuse he may set them in the stocks. If any be found unlawfully cutting corn, breaking fences or uprooting fruit trees, they may be committed to the constable to be whipped. The constable may take and imprison all madmen, and if they die there, why, it is not his fault. He may levy fines for profane swearing ; to wit, for each labourer or servant, 1*s.* ; for others under the degree of a gentleman, 2*s.* ; for gentlemen, 5*s.* per time. If any gentleman swear twice, the fine shall be doubled. Truly the Constable is a potent man, and in addition to all these his powers, it is his prerogative to raise the Hue and Cry.

Now, before the days of police forces, when constables were few and most towns possessed but one or two, the odds were heavily in favour of the criminal who took to his heels. Naturally the victim of the crime was only too happy to join the constable in pursuit, as were all bystanders whose sporting instincts were aroused. But this was a haphazard method of dealing with crime ; and as the community grew, the increase of law-breaking demanded better measures for coping with it. I have already mentioned the Statute of Winchester passed in 1285. This statute directed that henceforth each county should be so well organized that immediately upon a robbery or felony being committed the Hue and Cry should be raised and carried from town to town and from county to county till the law-breaker be taken. ' And they that keep the town shall follow with Hue and Cry, with all the town and the towns near ; and so Hue and Cry shall be made from town to town until they (*i.e.* the felons) be taken and delivered to the Sheriff.' And in order that the Hue and Cry should be properly taken up, the Hundred (county division) was bound to answer for all robberies therein committed, unless they took the felon. A further statute passed in 27 Eliz. (1585) ordained that no Hue and Cry should be considered sufficient unless made with both horsemen and footmen ; while in 1744–5 the constable was made liable to a fine of £5 if he refused or neglected to raise the Hue and Cry properly.[1]

I may here interject that *Hue* is derived from the old French word *huer*, which means to shout. Originally ' hue ' seems to have signified the complaint of the party aggrieved, and ' cry ' the pursuit of the felon. There is a whole parcel of statutes dealing with this particular form of repressing crime ; but their

---

[1] But fines for neglect to raise the Hue and Cry were levied centuries before this. The Pipe Roll for 1176 records that Walter the Taverner was fined half a mark (6s. 8d.) for this neglect.

THE OLD-TIME CONSTABLE 659

interest is rather for the legal antiquary than for readers of *The Police Journal*.

An excellent account of raising the Hue and Cry is contained in an Elizabethan play entitled *The Contention betweene Liberalitie and Prodigalitie*, printed in 1602.

Enter a Constable, *making hue and cry*.

Con. : Thieves, neighbours, thieves ! Come forth ; beset the
    country.
1 Fel. : 'Zwounds, we are undone ; the constables come after
    with hue and cry.
2 Fel. : Stand back ; lie close, and let them pass by.
Con. : Thieves, thieves ! O vile, O detestable deed ! Thieves,
    neighbours ! Come forth, away ! Abroad with speed.
Host : Why, what's the matter, friend, I pray ?
Con. : Why, thieves, man, I tell thee ; come away.
Host : Thieves, i'faith ! Wife, my scull, my jack, my brown
    bill.[1]
Con. : Come away quickly.
Host : Dick, Tom, Will, ye whoresons, make ye all ready, and
    haste. But let me hear, how stands the case ?
Con. : Marry, sir, here-by. Not far from this place
    A plain simple man, riding on his ass,
    Meaning home to his country in God's peace to pass,
    By certain roisters, most furious and mad,
    Is spoiled and robbed of all that he had.
    And yet not contented, when they had his money,
    But the villains have also murdered him most cruelly.
Host : Good God, for his mercy !
Con. : It was my hap to come then presently by him
    And found him dead, with twenty pounds upon him.
Host : What became of them ?
Con. : They fled this way.
Host : Then, neighbour, let us here no longer stay,
    But hence and lay the country round about :
    They shall be quickly found, I have no doubt.

To assist him in his duties the constable had command of a squad known as ' the watch.' Strictly speaking the watch

[1] *i.e.* my ' tin helmet,' my leather jerkin, my pike.

were on duty only at night, their task being to apprehend all rogues who practised their profession after nightfall. By day a squad known as ' the ward ' dealt with evildoers. By statute of the realm every city had to furnish a watch between Ascension Day and Michaelmas, with six men at each gate ; every borough to have twelve men on watch from sunset to sunrise, to arrest suspected strangers, or make hue and cry after them, and detain them until morning.

Now for the composition of the watch. Justices of the Peace were instructed to require annually from the overseers of parishes a list of those within the parish qualified and liable to serve as watchmen. Every able-bodied man between the ages of twenty-five and fifty-five years rated at £4 per annum was liable. Those appointed were bound to serve or find substitutes, or they could be indicted. Indeed, on refusal, the constable could set them in the stocks. They enjoyed the protection of the law, and if they were killed in the execution of their duty, why, it was flat murder.

It is not to be wondered, then, that the watch was not always taken very seriously. Able-bodied men could always find an excuse for not serving—and indeed it was not every able-bodied young man whom the parishioners cared to entrust with a ' brown bill ' and summary powers. So for the most part the watch—I am thinking of Queen Bess's days—consisted of the lesser tradesfolk, their assistants, and harmless unemployed. But their commander, the constable, if he is treated roughly by the dramatists, was at least a man of character, often of intrepidity, always with a good knowledge of the world and its ways, though sometimes burdened a little with the weight of his own importance. But he was such an integral part of civil life that most of the greater dramatists have introduced him into one or more of their plays.

Probably the best known constable in fiction is Dogberry, and certainly in *Much Ado About Nothing* (printed in 1600) Shakespeare has given us the most complete character sketch of the Elizabethan constable that has come down to us. The scene is laid in Sicily, and Dogberry is a native of that country ; but he bears about as much resemblance to a Sicilian as a Hottentot does to an Eskimo. He is a Cockney of the Cockneys, and he is of a type (with Corporal Bardolph, Nym, and Pistol) that survives to-day and makes the Londoner of the sixteenth century so familiar to us. Dogberry is illiterate, but greatly filled with the importance of his office. Words of three syllables are usually beyond his ken, but he loves the sound of imposing words and uses them on every possible occasion, regardless of their meaning.

Scene : A Street. *Enter* Constables Dogberry and Verges, in order to inspect the watch, who are drawn up in line, and instruct them in their duties. From what follows we can gather that this particular watch was not a particularly smart body of men, and it is probable that their entry was greeted with shouts of laughter by the audience.

VERGES : Well, give them their charge, neighbour Dogberry.

DOG. : First, who think you the most desartless man to be constable ?

1st WATCH. : Hugh Oatcake, Sir, or George Seacoal ; for they can write and read.

DOG. : Come hither, neighbour Seacoal : God hath blessed you with a good name ; to be a well-favoured man is the gift of fortune ; but to write and read comes by nature ... You are thought here to be the most senseless and fit man for the constable of the watch ; therefore bear you the lantern. This is your charge : you shall comprehend all vagrom men ; you are to bid any man stand, in the prince's name.

2ND WATCH. : How if he will not stand ?

DOG. : Why then, take no note of him, but let him go ; and presently call the rest of the watch together, and thank God you are rid of a knave. . . . You shall also make no noise in the streets ; for, for the watch to babble and talk is most tolerable and not to be endured.

2ND WATCH. : We will rather sleep than talk ; we know what belongs to a watch.

DOG. : Why, you speak like an ancient and most quiet watch-man ; for I cannot see how sleeping should offend ; only, have a care that your bills be not stolen. Well, you are to call at all the ale-houses, and bid those that are drunk get them to bed.

2ND WATCH. : How if they will not ?

DOG. : Why, then, let them alone till they are sober ; if they
make you not then the better answer, you may say they
are not the men you took them for.

2ND WATCH. : [Very] Well, sir.

DOG. : If you meet a thief, you may suspect him, by virtue of
your office, to be no true man : and, for such kind of
men, the less you meddle or make with them, why, the
more is for your honesty.

2ND WATCH. : If we know him to be a thief, shall we not lay
hands on him ?

DOG. : Truly by your office, you may ; but, I think, they that
touch pitch will be defiled : the most peaceable way for
you, if you do take a thief, is, to let him show himself
what he is, and steal out of your company.

VERG. : You have been always called a merciful man, partner.

DOG. : Truly, I would not hang a dog by my will ; much more a
man who hath any honesty in him.

VERG. : If you hear a child cry in the night, you must call to
the nurse, and bid her still it.

2ND WATCH. : How if the nurse be asleep, and will not hear us ?

DOG. : Why, then, depart in peace, and let the child wake her
with crying. . . . That is the end of the charge. . . .
Well, masters, good night ; an there be any matter of
weight chances, call up me. Keep your fellows' counsels
and your own, and good-night. Come, neighbour.

2ND WATCH. : Well, masters, we hear our charge. Let us go sit
here upon the church-bench till two, and then all to bed.

DOG. : One word more, honest neighbours : be vigitant, I
beseech you.

What a character sketch it is ! One can picture the whole
scene, and the characters too. Dogberry's red nose absolutely
shines through the words.

Next comes a truly up-to-date scene : the examination of
a suspected man under arrest. Dogberry reports to Leonato,
Governor of Messina, that his watch have arrested two suspicious characters during the night.

DOG. : Our watch, sir, have, indeed, comprehended two

THE OLD-TIME CONSTABLE   663

aspicious persons, and we would have them this morning examined before your worship.

LEON. : Take their examination yourself, and bring it me ; I am now in great haste. . . .

DOG. : It shall be suffigance. (*To Verges*) Go, good partner, go, get you to Francis Seacoal, bid him bring his pen and inkhorn to the gaol : we are now to examine these men.

VERG. : And we must do it wisely.

DOG. : We will spare for no wit, I warrant you. Here's that (*touching his forehead*) shall drive some of them to a *non com*. Only get the learned writer to set down our excommunication, and meet me at the gaol.

Arrived at the gaol, Dogberry, Verges and a Sexton (!) proceed to examine the prisoners, Conrade and Borachio.

DOG. : Is our whole dissembly appeared ?

SEXT. : Which be the malefactors ?

DOG. : Marry, that am I and my partner.

VERG. : Nay, that's certain ; we have the exhibition to examine.

SEXT. : But which are the offenders that are to be examined ? Let them come before Master Constable.

DOG. : Yea, marry, let them come before me.—What is your name, friend ?

BORA. : Borachio.

DOG. : Pray write down, ' Borachio.'—Yours, sirrah ?

CON. : I am a gentleman, sir, and my name is Conrade.

DOG. : Write down, ' master gentleman Conrade.' Masters, do you serve God ?

CON. and BORA. : Yea, sir, we hope.

DOG. : Write down that ' they hope they serve God '—and write God first ; for God defend but God should go before such villains. Masters, it is proved already that you are little better than false knaves. . . . How answer you for yourselves ?

CON. : Marry, sir, we say we are none.

DOG. : A marvellous witty fellow, I assure you. . . . Come you hither, sirrah, a word in your ear, sir. I say to you, it is *thought* you are false knaves.

BORA. : Sir, I say to you, we are none.

DOG. : Well, stand aside. 'Fore God they are both in a tale. Have you writ down ' that they are none ' ?

SEXT. : Master Constable, you go not the way to examine. You must call forth the watch that are their accusers.

DOG. : Yea, marry, that's the eftest way. Let the watch come forth. Masters, I charge you, in the prince's name, accuse these men.

IST WATCH. : This man said, sir, that Don John, the prince's brother, was a villain.

DOG. : Write down, ' prince John a villain.' Why this is flat perjury, to call a prince's brother ' villain.'

SEXT. : What heard you him say else ?

2ND WATCH. : Marry, that he had received a thousand ducats of Don John for accusing the lady Hero wrongfully.

DOG. : Flat burglary, as ever was committed.

VERG. : Yea, by the mass, that it is.

SEXT. : What else, fellow ?

IST WATCH. : And that Count Claudio did mean, upon his words, to disgrace Hero before the whole assembly, and not marry her.

DOG. : O villain ! Thou wilt be condemned into everlasting redemption for this.

SEXT. : What else ?

2ND WATCH. : This is all.

DOG. : Come, let them be opinioned (*i.e.* pinioned).

CON. : Off, coxcomb !

DOG. : God's my life ! Where's the sexton ? Let him write down, ' the prince's officer, coxcomb.' Come, bind them. —Thou naughty varlet.

CON. : Away ! You are an ass, you are an ass !

DOG. : Dost thou not suspect my place ? Dost thou not suspect my years ? Oh, that he were here to write me down ' an ass ' ! But, masters, remember that I am an ass ; though it be not written down, yet forget not that I am an ass ! No, thou villain, thou art full of piety, as shall be proved upon thee by good witness. I am a wise fellow, and, which is more, an officer ; and, which is more, a householder ; and, which is more, as pretty a piece of flesh as any is in Messina ; and one that knows the law, go to ; and a rich fellow enough, go to ; and a fellow that hath had losses ; and one that hath two gowns, and everything handsome about him. Bring him away. Oh, that I had been writ down ' an ass ' !

Another of Shakespeare's constables is Elbow in *Measure for Measure*, performed in 1604. He is described in the list of characters prefixed to the play as ' a simple Constable,' and he too indulges in the luxury of using words he does not understand. The scene here is laid in Vienna, but Constable Elbow is no more an Austrian than Dogberry. He presents himself before Angelo, the Duke of Vienna's deputy, having ' run in ' two delinquents.

ELBOW : If it please your honour, I am the poor Duke's constable, and my name is Elbow. I do lean upon justice, sir, and do bring in here before your good honour two notorious benefactors.

ANG.: Benefactors ? Well, what benefactors are they ? Are they not malefactors ?

ELBOW : If it please your honour I know not well what they are. But precise villains they are, that I am sure of ; and void of all profanation in the world, that good Christians ought to have.

And so on throughout a somewhat tedious scene, distinguished rather for its coarseness than its wit, in which the constable continually trips himself up by using the wrong word.

The constable in another play of Shakespeare's day, *The Heir*, by Thomas May (1620), is clearly a descendant of Dogberry ; indeed, the whole scene in which he appears is redolent of Shakespeare's creation. The scene also is laid in Sicily and the characters are likewise Cockneys.

CON. : Come, fellow-watchmen, for now you are my fellows.

1ST WATCH. : It pleases you to call us so, Master Constable.

CON.: I do it to encourage you in your office—it is a trick that we commanders have : your great captains call your soldiers ' fellow-soldiers ' to encourage them.

2ND WATCH. : Indeed, and so they do. I heard Master Curate reading a story-book t'other day to that purpose.

CON. : Well, I must show you what you have to do, for I myself, before I came to this prefermity, was as simple as one of you ; and, for your better destruction, I will deride my speech into two parts. First, what is a watchman ? Secondly, what is the office of a watchman ? For the first, if any man ask me what is a watchman, I may answer him, he is a man, as others are ; nay, a tradesman, as a vintner, a tailor, or the like, for they have long bills.

3RD WATCH. : He tells us true, neighbour ; we have bills indeed.

CON. : For the second, what is his office, I answer he may, by virtue of his office, reprehend any person or persons that walk the streets too late at a seasonable hour.

4TH WATCH. : May we indeed, Master Constable ?

CON. : Nay, if you meet any of those rogues at seasonable hours, you may, by virtue of your office, commit him to prison, and then ask him whither he was going.

1ST WATCH. : Why, that's as much as my lord Mayor does.

CON. : True, my lord Mayor can do no more than you in that point.

2ND WATCH. : But, Master Constable, what if he should resist us ?

CON. : Why, if he do resist, you may knock him down, and then bid him stand, and come before the constable. So now I think you are sufficiently instructed concerning your office. Take your stands : you shall hear rogues walking at these seasonable hours, I warrant you. Stand close.

However, in spite of his verbal shortcomings the constable soon shows his mettle and makes an arrest for which the judge subsequently commends him.

JUDGE : What's his offence ?
CON. : Murder.
WATCH. : No, Master Constable, 'twas but poisoning of a man.
CON. : Go, thou art a fool.
JUDGE : What proofs have you against him ?
CON. : His own profession, if it please your Honour.
JUDGE : And that's an ill profession, to be a murderer. Thou meanest he has confessed the fact. . . . You have been

THE OLD-TIME CONSTABLE   667

careful in your office, Constable ; you may now leave your prisoner.   Murder, I see, will out.

Another London constable, disguised as a Spaniard, appears in Beaumont and Fletcher's play, *The Maid in the Mill* (1623), and here the dramatists have taken every inch of the rope of poetical licence by making the watch hale their victim before the King himself !

KING : What's that ?

CON. : This is a man suspected of murther, if it please your Grace.

KING : It pleases me not, friend.   But who suspects him ?

CON. : We that are your Highness's extraordinary officers, we that have taken our oaths to maintain you in peace.

KING : 'Twill be a great charge to you.

CON. : 'Tis a great charge indeed ; but then we call our neighbours to help us. This gentleman and another were fallen out (yet that's more than I am able to say, for I heard no words between 'em but what their weapons spoke, clash and clatter) ; which we seeing, came with our bills of government and first knocked down their weapons and then the men.

KING : And this you did to keep the peace ?

CON. : Yes, an't like your Grace, we knocked 'em down to keep the peace.   This we laid hold on, the other we set in the stocks.   That I could do by mine own power, without your Majesty.

A later play, *Lady Alimony* (1659), also makes fun of the constable, who, again, is clearly of the Dogberry breed, though not nearly so convincing a character as that immortal officer. The scene here is Seville—how far afield these London constables do travel !

Enter Constable *and* Watch, *in rug gowns, bills and dark lanthorns*.

CON. : Come along with your horns,[1] my lads of metal. It was the duke's pleasure before his departure that we should

---

[1] Lanthorns.

be appointed the sinks and sentinels of the city, and that none shall have ingress, egress or regress but by our special authority and favour. But, harm watch, harm catch ; for my part, since I crept into this office I am woven into such a knot of goodfellowship as I can watch no more than a dormouse. Nay, I am verily persuaded, if I hold constable long, the deputy of the ward will return me one of the Seven Sleepers. But let me advise you, my birds of the Capitol, that you walk not after my example : be it your care to watch, while I sleep. Many eyes are upon you ; but my eyes grow heavy ; my day's society bids me take a nap.

WATCH. : But one word, good master, before you drop into your slumber : report goes that there be spirits that patrol familiarly in this sentry : what shall we say to them if they pass by ?

CON. : Bid them stand.

WATCH. : But what if they either cannot or will not ?

CON. : Let them then take themselves to their heels, and thank God you are so well rid of them.

Which last sentence is so near Dogberry's words that we are not surprised the author of *Lady Alimony* did not affix his name to the play.

Although the foregoing examples show that the constable was sometimes introduced into their plays by the Elizabethan dramatists in order to provide ' the lighter element,' this was by no means always the case. Often the stage constable was a very efficient officer indeed. Witness the scene in *Eastward Ho* (1605), where the constable has ' run in ' a couple of knights and duly parades them before Golding, J.P. Incidentally it shows the constable performing a duty not usually associated with his office—the impressing of recruits for the army.

GOLDING : What are those, Master Constable ?

CON. : An't please your worship, a couple of masterless men I pressed for the Low Countries, sir.

GOLD. : Why do you not carry 'em to Bridewell, according to your order, [that] they may be shipped away ?

THE OLD-TIME CONSTABLE 669

CON.: An't please your worship, one of 'em says he is a knight; and we thought good to show him to your worship, for our discharge.

GOLD.: And what's the other?

CON.: A knight's fellow, sir, an't please you.

GOLD.: What! a knight and his fellow thus accoutred? Where are their hats and feathers, their rapiers and their cloaks?

CON.: Nay, truly, sir, they had cast both their feathers and hats too before we see 'em. Here's all their furniture, an't please you, that we found. They say knights are now to be known without feathers, like cockerels by their spurs, sir.

So also in *The Witch of Edmonton* by Thomas Dekker (1658). The scene is Sir Arthur Clarington's country house. Revels are in progress. Enter a constable.

CON.: Away with jollity! 'Tis too sad an hour. Sir Arthur Clarington, your own assistance, in the King's name, I charge, for apprehension of these two murderers, Warbeck and Somerton.

SIR A.: Ha! flat murderers?

CON.: The accusation's flat against you, gentlemen. Sir, you may be satisfied with this (*shows his warrant*). I hope you'll quietly obey my power; 'twill make your cause the fairer.

Whereupon Warbeck and Somerton, being model murderers, reply, ' with all our hearts, sir.'

But if Shakespeare has given us a perfect portrait of a sixteenth century London constable of the less efficient sort, Ben Jonson has provided us with an admirable picture of the opposite kind of officer. Constable Turfe, one of the principal characters in *A Tale of a Tub*, is High Constable of Kentish Town and an excellent type of Englishman. Scantily educated, amusing in his efforts to acquire book-learning, nevertheless he stands four-square to the world. He is beset with troubles, and at the most critical moments, such as his daughter's wedding day, warrants arrive from the justices ordering him, at his peril, to raise the hue and cry immediately. Poor man, no wonder he thus apostrophises his fate :

> Passion of me, was ever a man thus crossed ?
> All things run arsie-versie, upside down.
> High Constable ! Now, by our Lady o' Walsingham,
> I had rather be marked out Tom Scavenger
> And with a shovel make clean the highways
> Than have this office of a constable.

However, all comes right in the end, and we leave him dancing at his daughter's wedding.

As good a character sketch as any occurs in Ben Jonson's famous play, *Every Man Out of his Humour*, acted in 1599. There is a tavern brawl and the constable is quickly on the scene.

CON. : (*calling from outside*) Here's the constable ; open the doors.

KNIGHT : Open no door. If the Adalantado of Spain were here he should not enter. One help me with the light, gentlemen. You knock in vain, sir officer.

CON. : Open the door, or I will break it open.

SCHOLAR : Nay, good constable, have patience a little ; you shall come in presently, we have almost done.

Enter Constable *with* Watch.

CON. : Lay hold upon this gallant and pursue the rest.

BEAU : Lay hold on me, sir ? For what ?

CON. : Marry, for your riot here, sir, with the rest of your companions.

BEAU : My riot ! Master Constable, take heed what you do. Carlo, did I offer any violence ?

CON. : O sir, you see he is not in case to answer you, and that makes you so peremptory.

BEAU : Peremptory ? 'Slife, I appeal to the drawers[1] if I did him any hard measure.

GEORGE : They are all gone, there's none of them will be laid any hold on.

CON. : Well, sir, you are like to answer till the rest can be found out.

---

[1] Tap-boys.

THE OLD-TIME CONSTABLE 671

BEAU : 'Slid, I appeal to George, here.

CON. : Tut, George was not here.   Away with him to the Counter,[1] sirs.

A very realistic scene, and a very efficient officer.

The constable in Robert Greene's play, *The Honorable Historie of frier Bacon and frier Bongay* (1594), is also a man of action ; but beyond arresting ' a companie of rufflers that, drinking in the taverne, have made a great brawle and almost kill'd the vintner ' he has no more to do.   Still, a man of action and an upholder of the law.

An excellent little character sketch occurs in Ford's play, *Perkin Warbeck* (1634).   Here again the constable is an efficient officer—a little pompous, perhaps, but clearly a man who means to be obeyed.   The scene is Tower Hill, and a crowd has collected to see Warbeck put in the stocks.

CON. : Make room there !   Keep off, I require you ; and none come within twelve foot of his Majesty's new stocks, upon pain of displeasure.   Bring forward the malefactor. Friend, you must to this gear, no remedy.   Open the hole and in with the legs, just in the middle hole ; there, that hole.   Keep off, or I'll commit you all !   Shall not a man in authority be obeyed ?   So, so, there ; 'tis as it should be ; put on the padlock, and give me the key. Off, I say ; keep off !

The watch, however, as I have said, is seldom taken very seriously by the dramatists.   In nine cases out of ten they appear only to provoke laughter, and on one occasion at least they are the worse for liquor.   Here are some lines from John Lilly's play, *Endimion, or The Man in the Moone* (1591).

Enter the Watch.

1ST PAGEBOY : Masters, God speed you.

1ST WATCH : Sir boy, we are all sped already.

2ND PAGE : So methinks, for they smell all of drink like a beggar's beard.

---

[1] Properly ' Compter ' ; a debtors' jail.   One was attached to each of the Sheriffs' Courts.   The last of them—that in Giltspur Street—was closed so lately as 1854.

THE POLICE JOURNAL

Then follows some amusing back-chat, ending with one of the Watch singing the following song :

> Stand, who goes there ?
> We charge you appear
> 'Fore our constable here,
> In the name of the Man in the Moon :
> To us billmen relate
> Why you stagger so late
> And how you come drunk so soon.

The watch in *Romeo and Juliet* (1594), on the other hand, act with vigour—so much so that one suspects Shakespeare to have had a military watch, a squad of soldiers, in mind when he drew them. The watch is undoubtedly of a military character in Markham's play, *The Dumb Knight* (1608), although, strangely enough, it is a merchant who gives them their charge :

MER. : You must perform your office, or else expect to taste sharp punishment.

IST WATCH. : Tut, fear not, my lord : we that have had Cerberus' office so many years under a gate are not to learn now to play either devils or tyrants.

From the expression ' under a gate ' it is evident that the watchmen in this case were soldiers or at least professional guards. A somewhat unpleasant character is given to the watch in Beaumont and Fletcher's play, *The Coxcomb*, first acted in 1610.

RICARDO : Stand further off, the watch ; you are full of fleas.

CON. : Gentlemen, either be quiet, or we must make you quiet.

A very proper retort.

Throughout the seventeenth century the constable changed very little, if we may judge by the dramatists ; he gave up using the wrong words, but he remained in essentials the Cockney of the type that endures. So I will bring this paper to a close with a quotation from *The Constant Couple*, by George Farquhar, written in the last year of the century and produced in 1700.

THE OLD-TIME CONSTABLE   673

The scene is Covent Garden. Clincher, a young man about town, has been painting the city red.

Enter Constable.

CON.: Hold, neighbours, I command the peace.

WIFE: O, Mr. Constable, here's a rogue that has murdered my husband and robb'd him of his clothes.

CON.: Murder and robbery! then he must be a gentleman. Hands off, there; he must not be abused. Give an account of yourself. Are you a gentleman?

CLIN.: No, sir, I am a beau.

CON.: A beau! Then you have kill'd nobody, I'm persuaded. How came you by these clothes, sir?

CLIN.: You must know, sir, that walking along, sir, I don't know how, sir; I can't tell where, sir; and—so the porter and I changed clothes, sir.

CON.: Very well. The man speaks reason, and like a gentleman.

WIFE: But pray, Mr. Constable, ask him how he changed clothes with him.

CON.: Silence, woman! and don't disturb the court. Well, sir, how did you change clothes?

CLIN.: Why, sir, he pull'd off my coat, and I drew off his; so I put on his coat, and he put on mine.

CON.: Why, neighbour, I don't find that he's guilty. Search him, and if he carries no arms about him, we'll let him go.
(*They search his pockets and pull out his pistols.*)

CON.: What, a case of pistols! Then the case is plain. Speak, what are you, sir? Whence came you, and whither go you?

CLIN.: Sir, I came from Russell Street, and I am going to the Jubilee.

WIFE: You shall go to the gallows, you rogue.

CON.: Away with him, away with him to Newgate, straight.

A. M. P.

[11]

The English Village Constable, 1580-1642: The Nature and Dilemmas of the Office

JOAN KENT

Dogberry: This is your charge: you shall comprehend all vagrom men; you are to bid any man stand, in the prince's name.
Watch: How if a' will not stand?
Dogberry: Why, then take no note of him, but let him go; and presently call the rest of the watch together, and thank God you are rid of a knave.

(*Much Ado About Nothing*, Act III, Scene iii)

Modern historians who have described the English village constable of the late sixteenth and early seventeenth centuries have largely accepted Shakespeare's Dogberry as an accurate portrayal of this official. They are almost unanimous in regarding the constable as an incompetent agent of royal authority, and like many of his seventeenth-century critics they depict him as uneducated, unprofessional, lazy, and disobedient. A recent study has also revealed that some of the men chosen as constable had "criminal" records. In one Essex village a number of these officials had previously been "in trouble with the courts," sometimes having broken laws that it would be their duty to enforce when they became constables. Both historians and seventeenth-century commentators frequently attribute such failings to the social unsuitability of the men selected for the office. They claim that the substantial inhabitants of the village sought to avoid such a lowly position, and that it was thus filled by the "meaner sort" of residents who were attracted by its perquisites or were too poor to hire substitutes. Such men, it is contended, were not only ignorant and unable to spare time for

The research for this article was initially made possible by a Canada Council grant and later supported by grants from Sweet Briar College. I wish to express special appreciation to Miss Margaret Henderson, Chief Archivist at St. Helen's, for her many kindnesses during my visits to the Hereford and Worcester Record Office, to the Reverend C.J.L. Waters for making available to me the Pattingham Constables' Accounts; to F.B. Stitt and the members of his staff at the Staffordshire Record Office for their cooperation and helpfulness over many years; to the Reverend Peter Bradshaw for making it possible for me to examine the Shelton Constables' Accounts; and to the Reverend A.C.C. Heigham for allowing me to examine materials in Bunwell and Carleton Rode.

their duties but also so lacking in social status that they were easily intimidated and commanded little respect.[1]

Several studies of county government do suggest alternative approaches to understanding the constable's alleged incompetence. T.G. Barnes and A. Hassell Smith, for example, attribute the constable's weaknesses not

---

[1]Official documents of the seventeenth century often implied, if they did not directly state, that constables were being chosen from the "meaner sort" of inhabitants who were incapable of fulfilling the duties of the office; see, for example, British Library (hereafter B.L.), Add. MS. 12496, f. 287v.; Staffordshire Record Office (hereafter Staffs. R.O.) Quarter Sessions Order Book, V, f. 47. Also see William Lambard, *The Dueties of Constables, Borsholders, Tythingmen, and such other lowe and Lay Ministers of the Peace.* (London, 1599), Preface, pp. 3-4; Francis Bacon, "The Answers to Questions Touching the Office of Constable" (1608), in J. Spedding et al, eds., *The Works of Francis Bacon* VII (London, 1859), p. 751; Michael Dalton, *The Countrey Justice* (London, 1635), p. 47; William Sheppard, *The Offices and Duties of Constables, Borsholders, Tything-men, Treasurers of the County-Stock, Overseers of the Poore and other lay-Ministers* (London, 1641), pp. A3-A3v., 16-17; R[obert] G[ardiner], *The Compleat Constable* (2nd ed., London, 1700), p. 7; E.W., *The Exact Constable: with his Original and Power in the Offices of Church wardens, Overseers of the Poor, Surveyors of the Highways, Treasurers of the County Stock, and other inferior officers as they are established, both by the Common Laws and Statutes of this Realm* (2nd ed., London, 1660), pp. 8-10; Conyers Read, ed., *William Lambarde and Local Government* (Folger Documents of Tudor and Stuart Civilization, Ithaca, 1962), pp. 107, 115, 141. J.A. Sharpe, "Crime and Delinquency in an Essex Parish, 1600-1640," in J.S. Cockburn, ed., *Crime in England, 1550-1800* (Princeton, 1977), pp. 90-109 discusses the "criminal" records of some constables. Despite their records of wrongdoing, however, Sharpe argues that they were men "of middling fortune," of some "economic and social standing." The modern characterization of the constable is based largely on Edward P. Cheyney, *A History of England from the Defeat of the Armada to the Death of Elizabeth* (New York, 1926), II, p. 408; W.E. Tait, *The Parish Chest* (3rd ed., Cambridge, 1969), p. 187; T.A. Critchley, *A History of Police in England and Wales* (rev. ed., London, 1978), pp. 10-11; Sidney and Beatrice Webb, *English Local Government from the Revolution to the Municipal Corporations Act: The Parish and the County* (London, 1906), pp. 18-19; Joel Hurstfield, "County Government: Wiltshire c. 1530—c. 1660," in *Freedom Corruption and Government in Elizabethan England* (Cambridge, Mass., 1973), p. 283 [first published in R.B. Pugh and Elizabeth Critall, eds., *Victoria History of the Counties of England: Wiltshire*, V (1957)]; T.G. Barnes, *Somerset, 1625-40* (London, 1961), pp. 76-77; A. Hassell Smith, *County and Court: Government and Politics in Norfolk, 1558-1603* (Oxford, 1974), pp. 112-13; Anthony Fletcher, *A County Community in Peace and War: Sussex, 1600-1660* (London, 1975), pp. 226-27; William B. Willcox, *Gloucestershire, A Study in Local Government, 1590-1640* (New Haven, 1940), pp. 50, 54-55. However, Fletcher concludes (p. 223) that "negligence and inefficiency" were "the exception rather than the rule" amongst local officials, while Willcox (p. 55) suggests that the constable is deserving of greater sympathy than he has received. Joel Samaha, *Law and Order in Historical Perspective* (New York, 1974), pp. 84-88 regards the constable as an effective law enforcement officer, and suggests that these officials were of higher social status than earlier writers had assumed. More positive evaluations of the constable are also found in two other brief treatments of the office, Eleanor Trotter, *Seventeenth Century Life in the Country Parish* (Cambridge, 1919), ch. 5, and Mildred Campbell, *The English Yeoman under Elizabeth and the Early Stuarts* (New Haven, 1942), pp. 318-25, while W.G. Hoskins, *The Midland Peasant* (London, 1957), p. 208, claims that constables of Wigston Magna, Leicestershire, were drawn from "the leading yeomen, husbandmen and craftsmen of the village."

only to the personal and social defects of the men selected for the position; they also suggest that divided allegiances often rendered such officials incapable of action. They describe constables as being "torn between loyalty to the community in which they lived and their obligations to implement the dictates of superior officials."[2] Although the constable is not central to such studies, which are concerned primarily with county officials, they do indicate the need for a more detailed examination of the constableship in which the nature of the position and not merely the qualifications of those who held it is considered.

A study of the constable based on village records,[3] as well as on those of the county and the central government, suggests that the accepted picture of this official is in need of revision. Anecdotal accounts of the behavior of individual constables have focused too much attention on the failings of such officials. "Comic constables" who were a match for Dogberry, Dull, and Elbow can be found in historical records,[4] and ignorance, stupidity, and even laziness on some occasions probably contributed to a constable's inadequacies as a royal official. However, evidence in local records of their busy round of duties within the village, and of their many journeys to neighboring villages or the county town to answer the summons of higher officials, makes it difficult to accept that they were normally either dilatory or willfully disobedient.[5] The heavy demands of the position, and the extent to which constables attempted to fulfill them, are far more evident in such records than their supposed lack of responsibility.

Furthermore, the constable's weaknesses as royal agents cannot be explained entirely by the personal and social deficiencies of those selected for the position. Materials from the villages included in this study do not support claims that constables were usually chosen from among "the meaner sort" while the more prosperous inhabitants escaped office by hiring substitutes. It is true that a record of offenses, at least of the sort punished by fines in the manorial courts, was apparently no bar to office; but this did not reflect upon the status of those selected for the position. Although few gentlemen served as constables, these officials were most often chosen from the more substantial families just below that rank. In Pattingham, Staffordshire, for example, a total of sixty-three of the eighty-one constables who held office between 1583 and 1642 were large- or middling-size farmers, in terms of the standards existing in that community. An additional nine men can be identified as craftsmen or tradesmen, seem-

[2]Barnes, *Somerset,* p. 77, 222, 230; Hassell Smith, *County and Court,* pp. 112-13 from which the quotation is taken. Also see Cheyney, *History of England,* II, pp. 415-16; J.S. Morrill, *The Cheshire Grand Jury, 1625-59* (Leicester, 1976), pp. 30-32, 46.

[3]For a description of the nature and location of the local records, and other sources consulted, see the Bibliographical Note in the Appendix.

[4]See Hugh C. Evans, "Comic Constables-Fictional and Historical," *Shakespeare Quarterly,* XX (1969), pp. 427-33 for some comparisons of literary and historical officers.

[5]The nature and extent of the constable's duties will be discussed more fully in a monograph on the constable.

ingly the more prosperous and more stable elements among the"cottage" population of the village. The same men filled other local offices as well, including that of churchwarden, a position sometimes assumed to have been more elevated and more desirable than the constableship. Many of them were among the leaders of the parish or manor, men who regularly put their names or their marks to important decisions of the vestry or township and who sat year after year on the leet jury. Forty-nine of the Pattingham constables are known to have served as churchwardens. The overlap on the two lists would almost certainly be greater were it not for early deaths and removals from the parish of some who would otherwise have served as churchwardens, and for the fact that some of the church-wardens were tenants of a second manor in the parish, Rudge, and there-fore not eligible to serve as constables of the manor of Pattingham. In addition, some of the constables were probably churchwardens before 1584 and after 1646-47, periods for which the names of the churchwardens do survive. Although jury lists for the manor of Pattingham are rather incom-plete before the 1620s, at least sixty-two of the eighty-one constables are known to have served on the jury at least once, and at least thirty-four of them appear to have done so with some regularity. Just over half of the constables, forty-two of them, can be found among the dozen or so men whose names appear on documents authorizing various actions on behalf of the manor or the parish, and they can probably be regarded as belonging to the inner circles of parish and manorial government. Such inhabitants enjoyed positions of power and respect within the local community, and their inadequacies as constables cannot be explained as a product of lowly social position within the village or of lack of experience in its affairs.[6]

The character of the constable's office seems to provide a better explana-tion of the constable's weaknesses, and also of his strengths, than do the qualifications of individual incumbents. His role during the late sixteenth and early seventeenth centuries was a dual one, requiring him to function in two different capacities. On the one hand, the constable was the lowest officer in a hierarchy of authority that stretched from the monarchy to the village and was bound by his oath of office to serve the king and higher officials of the crown. He was required to represent the state to his subor-dinates and was legally responsible to higher authorities for many of the

---

[6]The Pattingham evidence is derived from constables' and churchwardens' ac-counts, local tax lists, and other parish documents included with the accounts, jury lists, land transfers, and other materials in the Pattingham Court Rolls (see Appen-dix for location of these materials), lay subsidy rolls in the Public Record Office (hereafter P.R.O.), E. 179/nos. 178/225, 178/248, 178/280, 178/284, 178/292, 179/ 299, 179/305, 179/308, 241/343, and a few surviving wills and inventories in the Staff. Joint Record Office in Lichfield. Parish registers were used to try to reconsti-tute village families. The economic and social structure of villages varied consider-ably so it is difficult to generalize, in absolute terms, about the status of constables. However, relative to their own communities, constables were usually drawn from the leading yeomen, husbandmen, and craftsmen. The status and qualifications of constables will be explored more fully in a monograph on the constable.

villagers' actions. On the other hand, the constable also had to represent the village's interests to his superiors. He was the township's agent in its dealings with the crown's officials, and to its inhabitants he also had to render account, formally at the end of his term and no doubt informally during the course of his duties. The constable was thus subject to dual pressures, and when the interests of the state and those of the village diverged his office would be a focus of conflict. Although other officials, such as sheriffs and justices of the peace and high constables, probably found themselves caught in similar dilemmas, such tensions were particularly acute in the case of the village constable. As long as government in the provinces was staffed by unpaid local men closely identified with the areas in which they also held office, such positions were likely to be subject to conflict; but in the case of the constable the tensions were exacerbated by the fact that the office began as a local one, and that he continued to be chosen by a local body even after he was given royal duties.

In origin, the English constable was an officer of the village, tithing, or township and known variously as tithingman, headborough, borsholder, or even reeve.[7] Like the village headman in other parts of Europe[8] or in nonwestern societies,[9] he was the chief officer and representative of a local

---

[7]The discussion of the origin of the constable's office is based on Lambard, *Dueties of Constables*, pp. 6-9; Bacon, "Answers to Questions," pp. 749-50; Dalton, *Countrey Justice*, pp. 46-47; Sheppard, *Offices and Duties of Constables*, pp. 11-13, 26-32; G[ardiner], *Compleat Constable*, pp. 1-5; E.W., *Exact Constable*, pp. 4-6; Edward Coke, *The Fourth Part of the Institutes of the Laws of England* (London, 1671), p. 265; F.W. Maitland, *The Constitutional History of England* (Paper ed., Cambridge, 1961), pp. 47-52, 276; George C. Homans, *English Villagers in the Thirteenth Century* (Harper Torchbook, New York, 1970), pp. 297, 324-26, 333-37; Helen M. Cam, *The Hundred and the Hundred Rolls* (New York, 1930), pp. 19, 189, 192-93; Helen Jewell, *English Local Administration in the Middle Ages* (New York, 1972), pp. 60-61, 129-33, 158-69; Critchley, *History of Police*, pp. 1-8. Also see H.B. Simpson, "The Office of Constable," *English Historical Review*, X (1895), pp. 625-36, and W.S. Holdsworth, *A History of English Law*, IV (London, 1924), p. 123.

[8]The position of village headmen in various parts of Europe, including England, receives brief treatment in Jerome Blum, "The Internal Structure and Polity of the European Village Community from the Fifteenth to the Nineteenth Century," *Journal of Modern History*, XLIII (1971), pp. 556-62, 568-69.

[9]The approach to the constable's position developed in this article owes much to the work of anthropologists on village headmen in nonwestern societies, particularly in central and southern Africa, and to Max Gluckman's formulation of the concept of the "interhierarchical role." See Gluckman, "Interhierarchical Roles: Professional and Party Ethics in Tribal Areas in South and Central Africa," in Marc J. Swartz, ed., *Local-Level Politics* (Chicago, 1968), pp. 70-72; *Custom and Conflict in Africa* (rep. Oxford, 1970), esp. pp. 34-37, 51-52; *Politics, Law and Ritual in Tribal Society* (Oxford, 1965), pp. 165-66; J.A. Barnes, J.C. Mitchell and Max Gluckman, "The Village Headman in British Central Africa," in Gluckman, *Order and Rebellion in Tribal Africa* (London, 1963), pp. 146-70. Similar approaches are found in J.A. Barnes, *Politics in a Changing Society* (rep. Manchester, 1967) and J.C. Mitchell, *The Yao Village* (Manchester, 1956). Also see Elizabeth Colson, "Modern Political Organization of the Plateau Tonga," *African Studies*, VII (1948), pp. 85-98. A somewhat different perspective is employed in studying similar positions in Lloyd Fallers, "The Predicament of the Modern African Chief: An Instance from

self-governing body and in European villages he was selected for office by his fellow inhabitants. As leader of the township, he not only enjoyed various responsibilities within its bounds, but he also acted as the village's executive agent in its dealings with outsiders. As a result of the expansion of royal government during the medieval and early modern periods, however, village chiefs in England became subordinated to higher authorities and in many cases acquired a new title, constable. While retaining their earlier functions as leaders and representatives of local communities, they also acquired new "royal" duties, as did headmen in nonwestern societies who became agents of colonial powers during the nineteenth and twentieth centuries.

The constable's subordination to the state was achieved by two means and over the course of several centuries. In the first place, his position was altered by legislation. He may have acquired new police duties as early as the reign of Edward I, but it was under Edward III that the collective responsibility of the bill for peacekeeping was transferred by statute to its executive agent, the constable.[10] Later statutes not only extended his police functions, but conferred on him many other responsibilities, ranging from the collection of a wide variety of taxes and rates to the implementation of social and economic legislation. His duties were still being expanded during the early seventeenth century.[11] Secondly, the constable was subordinated to the state and his duties further enlarged when he bacame a servant to higher officials of the crown, the lords lieutenant, the sheriff, the coroner, and particularly the justices of the peace. He was also attendant upon a host of lesser officials, such as high constables, bailiffs, salt petre men, postmasters, and clerks of the market. His obligations to execute the justices' warrants received statutory confirmation during the sixteenth century, and by 1600 his royal powers owed as much to his being a general agent of these officials as to the statutory duties with which he was directly entrusted.[12]

The gradual transformation of the constable into a royal official is also reflected in changes in the content and administration of his oath of office. A copy of an oath found among the North Riding Sessions papers may be the original oath taken by the constable when he first became a royal

---

Uganda," *American Anthropologist*, LVII (1955), pp. 290-302, and in his *Bantu Bureaucracy* (Cambridge, n.d.), esp. pp. 17-19, 141-43, 155-78. Yet another viewpoint is found in Harriet J. Kupferer's study of Cree chiefs and New Guinea headmen, "Impotency and Power: A Cross-Cultural Comparison of the Effects of Alien Rule," in Marc J. Swartz, Victor Turner, and Arthur Tuden, eds., *Political Anthropology* (Chicago, 1966), pp. 61-71.

[10]13 Ed. I (Statute of Winchester); 4 Ed. III, c. 10; 5 Ed. III, c. 14; 25 Ed. III, Stat. 2, c. 5. Also see Simpson, "Office of Constable," pp. 633, 638, and Trotter, *Seventeenth Century Life*, pp. 83-84.

[11]The statutes that extended the constable's powers are too numerous to list, but a discussion of most of them can be found in Lambard, *Dueties of Constables* (1631 ed.).

[12]1 H. VII, c. 7; 27 H. VIII, c. 5; also see Simpson, "Office of Constable," p. 635; Holdsworth, *History of English Law*, IV, pp. 123-25.

official.[13] It stated only that he should exercise his office in the township, present all breaches of the king's peace, execute all writs lawfully directed to him, and personally do all in his power to conserve the peace. The oath was revised and expanded as his position changed and his duties increased. His obligations as a royal official were clarified, new statutory duties were incorporated into the oath, and he was specifically bound to execute the precepts of the justices of the peace.[14] Changes in the administration of the oath also bear witness to the constable's conversion from a local officer to a servant of the state and its officials. Originally he had been sworn in the court leet, and sometimes he continued to take his oath there even during the early seventeenth century, but it became increasingly common for the justices to administer the oath. In the 1630s this procedure received the endorsement of the judges of assize who claimed that the justices could fine or imprison a constable who had not appeared before them to be sworn into office.[15]

Although on the one hand the constable had become "the king's man" in the village, on the other hand he continued to represent the local community to the state and its officials and some of his power derived from his position as the executive agent of the township. In his presentments to Quarter Sessions and Assizes and to the justices in their monthly meetings, there survived traces of his function as the village's elected representative to higher authority. His powers to call upon neighbors to keep watch, to pursue hue and cry, and to assist him in making arrests are also reminders of the collective responsibility of the vill for peacekeeping when the constable was merely its head man. The constable, sometimes accompanied by several neighbors, also represented the township in negotia-

---

[13]J.C. Atkinson, ed., *Quarter Sessions Records* (The North Riding Record Society, 1884), I, p. 183; Trotter, *Seventeenth Century Life*, p. 85.

[14]See the oaths printed in Bacon, "Answers to Questions," pp. 753-54, and Dalton, *Countrey Justice*, pp. 363-64.

[15]There are many references in Quarter Sessions records to the justices swearing constables. Such evidence is also found occasionally in constables' accounts, for example, Pattingham Constables' Accounts, 1625/6 (this volume lacks pagination and references will be given to the year in which an entry occurs); Norfolk and Norwich Record Office (hereafter N. & N.R.O.) PD 50/36H, no. 89; Staffs. R.O., D 705/PC/1/1, p/ 25; Leicestershire Record Office (hereafter Leics. R.O.) DE 720/30, ff. 9, 13, 18v.; Shelton Parish Book, 1621 (this volume lacks pagination and references will be given to the year in which an entry occurs). For constables sworn in the leet, see Leics. R.O., DE 720/30, ff. 11v., 45v., 47v.; and for orders by the justices that they be sworn in the leet, Atkinson, *Quarter Sessions Records*, III, p. 150; H. Hampton Copnall, ed., *Notes and Extracts from the Nottinghamshire County Records of the Seventeenth Century* (Nottingham, 1915), p. 20; E.H. Bates Harbin, ed., *Quarter Sessions Records for the County of Somerset* (Somerset Record Society, XXIV, 1908), II, pp. 87-88 (the hundred court, presumably enjoying leet jurisdiction); Staffs. R.O., QS/O, IV, ff. 226-226v.; V, ff. 31-32. For the judges opinions, see T.G. Barnes, ed., *Somerset Assize Orders*, 1629-40, (Somerset Record Society, LXV, 1959), p. 69. Also see Simpson, "Office of Constable," p. 639; and for contemporary opinions about where the oath was to be taken, Bacon, "Answers to Questions," p. 750, and Dalton, *Countrey Justice*, p. 47.

tions with higher authorities about the assessment and collection of a wide variety of taxes and rates. His military duties too continued to reflect his position as executive agent of the village. He was not only responsible to the lords lieutenant and the justices in their capacity as commissioners of musters, but he also inherited the collective responsibilities of the vill for the maintenance of common armor and for the upkeep of the shooting butts.[16]

The constable also retained a number of purely local functions, which further reinforced his position as an officer of the village. Such duties varied from township to township and were more numerous in some communities than in others. In some instances the churchwardens had become responsible for local tasks that in other villages still devolved upon the constable. It is possible that in pastoral and forest areas, with their scattered settlements and weak manorial structure, the constable had never functioned as the leader of an agricultural community to the same extent that he did, even in the early seventeenth century, in open-field villages.[17] In Branston and Waltham-on-the-Wolds, for example, the constable's accounts indicate that a wide variety of local concerns fell within his jurisdiction, although he did not personally undertake all such tasks. His duties included custody of the communal bull; maintenance of village gates, waterings, weirs, sheep dams, hedges, and the pinfold; fetching "setts," that is, slips or shoots for planting; "trenching" and even sowing certain fields and thatching the herdsman's house. Sometimes he was also responsible for guarding the crops from village animals and from deer and crows and for the eradication of vermin such as foxes and moles. Other payments from his accounts "for drawing the field on Plow Monday" or "when we came from the perambulation" or "for wood for a bonfire on the king's holiday" also reflect the constable's 1position of leadership within the village and his role in its communal rituals.[18]

---

[16]The material in this paragraph is based on evidence in constables' accounts and in the Quarter Sessions Records listed in the Appendix.

[17]For a discussion of some of the differences in settlement patterns and social organization, as well as in economic structures, between "champion" and "pastoral" areas, see Joan Thirsk, ed., *The Agrarian History of England and Wales*, IV (Cambridge, 1967), pp. 1-15, 109-112, and her "Seventeenth-Century Agriculture and Social Change," in Paul Seaver, ed., *Seventeenth Century England* (New York, 1976). For a more specialized study of pastoral farming in one of the counties included in this paper see Joan Thirsk, "Horn and Thorn in Staffordshire: The Economy of a Pastoral County," *North Staffordshire Journal of Field Studies*, IX (1969), pp. 1-16.

[18]The discussion above is based primarily on repeated entries in the constables' accounts of Branston and Waltham (Leics. R.O., DE 720/30 and DE 625/60), though similar entries occur in the accounts of Wimeswold, Leics. (B.L., Add. MS. 10457) and in the fragmentary accounts of Stathern, Leics. (Everard L. Guilford, "The Accounts of the Constables of the Village of Stathern, Leicestershire," *The Archaeological Journal*, LXIX (1912), pp. 128-32), and some such entries are also found in the accounts of Stockton, Salop (Salop Record Office, 3067/3/1) and Millington, Yorks. (Borthwick Institute, PR MIL. 10). Also see Hoskins, *Midland Peasant*, p. 208; Trotter, *Seventeenth Century Life*, p. 89; Peter Laslett, *The World We Have Lost* (2nd ed., New York, 1971), p. 77.

Although the constable's recognition as an agent of the central government had partially transformed the character of his office it had not, even by the early seventeenth century, altered the method of his appointment. Unlike the justices of the peace he was not chosen by the central government. Nor was he, like the high constable, usually appointed by his administrative superiors. Although he was responsible to the justices, and often sworn into office by them, they had no legal right in his selection, which continued to rest with the local community. A case tried in King's Bench in 1612 was decided against the justices who had removed a constable of Stepney and appointed a new officer. The judges declared that the justices could choose and remove high constables but that they had "no power nor authority" to elect or displace petty constables.[19]

Some variation in the term of office and a diversity of customs governing the constable's selection further attest to the fact that this "appointment" remained a local matter. The office was most often one for a year with constables being selected at either Michaelmas or Easter, but in some villages with two constables, two-year staggered terms were usual. There were many differences from village to village, even within a county, in the proportion of villagers eligible to serve as constable and in the procedures for choosing someone to fill the office. Where courts leet continued to meet, constables were normally selected there; sometimes chosen by those owing suit to the court, or the jury, from among those eligible for the post, while in cases the office followed a regular rotation among certain houses in the village and the leet merely confirmed in the position the man whose turn it was to serve. Occasionally the incumbent proposed several names and his successor was selected from among them. In a few instances a particular property holder or the steward of the court seems to have enjoyed the right to choose a constable. In manors where leets had ceased to meet, the inhabitants of the village sometimes assembled for the specific purpose of choosing a constable, and in some cases they were ordered to do so by the justices. In other instances it was the parish vestry that fell heir to the leet's powers to choose a constable, though this body had no legal right to appoint him and he was not, strictly speaking, an officer of the parish. Sometimes he appears to have been nominated in the vestry even though he was formally confirmed in office in the court leet. His contemporaries did not draw clear distinctions between township and parish, even when the two were not coterminous. Even when the constable was selected in the leet he was often termed "parish constable," and his accounts are sometimes found in the same book with those of the churchwardens. In the selection of city constables, there seems to have been a similar confusion between the precinct and the parish. Although constables in both Norwich and London were formally officers of the ward and its subdivision, the precinct, in

---

[19]*The Reports of Edward Bulstrode, Court of King's Bench, 1609-26* (London, 1657), p. 174.

London at least they came to be chosen by parish vestries though they continued to be confirmed in the wardmotes.[20]

The constable was legally the appointee of a local body until 1662 when an act of Parliament authorized the justices to fill the office if a leet had not been held or if an incumbent had died or moved from the village.[21] Some historians have argued that the statute resulted in little real change because the justices had been appointing constables for some time, either in their official capacities or as lords of manors.[22] There is some indication that the justices in the 1630s, under growing pressure from the central government to create a more effective local administration, wanted a voice in the selection of constables. At the same time, they also began to deny the validity of local customs that had governed eligibility for the office. Encouraged by the council and the judges of assize, the justices probably did make some inroads into the rights of local bodies to select the constable during the 1630s.[23] Prior to that decade, however, the justices of most

---

[20]This discussion of the selection of constables is based on information found in the Quarter Sessions records listed in the Appendix; in constables' papers for the villages under consideration; and in court rolls for the manor of Pattingham (Staffs. R.O., Transcripts of Pattingham Court Rolls, D 1807/ 159-293) and the manor of Bushey (Hertfordshire Record Office, [hereafter Herts. R.O.], Bushey Court Rolls, esp. no. 6403). The vestry seems to have played a prominent role in the selection of constables in Essex; see B.W. Quintrell, "The Government of the County of Essex, 1603-42," (London, Ph.D. thesis, 1965), pp. 195, 198, and F.G. Emmison, *Catalogue of Essex Parish Records* (2nd ed., Chelmsford, 1966), p. 17. John T. Evans, *Seventeenth Century Norwich, Politics, Religion and Government* (Oxford, 1979), p. 58, indicates that constables in that city were officials of the ward; and further evidence to this effect is found in *Norfolk Archaeology*, I (1847), pp. 1-4, 28. For a discussion of the relative roles of the ward/precinct and the parish in the selection of London constables see Frank F. Foster, *The Politics of Stability—A Portrait of the Rulers of Elizabethan London* (The Royal Historical Society, London, 1977), pp. 29-32, 37-38. G[ardiner], *Compleat Constable*, contains a separate chapter (XXIII on London constables which also indicates that they were nominated in the vestry though confirmed in the wardmote. Lynda Price is currently engaged in a study of the constableship in London and Middlesex during the Jacobean period and her work should provide more detailed information about city constables.

[21]14 Car. I, c. 12, # XV.

[22]For a summary of the debate on this question see Critchley, *History of Police*, p. 17.

[23]Barnes, Somerset Assize Orders, p. 69; P.R.O., SP 16/255/48, also reprinted in *Ibid.*, p. 71; B.L., Add. MS. 12496, f. 287v. (The Book of Orders, 1631); Staffs. R.O., QS/O, V, f. 47. Also see Staffs. R.O., QS/O, V, ff. 11, 116; Copnall, *Notes and Extracts*, p. 18; Barnes, *Somerset Assize Orders*, pp. 35, 39, 40; and for a recent discussion of the origins of the Book of Orders, B.W. Quintrell, "The Making of Charles I's Book of Orders," *EHR*, XCV (1980), pp. 553-72. The handbooks on the office of constable record the judges' decisions of the 1630s, which accorded greater power to the justices of the peace in the selection of constables, but they also suggest the confusion and disagreement that existed as to the relative powers of the justices and local bodies such as the leet. See Sheppard, *Offices and Duties of Constables*, pp. 14-15, 22-24; E.W., *Exact Constable*, pp. 7, 12-13, 96-99, 101-102; G[ardiner], *Compleat Constable*, pp. 8-9.

counties do not appear to have selected constables; Hertfordshire, where a number of such appointments are recorded in Quarter Sessions records, seems to be an exception, one perhaps explained by the unusual diligence that seems to have characterized the Hertfordshire justices.[24] The justices of the North Riding of Yorkshire did not even know the number, let alone the names, of the constables in their jurisdiction in 1612 and they requested the high constables to bring a list of these officers to the next sessions.[25] Other records too suggest that the justices were concerned primarily with assuring that every village had a constable, and that they made appointments only as a last resort when other more traditional means of filling the office had failed. When they did make orders concerning a constableship, their action usually seems to have been prompted by a village petition or by a plea from an incumbent who had served his term and wished to be relieved of his office, or because of a protest from someone selected for the position who claimed to be exempt from service. In such cases the justices until the 1630s were usually careful to uphold custom, even if this resulted in lengthy investigations and sometimes in long delays in selecting a new official, delays that often obliged an incumbent to remain in office well beyond his term[26]. The justices in their private capacities as large landowners and lords of leets may have selected constables,[27] but there is little evidence of this in the records consulted. This action would also have been very much at odds with the respect for village customs that they displayed as magistrates. Furthermore, it seems probable that villagers would have resisted any interference with traditional arrangements for choosing a constable. Their petitions to the justices indicate that they did take an interest in his selection and while such petitions sometimes called for innovations, usually a broadening of the eligibility for office, they most often reflect a concern about the maintenance of customary procedures. Moreover, if ordinary farmers and craftsmen could display independence in voting for members of Parliament in the early seventeenth century, as a recent study has suggested,[28] there is no reason to believe that they were more subservient to their landlords in the selection of officers within the manor.

---

[24]Herts. R.O., Quarter Sessions Books, 2A, ff. 32v., 36-36v., 42v., 54v., 60, 67, 78, 108, 109, 120, 139, 150, 153v., 163, 182, 194, 211; 2B, ff. 8v., 9, 14, 28v. The special diligence of the Hertfordshire bench is analyzed in Julie Calnan, "County Society and Local Government in the County of Hertford, c. 1580-c. 1630, with special reference to the Commission of the Peace," (Cambridge, Ph.D. thesis, 1979). There are also a few cases of justices appointing constables in the Warwickshire records, for example, S.C. Ratcliffe and H.C. Johnson, eds., *Quarter Sessions Order Books* (Warwick County Records, 1935-6), I, pp. 12, 17, 196, 231-32; II, pp. 7, 40-41.

[25]Atkinson, *Quarter Sessions Records*, I, p. 256.

[26]This discussion is based on a study of the Quarter Sessions records listed in the Appendix. Also see Fletcher, *Sussex*, p. 141; Trotter, *Seventeenth Century Life*, pp. 106-11.

[27]This is the argument of A. Hassell Smith in "Justices at Work in Elizabethan Norfolk," *Norfolk Archaeology*, XXXIV (1967), p. 105.

[28]Derek Hirst, *The Representative of the People? Voters and Voting in England Under the Early Stuarts* (Cambridge, 1975), esp. chs. 6, 7, and 9.

Constables were not only in most cases locally appointed, but they were bound to their subordinates within the village by different kinds of ties than those that governed their relations with their administrative superiors. Their relationships with higher authorities usually seem to have been official in nature, and the records provide little evidence of personal bonds between constables and their superiors.[29] While their ties to higher officials normally seem to have been "single-interest linkages" to men with whom they were brought into temporary contact by virtue of their office, their local political position, like that of other village headmen, was deeply enmeshed in the "multiplex relationships" of the village community.[30] Although their local public was not a kin group, as often was the case with village headmen in nonwestern societies, constables too had to represent higher authority to communities of which they were "in other respects full members."[31] English villages of the late sixteenth and early seventeenth centuries were no longer always highly integrated communities and relationships among their residents were not always harmonious, as evidenced by the number and nature of affrays recorded in court leet rolls and by the tensions that surfaced in witchcraft accusations.[32] Constables, like other

---

[29]Despite the importance that historians have attached to interpersonal networks of relations, such as clientage, in the political system of Tudor-Stuart England, more evidence is needed before it can be assumed that such bonds were as significant in linking village and county officials as they were in cementing relations at higher levels of government. There is little evidence of such ties between constables and their superiors in the records consulted, though it is possible that such relationships escaped the records. For a recent discussion of interpersonal networks that suggests that they *did* provide the means of linking village and county hierarchies, but which gives no evidence to support this contention, see Paul Christianson, "The Causes of the English Revolution: A Reappraisal," *Journal of British Studies*, XV (1976), pp. 40-75 and esp. pp. 52-65. Some of J.H. Hexter's criticisms in "Power Struggle, Parliament and Liberty in Early Stuart England," *J. of Mod. Hist.*, LV (1978), pp. 16-21, are applicable to Christianson's discussion of personal networks at the local level as well as to those involving peers and gentlemen.

[30]For a further elaboration of the concepts of "multiplex relationships" and of "single-interest linkages," see Max Gluckman, *The Judicial Process among the Barotse of Northern Rhodesia* (Manchester, 1955), pp. 18-19.

[31]Gluckman, *Order and Rebellion*, p. 42.

[32]Evidence about affrays is derived from the Pattingham Court Rolls, Staffs R.O., Transcripts D1807/159-293. For a discussion of the importance attached to social harmony, but also suggestions that witchcraft accusations reflected a breakdown in such harmony, see Keith Thomas, *Religion and the Decline of Magic* (New York, 1971), chs. 16 and 17, and A.D.J. Macfarlane, *Witchcraft in Tudor and Stuart England* (Harper Torchbook, New York, 1970), chs. 15 and 16. Also see M.J. Ingram, "Communities and Courts: Law and Disorder in Early Seventeenth-Century Wiltshire," in Cockburn, *Crime in England*, pp. 110-34 for a discussion of "ideals of neighbourly harmony" reflected in arbitration mechanisms and in the apparent bias in favor of local residents reflected in legal proceedings. Ingram too suggests that such ideals were being subjected to strains during the early seventeenth century. Historians still have much to learn about the structure of village communities in the early modern period and about the nature of interrelationships among their inhabitants. The reconstruction of villages along the lines being pursued by Alan Macfarlane should provide further information of this kind; for the methodology

men, could be at odds with their fellow villagers and sometimes they apparently tried to use their powers as "king's man" in the village to lord it over other inhabitants, to pursue existing quarrels or settle old scores, or to favor a few friends. However, such instances are rather rare in the records.[33] The constable's ties with the village, where communal cooperation and harmony remained accepted *ideals,* usually seem to have been more important to him than his relations with higher officials and the powers he derived from being an agent of royal authority. This is not surprising because the constable was normally in office for only a year, while he might remain in the village for the rest of his life. He was bound to his fellow villagers by ties other than those of office—as kinsman, affine, neighbor, or fellow farmer—and such relationships would continue to be important long after his term as constable had ended. Even while he was in office his position as constable would not be completely differentiated from these other social identities and the rights and duties that they entailed. As a local man, involved in the day-to-day life of the community and immediately subject to pressures from his neighbors, the constable would thus be "closely involved in every matter over which he should preside impartially."[34]

The ways in which local ties and neighborly pressures could lead to confusion between an officer's public and private roles within the village are well illustrated by the activities of an early seventeenth-century constable of Burton-on-Trent. The constable made use of his official position 0to lead some of his neighbors in inflicting a traditional form of village justice on two of the inhabitants. The group, apparently numbering about forty, broke into the house of a couple whom they accused of irregular and immoral behavior, of cohabiting, and having sexual relations without being married. They dragged the couple into the street and subjected them to a noisy procession through the town, their cries of "A Whore and a Knave" accompanied by "ringing of cow bells, basons, candlesticks, frying pannes and . . . the sounde of a drumme." The incident matches other descriptions of "rough music" or "charivaris" in which villagers took it upon themselves to ridicule deviant behavior in their neighbors; but the Burton case passed beyond ridcule to punishment, and the goal was probably to drive the couple from the town.[35] However, the constable who led

and goals of this research, see Macfarlane, "History, anthropology and the study of communities," *Social History,* V (1977), pp. 631-52; and his *Reconstructing Historical Communities* (Cambridge, 1977).

[33]These claims are based on complaints to the justices or cases before the courts, and it is not usually possible to discover whether the constable was in the wrong; but see, for example, Staffs. R.O., QS/O, III, f. 190; V, f. 83; Transcripts of Quarter Sessions Rolls, Charles I, Roll 32, #35; Bates Harbin, *Somerset Quarter Sessions,* II, p. 249; P.R.O., Star Chamber Proceedings, James I (hereafter STAC 8), 218/23; *Calendar of State Papers Domestic,* Charles I, 1636-37, p. 408.

[34]Barnes, Mitchell, and Gluckman, "Village headman," p. 152.

[35]The information about this case is derived from a petition by the two inhabitants to Star Chamber and the response to the petition by the constable and one other villager, P.R.O., STAC 8/ 104/ 20. Also see Natalie Zemon Davis, "The Rea-

his neighbors in these activities was not acting in his official capacity nor at the behest of the state when he punished the couple by placing them in the stocks. He and his neighbors had acted as both accusers and judges, operating outside the legal channels provided by either the secular or the ecclesiastical courts.[36] The complainants' petition does have to be treated with caution because they were probably trying to establish that the behavior had been riotous in order to gain a hearing in Star Chamber, but the constable did not deny his participation nor challenge their account of the events. He provided no evidence, however, that his office empowered him to take such action, claiming only that the punishment was traditional, that he had acted because he was *pressed to do so by some of his neighbors*, and that the justices had, after the event, upheld his action and denied the grievances alleged by the petitioners. The couple, whether or not they were guilty of the charges, were not entirely unjustified in their claim that the constable had disregarded "his othe formerly taken duly and justly to execute the office of a constable," having failed to enforce the peace, and that he abused the powers of his office when he became "ring leader" and charged the townsmen in the king's name "to goe with and aide him." The villagers probably did believe, as the complainants suggested, that the constable's leadership would lend greater legitimacy to their actions. In accepting that leadership, however, the constable had failed to differentiate between his position as a concerned townsman and his official responsibilities as an agent of the state.[37]

---

sons of Misrule: Youth Groups and Charivaris in Sixteenth-Century France," *Past and Present*, L (1971), pp. 41-75; E.P. Thompson, "Rough Music: Le Charivari anglais," *Annales*, XXVII (1972), pp. 285-312. I am grateful to Natalie Davis for allowing me to read, before publication, a paper that she delivered to the Burg Wartenstein Symposium, "Charivari, Honor and Community in Seventeenth-Century Lyon and Geneva."

[36]Lawrence Stone, *The Family, Sex and Marriage in England, 1500-1800* (New York 1977), p. 145, argues that in the late Elizabethan period a constable could break into any house where he suspected fornication or adultery to be occurring and that if his suspicions were confirmed he could take the offenders to jail or before a justice. Stone cites as the authority for this statement the 1622 edition of Dalton's *Countrey Justice*. Lambarde, *Dueties of Constables*, p. 18, also makes reference to such a situation, but the legal basis for the constable's action is not clear. Lambarde declares that "I like well of their opinion which do hold that if information be given to any such officer that a man and woman bee in adulterie or fornication together, then the officer may take companie with him, and that if he find them so, hee may carie them to prison." None of these authorities suggest, however, that the constable had the power to *punish* such offenders.

[37]For another case in which a constable apparently yielded to village pressures, arresting a man and placing him in the stocks without any warrant from higher authorities, and then allowed his neighbors to determine the additional punishment to be inflicted, see P.R.O., STAC 8/ 95/ 11. Also see the discussion of village arbitration mechanisms and of the community pressures brought to bear on local officials in Ingram, "Communities and Courts," pp. 116-18, 125-34; T.C. Curtis, "Quarter Sessions Appearances and Their Background: A Seventeenth Century Regional Study," in Cockburn, ed., *Crime in England*, pp. 135-54.

The constable, due to the very nature of his office, was thus caught between conflicting pressures from his superiors and his fellow villagers. A Surrey constable who wrote a ballad about the office in 1626 vividly described the dilemmas of such a dual position when he wrote:

> The Justices will set us by the heels,
> If we do not as we should;
> Which if we perform, the townsmen will storm
> Some of them hang's [hang us] if they could.[38]

The incompatible demands placed upon the constable as a result of the duality of his position can be explored in further detail by examining one facet of his office, his duties as a tax collector. The government's demands upon him to collect its revenues were often matched by the resistance of his fellow villagers to the payment of such levies. In his capacity as a tax collector, the constable was pushed and pulled in opposing directions, and he was frequently faced with a choice of "damned if I do, damned if I don't."[39]

As the government's agents, constables were pressed to draw up local assessments, collect the levies, and meet the deadlines for payment established by their superiors. If they did not do so, the regular precepts by which higher officials ordered them to levy such revenues could become quite threatening in tone, warning constables of the punishments that awaited them. The directives received by constables of Salwarpe, particularly those of 1639-40 concerning ship money, provide a good illustration of the written harassments to which such officers were subjected by their administrative superiors. The constable had apparently failed to return ship money assessments for the township, and in a precept of January 1639-40 the high constable once again ordered him to do so, all excuses aside, or to appear personally before the sheriff. By March the high constable's patience was wearing thin. He claimed that many precepts had been sent to the constable who, by refusing to perform his duties, had displayed his disregard for the king's service as well as contempt for the authority of the sheriff. The constable was warned that his willful neglect would no longer be tolerated and that no further excuses would be accepted. He received further reproof in April because the money had not yet been paid, and the pressures continued through June and July because he was still in arrears for part of the tax. Angry precepts from their superiors may have reached their height in the case of ship money, but constables of Salwarpe were also threatened with fines or warned that their names would be returned to higher officials when they were in arrears for other taxes and rates; provision for the household; "quarteridge" for the

---

[38]James Gyffon, "The Song of a Constable," (1626), in A.V. Judges, *The Elizabethan Underworld* (London, 1930), p. 489. These lines are also cited in Campbell, *English Yeoman*, p. 322, while other portions of the ballad are quoted in Trotter, *Seventeenth Century Life*, p. 105.

[39]Hassell Smith, *County and Court*, p. 113.

jail, maimed soldiers, and the house of correction; money for the maintenance of the beacons; and the "forced loan" of 1627-28.[40]

Although written rebukes apparently could be ignored, at least for a time, the threats of punishment sometimes were carried out. A number of constables who were negligent in making assessments and collections were called to answer before higher officials or were fined by the courts for failure to carry out their duties. Those deemed remiss in the collection of ship money were sometimes summoned before the sheriff or his undersheriff. Pattingham constables, for example, were called before the undersheriff in 1636; in 1638-39 they had to answer to the sheriff for their negligence on three occasions and they were also hauled before the assizes; and in 1640-41 they again were summoned before the sheriff three times.[41] Quarter Sessions records contain many orders for constables to appear before the justices to answer for their neglect, and indictments charging them with failure to pay a wide variety of levies, ranging from county rates to provision, subsidies, and ship money.[42] Some who were negligent in collecting ship money were imprisoned, or threatened with imprisonment, in the county jail. Others faced even higher tribunals, being attached by messengers and brought before the privy council to answer for their refusal to levy ship money.[43]

Constables were not excused by claims that they had been unable to collect a levy. In that case the government expected them to resort to distraint, though this action was not likely to endear them to the neighbor whose cattle or goods had been seized. Sometimes warrants from higher officials obliged constables to convey before them recalcitrant villagers who had not paid their levies. Constables themselves were occasionally subject to distraint when they had failed to make payments or they had to dip into their own pockets to meet their financial obligations.[44]

---

[40]Hereford and Worcester Record Office (hereafter H. & W.R.O.), 850 SALWARPE, BA 1054/1, Bundle A, nos. 147, 169, 171, 180 (ship money); *Ibid.*, Bundle A, nos. 21, 65, 97, 99, 114, 117, 133, 147, 174, 183; Bundle H, 20 March 1613-14 (other taxes and rates).

[41]See Pattingham Constables' Accounts for the years cited.

[42]For example, Staffs. R.O., QS/O, II, ff. 13v., 50v., 67; III, ff. 15, 98v., 155v., 185v.; IV, ff. 157, 231, 259; Atkinson, *Quarter Sessions Records*, I, pp. 17, 24, 27, 33, 61, 69, 165-66, 191, 205, 207, 227, 238, 244, 250, 253; II, pp. 57, 112, 159, 166, 179-80, 194, 234; III, pp. 111, 112, 126, 129, 164, 189, 191, 195, 235, 269, 354, 359, IV, pp. 28, 177, 205. References could be given to many other Quarter Sessions records from other counties.

[43]For example, P.R.O, SP 16/306/55; 352/24; 381/71; 457/22; 387/46; 452/10.

[44]For example, Staffs R.O., QS/O, V, f. 16; Leics. R.O., DE 720/30, f. 45v.; DE 625/60, ff. 42v., 49v., 50, 53, 56; H. & W.R.O., 850 SALWARPE, BA 1054/2, D8; Pattingham Constables' Accounts, 1619-20, 1637-38, 1640-41. There is evidence in Quarter Sessions records of constables being out of pocket in order to meet the collections for which they were responsible; for example, J. Willis Bund, ed., *Calendar of Quarter Sessions Papers, 1591-1643* (Worcestershire Historical Society, 1900), II, pp. 461-62; Staffs. R.O., QS/O, III, ff. 27-27v., 39, 155v., 158v.; IV, ff. 258v.-259; Staffs. R.O., Transcripts of Quarter Sessions Rolls, James I, Roll 66, nos., 26, 27; Roll 75, nos 34, 35, 70; Herts. R.O., Quarter Sessions Book, 2A, ff. 49-49v., 53v.-54, 87-87v., 91, 112; 2B, ff. 13, 26v.

The pressures and threats from the constable's superiors were matched by those from within the village. There is considerable evidence of villagers' reluctance to pay a wide variety of levies, ranging from the constable's own "lewne" to provision money (which in Pattingham fell short of the assessment in twenty-one of the twenty-four years between 1616 and 1640 and by increasingly large amounts) to benevolences, contributions for the repair of St. Paul's, and ship money.[45] Villagers too could inflict punishment on a constable when they disagreed with local assessments or when they opposed a tax and refused to pay it. A constable might be ostracized by his neighbors, probably a rather unpleasant experience in a small village community, but some officials also faced more overt resistance, particularly in instances when they resorted to distraint. Sometimes a constable was physically driven from the door and occasionally wounded in the scuffle, or cattle and goods were forcefully repossessed by their owners. On other occasions they faced only threats of violence or were heaped with merely verbal abuse, being called "fool" or "slave." In a few instances a constable had some of his beard torn from his chin by an angry villager, a form of assault that probably had symbolic significance and was as degrading as it was physically painful.[46] Such evidence of villagers' resistance to the constable's demands would suggest that ship money sheriffs were not merely offering excuses for their own delinquency when they claimed that constables "dare doe nothinge but what the parishe alowe of," or that these officials failed to distrain because "they were soe menaced by theire neighbors." If many officers heard rumors like the one being circulated in Northamptonshire in 1636, in which it was alleged that sixty-six constables in that county had been hanged by the inhabitants for attempting to collect ship money, the temptation to bow to village pressures must have been rather great.[47] The "folk justice" of the village, with its immediacy and its probable damage to a man's local position and reputation, probably held as much terror for the constable as a fine im-

---

[45]For example, Staffs. R.O., QS/O, II, ff. 63, 81-2; III, ff. 19-19v., 36v., 56v., 85, 117-117v., 132; IV, ff. 24, 56, 100-100v., 143v., 196, 231, 234; V, ff. 97, 139; Atkinson, *Quarter Sessions Records*, I, p. 244; III, p. 342; Leics. R.O. DG36/187, f. 1v.; DG 36/188, DD2; DG 36/189; DE 332/1, p. 12; DE 625/60, ff. 26v., 49v., 50v.; N. & N.R.O., PD 50/36H, no. 53; Shelton Parish Book, 1616, 1621, 1622. In addition to the difficulties of the Pattingham constable in collecting provision money, see their problems in levying their own "lewnes," Pattingham Constables' Accounts, 1583/4, 1584/5, 1587/8, 1592/3, 1593/4, 1602/3, 1610/11, 1611/12; and in collecting ship money, *Ibid.*, 1634/5, 1636/7, 1637/8.

[46]The records often do not indicate which of his duties the constable was attempting to fullfill when he met with resistance and violence; but for instance when tax and rate collecting is specified, see Atkinson, *Quarter Sessions Records*, I, pp. 213, 237, 244; III, p. 342; P.R.O., SP 16/351/20; 367/83 (I.); 380/35; 398/19. For a few other interesting instances of attacks on the constable, when the cause is not specified, see Atkinson, *Quarter Sessions Records*, I, p. 210; S.C. Ratcliffe and H.C. Johnson, eds., *Quarter Sessions Indictment Book* (Warwick County Records, 1941), VI, p. 48; S.A.H. Burne, ed., *Staffordshire Quarter Sessions Rolls* (Staffordshire Historical Collections, 1932), III, p. 102.

[47]P.R.O., Sp 16/ 385/1; 452/10; 467/58; 313/11.

posed by the justice or the more distant threat of a summons before the council.

In view of the conflicts attendant upon the constable's office, and the difficulties he thus encountered in carrying out his duties, it is perhaps surprising that local government did not come to a complete standstill. The tensions that had accumulated by the late 1630s may very nearly have produced this result in some areas. There is a growing amount of evidence from this period that men were reluctant to hold the office of constable, that some agreed to do so only on certain conditions, and that those chosen for the position more often attempted to hire substitutes. A larger number of cases of disputed constableships came before the justices in sessions in the later 1630s than during earlier periods, and in some of the villages included in this study there are also hints of a new reluctance to serve as constable. Two Pattingham men selected for the office in 1638-39 and 1639-40, respectively, procured others to serve for them, while no such substitutions are recorded during the previous fifty years. A widow in the same village was obliged to provide a constable in 1642-43, though a number of other women holding substantial properties apparently had been passed over in the selection of a constable during earlier years. A Little Munden man chosen as constable in 1639, probably just a cottager since he was taxed locally only as an "inhabitant" and not for any lands, agreed to serve only on the condition that he be excused from the office for the next four years.[48] This evidence, though fragmentary, suggests that a Worcestershire sheriff did not exaggerate when he reported in 1640 that many constables imprisoned for their failure to collect ship money were content to remain in jail in order "to avoid all other services."[49] The "services" that accumulated under Charles I, and the more frequent occasions for conflict between villagers and the state to which his policies gave rise, had made the constable's position one of of increasing difficulty.

It would be wrong to see the relations between the village and higher authorities only in terms of conflict, however, even during the 1630s, or to leave the impression that the dual pressures on the constable usually led him to fail completely in his duties. Anthropologists have tended to focus on the structural conflicts inherent in such offices, but such conflicts did not preclude the existence of relative cohesion within the political system as a whole. In sixteenth- and seventeenth-century England, periodic clashes between the village and higher authorities could produce compromise, despite the pressures that they imposed on the constable, because neither side had a monopoly of power. Constables' accounts show that on

---

[48]See Barnes, *Somerset*, p. 241, who points out that the justices in that county dealt with twelve cases of men unwilling to be constables between 1635 and 1638, nine of them between Epiphany 1637-38 and Epiphany 1638-39, twice as many as during the previous ten years. Also see Hurstfield, "Wiltshire," p. 288; Pattingham Constables' Accounts, 1638-39, 1639-40, 1642-43; Herts. R.O., D/ P 71. 5/ 2.

[49]P.R.O., SP 16/ 457/22.

many occasions they did gain the cooperation of the local community in meeting the demands imposed on them by their superiors, and that they successfully called upon other villagers to assist them in carrying out their duties. However, this had its price because in other instances higher authorities were obliged to meet the demands that the constable made on behalf of the village. There was a degree of reciprocity in the relations between local communities and superior officials; if villagers sometimes acquiesced in demands from above on other occasions, they had an ability to arouse caution in higher authorities, to force negotiation upon them, and to obtain concessions.[50]

When county officials met united resistance from local communities represented by their constables, they often seem to have realized the limitations of their power and to have become cautious and conciliatory. Such a tone is sometimes reflected in the letters of ship money sheriffs. Their reports to the council about their difficulties in collecting the money need to be treated with caution since higher officials themselves sometimes were opposed to the tax, encouraged resistance among their inferiors, and then offered excuses for their failure to make payment.[51] There is a ring of truth in their expressions of helplessness, however, and in their advocacy of moderation in the face of constables whose opposition to ship money reflected the solid resistance of their fellow villagers. Several sheriffs admitted that they could have accused most of the constables of negligence, but they defended the wisdom of making an example of only a few of them. They pointed out that they were dependent upon the cooperation of these officers without whose local knowledge and authority they could not obtain village assessments or identify the lands and goods of recalcitrant villagers whom they wished to distrain. Moreover, they contended, the incarceration of constables for negligence in levying ship money prevented these officers from carrying out other important responsibilities. In 1639-40, when the opposition to ship money reached its height, higher officials urgently needed constables' assistance in mustering troops for service on the northern borders. It is not surprising that several sheriffs urged moderation in dealing with delinquent constables and the villagers "who promised to bear them out"; such situations must have left room for little but negotiation and compromise.[52]

[50]See E.P. Thompson, "Patrician Society, Plebien Culture," *Journal of Social History* (1974), pp. 382-405, to which this section is indebted; and also Christianson, "English Revolution," pp. 62-64. Christianson, however, assumes that such reciprocity was based on clientage.

[51]See especially the evidence from Somerset presented in Barnes, *Somerset*, pp. 209-41.

[52]For example, P.R.O., SP 16/ 266/21; 346/108; 387/46; 418/51; 455/85; 456/21, 49; 457/22; 467/58. A somewhat similar caution and awareness of the limits of their power seems to have characterized the attitude of magistrates and gentlemen toward the application of the criminal law in the eighteenth century; see Douglas Hay, "Property, Authority and the Criminal Law," in Hay et al, eds., *Albion's Fatal Tree* (New York, 1975), pp. 17-63. Also see J.S. Morrill, *The Revolt of the Provinces* (London, 1976), pp. 24-29.

In some instances, constables' accounts reveal that they succeeded in gaining concessions from higher authorities to the demands they made on behalf of the village, and such compromises were probably part of the normal give and take of relations between the two levels of government. Most of the evidence concerns burdens in kind, such as the carriage of royal provisions, requisitions by the salt petre man, or the postmaster's request for horses, probably because such items were more negotiable than monetary levies.[53] Constables of Branston, for example, represented the village before the salt petre man to "procure ease of our carraiges" and to get the town excused from carrying ashes to Nottingham. They also negotiated about carriage to Derby, journeyed to Belvoir "to gett some parte of our gose abated," and several times made small payments to officials for "excusing the post horses." In 1643-44 the constable, accompanied by several villagers, traveled twice to Melton Mowbray "to make friends for the tax."[54] Waltham constables too represented the village's interests to higher authorities and secured reductions in its burdens. They negotiated with the high constable to spare a cart from Nottingham to Derby and to excuse other carts to Ashby. Along with several neighbors they made three other arrangements with the high constable that entailed the release of six horses and a cart and excused them from drawing a wagon to Newark. They persuaded the salt petre man to overlook the village's obligation to provide him with three carts to carry coals.[55] Similarly, the Melton Mowbray constables sought concessions from the postmaster. They had just taken ten post horses to Witham and attended them a day and a night when they retraced their steps to "intreat Mr. Crapper to excuse our town, hearing that he would send for many more post horses." If their entreaty was supported by a shilling or two it also probably met with success.[56]

The dual nature of the constable's position made him well suited to such mediatory functions and enhanced the possibilities of achieving compromise out of the conflicting interests of the village and those of higher officials. As a local man with many ties to the villagers, who could call upon the personal obligations involved in these relationships, he was more likely than an outsider to be successful in gaining the acquiescence of the local community to the demands of the state. At the same time, as "village headman" chosen by and representing his fellow inhabitants, he was in a position to carry weight in expressing their demands to higher authorities. The use of an existing local official to interrelate local communities and the state thus had certain advantages. Despite the conflicts to which the constable's office was subject in the political context of sixteenth- and sev-

---

[53]Such burdens do seem to have been considered particularly onerous and to have occasioned considerable protest, partly because they offered ready opportunities for corrupt dealings; see, for example, P.R.O., SP 16/ 388/77; 395/9, 89; 399/51; 400/127 (postmasters) and SP 16/ 103/ 31; 192/ 89; 395/9 (salt petre men).

[54]Leics. R.O., DE 720/30, ff. 15v., 16, 31, 46, 50, 54.

[55]Leics. R.O., DE 625/60, ff. 23v., 45v., 48v., 61.

[56]Leics. R.O., DE 332/44/

enteenth-century England, such a position probably offered the most effective means available of linking villages to the national government.

The subordination of somewhat autonomous local communities to the rule of a central administration and a national code of law was no easy task in early modern Europe. In England, the weakness of the state during this period has sometimes been attributed in part to the lack of a paid bureaucracy in the provinces.[57] Attention has usually been focused on the county where administration rested largely on the shoulders of unpaid local gentlemen, the justices of the peace; and historians have pointed out the frequency with which these officials defended local interests in defiance of the commands being issued from Whitehall.[58] Although justices were local men, amateurs by modern standards of bureacratic government, and bound to other gentry of the shire by ties that probably often overrode their loyalty to the state, they were appointed, and could be removed, by the central government. They were formally responsible to the crown alone. At a lower level of government, the implementation of most of the crown's policies, whether the maintenance of law and order, the collection of its revenues, or the country's defense, was no less dependent on other unpaid local men, the yeomen, husbandmen, and craftsmen who served as constables. In the village, the government employed as its agents existing local officials and gave them new duties, and by the late sixteenth and early seventeenth centuries they were the state's "men of all work" in the local community much as were the justices in the county.[59] However, the constables were not only inhabitants of the villages in which they held office, and probably even more subject than the justices to local pressures deriving from bonds of kinship, friendship, and neighborliness, but they were also in most cases selected for office by their fellow villagers and formally responsible to them as well as to their administrative superiors. This was both the strength and the frailty of their position as agents of the central government. The dual nature of the office made it possible for them to link together otherwise distinct, and often incompatible, hierarchies of author-

---

[57]For example, Lawrence Stone, *The Causes of the English Revolution, 1529-1642* (London, 1972), pp. 63-64 for a recent statement; but also see H.G. Koenigsberger's comments in his review in *J. Mod. Hist.*, XLVI, (1974), pp. 104-105.

[58]See the county studies cited in n. 2, and in addition, Alan Everitt, *The Community of Kent and the Great Rebellion* (paper ed., Leicester, 1973); J.S. Morrill, *Cheshire, 1630-60* (Oxford, 1974); Peter Clark, *English Provincial Society from the Reformation to the Revolution* (Hassocks, Sussex, 1977).

[59]Although the parish officers (the churchwardens, the overseers of the poor, and the surveyors of the highways) were increasingly important within certain spheres of activity, the constable remained the chief local officer even during the early seventeenth century. Holdsworth, *History of English Law*, IV, pp. 123-25, recognizes the importance of the constable's position in interrelating local communities and the justices of the county, but both he and Cheyney, *History of England*, II, pp. 403-404 overestimate the extent to which the constable's function as representative of the village had declined by the end of the sixteenth century. The Webbs, *Local Government*, pp. 18-19 and n. 3, 30-21, 25-26 also overstate the importance of the parish officers, and especially the churchwardens, in relation to the constable.

ity and to achieve some measure of accommodation between them; but the "dual pulls of political representation"[60] to which they were subject also made the position a focus of conflict. As long as English local government remained largely "self-government at the king's command," however, it seems unlikely that other men would have achieved any greater success in linking the village and the state than did the relatively substantial villagers who usually filled the constableship.

SWEET BRIAR COLLEGE

Appendix: Bibliographical Note

This analysis of the constable's position, which is preliminary to a more detailed study of the office and its occupants, is based primarily on an examination of the constableship in nine villages: Salwarpe, Worchestershire; Pattingham, Staffordshire; Branston, Melton Mowbray, and Waltham-on-the-Wolds, Leicestershire; Bushey and Little Munden, Hertfordshire; and Gissing and Shelton, Norfolk. These villages have been selected largely because they are among the few for which relevant documents have survived for the period 1580-1642; but geographical diversity was considered to the extent that the sources permitted. Materials from these villages include constables' accounts and other papers such as precepts and receipts; churchwardens' accounts; local tax and rating lists; parish or town books, which often record the selection of local officials and summaries of their accounts; parish registers or bishop's transcripts of the registers; wills and inventories; manorial court rolls, particularly those of the leet. The materials are very uneven in quantity and quality from village to village, and in no case do all these sources survive for a single village. Information from these communities has been supplemented by a few materials from some other villages in the same counties, Stone, Worchestershire; Gayton and Hatherton, Staffordshire; Bunwell and Carleton Rode, Norfolk; Wimeswold, Leichestershire; and by constables' accounts only from several villages in other counties, West Monckton, Somerset; Millington, Yorks; Stockton, Shropshire; and Great Easton, Essex.

The Salwarpe and Stone materials are found in the Hereford and Worcester Record Office; those for Branston, Melton Mowbray, and Waltham-on-the Wolds in the Leicestershire Record Office, while the Wimeswold accounts are among the Additional MSS. in the British Library; those for Bushey and Little Munden in the Hertfordshire Record Office; those for Gayton and Hatherton in the Staffordshire Record Office, those for Gissing in the Norfolk and Norwich Record Office. The constables' accounts of Stockton are in the Salop Record Office and those of Great Easton in the

---

[60]Gluckman, *Custom and Conflict*, p. 52.

Essex Record Office, while those of Millington, Yorkshire, are in the Borthwick Institute, York. The parish book of Shelton, Norfolk, is in the parish church and a few constables' papers for Bunwell and Carleton Rode, Norfolk, are also found in the churches of those parishes. The constables' accounts of Pattingham, included in a volume with those of the churchwardens for the same period, are also found in the churches of those parishes. The constables' accounts of Pattingham, included in a volume with those of the churchwardens for the same period, are also in the parish church. The Pattingham court rolls are in the Staffordshire Record Office, which also possesses manuscripts of these rolls; in most cases the transcripts have been used rather than the original rolls because it was possible to have them copied. *The Pattingham Parish Register, 1559-1812* has been edited by H.R. Thomas for the Staffordshire Parish Registers Society (1934). A few surviving Pattingham wills are found in the Staffordshire Joint Record Office in Lichfield.

Other sources include State Papers; Acts of the Privy Council; Statutes of the Realm; lay subsidy rolls; Jacobean Star Chamber cases that involved constables; printed assize records; and Quarter Sessions records, particularly order books. Sessions records for Leicestershire are not extant for the late sixteenth and early seventeenth centuries, and those for Norfolk have not yet been examined; but those for three of the five major counties under consideration have been used, in printed catalogues, in transcripts or in manuscript:

Hertford: W.J. Hardy, ed., *Notes and Extracts from the Sessions Rolls, 1581 to 1689,* Hertford County Records, I, Hertford, 1905).

William Le Hardy, ed., *Calendar to the Sessions Books and Sessions Minute Books, 1619-57,* (Hertford County Records, V, Hertford, 1928). Herts. R.O., Quarter Sessions Books, 2A and 2B.

Staffordshire: S.A.H. Burne, ed., *The Staffordshire Quarter Sessions Roll for 1586,* (Staffordshire Historical Collections, 1927).

S.A.H. Burne, ed., *Staffordshire Quarter Sessions Rolls,* I-V, (1590-1606), (Staffordshire Historical Collections, 1929-40).

D.G.H. Salt, ed., *Staffordshire Quarter Sessions Rolls,* Easter 1608-Trinity 1609, (Staffordshire Historical Collections, 1948-49).

Staffs R.O., Quarter Sessions Order Books, II-V.

Staffs. R.O., Transcripts of Quarter Sessions Rolls, 7 Jac. I (Roll 16) to 9 Car. I (Roll 34).

Worchestershire: J. Willis Bund, ed., *Calendar of Quarter Sessions Papers, 1591-1643,* (Worchestershire Historical Society, 1900).

The following additional printed sessions records have been consulted:
Cheshire: J.H.E. Bennett and J.C. Dewhurst, eds., *Quarter Sessions Records, County Palatinate of Chester, 1559-1760* (Record Society of Lancashire and Cheshire, XCIV, 1940.

Lancashire: James Tait, ed., *Lancashire Quarter Sessions Records,* I (Chetham Society, LXXVII, 1917).

Nottinghamshire: H. Hampton Copnall, ed., *Notes and Extracts from the Nottinghamshire County Records of the Seventeenth Century* (Nottingham, 1915).

Somerset: E.H. Bates Harbin, ed., *Quarter Sessions Records for the County of Somerset,* I and II, (Somerset Record Society XXIII, XXIV. 1907-08).

Warwickshire: S.C. Ratcliffe and H C. Johnson, eds., *Quarter Sessions Order Books* (Warwick County Records, I and II, 1935-36).
S.C. Ratcliffe and H.C. Johnson, eds., *Quarter Sessions Indictment Book, Easter 1631 to Epiphany 1674,* (Warwick County Records, VI 1941).

Wiltshire: H.C. Johnson, ed., *Minutes and Proceedings in Sessions* (Wiltshire Archaeological and Natural History Society, Records Branch, IV, 1948).

B. Howard Cunnington, ed., *Records of the County of Wiltshire, being extracts from the Quarter Sessions Great Rolls of the Seventeenth Century* (Devizes, 1932).

Wiltshire Quarter Sessions Great Rolls, Historical Manuscripts Commissions, Various Collections, I, 65-176.

Yorkshire: J.C. Atkinson, ed., *Quarter Sessions Records* (The North Riding Record Society, I-IV, 1884-86.)

John Lister, ed., *West Riding Sessions Records,* I and II (The Yorkshire Archaeological Topographical Association, Record Series, II and LIV, 1888 and 1915).

[12]

Two concepts of order: justices, constables and jurymen in seventeenth-century England

Keith Wrightson, University of St Andrews

The Justices will set us by the heels
If we do not as we should,
Which if we perform, the townsmen will storm,
Some of them hang's if they could.

The song of James Gyffon, Constable of Albury (1626)[1]

At about midnight on the night of Saturday 14 August 1652, the watchmen of West Leigh, Lancashire, Robert Sweetlove, a twenty-three-year-old husbandman, and Humphrey Whittall, a thirty-five-year-old buttonmaker, were proceeding on their patrol when they heard 'a great noyse' and saw 'a great light' in the house of Nicholas Rannicar, alehousekeeper. They stopped, entered the house and there 'found William Corfe and Robert Bradshaw of Abraham, John Urmeston and Robert Rigbie of Hindley and John Hurst of West Leigh drinkeing healths singinge and swereinge in a most disorderly manner'. Advancing on this company of 'goodfellows', the watchmen 'urged them to depart and to forbeare these their disorderly courses', saying, 'Gentlemen ye know there is an Acte that none shall continue drinkings after Nyne of the Clock in the night and that no Alewife should fill any drinke after that hower.' To this Rigby and Bradshaw replied, 'Wee know there is such an Acte but weele not obey it, for weele drinke as long as wee please', subsequently threatening the watchmen 'that if they would not goe out of the house they would send them out, for they had nothing to doe with them'. The watchmen went their way.[2]

This unremarkable incident serves to introduce some of the themes which I wish to discuss briefly in this paper. For these exchanges reveal nicely a conflict between the concept of order of the governing magistracy of seventeenth-century England as embodied in legislation and the somewhat broader area of behaviour permitted to themselves by a group of villagers. Ensnared at the point where

22   *Two concepts of order*

national legislative prescription and local customary norms inter-
sected were the wretched village officers, the much tried, sorely abused,
essential work-horses of seventeenth-century local administration.

No student of the period is likely to underestimate the ubiquity
and the emotional force of the concept of order in the England of the
Tudors and early Stuarts. Contemporary moralists, administrators
and legislators persistently employed the word in their discussions of
political, social and economic relationships. Humbler and less articulate Englishmen used it no less in their denunciations of inebriate
and foul-mouthed neighbours than did their betters in their sublime
articulations of the structure of the universe. The concept of order
was ubiquitous, but this is not to say that it was monolithic. For the
notion of order embodied in the stacks of regulative statutes passed
by Tudor and early Stuart parliaments should not be identified too
readily with that implicit in the norms and attitudes which governed
social behaviour in the village community. While both had their
origin in a shared concern with the maintenance of social harmony,
order might have markedly different implications in different situations. In particular, the very process of definition and statutory regulation which was involved in the legislative initiative might ultimately
threaten to create new problems of order and obedience at the point
at which precise national legislation came into contact with less
defined local custom.

This simple fact has perhaps been obscured by the tendency among
historians to conduct discussions of the problem of order primarily
at the elevated level of official ideology. The 'order' discussed is that
of conventional moralists and political thinkers, of the preachers of
assize sermons and the writers of preambles to statutes. It is the order
of the 'Homily on Obedience' and of Wentworth's speech to the
Council of the North. This was order as a coherent structure of social
relationships and moral values, as an aspiration towards a condition
of universal harmony which was, as Christopher Hudson preached
to the magistrates of Lancashire in 1632, a glorification of God, the
orderer of all things.[3] Order thus conceived was at once an ideal
arrangement of human institutions, a pattern of authority and an
ultimate scheme of values. It projected a stable and harmonious ideal
of human affairs which eliminated the possibility of rebellion, of
social conflict, of the sins which might stimulate a stern deity to
chastise his disordered people with his judgements of dearth, pesti-
lence and war.

This concept of order as a positive ideal to be achieved and defended was repeatedly elaborated by statesmen and moralists endeavouring to contain the perplexing problems of a fluid social reality within the framework of a uniform and enduring structure of traditional values and social relationships. John Downame, the Jacobean divine, urged his readers to make the establishment of a righteous order

the principal scope of all their actions, using all good means whereby it may be furthered and advanced. As Princes and Magistrates by enacting good lawes and seeing them duely executed. . . . Ministers by leading those which are committed unto their charge in the waies of truth and godlinesse. . . . Finally the people, by yeelding their cheerfull obedience to the godly lawes of Governors and by embracing the sound and profitable doctrine and imitating the Christian and religious examples of their godly teachers.[4]

Arthur Dent, one of the most popular moralists of the early seventeenth century, argued that in a properly ordered Christian commonwealth,

doubtlesse, doubtlesse we should live and see good dayes: all future dangers should be prevented, our peace prolonged, our state established, our king preserved and the Gospel continued. Then should we still enjoy our lives, our goods, our landes, our livinges . . . Yea . . . we should eat the good things of the land, spending our days in much comfort, peace and tranquility and leave great blessings unto our children and posterity from age to age, from generation to generation.[5]

Downame and Dent, of course, were both Puritans. As such they were more acutely aware of England's disorders than many of their contemporaries, more intoxicated with the poetry of the Bible in their projection of the imagined future. Yet only their enthusiasm and the consistency of their idealism distinguished their statements from those of England's secular and ecclesiastical governors. The ideal of order was more prosaically but no less firmly embodied in the regulative penal legislation to which the parliaments of the time devoted so much energy. On the one hand were the Acts which defined, codified, elaborated and generalized existing good practice in the ordering of social and economic life. On the other was the series of enactments pushed through by such moral entrepreneurs as the Puritan gentry to regulate the 'common country disorders' of drunkenness, profanity, sabbath-breaking and the like; legislative support was obtained by an appeal to the generalized concept of order.[6]

Some way removed from the notion of order espoused by moralists and legislators, the order of the study and of the debating chamber,

24   *Two concepts of order*

lay the complex of attitudes which surrounded the maintenance of harmony not so much between God and man, or even prince and people, as between neighbours in the face-to-face and day-to-day relationships of the village community. Order, as it was conceived of at this most intimate local level, was less a positive aspiration towards a national condition of disciplined social harmony than a negative absence of disruptive conflict locally. One would not wish to sentimentalize the social relationships of a seventeenth-century village into a picture of neighbourly solidarity and harmony. Villages were riddled with petty conflicts and rivalries of interest. But for this very reason order at this level was characterized by an impulse to avoid, or at any rate contain, such conflict, while at the same time allowing a considerably larger area of ambivalent permitted behaviour than was compatible with the nice definitions of moralists and legislators. 'Order' meant little more than conformity to a fairly malleable local custom which was considerably more flexible than statute law. The maintenance of order meant less the enforcement of impersonal regulations than the restraint of conflict among known individuals in a specific local context. It concentrated above all on the dual task of resolving the more poisonous kinds of dissension, while at the same time avoiding if possible the nuisances and expenses which might endanger the precarious livelihood and marginal surplus of a predominantly peasant population.

Thus the inhabitants of a village might take action, formally or informally, against such a 'daily practiser of mischief' as Robert Wilson of Ashwell in Hertfordshire. His neighbours reported him to the justices as one who pilfered their wood and corn, sowed discord among them by his 'perverse humour and bould speech' and was 'ready to lay hould upon any occasion to enter into tumult'. They might draw up an 'order' for their township, as did the inhabitants of Aughton, Lancashire, in 1630, to avoid the expense of bastard children or of squatters who might inflate the poor rates, and to stipulate the contributions for highway repair and poor relief.[7] They might even welcome a new statute which allowed them to proceed firmly against squatters or vagrants. They were less likely to embrace the full panoply of the penal laws. For a vigorous application of the laws could excite conflict within the local community.

Time after time in the later sixteenth and earlier seventeenth centuries the statutory proscription of established local customs resulted in popular reluctance either to accept the law's definition of an offence, or to enforce it where it ran counter to local needs. The

Edwardian Act for the licensing of alehouses, for example, attempted, in the interests of preventing 'hurts and trobles . . . abuses and disorders', to restrict participation in a trade which had been a customary by-employment of the poor since at least the thirteenth century. Enforcement of the Elizabethan Statute of Artificers might threaten, in some localities, to interfere with the unapprenticed participation in trades and manufactures which was of considerable local economic importance.[8] In the case of laws intended to regulate personal conduct, the common people might enjoy a radically different perception of the value of the behaviour proscribed. 'Unlawful gaming' and 'inordinate tippling' in a 'disorderly alehouse' in the eyes of the law might be 'good fellowship and a good means to increase a love amongst neighbours' in the eyes of villagers. Indeed, one moralist of the time actually complained that linguistic conventions among country people restrained their perception of the disorderly nature of many aspects of their behaviour. A man who supported his word with profane oaths (an offence legislated against in 1623 and 1650), might be regarded locally as 'of stout courage'. A frequenter of 'disordered and unlawfull exercises and pastimes' on the sabbath (legislated against in 1625, 1644, 1650 and 1657) might be 'a fine proper and a nimble man' to admiring locals. Pre-marital sexual lapses which did not result in bastard births were 'the tricke of youth'. A man prepared to stand and fight if need be was 'a tall man'.[9] Above all, the tension between the order of the law and that of the neighbourhood was a question of scale. For the very complexity of relationships within small communities made it exceedingly difficult to judge the behaviour of an individual without bringing into play a host of personal considerations. If a widow eked out a living by selling ale unlicensed, why should the neighbourhood be troubled with a prosecution which might foment local resentment? The order of the village community could survive occasional drunkenness, erratic church attendance, profane language, neglect of the licensing and apprenticeship laws. It was more likely to be disturbed by the enforcement of the host of penal laws which might excite new conflicts and drain, in fines, its resources. What really mattered was the maintenance of specific, local, personal relationships, not conformity to impersonal law.

In this situation the vital area became that of enforcement, for the degree of law enforcement was the factor which could determine whether central regulation and local customary practice were to enjoy a precarious co-existence or to come into disruptive conflict.

26 *Two concepts of order*

Mediating between the national legislative ideal and ambivalent local realities was the whole apparatus of Tudor and Stuart local government. Upon its officers was devolved the essential task of balancing out the needs and requirements of both provincial society and the royal government. In the case of secular administration, this problem was solved by the justices of the peace, who adopted what has been called a 'doubly passive' stance.[10] On the one hand they seem rarely to have acted vigorously to enforce penal legislation except when stimulated by direct and unambiguous commands from the Privy Council, by crisis conditions, or by both, as for example in their energetic enforcement of famine regulations in 1622 and 1630–1. On the other hand, their characteristic form of procedure was to require the high constables of the hundreds, into which each county was divided, to order the petty constables and presentment jurymen of the townships and villages to make their 'presentments' of local offenders. The 'stacks of statutes' laid upon the shoulders of the justices of the peace were more lightly borne by passing on both the final responsibility for their enforcement, and the strains which that enforcement entailed, to these humbler local officers. Who were they?

All that can be said of the petty constables and hundredal jurymen of England as a body is that they were ordinary members of their communities, subject to the prejudices, the strengths and weaknesses of their society. Officially, petty constables were elected for the year by the courts leet of their manors and often this practice continued. Elsewhere the leet might merely confirm the nomination of the parish vestry, or the office might pass round the villagers in rotation by 'the ancient custom of Houserow'. The parish representatives who sat on the presentment juries of the hundreds of a county were selected by undersheriffs before each meeting of quarter sessions and were later sworn in at sessions, before making their presentment of offenders from their district.[11] None of these systems of appointment could be guaranteed to supply the 'honest and substantiall', 'fitt and serviceable', men repeatedly demanded by the Privy Council and local justices to fill these vitally important offices. Indeed, in the case of that of petty constable, villagers were notoriously reluctant to accept the onerous responsibility of office if they could avoid it. Not infrequently this job was pushed on to a poor man or given to a paid substitute by the person elected, if he had the means. The township of Goldhanger, Essex, for example, elected in 1626 one Henry Motte, 'a poore man . . . haveing no estate to live by but only his day labour'. Aspull, Lancashire, chose in 1638 one Thomas Tinckler who had 'little over two acres of ground' and was indebted, having 'a verye small personall estate whereupon to subsist'. When he appealed to the justices and was excused service, his neighbours took their revenge by prosecuting him for taking in an aged widow as a lodger! What could happen is further illustrated by the case in Little Hulme, Lancashire, in 1651 when John Mosse, Christopher Walton and Humphrey Bradshaw were charged with finding a constable in respect of the subdivided holding which they shared. Mosse and Walton held nine acres each, Bradshaw only half an acre. Predictably, the two larger men were able to use their influence to get Bradshaw chosen and an appeal to the justices was necessary before they even consented to share his expenses in office.[12]

How typical such examples were is difficult to assess. We know of these cases only because of successful appeals to the justices of the peace. Probably they were common enough, but it would be unwise to make too sweeping a dismissal of the petty constables as shanghaied village paupers. At least a quarter of the constables of Elizabethan Essex surveyed by Professor Samaha were men of 'considerable substance' and yeomen served commonly enough elsewhere. In the case of presentment jurymen the picture is much clearer. This office carried some prestige and the jurymen's ranks were filled up by village notables, men of yeoman status predominating.[13]

The constant fretting of the authorities about the social standing of local officers derived largely from their association of ignorance and negligence with low social position. Michael Dalton summed up the situation with his opinion that 'constables chosen out of the meaner sort are either ignorant what to do; or dare not do as they should; and are not able to spare the time to execute this office'. All this was fair enough in itself. Illiteracy and ignorance of the law undoubtedly struck against the efficiency desired by the authorities. The justices of Hertfordshire complained in 1657 of the unfitness for their duties of illiterate constables and there are examples enough of the inability of such men to read the warrants and precepts sent down to them. One Wiltshire constable in 1616 had to walk two miles every time he received written instructions in order to have them read to him. One Worcestershire man was sufficiently baffled and impressed by 'a leaf of paper written folded up', handed to him by a servant girl who had 'a purpose to be merry' at his expense, that he thought the hue and cry was raised. As regards legal expertise, even the justices of the period had increasingly to rely on frequently updated textbooks of their duties in order to keep abreast of the law. Few villagers can be

28 *Two concepts of order*

expected to have possessed Lambarde's *The duties of constables* or Dalton's *The Country Justice*. The law was a maze to the unwary officer. As Major-General Worsley was to complain in 1655, many constables were 'doubtful of what power they have', for the simple reason that 'the law is very dark'.[14]

Both the illiteracy and legal ignorance of local officers, of course, varied widely. In the Protestation Oath returns of 1642, only 7 per cent of the constables of Somerset were illiterate, a level almost matched by the constables of Dorset. Illiteracy among the constables of Nottinghamshire, Sussex, Warwickshire and Buckinghamshire ran between 50 and 53 per cent, while Cheshire and Westmorland constables had the dubious distinction of being 100 per cent illiterate. In a society in which adult male illiteracy was heavily concentrated in the lower reaches of the social hierarchy, the relative performance of constables doubtless depended on the degree to which they were selected from literate village notables or from the population as a whole. Presentment jurymen, as might be expected given their social composition, did rather well. Of the forty-four jurors from Terling, Essex, who signed or marked their presentments between 1612 and 1687, for example, only six could not sign their names.[15] Knowledge of the law, on the other hand, probably greatly depended on the extent to which justices of the peace informed local men of their duties by either putting detailed 'charges' to them at sessions, or issuing to them 'articles' as guides for presentment. Where this was done, regular service could familiarize constables and jurymen with at least those statutes which the local bench regarded as most significant. Among jurymen or constables selected from a small pool of parish notables such regular service was not uncommon. Where the office of constable passed round a village in rotation it was correspondingly rare.[16]

The qualifications of local men for their key role in the policing of the countryside thus varied. From time to time very able and conscientious men were thrown up. The constable of Hampton Lovell, Worcestershire, in 1634 must have paid close attention to the 'charge', for example. He referred specifically to several Acts of Parliament in making his presentment. Again, the jurymen of West Mersea, Essex, were sufficiently conscious of their duties to upbraid the justices for negligent law enforcement, complaining that this 'doth discorige us to make presentment'.[17] At the other extreme, however, were those petty constables who surpassed in their disorders the very miscreants whom they were charged to keep in order. The substitutes hired to serve as constables in one Lancashire village in 1632 were so drunken that they had to be clapped in the stocks themselves. The constable of Chelmsford in 1628 'withdrewe his watchmen to drinkeinge' and then led them in an affray with the watchmen of neighbouring Moulsham. Some officers might abuse their public office by maliciously prosecuting private enemies or rivals or by otherwise turning their brief authority to private advantage. The constable of one Essex village, for example, took advantage of his period of office in 1625 to run a disorderly alehouse. There he entertained the men of nearby townships day and night, innocently informing the constables of their home parishes that he had impressed them for the king's service![18]

Such examples of negligent, drunken and disorderly constables are easy enough to find in sessions files. They can be introduced as evidence of the unsteady legs upon which magisterial authority too often swayed. But they are scarcely typical of the norm. The majority of constables were no worse, and the majority of jurymen probably somewhat better, than their peers in these respects. Both, however, were placed in the intolerable position of having to enforce against their neighbours penal legislation which must frequently have seemed excessively severe, save in the most extreme cases. As a result, they risked not only the loss of time and money in pursuing prosecutions, but also the likelihood of arousing the antipathy of the neighbourhood, accusations of officiousness and malice and even physical danger. The efficient constable or juryman in the eyes of the law would be very likely to turn every tongue, if not every hand, against himself. The villages of the period contained sufficient elements of conflict to ensure that a high premium was placed by the local community upon the maintenance of harmony. Yet a diligent local officer threatened to provoke conflict and drag it out of the neighbourhood to the judicial bench, thus triggering a chain reaction of enmity which might be stabilized only with difficulty.

Thus one finds a reluctance of village officers to present to the justices offenders other than those who had scandalized, threatened or alienated the greater part of the community; who had stepped outside the moral community as it were. The constables of Tarleton, Lancashire, were not unusual in presenting with alacrity two girls who had had bastard children which were unfiliated 'and thereby likely to be chargeable to this parish'. The parish officers of North Mynes, Hertfordshire, lost patience with the persistent drunkard and 'abuser of his neighbours', Harrington Bickley, who had called two good women whores and a village patriarch an 'ould fatbacked

30 *Two concepts of order*

rogue'. The inhabitants of Waltham Cross presented 'our neighbour' John Bowden, who persistently harboured vagrants in his disorderly alehouse 'to the great disquiet of his neighbours so that unlesse hee bee . . . dealt with according to lawe and justice there will bee noe living by him'.[19] The occasional swearer, tippler, unapprenticed artisan or unlicensed aleseller, however, was fairly safe unless a local informer or zealous minister took a hand in securing prosecution.

Formal prosecution in the courts was by no means the only, or even the preferred, method of settling such conflicts as arose within villages. This is not simply to say that many petty offences were tolerated (which they were), but that a preference existed for less formal sanctions which might be kept under the control of the community. Thus the villagers of Myddle in Shropshire preferred the cudgelling of a petty thief to his indictment. One Worcestershire man requested the justices that a thief be simply bound to her good behaviour (a condition which would be judged satisfied or otherwise by local opinion), since 'he would not charge her with felony being so small a matter'. Wherever possible mediation was preferred, though it was not always successful. When Adam Martindale fell out with one of his Cheshire parishioners, 'some interposed for peace between us, but to no purpose'. The result was an affray in which Martindale was badly beaten up, but he still refused to take the matter to court, since he 'took all such courses for pure revenge and would make no use of them'.[20]

This attitude towards the law could be so extended that village officers who presented cases to the courts might find the informal sanctions of village opinion turned against themselves. When the constables of Moulsham, Essex, presented Peter Decort for allowing gaming in his alehouse, they were accused of being 'too busie' and of making the presentment through 'spit[e] or malis'. A rumour was spread that they 'desired an offis' and they were mocked at as 'our worships'. When the constable of Bury found a group of men drinking illegally one night in 1649 and asked whether they knew 'what the lawes were', one showed his dislike of the law by replying that 'he now knew not, they were new modelised and Cromwellysed'. For this shaft of wit he found himself in court, but even there continued to belittle the constable by approaching him 'in a feareinge manner askinge howe his worship did' and 'calling him knave in open court'. The presentment officers of another Lancashire village who put forward the names of several local recusants were generally maligned as being too 'presyce'.[21]

Gossip and ridicule were a hazard of office. There were others, less subtle. When the constable of one Worcestershire township rushed into a drunkard's house to keep the peace he had the clothes torn off his back for his pains. Another who tried to break up traditional May Games was knocked over by the revellers, who then threatened to break his neck. A Lancashire constable who entered an alehouse to clear it of Welsh vagrants left hurriedly after being attacked with a chopping knife. Some village officers might even find themselves called into court by cunning adversaries and accused of malicious prosecutions, libel, or illegal entry.[22]

Not surprisingly, these circumstances could make village officers extremely wary about presenting those misdemeanours with which they came into contact and complaints of constabular negligence, in particular, were a commonplace of the period. This reluctance to prosecute, however, cannot be adequately explained simply in terms of the personal inadequacy, parsimoniousness, or liability to intimidation of village officers. There is a more positive logic in the studied negligence of some officers, which derived ultimately from the strains of their mediating position between their communities and the law. Robert Fazakerley of West Derby, Lancashire, when charged with the serving of warrants upon several neighbours conscientiously attempted to do so, but only after first advertising the fact in the hope that they would keep out of his way. Another northern officer allowed persons placed in the stocks to escape while he absented himself 'to fetch a locke to sett upon the same stocks'. The constable of Braintree, Essex, performed his duty, while at the same time preserving good relationships, when he removed a drunk from an alehouse, but 'would not give his consent to have him punished according to the lawe but let him gooe paieinge 1s when he should have paid 5s'. Richard Kay of Middleton, Lancashire, neglected to serve a warrant on a man in a bastardy case – one, significantly, in which the pregnant girl was from another parish – 'in regard of their nere neighbourhood and other allyance'.[23]

These and other cases highlight the conflict raised in the mind of the man who was both neighbour and officer of the law. When John King, an Essex villager, stole eight hens in 1636 he was rapidly taken by the constable Thomas Burrowes, but then 'did falle downe on his knees . . . and did desire him that he would not be the meanes to cast him away for a few hennes, for it was the first offence that ever he had donne'. Burrowes, taking it upon himself to act as mediator, talked the matter over with the victim of the theft and having decided that

32   *Two concepts of order*

it was the lesser of two evils, released the thief. The constables of
Hatfield Peverel refused to execute orders to whip an unlicensed aleseller too poor to pay his fine, while those of Wethersfield would not
serve process on illegal cottagers 'because they are poor'. Some even
tried to plead the case of offenders while at the same time presenting
them. The juryman who presented Widow Reynolds of Birchanger for
unlicensed aleselling included the excuse that she was 'a very poore
woman and takes almes'. Similarly, the presentment of Josias Barritt
of Prittlewell, who had neglected to perform his work on the highways, explained: 'but he is a verie poore man and hath foure small
children'. In an extraordinarily tortured presentment, the constable
of Worsley, Lancashire in 1651 informed the justices, who were conducting a rigorous purge of alehouses, that

We have one in our township by name Jony Horridge who breweth and
selleth alehouse continually without licens and therefore I could not omit
to present her as a misdoer and likewise Richard Princeton who brewes at
some times when god makes him able; who though he be a poore man I
could not omit to expres him a misdoer And also John Man who brewes
ale some times.

This valiant attempt to distinguish degrees of culpability failed to
pass the clerk of the peace. He, in an action which admirably sym-
bolizes the distinction between the order of the law and that of the
community, struck through the excusing clauses and neatly substituted the simple legal formula of an indictment for unlicensed aleselling.[24]

These various factors could combine to produce a situation in
which, as James I's Privy Council complained to the justices of
Essex, the public service might be 'carried soe confusedly or executed
soe remisslie as the vulgar sort of people will in tyme gett a custome
of disobedience'.[25] A situation might develop in which the local
courts contributed little more to the enforcement of the law than the
provision of machinery for prosecutions initiated by private persons
or common informers. Indeed, this was very probably the norm in
many English counties prior to the tightening up of local government, which was so marked a feature of the late sixteenth and early
seventeenth centuries. By the beginning of the reign of Charles I in
1625 it persisted in some counties. In others, the justices of the peace
had succeeded in establishing at least an acceptable level of regulative
control. The situation obtaining as the 'increase of governance'
peaked in the years after 1625 can best be illustrated by comparing

the experience of two very different areas: Essex and south Lancashire.

In the early and central decades of the seventeenth century, Essex and south Lancashire might appear to have had little enough in common. Essex was a fertile lowland county, one of the principal grain-producing counties of England. Moreover, it was a home county, deeply influenced in its economy, its religious life and its administration by its proximity to the markets and radical pulpits of London and the seat of government in Westminster. Essex was comparatively wealthy, closely governed and solidly Protestant. South Lancashire, in contrast, was comparatively poor. Economically, the area embraced not only the lowland triangle between Preston, Warrington and Manchester, but also the pastoral economies of the extensive coastal marshlands and of the hill country of the east. Lancashire lay far from the hub of secular and ecclesiastical government, was comparatively laxly administered and was notorious (save for the Puritan cloth towns around Manchester) for its religious conservatism.

This baldly stated contrast, while it was as much a commonplace among contemporaries as it has become among historians, might on further reflection be considered more apparent than real. Within each county there were local variations in economy and social structure, which, together with local differentials in administrative effectiveness and in religious complexion, went far to modify their stereotyped images. Essex had its dark corners. Lancashire had its radical oases. Moreover, while the localism of English society in the seventeenth century was considerable, we must also remember that there were strong elements of social and cultural homogeneity by comparison with the more diverse societies of the great continental kingdoms. Again, within our period there were strongly integrative forces at work within the relatively small compass of the kingdom. Not least among these was the influence of the increasingly aggressive central government, expressed above all through the activities of the justices of the peace. By comparing the experience of south Lancashire and Essex in this respect we can detect both the local variations which existed within the overall national chronology of administrative change and the extent to which similar processes of change were active within the nation at large. How far, then, did the two areas differ in the nature and volume of the business handled by their governors in their courts of quarter sessions?

34 *Two concepts of order*

The short answer would be that they differed to a significant degree, but that these differences were diminishing steadily over time.

Let us look first at the volume of prosecutions handled by the justices of the peace. In seven sample years of court business between 1626 and 1639, the justices of Essex handled an average of some fifty-one cases per 10,000 population per year. The comparable rate for the seven years, 1626–38, in south Lancashire was thirty-three. In seven sample years for the period 1646 to 1658, however, the rate of prosecutions handled in Essex fell to thirty-three, while in south Lancashire it rose to sixty-two. In three final sample years, 1662–6, the Essex rate remained stable at thirty-three, while that of south Lancashire returned to its pre-civil war level at thirty-four per 10,000 population per annum. The courts of Essex were declining from a peak of activity in the reign of Charles I, while those of south Lancashire witnessed an interregnum boom in court business which was not sustained thereafter.[26]

The reasons for these changes and fluctuations become apparent only when we examine the actual composition of the cases handled by the justices. Tables 1 and 2 in the appendix (pages 300–3) give detailed breakdowns of court business in both counties. Their message is quite clear. From 1626 to 1640 the sessions of south Lancashire dealt primarily with cases which I have categorized as 'interpersonal disputes'. These cases of theft, assault, trespass, disseisin (dispossession) and poaching represent disputes within particular localities which had resulted in private prosecutions before the justices. In addition, the justices handled a smaller number of cases categorized as 'obligation enforcement'. These cases involved the prosecution of individuals, or even whole communities, for neglect or abuse of local office and failure to perform their obligations in the maintenance of roads and bridges. They were usually initiated by the justices themselves, by the grand jury, or by surveyors of the highways. Finally, came a trickle of cases classed as 'regulative prosecutions'. This category represents the regulative jurisdiction of the justices of the peace, the sphere of the penal statutes and of public presentment by constables and jurymen. In south Lancashire prior to 1640 it was distinguished by its emptiness. From 1646, however, this pattern changed. From that year through to the early 1650s the justices dealt with massive numbers of regulative prosecutions. Thereafter cases of this nature continued to form the principal element in court business.

In Essex, by way of contrast, substantial numbers of regulative prosecutions initiated by constables and jurymen always made up the most significant element of court business, prosecution of this kind reaching a peak in 1630/31. Close behind came prosecutions relating to obligation enforcement, while cases originating in interpersonal disputes came a poor third. In the sphere of regulative prosecution the courts of Essex performed much more consistently than did those of south Lancashire. Unlicensed and disorderly alehousekeepers and persons neglecting church attendance were much more regularly presented in Essex, these offences alone going far to account for the predominance of regulative business. In addition a number of other offences – the illegal erection of cottages, swearing, drunkenness and breaches of the Statute of Artificers relating to servants and apprentices – were more commonly dealt with in the southern county. In Lancashire the swing towards regulative activity after 1646 can be accounted for largely by a novel concern with such offences and with the activities of unlicensed dealers in the victuals trade.

One might infer from these findings that the courts of south Lancashire prior to 1646 functioned primarily as passive instruments for the settlement of disputes arising in local communities and brought privately to the justices for adjudication. From 1646 their character had changed. They developed new teeth as courts of aggressive regulation. The sessions of Essex, however, functioned throughout the period as a court of regulation and obligation enforcement. The character of the court remained unchanged over time, though the volume of its regulative activity could intensify in certain years.

We have, then, two points of contrast in the enforcement of Tudor and Stuart regulative statutes by these crucial local courts. The one contrast is regional, between Essex and Lancashire; the other, chronological, between periods of normal, or even lax, prosecution and periods of intense activity. Both of these matters turned upon the vital issue of how business was brought to court and most particularly upon the steps taken to secure the co-operation of village officers.

Regionally, one finds that the quarter sessions rolls of Essex contain five distinct types of document relating to the initiation of prosecutions. These include on the one hand the individual indictments initiated by private members of the community and on the other hand public presentments by a grand jury of minor gentry, by surveyors of the highways, by petty constables and by hundredal presentment juries. Individual presentments by petty constables were rare save in certain years. Regulative prosecutions were usually initiated by hundredal jurymen replying to charges or articles put to them directly

36   *Two concepts of order*

by the high constables of the hundreds. The sessions of Essex thus employed a procedure by which the presentment of minor offences at a local level was institutionalized, built into the normal functioning of the court. This in itself goes some way towards explaining the high level of regulative prosecution in Essex even in normal years.

In Lancashire, for reasons of geography, four distinct courts of quarter sessions were in operation. The justices of the different hundreds of the county met, every quarter, at Lancaster, Preston, Manchester and alternately Ormskirk or Wigan. The grand juries of these distinct courts were in themselves hundredal juries. These Lancashire hundredal juries, however, consisted, like the Essex grand jury, of minor gentlemen rather than villagers. Distanced as they were from village life, they confined their activities largely to the vetting of indictments initiated by private persons. Presentments by petty constables or other village officers were rarely requested and rarely brought before them. This peculiarity of procedure largely accounts for the predominance of interpersonal disputes and the low level of regulative business in Lancashire courts prior to 1646.

The institution of hundredal juries composed of village notables could thus go far to improve regulative efficiency. Nevertheless, the actual performance of such juries depended a great deal upon both their composition from session to session and the rigour with which they were examined by the high constables. On occasion, for example, juries explained that they could not report on particular parishes 'by reason there is none of the jury'.[27] Alternatively, jurors could be singularly unwilling to present offenders. When the high constable of Barstable hundred, Essex, took the presentments of the representatives of thirty-four parishes in 1573, he learned only that a few archery butts, a ducking stool and a bridge needed repairing and that five singlemen were living out of service. For the rest the jury chorused, 'all well'.[28] Such replies were common enough in Essex before 1600. The chronology of change can be illustrated from the presentments of the half-hundred of Witham and the various hundreds associated with it on presentment juries. Before 1590, the jurors presented only occasional decayed roads and bridges and very occasional neglectors of church attendance. From the early 1590s, however, they were more closely questioned, one presentment of 1592, for example, being prefaced,

As touching the rules given us in charge this day we have duly made enquiry of them and either of them and have not anything at this present worthy of reformation.

This initial unwillingness persisted through the 1590s, but from 1602 the juries began to expand the scope of their presentments. They soon evolved the pattern of prosecution of alehouse offences, non-attendance at church and other misdemeanours which became such a pronounced feature of Essex sessions business by 1625.[29] The motivation of this more co-operative spirit is an issue to which we will return.

Efficient presentment juries could thus go some way towards the establishment of regulative rigour, though the marginal nature of the persons commonly presented – occasional alehouse offenders, persistent neglectors of church, unwelcome inmates and cottagers – suggests that presentments could be so contrived as to cut only selectively into local life. This point may be reinforced when we consider the activities of petty constables in presenting cases to the petty sessions or 'monthly meetings' of justices which, after earlier attempts, were regularly established in the years after 1631. These sessions were intended to bring a closer control over the parishes. Petty constables were required to appear at them and were fined for neglect of their duties. It was an uphill struggle for the justices. In the Bolton and Deane division of Lancashire in 1634 negligent constables in fact formed the main group of offenders punished. By 1637/38, however, the constables had been disciplined into reporting on vagrancy and disorderly alehouses. Examination of the actual business dealt with in other divisions of Lancashire and of Essex in the 1630s, reveals how eager the constables became to report on the repression of vagrants, how relatively unwilling they remained to present other types of offender among their neighbours. Little enthusiasm was to be found for the presentment of the moral offences which preoccupied the justices who presided over the petty sessions of the 1640s and 1650s (see Tables 3–7, pages 304–6).

Whatever the achievements of the justices with presentment juries and petty sessions and whatever the personal activity of unusually severe individual justices out of court, real regulative efficiency of the type which produced massive crops of offenders in Essex in 1629–31 and in Lancashire from 1646 required something more. It required, above all, steps to overcome the unwillingness and inefficiency of petty constables by more closely regulating their appointment and by prosecuting their neglect, while at the same time instituting a more systematic presentment of offenders. In Essex at the time of the dearth crisis and disorders of 1629–31 and in Lancashire under the rule of Puritan justices struggling against both economic crisis and ungodliness after 1646, this is exactly what the justices did. Orders

38   *Two concepts of order*

flowed out for the appointment of 'sufficient', and the replacement of
'insufficient' or incompetent, constables. Negligent local officers were
hauled before the justices, punished and dismissed. The slack in the
whole apparatus of social regulation was vigorously drawn in. Years
of peculiar concern with and harassment of the village officers
corresponded exactly with those of towering peaks of regulative
prosecutions (see Table 8, page 307).

Nor was this all. Attempting to make sure that fit constables were
appointed and negligent men prosecuted was less than half the battle
for the enforcement of the justices' conception of order. Action was
also needed, as a petition of Lancashire Puritans in 1647 pointed out,
'to cause the Constables to execute their office'.[30] This end was
achieved by the novel insistence that the petty constables of individual
parishes and townships return not simply their occasional verbal or
written presentments, but also written replies to specifically enumer-
ated articles of inquiry. Precepts listing the articles were sent out to
the high constables of the hundreds and communicated by them to
the petty constables. They in turn were obliged to bring in their
detailed replies, commonly repeating in these the date of the original
order of quarter sessions and following the form of the precepts issued
to them in making their presentments.

Articles of inquiry were in themselves no novelty. They had been
issued by central governments since at least the 1590s as guides to the
justices of the peace.[31] But the enforcement of written answers to such
articles by village officers was something new in both Essex and
Lancashire in the years concerned. Where it was enforced the results
were spectacular. The transformation of the structure of sessions
business in south Lancashire, for example, was wholly the result of a
series of regulative initiatives of this kind. In 1646 and 1647 the drive
was against alehouse offences; in 1648 against the alehouses, failure
to attend church, and marketing offences. Later years saw attacks on
such offences repeated, while the articles were expanded to include
other misdemeanours – taking in inmates or lodgers, for example. In
almost every year of the interregnum the constables were sent scurry-
ing about their duties and still the justices were unsatisfied. In 1659
they announced at Manchester a new programme. Fearing 'the
encouragement of offenders . . . for want of puting in execucon those
good penall Lawes made against them', they ordered the constables
to draw up indictments and presentments at their townships' expense
against 'all offenders comittinge any misdemeanours . . . and prosecute the same and see the said parties brought to condigne punish-

ment'.[32] The justices wanted order, whatever the cost. Fortunately for the constables the restoration intervened before this new policy bore fruit. Though the justices of the early years of Charles II's reign made some efforts to control the victuals trade, intense constabular activity of the type maintained during the interregnum was not renewed.

In the case of Essex, the peak of regulative activity in 1630/31 was the result of an exactly comparable policy of requiring petty constables to produce their written returns to articles of inquiry. Essex was to see later inquiries into popish recusancy in 1641 and the numbers of alehouses in 1644, but activity on the scale of 1630/31 would appear to have been unique.[33]

The key to effective social regulation in this period was thus the securing of efficient presentment of offenders to the local courts of provincial England. Prosecution of this kind, however, placed the presenting officers, the jurymen and petty constables, in a position of considerable difficulty. Fortunately for them, vigorous action was rarely required of them, though they were put under a mounting pressure throughout the early seventeenth century. Again, on occasion, the reserves of energy which lay dormant in the apparatus of social regulation could be drawn upon to intensify the control exercised by the magistrates over the local communities within their jurisdictions. Such regulative initiatives, however, required an enormous and exhausting effort and placed a considerable strain upon the machinery of local administration. As a result they were rarely undertaken, save in conditions of acute economic crisis or when magistrates were motivated by a peculiar zeal for social discipline and godly reformation.

In Lancashire only such major drives initiated from above could achieve the order desired by the justices of the peace. Where they were less zealous and relaxed their hands, little business came up to them freely from below. In Essex, however, the situation was somewhat different, for the gentler pressure placed on the presentment jurymen produced in the earlier seventeenth century a limited willingness to co-operate more regularly with the magistrates. This co-operation was selective in two senses; it involved only certain parishes and only certain offences. Taking the example of prosecutions for unlicensed aleselling (something of a litmus test in these matters), we find that in the years between 1616 and the great purges of 1630/31, fewer than sixty out of over 400 parishes and hamlets in Essex freely presented offenders on three or more occasions. Again, the offences which Essex jurymen prosecuted with any regularity were highly

40   *Two concepts of order*

selective – alehouse offences, failure to attend church, cottaging, taking in unwanted inmates. If we are to understand why some parishes chose to co-operate and why they did so in such a limited way, we must understand the little dynamic of change in the villages which proceeded alongside the greater dynamic of national and provincial administration. Let us look briefly at a single parish: Burnham-on-Crouch.[34]

The parish of Burnham lies on the Crouch Estuary in south-east Essex, sixteen miles from Chelmsford where the courts met. In the mid seventeenth century the parish had a population of about 500, supported by agriculture, rural crafts and fishing. There was no resident gentry family and parish society was led instead by the minister and a dozen yeoman families. Below them came a somewhat larger group of substantial husbandmen and craftsmen and below these families came those of the cottagers, labourers and fishermen who made up almost two-thirds of the population. Though Burnham was prosperous by comparison with many Essex villages, it had considerable poverty. In 1671 some 20 per cent of householders were excused payment of the hearth tax on the grounds of chronic poverty. Many of the labourers, fishermen and cottagers were probably little better off.

The manor of Burnham-with-Mangapp possessed a manor court throughout our period of study. By the early seventeenth century, however, it had come to confine its activities to the registration of land transactions, the appointment of local officers and the regulation of minor nuisances. In the absence of any local forum for conflict resolution, such disputes as arose were either settled informally or taken to quarter sessions and assizes. Over the whole period 1603–62 only six cases, all of theft, are known to have been brought before the assizes, most of the accused being labourers. In the same period, however, at least eighty-nine cases were brought before the justices of the peace in quarter sessions, in addition to which a number of villagers were bound over to keep the peace without any formal prosecution being made.

These Burnham cases involved comparatively few interpersonal disputes. There were scattered cases of theft or assault and from time to time villagers were bound over to keep the peace to one another. The latter seems to have been a favoured form of pre-emptive action, which probably went far to defuse potential violence. Obligation enforcement was also little looked to save in 1641/42, when a number of villagers were presented for failing to maintain the highways. Over three-quarters of the known Burnham cases were concerned with social regulation and were publicly presented. The vast majority of these were prosecutions of alehousekeepers and their disorderly customers, to which can be added a scattering of cases of illegal cottaging, taking inmates, failure to attend church and the misdeeds of servants and apprentices. Two points must be made about these cases. First, they were essentially misdemeanours of the poor or of those who countenanced their offences. Secondly, they differed from the occasional interpersonal disputes in that they were not evenly spread over time. In fact their chronology, when traced, reveals a great deal about the relationships of the villagers both with the authorities and with one another.[35]

Between 1603 and 1620 the villagers of Burnham had little enough to do with the justices. There were only five regulative prosecutions in the whole period and two of these concerned a single man – Robert Sampson, a persistently disorderly alehousekeeper, who was twice prosecuted and subsequently bound over to keep the peace to the yeoman who had secured his presentment. After 1620 there was rather more activity. A group of unlicensed alesellers were presented in 1623/24. In the years 1629 to 1631 the parish was caught up in the regulative drive of the Essex justices. Burnham jurymen duly reported on their disorderly alehouses, while the constables prepared their written presentments. Though replying in the negative to most of the articles, they named a handful of swearers, 'alehouse-haunters' and neglectors of church services. When magisterial pressure relaxed, so too did Burnham presentments. From 1639, however, things began to change. That year saw the beginning of a spate of prosecutions for alehouse disorders which continued into the early 1640s and was consolidated during the county-wide purge of alehouses in 1644. Then, in 1647, came a parish petition to the justices concerning alehouse disorders; there was a further flurry of prosecutions through into the 1650s. Both before and after the purge of 1644 this activity directed against the alehouses was a movement from below. The justices were not at this time showing the kind of aggression shown in 1630/31. What was going on in Burnham?

As we assemble the information available in the whole range of local sources relating to the parish, a clear picture slowly emerges. The initial burst of activity in 1639 turns out to have been provoked by the actions of a yeoman churchwarden, John Hills. Back in February 1638 Hills had presented Harrison Lattilaw, a tavern keeper, and several of his customers to the court of the Archdeacon of Essex for drinking and disorders in church service time. Hills's action was

42   *Two concepts of order*

something of a novelty, since previous churchwardens had preferred
to confine their attentions largely to sexual offences when making
presentments to the 'bawdy courts'. It may have been inspired by a
newcomer to Burnham, the curate Anthony Sammes. He was a
notable Puritan and was soon to be appointed vicar by the Puritan
magnate, the Earl of Warwick (in succession to a man who had been
happier on the alebench than in the pulpit). Whether or not Sammes's
influence was there, the presentment infuriated Lattilaw. Not long
before, in December 1637, Hills had presented him to the archdeacon
for fornication with his maidservant. Probably he was guilty. His
wife had recently died and he was shortly to marry the girl. But he
was lucky. The case was dismissed, though not before he had been
obliged to pay fees. Only a month after the dismissal Hills presented
him again for this offence in addition to the charge of tolerating disorders in his house in service time.

Three days later Lattilaw retaliated. With splendid irony he prosecuted John Hills before the court of the Bishop of London for drunkenness. In this he was supported by two yeomen, Robert Brown and
John Clements. They may have had good reason to dislike John
Hills's activity against village disorders. Both were on the point of
taking office for the year as constables, and Clements had a personal
axe to grind. He had been prosecuted by Hills for failing to attend
church. The case against Hills, however, was dismissed. He bided his
time, then six months later presented Lattilaw and his now wife for
pre-nuptial fornication. This time the girl's obvious pregnancy proved
the case to anyone with fingers to count upon and Lattilaw was
obliged both to pay fees and to undergo penance before the minister
and churchwardens. These included, of course, the triumphant
John Hills.

There the matter might have ended had not Lattilaw decided to take
the offensive against trade rivals. In July 1639 he and John Botting,
a customs officer, brought private indictments in quarter sessions
against four villagers for unlicensed aleselling. Two of those prosecuted merely submitted and we hear no more of them. The other two,
however, were William Philby and his son Thomas. They were poor
men, but were tenants of the manor and had powerful connections
among the manorial jurymen. Petitions in their defence were quickly
got up, led by John Hills and supported by eight leading inhabitants
of the parish. Interestingly, the petitioners did not try to deny the
Philbys' offences. Instead they excused them and asked for the
remission of their fines. They explained that the Philbys were poor

and that William had recently suffered losses at sea. They pleaded that the offences were committed 'ignorantly', from 'forgetfulness', and would not be repeated, adding for good measure that the prosecutions had been brought 'upon neighbours malice', 'out of a malicious and envious mind'. The churchwardens among the petitioners expressed a generous willingness to remit that part of the fines due to the parish and urged the nearest justice 'to be a mediator' for them with the court. Whether or not these revealing petitions were successful is uncertain. What is certain is that John Hills went on to complete the discomfiture of the prosecutors by presenting John Botting to the archdeacon in April 1640 for failing to attend church and running a disorderly house on the sabbath. He secured Botting's conviction and the payment of a fine to the parish poor.

This case sufficiently demonstrates the complexity of the circumstances underlying prosecutions. Here we see also the conflict they could arouse, the crucial role of village notables in either promoting or resisting prosecution and their extremely ambivalent attitude towards the law. Equally striking, however, is the fact that the conflict of loyalties evidenced in this dispute seems soon to have been resolved. From 1641 the parish officers regularly presented unlicensed and disorderly alehousekeepers themselves. They prosecuted both the Philbys, who had repeated their offence, and Harrison Lattilaw. Times had changed. Why?

One influence may have been the fact that the initiation of prosecutions was now firmly back in the hands of the parish notables. The selection of offenders for prosecution was no longer complicated by the cross-currents introduced by the activities of Lattilaw and Botting. Yet this explains only the smoothness of prosecution, not the willingness to undertake it. I have argued elsewhere that the growing readiness to regulate the offences of alehousekeepers in Essex in this period stemmed ultimately from a growing concern to discipline the parish poor.[36] This concern had its economic element in the desire to keep down the poor rates and prevent further impoverishment in a period of economic polarization in rural society. It also had its ideological element, partly in religiously inspired hostility to the 'disorders' of the popular culture, partly in the slow assimilation of leading villagers to the concept of order proclaimed from the judicial bench. Such influences may very well have been at work in Burnham. The problem of poverty was severe enough and the burden of supporting the parish poor fell upon the same parish ratepayers who also served as parish officers. Again, their concern with the alehouses was

44 *Two concepts of order*

soon augmented with a new preoccupation with preventing the taking in of inmates and unlicensed cottaging in their parish. Shifts in attitudes may have been accelerated by the influence of Anthony Sammes. He was now actively laying the Puritan foundations of what was to become one of the strongest nonconformist congregations in Essex.

This compounding of concern for the authority of the parish's 'natural' leaders, the disorders of the poor and the reformation of manners was made explicit in the parish petition of 1647. It was written by Sammes and supported by six leading landholders and two humbler men. Four of the petitioners were recent constables, two churchwardens. All were literate. They complained against a number of 'very poore people . . . of very lewde livinge and conversation' who were guilty of enticing

farmers servants and other poore people to tipple . . . whole or most part of publicke fast and other dayes and nights togeather causeing them to spend their tyme and moneyes there and to neglect their Masters service.

This petition suggests a consolidation of attitudes among a group of yeomen in the parish and an element of group conflict within the community of a kind not evident eight years before. Attitudes had clarified. Ground won against the petty disorders of village life since 1640 was being defended. The perception of such behaviour had been modified. If this was indeed the case, then the critical point had been reached when the yeomen of the parish were prepared to give consistent and voluntary support to the enforcement of the law, even though that support might extend no further than the selection for prosecution of those offenders who seemed to threaten their own position as masters, employers, ratepayers and pillars of the church.

The experience of a single small parish cannot be used to prove a general case. But it may be suggestive in the light of the broader national and regional trends discussed in this essay. Above all, it may suggest a process of change which may have been more common, though subject to variations in chronology and local peculiarities of circumstance. The initial unwillingness to make regular prosecutions and the intense conflict which prosecutions could touch off are by now familiar. The manner in which the authorities could on occasion cut down into village life, sharply reminding men of the demands of the law, has been witnessed in both Essex and Lancashire. The role of parish notables as brokers between the demands of their governors and those of their neighbours has been observed. The selective nature of their support when they chose to give it to the magistrates is strongly suggestive of the combination of factors which could stimulate their co-operation.

One would not expect such a process of change to be either uniform or universal. There were more egalitarian local communities in England where there was less chance of open conflict between the interests of a yeoman elite and the labouring poor. There were also villages where conflict continued to be expressed in a rustic vernacular free from the legitimizing rhetoric of sermon or statute. Yet elsewhere, the proponents of change may have remained a relatively powerless minority unable to call the tune in village affairs. As we have seen, the evidence of change belongs to central, precocious, Essex rather than to peripheral, backward, Lancashire. In the north, significant change at the village level may well have awaited another time, different circumstances.

Nor were such processes of change necessarily ongoing. They might be slowed, even reversed. As the seventeenth century closed, the regulative initiative described in this essay was losing force. Governmental pressure upon local magistrates relaxed. Enthusiasm for new standards of order and reformation waned both at the level of the nation and of the parish when it became evident that despite its conservative intentions it might have revolutionary implications. In many counties, presentment juries became inactive and disappeared. Formal presentments, where they were required, became increasingly ritualized and empty. In a sense, the manipulation of the courts for local ends by parish oligarchies may have been less needed. New instruments of parish government – the vestry, the poor laws, the settlement laws – had matured and introduced new possibilities for the entirely local settlement of conflict and disciplining of offenders. The courts could return to their accustomed role in defending the property of the propertied.

Nevertheless, the developments of the earlier seventeenth century, however halting and incomplete, were matters of some significance. It has been suggested here that the village communities of the period between the Armada and the restoration were to some extent moral communities, in the sense that they placed a premium upon good neighbourliness and preferred local opinion to the impersonal values of the larger society. The developments in local government and law enforcement of the earlier seventeenth century may have both furthered and reflected the weakening of this particular form of localism. For however conservative in intention, the pulsating search for order

46   *Two concepts of order*

could play its part in the slow assimilation of the village notables of
some rural areas to the values of their social superiors and religious
mentors. Where this was achieved, they were encouraged to identify
their interests with those of the magistracy and to express in action
their dissociation from the vernacular tradition of their neighbours.

In January 1629 the ministers and seven leading inhabitants of
Stock and Butsbury, Essex, petitioned the justices for the suppression
of six out of the eight local alehouses. They praised the 'most excellent
lawes' passed by Parliament for the suppression of alehouse disorders. They condemned

the slacknes of inferiour officers and other inhabitants of parishes (where
these evills abound) to informe the magistrates of the delinquents that such
good lawes might be executed.

In a crescendo of righteous indignation, they denounced the drunkenness and idleness bred among poor men and servants and urged the
justices to root out these 'styes for such swyne and cages of these
uncleane birds'.[37] Where such language could be used, a wedge had
been inserted between the 'better sort' of the parishes and their
poorer neighbours far more subtle and significant than their age-old
inequalities of wealth. For it affected their perception of their social
world. It edged forward the slow processes of national incorporation
and cultural differentiation which marked one stage of the evolution
of pre-industrial society in England.

1 Two concepts of order

1 Quoted in F. Aydelotte, *Elizabethan rogues and vagabonds* (Oxford, 1913), p. 489.

2 Lancashire RO QSB/1/1652 unsorted.

3 'MSS sermons of Christopher Hudson', Lancashire RO DP 353, fo. 55. The 'Homily on Obedience' and Wentworth's speech can be most conveniently found in G. R. Elton (ed.), *The Tudor Constitution* (Cambridge, 1960), pp. 15–16, and J. P. Kenyon (ed.), *The Stuart Constitution* (Cambridge, 1966), pp. 18–19, respectively. For two interesting recent discussions of the concept of order, see E. W. Talbert, *The problem of order* (Chapel Hill, N.C., 1962) and D. Little, *Religion, Order and Law* (Oxford, 1970).

4 John Downame, *A Guide to Godlynesse* (London, 1622), preface.

5 Arthur Dent, *The plaine mans path-way to Heaven* (London, 1601), p. 228. This work went through twenty-five editions up to 1640.

6 M. W. Beresford, 'The common informer, the penal statutes and economic regulation', *Economic History Review*, 2nd series, vol. 10 (1957–8), p. 222; J. R. Kent, 'Attitudes of members of the House of Commons to the regulation of "personal conduct" in late Elizabethan and early Stuart England', *Bulletin of the Institute of Historical Research*, vol. 46 (1973), *passim*; J. B. H.

Jones, 'Puritanism and moral legislation before the civil war' (Unpublished MA thesis, University of Wales, 1954).

7 Hertfordshire RO QSR/7; Lancashire RO QSB/1/70/48.

8 5 & 6 Edw. VI c. 25. See al so K. Wrightson, 'Alehouses, order and reformation in rural England 1590–1660', in E. and S. Yeo (eds.), *Class relations and cultural forms: Essays on the working class and leisure* (forthcoming); M. G. Davies, *The Enforcement of English Apprenticeship. A Study in Applied Mercantilism* (Cambridge, Mass., 1956).

9 Dent, *Plaine mans path-way*, pp. 165–6; John Northbrooke, 'To the Christian and Faithful Reader', in *Spiritus est Vicarius Christi in Terra: A treatise wherein dicing, dauncing etc. are reproved* (London, 1579).

10 Davies, *Apprenticeship*, p. 220.

11 H. B. Simpson, 'The office of constable', *English Historical Review*, vol. 10 (1895), *passim*; Davies, *Apprenticeship*, pp. 199–200; Lancashire RO QSR/22. As an increasing number of courts leet ceased to meet in the course of the seventeenth century petty constables came often to be appointed directly by the justices, a practice confirmed in law in 1662.

12 Essex RO Q/SR243/24; Lancashire RO QSR/34, 45.

13 J. Samaha, *Law and Order in Historical Perspective: The case of Elizabethan Essex* (New York and London, 1974), pp. 45–50, 87; M. Campbell, *The English Yeoman under Elizabeth and the early Stuarts* (New Haven, Conn. 1942), pp. 318, 341; Davies, *Apprenticeship*, pp. 168–9, 199; W. G. Hoskins, *The Midland Peasant: The economic and social history of a Leicestershire village* (London, 1957), p. 208.

14 Dalton quoted in Davies, *Apprenticeship*, p. 167; W. J. Hardy (ed.), *Hertford County Records*, vol. 1: *Notes and Extracts from the Sessions Rolls, 1581 to 1698* (Hertford, 1905), p. 149; Campbell, *Yeoman*, p. 324; *Worcs. Q/S*, p. 161; T. Birch (ed.), *A collection of state papers of John Thurloe Esq.* (7 vols., London, 1742), vol. 4, p. 315.

15 The information on the literacy of constables taking the Protestation Oath is drawn from the Literacy File of the Cambridge Group for the History of Population and Social Structure. I wish to express my gratitude to the Cambridge Group and in particular to Dr R. S. Schofield for permission to use this material. The literacy of Terling jurors was determined from signed presentments in Essex RO Q/SR 198–453, *passim*.

16 e.g. in Burnham-on-Crouch, Essex, from 1626 to 1643, one man served three times as constable while three men served twice each. Essex RO D/DGe M 170. Of the forty-two hundredal jurymen from Terling, Essex, 1580–1609, sixteen served once only, eighteen from two to four times and eight on five or more occasions. Essex RO Q/SR 73–185 *passim.*

17 *Worcs. Q/S*, pp. 564–5; Essex RO Q/SR 277/42.

18 Lancashire RO QSR/29; Essex RO Q/SR 263/18, 247/48.

19 Lancashire RO QSP/158/25; Hertfordshire RO QSR/10/984, QSR/9/830.

20 R. Gough, *The History of Myddle* (Fontwell 1968), p. 89; *Worcs. Q/S.*, p. 544; *R. Parkinson* (ed.), *The Life of Adam Martindale*, Chetham Society, old series, vol. 4, (1875) pp. 46–8.

21 Essex RO Q/SR 267/20; Lancashire RO QSB/24/27, QSR/15.

22 *Worcs. Q/S*, pp. 32, 249, 254; Lancashire RO QSB/1/71/10; Samaha, *Law and Order*, p. 86; Davies, *Apprenticeship*, p. 186.

23 Lancashire RO QSB/1/78/78, QSR/33; Essex RO QSR/230/24; Lancashire RO QSB/1/123/67.

24 Essex RO Q/S Ba 2/24, Q/SR 352/30, 273/15, 292/21, 276/25; Lancashire RO QJI/1/1651 unsorted.

25 Essex RO T/A 278, fo. 545.

26 The population estimate for rural Essex, based upon hearth tax returns, is taken from F. Hull, 'Agriculture and rural society in Essex, 1560–1640 (Unpublished PhD thesis, University of London, 1950), p. 121. The Lancashire estimate is based upon hearth tax returns for 1663 and 1666, PRO E 179 250/6, 8, 9. Since the Lancashire returns did not systematically record exempted paupers they have been corrected upwards considerably. The years sampled for the two counties were Essex: 1626, 1628, 1630, 1632, 1634/35, 1636/37, 1639, 1646, 1648, 1650, 1652, 1654, 1656, 1658, 1662, 1664, 1666. Lancashire: 1626, 1628, 1630, 1632, 1634, 1636, 1638, 1646, 1648, 1650, 1652, 1654, 1656, 1658, 1662, 1664, 1666. For the detailed figures see Tables 1 and 2 (pages 300–3). These rates are of course approximate and have been calculated simply as a means of establishing a basis for comparison. If anything, the population estimate for Essex may be rather high and that for south Lancashire rather low. If this is so then the contrast between the counties would be even greater.

27 Essex RO Q/SR 74/50. cf. Q/SR 105/31.

28 Essex RO Q/SR 44/61.

29   Essex RO Q/SR 7–251. Quotation from Q/SR 121/20. cf. 130/ 17, 134/35.

30   Lancashire RO QSB/1/288/22.

31   Davies, *Apprenticeship*, pp. 230–4. J. S. Cockburn, *A History of English Assizes, 1558–1714* (Cambridge, 1972), p. 116.

32   Lancashire RO QSR/53. The discussion of the regulative drives in Lancashire is based upon comparison of the prosecutions enrolled in Lancashire RO QSR/26–60 with the rolls of indictments and presentments, Lancashire RO QJI/1/7–40.

33   Essex RO Q/SR 264–276, Q/S Ba 5, Q/S Ba 6.

34   The discussion of Burnham-on-Crouch is based upon the following records: N. McNeil O'Farrell (ed.), 'Calendar of Essex assize files in the Public Record Office' (Essex RO typescript); Essex Quarter Sessions, Essex RO Q/SR 160–394, Q/S O 1, Q/S Ba 1/24–39, Q/S Ba 2/1–102, Q/S Ba 6/3/3. Ecclesiastical court records: Archdeacon of Essex, Essex RO D/AEA 35–44, D/AEV 6–7; Bishop of London's Commissary in Essex and Herts., Essex RO D/ABA 1–12; Bishop of London's Consistory Court, Essex RO D/ALV 1–2, Greater London Council RO DL/C/305, 308, 323, 324, 325, 624. Parish Registers of Burnham, 1559–1759, Essex RO D/P 162/1/1; Records of the Manor of Burnham with Mangapp, Essex RO D/DGE M, 158–67, 170, 184, 186, 187; Hearth Tax, 1671, Essex RO Q/R Th 5.

35   Occasional gaps in record survival preclude the assumption that we have a complete record of Burnham business brought to quarter sessions. Nevertheless, record survival is generally so good that one may have some confidence that the broad patterns and chronology of Burnham prosecutions have been accurately established. Had detailed records of the petty sessions meeting in the district from the early 1630s onwards survived, the trend towards increasing regulative activity in the later 1630s, 1640s and 1650s would very possibly be accentuated.

36   These issues are discussed at some length in Wrightson, 'Alehouses, order and reformation'.

37   Essex RO Q/SR 264/103.

Part IV
Policing Eighteenth-Century England

[13]

'Civic' police and the condition of liberty: the rationality of governance in eighteenth-century England[1]

Francis M. Dodsworth

The nature of the 'old' police of the 'long eighteenth century', which in this context lasts until the 1829 Metropolitan Police Act in London and the 1835 Municipal Corporations Act or the 1856 County and Borough Police Act elsewhere, has been a controversial subject.[2] Given the nature of police at this time as a broad mechanism of local, urban government for the cultivation of the health, wealth and welfare of the population, as well as the control of law and order, the subject has implications for our understanding of eighteenth-century governmental organization in general.

This article places the 'old' police in the context in which they were debated, arguing that opposition to its reform revolved around a particular conception of the nature of freedom in a free state. It becomes apparent that those arguing for police reform were actually instigating a radical reconfiguration of liberty. Opposition to change was not, therefore, simply about the protection of vested interest; rather it reflected a classical understanding of the nature of freedom and its relation to the structure of government. This did not only define opposition to the police, but more generally established what was at stake in the debate about wider governmental reform. There is an unexplored relationship between the legitimating categories long understood as central to defences of the 'old' police, the wider political meanings they carried that have largely been ignored in the historiography, and the structure of government itself. What seem to the historian to be practical matters of organizational structure that can be assessed according to the criteria of efficiency and efficacy are actually aspects of the condition of liberty and thus carry significant political implications.

[1] Thanks to Clive Emsley, Patrick Joyce, Matthew McCormack, Thomas Osborne, Bertrand Taithe and Chris Williams who all commented on drafts of this article. Particular thanks to Kay, Martin, Olwen and Philip Dodsworth, Elizabeth Millington and Rebeca Sanmartín Bastida.

[2] See particularly D. Hay, 'Property, authority and the criminal law' in D. Hay, P. Linebaugh, J. Rule, E. P. Thompson and C. Winslow, *Albion's Fatal Tree: Crime and Society in Eighteenth-Century England* (London, 1975); D. Hay, 'Prosecution and power: malicious prosecution and the English courts, 1750–1850' in D. Hay and F. Snyder (eds), *Policing and Prosecution in Britain 1750–1850* (Oxford, 1989); D. Hay and F. Snyder, 'Using the criminal law, 1750–1850: policing, private prosecution and the state' in Hay and Snyder, *op. cit.*; P. King, *Crime, Justice, and Discretion in England 1740–1820* (Oxford, 2000); and J. Langbein, 'Albion's fatal flaws', *Past and Present*, XCVIII (1983), 96–120.

200   Social History   VOL. 29 : NO. 2

I

Traditional police histories took contemporary criticisms of corruption, vested interest and inefficiency in the 'old' police at face value and assumed that Lord Shelburne's condemnation of the system as 'imperfect, inadequate and wretched' was accurate.[3] Recent historical work has suggested that this was not, in fact, the case.[4] An equally pervasive, yet less prominent assumption, however, remains. It is commonly assumed that the old police were illogical as a form of organization. Paley writes:

> One of the myths of eighteenth-century constitutional thought was that the English legal system, with its emphasis on decentralized procedures and private prosecution, provided a far better safeguard for the liberties of the subject than the centralized, inquisitorial system of continental Europe.[5]

This, she concedes, 'may have been true in an abstract sense, but what few people seem to have been willing to recognize was that there was a high price to be paid for the protection of English liberties'.[6] This entirely misunderstands the nature of the 'English liberty' that the system of police was designed to protect. Paley is making the liberal assumption that the only real constraint on freedom is interference in action, whereas those defending the 'old' police understood freedom not 'merely as a predicate of our actions but as an *existential condition* in contrast with that of servitude'.[7] Liberty did not lie in freedom from criminal interference alone, but in the form of governance of the institutions of government themselves; that is to say the lack of a free state, the potential for arbitrary rule, was as much of a constraint on freedom as practical interference. The purpose of this article is to establish the relevance of this notion of civil liberty for the eighteenth-century police and to develop the consequences of this view for our understanding of police organization. It will be argued that there is a direct relationship between this fundamentally classical view of liberty and the structure of police governance.[8] Classical – particularly Roman – writers understood freedom to be a property of the *civis*, the citizen, living in a *civitas libera*, or free state.[9] One of the conditions of liberty was that the citizens were obliged to be active in their own government, which we term, following the classical terminology, 'civic' engagement. For this reason, I term the 'old police' system of government based on the activity of the citizens in the free state 'civic' police.

Cornelius Castoriadis suggests that in order to understand social change we need to appreciate the 'social imaginary' of the period we are studying, which in the eighteenth century

[3] Quoted in D. Philips, '"A New Engine of Power and Autority": the institutionalization of law-enforcement in England 1780–1830' in V. A. C. Gatrell, B. Lenman and G. Parker (eds), *Crime and the Law: The Social History of Crime in Western Europe since 1500* (London, 1980), 164.

[4] See R. Paley, '"An Imperfect, Inadequate and Wretched System"? Policing in London before Peel', *Criminal Justice History*, X (1989) and E. A. Reynolds, *Before the Bobbies: The Night Watch and Police Reform in Metropolitan London, 1720–1830* (London, 1998).

[5] R. Paley, 'Thief-takers in London in the age of the McDaniel gang, *c.* 1745–1754' in Hay and Snyder, *op. cit.*, 337–8.

[6] *ibid.*, 339.

[7] Q. Skinner, *Visions of Politics: Volume I: Questions of Method* (Cambridge, 2002), 178, my emphasis, and see Q. Skinner, *Liberty Before Liberalism* (Cambridge, 1998), 59–99 and throughout.

[8] Skinner, *Liberty Before Liberalism, op. cit.*, 11, 54 n. 174, 55 n. 176 terms this a 'neo-roman' understanding of freedom; the Aristotelian heritage of classical liberty is stressed in J. G. A. Pocock, *The Machiavellian Moment: Florentine Political Thought and the Atlantic Republican Tradition* (Princeton, N.J., 1975) and *Virtue, Commerce, and History: Essays in the History of Political Thought and History, Chiefly in the Eighteenth Century* (Cambridge, 1985) throughout.

[9] Skinner, *Liberty Before Liberalism, op. cit.*, 10.

was structured according to classical ideals.[10] I wish to contribute to the historical reconstruction of the English 'governmental imaginary' in order to further our understanding of the eighteenth-century 'rationality' of police, where 'rationality' means

> a way or system of thinking about the nature of the practice of government (who can govern; what governing is; what or who is governed), capable of making some form of that activity thinkable and practicable both to its practitioners and to those upon whom it was practised.[11]

It is clear that there was a coherent system of thought behind the English police. Understanding this illuminates the debate and practice of the time and allows us to rethink the nature of the change that took place in the police between 1792 and 1856, from the first state-appointed magistrates and police offices to the compulsory introduction of the 'new' police throughout the country. Such an understanding will provide an historical foundation for the genealogy of government as we engage in the ongoing critique of modern governance and attempt to draw attention to the radical difference in previous conceptions of police.[12] This, as Quentin Skinner has noted, is the basis for any attempt to rethink the nature of the apparatus of rule and the ethics that govern our society.[13]

David Philips suggests opposition to police reform centred on the Country faction in parliament, opposing any governmental reform presented by the 'Court'; however he has failed to appreciate the full logic of the 'Country' position.[14] As the work of Pocock and Skinner has shown the Country position was an aspect of a wider 'civic humanist' or 'neo-roman' view of governmental legitimacy that defined the structure of government as the foundation of civil liberty.[15] This classical view of government pervaded both Court and Country writing and lay

[10] C. Castoriadis, *The Imaginary Institution of Society*, trans. K. Blamey (Cambridge, 1987).

[11] C. Gordon, 'Governmental rationality: an introduction' in G. Burchell, C. Gordon and P. Miller (eds), *The Foucault Effect: Studies in Governmentality* (Hemel Hempstead, 1991), 3.

[12] The genealogy of government is at its most developed in the work of Michel Foucault and his followers in the 'governmentality' field. For Foucault's work see M. Foucault, 'Politics and reason' in L. D. Kritman (ed.), *Politics, Philosophy, Culture: Interviews and Other Writings, 1977–1984* (London, 1988); 'Governmentality' in Burchell, Gordon and Miller (eds), *op. cit.*; 'The birth of biopolitics' in P. Rabinow (ed.), *Ethics, Subjectivity and Truth: Essential Works of Foucault 1954–1984*, vol. I, trans. R. Hurley and others (Harmondsworth, 2000); and 'The politics of health in the eighteenth century' in J. D. Faubion (ed.), *Power: Essential Works of Foucault 1954–1984*, vol. III, trans. R. Hurley and others (Harmondsworth, 2002). On 'governmentality' see the collected essays in A. Barry, T. Osborne and N. Rose (eds), *Foucault and Political Reason: Liberalism, Neo-Liberalism and Rationalities of Government* (London, 1996); Burchell, Gordon and Miller (eds), *op. cit.*; see also M. Dean, *Governmentality:*

Power and Rule in Modern Society (London, 1999) and N. Rose, *Powers of Freedom: Reframing Political Thought* (Cambridge, 1999). For an historical approach to this subject see P. Joyce, *Democratic Subjects: The Self and the Social in Nineteenth Century England* (Cambridge, 1994) and *The Rule of Freedom: The City and Modern Liberalism* (London, 2003).

[13] Skinner, *Liberty Before Liberalism*, *op. cit.*, 116–17 and *Visions of Politics: Volume I*, *op. cit.*, 6–7 and 88–9.

[14] Philips, '"A New Engine of Power and Authority"', *op. cit.*, 169. The Court faction were those who could be relied upon, through patronage, to support the actions of the incumbent administration. The Country faction were gentlemen who were opposed to the system of government place-men and patronage in general and pushed for moderate reform. On eighteenth-century politics generally, see H. T. Dickinson, *Liberty and Property: Political Ideology in Eighteenth-Century Britain* (London, 1977).

[15] Pocock, *Virtue, Commerce, and History*, *op. cit.*, 215–310 and throughout, and *Machiavellian Moment*, *op. cit.*, 401–22; Skinner, *Liberty Before Liberalism*, *op. cit.*

202   Social History   VOL. 29 : NO. 2

at the heart of the system of police and was opposed to corruption, the danger that could propel society backwards into barbarism.[16] Philips's limited understanding of the classical basis of the Country position is demonstrated by his reaction to the following statement by David Robinson in *Blackwood's* magazine in 1831. Robinson wrote:

> Let the system of stipendiary magistrates be carried to perfection, and the case will stand thus. The blue army, almost unlimited in numbers and powers, will be the servile instrument of the Executive; it will continually increase its encroachments on popular rights and the liberty of the subject.[17]

This critique of corruption in the form of a standing army, tied by salaries to the Executive, where liberty is opposed to slavery, is described by Philips as 'extreme and rather eccentric'.[18]

The classical basis of eighteenth-century police organization is crucial since, as Skinner has noted, the discursive context within which police exists has a limiting impact on its practice as 'what it is possible to do ... is generally limited by what it is possible to legitimize', which depends upon 'what courses of action you can plausibly range under existing normative principles'.[19] The 'civic' nature of police established the basis upon which its use and reform could be discussed. As Thompson shows 'the rulers were, in serious senses, the prisoners of their own rhetoric; they played the games of power according to rules which suited them; but they could not break those rules or the whole game would be thrown away.'[20] In fact, this classical language was taken up by those advocating the rights of the 'free-born Englishman' and was turned against those in authority as well as used by them.[21] The influence of classical learning since the Renaissance, in the police as elsewhere, meant that the structure of government was already understood and described in classical terms as a system of local government, independent of the state, practised through annually rotated, elected or publicly appointed offices by 'independent' men possessing landed property.[22] The system of police was

[16] Skinner and Pocock have shown that Tories and independent Whigs deployed and understood freedom and government in classical terms. S. Burtt, *Virtue Transformed: Political Argument in England, 1688–1740* (Cambridge, 1992), 110–27 and R. Browning, *Political and Constitutional Ideas of the Court Whigs* (Baton Rouge, 1982) show that classical, specifically Roman discourse was central to Court argument. P. K. Monod, *Jacobitism and the English People, 1688–1788* (Cambridge, 1989) shows that not only Tories but Jacobites also deployed classical 'Country' language.

[17] Philips, '"A New Engine of Power and Authority"', *op. cit.*, 155–6.

[18] *ibid.*, 156.

[19] Skinner, *Liberty Before Liberalism, op. cit.*, 105.

[20] E. P. Thompson, *Whigs and Hunters: The Origin of the Waltham Black Act* (Harmondsworth, 1977), 263.

[21] *ibid.*, 264. Classical language is prominent in complaints against the introduction of the 'new' police in the 1830s. See Anon., *The Devil's Visit; A Poem, From the Original Manuscript. With notes by a*

Barrister (London, 1830); A. Hypochondriac, *The Blue Devils; or, New Police. A Poem: in three Cantos* (London, 1830); and 'Fidget', *A Letter to the lord Mayor and Citizens of London, Respecting the Introduction of the New Police* (London, 1838).

[22] On the influence of classical political thought in the early modern period see P. Collinson, 'The monarchical republic of Queen Elizabeth I', *Bulletin of the John Rylands University Library of Manchester*, LXIX (1987), 394–424 and M. Peltonen, *Classical Humanism and Republicanism in English Political Thought, 1570–1640* (Cambridge, 1995). A classical interpretation is applied to police by Sir Francis Bacon, 'The Office of Constables' [1610] in G. Jacob, *The Complete Parish Officer*, 16th edn (London, 1772), *Addenda*. On the structure of the 'old' police see C. Emsley, *Policing and its Contexts, 1750–1850* (London, 1983), 21–9. On the way English local government was understood as a patriarchal duty, justified through property, see P. Langford, *Public Life and the Propertied Englishman 1689–1798* (Oxford, 1991), 367–509.

organized by the parish or, in the case of Manchester, the Manor, and David Eastwood has argued, without recourse to the literature on civic humanism, that

> Until their slow emasculation in the nineteenth century, the political institutions of the parish were representative, participatory, and accountable. The theatre in which the political life of the parish was forged was the vestry, which all ratepayers were entitled to attend and at which each ratepayer enjoyed the right to vote. As with parliament, property and wealth constituted the basis through which participation in the local institutions of the state was regulated.

Indeed, he has gone further: 'in terms of its formal construction, the parish was a ratepayers' republic.'[23] Likewise the Manor was both patriarchal and participatory. It was assumed that all males over twelve would attend the Manchester Court Leet, giving it a communal basis. However, the Leet was presided over by the Steward of the Lord of the Manor and he selected the jurors of the court and its officers from the propertied men of the township.[24]

Government in eighteenth-century England was understood in terms of the equal government of the community by the citizens, a series of family heads, each of whom could be described as 'independent', that is not subject to domination.[25] In order to understand this rationality of government, it is necessary to attend to the contemporary meanings carried by eighteenth-century police organization. It would seem impossible to understand a governmental rationality without paying attention to the ways in which its practitioners described it. That some understood it in terms of a classical system of civic duty will be seen to be crucial for the form of police governance. However, even where the eighteenth-century police officers did not describe their role in classical terms, it can be seen that the system in which they participated was already structured for them according to the logic of civic participation.

II

J. G. A. Pocock has argued that in the eighteenth century 'The Englishman had begun to envisage himself as a civic individual through the use of Aristotelian and civic humanist categories.'[26] By imagining himself in this way the Augustan Englishman was constituting himself as a citizen in the Roman mould, as a patrician or a member of the public in its restricted sense. This was fundamentally an ethical subjectivity in relation to fellow citizens and their mutual government, which was defined as 'civic virtue', that is *virtus* in Latin, *virtù* in Machiavelli's Italian. This was not simply moral virtue, but a capacity for political action. According to the most prominent English 'neo-roman' or 'civic humanist' theorist James Harrington, 'those actions of a man that are virtue, acquire unto himself honour, and upon

[23] D. Eastwood, *Government and Community in the English Provinces, 1700–1870* (Basingstoke, 1997), 43.

[24] S. and B. Webb, *English Local Government, Volume II: The Manor and the Borough*, vol. I (London, 1963 [1908]), 21–4, 100–2.

[25] For the full logic of freedom from domination see Skinner, *Liberty Before Liberalism*, op. cit., throughout and P. Pettit, *Republicanism: A Theory of*

Freedom and Government, 2nd edn (Oxford, 1999), 19–79.

[26] Pocock, *Machiavellian Moment*, op. cit., 450. Skinner has redefined these categories as fundamentally Roman in form: see Skinner, *Liberty Before Liberalism*, op. cit. and Q. Skinner, *Visions of Politics: Vol. II: Renaissance Virtues* (Cambridge, 2002) throughout.

204   Social History   VOL. 29 : NO. 2

others authority.'[27] The form of the eighteenth-century police can be directly related to this classical ethic of duty and authority. Definitions of the nature and practice of the old police resonate with civic concerns and language, and the classical sources (Aristotle, Cicero, Justinian's *Digest* and Livy) that underpinned this ethos. Of course, as the century developed this was not the only way in which policing was understood. However, even in such apparently unrelated systems of thought as utilitarianism, traces of classical ethics, particularly in terms of the tropes mobilized to describe ideal structures, can be seen throughout the debate.[28] The movement for economical reform in general addressed, in its own distinctive way, the problem of corruption and, as Pocock argues, 'corruption was a problem in virtue, not in right, which could never be resolved by asserting a right of resistance.'[29]

In the eighteenth century traditional offices of English government were often described in classical terms, indeed some saw the offices of police themselves as part of the Roman heritage, descended from the *Comes Stabuli* of the Eastern Empire.[30] Even when those such as 'Philonomos' saw police as descended from the Saxon system of government, this was imagined in terms reminiscent of Roman liberty, the Saxon spirit being 'the desire of living under the obedience of known laws, made by the consent of our representatives, executed in the ancient and legal manner, binding equally on all ranks and degrees of people'.[31] Philonomos's view that this was 'a spirit of liberty if considered in opposition to tyranny' but 'a spirit of obedience when referred to the constitution' and where 'the people really loved the laws' to which the king was also subject sounds remarkably like the classical view of freedom as an existential condition.[32]

Quentin Skinner has identified two aspects of 'neo-roman' thought which render its conception of civil liberty distinctive: the necessity of self-government 'whereby a civil society of men is instituted and preserved upon the foundation of common right or interest', and the opposition between freedom and servitude, otherwise expressed as an opposition between independence and domination, obligation or dependence.[33] Self-government could carry a whole range of implications in the eighteenth century, but the most important for civic virtue was the *vivere civile*, or active civic life involving participation in government and the annual rotation of local office. Public service was not a vocation, a calling to permanent office, but an obligation, one that if necessary citizens could be coerced into through fines.[34] It was necessary that if a state was to be free (and it was considered that citizens could only be free in a free

---

[27] J. Harrington, *The Commonwealth of Oceana and A System of Politics*, ed. J. G. A. Pocock (Cambridge, 1992 [1656]), 19.

[28] Utilitarian sources of police reform that utilized classical tropes are P. Colquhoun, *A Treatise on the Police of the Metropolis . . .* , 6th edn (London, 1806) and [J. Wade], *A Treatise on the Police and Crimes of the Metropolis . . .* (London, 1829).

[29] See P. Harling, 'Rethinking "Old Corruption"', *Past and Present*, CXLVII (1995), 127–58 and *The Waning of 'Old Corruption': The Politics of Economical Reform in Britain, 1779–1846* (Oxford, 1996). See also P. Harling and P. Mandler, 'From "fiscal-military" state to laissez-faire state, 1760–1850', *Journal of British Studies*, XXXII, 1 (1993), 44–70; Pocock, *Virtue, Commerce, and History, op. cit.*, 48.

[30] J. Ritson, *The Office of Constable: Being an Entirely New Compendium of the Law Concerning that Ancient Minister for the Conservation of the Peace*, 2nd edn (London, 1815), 7.

[31] 'Philonomos', *The Right Method of Maintaining Security in Person and Property to all the Subjects of Great Britain: By a vigorous Execution of the present LAWS OF THE LAND . . .* (London, 1751), 10.

[32] *ibid.*, 10, 14–15.

[33] Quotation in Harrington, *op. cit.*, 8; Skinner, *Liberty Before Liberalism, op. cit.*, 26, 36.

[34] On the Machiavellian interpretation of the relationship between liberty and the obligations of public service that was so influential in the eighteenth century see particularly Skinner, *Visions of Politics: Volume II, op. cit.*, 160–212.

state) 'the laws that govern it – the rules that regulate its bodily movements – must be enacted with the consent of all its citizens, the members of the body politic as a whole'.[35] The citizens were to be those persons free from the influence of another, that is 'within their own jurisdiction or right', or independent.[36] In contrast loss of freedom was defined by dependence. In practice

> the realities of the seventeenth-century social structure established as paradigmatic the image of the freeholder, founded upon real or landed property which was inheritable rather than marketable, was protected by the ancient customs of the common law, and brought with it membership of the related structures of the militia and the parliamentary electorate, thus guaranteeing civic virtue.[37]

Civic virtue, then, was both the qualification and practice of public duty and the foundation of a system of citizenship based upon certain material conditions: the possession of real property (defined by Harrington) and the right of the citizens to bear arms (developed in Machiavelli).[38] The opposite to this (masculine) civic duty was an eighteenth-century reading of (feminine) *fortuna*, or corruption that was equivalent to instability and decline.[39]

Negligence of public duty implied far more than bad government: it implied an end to the condition of liberty. It was this negligence that constituted the greatest threat to freedom, commonly termed corruption and identified as anything that could cause imbalance in the constitution, which was commonly represented as a body in balance.[40] Henry Fielding, in his *Enquiry into the Cause of the Late Increase of Robbers* (1751), the statement which was to influence the form of police debate for many years to come, wrote of the constitution as a balanced body, whose equilibrium had been destroyed by the emergence of trade, which held out the danger of the rise of luxury.[41] Luxury could lead to neglect of public duty and could result in England

> running the same Course, which *Rome* itself had run before it; from virtuous industry to Wealth; from Wealth to Luxury; from Luxury to Impatience of Discipline and Corruption of Morals; till by a total Degeneracy and Loss of Virtue, being grown ripe for Destruction, it falls a Prey at last to some hardy Oppressor, and, with the Loss of Liberty, losing everything else that is valuable, sinks gradually into its original Barbarism.[42]

This direct quotation from Middleton's *The Life of Marcus Tullius Cicero* (1741), traditional hero of the civic humanists and neo-roman theorists, was made more apposite in the context of the continuous wars between the 'free state' of Britain and 'despotic' continental regimes in the eighteenth century.[43] The failure of police to stem the tide of luxury would destroy the

---

[35] Skinner, *Liberty Before Liberalism, op. cit.*, 27.

[36] *ibid.*, 40–1.

[37] Pocock, *Machiavellian Moment, op. cit.*, 450.

[38] *ibid.*, 450.

[39] *ibid.*, viii, 486. On the relationship between *virtus* and the masculine root *vir* see *ibid.*, 37.

[40] On negligence and the threat to freedom see the reference in n. 34. On the metaphor of the body politic, see Skinner, *Liberty Before Liberalism, op. cit.*, 24.

[41] H. Fielding, *An Enquiry into the Cause of the Late Increase of Robbers and Related Writings*, ed. M. Zirker (Oxford, 1988 [1751]), 69–70. For a detailed reading of the way in which luxury (an aspect of

corruption) was pictured in the eighteenth-century social imagination see J. Sekora, *Luxury: The Concept in Western Thought, Eden to Smollet* (London, 1977).

[42] H. Fielding, *Enquiry, op. cit.*, 74.

[43] Middleton was a Court propagandist who likened Walpole to Cicero. Fielding wavered between support for Court and Country. On the relationship between police, internal order and the European state system, particularly the necessity of securing a stable state for the purposes of international recognition, negotiation and security, see H.-H. Liang, *The Rise of Modern Police and the European State System from Metternich to the Second World War* (Cambridge, 1992).

free state, and thus individual liberty, and reduce the nation to slavery by some foreign competitor with an arbitrary government. Significantly in this context, 'The danger of luxury ... is not that it produces effeminacy of taste or even mutability of fashion, so much as that it leads to choice and consequently to specialization'.[44] Specialization was a problem because, following the logic of Pocock, the citizen who allowed another to govern for him 'parted with a vital element of his *virtus*'.[45] Specialization made the police officer a servant of others and equally made others dependent upon him in their turn. Some, such as Fielding, however, were beginning to accept specialization as a necessary evil to ward against more pressing causes of corruption: negligent and dishonest officers.[46]

The supposedly 'functional' characteristics of the police – vigour, trustworthiness and independent status – were far from neutral in their meaning, they defined civic virtue and thus freedom. This identified parish officers as public servants in a classical sense, where every constable was required to be

> *idoneus homo*, i.e. apt and fit to execute the said office; and he is said in law to be *idoneus* who has these three things, – honesty, knowledge and ability; honesty, to execute his office truly, without malice, affection, or partiality; knowledge, to know what he ought to do; and ability, as well in estate as in body, that he may intend and execute his office, when need is, diligently, and not for impotence or poverty to neglect it.[47]

It had, however, become common for police officers to pass their duty on to a deputy charged (and paid) to execute this onerous task for them. Since the 1735 Westminster Watch Act it had become common to pay watchmen for their services and it was equally common for more senior police offices to be deputized to salaried replacements. This did not necessarily mean that these men were actually inefficient or corrupt, but it opened up the possibility for those attempting to reform the system to criticize them on those terms. It was the independent status of the men and the unpaid nature of the office that supposedly underpinned the virtue of the officer. The fact that they were open to criticism, by virtue of the fact that they were specialists, destabilized the system of itself.

One of the most famous paid systems of police was the Bow Street system established by Thomas de Veil and developed by Henry and John Fielding. Writing in 1755, after the scandal where the McDaniel gang of thief-takers had been exposed as criminals (implicating the Bow Street Runners), John Fielding was forced to defend his men against accusations of corruption, 'the perjuries of M'Daniel and his crew having raised a strong prepossession against thief-takers in general'.[48] He encouraged the use of the Bow Street Office to counteract the current system

[44] Pocock, *Machiavellian Moment, op. cit.*, 430.

[45] *ibid.*, 499.

[46] Many watch committees used paid watchmen following the 1735 Westminster Watch Act. See Emsley, *op. cit.*, 20–9, Reynolds, *op. cit.*, throughout and J. Styles, 'Sir John Fielding and the problem of criminal investigation in eighteenth-century England', *Transactions of the Royal Historical Society*, 5th series, XXIII (1983), 127–49.

[47] Ritson, *op. cit.*, 29–30. This definition had its source in a charge by the king in 1630 for constables to be fit men: W. Sheppard, *The Offices and Duties of Constables, Borsholders, Tythingmen. . .* (London,

1641), 17. This phrase was repeated in constabulary handbooks from Sheppard up to the nineteenth century, for example see P. Colquhoun, *A Treatise on the Functions and Duties of A Constable* (London, 1803), xiii and Ritson, quoted above.

[48] J. Fielding, *A Plan For Preventing Robberies within Twenty Miles of London. With an Account of the Rise and Establishment of the Real Thieftakers. . .* (London, 1755), no pagination. For an in-depth study of the McDaniel gang and the phenomenon of thief-takers in general see Paley, 'Thief-takers', *op. cit.*, throughout.

of rewards for the return of stolen goods which, it was felt, encouraged corruption. It was common to advertise property stolen and thief-takers would attempt to recover it for a fee; alternatively the thief-takers would advertise property they had recovered from criminals and the owner would have to pay to collect it. In practice the thief-takers were often portrayed as organizing the theft of goods to provide a market for their services and

> instead of being an encouragement to honest men, of bold and daring spirits, to pursue, attack, and apprehend robbers [financial rewards] have been a temptation to a body of villains, who disgrace human nature, to contrive robberies, and to make robbers, in order to destroy the latter for the sake of the reward.[49]

Henry Fielding had himself written a life of the notorious thief-taker Jonathan Wild, immortalized by Defoe.[50] This is particularly significant as Fielding's version is a fictionalized account that operates as a satire on Walpolean corruption, with Wild identified with Walpole.[51] The significance of this is that the classical criticism of corruption figured most prominently in Bolingbroke's critique of Walpole's use of patronage in government, a critique in which Fielding participated.[52] This not only links 'political' to 'social' corruption (a distinction that was not in operation at the time) but does so with recognizably classical concerns. Such portrayals of the corruption of criminal life and the offices supposed to protect the public became a staple of the debate about police ethics.

The importance of voluntary duty was heavily stressed by John Cross in his appeal to the Manchester Court Leet – the manorial governing body of the township of Manchester – and by proxy, being the same men, to the Police Commission, the improved governmental system introduced in 1792:

> futile and unavailing [is] the best system of regulations that human ingenuity can devise: alike useless and unwieldy every body politic or physical, unanimated by the *voluntary exertions* of those to whom are committed the management and direction of their power.[53]

Cross was the Steward of the Lord of the Manor and, as such, director of the Leet and was well aware that public, particularly voluntary, service was only as effective as its agents were active. Effective government is thus not simply a system of regulations, but dependent upon an ethic of activity. The performance of the duty of governing had not 'of late attracted their due of attention', but he wished to rouse them out of their 'apathy': 'We should all, undoubtedly, best consult our immediate personal ease and convenience on this occasion, by a supine and merely formal discharge of our respective duties'; however, 'this kind of public service' was essential.[54]

---

[49] J. Fielding, *op. cit.*, 8.

[50] On Wild see G. Howson, *Thief-Taker General: The Rise and Fall of Jonathan Wild* (London, 1970) and D. Defoe, *The True and Genuine Account of the Life and Actions of the Late Jonathan Wild* [1725] in H. Fielding, *Jonathan Wild*, ed. D. Nokes (Harmondsworth, 1986).

[51] H. Fielding, *Jonathan Wild*, *op. cit.* [1743]; see Nokes's introduction, 12, 18.

[52] See Henry St John, Viscount Bolingbroke, *A Dissertation on Parties* [1735] in D. Armitage (ed.),

Political Writings (Cambridge, 1997) and Skinner, *Liberty Before Liberalism*, *op. cit.*, 12, 72 and *Visions of Politics: Volume II*, *op. cit.*, 344–67.

[53] J. Cross, 'Manchester in 1799 – a charge to the Grand Jury of the Court Leet by John Cross Esq.' in J. P. Earwaker (ed.), *The Court Leet Records of the Manor of Manchester (from the Year 1552 to the Year 1686, and from the Year 1731 to the Year 1846)*, Vol. IX, 1787–1805, Appendix II (Manchester, 1889), 257.

[54] *ibid.*, 255, 258.

The neglect of duty, despite the introduction of new legal powers in 1792, had led to a decline in local government:

> During many dark and wet winter months, the streets have remained uncleaned and without lights; for some time no watchmen or patroles were appointed – Security and temptation were thus afforded to plunder: and none could pass through the streets in safety – Escaping personal violence, they were still in imminent personal danger, from the numerous unguarded cellars, pits, and various obstructions that everywhere interrupted their passage.[55]

Thus the neglect of the voluntary public duty of the Leet and Police Commission had led directly to the social problems of crime and disorder.

William Blizzard, from a metropolitan perspective, was equally clear about the relationship between the condition of the government and the wider social order, relating political corruption directly to crime: 'The EVILS, that branch from *ministerial arts and intrigues for obtaining majorities in parliament*, have nearly ruined this country. They pervade all ranks: the VICES of the GREAT, and CRIMES of the VULGAR, have hence their radical cause.'[56] The factional politics at the heart of government had led to the neglect of the real needs of society and to its improper government. Blizzard was a member of the Honourable Artillery Company, an offshoot of the London Military and Foot Association, formed as a kind of Home Guard to ward off invasion from the continent.[57] This group of volunteers patrolled London at night, seeking to prevent crime and discover criminals, investigating their lifestyle and places of refuge. Blizzard clearly saw this activity in classical terms. Aware that Pitt's government was about to introduce a bill to reduce crime he wrote: 'The King has ever been a friend to VIRTUE and JUSTICE; we have *now* a minister, virtuous as well as able and active; and it is understood to be the intention of the government to form a plan for the security and happiness of the community.'[58] He saw his own role as a volunteer patrol to assist in this programme 'and, if possible, promote public virtue'.[59] In order to do this it was necessary to reform the existing system which was damaging in itself for 'when you shall be led to reflect with me on the nature and magnitude of iniquity in this town. . . . When VICE shall appear to be the foundation of plans and systems bearing the fair titles of *virtue* and *justice*, you will shudder and exclaim, *It is too much!*'[60]

Blizzard's desire was to remove 'obnoxious persons' operating according to their own (rather than the public) interest in the criminal justice system. This is not simply a matter of financial corruption for, as Skinner has noted, the term 'obnoxious' carried connotations of flattery and political intrigue of the kind condemned above and was used to refer to 'servile supporters of absolute power', originally meaning 'those who live at the mercy of other people'.[61] Blizzard is thus arguing for independence for the officers of police, and for their attention to public duty, not self-serving practices. The best way to do this was to rebuild the self-esteem of police officers and thereby public confidence in them. He notes:

---

[55] *ibid.*, 256.
[56] W. Blizzard, *Desultory Reflections on Police: with an Essay On the Means of Preventing Crimes and Amending Criminals* (London, 1785), 75.
[57] *ibid.*, v–vi.

[58] *ibid.*, vi.
[59] *ibid.*, vii.
[60] *ibid.*, 2.
[61] Skinner, *Liberty Before Liberalism*, *op. cit.*, 94.

> The ancients had a just veneration of those men by whose conduct they obtained domestic security. The Greek and Roman historians have recorded, in the most honourable terms, the patriotic citizens, who, either by their judgement or bravery, freed cities and countries from robbers and disturbances of the community.[62]

As such he is arguing that police activity can be seen as patriotism in the classical sense of public service, taken up by both the Country opposition to the government and the Court writers defending them. More public appreciation of police officers would encourage better men to come forward for the duty and were 'more attention . . . paid to this observation, there would be a greater degree of *active* virtue in the nation'.[63]

The government's response was rather different, but articulated in relation to the same concerns about the corruption of police officers. In June 1785 Pitt's Solicitor-General, Mac-Donald, attempted to introduce a new police system into London, covering the whole metropolitan area, with new powers of arrest. It was acknowledged by one *opponent* of the bill 'that they were got into a lamentable state of police, and . . . thieves and rogues of all denominations had increased to an almost incalculable number', which he attributed to the prevalence of 'trading justices', that is, those generating revenue through their dispensation of justice.[64] Here the state of crime is linked directly to corruption in the same way: the malformed offices of law and order encourage neglect of duty in favour of personal gain and actively promote crime. However, the bill was opposed on the grounds that it would introduce a law

> which, under colour of correcting abuses, overturns the forms established by the wisdom of our ancestors . . . and goes to the entire subversion of the chartered rights of the greatest city in the world, and the destruction of the constitutional liberties of above a million of his Majesty's subjects.[65]

It was also claimed to be 'altogether new and arbitrary in the extreme' creating 'without necessity, new offices, invested with extraordinary and dangerous powers . . . and expressly exempted from those checks and that responsibility, which the wisdom of the law has hitherto thought necessary to accompany every extraordinary power'.[66] This was, no doubt, as it is often portrayed, the City of London defending its privileges. However, it was necessary to deploy classical tropes to do so. In the eighteenth-century context the rights of the City were clearly related to freedom understood as direct self-government, which the new system would remove with its uniform coverage of the city. Likewise the opposition of arbitrary power, exercised without redress, is clearly an argument against domination. The bill, it was argued, should be rejected 'to quiet the minds of His Majesty's subjects, and relieve them from the dread of being reduced under the scourge of such a system'.[67] As Skinner has shown, the condition of *potential* oppression constituted a constraint on freedom as much as any actual practical restriction on action.[68] Whether or not these rhetorical devices were sincerely meant, or merely tools to argue for a preservation of privilege, is immaterial. The fact remains that to argue against the police

---

[62] Blizzard, *op. cit.*, 22.

[63] *ibid.*, 24.

[64] W. Cobbett and T. C. Hansard (eds), *The Parliamentary History of England From the Earliest Period to the Year 1803*, XXV, 1st February 1785–5th May 1786 (London, 1815), 902.

[65] *ibid.*, 900.

[66] *ibid.*, 900, 900–1.

[67] *ibid.*, 901.

[68] Skinner, *Liberty Before Liberalism*, *op. cit.*, 84–95.

bill it was necessary, or at least considered most effective, to do so in classical language. That the bill did not pass suggests this was still a persuasive argument.

III

This reading of liberty as a condition was felt to necessitate a certain form of organization and, indeed, consciously or not, the system of police embodied civic virtue in terms of the obligations of the citizen. It was necessary that, however the police was organized, it was able to be described as consonant with these ideals. It was quite specifically stated that constables must be

> Men qualified for the Execution of their Office, and therefore to be chosen out of the honestest, ablest and most understanding Men, not feeble with old Age, nor otherwise weak, sick, poor or impotent; that so the Office may be perform'd truly and diligently, and without Malice, Affection or Partiality.[69]

This office was explicitly 'not to be put upon the poorer Sort, for they are usually most ignorant and fearful, and less able to attend this Office; their Necessity requiring them to mind their own Trade and Employment'.[70] It is clear that the constable was to be a man 'at Leisure to attend upon this Office', which excluded anyone who needed to work for a living or was rendered busy by their calling, such as doctors, lawyers, clergymen and of course 'Women, whether Maids or Widows, ought not to be chosen; neither Madmen, or Ideots [sic], nor Infants under 21 Years of Age, nor old Men above Seventy', all of whom lacked the social and financial independence necessary to discharge a civic duty according to the prevailing notions of authority.[71] This was the standard argument from 1610 – when Sir Francis Bacon argued that petty constables should be 'of the better sort of resiants of the said town' and 'the high constable ought to be of the ablest of freeholders, and of the most substantial sort of yeomen, next to the degree of gentlemen' – to the nineteenth century, when government could only be carried out by propertied men of leisure, men 'of the better sort of resiants', 'for constables chosen out of the meaner sort, they are either ignorant what to do, or dare not do what they should, or are not able to spare the time'.[72] This echoed Aristotle: 'The citizen excellence of which we have spoken cannot be attained by every citizen, by all those who are simply free men, but can only be achieved by those who are free from the necessary tasks of life.'[73] Thus a distinction could be made between those who were simply too busy to carry out the task because of their other public obligations and those whom necessity rendered dependent and corruptible, and therefore unfit for public office. The freemen, those who were independent, were explicitly defined by Harrington as the citizens in his neo-classical landscape: 'distributing the people into freemen or citizens, and servants, while such; for if they attain unto liberty, that is to live of themselves, they are freemen or citizens'.[74]

The most important aspect of citizenship was that it designated its bearer a free man. Freedom in this sense was understood as independence, that is, freedom from obligation, domination or

[69] [Robert Gardiner], *The Complete Constable. . . ,* 6th edn (London, 1724), 6.
[70] *ibid.*, 6.
[71] *ibid.*, 7.

[72] Bacon, *op. cit.*, 3–4; Ritson, *op. cit.*, 30.
[73] Aristotle, *Politics*, trans. E. Baker and R. F. Stalley (Oxford, 1998), 95.
[74] Harrington, *op. cit.*, 75.

arbitrary interference.[75] This was a condition and a duty, not a right, and in order to possess his freedom (for only a limited number of mature, wealthy, landed, usually English, *men* could qualify as independent)[76] it was necessary that the citizen actively participate in the civic life of the community. Otherwise, some groups or individuals might come to dominate it and to 'become the dependent of another was as great a crime as to reduce another to dependence on oneself'.[77] In the same way, to allow crime and disorder to gain a foothold in society was an offence against one's civic duty, which was to uphold the law and thus maintain the condition of liberty, 'that is, liberty stated and ascertained by law, in equal opposition to popular license and arbitrary will'.[78] In a free state the system of government should 'ideally enable each individual citizen to exercise an equal right of participation in the making of laws'.[79] This could take place on a national level in parliament or, more commonly, on a local level where individuals could actually participate in the framing and execution of by-laws. The act of governing was to be practised among equals according to laws they had made or consented to: 'it consisted in a partnership of ruling and being ruled with others who must be as morally autonomous as oneself.'[80] The office of constable was particularly significant in this respect as he supposedly held his position not through the power of the crown but as an equal among citizens under the Common Law.[81] According to Aristotle, 'The citizen in this strict sense is best defined by the one criterion that he shares in the administration of justice and the holding of office.'[82] Thus engagement in police duties could be seen as one of the defining characteristics of civic virtue.

Self-government in the eighteenth century was, then, understood to mean local government and its officers must necessarily 'be an inhabitant of the place for which he is chosen'.[83] This not only ensured there was no government from outside the community (hence not appointed and directed by them, rendering them dependent on it), but also ensured the officers of police had an interest in the activities they were undertaking which came from their local security, not possible rewards. It was specifically stated that the qualification for service in a parish was residency there, as opposed to the simple ownership of lands in the area.[84] Police officers were also in charge of the forces of order and the militia, which were crucial to public freedom. It was fundamental that the local polity be in charge of a body of 'citizen-soldiers' who were outside the sway of any arbitrary authority and acted according to the will of the governed, indeed were made up themselves of volunteers from the public. Following Aristotelian logic, 'the members of a city must bear arms in person, partly in order to maintain their rule over those who disobey, and partly in order to meet any threat of external aggression.'[85] This would prevent the seizing of power by any ambitious individual in the manner of Julius Caesar, who

[75] My understanding of independence, and particularly its changing meanings has been aided by discussions with Matthew McCormack and reading his unpublished thesis '"The Independent Man" in English Political Culture, *c.* 1760–1832' (Ph.D., University of Manchester, 2002).

[76] M. McCormack, 'The independent man: gender, obligation and virtue in England, *c.* 1750–1850' (unpublished paper delivered at *Vice and Virtue*, annual conference of the Social History Society, Manchester, 4 January 2002).

[77] Pocock, *Machiavellian Moment, op. cit.*, 75.

[78] Bolingbroke, *op. cit.*, 112.

[79] Skinner, *Liberty Before Liberalism, op. cit.*, 30.

[80] Pocock, *Machiavellian Moment, op. cit.*, 75.

[81] H. B. Simpson, 'The office of constable', *English Historical Review*, XL (1895), 635.

[82] Aristotle, *op. cit.*, 85.

[83] Ritson, *op. cit.*, 31.

[84] W. Sheppard, *The Offices of Constables, Churchwardens, Overseers of the Poor. . .* (London, 1652), A4.

[85] Aristotle, *op. cit.*, 269.

212   Social History   VOL. 29 : NO. 2

'undermined all laws, divine and human, in order to establish that dominance which his erroneous belief had targeted for itself'.[86] Domination was, of course, unfreedom. The yeomanry under the control of the constables and the magistrate are the most obvious manifestations of this; however, on the side of public order, the watchmen and other officers of the police also embodied these ideals, made up as they were of (often paid) volunteers from the public itself, supervised by the citizens, the constables.

As a sign of their authority the officers of the police wore a traditional uniform. In Manchester the Beadle or Marshall wore a hat and coat with four-dozen buttons and carried a gilded staff.[87] By the early years of George III's reign a gold cap had been added, and the Beadle was also decked out with gold lace and a tassel and shoes and scarlet stockings.[88] This persisted into the Police Commission uniform for its officers whose 'suit of livery' included a 'staff of office'.[89] These marks of office are significant as they designated the bearer as a civic official carrying out a public trust. All the 'old' police officers, including those of Manchester, the City of London and the City of Westminster, as well as the officers of the Bow Street patrols and the various watchmen, carried a truncheon as a weapon and a symbol of their office that usually bore the crown and the royal arms, but also the arms of the city or the mark of the borough or parish they represented.[90]

This staff of office seems to have held some significance, for Bacon felt obliged to remind constables that they were entitled to be obeyed 'as well without their staff of authority, as with it', 'For it is not the staff that makes the constable, but the office which he is sworn unto'.[91] In Glasgow the Manchester Police Commission discovered that the '34 Sergeants wear a uniform of blue with red Collar and buttons Stampt with the City Arms'.[92] The wearing of the City arms on the buttons prefigures the wearing of the corporation or borough arms on the uniform of most borough police forces, demonstrating the direct link between the officers and the legitimate civic authority whose power, and thus that of the citizens who elected its governors, they were enacting. In the eighteenth century the constables of the City of London were to 'place the City Arms over their doors' to identify them and link their personal authority to that of the City whose inhabitants had elected them.[93] Although there was a constant fear of a standing army controlled by the Executive that could enforce its will, this did not preclude local bodies of 'citizen-soldiers'.[94] According to the Machiavellian logic that underpinned the classical imagination of the eighteenth century, such a force was central to the maintenance of the condition of liberty, and police officers could wear a uniform and carry arms in this role.[95]

John Cross, in a Platonic variation on classical duty, wrote explicitly about the function of the Court Leet and the Police Commission as 'this kind of public service' which had been carried out by 'A few respectable and active persons'.[96] Roberts wrote of the failure of the

[86] Cicero, *On Obligations [De Officiis]*, trans. P. G. Walsh (Oxford, 2000), 11.

[87] A. Redford, *The History of Local Government in Manchester*, vol. I (London, 1939), 52.

[88] *ibid.*, 86.

[89] Anon., *The Orders and Instructions to be Observed by the Officers of the Manchester Police* (Manchester, 1836), 5–6.

[90] E. R. H. Dicken, *The History of Truncheons* (Ilfracombe, Devon, 1952), 13–14, 29–30, 40, 82, 84, 104,108 and plates 3, 5, 15, 20 nos 1–5 and 21

nos 4 and 5.

[91] Bacon, *op. cit.*, 8.

[92] Manchester Central Reference Library, Local Studies Unit, Archive Service, M9/30/9/1, *Reports of the Police Establishments in Various Towns*, 28.

[93] J. Paul, *The Parish Officer's Complete Guide . . .* , 3rd edn (London, 1776), 61.

[94] Skinner, *Liberty Before Liberalism, op. cit.*, 74.

[95] Pocock, *Machiavellian Moment, op. cit.*, 381–3.

[96] Cross, *op. cit.*, 258.

Court Leet to pursue a 'vigilant and active performance of the trusts reposed in them'.[97] In general he felt that 'When any man is entrusted with an office, he ought to consider himself as one of the Guardians of the Repose of his Fellow-Citizens',

> These Observations tend to shew the necessity of appointing such Officers only who *from their good sense, and their respectability, derive their Title to preside over the Town*, and *from their integrity, activity, and regards for its welfare, their title to officiate* in those various departments, to which you have the power of appointment.[98]

It is clear that it is from their respectability, integrity, energy and sense of duty that they draw their authority. This is the model of the virtuous citizen practising his public duty to govern in order to *create* the freedom of the community. This extended as far as requiring an active governing power to create liberty. It was not sufficient to have a system that prevented incursions upon peoples' rights: 'if civic virtue is to be encouraged (and public liberty thereby upheld), there will have to be laws designed to coerce the people out of their natural but self-defeating tendency to undermine the conditions necessary for sustaining their own liberty.'[99] In this sense it was necessary to establish freedom *through* government according to the law, to encourage virtue in the citizens and guard against the corruption which could undermine it.[100] This notion of establishing the condition of liberty is radically different from the Hobbesian assumption that any interference (and hence any law) is a restraint and that freedom can be maximized by having as few laws and as little interference as possible. From the neo-classical perspective liberty was not (or not only) defined by non-interference but as independence, and thus the law could be positive in nature, preventing domination; it could be a 'non-mastering interferer'.[101] Law was not antipathetic to, but constitutive of liberty: 'the laws of a suitable state, in particular the laws of a republic, create the freedom enjoyed by citizens.'[102] For Harrington, 'government . . . is an art whereby a civil society of men is instituted and preserved upon the foundations of a common right or interest, or (to follow Aristotle and Livy) it is the empire of laws and not of men'.[103] This was 'a state where the laws are fitted to create freedom for their citizens', which was taken up by Locke: 'that ill deserves the Name of Confinement which serves to hedge us in only from Bogs and Precipices . . . the end of Law is not to abolish or restrain, but to preserve and enlarge freedom'.[104]

The virtuous citizen was by nature independent, free from political, financial or social obligation or influence: 'if any party motives whatever, either of Religion or Politicks, or of Trade, bias your election [of police officers], you are forgetful of the sacred obligation you are under of acting only for the publick welfare, and not from private inclination'; indeed, Roberts notes that the Test Act did not expressly extend to Constables, Tythingmen or Headboroughs.[105] John Paul identified the idea that the Constables must be 'Freemen of the City, and are

---

[97] W. Roberts, 'A charge to the Grand Jury of the Court Leet, for the Manor of Manchester, by William Roberts Esq. Delivered at Michelmas Court on 15th October 1788' in J. P. Earwaker (ed.), *The Court Leet Records of the Manor of Manchester (from the Year 1552 to the Year 1686, and from the Year 1731 to the Year 1846)*, Vol. IX, 1787–1805, Appendix I (Manchester, 1889), 251–2.

[98] *ibid.*, 252, my emphasis.

[99] Skinner, *Liberty Before Liberalism*, *op. cit.*, 33

n. 103.

[100] This makes an interesting contrast to the government *through* freedom highlighted in Rose, *op. cit.*, 72.

[101] Pettit, *op. cit.*, 35.

[102] *ibid.*, 36.

[103] Harrington, *op. cit.*, 8.

[104] Pettit, *op. cit.*, 38, 40.

[105] Roberts, *op. cit.*, 252.

nominated by the Inhabitants'.[106] Thus the community governed itself directly by electing those with power over it and by actually sharing in that power by rotating the offices among themselves. The traditional offices of police, the constable and his officers, like his judicial counterpart the Justice of the Peace, along with the watchmen and Beadles, were unpaid offices and were either elected by the leypayers (the 'citizens') or selected by the Justice, 'so that High Constables are by Appointment of the Justices, and Petty Constables elected by the People'.[107] Ideally the office was actually rotated among the citizens themselves: 'it may be a good custom, That every Man, sufficiently qualified, shall serve or find one to do it.'[108] This was to prevent too much power being accrued to the office and its incumbent over time, and people

> were brought up in an habitual respect to the laws, and to those who were entrusted to the administration of them, as by the frequent change of these officers they could not help seeing that they obey'd the men for the sake of the law, and not the law through the power of the men.[109]

It was one of the most important aspects of public duty that it be unpaid service, free from the possibility of influence through 'emoluments', 'neither must they be in any man's livery'.[110] This guarded against corruption, particularly patronage and its use to increase the power of the Executive against the people and other branches of the state and the assumption of offices for financial benefit alone.[111] The criterion of independence was central to the legitimacy of the police.

It is clear that the system of propertied independence that characterized local government in the eighteenth century was organized, consciously or otherwise, in accordance with classical principles of government which saw liberty as secured by a system of civic obligation. In order to understand the logic of the eighteenth-century police and the context within which debates about its use or reform took place it is useful to pay attention to the wider implications of neo-classical thought and the way it defined the limits of government and governance. It is clear from the way the eighteenth-century police was organized, and the way its nature and use were discussed, that we need to rethink the distinctions we make between 'social', 'organizational' and 'political' activities at that time and recognize that what we view as social or institutional matters often had political implications.

CONCLUSION

It is clear that the 'old' police were described and debated in classical terms that defined the obligation to engage in the activity of policing as one aspect of civic virtue, that is, one of the key securities for the perpetuation of the free state and as such the liberty of the citizens. From at least the 1730s, however, following the 1735 Westminster Watch Act, watchmen were being paid to undertake policing duties. From the late eighteenth century, particularly from 1792 which saw the Middlesex Justices Act that introduced a state-appointed, stipendiary magistracy in London and the Police Commission in Manchester, the supervisors of these watchmen were also becoming increasingly bureaucratized. The extension of a paid, hierarchical system of police

---

[106] Paul, *op. cit.*, 59.
[107] [Gardiner], *The Complete Constable, op. cit.*, 7.
[108] *ibid.*, 7.

[109] 'Philonomos', *op. cit.*, 8.
[110] Ritson, *op. cit.*, 30.
[111] Pocock, *Machiavellian Moment, op. cit.*, 407.

gathered pace in the early nineteenth century, most notably with the reform of the Manchester Police Commission and the Metropolitan Police Act in 1829, the Municipal Corporations Act of 1835 that made a 'new' police force compulsory for all incorporated boroughs, and the County and Borough Police Act of 1856 that made a bureaucratic force compulsory for all of England and Wales. This process, which saw the system of 'civic' police, based on the rotation of office and the participation of the citizens in their own government, dismantled and replaced with a permanent, paid bureaucracy, constitutes a significant change in security for the condition of liberty.

Nevertheless, although the participatory system of police was replaced with a bureaucratic alternative, this specialized system was introduced as a new response to a traditional problem. The bureaucratic organization of police was a solution to problems of negligence and corruption in the officers and police system and, as such, constitutes a modern response to a classical problematic. The crucial debates in the emergence of the modern police – if not exclusively, then in very significant measure – all revolved around the problem of crime as a product of incompetent, lazy and unfit men. The accusation, then, was that the 'old' police were 'imperfect, inadequate, and wretched', and that the well-known reforms that established the 'new' police, appear in a new light.

Advocates of an improved system of police from the mid-eighteenth century onwards made their case by arguing that the existing system of police was actually contributing to the problems that civic participation was intended to prevent.[112] Bureaucracy, according to the police propagandists, would introduce energy, virtue and independence into the system of police. Independence was to be achieved by separating the institutions of police, and its officers, from political involvement, creating organizations staffed not by office-holders introduced through political patronage but specialists who graduated from the ranks with experience in the job. These independent men would direct the practice of policing without regard for party political aims, but solely according to the dictates of 'order'. Likewise, the officers of the police themselves would be separated from politics by excluding them from the franchise and forbidding them any political activity. The distinctive uniforms introduced would supposedly render the officers visible and, as such, immune from the allegations of political spying common on the continent. Equally, the classical virtues of temperance, fortitude, wisdom and justice were encouraged in the men through the handbooks written for them and the code of conduct they prescribed. The character of the men was ascertained by the use of references on recruitment and their virtue was secured by the system of surveillance and discipline that was intended to prevent corruption and negligence. Equally important was the emphasis on the impartiality of the officers and the concentration on the rule of law: this was central to the condition of liberty, understood in classical terms. The importance of citizens' participation in their own government remained: the 'new' police forces – with the exception of the Metropolitan Police, governed by the Home Office – were governed by watch committees, appointed by the elected representatives of the local council. The connection with locality was preserved in the Manchester Police Commission and later the borough forces by a preference for men

---

[112] In addition to the works cited see M. Madan, *Thoughts on Executive Justice. . .* , 2nd edn (London, 1785), 3; G. Barrett, *An Essay Towards Establishing a System of Police, on Constitutional Principles* (London, 1785), 3–4; J. Donaldson, *Sketch of a Plan to Prevent Crimes* (London, 1792), 9; G. B. Mainwaring, *Observations on the Present State of the Police of the Metropolis* (London, 1821), 11, 23, 30–3, 39–40; [J. Wade], *op. cit.*, 11–12, 75–9.

216   Social History   VOL. 29 : NO. 2

from their own locality as officers. The Metropolitan Police thought this encouraged a lack of impartiality, but did require their recruits to reside wherever they worked.[113]

Ultimately, then, the bureaucratic, disciplinary system that was introduced into the police over the course of the late eighteenth and early nineteenth centuries can be seen as a new solution to the traditional classical problems of corruption, negligence and dependence. For police reform to be successful, it was necessary that the preferred system should address this problematic and be capable of description in terms of independence, virtue and activity. The condition of liberty was being institutionalized, but classical ideals were still active in the formation of the 'new' police in the early nineteenth century and as such they provided the foundation for the distinctive ethos of the English police.

University of Manchester

---

[113] F. M. Dodsworth, 'The Institution of Police in Britain, *c.* 1750–1856: A Study in Historical Governmentality' (Ph.D., University of Manchester, 2002), 49–130.

[14]

SOCIAL POLICE AND THE MECHANISMS
OF PREVENTION

Patrick Colquhoun and the Condition of Poverty

MARK NEOCLEOUS*

This article reassesses the work of Patrick Colquhoun by reconsidering his notion of prevention. It argues that Colquhoun has been badly served by having his notion of prevention understood in the light of the emergence of the new police in 1829. This has obscured the importance of poverty, indigence and political economy to Colquhoun's understanding of police. I suggest that Colquhoun's work should be of interest as much to the discipline of social policy as police studies, and use this argument as a springboard into a wider argument concerning the historical, political, and conceptual links between police and social policy as mechanisms for the fashioning of the market. The major suggestion is that the concept of a 'social police' may be a useful way to understand these links.

In a recent article on 'The Limits of the Sovereign State' David Garland ended an interesting account of recent trends in crime control by pointing to the relevance of the work of the late 18th and early 19th century magistrate and writer Patrick Colquhoun. Colquhoun's ideas, Garland claimed, are 'remarkably similar to the thinking which has recently re-emerged in official circles' (Garland 1996: 464). Garland's discussion of Colquhoun was short and in itself thought provoking. Though a discussion of Colquhoun was an original way to end a discussion of recent trends in the politics of crime control, Garland was latching on to an existing interest in Colquhoun's work. Colquhoun has long been a key figure for British 'police studies', in which he is frequently cited as one of the key thinkers behind the emergence of the New Police in 1829, or at least a thinker who put police and policing on the political agenda by writing about it at great length. Leon Radzinowicz, for example, gives Colquhoun a central role in the volume on police in his *History of English Criminal Law*. 'Colquhoun was the first major writer on public order and the machinery of justice to use "police" in a strict sense closely akin to modern usage' (1956b: 247). For T. A. Critchley, Colquhoun's ideas 'represent an important link between the old and the new', whereas for Charles Reith Colquhoun is the second of three of the 'outstanding creators of the British police' (Critchley 1967: 40; Reith 1952: 136).

Radzinowicz's and Critchley's references to the 'modern' and 'new' here are partly attempts to highlight the idea of prevention in Colquhoun's work. Although more recent interest in Colquhoun's work has been among those developing new ways of understanding power and poverty (Dean 1991: 194–9) or those investigating the nature of 'private' policing (Johnston 1992: 5–6; Jones and Newburn 1998: 3), the main reason for the attention given to Colquhoun by writers in mainstream British police studies has centred firmly on the idea of prevention (Reith 1952: 155; Reith 1956: 24–7; Stead 1977:

* Department of Government, Brunel University, Uxbridge.

48; Emsley 1996: 21–2; Whitaker 1979: 40; Hardwicke n.d.: 30–1; also Dean 1991: 66). This is partly because of the way the New Police from 1829 has been understood. Since the New Police is commonly said to have involved the emergence of preventive policing, commentators searching for the origins of the New Police have focused on the preventive principle in Colquhoun's work. In this article I shall argue that although the general attention to Colquhoun's work is warranted, and specific attention to his notion of prevention especially so, his understanding of prevention has been misunderstood. Commentators have tended to assume that since the New Police emerged as an agency for the prevention of crime, so those working on preventive policing before 1829 must have had in mind the kind of force that emerged in 1829. But in reading Colquhoun through the lens of 1829, they have created a distorted view. In particular, they have obscured the relation Colquhoun sees between prevention, property, poverty and indigence. The more modest aim of this article is thus to present Colquhoun in a way that makes better sense of his place in police history and to give credit to him as a thinker who should remain of interest, as Garland suggests, not only to those interested in policing, but also to those interested in questions of poverty and state power more generally. More ambitiously, the article also aims to use Colquhoun's work as a springboard into making some wider historical and theoretical links between police and social policy, and to situate both in relation to the question of poverty and the condition of the working class. The purpose is to suggest that perhaps we need to rethink research into the nature of policing and social policy by linking them through the idea of 'social police'.

Towards a Preventive Police

Colquhoun's starting point is the insecurity of property, which he believes is a result of the combination of imperfections in the criminal law and the lack of an 'active principle' regarding the police of the metropolis (Colquhoun 1796: 28, 33). Estimating that in 1795 there were some 150 offences on the statute books with execution as their punishment, Colquhoun notes that the rationale for this is prevention, yet this is precisely what severe punishment fails to achieve. Despite a 'bloody code', which saw the execution of large numbers of people for increasingly petty crimes, the crime rate in London was still high; according to Colquhoun there were some 115,000 people in London supporting themselves by criminal or immoral means, resulting in a net loss to the metropolis of over £2 million a year. The criminal law merely punished the inexperienced criminal severely while leaving the experienced criminal free to commit more crimes (1796: vi, 3–6, 45–7, 188).

Colquhoun suggests a number of solutions. One is a Beccarian argument that instead of severity, the criminal law should be based on certainty. Another is a shift in the style of punishment, focused on the use of the penitentiary (Colquhoun 1796: 7, 282, 299, 334–52). But the main way to reduce crimes, Colquhoun argues, is less through the style of punishment and more through the prevention of crimes in the first place. While in England property is ravaged and threatened, Colquhoun points out that in many European countries this is not the case—he claims that in many European cities people rarely bolt their doors or windows at night. Thus 'security [of property] does not proceed from *severe punishments,* for in very few countries are they more sanguinary than in England. It is to be attributed to a more correct and energetic system of Police, joined to an early and general attention to the education and morals of the lower orders of the people; aided by a system of industry and sobriety'. Society needs not just sensible laws but also 'a watchful police, aided by a correct system of restraints'. This would *prevent* crimes occurring and thus obviate the need for punishment: wise legislatures know that it is better to prevent rather than punish crimes: 'the prevention of crimes and misdemeanours is the true essence of Police' (1796: 14, 18, 94–5, 259).

On this score Colquhoun's proposals are radical and wide-ranging, including breaking with the five separate jurisdictions in London in which a few watchmen and constables were expected to prevent crime and keep the peace, and establishing a uniform and centralized system. This police—which Colquhoun calls 'the Criminal Police', a significant point to which we shall return—would carry out many of the functions of the magistrates. It would license and regulate those activities which encouraged frauds, such as hawkers and peddlers, pawnbrokers, hackney coaches, fortune tellers, and alehouses, and regulate those areas the proper supervision of which would prevent crime, such as customs and excise, stamps, game laws, friendly societies, the highways, and vagrancy. Aside from this, the police would compile a register 'of all or most of the criminal or fraudulent persons who resort to the Metropolis'—'a general and complete register of every known offender'—as well as a register of stolen property— enabling a complete knowledge of the state of the criminal population and their activities. He approvingly cites the fact that 'at the commencement of the troubles in France' the Lieutenant General of the National Police there had no less than 20,000 suspect or depraved characters of the criminal variety on his register (1796: 28, 381, 394). These activities would be carried out by a group of men 'who would give *their whole attention to* the criminal department of the Police' on a centralized and national basis, with a Board of Commissioners of police maintaining the registers and managing the force overall in terms of salaries and uniforms. This Board would in turn operate under a 'Minister of the National Police', the Home Secretary (1796: xviii, 368, 374; 1800: 245–51).

Clearly then Colquhoun's work must be understood as an argument for the protection of liberty and security of property via the prevention of crime, as we have seen many commentators note. But the focus on crime prevention disguises the breadth and originality of Colquhoun's thought. Narrowing his work down to the preventive principle obscures the wider aspects of his work through which his ideas concerning prevention have to be understood.

The Genuine Character of Police

The problem lies in the meaning of 'prevention' and the instruments used to achieve it, and the key to understanding it lies in the definition of police Colquhoun introduced in later editions of his *Treatise on the Police*. Here is the often cited opening of the later editions:

Police in this country may be considered as a *new Science*; the properties of which consist not in the Judicial Powers which lead to *Punishment*, and which belong to Magistrates alone; but in the PREVENTION AND DETECTION OF CRIMES, and in those other Functions which relate to INTERNAL REGULATIONS for the well ordering and comfort of Civil Society. (1806c)

Colquhoun's emphases here are significant. As we have noted above, Colquhoun understands one aspect or branch of the police as 'the Criminal Police'. It is essentially this aspect or branch which became institutionalized as *the* police from 1829. The uniformed force for the prevention and detection of crime, the keeping of registers of known offenders and enforcing the criminal law in conjunction with the courts, is only one part of the police system. The other integral part is the Municipal Police. Noting that various Acts of Parliament have established a system 'which may be denominated *municipal regulations*, such as *paving, watching, lighting, cleaning, and removing nuisances; furnishing water; the mode of building houses;* the system *established* for *extinguishing fires*, and for regulating *coaches, carts*, and *other carriages*; with a variety of other useful improvements, tending to the comfort and convenience of the inhabitants', a list to which he later adds the sewage system, signs and signposts, and gutters and balconies, Colquhoun makes the point that these regulations are part of the system of police: he describes Acts of Parliament outlining the management of the city as containing 'a complete and masterly system of *that branch of the Police* which is connected with municipal regulations'; the regulations explain 'by what means *the system of Police*, in most of its great features, is conducted in the metropolis' (Colquhoun 1796: 357, 428–35, last two emphases added; 1806c: 567, 591–601). In fact, Colquhoun's more subtle point is that till now there has been no real police system to speak of in England (1816: 56, 90), and that thinking of such regulations as part of the police would require a thorough rethinking through of what it means to have a proper police system. And for Colquhoun, what it means to have a proper police system extends well beyond a law enforcement agency for the prevention of crime.

The crux of this lies in the connection Colquhoun makes between crime and indigence and thus, indirectly, between crime and poverty. It is significant that Colquhoun presents *The State of Indigence* of 1799 and the later *Treatise on Indigence* of 1806 as part of the overall argument found in his *Treatise on the Police*: his continual cross-referencing between the texts is indicative of his basic working assumption that the problem of poverty is part of the wider problem of police (1799b: 5; 1806b: 251). Colquhoun's initial thoughts on this, in *The State of Indigence*, are that the poor be put 'under the review of certain persons' within Houses of Industry, or Work-rooms, where they 'should receive whole of their earnings and a meal besides'. This would cut the expense to the parish and end begging. The modest and deserving poor would receive relief while the idle and profligate would be compelled to labour for their subsistence (Colquhoun 1799b: 16). The 'certain persons' would be Chief Officers, or Commissioners, who would examine applications for relief, oversee the provision of relief and management of the casual poor, provide work-rooms in key locations in the metropolis where those without employment can receive subsistence for labour, give temporary relief to families, assist in binding out the children of the poor and preventing the females from becoming prostitutes and the males from developing loose or immoral habits, keep a register of those applying for relief and in receipt of it, and exercise legal powers through constables to compel the idle and destitute to come before the Commissioners for examination (1799b: 25–8). In other words, in his earlier attempts to grapple with the policing of the poor Colquhoun was a fully-fledged supporter of early arguments for a workhouse system operating a test of eligibility for work. Given the five classes of the poor identified by Colquhoun—useful poor, vagrant poor, indigent poor, aged and infirm, and poor infants—the 'great art' is to establish a system whereby those verging on indigence may be kept in the class of useful labour and those who are able but not willing to work (vagrants) be compelled to do so. At this stage in his work then, Colquhoun's criticism that in the present system 'the Police . . . has provided no place of industry in which those who were disposed to reform might find subsistence in return for labour' should be seen in the light of his proposals in *The State of Indigence* for work-rooms and tests of ability to labour as 'a most important branch of Police' (1796: 99; 1799b: p. 29). Indeed, it is the very core of the police system, since if this part of the system is effective then crimes will reduce and the Criminal Police will be as little active as possible.

In the later *Treatise on Indigence*, however, the concern with the workhouse has diminished somewhat. He criticizes the workhouse for debasing the mind of the labouring people, being 'gaols without guilt, punishment without crime', and for rewarding in a roundabout way vice and idleness. Although in 'the present state of society' workhouses are 'indispensably necessary' they are in dire need of improvement (1806b: 219–23, 270). His failure to suggest what kind of reforms would constitute improvement is because by the time of the *Treatise on Indigence* he has developed a key theoretical presupposition which comes to determine his approach to poverty and thus his overall approach to police in later editions of the *Treatise on Police*: namely, the distinction between poverty and indigence.

In Colquhoun's writings from the 1790s the distinction between poverty and indigence lacks any real theoretical importance. Sometimes he works without the distinction at all, distinguishing instead between 'the *noxious* and the *blameless* and useful part of the community' (1799a: 25). At other times he refers to the differences between the poor and the indigent but without spelling out the theoretical, or indeed practical, importance of the distinction: 'The principle object of this [meat and soup] Charity is not only to afford a temporary relief to the indigent, sober and industrious' (1797: 13). Once he starts dealing with the issue of indigence more directly, however, in the 1799 text on *The State of Indigence* he begins to recognize the importance of labour to the production of wealth, and thus the importance of poverty, and starts to separate poverty from indigence. 'Labour is absolutely requisite to the existence of all Governments; and it is from the Poor only that labour can be expected . . . It is not *Poverty* therefore, that is itself an evil'. Instead 'the evil is to be found only in *Indigence*, where the strength fails, where disease, age, or infancy, deprive the individual of the means of subsistence, or where he knows not how to find employment when willing and able to work' (1799b: 18; 1800: 155). By the 1806 *Treatise on Indigence* this has become a categorical distinction between poverty and indigence of fundamental theoretical importance.

Poverty is that state and condition in society where the individual has no surplus labour in store, and, consequently, no property but what is derived from the constant exercise of industry in the various occupations of life; or, in other words, it is the state of every one who must labour for subsistence.

Poverty is therefore a most necessary and indispensable ingredient of society, without which nations and communities could not exist in a state of civilization. It is the lot of man—it is the source of *wealth*, since without *labour* there would be *no riches*, no *refinement*, no *comfort*, and no *benefit* to those who may be possessed of wealth.

Indigence therefore, and not *poverty*, is the evil . . . It is the state of any one who is destitute of the means of subsistence, and is unable to labour to procure it to the extent nature requires. The natural source of subsistence is the labour of the individual; while that remains with him he is denominated *poor*; when it fails in whole or in part he becomes *indigent* (1806b: 7–8).[1]

Although some have rightly pointed to Bentham's prior use of this distinction (Poynter 1969: 200–2; cf. Himmelfarb 1984: 85), to present Colquhoun as doing little more than following Bentham here is misleading. Colquhoun has been badly served by being presented as a 'Benthamite', a label that often obscures more than it reveals. In this context Colquhoun is in fact more Malthusian than Benthamite—it is significant that the *Treatise on Indigence* and the later editions of the *Treatise on Police* appear after the publication of Malthus's hugely influential *Essay on Population* (1798). Following Malthus rather than Bentham, Colquhoun was a key figure in effecting a conceptual break in the notion of the 'labouring poor' that was to become a crucial conceptual device in ruling class strategies thereafter—it is at the heart of the Poor Law Report of 1834 for example, as we shall see. The point here is that this distinction between poverty and indigence not only forms the theoretical foundation of Colquhoun's understanding of poverty, *it also shapes his conception of police*. It is thus the key to understanding his idea of the Municipal Police and, as such, his notion of prevention.

This is due to Colquhoun's fundamental belief that 'From indigence is to be traced the great Origin and the Progress of Crimes' (1796: 95; 1799b: 5, 8; 1806b: 43–9; 1816: 55). The key to Colquhoun's science of police is that the Criminal Police deals with the criminal underclass, those who have fallen from indigence into crime. The Municipal Police is there to prevent the class of poverty from falling into indigence. The overall project of the science of police is to identify and implement the mechanisms necessary to prevent the poverty-stricken class from falling into indigence and from there into crime. 'The great desideratum, therefore, is to prop up *poverty* by judicious arrangements at those critical periods when it is in danger of descending into indigence. The barrier between these two conditions in society is often slender, and the public interest requires that it should be narrowly guarded' (1806b: 8–9). Hence the two 'sides' of police: whereas the potentially criminal indigent class are to be the main object of the Criminal Police, the class of poverty—the working class—are to be the main object of Municipal Police. The key to prevention is thus not directly preventing crime, but preventing the class of poverty from falling into indigence. Not for nothing do later editions of the *Treatise on Police* include a section called 'The Origin of Crimes: State of the Poor' and the *Treatise on Indigence* a section on 'A Board of General and Internal Police'; and not for nothing did Colquhoun earlier describe the Board of General and Internal Police as 'Commissioners of the Poor' (1806c: 351–80; 1806b: 79–110; also see 1816: 55). 'The

---

[1] The increased importance of this distinction to Colquhoun's work is notable from the change in the titles from the *State of Indigence* (1799) to the *Treatise on Indigence* (1806). The full title of the earlier work is *The State of Indigence and the Situation of the Casual Poor in the Metropolis, explained; with reasons assigned why the prevailing system, with respect to This Unfortunate Class of the Community, contributes, in a considerable degree, to the increase and multiplication of crimes: with suggestion, shewing the necessity and utility of an establishment of pauper police, immediately applicable to the casual poor, under the management of responsible commissioners, with their functions explained.* Here the concern is merely with the relationship between the 'unfortunate class' and crime. In the later work, however, the full title makes explicit not only the link between indigence and crime, but also the importance of distinguishing between poverty and indigence. The title is *A Treatise on Indigence; exhibiting A General View of the National Resources for Productive Labour; with Proposition for Ameliorating the Condition of the Poor, and Improving the moral Habits and increasing the Comforts of the Labouring People, particularly the Rising Generation; by regulations of Political Economy, calculated to prevent Poverty from descending into Indigence, To Produce Sobriety and Industry, to reduce the Parochial Rates of the Kingdom, and generally to promote the Happiness and Security of the Community at Large, by the Diminution of moral and penal Offences, and the future Prevention of Crimes.*

Board of General and Internal Police is to embrace all objects in any degree connected with the casualties of life or a retrograde state of morals, producing *indigence, vagrancy,* or *criminal offences*'. It is in fact part of the system of police to 'relieve the indigent requiring assistance [and] to prop up the industrious poor ready to descend into indigence'. This is not an optional extra of police but its very essence, for it would have the effect of 'returning to police its genuine character, unmixed with those judicial powers which lead to punishment, and properly belong to magistracy alone' (1806b: 69, 82, 87, 90, 94, 109; also 1799b: 12–15). In this sense the poor law is the main component of municipal policing.

Since crime is so closely associated with the condition of poverty, the police has no option but to employ a whole panoply of measures and techniques to manage this condition, extending well beyond the management of relief into the morality, profligacy, and propriety of the working class. For Colquhoun, part of the problem is the tendency to idleness, immorality, and depravity among the indigent working class. 'Crimes of every description have their origins in the vicious and immoral habits of the people; in the want of attention to the education of the inferior orders of society; and in the deficiency of the system which has been established for guarding the morals of this useful class of the community.' Thus 'the first object, with a view to the prevention of crime in great societies, is to look accurately at whatever has a tendency to the corruption of morals'. Like many police writers before him, Colquhoun sees the 'corruption of morals' as inextricably linked with drink and gambling. 'A moment's reflection will show how much these unfortunate habits tend to destroy the moral principle, and to engender crimes.' Through drinking the working class squander their money, unaware of the immorality of doing so and are slowly dragged into yet more immoral behaviour such as crime, cohabitation, prostitution, political subversion, and trade unionism. One answer to this is for the police to regulate properly public houses and gambling. Not only do the working class get drunk there, but criminals learn, find asylum, and commit crimes there. The number of pubs should be limited, with licences given only to responsible men of sober manners and good moral character, and it is the task of police to keep a watchful eye on them and remove the licence should the landlord allow 'misconduct' in the form of games, gambling, or political meetings, or tolerate disorderly people such as prostitutes, thieves or vagabonds (1796b: 34, 37–9, 42–3, 361, 449; 1816: 56; 1794: 16, 23, 38; 1803). He similarly points to the way that any money the poor receive can be spent in gin shops, the way recipients of poor relief are not compelled to redeem their possessions from the pawnshop, and the fact that no questions are asked about the extent or manner in which they are seeking labour. In this context it is worth noting that Colquhoun's proposed Police Gazette is very different from the earlier and better-known Gazette of John Fielding, for Colquhoun sees the Gazette as a moralizing force. Not only should the Gazette detail crimes committed, list stolen goods, and provide criminal statistics in the way Fielding had envisaged, but it should also be used to 'excite in the minds of the labouring people a strong sense of moral virtue, loyalty and love of their country'. Short essays, articles, and selections from the more moral sections of statutes should be printed to show the importance of industrious activity and good behaviour (1806b: 97–107).

Alongside the careful watch on the habits of the poor by police, the clergy and teachers should also ensure that morality is maintained. Colquhoun's recommendations for the reform of the education of the poor rest on his belief that the children of the poor should not 'be educated in such a manner to elevate their minds above the rank they are destined to fill in society', but rather in such a way as to 'fortify their minds as, if possible, to render them proof against those vices and temptations to which their situations, particularly in large cities, expose them'. Hence his recommendations for teaching to begin with spelling and move to writing, arithmetic and then end with religious and moral instruction. The last of these constitutes 'the great and primary object of this institution' and should thus be carried out in conjunction with the established church. Interestingly, Colquhoun adds that because this kind of institution is also intended to 'contribute to the reform of the parents' too, its knock-on effect is of crucial importance to the prosperity of the nation; as such it should be central to the concerns of political economy (1806a: 12, 17–18, 39–40, 64–5, 68; 1806b: 139–56).

Political Economy, Police Science and Wage Labour

Like most writers on police, it is crime against property that so concerns Colquhoun, and as the distinction between poverty and indigence is sharpened so his account of property is also refined. In doing so it comes to focus on the general *public* effect of crimes and the damage done to the state or community *as a whole* by crime. Significant here is the change in title between the earlier and later editions of his *Treatise on Police*. In the title of the earlier edition Colquhoun fails to mention property at all: it is presented as *A Treatise on the Police of the Metropolis, explaining the various crimes and misdemeanours Which at present are felt as a Pressure on the Community; and suggesting remedies for their prevention.* By the seventh edition ten years later not only does property come to dominate the discussion, but the importance of property as a question of *public* concern has also become central. The work had therefore become *A Treatise on the Police of the Metropolis; containing a detail of the various crimes and misdemeanours by which Public and Private Property and Security are, at present, injured and endangered: and suggesting remedies for their prevention.* And it is for this reason that in trying to show that theft is a serious matter he gives figures for the total loss to the community and not just to any single individual or group of individuals.

Since the labour of the class of poverty was clearly central to the wealth of the nation, and since this wealth was also understood as consisting in property, Colquhoun presents his vision of police as a contribution to political economy. The distinction between poverty and indigence is the crux of his contribution to *both* political economy and his science of police, and both have the condition of labour at their core. Since for Colquhoun the acceleration of wealth can only be achieved 'by establishing a correct system of police', political economy must concern itself with this. Yet the science of wealth has failed to grasp this point. 'In all the branches of the Science of Political Oeconomy, there is none which requires so much skill and knowledge of men and manners, as that which relates to this particular object [the poor]'. Thus the main concern of his proposal for a Pauper Police Institution and a Board of General Internal Police should be seen as his contribution to the political economy of the wealth of nations, and the set of measures which Colquhoun subsumes under the police idea should also be seen as, in a roundabout way, Colquhoun's contribution to *political economy* in the form of a *science of police* (1799b: 11, 17, 28; 1796: 76; 1806b: 90). In Colquhoun's case then, it is not that the discourse of police is displaced by the discourse of political economy and the system of natural liberty, as it is in the work of political economists such as Adam Smith (see Neocleous 1998a, 1998b, 2000), but that police and political economy are the two sides of the same discursive coin. Colquhoun's contribution to political economy was to develop an account of the role of police as a *complement* to the political economy of commercial society rather than its opposite.

As with political economy more generally in this period, Colquhoun's objective was the development of a free market economy and, concomitantly, the commodification of labour. But in contrast to classical political economy, Colquhoun's belief was that the police is the prime mobilizing force to achieve this objective. The police, on this score, would not only oversee the disciplinary nature of the market and step in where that discipline fails, but would help shape the market in the first place. Significant here is Colquhoun's first practical success in introducing a police for the Thames in the late-1790s. This event has been understood as merely a limited precursor of the more widespread introduction of police forces from 1829, or as a pointer to the tension between 'private' and 'public' policing in the period. But these ways of understanding it have obscured the fact that the introduction of this force was deliberately designed not only to end commercial losses on the river and docks, but to do so by consolidating the money wage as the form of subsistence for the workers in question.

In the 18th century the worker was not yet fully tied to the money wage. Many workers during this period were paid partly in money wages and partly in kind. This was often seen in terms of ancient entitlements. The thresher was partly paid with part of the harvest, the coal worker by part of the coal he handled. In the docks the ships' carpenters were still entitled to some of the spare timber, while dock workers generally claimed to be entitled to any sugar that was spilt. T. S. Ashton notes that

Both the coal-hewers of the north and the coal-meters of the Thames received by custom an allowance of fuel; and ironworks and other establishments that used coal often supplied it on special terms to their workers. The mates of the West Indiamen had a right to the sweepings of sugar and coffee from the hold of the ship; the gangsmen and coopers established a claim to the drainings of molasses and spilt sugar on the floor of the warehouse; and the labourers in the corn ships believed themselves to be similarly entitled to the grain that had been removed as samples. At the Royal Yards, the shipwrights were allowed to take for firewood the chips that fell from the axe, and their womenfolk were permitted to do the gleaning (1955: 208).

Though not a part of the actual wage, such customary rights formed an important part of a labourer's income. Workers therefore ensured that such 'extras' were always available and in plentiful supply, appropriating whatever they could as part of such 'ancient entitlement' and the customary 'right' to their share of the product of their labour: 'the workers saw to it that the crumbs from the master's table were ample', as Ashton puts it. In such conditions the line between established rights and theft was difficult to draw. From the mid-century many of the non-monetary forms of the wage were coming within the criminal sanction, yet the deeply embedded notion of customary right was so entrenched that the moral sanction against such crimes was lacking (Linebaugh 1972: 13). Towards the end of the 18th and into the 19th century employers therefore began a more concerted attempt to enforce the moral sanction against such perks and to ensure that such activities were properly criminalized. For example, in 1777 the Worsted Committee had been established by legislation to limit appropriation in the textile industry in Yorkshire, Lancashire, and Cheshire, and in 1790 the West India merchants introduced regulations prohibiting the allowance of sweepings or molasses to the

Gangsmen (Godfrey 1999; Colquhoun 1800: 80). The increasingly dominant bourgeois class felt that the activities in question jarred with the fundamental purpose of labour, which was to earn a wage and be paid in money. The thefts in general raised a fundamental question: are those who labour entitled to appropriate the products of their own labour, other than through the wage received? The answer given by capital was increasingly a firm 'no'. Thus the increased prosecution for such 'thefts' in the 19th century 'mark an offensive by the employers designed to eliminate popular ideas about the legitimate taking of property, which the employers now wanted to be clearly defined as unlawful and liable to be punished' (Philips 1977: 188–9; also Linebaugh 1972). Moreover, it was an attempt to stamp out crimes that were taking place at the very heart of the circuit of capital. It is this broader context in which the significance of Colquhoun's work—and the police project more generally—becomes clear.

Colquhoun estimated that nine tenths of all crimes in the port were committed by persons whose presence in the area was justified—that is, by workers—and that in some groups of workers up to half were delinquents (1800: 198). For Colquhoun, the major task of the new preventive police was not just to halt the losses but to break the notion that the appropriation of goods on which workers labour was 'sanctioned by custom'. 'The transition from innocence to acts of turpitude . . . is easy and obvious', he notes.

An indulgent Master, at first, grants the privilege of a few samples or a trifling quantity of foul Corn, on the solicitation of an industrious servant, under the pretence of feeding a pig, or a few poultry. The stock of poultry or pigs is increased, and additional quantities of grain become necessary. The indulgence of the Master in a few instances is, at length, constituted into a sanction to appropriate Sweepings of foul Grain. These Sweepings are presently increased by previous concert among the Labourers. Corn becomes foul, which might have been preserved in a clean and Merchantable state.

This process is then extended to other commodities and industries (1800: 80, 139, 141, 163). For this reason, Colquhoun argues, workers agreed to work without wages because they knew this would provide them with opportunities for taking what they considered to be justifiably theirs: they would agree 'to be admitted to work . . . without any pay, trusting to the chance of Plunder for remuneration' (1800: 63). Introducing the river police therefore meant that not only would commodities being transported be better secured, but the improvement in the security of property would also have the deliberate effect of reducing 'wastage' and 'loss'. This would mean that payments of money wages could be regularized as well. Such decisions were consolidated in 1798 with the issuing of a public notice of a new 'Marine Police Establishment . . . under the sanction of Government', by the West India merchants. Its fourth department—the 'Discharging Department', but which Colquhoun described as an 'Establishment for Protection and Labour'—was charged with controlling dock labour, especially of the lumpers (Colquhoun 1800: 80–9, 159; Radzinowicz 1956a: 369). Eight hundred and twenty lumpers were enlisted to perform their duties in accordance with instructions issued by the Marine Police. Master lumpers were appointed to restrain the lumpers from pillage and wilful breakage, and to search the lumpers regularly with the help of other police. Not only was the unloading of ships overseen by the Marine Police, but rates of pay were set by it too. Thus a force designed to protect property was also at the heart of imposing the money wage on the foundation stone of capital accumulation, namely the working class, and of enforcing the discipline of labour on the same group. This 'virtual conscription', as Radzinowicz describes it, was not just to the discipline of police but to the discipline of the wage too.

The net effect of the first preventive police system was the consolidation of the money wage and thus the commodification of labour.[2]

The roots of this attempt to help shape a commercial society by using the power of police to accelerate the commodification of wage labour returns us to the importance of Colquhoun's categorical distinction between poverty and indigence. His claim that poverty 'is the state of every one who must labour for subsistence' and is 'a most necessary and indispensable ingredient of society' for without it 'there would be no riches, no refinement, no comfort, and no benefit to those who may be possessed of wealth', feeds into every aspect of his work. For example, as much as his opposition to capital punishment for all crimes except murder is an outcome of his opposition to an excessively severe criminal code, it is equally an outcome of his obsession with productive labour and the waste of human resources. The penitentiary, on this score, operates not only as the most effective and useful punishment but also as a mechanism within which the confined are put to work. Prison labour benefits both the state and the criminal: the former finds its wealth increased through the labour of the convicted; the latter learns the importance of labouring for one's subsistence and the requisite discipline that this requires (Colquhoun 1796: 9–10, 334–6, 350–2; 1806c: 364–5). And his vision of an educational system for the poor is based on the view that education is to 'rouse the indolent, and to correct the slothfulness of the idle' (1806a: 17, 21).

Social Police and the Government of Poverty

I suggested above that commentators on police who have focused on Colquhoun's contribution to the idea of prevention have tended to narrow the idea of 'preventive police' down to what Colquhoun actually thought of as Criminal Police, and to thereby reduce his idea of prevention to the kind of police that emerged after 1829 in Britain. In the light of Garland's comment (1996: 466) that to refer to Colquhoun's 'criminology' would be to use an anachronism I suggest that, given Colquhoun's understanding that 'by the term *police* we are to understand *all those regulations in a country which apply to the comfort, convenience, and safety of the inhabitants*' (1806b: 82), and given the centrality of the condition of the poor to these regulations, a better anachronism would perhaps be to refer to Colquhoun's 'social policy'. In other words, Colquhoun's conception of prevention has less to do with what we now call 'police' and much more with what we call 'social policy'. I am arguing, in effect, that since the heart of Colquhoun's proposals is the overseeing of the condition of labour through the political management of poverty, he should be remembered for being a forerunner of the new poor law as much as a forerunner of the New Police—a forerunner of preventive *social policy* as well as preventive *criminal policing*. Those figures which emerged following the 'birth of the welfare state' and which became central to social policy—poor law and social security

---

[2] My comments here have been partly generated by comments by Macdonald (1973: 331-3) and Bunyan (1977: 61). It is also clear from Philips's (1977) study of crime in the Black Country that there was a concerted effort on the part of industrial capital, police, and magistrates to impose the money wage on the working class, while in Liverpool merchants complained of the way the secondary economy of the streets threatened their own welfare and property by creating alternative points of sale, draining wages, and taking the time of those who should more properly be engaged in wage labour (Brogden 1982: 44-55; Brogden and Brogden 1984: 45). The use of police street powers to end this secondary economy can thus be seen as an attempt to impose the discipline of wage labour.

officers, social workers, probation officers and the 'official' administrators of policy—are on this view as much a part of the policing of the system as uniformed police officers. It is indicative of the skewed focus of police studies that this aspect of Colquhoun's work has been largely ignored. And, one might add, it is indicative of the skewed nature of political economy and social policy that these disciplines have also failed to note Colquhoun's importance.[3]

Now, 'social policy' may be a little too anachronistic, and I am aware that there are many within the discipline of social policy who would perhaps defend it by claiming that its central concern with the welfare of the population distances it from police and the coercive connotations of the latter. So I suggest that perhaps another term, first used by A. P. Donajgrodzki (1977) over 20 years ago but never really developed, may be more appropriate: 'social police'. Not only is this term more useful for understanding Colquhoun's work, but it may well be useful in understanding the nature of policing more generally, including the policing that goes under the title of 'social policy'. To sustain this view I shall explore at a little more length the reasons why it might be useful to draw together 'police' and 'policy' in this way (the fuller version of this argument can be found in Neocleous (2000)).

The concept of police entered the political language from the late 15th century, and came to be associated with the activities of rulers as they responded to social disorder which traditional authority appeared unable to deal with. Originating in French-Burgundian *policie* in the fifteenth century, the word 'police' spread across continental Europe. In the German language, although the word *Polizei* eventually came to designate police, it originally had a range of words adopted from the French-Burgundian: 'Policei', 'Pollicei', 'Policey', 'Pollicey', 'Pollizey', 'Pollizei', 'Politzey', 'Pollucey', and 'Pullucey'. Though the spelling of the word varied, the meaning remained constant, denoting the legislative and administrative regulation of the internal life of a community to promote general welfare and the condition of good order (as encapsulated in phrases such as 'police and good order' or 'good police and order'), and the regimenting of social life (as in 'regiment and police'). In the 16th century 'policey' or '*Polizei*' came into widespread use, especially in instructions and activities considered necessary for the maintenance of good order. These were known as *Policey Ordnung*, or *Polizeiordnungen*—police ordinances—and referred to the management and direction of the population by the state. In giving rise to the *Polizeistaat* they referred, in effect, to what Marc Raeff has described as the 'well-ordered police state' (Raeff 1983; Foucault 1991).

In this sense we can say that early discourse on policing was simultaneously a discourse on *Polizeistaat* or 'police state', implying a state which engages in wide-ranging internal administration, welfare and surveillance. Given the negative connotations of the phrase 'police state' in the 20th century, it might be argued that a far better means of understanding *Polizeistaat* is as an early *welfare* state. As Brian Chapman points out (1971: 15–6), the first 'police states' were dedicated to three purposes not dissimilar to modern welfare states: the protection of the population, the welfare of the state and its citizens, and the improvement of society. And Reinhold August Dorwart suggests that the only reason we do not equate *Polizeistaat* with *Wohlfahrsstaat* is because we are captives of 20th century

---

[3] See for example Cowherd (1977), in which Colquhoun is mentioned only in passing. This is generally true for texts on the history of social policy.

definitions of police state and welfare state. He notes that the definition of the early welfare state as a *Polizeistaat* may best be understood in relation to the German phrases, *gemeine Nutz* and *gemeine Beste*. As there was no German equivalent to the relevant French word for police it could not be translated precisely; it connoted order, welfare, security. By the 18th century *Polizei* had become synonymous with *Wohlfahrt* or *gemeine Nutz* (Dorwart 1971: 4, 14).

Now, it is of course widely claimed that the idea of 'police' was for centuries alien to British yet common to Continental political discourse, and that this is why Britain had no 'organized' police to speak of. But this obscures the fact that the meaning of 'police' did in fact have an English equivalent: 'policy'. Both 'police' and 'policy' were used in rather undifferentiated but broadly parallel ways across Europe into the 16th century and after. Hence the meanings given to the earliest mentions of 'policy' in the *Oxford English Dictionary*—ranging from 'an organized state' or 'an organized and established system or form of government or administration', with particular reference to the decisions of rulers, urban conditions, and good conduct—are more or less identical to the definitions of police in continental languages at the time. Francis Bacon, for example, uses 'policy' as interchangeable with 'government' in *The Advancement of Learning* (1605), and on one occasion refers to government as 'the policing of cities and commonalties'.[4] Given that the 20th century 'welfare state' is also characterized by and understood in terms of its wide-ranging social policy, and given that it is generally accepted that 'social policy' refers to 'the policy of governments with regard to actions having a direct impact on the welfare of the citizens' (Marshall 1970: 9), it makes as much sense to think of the policing of the common good or general welfare as a form of policy, and to think of *Polizeistaat* as 'policy state'. For like police, 'policy' relies on the notion of what is to be policed (as opposed to 'policied'). It is for this reason that historians often slip between 'police' and 'policy'—as in John LeDonne's comment (1984: 115) on policing in Russian towns that 'to administer the collectivity was to police it, to formulate a single *policy* of interdependent parts', or the way G. R. Elton (1972) uses 'police' and 'policy' more or less interchangeably in his work on the enforcement of the Reformation under Thomas Cromwell—and why historians of ideas often translate the idea of *Polizeistaat* as 'policy state' rather than 'police state' (Dyson 1980: 118; Johnson 1964: 391). In practical terms what this also means is that England in the 17th and 18th centuries was not an 'unpoliced' society (Emsley 1983: 30), merely that the agents of policing were often understood as carrying out *policy* rather than being *police*.

The reasons for the adoption of the different terms in different countries is partly due to the nature of translations of Aristotle's *Politics* from the 13th century onwards. In France and Germany the key terms of Aristotle's text—*polis* and *politeia*—were often translated as 'police', whereas in England they were translated as 'Commonwealth' or 'policy'. The first English translation of Aristotle's *Politics* in 1598 translated *politeia* as 'policy' and defined it as 'the order and description, as of other offices in a city, so of that which hath the greatest and most soveraine authority: for the rule and administration of a Commonweale, hath evermore power and authority joined with it: which administration is called policie in Greek, and in English a Commonweale'. That the meaning of the term 'policy' was more or less the same as that of the French term 'police' is

---

[4] In the 1605 and 1629 editions 'policing' was spelt 'pollicing'; in the 1633 edition it was rendered 'pollishing'.

unsurprising, given that the first English translations of Aristotle's text were from an earlier French translation of the Latin version. It was only later, with the first direct translation into English from Greek, that *politeia* was defined independently of either the concepts police or policy, as the 'form of government . . . the ordering and regulating of the city' (Stourzh 1988; the relevant paragraph is 1278b of Aristotle's *Politics*).

Now, this helps make some sense of Colquhoun's definition of police in later editions of his *Treatise*. British police studies has made much of his reference to the 'new science' of the prevention and detection of crimes (police in the narrow sense), but has tended to ignore his reference straight after this to the new science including all those functions which relate to internal regulations for the well ordering and comfort of society, a reference to police in the wider sense of 'policy'.[5] Moreover, if my argument has any substance then it helps make sense of the many ways in which the activities of the police from 1829 onwards were clearly *not* restricted to the prevention and detection of crime.

That the police came to operate as 'domestic missionaries', suppressing 'vice' and 'immorality' among the working class, has been well-documented (Storch 1975; 1976). More important, however, are the activities of police in relation to the poor and the exercise of the poor law. It is clear that those behind the new poor law recognized the need for a police force (rather than the military) to crush any anti-poor law disturbances (see Knott 1986), but the links between police and poor law run far deeper than the need to suppress riots and resistance. To function properly the new poor law required an intensification of the policing of vagrancy. The police had responsibility under common law and the Vagrancy Act (1824) for controlling vagrants, and the extension of the police to the boroughs in the County and Borough Police Act of 1856 was justified by the need to suppress vagrancy (Steedman 1984: 56). The omnibus mandate contained in police street powers helped remove the possibility of obtaining the means of subsistence other than the wage. Not only was begging severely curtailed, but customs and common rights such as casual labour for payment in kind, grazing cattle on public byways, pilfering wood, picking fruit or vegetables for either consumption or sale, fishing from rivers without licence, hawking, peddling and street selling, all became subject to the social police and eventually eliminated (Carson 1985: 8). In conjunction with the New Police, the new poor law was explicitly designed to enforce wage-labour on the working population by disallowing out-relief to all but the truly destitute and suppressing subsistence practices antithetical to the development of the new relations of production. In doing so it distinguished between poverty and indigence in terms almost identical to Colquhoun's:

In no part of Europe except England has it been thought fit that the provision, whether compulsory or voluntary, should it be applied to more than the relief of *indigence*, the state of a person unable to labour, or unable to obtain, in return for his labour, the means of subsistence. It has never been deemed

---

[5] It is also the case that Colquhoun's admiration for Continental police systems—Radzinowicz describes his work as a eulogy of the Paris police—lies less in their use of police surveillance, though this aspect is undoubtedly important, than in the activities of police concerning the poor. His discussion of the usefulness surveillance techniques of the French police is intended to placate British concerns over 'French spies and despotism'. It is for this reason that he continually insists that his proposed reforms will not affect the 'liberty of the subject' and are 'perfectly consistent with the spirit of our national laws' (1796: 16–17, 145, 259, 282, 380–1, 387; 1800: 38). Having his readers buy this argument is a strategy for having them buy the argument that the relief of the poor should be in the hands of police, just as it was in Paris. It is perhaps worth mentioning that previous British writers who had argued that the relief of the poor should be an aspect of police, such as Hanway (1775), had also tended to adopt their ideas on police from the Continent.

expedient that the provision should extend to the relief of *poverty*; that is, the state of one who, in order to obtain a mere subsistence, is forced to have recourse to labour. (Checkland and Checkland 1974: 334)

In other words, the new poor law and the new system of police shared the same conceptual foundations. Moreover, the central Poor Law Board encouraged the use of police as poor law relieving officers and from the 1860s many policemen who acted as assistant poor law relieving officers were empowered to grant food as well as shelter (Steedman 1984: 56–9; Knott 1986). This was built into the very origins of the poor law. Chadwick argued that 'the view generally taken of a Police force have always appeared to extremely narrow. Popularly they are for the most part viewed as a mere agency for the apprehension of criminals'. Instead he suggested that 'the complete operation of the principles of the poor law Amendment Act is largely dependent on the aid of a rural Police whose chief functions would necessarily be clearly connected with the poor law business of a Board of Guardians' (cited in Knott 1986: 258). And when he came to write the *Constabulary Forces Commission Report* in 1839, Chadwick obtained much of his evidence through the agency of the Poor Law Commission.

That the founding institution of modern social policy was so integrally linked with the founding of the new police is no coincidence, since they were both ultimately ranged against the same group—the nascent working class—and had the same aim: the commodification of labour through the enforcement of the wage and thus the fashioning of the market (Neocleous 1996: 117–26). In working together towards this aim—as a system of social police—they closed off any access to the means by which the class of poverty might obtain subsistence other than through the sale of its labour. In doing so social police consolidated the existence of a class of wage labour. Social police, then, played a crucial role in the making of the working class.

The conclusion to draw from this in terms of Colquhoun's work is that he was indeed a major influence on the emergence of the new police, though for reasons different to those usually given within British police studies. Moreover, Colquhoun has been badly served by the intellectual poverty induced by the excessive specialization within the social sciences: he should be read for his influence on the new poor law and the history of social policy as much as he is for his influence on the new police, though convincing those interested in social policy of this may take some doing. The more ambitious conclusion to draw is that although the new poor law and the new police have tended to be studied separately within the 'disciplines' of social policy and police studies, they should in fact be studied together, in the light of both their historical, conceptual and political concordance. This would lead to a better understanding of what I am calling 'social police', the main aim of which is to understand the ways in which policing extends well beyond a uniformed force for the prevention and detection of crime.

REFERENCES

ASHTON, T. S. (1955), *An Economic History of England: The Eighteenth Century.* London: Methuen.

BACON, F. (1605), *The Advancement of Learning.* London: Dent & Sons.

BROGDEN, M. (1982), *The Police: Autonomy and Consent.* London: Academic Press.

BROGDEN, M. and BROGDEN, A. (1984), 'From Henry III to Liverpool 8: The Unity of Police Street Powers', *International Journal of the Sociology of Law*, 12: 1.

BUNYAN, T. (1977), *The History and Practice of the Political Police in Britain*. London: Quartet.

CARSON, W. G. (1985), 'Policing the Periphery: The Development of Scottish Policing 1795–1900. Part II—Policing and the Production of Social Order', *Australian and New Zealand Journal of Criminology*, 18.

CHAPMAN, B. (1971), *Police State*. London: Macmillan.

CHECKLAND, S. G. and CHECKLAND, E. O. A. (eds.) (1974), *The Poor Law Report of 1834*. Harmondsworth: Penguin.

COLQUHOUN, P. (1794), *Observations and Facts Relative to Public Houses in the City of London and its Environs*. London: Henry Fry.

——(1796), *A Treatise on the Police of the Metropolis, etc.*, 2nd edn. London: H. Fry.

——(1797), *An Account of a Meat and Soup Charity, etc.* London: H. Fry.

——(1799a), *A General View of the National Police System, etc.* London: H. Baldwin and Son.

——(1799b), *The State of Indigence and the Situation of the Casual Poor in the Metropolis, explained, etc.* London: H. Baldwin and Son.

——(1800), *A Treatise on the Commerce and Police of the River Thames, etc.* London: Joseph Mawman.

——(1806a), *A New and Appropriate System of Education for the Labouring People, etc.* London: J. Hatchard.

——(1806b), *A Treatise on Indigence, etc.* London: J. Hatchard.

——(1806c), *A Treatise on the Police of the Metropolis, etc.*, 7th edn. London: J. Mawman.

——(1803), *A Treatise on the Functions and Duties of a Constable, etc.* London: J. Mawman.

——(1816), *Minutes of Evidence Taken Before a Select Committee Appointed by the House of Commons, to Inquire Into the State of the Police of the Metropolis*. London: Sherwood, Neely and Jones.

COWHERD, R. (1977), *Political Economists and the English Poor Laws: A Historical Study of the Influence of Classical Economics on the Formation of Social Welfare Policy*. Ohio University Press.

CRITCHLEY, T. A. (1967), *A History of Police in England and Wales 900–1966*. London: Constable.

DEAN, M. (1991), *The Constitution of Poverty: Toward a Genealogy of Liberal Governance*. London: Routledge.

DONAJGRODZKI, A. P. (1977), '"Social Police" and the Bureaucratic Elite: A Vision of Order in the Age of Reform', in A. P. Donajgrodzki, ed., *Social Control in Nineteenth Century Britain*. London: Croom Helm.

DORWART, R. A. (1971), *The Prussian Welfare State before 1740*. Cambridge, MA: Harvard University Press.

DYSON, K. (1980), *The State Tradition in Western Europe: A Study of an Idea and Institution*. Oxford: Martin Robertson.

ELTON, G. R. (1972), *Policy and Police: The Enforcement of the Reformation in the Age of Thomas Cromwell*. Cambridge: Cambridge University Press.

EMSLEY, C. (1983), *Policing and its Context 1750–1870*. London: Macmillan.

——(1996), *The English Police: A Political and Social History*. London: Longman.

FOUCAULT, M. (1991), 'Governmentality', in G. Burchell, C. Gordon and P. Miller, eds., *The Foucault Effect: Studies in Governmentality*. Hemel Hempstead: Harvester.

GARLAND, D. (1996), 'The Limits of the Sovereign State: Strategies of Crime Control in Contemporary Society', *British Journal of Criminology*, 36/1: 4.

GODFREY, B. (1999), 'Law, Factory Discipline and "Theft": The Impact of the Factory on Workplace Appropriation in Mid to Late Nineteenth-Century Yorkshire', *British Journal of Criminology*, 39/1: 1.

HANWAY, J. (1775), *The Defects of Police, etc.* London: J. Dodsley.

HARDWICKE, G. (n.d), *Keepers of the Door: The History of the Port of London Authority Police*. London: Peel Press.

HIMMELFARB, G. (1984), *The Idea of Poverty: England in the Early Industrial Age*. London: Faber and Faber.

JOHNSON, H. (1964), 'The Concept of Bureaucracy in Cameralism', *Political Science Quarterly*, 79.

JOHNSTON, L. (1992), *The Rebirth of Private Policing*. London: Routledge.

JONES, T. and NEWBURN, T. (1998), *Private Security and Public Policing*. Oxford: Clarendon Press.

KNOTT, J. (1986), *Popular Opposition to the 1834 Poor Law*. London: Croom Helm.

LEDONNE, J. (1984), *Ruling Russia: Politics and Administration in the Age of Absolutism 1762–1796*. Princeton, NJ: Princeton University Press.

LINEBAUGH, P. (1972), 'Eighteenth-century Crime, Popular Movements and Social Control', *Bulletin of the Society for the Study of Labour History*, 25.

MACDONALD, I. (1973), 'The Creation of the British Police', *Race Today*, 5: 11.

MARSHALL, T. H. (1970), *Social Policy*. London: Hutchinson.

NEOCLEOUS, M. (1996), *Administering Civil Society: Towards a Theory of State Power*. London: Macmillan.

——(1998a), 'Policing and Pin-Making: Adam Smith, Police and the State of Prosperity', *Policing and Society*, 8: 4.

——(1998b), 'Policing the System of Needs: Hegel, Political Economy, and the Police of the Market', *History of European Ideas*, 24: 1.

——(2000), *The Fabrication of Social Order*. London: Pluto Press.

PHILIPS, D. (1977), *Crime and Authority in Victorian England: The Black Country 1835–1860*. London: Croom Helm.

POYNTER, J. R. (1969), *Society and Pauperism: English Ideas on Poor Relief, 1795–1834*. London: Routledge.

RADZINOWICZ, L. (1956a), *A History of English Criminal Law and its Administration from 1750*, Vol. 2. London: Stevens and Sons.

—— (1956b), *A History of English Criminal Law and its Administration from 1750*, Vol. 3. London: Stevens and Sons.

RAEFF, M. (1983), *The Well-Ordered Police State: Social and Institutional Change Through Law in the Germanies and Russia, 1600–1800*. New Haven: Yale University Press.

REITH, C. (1952), *The Blind Eye of History* London: Faber and Faber.

—— (1956), *A New Study of Police History*. London: Oliver and Boyd.

STEAD, P. J. (1977), 'Patrick Colquhoun: Preventive Police', in P. J. Stead, ed., *Pioneers in Policing*. Montclair, NJ: Patterson Smith.

STEEDMAN, C. (1984), *Policing the Victorian Community: The Formation of English Provincial Police Forces, 1856–80*, London: Routledge.

STORCH, R. (1975), 'The Plague of Blue Locusts: Police Reform and Popular Resistance in Northern England, 1840–57', *International Review of Social History*, 20.

——(1976), 'The Policeman as Domestic Missionary: Urban Discipline and Popular Culture in Northern England, 1850–1880', *Journal of Social History*, 9: 4.

STOURZH, G. (1988), 'Constitution: Changing Meanings of the Term from the Early Seventeenth to the Late Eighteenth Century', in T. Ball and J. G. A. Pocock, eds., *Conceptual Change and the Constitution*. Lawrence: University Press of Kansas.

WHITAKER, B. (1979), *The Police in Society*. London: Eyre Methuen.

[15]

Good men to Associate and Bad Men to Conspire

Associations for the Prosecution of Felons in England 1760–1860*

DAVID PHILIPS

This Society and may there always be good men to associate while
there are bad men to conspire. Toast of Society for Prosecuting Felons,
Forgers etc. at Anniversary Dinner, 18 April 1798.

The OBJECT of this ASSOCIATION is the prevention, as far as
may be, of the Commission of Crime, rather than the punishment of
Offenders.

The evil dispositions of the corrupt and dissolute, however, but too
frequently lead to Offences against Society, and as such cannot be
altogether prevented, it becomes a matter of prudence for those interested in the preservation of Good Government and Social Order, and
anxious for the Security of Person and Property, to take measures for
the due and speedy punishment of such as may be found offending
against the Laws.

To this end, no course seems more proper, or more likely to lead to
the desired result, than that held out by the formation of Associations.

By becoming Members of such a Union, those Classes of Society
whose employments and situations more particularly place them at
the mercy of the evil-disposed, ensure that assistance towards defray-
ing the unavoidable and necessary cost of effectually pursuing after,
and prosecuting to conviction, the guilty Parties, which would otherwise, in many instances, fall heavily upon Individuals; and the consideration of which not unfrequently makes one of the many chances
of escape from punishment which the Offender already possesses.

There can be no greater check upon the conduct of the vicious,
than that, which the certainty of discovery and punishment, affords.

* Earlier versions of this paper were presented at the Australasian Modern British History Association conference in Adelaide in August 1983, and at the Conference on the History of Law, Labour,
and Crime at the University of Warwick in September 1983. I am grateful for the comments and
suggestions which I received from participants in those two discussions, and grateful also to John
Langbein and Iain McCalman for their comments on the paper. I gratefully acknowledge the permission
of the Calderdale District Archives and the Halifax Antiquarian Society to quote from material held
in the Calderdale District Archives relating to local associations for prosecution.

114   *David Philips*

The main object therefore of this Association is to ensure that *strict enforcement* of that wholesome and salutary Code of Criminal Law, which the Legislature of this Country has from time to time so wisely enacted, against all such as shall violate these Laws, by the Commission of Offences against either the Person or Property of members of this association.

Market Rasen Association for Prosecuting Felons, Poster 16 January 1840.

I ORGANIZING PROSECUTION

In the period from the late eighteenth to the middle of the nineteenth century, the advanced nations of Western Europe and the United States made significant changes to their institutions and philosophies of law enforcement and punishment. Perhaps the most important of these was the establishment and development of what Allan Silver has called 'the policed society'. This change was probably most dramatic in England, where the establishment of new police forces from 1829 onwards signalled the change from a law-enforcement system dependent on unpaid JPs, parish constables, and *ad hoc* watch forces, to one reliant on bureaucratic, uniformed, paid police forces. This coincided with a change in the central philosophy of punishment from a system based on a wide use of capital punishment to one based on imprisonment. And the police forces, in time, took over more than just the duties of arresting offenders and preserving the peace; they also came to exercise—and quite soon monopolize—the function of prosecuting accused persons in court.[1]

Recent studies of the changes in policing have brought out the complexities of developments in the period from the 1770s and 1780s—when the first serious attempts were made by the British state to reform its police apparatus—until 1856, when the government finally legislated to make it compulsory for all parts of England and Wales to have new police forces.[2] The change from old agencies of law enforcement to new police was neither simple nor straightforward. Many groups resisted the imposition of state-

---

[1] See A. Silver, 'The Demand for Order in Civil Society: A Review of Some Themes in the History of Urban Crime, Police and Riot', in D. Bordua (ed.), *The Police: Six Sociological Essays* (New York, 1967), pp. 1–24; M. Foucault, *Discipline and Punish: The Birth of the Prison*, trans. A. Sheridan (London, 1977); M. Ignatieff, *A Just Measure of Pain: The Penitentiary in the Industrial Revolution 1750–1850* (London, 1978); D. Philips, ' "A New Engine of Power and Authority": The Institutionalisation of Law-Enforcement in England 1780–1830', in V. A. C. Gatrell, G. Parker, B. Lenman (eds.), *Crime and the Law: The Social History of Crime in Western Europe since 1500* (London, 1980), pp. 155–89.

[2] C. Emsley, *Policing and its Context 1750–1850* (London, 1983); V. Bailey (ed.), *Policing and Punishment in Nineteenth-Century Britain* (London, 1981); Philips, 'A New Engine of Power and Authority'.

run police forces, even while acknowledging defects in the old policing system. During this long transitional period, many forms of intermediate law enforcement were tried—attempts to improve the old machinery, but still stopping short of a fully state-run, tax-funded police.[3] These included a variety of private enterprise voluntary associations, funded by individual subscriptions. Prominent among these, for almost a hundred years, were the numerous Associations for the Prosecution of Felons, established in large numbers throughout England.

In December 1833, Mr James Bailey, a resident of Southwell in Nottinghamshire, and a member of the local Association for the Prosecution of Felons, had his horse stolen. He reported this to the treasurer of the association, who advertised it with handbills, and subsequently with advertisements in the *Stamford Mercury, Nottingham Journal,* and *Nottingham Mercury*. A report came from a Doncaster police officer about a horse which had been ridden through there on 3 January 1834, but after investigation, this proved not to be Bailey's horse. On 12 February, Bailey 'received an anonimous letter informing him that his Horse was in the Neighbourhood of Macclesfield'; he was able to get further particulars from the Chief Constable of Macclesfield confirming that it was, indeed, his horse. By agreeing to pay a hefty bill of expenses (£13. 7s. 6d.) to the Macclesfield constable, Bailey was able to have the necessary witnesses in Macclesfield found and examined, and he brought one James Widdowson to trial at the assizes, for the theft of the horse. His expenses in this case included the initial advertisements; correspondence and travel (by him and others) to Doncaster, Macclesfield, Bingham, Belvoir, Grantham, Leicester, Lincoln, and Chesterfield, in search of the horse, Widdowson, and witnesses; and the expenses of getting himself, witnesses, and solicitor to the assizes for two days. Including £2. 10s paid as half the reward offered for finding the horse and convicting the thief, the total outlay on this case came to £66. 9s. 7d. The prosecutor could reclaim his expenses from the court; in this case, the county allowance awarded was £38. 8s. 6d.— or just over half of what it had cost to find the horse and convict the thief.[4]

The case of Mr Bailey's horse offers a good insight into why Associations for the Prosecution of Felons were established in such large numbers in England, and continued to flourish until at least the 1850s. The crux of the issue lay in the English system of law enforcement and prosecution, which was essentially dependent on private initiative; and, until the establishment of the paid, uniformed, new police forces throughout the country,

---

[3] Robert Storch's essay in this volume (ch. 5) discusses the types of intermediate policing tried in many rural areas before 1856.

[4] The events of this case, and the various detailed expenses, are set out fully in Notts. RO, DD.M 71/201, a collection of loose vouchers and accounts from the Southwell Association.

there was very little official help offered to the private prosecutor[5]. This system, as Douglas Hay has shown[6], allowed a great deal of discretion to those with the power and opportunity to exercise it; but it also raised a number of problems for the victims of offences—problems which became increasingly apparent from the late eighteenth century onwards. These problems were essentially those of the difficulty and cost of finding and apprehending the offender and prosecuting successfully.

In Bailey's case, the victim/prosecutor had to be able to lay out £66, and still be £30 out of pocket once the prosecution was over: this at a time when agricultural labourers were earning about 10s., factory workers 20s., and skilled workers perhaps 30s. a week. Bailey's case, being one of horse theft, was likely to prove particularly expensive. A horse was a very valuable piece of property, worth from £10 to £50; and, since the stolen animal could be used to travel far and fast, recovering it and finding the thief was likely to involve having to search over a wide area and having to pay large travel expenses.[7] Cases involving other offences, such as sheep-stealing, burglary, and arson, could also prove very expensive to prosecute.[8] Even prosecutions for lesser offences could easily cost £5 to £10 at quarter sessions and £10 to £20 at assizes—including the costs of finding and apprehending the suspect (paying for the time, trouble, and travel expenses of local constables); keeping the prisoner in custody; transporting him and the necessary witnesses to the appropriate town for the sessions or assizes; employing a solicitor, and possibly a barrister, to prosecute the case; and

---

[5] See F. W. Maitland, *Justice and Police* (London, 1885), and D. Phillips, *Crime and Authority in Victorian England: The Black Country 1835–1860* (London, 1977), ch. 3, 4. See also ch. 1 above.

[6] D. Hay, 'Property, Authority and the Criminal Law', in D. Hay, P. Linebaugh, E. P. Thompson (eds.), *Albion's Fatal Tree: Crime and Society in Eighteenth-Century England* (London, 1975), pp. 17–63.

[7] For similar expensive cases of horse-stealing, see: (1) *North Shields and Tynemouth Association* July 1811–Nov. 1813. Recovering the horse from London and convicting the thief at Newcastle cost the Association more than £95; only £22. 1s. 2d. was reimbursed by the county: Tyne and Wear Arch., LIB 429, mins. and accounts, and LIB 32, correspondence. (2) *Salt Hill Society* (Bucks.) 1810–11: The stolen horse had to be traced through London, with the expensive help of a Bow Street officer, and the thief found and prosecuted in Sussex. The Society had to pay out £110. 2s. 8d. *over and above* the county allowance: Bucks. RO, D/X 69. (3) *Notts. Association* Aug. 1843–Mar. 1844: This case required travel into Yorks., Lancs., and Lincs., and getting the co-operation of the Notts., Lancs., and Metropolitan Police; it cost the Association £87. 16s. 4d., of which the county allowance reimbursed £60. 12s. 8d.: Notts. RO, DD.T 11/14.

[8] e.g. (1) *Dursley etc. Association* (Glos.): (a) Stealing sheep and bacon, 1796—total cost £70. 7s. 2d., of which county allowance paid £18. 15s. 6d.; (b) 2 cases of burglary Sept. 1828–Apr. 1829 cost the Association over £200, of which the county paid £158: Gloucester Lib., JF 11.26, 11.27(2), 11.27(23). (2) *Doncaster Borough and Soke Association:* Burglary July 1822 cost £120. 6s.; county allowance paid £49. 15s.: Doncaster Arch., AB 8/2 constables and constabulary. (3) *Earl Manvers Association* (Notts.): Sheep-stealing 1814–15 cost £69. 13s. 8d.; county allowance paid £29. 2s. 8d.: Notts. RO, DD 54/2. (4) *Charing Society* (Kent): Breaking and entering granary and stealing wool, 1825–6; Association paid out £87. 14s. 11d. for the search and the prosecution costs; county allowance refunded £26. 3s. Kent RO, U442 066. (5) *Linton etc. Association* (Cambs.): Arson of premises 1829; cost Association £71. 4s. 8d. (including £20 reward) *over and above* the county allowance Cambs. RO, L95/18(b).

Associations for Prosecution of Felons 117

paying all the required fees to the Clerk of the Peace or of Assize. For example, for the Goudhurst Association (Kent) to convict Thomas Roberts of stealing peas from one of their members in 1847, they had to pay: a solicitor's bill of £15. 14s. 8d.; £1. 7s. to the local constable for watching the premises at night; £3 as a reward to the two police constables who arrested Roberts; and 9s. 3d. for additional expenses of the prosecutor.[9]

In 1840, a Mr Kendall, a member of the Olney Turvey and Harrold Association, on the Bedfordshire–Buckinghamshire border, claimed from them the £44. 5s. he had spent in pursuing and recovering his two horses; they gave him £30 'he not having a claim, on account of the thief not being discovered and prosecuted to conviction'.[10] Like Kendall, many property-owners had great difficulty finding and arresting offenders against them in the days before organized professional police forces—particularly if the offenders had travelled any distance from the scene of the crime.[11] Two examples from the records of the Dursley Association in Gloucestershire convey some sense of the hit-or-miss nature of the early police system in such cases. On 2 August 1833, the house of Mr John Jenkins at Dursley, an association member, was burgled and some silver spoons stolen. Four days later, Louis Alman, a pawnbroker in Bristol (some 20 miles away), was offered some broken silver spoons by George and John Pegler. The Peglers were dealers in iron 'well known to the police', and Alman was suspicious of them; he advertised the spoons in the *Bristol Mirror*. Jenkins had notified the association solicitor of his loss; the solicitor saw Alman's advertisement, and wrote, giving an impression of the crest on two of the stolen spoons. They proved to be the same spoons, and, as a result of Alman's advertisement and the association response, the Peglers were caught, prosecuted, and convicted at the Gloucestershire assizes.

The second example, from September 1828, was the burglary of the Rectory of the Revd Mr Pruen, association member. Pruen suspected his former servant, Joseph Fletcher, but, by the time he had secured a warrant to search Fletcher's premises, Fletcher had gone to Birmingham. The association solicitor wrote to the High Constables in Birmingham and Worcester, asking them to spread the word. A few days later, Fletcher was

---

[9] Kent RO, U769 L6, mins. and accounts. See also Notts. RO, DD.T 25/6: the Notts. Association paid a similar series of amounts in prosecutions for stealing a saddle, in 1790, and for stealing wool, in 1827. The runs of minutes and accounts, vouchers, bills, and correspondence of most associations offer a wealth of detail on this topic. For a discussion of all the expenses involved in a normal prosecution, see Philips, *Crime and Authority*, ch. 4.   [10] Beds. RO, GA 1108/1, mins. 1840.

[11] For a good discussion of these problems in the mid-to-late 18th c., see J. Styles, 'An Eighteenth-Century Magistrate as Detective: Samuel Lister of Little Horton', *Bradford Antiquary*, NS, 47 (1982), pp. 98–117; and 'Sir John Fielding and the Problem of Criminal Investigation in Eighteenth-Century England', *Transactions of the Royal Historical Society*, 5th ser., 33 (1983), pp. 127–49.

118   *David Philips*

caught by Samuel Haines, a Birmingham silversmith, when he tried to sell a gold watch and other stolen articles. He was tried and convicted at the Gloucestershire assizes, and sentenced to transportation for life.[12]

II ORIGINS

It is these two problems—the difficulty and cost of detection and arrest, and the cost of prosecution—which explain why so many property-owners established and joined associations for the prosecution of felons in England, especially from the 1780s onwards. The associations offered some assistance towards solving these problems. As institutions, they appear to arise uniquely from the English common law tradition, and to owe their existence largely to the fact that the English system placed the onus of prosecuting an offence on the victim himself. England had no state official—like the public prosecutors of France, USA, or Scotland—charged with prosecuting criminal offences.[13] The only form of state assistance was the reimbursement, after the event, of the expenses of the various stages of prosecution—by means of the county allowance, awarded by the courts, whose scope was gradually extended by a series of statutes between 1752 and 1826.[14] The Associations (sometimes Societies) for the Prosecution of Felons were private institutions, made up of local property-owners, who came together t form an organization and raise a fund in order to find, arrest, and pros cute, at common expense, offenders against themselves and their property.

The modern analogy which these associations might immediately call to mind is that of privately run security services or other forms of 'private police'.[15] As we shall see, a number of associations *did* establish their own private police forces or patrols; but the majority did not go to this extent, preferring to work through their relationship with the parish constables,

---

[12] Gloucester Lib., JF 11.29 and 11.30 (correspondence 1829, 1833–4), 11.26 (accounts), 11.27 (solicitors' accounts), 11.28 (reward handbills), and 15409 (mins.). The Association proved to be very mean in their payment of their advertised rewards. They tried to browbeat Alman, a Jewish pawnbroker, into forgoing his claim to the £5 reward advertised, claiming (falsely, as their accounts show) that their funds were very low, and that he should be content with the allowance made to him at the assizes. He persisted, 'knowing that I have Gentlemen to deal with', and was eventually given £2. 10s. Haines claimed the 20 guineas reward for apprehending Fletcher, which the Association tried to refuse, hoping 'you will authorize us in your reply to pay some portion of the *Reward* to the poor of this Parish'. (There is no evidence that this, or any other, association ever did such a thing!) Only when Haines had two solicitors' letters sent demanding the reward, did the Association yield.

[13] Many associations for prosecution were established in England and Wales. For Ireland and Scotland, see ch. 1 above. This chapter deals only with English associations.

[14] See Philips, *Crime and Authority*, pp. 112–13.

[15] See S. Spitzer and A. T. Scull, 'Privatization and Capitalist Development: The Case of the Private Police', *Social Problems* 25/1 (1977), pp. 18–29; and H. Draper, *Private Police* (Harmondsworth, 1978).

or, later, with the new police forces. A closer historical analogy is that of the vigilante movement in the United States.[16]

The first recorded vigilantes, the South Carolina Regulators, began in 1767, coinciding with the first wave of foundation of English associations for prosecution. Both movements established private self-help organizations to replace or supplement state action in order to resolve what their members perceived as a crisis in the enforcement of law and order. A crucial difference, however, is that the mainstream nineteenth-century vigilante movements, especially in frontier areas, took the whole process of law enforcement into their own hands—arrest, trial, and punishment (often capital). This was never a feature of the English associations, whose efforts were directed only towards the pursuit, arrest, and prosecution of offenders against them; once the offenders were caught, prosecution was carried out through the normal legal channels of the courts, and punishment was left to the authorities. English associations never took the law into their own hands in the way which made American frontier vigilante groups notorious.[17]

However, there were strands of the American vigilante movement which were very similar to the English associations. Large numbers of 'anti-horsethief societies' were established in the USA, first in the North-east from 1782 onwards, and subsequently in the Midwest and South-west. These societies did not take the law into their own hands. Like the English associations, they pursued horse-thieves, and, if they found them, handed them over to law-enforcement officers for regular prosecution and punishment. The early anti-horsethief societies were established in the decade that English associations aimed especially against horse-thieves were being set up in large numbers, and the names of the American societies show a resemblance to those used for English associations. This suggests a common origin of both sets of societies in the possibilities which the English common law tradition offered for this sort of self-help private enterprise in law enforcement. It also suggests some transatlantic communication of ideas about the utility of such associations.[18]

---

[16] See R. M. Brown, 'The American Vigilante Tradition', in H. D. Graham and T. R. Gurr (eds.), *The History of Violence in America* (New York, 1969), pp. 154–226, and *Strain of Violence: Historical Studies of American Violence and Vigilantism* (New York, 1975), chs. 1, 4–6. An explicit comparison of English associations for prosecution and American Vigilante groups has been attempted by C. B. Little and C. P. Sheffield, 'Frontiers and Criminal Justice: English Private Prosecution Societies and American Vigilantism in the 18th and 19th Centuries', *American Sociological Review*, 48 (Dec. 1983), pp. 796–808. (I am grateful to Michael Sturma for drawing to my attention this article, which appeared after I had presented the original version of this paper to the Warwick conference.)

[17] There are occasional suggestions that associations may not always have bothered to ensure that their members' actions were fully within both the letter and the spirit of the law. John Billing, a member of the Olney, Turvey, and Harrold Association, arrested a Mr Johnson, and was then sued for false imprisonment. The Association agreed to pay £30 towards the cost of Billing's defence: Beds. RO, GA 1108/1, mins. 1857–8.

[18] See A. N. Nicolosi, 'The Rise and Fall of the New Jersey Vigilant Societies', *New Jersey History*,

The English associations for prosecution were founded, and operated actively, in large numbers, particularly in the period 1780–1850. An 1836 Parliamentary inquiry listed 189 associations active in the period 1830–4, and it is easy to show that that list is far from comprehensive, even for that five-year period. The report of the Royal Commission on a Constabulary Force for England and Wales, published in 1839, stated 'it appears that there are upwards of 500 voluntary associations for promoting the apprehension and prosecution of felons'; the Commissioners (or, rather, Edwin Chadwick, who wrote the report on behalf of all three Commissioners) adduced this figure as 'proof of the prostrate condition of the penal administration of the country' and said that the associations might subsequently 'be cited to prove that the community in which they arose was relapsing into a state of barbarism'. The clerk to the Royal Commission informed Chadwick that this figure was a serious underestimate of the total number of associations: 'The number of Societies for the Prosecution of Crime mentioned in the Magistrates returns is 575 and for the Suppression of Vagrancy 37—but these numbers are far short of what they should be as in many Returns the words "several" are used where the number is unknown.'[19] Adrian Shubert has estimated that over this whole period there were 750 to 1,000 associations in existence in England; Peter King has calculated, from his Essex findings, that the figure for England must have been well over 1,000, and possibly as high as 4,000 associations. We will never know for certain exactly how many associations there were, but we can take a figure of at least 1,000 as a good working estimate.[20] This

---

86 (1968), pp. 29–53. Little and Sheffield similarly suggest the possible value of looking for such English–American links ('Frontiers and Criminal Justice', p. 805 n. 19). For the 19th c., there is an elusive and tantalizing suggestion of a 'Dimsdale connection' in self-help law enforcement. The author of the classic account of American vigilantism, *The Vigilantes of Montana* (Montana, 1866; Univ. of Oklahoma Press, 1953), was one Thomas J. Dimsdale (b. 1831), an Englishman and Oxford graduate (see the introduction to the 1953 edn.). The great publicist of the value of English associations, especially those which ran their own police forces, was Thomas Dimsdale, secretary of the Barnet General Association (see sect. VI below).

[19] *Report of the Commissioners for inquiring into County Rates* PP 1836, xxvii, pp. 1–383, Appendix C, pp. 37a–45a; *First Report of the Commissioners appointed to inquire as to the Best Means of establishing an Efficient Constabulary Force in the Counties of England and Wales* PP 1839, xix (169), p. 97; Chadwick Papers (Univ. College, London), item 1657, Redgrave to Chadwick 28 Mar. 1839.

[20] A. Shubert, ' "Lest the Law Slumber in Action": Associations for the Prosecution of Felons' (M.A. thesis, Univ. of Warwick, 1978), p. 12. (Shubert's article 'Private Initiative in Law Enforcement: Associations for the Prosecution of Felons, 1744–1856', in V. Bailey (ed.) *Policing and Punishment in 19th-Century Britain* (London, 1981), pp. 25–41, summarizes this thesis, but omits this estimate); P. King, 'Prosecution Associations in Essex 1740–1800', ch. 4 below. We are unlikely ever to know the full number of associations, since they were private organizations and survival of their records is capricious. People such as Peter King, John Styles, and Douglas Hay, who have done detailed studies of particular counties (Essex, Yorks., and Staffs. respectively) for the 18th c., making intensive use of the local newspapers, invariably come up with higher figures than the general surveys do, and one often catches a reference to an association for which no material appears to have survived.

chapter is based on a study of the surviving records of 213 associations, or agreements to prosecute, from 26 counties of England, in the period 1760–1860.[21]

The idea of forming private societies for a purpose such as mutual assistance and cost-sharing in the arrest and prosecution of offenders, did not arise as something totally new or unknown in the late eighteenth century. England already had a tradition of voluntary associations for a variety of charitable and other purposes, including reforming the morals of the lower orders through the enforcement of some of the criminal laws. This went back at least as far as the Societies for the Reformation of Manners, in the late seventeenth century, and was revived by the Evangelicals' 'Society for the Suppression of Vice', in the early nineteenth. A system which placed the onus of initiative on the individual prosecutor, as the English system did, was ripe for exploitation by this style of organization.

Hanoverian England also saw the flowering of many other sorts of voluntary associations. Friendly Societies, formed by mutual agreement to provide some insurance for members against future dangers, grew in numbers during the eighteenth century, and their growth was especially rapid from the 1760s onward. The commercial insurance industry also developed rapidly, and the principle of insurance against possible future loss became widely accepted. Mutual assurance companies were formed by a number of property-owners coming together and binding themselves by a list of rules and regulations set out in a deed of settlement or articles of association. As we shall see, the prosecution associations similarly offered their members a degree of mutual insurance against the costs of theft or arson, in return for their subscriptions. And the eighteenth century was the great era of the English club. Clubs were established by men (it was largely a male phenomenon) at almost all social levels, both for entertainment and for more serious purposes. Samuel Johnson, himself a preeminently clubbable man, defined 'club' in his *Dictionary* as 'an assembly of good fellows, meeting under certain conditions'. This convivial aspect helped to launch and sustain the prosecution associations. Certainly, by the time of the first great waves of foundation, in the 1770s and 1780s, the idea was well established in English minds of the utility of voluntary associations formed for mutual self-help and/or the enforcement of the law. During the anti-Jacobin panic of 1792–3, when conservatives organized to suppress the threat from popular radical societies, it was easy for John Reeves to initiate a national movement of volunteer 'loyalist associations' pledged to the support of the British king and constitution.[22]

---

[21] See Appendix 1 for full details.
[22] T. C. Curtis and W. A. Speck, 'The Societies for the Reformation of Manners: A Case Study in the Theory and Practice of Moral Reform', *Literature and History*, 3 (Mar. 1976), pp. 45–64; L.

It is not clear exactly when the first mutual agreements to share the costs of prosecution began. Douglas Hay has found an agreement made by the inhabitants of Stoke-on-Trent in 1693, to prosecute horse-thieves at mutual expense; and the township of Maghull, Lancashire, recorded a similar agreement in 1699.[23] During the eighteenth century, similar such agreements to raise a local rate to prosecute at common expense, made by the inhabitants of townships and parishes and usually designed to last only a limited period, can be found; and these limited *agreements* continued into the early nineteenth century.[24] But from an early date we also see the development of organizations of a more permanent nature. From the 1740s, associations were established to enforce the game laws, and from the 1760s, associations for the prosecution of felons began to be set up in both London and the provinces.[25] In London, the Society for Prosecuting Felons, Forgers etc. was founded in 1767, with the advice and help of Sir John Fielding who had succeeded his half-brother Henry as chief magistrate at Bow Street. The two Fieldings had, since the 1740s, been attacking the inadequacy of the existing official institutions to cope with the problems of crime and disorder in the metropolis, and Sir John now urged the formation of prosecution societies as a measure to help relieve these problems.[26]

In the 1770s, associations were established all over England, and there was a marked acceleration in the pace of new foundations in the 1780s (see Appendix 2). New associations continued to be set up steadily, from the 1780s well into the nineteenth century. After the initial wave of the 1770s and 1780s, there was a noticeable second wave of foundations (and, sometimes, re-foundations of associations which had become moribund) between 1810 and 1840 (Appendix 2). They were established in both urban

Radzinowicz and R. Hood, *A History of English Criminal Law and its Administration from 1750* (5 vols., London, 1948–86), iv, ch. 2; M. J. D. Roberts, 'Making Victorian Morals? The Society for the Suppression of Vice and its Critics, 1802–1866', *Historical Studies* (Melbourne), 21/83 (Oct. 1984), pp. 157–73. On Friendly Societies, see P. H. J. H. Gosden, *Self Help: Voluntary Associations in the 19th Century* (London, 1973), chap. 1–2; on insurance, H. E. Raynes, *A History of British Insurance* (London 1948). On the 18th-c. development of the word and institution of the club, see *Oxford English Dictionary*, 'Club'; James Boswell, *Life of Johnson* (OUP World's Classics edn., 1980), pp. 338–9, 798, 1260–2; D. George, *London Life in the 18th Century* (London, 1966), pp. 266–7; J. Money, 'Taverns, Coffee Houses and Clubs: Local Politics and Popular Articulacy in the Birmingham Area, in the Age of the American Revolution', *Historical Journal*, 14/1 (1971), pp. 15–47, and *Experience and Identity: Birmingham and the West Midlands 1760–1800* (Manchester, 1977). ch. 5. On Loyalist associations, see A. Mitchell, 'The Association Movement of 1792–3', *Historical Journal*, 4/1 (1961), pp. 56–77, and D. E. Ginter, 'The Loyalist Association Movement of 1792–3 and British Public Opinion', *Historical Journal*, 9/2 (1966), pp. 179–190.

[23] D. Hay, 'Crime, Authority and the Criminal Law: Staffordshire 1750–1800' (Ph.D thesis, Univ. of Warwick, 1975), p. 355; Lancs. RO, PR 2814/1.   [24] See Appendix 1 and Appendix 2.

[25] See King, ch. 4 below, and Hay, 'Crime, Authority', pp. 355–7.

[26] CLRO Misc. Mss. 115.9; *Times*, 7 Sept. 1795, letter from member of committee of Society; Radzinowicz and Hood, *History of English Criminal Law*, iii, chs. 2–3; Styles, 'Sir John Fielding'.

Associations for Prosecution of Felons 123

and rural areas—there is nothing distinctively either urban or rural about these societies. After 1840, there was a sharp decline in the number of new associations being founded; and many of the existing associations dissolved themselves. This happened as the new police forces were making their influence felt throughout the country, and were progressively taking over responsibility for pursuit, arrest, and prosecution of offenders—those problems which the associations had been set up to solve. However, by no means all associations went out of existence with the coming of the police; many continued an active existence for a while, extending to the new policemen a similar relationship to the one they had maintained with the parish constables.[27] But the volume of business and activity of these associations diminished noticeably from the 1850s onward; some of these associations continued until the 1890s; a number of others were brought to an end by the First World War; and a few have lingered on to preserve a formal existence still today—though most of them now operate as a club offering a convivial annual dinner rather than in their original role. The great period of activity and importance of the associations was *c*.1770–1850.

Why was it in the 1770s and 1780s that associations were first established in large numbers? Those decades were marked by a growing public concern, expressed particularly by influential magistrates in London and the provinces, about the perceived inadequacy of England's system of police, prosecution, and punishment. Reactions to the two phases of Sir John Fielding's ambitious General Preventative Plan (1772–3 and 1775) to improve policing and the communication of police information, showed a widely held belief among local authorities that the existing institutions were inadequate. Even though most magistrates rejected the solutions Fielding proposed in his second phase (1775), they clearly shared his view that the problems were real.[28] The 1780s saw the growth of an atmosphere of crisis in England's law-enforcement system. Serious symptoms included the scale of destruction in the Gordon Riots in London in 1780, the 'crime wave' which followed the end of the American War, and (as a result of that war) the increasing number of convicts building up in the hulks and prisons until transportation to Australia began in 1787. It was in 1785 that the first serious government attempt was made to establish a police force for London; the attempt failed, but the arguments used in favour of it all stressed this sense of the inadequacy of the existing institutions to cope with the crisis.[29] Within this general climate of crisis, the actions of a

---

[27] See sect. VI below.   [28] Styles, 'Sir John Fielding'.

[29] See D. Hay, 'War, Dearth and Theft in the Eighteenth Century: The Record of the English Courts', *Past and Present*, no. 95 (May 1982), pp. 117–60; King, 'Prosecution Associations'; J. Beattie, *Crime and the Courts in England* (Princeton, NJ., 1986), ch. 10; Radzinowicz and Hood, *History of English Criminal Law*, iii, chs. 3–5; Philips, 'A New Engine'; D. Mackay, *A Place of Exile: The European Settlement of New South Wales* (Melbourne, 1985).

few determined 'moral entrepreneurs' could have a considerable impact. Among the measures which Fielding urged, as part of his plan, was the establishment of private associations to assist victims of offences to apprehend and prosecute the offenders. A number of Essex magistrates set up the Essex Association in 1775, designed to implement Fielding's suggestions. The Nottinghamshire Association, started in 1770 (initially as a society aimed just against horse-stealers), sought Fielding's help and advice about the rules and orders of their group. Twelve years later, when they decided to turn it into a general association against all felonies, they asked the advice of Fielding's successor at Bow Street, Sir Sampson Wright. Wright replied, offering strong support to the association and endorsing fully its aims:

> Societies of this Kind appear to me to have but two Objects for their Attention— Prevention and Prosecution—and their Rules and Orders should be so calculated as best to answer those Ends.
> The settling a Mode of a speedy Communication throughout the Country in all Cases of Theft & Robbery seems very essential to those Purposes, as well as the Activity of the members in their respective Divisions or Parishes on receiving such Information.... And I would likewise beg Leave to recommend that all Prosecution should be carried on under the Direction of the Society, and that the injured Party should only consider himself as a Witness. I mention this because daily experience proves that Individuals are too apt to relax in this sort of prosecution—especially if they have got back their Property—to the no small Encouragement of Thefts & Robberies....
> P.S. Care should be taken to have it propagated thro' the County what spirited Exertions will take Place in all Cases of Theft and Robbery.[30]

Wright's letter sets out the main objectives and methods which the Nottinghamshire Association—and most similar associations—set for themselves. Energetic Justices in the provinces could play a similar role in stimulating the establishment of associations. John Hewitt, alderman, mayor, and very active magistrate in Coventry, was responsible for getting a Coventry Association started in 1773; and a number of very active Staffordshire magistrates played important parts in the Staffordshire associations in the 1770s and 1780s.[31] In April 1786, the West Riding quarter sessions passed a series of ten resolutions, which they published and distributed, to deal with the problems of 'the Commission of Crimes and Offences [which] hath increased to an alarming Degree'. The chairman of that sessions was the Earl of Effingham, who was already an active member of the Strafforth and Tickhill Association for prosecuting Stealers of

---

[30] King, ch. 5 below; Notts. RO, DD.T 25/1 mins. 1773, DD.T 25/5 Wright to Job Brough, 25 Nov. 1785.

[31] Shubert, ' "Lest the Law Slumber" ', pp. 13–14; Hay, 'Crime, Authority', pp. 364, 389–90.

Horses; the first resolution recommended to the principal inhabitants of all places 'to agree *in uniting together*, under certain Rules and Regulations, for the better Purpose of detecting Felons, Cheats, Vagrants, Night-Walkers and Night-Poachers, Pawn-brokers, who are often guilty of Male-practices, and particularly in receiving Stolen Goods, knowing them to be such ...'. These resolutions were followed by another ten, similarly published, in April 1787, which required all constables to call meetings of local inhabitants and urge on them 'the Necessity there now is for all honest Men to form themselves into Committees, or otherwise associate themselves, as well in Aid of the Civil Magistrate, as to superintend and regulate all parochial matters.'[32] Most associations included a number of county magistrates among their membership, and could count on a fairly close relationship between them and the magistrates when it came to getting warrants issued and arrested persons committed for trial.[33]

This period of initial rapid growth of associations (1770s and 1780s) is also the time when lawyers were coming to play a much more significant role in the English criminal trial—an increasing use of prosecution counsel at assizes and quarter sessions, and a greatly enlarged role for solicitors in pre-trial proceedings and in appearances at quarter sessions. This development considerably increased the normal cost of a criminal prosecution for the prosecutor. Associations (as their accounts show) paid a large part of these increased expenses; their rapid growth in the 1770s and 1780s may reflect a move by many property-owners to insure themselves against the greater costs.[34]

Once the initial associations had been set up, the idea spread rapidly. A number of the early societies were aimed specifically against horse-thieves—horses being very valuable property (worth £10 to £50) which were easy to steal and easy to move away very quickly. Most of these groups subsequently broadened their base to become general associations prosecuting all offences.[35] Copies of the articles and rules of the early

---

[32] Wakefield Lib., Goodchild Loan MSS M45 and resolutions in Local Govt. drawer, in section of mounted maps etc. (emphasis in original).

[33] e.g. the Dursley Association (Glos.) included a number of JPs from the Paul and Purnell families, and made use of them for committals etc.; the North Elham (Norfolk), Blockley (Glos.), and Hammersmith Associations all included active JPs who exercised their magisterial functions on behalf of the Association. In 1840, the Market Rasen Association (Lincs.) included among its members 6 county magistrates for the Parts of Lindsey.

[34] I owe this suggestion to John Langbein. For the gradual 'lawyerization' of the 18th-c. English criminal trial, see his 'The Criminal Trial before the Lawyers', *Univ. of Chicago Law Review*, 45/2 (Winter 1978), pp. 263–316, and 'Shaping the Eighteenth-Century Criminal Trial: A View from the Ryder Sources', *Univ. of Chicago Law Review*, 50/1 (Winter 1983), pp. 1–136, and Beattie, *Crime and the Courts*, ch. 7.

[35] e.g. Nottingham Association for the Prosecution of Horse-Stealers (founded 24 Oct. 1770—became the general Nottingham Association in 1788); Strafforth and Tickhill Association for prosecuting Stealers of Horses (Yorks.) (1779—discontinued in 1782); North Elmham Association for the Prosecution of Horse Stealers and other Felons (1787); Great Bealings Association for Apprehending

126 *David Philips*

associations were widely diffused, and their models followed by many others; examination of a large number of printed articles of association, and rules and regulations of associations, over this whole period, shows that they followed very similar patterns, often using identically worded clauses. Enthusiastic association members disseminated their articles widely to encourage others to associate; new or re-founded associations sought the rules of existing societies as a model for themselves.[36] Within this general climate, at the turn of the eighteenth century, of anxiety about crime and law enforcement, and information widely diffused, particular local incidents—a frightening local burglary, an outbreak of arson, a string of unsolved thefts—could often be the precipitating factor leading to a particular association being founded or revived. The secretary of the Barnet General Association, Thomas Dimsdale, giving evidence to the Constabulary Force Commissioners, enunciated this point:

> What were the events that required an extension of the [association's private police] force as to number?—The increase of territory and the events that were of an alarming nature; incendiarism in particular . . .
>
> It is only, then, by such events operating upon the fears that will induce persons to come forward to form voluntary associations?—Yes.
>
> And some conspicuous events also are requisite?—Yes, in a great measure. It is like the fire-offices in London; a great fire in a neighbourhood increases the insurance all round.[37]

and Prosecuting Horse Stealers (Suffolk) (1789—merged with the Great Bealings Association for Apprehending and Prosecuting All Felonies etc., in 1802); Thorney and North Level Association for Prosecution of Horse Stealers and Other Felons (Cambs.) (1792). Hay records a number of anti-horse-thief societies among the early Staffs. associations, including the Lichfield Association, started in 1770, which had over 100 members within 10 months: 'Crime, Authority', p. 81. King, ch. 4 below, lists 7 early anti-horse-thief associations in Essex, and one in Suffolk which began in 1761—at least 2 of these subsequently broadened into general associations.

[36] John Hewitt recorded that he had got the idea in an association from hearing of others in existence; and he published the articles of his Coventry Association to make them available to others: Shubert, ' "Lest the Law Slumber" ', p. 14. The Dursley Association sent a copy of their articles to assist those setting up the Tetbury Association in 1801: Gloucester Lib., RX 300.2(5). The East Essex Association treasurer was asked in 1808, for a copy of his rules and any useful observations to assist the establishment of a Society for Prosecution in Saffron Walden: Essex RO, D/DE1 C.1. The Barkway and Reed Association used Cambs. models for its foundation in 1818: Herts. RO, D/P 13 29/5; the Bradford (Yorks.) Association, in drawing up new rules in 1829, collected as many copies as possible of the rules of associations in the neighbourhood, to use as a model: Bradford District Arch., DB. 6, case 44.

[37] Chadwick Papers, Univ. College London, item 13, evidence taken by the Constabulary Force Commissioners, p. 63. The Colchester Association was set up as a result of a 'crime wave' in Dec. 1765: King, ch. 4 below; the Stow-on-the Wold Association was established following a brutal robbery-murder: Storch, ch. 5 below.

III THE SOCIAL SIGNIFICANCE OF ASSOCIATIONS

From the fact that so many people set up or joined associations, what can we deduce about the members' attitudes towards the existing system of criminal law, police, and prosecution? Adrian Shubert has argued that the large numbers of people who founded and joined associations were attacking the inadequacies of that system and demanding its substantial reform. This, he says, contradicts Hay's argument that the eighteenth-century ruling class *valued*, and made use of, the large element of discretion and choice which that system allowed to them. On the contrary, that class was showing, by joining associations, that they wanted to *remove* this element of discretion from the prosecution process. Associations forbade their members to drop or compromise prosecutions, once begun; and they imposed penalties on any member who was found to have compounded a felony, i.e. agreed to drop a prosecution in return for some payment from the offender; technically, this act itself constituted an offence. Association members, Shubert suggests, favoured replacing the lax old system with a stricter Beccarian–Benthamite criminal law, in which detection of an offence would be followed by certainty of prosecution and punishment, in order to deter others from transgressing.[38]

It is certainly true that the existence and functioning of associations in large numbers between 1770 and 1850 is a sign of some dissatisfaction with the existing systems of police and prosecution. Many associations did include in their articles a provision prohibiting their members from refusing to carry through a prosecution, on pain of expulsion from the society. Some went further, and threatened that if a member compounded a felony, the association would compel the member to prosecute the case, and they would prosecute that member for compounding.[39] However, it is hard to know whether this provision against dropping or compounding a pro-secution was more than a pious admonition inserted into many sets of articles and rules. In all the long runs of minutes and accounts which I have examined, I have only been able to find *one* case in which this provision was actually put into force: since the minutes of associations record very carefully any members leaving the society—one usually needed to give a few months' notice in writing in order to do so—we can take it that this penalty against compounding was rarely enforced. The one case in which

---

[38] Shubert, 'Private Initiative', pp. 37–39, and '"Lest the Law Slumber"', pp. 47–50; Hay, 'Property, Authority'.

[39] I have found 41 associations whose articles or rules forbid compounding or concealing a felony; of these, 8 included a provision for the association to prosecute, at its own expense, any member caught compounding; the others simply threatened the errant member with expulsion or making him repay whatever money he had received from the association. Hay found 6 late 18th-c. Staffs. associations with provisions against their members compounding or refusing to prosecute: Hay, 'Crime, Authority', pp. 377–80; King found only 2 of his 84 Essex associations with such provisions: King, ch. 4 below.

it was invoked suggests a reluctance to push it to the logical conclusion: the Harleston Association (Norfolk) recorded in 1796: 'That Mr. Loftly of this Society having Compromised a Felony is excluded being a Member thereof any longer, agreeable to the Rules hereof, but from his Ignorance of the Business, the Society have given up their Power of Prosecuting him for making such Compromise '[40] It is also certainly true that the preambles to many sets of articles and rules stress the need to deter offenders by means of certainty of detection and prosecution, and the virtues of measures taken to prevent the commission of crimes rather than to punish them.[41]

But this does not mean—as Shubert seems to think it does—that the associations were in favour of wholehearted reform of the systems of criminal law, prosecution, and police in the way Bentham, Colquhoun, or Romilly were demanding. There is no evidence at all (and Shubert adduces none) that either associations as bodies, or active individuals within associations, ever lent their support to campaigns for reforms of the criminal law or prosecution (the issue of police reform is slightly different, as will be seen). Indeed, one of the few examples I have come across, goes the opposite way—the Clothiers' Association of Gloucestershire joined the Stroud Association in petitioning the government in 1821 to *increase* the penalty for buying or receiving embezzled goods, after a first conviction, to 14 years' transportation.[42]

More seriously, Shubert assumes that once someone joined an association, he gave up any power as an individual to control his own prosecution—which is quite wrong.[43] Members who wanted association help in a prosecution had to report the offence committed against themselves and apply for assistance and reimbursement; there was no automatic assumption of all members' cases by the societies—which were usually keen to avoid spending more money than they absolutely had to. Virtually the only real power which associations could exercise over their members was the financial one—to refuse reimbursement if the member went against the association's wishes. But they had no way of compelling a recalcitrant member, who was not asking for money, to do something.

Hay contended that eighteenth-century gentlemen could and did make use of the criminal law's element of discretion in order to bolster their own powers by means of informal sanctions, rather than formal prosecutions. He adduced examples of gentlemen agreeing not to prosecute in return for the offenders publicly admitting, and asking pardon for, their offences. He

---

[40] Norfolk·RO, SO 6/1 444X, mins. Apr. 1796.

[41] See the example from the Market Rasen Association quoted at the head of this chapter. There are many similar examples which could be quoted, especially from the opening paragraphs of associations' printed articles of association or rules.

[42] Gloucester Lib., JF 11.22(1), mins., Mar. 1821.

[43] Shubert, 'Private Initiative', p. 37. King. ch. 4 below, also finds Shubert to be wrong in this assumption.

argued that 'Such acts helped to create the mental structure of paternalism. ... Magnanimity could sometimes command submission, even gratitude, where a prosecution might rouse only hatred and a desire for revenge.'[44] If Shubert were correct in his assertion that association members determined to replace this old discretionary pattern with a stricter, uniform enforcement of the law, then associations would clearly have outlawed such practices for themselves and their members. Yet, as late as the 1820s, we can find the Skircoat Society, in the West Riding of Yorkshire, recording this incident:

Whereas we, Joseph Sutcliffe, Delver, Simeon Sutcliffe, Delver, and John Barrow, Delver,

All of Southowram, in the County of York, Did on the 25th Day of December 1821 take from the Premises of Joseph Blakey, of Exley, one Key from the Door of his Dwelling House and after being repeatedly asked for it, refused to deliver the same, the aforesaid Joseph Blakey being a member of the Prosecution Society held in Skircoat, for which offence the said Society has threatened us with a Prosecution, but on our agreeing to ask their Pardon publicly, at our Expence, and paying 10s. to the Halifax Dispensary, they have consented to forgoe the same.

We do therefore most humbly ask their Pardon, and thank them for their Lenity, and do promise never to be guilty of the like Offence again–to witness our Hands this 27th Day of December 1821.[45]

Other associations, in the 1820s and 1830s, have left behind printed posters which similarly record an offender's public confession of guilt and asking pardon—in return for a formal prosecution being dropped.[46]

The Barkway and Reed Association, Hertfordshire, from their foundation in 1818, resolved to use informal sanctions as well as formal prosecutions, to achieve their aims. They declared that it was

highly necessary and incumbent upon all owners of Cottages, for the effectual restoration of the morality and honest habits of the labouring Classes, that in every case where offences shall have been *satifactorily brought Home to any Individual, either by Prosecution or otherwise*, and where the Person does not belong to the Parish, that the Owner of the Cottage occupied by such offender should take instant and prompt Steps to free the Parish from so unworthy an Inmate.[47]

That phrase 'either by Prosecution or otherwise' makes it clear that the association was not planning to confine itself to a strict formal enforcement

---

[44] Hay, 'Crime, Authority', pp. 430–1; and see his 'Property, Authority', *passim*.

[45] Calderdale District Arch., HAS 1335 (769), mins., 1821.

[46] Tyne and Wear Arch., LIB 32 (North Shields and Tynemouth Association Oct., Nov., Dec. 1827); Bolton Lib., FP/1 (Turton Association Jan. 1831.)

[47] Herts. RO, D/P 13 29/5, mins. of meeting 24 Feb. 1818 (emphasis added).

of the law. Ironically, 20 years later, the association found itself trying to persuade one of its members to institute a formal prosecution rather than use informal methods. A member of a local sheep-stealing gang, Martin Tims, had been caught, and he had confessed, *inter alia*, to stealing a sheep from Sir William Clinton, an association member. But Sir William refused to prosecute, and his wife Louisa set out his reasons in a letter. Her argument for not prosecuting Tims owes nothing to any feeling of tenderness for the man, she fears that, despite his confession (which he can retract in court), he might be acquitted, because the main prosecution witness is a very poor one; and such an acquittal would have a very bad effect locally:

> A much better use might be made of Tims' confession respecting the Sheep by holding out to him the hope that it should not be brought against him if he would make full and clear confession as to the misdeeds of the rest of the gang, so that *they* might be convicted or forced to run away for good ... If this is well managed, the advantage gained will be tenfold greater than could be gained by transporting that one more fellow—especially as I think he will have got such a bad name both with honest men and Thieves that he will not think of continuing to reside in Barkway and he may just as well work out the rest of his livelihood at one of the distant English railways as on the public works at the Antipodes.

Lady Louisa's arguments (and those of her husband, in a supporting letter), though coming from an association member in 1838, are very much the eighteenth-century ones about the value of being able to exercise discretion in decisions to prosecute and being able to choose informal sanctions where appropriate.[48]

The formation of so many associations certainly shows that the people who founded and joined them were not satisfied with the protection offered to their property by the existing system. The formation of voluntary associations offered members a relatively cheap and easy way of plugging some of the worst gaps in the system of police and prosecution, by providing the individual prosecutor with the organization and money needed to make the system work fairly efficiently for him. Associations formed a *supplement* to the existing law-enforcement system, not a challenge to its basic principles nor a basis for far-reaching reform. They supplemented the system

---

[48] Herts, RO, D/P 13 29/5, L. D. Clinton to William White 21 May 1838 (emphasis in original); Sir William Clinton to Revd George Ainslie, 9 June 1838. The Association persisted, and convicted Tims at the Herts. midsummer quarter sessions for stealing the sheep from Clinton and 6 turkeys from William White (another member): *Herts. County Records: Calendar to the Sessions Books 1833–1843*, x (Herts. County Council, Hertford, 1957). In 1798, the Hundred of Ely Association found itself with 2 men who were implicated by the confession of an associate in a number of felonies. They decided to prosecute only for the lesser offence of a misdemeanor, claiming that they were doing so 'in consideration of their [wives?] and families': Cambs. RO, Ely UDC Records, committee meeting 17 Sept. 1798.

without in any way disturbing the existing structure of power and status, and without any of the potential upheavals and public expense which substantial reforms would involve. The local aristocracy and gentry could encourage and sponsor such societies without any fear that they posed any threat to their own positions. Indeed, when one notes, in most lists of subscribers to associations (both rural and urban), that they are headed by a number of local gentry and Anglican clergy, with sometimes an aristocrat or two, this suggests that they helped to reinforce the existing system of deference and patronage; certainly there is no evidence that they did anything to undermine it. Substantial reform of the criminal law, police, and prosecution systems, on the other hand, was seen, throughout the period 1780–1850, as posing potential threats of increased taxes, increased central government power, and an undermining of the power of the landed gentry.[49] Associations could offer their members some of the benefits of reform, without any of its disadvantages. As late as 1832, Thomas Dimsdale used a variant of this argument in his appeal for more subscribers to his Barnet General Association, which operated a private subscription-based police force:

It has before been urged that it is highly probable a general Police system will, at no distant period, be thought necessary for the whole Kingdom, except such places as shall prove they are competently guarded. How much more desirable, therefore, must it appear to subscribe, even liberally to our Establishment, which a two-penny rate will fully support, than be compelled to receive one at the expense of a sixpenny rate at least.

Similarly, the Gloucestershire magistrate T. J. Lloyd Baker objected to Chadwick's proposed Constabulary Force, to be paid for largely by county rates with one quarter of the cost coming from the government: 'Personal property only can be protected by a Police force, and a great deal of it, belonging to Merchants, Tradesmen and others, who pay little or nothing to the County rate, is protected by it. *Every one has personal property more or less*, and every one pays, either directly or indirectly, a share of the general taxation of the country. Why then is the land to be held liable to all the present expense of protecting what does not belong to it, and to the expense of a Police force in addition?' Baker belonged to an association with a private subscription police force. He approved its effects, but argued strongly against the landed ratepayers having to fund a force, which would have to protect property of everyone in the county.[50]

Shubert's handling of this issue is simplistic. He has to categorize everyone as either contented with the old system or else demanding

---

[49] See Philips, 'A New Engine'; and sect. IV below.
[50] Herts. RO, D/P 37 18/3, annual report, 27 Oct. 1832; Chadwick Papers, item 229, Baker to Chadwick, 5 June 1839 (emphasis in original).

132 *David Philips*

complete reform of it. He cannot deal with the complexities of groups such as the associations, which identified flaws in the system but tried to deal with them by adding to, and working within, the old system, rather than trying to achieve substantial reform of the system of police, prosecution, and criminal law.

IV THE STRUCTURE AND FUNCTIONING OF ASSOCIATIONS

Membership

Of the surviving material which I have consulted, more relates to rural than to urban-based associations, but there is enough on urban societies to be able to generalize about them. The membership of most associations can be summed up in a phrase which is used in the articles and posters of many of them: they were composed of the 'Gentlemen, Farmers and Tradesmen' of the local district.[51] In rural areas, the gentlemen and farmers predominated; in urban areas, the tradesmen and business firms; but most associations combined some element of both rural and urban and had some mix of both farmers and tradesmen. Gentlemen and Anglican clergy were often prominent in heading the subscription lists, and a number also boasted a few peers;[52] but the bulk of the active membership was always made up of lesser propertied men (and some women[53]); none of the peers[54] and few of the gentry played an active part in running the associations. Clergymen, on the other hand, were often to be found on the committees which ran associations, and most of the committee members were farmers, business men, and tradesmen. Most associations also had the important advice of one or more solicitors.[55]

Some particular groups of property-owners established more narrowly specialized associations. Game-preserving landowners set up Game Law

---

[51] This phrase, or something very similar, is found in the articles of association of, e.g., the Horncastle Association (Lincs.), the Southwold and Reydon Association (Suffolk), the Harleston Association (Norfolk), the Notts. Association, and the Dursley Association (Glos.).

[52] e.g. members of the Notts. Association included the Dukes of Newcastle, Norfolk, and Portland, and Lord Vernon; the Marquess of Salisbury, the Earl of Rosebery, and Lord Melbourne were among the subscribers to the Bishop's Hatfield Association (Herts.); the foundation members of the Salt Hill Society (Bucks.) included the Duke of Buccleuch, the Duchess of Cumberland, and Lords Orkney, Grenville, and Godolphin Osborne; Lords Dacre and Petre were foundation subscribers to the Barstable and Chafford Association (Essex); members of the Snaith Association (Yorks.) included Viscount Downe and Lord Beaumont.

[53] Women were found on the membership and subscription lists of many associations—though generally in small numbers. Usually, they are there as widows, taking over their late husband's subscriptions, but sometimes they are there in their own right and for their own property or business.

[54] Except in the Game Law Associations, where they sometimes played an active role.

[55] This analysis is based on the subscription lists, runs of minutes and accounts, posters, and handbills of most of the associations here dealt with. King, ch. 4 below, reaches similar conclusions about the membership of his 18th-c. Essex associations; so, too, does Shubert for a sample of nine 19th-c. Warks. associations: ' "Lest the Law Slumber" ', p. 18, Table 2.

Associations for Prosecution of Felons　　　　133

TABLE 3.1. *Members' Occupations in Three Associations*

(*a*) Rural Associations

	N. Elmham		Chillington			
	1853		1850		1851	
	No.	%	No.	%	No.	%
Gentlemen	—	—	2	10	2	8
Clergy	1	4	3	15	4	16
Other professional	1	4	3	15	3	12
Merchant	1	4	—	—	—	—
Farmer	13	55	12	60	13	52
Tradesman/Publican	8	33	—	—	3	12
TOTAL	24	100	20	100	25	100

(*b*) Urban Association: *North Shields and Tynemouth Association*—'*Property Insured*'

	1837		1838		1840		1842	
	No.	%	No.	%	No.	%	No.	%
Industrial enterprise	28	26	29	28	29	28	23	22
Commercial enterprise	6	6	6	6	9	9	9	8
Shop	36	33	33	33	30	29	30	28
Hotel/Pub	7	6	8	8	9	9	9	9
Farm	6	6	4	4	5	4	5	5
House only	24	22	21	21	22	21	26	25
Other	1	1	—	—	—	—	3	3
TOTAL	108	100	101	100	104	100	105	100

Sources: Norfolk CRO PD 209/446; Mins. 1853; Staffs. CRO D 590/741. Subscription lists 1850–51; Tyne and Wear Arch. Accession 1432/1, lists of members' property insured, 1837–42. Although no occupations are available for the association in 3.1(b), the types of property suggest the nature of the membership.

Associations from the 1740s on. Manufacturers and merchants—especially in the textile industry—formed associations to prosecute embezzlement by their workpeople and theft of their exposed products by anyone. And the 'Captain Swing' rickburning in 1830 resulted in Kent landowners setting up the Sevenoaks Association for the Detection of Incendiaries and Protection of Property.[56]

[56] For 18th-c. Game Law Associations, see P. B. Munsche 'The Game Laws in Wiltshire 1750–1800', in J. S. Cockburn (ed.), *Crime in England 1550–1800* (London, 1977), pp. 210–28; P. B. Munsche,

Associations were very much *local* institutions, usually covering only a relatively small area—a town, a township or parish and its rural hinterland, with a radius of no more than 10–20 miles, one or two hundreds of a county, or a parish of a large city like London. There are a few instances of attempts at geographically larger associations,[57] but most associations were deliberately restricted in geographical scope—many of them wrote such a provision into their articles of association—and small in size. It is difficult to generalize briefly about the size of membership of associations; even the numbers within one association might vary quite sharply over time, increasing markedly at some periods, and declining steeply at others— particularly in the period just before the society was formally dissolved. Some associations built up their membership to well over 100, and proved able to sustain their numbers at these high levels for fairly long periods.[58]

TABLE 3.2. *Size of Normal Membership of Associations (Based on membership information for 111 associations)*

Size of membership	No. of associations	%
20 or under	11	10
21–60	69	62
61–100	16	14
101 or over	15	14
TOTAL	111	100

A few kept fairly stable memberships with numbers between 10 and 20. But by far the commonest size for an association was in the range of 20 to 60 members (see Table 3.2).

Gentlemen and Poachers: The English Game Laws 1671–1831 (Cambridge, 1981), pp. 56–62, 90–3, 110–13; King, ch. 4 below. Two 19th-c. examples were the Bedfordshire Association for the Preservation of Game and Fish (Beds. RO, LL 17/314) and the Barnard Castle Game Association (Durham RO, D/HH/2/13/3 and 7/7/18). For a manufacturers' association, see the Gloucestershire Clothiers and Woollen Manufacturers' Association, set up in 1812 (Gloucester Lib., JF 11.21); see also J. Styles 'Embezzlement, Industry and the Law in England, 1500–1800', in M. Berg, P. Hudson, M. Sonnenscher (eds.), *Manufacture in Town and Country before the Factory* (Cambridge, 1983), pp. 173–210; Hay, 'Crime, Authority', pp. 368–9; King, ch. 4 below. For the Sevenoaks Association, see Kent RO, U 442 067. See also Shubert, ' "Lest the Law Slumber" ', pp. 33–7.

[57] See King, ch. 4 below, on the Essex Association 1775–84. The Nottinghamshire Association developed out of an association against horse-thieves, in 1788, with an initial membership of 220; the Bedfordshire Association began in 1790 and reached a membership of 167 in 1808. The Dursley Association became the Gloucestershire General Association in 1828; the Oxfordshire Association was established in 1828, and the Lincoln and Lincolnshire Association in 1802. Despite their titles, none of these associations covered the whole of its relevant county, and they all existed alongside many other local associations in their respective counties.   [58] See Appendix 4.

Subscriptions

The type of subscription paid by members of associations can be classified into four broad categories (Table 3.3). In category A, the commonest form, every member paid the same fixed annual subscription. In category B, all paid the same, but, after paying an entry fee, members only paid a subscription as and when the association's finances required it—this would depend on the association's degree of activity and the decisions of its committee. Categories C and D refined these further, by dividing members into classes paying different proportions of the amount levied; the classes were determined by rough indicators of the members' respective wealth—amount or value of land occupied, or poor rate assessment. Table 3.3 shows that nearly half the associations listed there charged an annual subscription of 10s. 6d. or less; for most members, whether paying a fixed annual subscription or an irregular levy, belonging to an association was a relatively cheap matter.

T ABLE 3.3. *Types of Subscription levied by Associations (Based on subscription information for 107 associations)*

	A	B	C	D	Total
5s. or less	31				
6s. to 10s. 6d.	17				
£1 or more	7				
TOTAL	55	33	10	9	107
PERCENTAGE	52	31	9	8	100

Notes: A = Regular annual subscription; B = Fixed entry fee plus irregular levies on members as needed; C = Subscribers divided into 2–4 classes, each paying a fixed ratio of a regular annual subscription; D = Subscribers divided into 2–7 classes, each paying a fixed ratio of irregular levies on members as needed. The different classes for categories C and D were normally determined by the amount or value of land occupied by, or by the poor rate assessment of, the members.

Budgets

The budgets of associations naturally varied greatly, depending on the number of members, the size and type of subscription, and the amount of activity in which the association engaged. The expenditure was great if the society ran its own patrols or police force, which were a heavy drain on resources. Normal administrative costs of running the association—paying their solicitors' and printers' bills, the cost of their dinner at the annual meeting, and the regular salary for the secretary or treasurer who usually doubled as the association's solicitor—were not usually very high; some of the smaller and less active associations went for year after year with expenditures of well under £10 a year. What would always send the expenditure sky-rocketing, and the association accounts into the red, would be having to pay the legal costs of one or more difficult cases. In 1828–9, the Dursley Association prosecuted two cases of burglary at assizes and one of larceny at quarter sessions; the burglary cases were complex ones, involving difficulties in apprehending the offenders; by the time the cases were over, the association faced a legal bill of £200. 18s. 6d., of which they were able to recover £157. 16s. 4d. from the county; but it still left them having to find £43. 2s. 2d., and plunged them heavily into a deficit. The Plomesgate Association, Suffolk, which was very active, brought 25 prosecutions between 1832 and 1836; they secured convictions in all of them, getting 17 people transported, five of them for life; but this effort, plus paying their own private watch force to watch members' properties, left them with a massive deficit of £150. One horse-stealing case in 1810 landed the Salt Hill Society, Buckinghamshire, with a deficit of more than £70; it cost the Society £110. 2s. 8d. to pay for the services of a Bow Street officer and pursue the thief to Sussex where he was caught and prosecuted.[59] From time to time, some associations would make efforts to keep down their costs by declaring that they would only employ solicitors and counsel who would charge just the amount of the county allowance; or they would try to manage what they felt to be simple prosecutions without employing counsel at all.[60] Sometimes this economy drive could misfire: in 1815, members of the Great Bealings Association Suffolk, feeling 'the uncomfortable state of affairs in this country, as to the low price of Corn these last 12 months as well as the burdensome nature of the taxes, that is likely to fall upon us', decided to discharge their paid solicitor-treasurer and appoint one of their own number, John Thompson, to act gratis. But, within a year Thompson had gone bankrupt, taking with him the association's funds and plunging the members into a bad deficit.[61]

Management

Most associations were run by elected committees, on which the most important person was always the secretary or treasurer (sometimes the same man), one of whom usually also acted as solicitor to the association. The solicitors invariably benefited most financially from the associations: they received a regular retainer from the society, and they handled all its

---

[59] Gloucester Lib., JF 11.32(23); Suffolk RO, HA 34:50/21/6, 1(c), Report 1836; Bucks. RO, D/X 69, mins. and accounts 1810–12.

[60] Such cost-cutting attempts figure prominently in the records of some Yorks. associations—Bradford, Doncaster, Bradfield, Sowerby Bridge, and Skircoat. They also appear in the records of the Salt Hill (Bucks.), Neithrop (Oxon.), Tanworth (Warks.), Chillington (Staffs.), Hinckley (Leics.), Carlton-in-Lindrick (Notts.), and Gateshead societies.

[61] Suffolk RO, HB 10: 50/20/34.2, letter to John Wood, 20 Mar. 1815; mins. 1815–18.

business, taking members' reports of offences committed and handling the subsequent prosecutions, advertising the society and its members, and collecting subscriptions. Reading through their itemized accounts (each interview at 3*s*. 4*d*. or 6*s*. 8*d*. a time, which quickly mounted up) one sees how good associations were for their business. Not surprisingly, they were the most active promoters of associations, urging local property-owners to set them up; and many of them acted as solicitor to more than one association.[62] Members would come together for a general meeting at least once a year (in some associations, more frequently); at this meeting, the treasurer's accounts would be examined and passed, and any motions which needed to be discussed, would be debated, rules amended, etc. But perhaps the most important aspect of the annual meeting was that it was always held at a local inn, accompanied by a dinner. The dinner brought together, in a sociable atmosphere, members who might otherwise not see one another during the year (and who might not otherwise attend the annual meeting). The minutes and accounts of many associations show that they lavished much thought and a fair bit of money on the food and drink (especially the drink) for these functions.[63] This convivial ritual played an important part in the initial foundation of associations and in keeping them running year after year. It was probably the annual dinner, more than anything else, which kept many associations in existence from the 1860s on, when their period of real significance in law enforcement was past. The dinners also ensured that innkeepers were a second group who profited financially from associations. Most associations included among their members one or more innkeepers, and confined their dinner venues to the inns of their members.

V ASSOCIATIONS IN ACTION

All associations offered their members at least two basic forms of assistance: in the detection and apprehension of suspected offenders, and in the

---

[62] See Gloucester Lib., RX 300.2(5), letter of John Vizard, Dursley, to Henry Vizard, Tetbury, 18 Jan. 1801, enclosing a copy of the regulations of the Dursley Association (of which John was the solicitor). J. W. Buchanan wrote to the 1836 *Commission on County Rates* (pp. 139–40) to state that he was the solicitor to 5 local associations around Nuneaton; William Mason was treasurer and clerk to at least 5 Essex associations; John Wood was treasurer and solicitor for the Loes and Wilford and Great Bealings Associations, in Suffolk, for many years; Messrs. Wheatley & Hoyle, of Rotherham, acted as treasurer and solicitors to the Laughton-en-le-Northern and Aston Associations, in the West Riding; Thomas Rhodes was secretary, treasurer, and solicitor to the Market Rasen and Binbrook Associations in Lincs.; Thomas Wheldon was secretary, treasurer, and solicitor to the Barnard Castle Game Association and Lartington Association (Durham).

[63] A good example is provided in the minutes and accounts of the Salt Hill Society 1783–1860, which are full of details of discussion of the amount and cost of the food and drink for the dinners: Bucks. RO, D/X 69.

prosecution of those arrested people. They differed in the details, and in what other help they made available; but these two were the essential services for which associations existed.

Detection and Apprehension

All associations made extensive use of advertisement, publicity, and money for this purpose. The standard way of reacting to a member's report of an offence committed against himself was to print handbills, and, often, to place advertisements in a number of local newspapers, advertising a reward for information leading to conviction for that offence. Most associations had standard graduated tables of rewards for conviction for a whole range of specific offences, which they published in their articles and rules, and circulated via posters and handbills. (Associations' accounts make it clear that local printers shared with solicitors and innkeepers in deriving a regular income from the societies.) Associations would also provide the money to send people in search of the stolen goods and the offender; they would pay the travel costs, expenses, and an allowance for time and trouble, for the victim, his employees, or the constables of that or a neighbouring place, to be sent in search and pursuit. Some associations imposed on their members an obligation, when a member's horse or cattle had been stolen, to ride a certain distance themselves (or pay for a servant or hired substitute to do so) along certain set routes in search of the animal and/or the offender.[64] Apart from the set rewards for information leading to conviction, the associations would also often pay rewards, and gratuities for time and trouble, to the people who apprehended suspects.

Prosecution

Once the suspect was apprehended the association's solicitor would ensure that he was taken before a magistrate and would try to get him committed for trial at quarter sessions or assizes. The association assumed all the trouble and expense of preparing the prosecution case. This involved taking the evidence; finding and subpoenaing the witnesses; travelling, if necessary, to find and identify stolen property; drawing up the brief; briefing counsel; paying all the numerous necessary legal fees; transporting the prosecutor and his witnesses to the county town for the trial; and paying for their accommodation until the trial was over. As much of this as possible was recovered from the county allowance, made at the end of

---

[64] e.g. the Chillington, Penkridge, Weston, and Trentham Associations (all Staffs.), the Loes and Wilford and Southwold and Reydon Associations (Suffolk), the Norton Association (Yorks.), and the Oxfordshire Association.

the trial, but it never covered all of the cost and frequently it covered less than half the total outlay on the prosecution from the time the offence was committed. This difference was paid by the association, from the fund which it built up from members' subscriptions.

These were the bread-and-butter services which the associations offered their members, and it was for these advantages that people paid their subscriptions. One could see it as a simple form of self-help insurance against the problems of apprehension of suspects, and the large costs of prosecutions, especially in the late eighteenth century. Associations naturally tended to restrict these benefits to paid-up members; this was the main incentive for anyone to join an association. The societies frequently advertised the names of their members, coupled with the warning that anyone who offended against them could expect to be prosecuted by the full weight of the association. This was designed (like the notices of modern security companies stating that a building is protected by them) to deter would-be wrongdoers from choosing association members as victims. W. A. Miles, collecting information for the Constabulary Commission in 1836, believed that this worked in practice:

I think however that no correct conclusion can be derived from the number of prosecutions by the Associations, because a person who has been robbed feels more inclined to prosecute if he be in the Association than the person who has not a similar benefit—and this is so well known among the Depredators that they are careful not to rob a Member of such Association—or at any rate they would rather rob any other person.[65]

However, some associations (I have found 20) included in their rules a specific provision enabling them to prosecute on behalf of *non-members* who might be too poor to be able to prosecute for themselves. Douglas Hay has suggested that this might have been designed to enable the associations to continue the paternalist, deference-inducing, practice of many eighteenth-century landed gentlemen paying the costs of poor

---

[65] Chadwick Papers, item 1398, Miles to Chadwick, 7 Nov. 1836. Thomas Dimsdale claimed that a local farmer, who did not belong to the Barnet Association, suffered badly from thefts: 'Well, he came in and said, "Sir, I hear I am a marked man because I am not in your circle." Some of his labourers had said that if he was in the Association they would not steal his things. He became a member of the Association; and now they do not take a single thing. The effect upon the depredators is just as if they had a list of us': *Royal Commission on Constabulary Force* (1839), p. 129. A member of the East Essex Association, whose garden was frequently robbed, asked the treasurer of the Association to issue handbills offering a 10-guinea reward to see 'whether the terror of your name will not prevent future inconvenience of a similar nature'. Another member, similarly offering a reward, wrote: 'I confess I have but little expectation of discovering the thief, but I think it may tend to prevent future depredations': Essex RO, D/DE1 c.1, J. Griggs to William Mason, 2 Sept. 1806; Revd W. Driffield to William Mason, 7 Oct. 1806.

labourers prosecuting in court.[66] The language of these clauses is generally couched in terms of local people who 'shall not be able on account of
poverty to prosecute' or 'such poor Persons as they judge proper Objects
of their Assistance, although not Subscribers',[67] but it is instructive to
examine this clause in action. Hay was unable to find any case in which this
provision was put in force by eighteenth-century Staffordshire associations.
The Hammersmith Association had no such provision in their rules, and
in 1819 refused to prosecute on behalf of a non-member for that reason;
but in 1821 they decided to prosecute a man in custody for an alleged
felony on a Mr James Cromwell: 'This Association feeling the necessity at
this time of putting a Stop to the Numerous Depredations almost Nightly
Committed within this Hamlet—do undertake to carry on the Prosecution
in the event of Mr. Jas. Cromwell's not coming forward'.[68] This suggests
a more utilitarian reason for an association allowing itself the freedom to
prosecute on behalf of non-members or reluctant prosecutors: to take the
opportunity to rid the neighbourhood of what they saw as dangerous or
troublesome criminals.

In any event, I have been able to find very few instances in which
associations *did* exercise this power. The North Elmham Association, in
1814 and 1836, offered rewards for offences committed against poor non-
members, but apparently with no result. In August 1828, however, the
Association agreed to pay for the prosecution of Chris Frost, who stole two
donkeys belonging to two men 'both poor persons belonging to the parish'.
Frost was convicted at the assizes, and given six months' hard labour, and
the association paid a solicitor's bill of £11. 2s. 8d. plus 17s. to the man
who apprehended Frost, and 13s. 6d. to the constable as his expenses
for attending before the magistrate. The North Shields and Tynemouth
Association, in 1813, agreed to pay for a prosecution by two 'very poor'
men against a woman who had stolen clothes and sheets from their houses,
and had finally been caught after great exertions. However, by 1840, they
must have toughened their attitude towards the expenditure of members'
money, because in that year they refused to take up various recent burglaries
and thefts 'the persons upon whom depredations have been committed not

---

[66] The relevant associations are: Ecclesfield, Midgley, Heptonstall, Kirkburton (Yorks.); the Halsall
and Poulton Agreements (Lancs.); North Shields and Tynemouth; Horncastle (Lincs.); Newark-upon-
Trent (Notts.), Lutterworth (Leics.); Corby, Huxloe, and Rowell (Northants); Handsworth (Staffs.);
Birmingham; North Elmham (Norfolk); Epping (Essex); Goudhurst (Kent); West Ham, St Mary
Rotherhithe, Enfield (London area); Olney, Turvey, and Harrold (Beds.). Hay found only three 18th-
c. Staffs. associations with this provision: Alrewas, Rugeley, and Bradley: Hay, 'Crime, Authority', pp.
375–77.

[67] These phrases come, respectively, from the 1829 articles of the Handsworth Association (Birmingham Ref. Lib., 64041), and the 1783 rules of the Corby, Huxloe, and Rowell Association (Notts.
RO. DDM 71/196). The Goudhurst Association defined 'poor person' for these purposes as someone
'assessed and rated to the poor ... at and under £4': Kent RO, U 769 L6, mins. 1817.

[68] GLRO, P 80/PAU/11.

being members of the Society'. The Goudhurst Society, which began with such a provision in their articles in 1815, specifically removed it in 1842. One can follow the stages of a similar development, and see the reasons for it, in the West Ham Society. They began in 1817 with strong provisions for the society to prosecute and offer specific rewards on behalf of non-members. By 1823, they found themselves running short of money:

> It appearing to the Members that by far the greater portion of the Sums paid for rewards, is upon the apprehending of persons for Robbery on nonsubscribers, it is resolved that no rewards be paid in future for the apprehending of Felons for committing Depredations upon any other than Members of this Society.

As their clerk. Mr George Dacre, told the Select Committee in 1828,

> ... we paid a full reward if a subscriber was plundered, and half for those who were not subscribers; we found the inducement to subscribe was not sufficient, that our funds would not enable us to pay the second species in protecting the property of those who were not subscribers.

However, they continued some assistance towards non-members' pro-secutions, awarding, in 1833, a 2-guinea gratuity to the local constable for arresting people 'for robbing etc. parties in this Parish who are not sub-scribers to the Association'.[69]

Apart from these few instances, the provision does not seem to have been made use of by those associations which included it in their rules; this is not too surprising when one considers that most members looked jealously at expenditure of their subscription money for any purpose other than their own benefit, and when we see the financial problems which the West Ham Society brought upon itself by its more open policy. Primarily the associations existed to protect their members' property, and were not charitable institutions, despite the ingenious attempt by the Nottingham-shire Association in 1843 to claim exemption from the new income tax on the grounds that it was 'a Charitable Society'![70]

A Cheshire JP, giving evidence to the Constabulary Commission,

---

[69] Norfolk RO, PD 209/445; Tyne and Wear Arch., LIB 429 (1813) and Accession 1432/1 (1840); Kent RO, U769 L6, mins. 1842; Newham Local Studies Lib., IV 68 mins. 1817, 1823, 1833; *Report from the Select Committee on the Police of the Metropolis* PP 1828 (533) vi, pp. 201–2. A semi-literate letter to the Secretary of the Birmingham Association, in 1785, claimed that prosecution on behalf of poor non-members had been used by an earlier association to *cheat* 'a Poor widow with a family of Fatherless Childern'! The judge had awarded her £13 county allowance plus a 'Tyburn ticket' (a certificate granting exemption from parish duties in return for securing a capital conviction) which the association had sold for £26 or more, of which they returned to her only £12 (Birmingham Ref. Lib., 259647).

[70] Notts. RO, DD.T 11/14, letter from Special Commissioner's Dept., Stamps and Taxes, to Isaac Palethorpe, 19 Dec. 1843.

described a fairly inactive association in his division as being 'a sort of mutual insurance against felonies',[71] and this 'mutual insurance' aspect was stressed by a number of associations. Some of the early associations against horse-stealing included provision to reimburse half the value of the stolen horse, if it was not recovered.[72] The North Shields and Tynemouth Association required each member to specify what was his 'Property Insured' with the association; while a number of West Riding associations in the woollen manufacture area imposed a double subscription on members who had property particularly exposed to theft from tenter-grounds, bleaching-grounds, mills, or warehouses. The Lincoln and Lincolnshire Association took this aspect to its logical conclusion: as the association's importance as an apprehending and prosecuting society declined, with the spread of the county police, they set up an 'Indemnity Fund', separate from their prosecution fund, to insure members against losses by theft.[73]

Rural associations most commonly prosecuted thefts of farm animals (especially sheep and poultry), farm produce, and woood taken from trees, hedges, fences, and stiles. Urban associations were more likely to prosecute thefts of raw materials from places of work, thefts from shops and houses, and garden produce, or laundry stolen from gardens. Most offenders were prosecuted on indictment at quarter sessions or assizes; but from the 1820s onwards, a number of associations made increasing use of the possibilities of the legislation which extended the range of summary jurisdiction, such as the Malicious Trespass Act 1820, the Vagrancy Act 1824, and those provisions of the Larceny Act 1827 which provided summary trial for stealing or damaging plants, fruit, and vegetables in gardens and orchards.[74] As David Jones has neatly put it, the Vagrancy Act of 1824 (5 Geo. IV, c. 83) 'proved to be one of the most flexible, useful and criminal-making statutes of the century', and the North Shields and Tynemouth Association made sharp use of those possibilities to overcome the problems of having to construct a sufficient case to justify committal to trial on indictment and

---

[71] Chadwick Papers, item 13, Evidence taken by the Constabulary Force Commissioners, p. 98.

[72] Notts. Association would reimburse half the value of the horse, up to £13, increased to £17. 10s. from 1795 (Notts. RO, DD.T. 25/7 and 25/1); Harleston and Bedfordshire Associations would pay half the value, up to £10 (Norfolk RO, SO 6/1 444X, 1799 rules; Beds. RO, AD 1087, resolutions 1790).

[73] Tyne and Wear Arch., Accession 1432/1, membership lists 1837–42, 1851; articles of association of Halifax, Heptonstall, Luddenden, Midgley, and Wakefield Associations; Lincs. RO, WG 8/1/1 and 8/7/6.

[74] Posters of the North Shields and Tynemouth Association and Earsdon and Horton Associations in the 1820s,: Tyne and Wear Arch., LIB 32 and Accession 1432/1; Gloucester Lib., JF 11.25(17), poster 2 July 1829; Great Baddow Association, Essex RO, D/DTU 270, poster 1837; Olney, Turvey and Harrold Association: Beds. RO, GA 1108/3, posters 1814 and n.d.; Salt Hill Society from the late 1830s onwards: Bucks. RO, D/X 69, Mins. and Accounts. On the effect of this summary jurisdiction legislation of the 1820s in widening greatly the pool of people arrested and committed to gaol, see S. Magarey, 'The Invention of Juvenile Delinquency in Early Nineteenth-Century England', *Labour History* (Canberra), 34 (May 1978), pp. 11–27.

then to satisfy a jury. In 1835, they brought several suspected thieves before the magistrates

and the facts were not clearly proved so as to send them to be tried by a Jury although there was no Doubt of their Guilt and on that account they were committed for various periods as Vagrants and reputed Thieves to hard labour in the House of Correction

By this means the parties have been severely punished at very trifling expense to the Association.

In 1837, working in close co-operation with the local Superintendent of Police, they got five suspected thieves sentenced summarily in this way. A magistrate, who was also an active member of the association, suggested a similar procedure to the Dursley Association, Gloucestershire, in 1828, in proceeding against someone whom they suspected of burglary; and the Loes and Wilford Association, Suffolk, in 1833, similarly convicted summarily, as an 'Idle and Disorderly Person', someone whom they had initially charged with felony.[75] Summary prosecution and conviction was much quicker and cheaper than going through the whole process of committal followed by trial by jury at quarter sessions or assizes; it was also much more certain, if one had only to convince a friendly magistrate (who was often a member of the association) rather than a grand jury and then a jury. It is notable that the North Shields and Tynemouth Association moved over to making use of summary jurisdiction, especially the Vagrancy Act of 1824, at a time when they were concerned about the poor 'clear up' rate of offences against their members (see below).

It is difficult to calculate the exact number of prosecutions for which associations were responsible, since the records are often fragmentary; Appendix 3 lists calculations, made from surviving materials, for a number of associations. However, the number of prosecutions brought by an association is not necessarily the best test of its effectiveness in protecting the property of its members. Appendix 3 shows that most of the associations listed there averaged no more than one or two prosecutions a year. It also shows that what modern police would call their 'clear up' rate (here, calculated as their ratio of prosecutions to offences reported) is a poor one, often less than one in four.[76] The annual reports of the North Shields and Tynemouth Association for 1832–5 record an unimpressive picture of 36

---

[75] Tyne and Wear Arch., Accession 1432/1, annual reports 1835, 1837; Gloucester Lib., JF 11.32(23); Suffolk RO, HB 10: 50/20/34.1, mins. 1833; D. Jones, *Crime, Protest, Community and Police in 19th-Century Britain* (1982), pp. 206–7.

[76] Properly, a clear-up rate should be the ratio of *convictions* to offences reported, but the data of convictions are incomplete, whereas most associations recorded the prosecutions which they brought and for which they paid, without necessarily recording the result. On measures of effectiveness see the testimony of W. A. Miles, n. 65 above.

offences reported and only seven convictions secured on indictment for these. It was at this point that they started making systematic use of the clauses of the Vagrancy Act which enabled people to be summarily committed to gaol as 'Rogues and Vagabonds'. On the other hand, the Plomesgate Association (Suffolk) proudly boasted, in its report for 1832–6, that it had brought 25 prosecutions in that period, and had secured convictions in all of them, leading to 17 sentences of transportation (five of them for life and six for 14 years) and 12 prison sentences. The Barnet General Association proclaimed that it had convicted more than 200 people in the 20 years 1813–32, and that in 1833 it had arrested 26 people and had 20 of them convicted and sentenced to transporation or imprisonment.[77]

These last two examples remind us that, though each association prosecuted relatively few offenders, all the associations together prosecuted large numbers of people, and were responsible for securing many severe sentences. I have noted at least 13 association cases in which death sentences were passed on one or more of the accused, between the years 1793 and 1827: for murder, horse theft, sheep-stealing, burglary, robbery, and stealing from a shop. In at least two of those cases we know that the sentence was executed. Men were hanged for a murder in Stafford in 1793 and another two for burglary in Doncaster in 1823. In at least four more cases, a formal death sentence was *recorded* and the prisoners sentenced to life transportation. In another case, in 1799, the Society for Prosecuting Felons (London) refused a strong request to intercede and ask for a pardon on behalf of a woman whom they had capitally convicted for stealing from her employer, on the grounds that 'it would be incompatible with the duty they owe to the Public and their Institution'.[78] Many more people prosecuted by associations received sentences of transportation for life, for 14 or 15 years, and for seven years. Indeed, the solicitor of the Dursley Association, in urging the formation of a Tetbury Association, boasted:

The beneficial Effects of an Assoc[iati]on of this description were strongly evinced in the Pros[ecutio]n of Gunston at the last Sessions. No Trouble or

---

[77] Tyne and Wear Arch., Accession 1432/1; Suffolk RO, HA 34: SO/21/6.1(c) (the sentences add up to more than the 25 prosecutions because some involved more than one accused); Herts. RO, D/P 37 18/3, annual reports 1832 and 1833. In his study of Staffs., Hay estimates that associations were responsible for 20–25% of local prosecutions 1780–1802: 'Crime, Authority', pp. 393–94. King, ch. 4 below, reaches a lower estimate, of about 15%, for Essex in a similar period.

[78] For the death sentences, see Notts. Association 1793, 1803, and 1808; Society for Prosecuting 1798 (2 cases), 1799 (2 cases)—quotation from mins. Feb. 1800; North Shields and Tynemouth Association 1811; Dursley Association 1796; Henley-in-Arden Association 1819; Doncaster Association 1823—2 men hanged for burgling a jeweller's shop; Hammersmith Association 1827. For the men hanged as a result of the Stafford Association prosecution 1793, see Hay, 'Crime, Authority', pp. 383–4. The 4 *recorded* death sentences: Coleshill Association 1796; Charing Society 1800; Earl Manvers Association 1815; Tenterden Society 1824. (By 4 Geo. IV, c. 48 (1823), courts outside the City of London did not need to pronounce the death sentence (except in cases of murder) if of the opinion that the convict was a proper subject for a full or conditional pardon.)

Expence you know were spared in having this Man convicted, & I am very happy in informing you we succeeded in gratifying the wishes of all the Country. There is no Doubt but he will be transported, so the Chairman informed us on our representing to him that this was the third time of his being br[ough]t before the Bar, that he wo[ul]d make an Example of him. After the Trial was over, he called Mr. Marsh forward & told him, the Country was very much indebted to him for the Trouble he had taken in this Business, . . . and that he merited the Thanks of the Public. Had not Marsh been in the Assoc[iatio]n, Gunston wo[ul]d probably have been acquitted, as no Individual wo[ul]d have risqued the Expence;[79]

I have found only two cases in which an association prosecuted for murder, the Stafford Association in 1793 and the Market Rasen Association, Lincolnshire, in 1843. But in the 1830s a number of associations offered very large rewards for the conviction of people guilty of arson, and the Sevenoaks Association was set up specifically to combat incendiarism in September 1830, while the fires of 'Captain Swing' were raging. It remained active until at least 1839.[80] However, the normal business of the typical, fairly small, association was concerned with less dramatic offences and less severe sentences. Theft made up the vast bulk of association criminal business, and, except when it was the theft of large and valuable animals, it was normally punished by fairly short local prison sentences.

VI ASSOCIATIONS AND POLICING

All associations offered their members help, in terms of money, organization, and manpower, in apprehending and prosecuting offenders; but some went further than this, and set up their own watch forces, patrols, or police forces. The most famous of these was the Barnet General Association, on London's northern outskirts. Their secretary, Thomas Dimsdale, was an indefatigable publicist for himself and the association. He reported their achievements in printed annual reports, and gave evidence to the parliamentary inquiries of 1828, 1836, and 1839. In all of these, he spoke of his association's achievements in the most glowing terms.[81] The associ-

---

[79] Gloucester Lib., RX 300.2(5) John Vizard, Dursley, to Henry Vizard, Tetbury, 18 Jan. 1801.

[80] Large arson rewards were offered by the Bishop's Stortford Association (Herts.) 1825; the North Shields and Tynemouth Association 1835 and 1839; Linton Association (Cambs.) 1830; Tickhill Association (Yorks.) 1836; Eyam Association (Derbys.) 1836 and 1848; Silsoe and Ampthill Association (Beds.) 1835; Sevenoaks Association—Kent RO, U442 067. On arson as a widespread form of rural protest in the 1830s and 1840s, see Jones, *Crime, Protest*, ch. 2.

[81] The annual reports for 1832–5 inclusive are in the Herts. RO, D/R 37 18/3; Dimsdale's evidence is in 1828 *SC on Police*, pp. 211–13, 1836 *Commission on County Rates*, Appendix, pp. 32–5, and 1839 *RC on Constabulary Force*, pp. 122–3, 129–31, 168–9. The 1839 RC publishes only extracts from Dimsdale's evidence; his full evidence, and that of Isaac Pye, the Barnet Association superintendent, can be found in the Chadwick Papers, item 13, pp. 52–79.

ation was established in 1813 (incorporating an earlier Barnet Association founded in 1784) as a conventional prosecuting society, but they soon decided to set up a paid patrol force for the area. Barnet, being on the edge of London, and on an important road to the North, was felt to be particularly vulnerable to depredators. The association began with a force of just two paid police officers, whose job was to patrol at night and on foot, but the impact of the 'Captain Swing' disturbances decided the subscribers to increase the force to five (a superintendent and four patrols) in 1831, and, in 1834, to a force of six. The success of this force in preventing crime and apprehending thieves was widely publicized by Dimsdale, and Edwin Chadwick (in the 1839 Royal Commission) used the Barnet General Association as an illustration of the validity of his plans for a paid rural constabulary. Dimsdale's evidence states unashamedly the modern policeman's assumption that 'it is sometimes necessary to act a little beyond the power which the law gives us, or do more than it defines', in describing his pursuit of the person who had killed and stolen a sheep. He sent one of his patrols to search 'every man's cottage' in the district, for signs of the stolen mutton, without having the slightest legal authority to do so. He defended his conduct on the grounds that 'the success justifies the act' and 'an honest man will never conceal anything. It is only the dishonest that raise any cry about the liberty of the subject, and interference and so on.'[82]

Other association forces were less well known. Another metropolitan society, the Hammersmith Association, founded in 1811, made no fewer than five attempts to set up their own watch force for protection, in 1811–12, 1816–17, 1818–19, 1824, and 1827. None of these lasted very long, and most seem to have foundered on the problem of collecting enough in subscriptions from the members to be able to pay for a force of reasonably competent patrols and watchmen.[83] The Linton, Hildersham, Bartlow and Hadstock Association, on the Cambridgeshire–Essex border, in 1820 established a roster of its members to patrol the parish (or pay for a deputy to do the duty for them). In 1821, they added a paid constable to this patrol. In 1838, they made use of the Lighting and Watching Act 1833 (3 & 4 Wm. IV, c. 90) to set up a police force, employing one constable and two assistants, paid from the association's subscriptions. Other associations in the 1830s made similar use of this Act, which enabled the ratepayers of any parish, or part of a parish, to decide to levy a rate to support a local

---

[82] Chadwick Papers, item 13, p. 67. On modern police attitudes, see M. Banton, *The Policeman in the Community* (London, 1964), and M. Cain, *Society and the Policeman's Role* (London, 1973).

[84] GLCRO, P 80/PAU/11. The 1816 plan employed 2 superintendents (at 15s. a week each) and 6 'Patroles' (at 10s. 6d. a week). The Patroles were all appointed from unemployed men (see list in mins., 1 Dec. 1816). The 1818–19 force had 2 Patroles and 5 watchmen; they immediately ran into problems about the character and honesty of the watchmen: mins. 13 and 20 May 1818. In 1827 they appointed 7 patroles at 21s. a week each: mins., Apr. 1827.

police force.[84] Some associations, while not going as far as establishing a full subscription police force, used a mixture of paid men and householders who were required to serve on a roster system;[85] or employed watchmen to watch, by night, the property of their members.[86]

Most associations, however, did not set up their own forces for policing or patrolling. They usually established a very close working relationship with the local parish constables, binding them to their members' service with ties of money. The minutes and accounts of associations are full of instances of the constables being paid, not only rewards and their expenses incurred, but also gifts or gratuities in appreciation of their services on behalf of members of the association. Every year, from 1828 until he died in 1838, the West Ham Society paid a gratuity of 2 guineas to John Wright, the constable of Stratford 'for his services in furthering the purposes of this Society'. (His widow received it in the year he died.)[87] Before the coming of the new police, the parish constables were theoretically meant to be available to serve everyone, but in fact they would not take any energetic action, or travel any distance in search of stolen goods, unless the complainant was prepared to guarantee payment of their expenses and fees.[88] With the associations advertising widely that they would pay constables' fees, expenses, and for their loss of time, and would also offer rewards for apprehension and conviction, *and* possible gratuities for good service, they could generally count on prompt and devoted attention being paid to their needs by the constables whenever they required it.[89]

The relationship of associations and their members to the whole question of policing is an important issue. Dr J. Tobias, in some brief remarks on associations, considered them as simply private attempts to remedy the absence of a professional police force, which lost all point once the new police were firmly established. In 1977, in a short discussion of associations

[84] Cambs. RO, L. 95/18—the force remained in existence till 1851. Two Glos. associations, Stow-on-the-Wold and Bourton-on-the-Water, set up such forces under the Lighting and Watching Act in 1834; and the Wickham Market Association (Suffolk) tried unsuccessfully to establish such a force: (Storch, ch. 5 below). B. J. Davey has described the policing of Horncastle (Lincs.) by a subscription police established under the Lighting and Watching Act, in *Lawless and Immoral: Policing a Country Town 1838–1857* (Leicester, 1983).

[85] e.g. Tenterden Association 1824 onwards: Kent RO, TE/Z 1 and 4; Great Bolton Special Constables Society 1797–1832: Bolton Reference Lib., B352.2.BOL; Stafford Association 1819 onwards: Hay, 'Crime, Authority', p. 373.

[86] e.g. Notts. Association, Gedling Association: Notts. RO, DDT 25/1mins. 1801, DD 296/1; Plomesgate Association: Suffolk RO, HA 28: 50/23/4, HA 34: 50/21/6. 1(c); Charing Society: Kent RO, U 1293 07, mins. 1801. The Barnard Castle Game Association employed a gamekeeper and 7 paid 'watchers': Durham RO, D/HH/2/13/3/2/1–2.

[87] Newham Local Studies Lib., IV 68, mins. 1828–38.

[88] See Philips, *Crime and Authority*, chs. 3 and 4.

[89] See evidence to *Select Committee on Police, 2nd Report*, of the Chief Constable of the hundred of Aveland, in the Parts of Kesteven, Lincs., about the difference it would make in his constables' response to a sheep-stealing if the victim was an association member: PP 1852–3, xxxvi (715), Q 3407.

within the context of the workings of the prosecution system, I suggested that property-owners who opposed their county adopting the permissive 1839 Rural Police Act, could oppose it with some sense of security. If they belonged to an association, they already paid a small subscription to protect themselves and their property, and they resisted the idea of having to pay a higher county rate for a police force designed to serve the entire population of the county. Adrian Shubert has taken issue with this point, claiming that support for an association usually also implied support for a police force.[90] Having now examined a good deal more evidence on associations than I had been able to see in 1977, I wish to reconsider the issue.

Shubert has over-simplified the issue by presenting it as one in which associations and their members have to be seen simply as being either for or against a new police. Certainly, the metropolitan associations seem generally to have favoured a government police. The clearest example here is the Hammersmith Association. Their frantic attempts to establish a paid police force of their own stemmed from a sense that their position (on the fringe of London and on an important route) made them particularly vulnerable to crime, 'infested and beset with a numerous Gang of Thieves and Depredators. That scarcely a night passes but some House is broken into, or Depredation committed.' Failing to sustain their own paid force, they petitioned the Home Secretary Peel in 1827 to ask for government protection. Unfortunately for them, this was two years before Peel's police reform; their petition was turned down. But we can be fairly certain that the members of the Hammersmith Association (which had to be dissolved in 1827 because of its financial troubles) welcomed the coming of the Metropolitan Police in 1829.[91] Similarly, Dimsdale's evidence of the activities of the Barnet General Association was used by the 1828 and 1839 inquiries as strong evidence in favour of a paid police force; and a number of other associations within the London area gave evidence to the 1828 Select Committee broadly in favour of a police force.[92] But it is worth noting, even here, that the West Ham vestry (comprising a large number of members of the West Ham Society for prosecuting) in May 1831 passed a motion opposing the 'recent attempt to introduce the New Police into this extensive Parish' on the grounds of the 'enormous expenditure' this would entail, and the orderly nature of the parish. And in 1832 even Thomas Dimsdale was not above urging people to subscribe to the Barnet

---

[90] J. J. Tobias, *Crime and Industrial Society in the 19th Century* (Harmondsworth, 1972), p. 262, and *Crime and Police in England 1700–1900* (Dublin 1979), pp. 126–8; Philips, *Crime and Authority*, pp. 119–23; Shubert, 'Private Initiative', pp. 34–9.

[91] GLRD, P 80/PAU/11, mins. 1811, 1814, 1821, 1824; the quotation is from the 1827 petition to the Home Secretary, in mins. 1827.

[92] *SC on Police* (1828). pp. 201, 206–9, 211–13, 229, 233, 240, 245–6, 248, 253; *RC on Constabulary Force* (1839), pp. 122–3, 129–31, 168–9.

Associations for Prosecution of Felons   149

Association on the grounds that they would have to have some sort of police, and it was much cheaper to pay the subscription than be forced to pay a police rate.[93]

With rural or semi-rural associations, the situation was rather different. Once the permissive 1839 Rural Police Act had been passed, county quarter sessions found themselves faced with a decision whether or not to adopt it. A fierce debate took place within most counties on this issue, usually revolving around the state of crime and disorder in the county, the cost of establishing a county police force, and the question of who would control the police. By the end of 1841, 24 quarter sessions had adopted the Act for all of part of their counties; another 11 seem to have adopted it between 1841 and 1856; in 1856 a police force was made compulsory for all counties.[94] Some rural associations expressed support for the idea of their county adopting the Act and acquiring a police force. The Chillington and Brewood Associations, having considered appointing their own sub-scription police in 1841, petitioned the Staffordshire quarter sessions in favour of a rural police, and in June 1853, the clerk and treasurer of the Caistor Association (Lincolnshire, a county which had still not adopted the Act) gave evidence to the Select Committee on Police about the problems of heavy depredation in the previous winter, and asked for a rural police.[95] But the Southwold and Reydon Association, in East Suffolk, in a unanimous motion in May 1841, strongly attacked the newly adopted East Suffolk county police force as 'totally uncalled for, and as a means for the prevention of crime quite inefficient', and called on their agricultural neighbours to join them in memorializing quarter sessions against the force.[96] And another Lincolnshire witness to that same 1853 Select Committee, a Chief Constable in the old system, argued that a rural police was not necessary, because his parish constables, working with the local associations, could cope with all serious local crime. However, he did admit, under questioning, that the associations only served the interests of their own members, and that it was very difficult for a poor man to bring a prosecution.[97] For many association members, it might still seem cheaper to pay the subscription of 5s. to 10s. rather than the much heavier county police rate.[98]

[93] Newham Local Studies Lib., vestry minute-book, no. 8 1814–33.

[94] D. Foster, *The Rural Constabulary Act 1839* (London, 1982), p. 19. Foster discusses the difficulties of discovering exactly how many counties adopted the Act 1842–56; his estimate is 11, which differs from the table in Emsley, *Policing*, p. 72, which lists only 4. On the debates in quarter sessions, see Storch, ch. 5 below.

[95] Staffs. RO, D590/741; *SC on Police, 1st Report* PP 1852–3, xxxvi (603), pp. 72–4.

[96] Suffolk RO, GC 25: 1381/2, mins. May 1841. See also Glos. RO, P 127a M12 and Q/AP 8—petition, Apr. 1842, by parish of Eastington, which had an association since 1834, protesting against the new rural police (which Glos. established in 1840) as too expensive, and asking for its abolition.

[97] *SC on Police* (1852–3), *2nd Report*, pp. 61–8.

[98] Even the Caistor Association clerk, while giving evidence in favour of a police force, agreed that a county rate of 2 1/2d. in the pound would be heavier than a 7s. association subscription, but argued

The point is that there was never a simple choice 'for or against' a police force, for the associations and their members. Their attitude towards a new police tended to be influenced by the particular circumstances (the current extent of fear about crime or disorder, the amount of expense involved), and circumstances could certainly change people's attitudes.[99] The existence of an association, as such, does not necessarily tell us how the members would react to the idea of the new police. Certainly, association members were not automatically in favour of a paid county or borough police, and, if they chose to resist the adoption of the 1839 Act for their own county, that resistance was made easier for association members by the knowledge that they already had their own organization to protect them and their property. The coming of the new police, especially of the county forces after 1839, certainly affected the activity of associations. In most cases, one can note a clear decline in prosecution activity shortly after the new police became firmly established in their area. Many associations formally dissolved themselves fairly soon after the establishment of the police, while the Lincoln and Lincolnshire Association began its insurance scheme.

But, equally, quite a number of associations continued in existence *after* the establishment of the police; most of them now tried to bring the police into the same sort of relationship which they had previously enjoyed with the old parish constables.[100] In theory, the new police were supposed to be distinguished from the old constables and thief-takers by the fact that they did not accept fees, expenses, and rewards from the public.[101] None the less, there are many entries in the minutes and accounts of associations in the 1840s and 1850s, recording the payment of expenses, rewards, and gratuities to policemen, and even quite senior policemen continued to claim rewards from associations for arrests and convictions for which they had been responsible. No doubt this ensured that the cases of association

---

that it would be worth it because it would diminish people's losses from theft: *SC on Police* (1852–3), *1st Report*, p. 75.

[99] Storch, ch. 5 below, makes a similar point in analysing the quarter sessions debates on adoption of the Rural Police Act. He gives the example of the wave of incendiarism in 1844 which caused the West Suffolk quarter sessions to change to adopting the Act; similarly, the disorders of Aug. 1842 changed the Staffs. Quarter sessions from anti-police in June 1842 to adoption of the Act in Nov. 1842: Philips, *Crime and Authority*, pp. 57–8.

[100] For example, as soon as the West Riding county force was set up, the Sowerby Bridge Society wrote to the Chief Constable at Wakefield stressing the membership of their society and their wish that they and the new police should 'act in conjunction with each other'. The Chief Constable sent a friendly reply: Calderdale Central Lib., SPL 284 mins. Feb. 1857.

[101] See *SC on Police* (1852–3), *1st Report*, evidence of Captain J. B. M'Hardy, Chief Constable of Essex, pp. 54–5, and of Captain J. Woodford, Chief Constable of Lancs., p. 103: 'There have been cases in which rewards have been offered by parties ... but I approve of none, and I discourage as much as possible the giving of rewards by private persons, being fearful that the constables might be disposed to pay too much attention to the property of those persons who would give money rather than turn their attention to the property of those unable to give.'

members continued to receive special consideration in the allocation of sparse police manpower, as had been the case with the parish constables.[102]

However, in the long run, the coming of the new police, especially once forces were established throughout the country after 1856 and were under government inspection with financial incentives for being rated 'efficient', inevitably meant the lessening in importance of the associations. Not only did the police now take on the role of searching for and apprehending offenders, but they also increasingly took responsibility for organizing and conducting the prosecution of cases. This removed the two main reasons for the existence of associations, and many of them formally dissolved. Others, which continued, did so on a diminished scale, becoming little more than convivial societies meeting for an annual dinner. The time of great importance and influence of the associations, their height in terms of numbers and activity, had been the period 1770 to 1850.

---

[102] Associations which record payment of one or more rewards and gratuities to policemen, in the 1840s and 1850s, include: Notts., Southwell, Earl Manvers, Five United Parishes, and Carlton-in-Lindrick (Notts.); Falkingham (Lincs.); Sowerby Bridge (Yorks.); North Shields and Tynemouth (Northumb.); Chillington (Staffs.); Tanworth (Warks.); Neithrop (Oxon.); Salt Hill (Bucks.); Olney, Turvey, and Harrold (Beds.); Hemel Hempstead (Herts.); Goudhurst (Kent). Shubert ('"Lest the Law Slumber"', pp. 45–7) details the close relationship which the Leamington Priors Association (Warks.) developed with the Leamington Spa police. In the 1860s, the Association came into conflict with the local superintendent over the extent to which his policemen were claiming, and receiving, rewards from the association.

Appendix 1

Associations for the Prosecution of Felons whose Records were consulted for this Chapter

County	Association
Bedfordshire	(1) Association for the Preservation of the Game and Fish within the County of Bedford (2) Bedfordshire Association for the Speedy Apprehension and Effectual Prosecution of Horse and Sheep Stealers, Felons and Thieves, of Every Denomination (3) Harrold and Sharnbrook Association for the Protection of Property and Punishment of Offenders (4) The Association of the Parishes of Hockliffe, Chalgrave, Battlesden, and Tilsworth ... for the Apprehension and Prosecution of Horse and Sheep Stealers, Felons and Thieves, of Every Denomination (5) Kimbolton Association for Prosecuting Felons (6) Olney, Turvey, and Harrold Association for the Protection of Property and the Prosecution of Felons and Robbers (7) Potton Association for the Prosecution of Felons (8) Silsoe and Ampthill Association for the Prosecution of Felons
Berkshire	(1) Aldermaston, Wasing, and Padworth Association for the Prosecution of Felons (2) East Hendred Association for the Prosecution of Felons (3) Thatcham Association (4) Borough of Wallingford Association for the Prosecution of Felons (5) Wokingham Association for the Detection and Prosecution of Felons etc.
Buckinghamshire	(1) Fenny Stratford Association for the Prosecution of Robbers etc. (2) Salt Hill Society for the Protection of Person and Property from Thieves etc. (3) Whitchurch Association for the Prosecution of Felons

Associations for Prosecution of Felons 153

Cambridgeshire	(1) Hundred of Ely, and South Part of Hundred of Witchford Association for the Prosecution of all kinds of Felons
	(2) Linton, Hildersham, Bartlow, and Hadstock Association for the Detection and Prosecution of Felonies and Misdemeanors
	(3) Soham Association for the Prosecution of Felons
	(4) Thorney and North Level Association for the Prosecution of Horse Stealers and other Felons
Derbyshire	(1) Eyam Association for the Prosecution of Felons and other Offenders

Agreements to Prosecute
(1) Township of Dore and Tetley 3 Mar. 1742

Durham	(1) Barnard Castle Game Association
	(2) Elvet Association for the Prosecution of Felons
	(3) Gateshead Society for the Prosecution of Felons
	(4) Hart Association for the Prosecution of Felons
	(5) Lartington Association for the Prosecution of Felons
	(6) Sunderland Bridge Association for the Prosecution of Felons
Essex	(1) Barstable and Chafford Association against Robbers . . .
	(2) Blackwater Association against Felonies . . .
	(3) Bocking and Braintree Association against Felonies . . .
	(4) Association for the Protection of Property and the Prosecution of Housebreakers and Thieves within the Borough of Colchester
	(5) East and West Mersea Association for Apprehending and Prosecuting Felons . . .
	(7) Association for the security of the Lives and Properties of the Inhabitants of the Epping Division
	(8) Great Baddow and Adjoining Parishes Association For the Prevention of Crime and for the Prosecution of Felons . . .
	(9) Halsted Association for the more speedy Detection and Punishment of Highwaymen, House-breakers, Sheep-stealers, Receivers of Stolen Goods etc.
	(10) Ongar Association for the Prosecution of Felons
	(11) Radwinter Association for the Prosecution of Felons, Thieves and Other Offenders against the Person and Property of the Subscribers
	(12) Saffron Walden Society for the Prosecution of Felons
	(13) Uttlesford and Clavering Association for the Prosecution of Felons, Thieves and Other Offenders

154   *David Philips*

Essex (*contd.*)   (14) Waltham Half Hundred Association for Prosecution
                              of Felons
                         (15) West Ham Society for the Prosecuting of Felons

Gloucestershire   (1) Berkeley Association for the Prosecution of Fel-
                             ons ...
                         (2) Blockley Association for the Prosecution of Felons
                         (3) The Bourn Society for the Protection of Persons and
                             Property and Punishing Felony
                         (4) Bristol General Association for the Prevention, Dis-
                             covery and Prosecution of Burglaries and other
                             Offences ...
                         (5) Association of Clothiers in Dursley and other par-
                             ishes in the County of Gloucester for prosecuting
                             Offenders
                         (6) Dursley etc. Association for the Prosecution of
                             Felons (from 1829, General Association for the Pre-
                             vention, Discovery and Prosecution of Felonies ...
                             committed within the County of Gloucester)
                         (7) Eastington Association for the Prosecution of Felons
                         (8) Association for Prosecuting Offenders in the Parishes
                             of Forthamptom, Tirley and Chaceley
                         (9) Kingswood Association for the Prosecution of
                             Thieves, House-breakers etc.
                        (10) Sandhurst Association for the Prosecuting of Felons
                        (11) Slimbridge Association for Prosecuting Felonies ...
                        (12) Tetbury etc. Association for Prosecuting Felons ...

                        Agreements to Prosecute
                         (1) Cirencester Inhabitants Feb. 1774
                         (2) Bisley area subscribers Jan. 1783
                         (3) Clothiers of Dursley, Wotton under Edge, Uley etc.
                             Nov. 1783, renewed each year to 1808

Hertfordshire   (1) Abbot's Langley and King's Langley Association for
                             the Preservation of the Peace and Protection of the
                             Persons and Property of the Subscribers
                         (2) Barkway and Reed Association for the Prosecution
                             of Felons ...
                         (3) Barnet etc. Association
                         (4) Barnet General Association for the Protection of
                             Property
                         (5) Association of the Gentlemen, Farmers, and other
                             inhabitants of the Parish of Bishop's Hatfield ... for
                             apprehending and prosecuting Felons of all Denomi-
                             nations
                         (6) Bishop's Stortford Association for Prosecuting
                             Felons

Associations for Prosecution of Felons   155

Hertfordshire (*contd.*)	(7) Hemel Hempstead Association for the Protection of Property
	(8) Association of the Gentlemen, Farmers, and other Inhabitants of the Parish and Neighbourhood of Stevenage ... for Apprehending and Prosecuting Felons and Thieves, of all Denominations
Kent	(1) Charing Society for Prosecuting Thieves
	(2) Cranbrooke Society for Prosecuting Thieves
	(3) Society for Prosecuting Felons and Other Offenders in the Parish of Goudhurst, in Kent
	(4) Leigh Prosecuting Society
	(5) Pembury Society for the Protection of Persons and Property and for the Prosecution of Felons and other Offenders
	(6) Association for the Purpose of Detecting Incendiaries and Protecting Property, in the Neighbourhood of Sevenoaks
	(7) Tenterden Society for Prosecuting Thieves, Felons, and Receivers of Stolen Goods
Lancashire	(1) Ashton Association for the Prosecution of Felons
	(2) Bolton Black Horse Society for the Prosecution of Felons
	(3) Great Bolton Special Constables' Society
	(4) Caton Association for the more effectual prevention of housebreaking, robbery, stealing of fowls and other felonies, etc.
	(5) Culcheth Association for the Prosecution of Felons
	(6) Leyland Association for the Prosecution of Felons
	(7) Little Hilton Prosecution Society
	(8) Lowton Association for the Prosecution of Felons
	(9) Maghull, Lydiate and Melling Association for the Prosecution of Felons
	(10) Manchester Society for the Prosecution of Felons and Receivers of Stolen Goods
	(11) Padiham Association for the Prosecution of Felons
	(12) Turton Prosecution Society

Agreements to Prosecute

(1) Maghull Township 1699
(2) Township of Bretherton 16 Feb. 1744 and 11 Dec. 1777
(3) Township of Freckleton 1754
(4) Township of Newton cum Scales 5 Apr. 1763 and 25 Sept. 1802
(5) Higham and West Close Booths 25 Aug. 1764
(6) Township of Halliwell 28 Jan. 1790

156   *David Philips*

Lancashire (*contd.*)   (7) Township of Heaton 28 Jan. 1790
                           (8) Township of Horwich 28 Jan. 1790
                           (9) Township of Bickerstaffe 4 Dec. 1792
                           (10) Townships of Pensortham and Howick 1801
                           (11) Township of Barton 6 Feb. 1802
                           (12) Township of Poulton 1 July 1805
                           (13) Borough and Town of Preston and vicinity 4 Jan. 1809
                           (14) Township of Prescot 22 Nov. 1814
                           (15) Township of Halsall 27 June 1829

Leicestershire   (1) Castle Donington Association for the Prosecution of Felons
                           (2) Hinckley New Association for the Prosecution of Felons
                           (3) Loughborough Association for the Prosecution of Felons
                           (4) Lutterworth Association for the Prosecution of Felons
                           (5) Melton Mowbray New Association for the Apprehension and Prosecution of Persons guilty of Felony and Misdemeanors
                           (6) Shepshed and District Association for the Prosecution of Robbers, Thieves etc.

Lincolnshire   (1) Binbrook Association for the Prosecution of all Persons who shall be Guilty of Felonies, Thefts, Crimes or Misdemeanors
                           (2) Caistor Association for the Prosecution of Felons
                           (3) Donington Association for the Prosecution of Felons
                           (4) Falkingham Association for Prosecuting Felons
                           (5) Horncastle Association for Prosecuting Felons ...
                           (6) Lincoln and Lincolnshire Association for the Prosecution of Felons
                           (7) Louth-Esk Marsh Association for Prosecuting Felons, Swindlers, and other Delinquents
                           (8) Market Rasen Association for the Prosecution of Felons
                           (9) Wroot Parish Association for Prosecuting Felons ...

                           Agreements to Prosecute
                           (1) Township of Owston 25 June 1796
                           (2) Parish of Bramston 12 May 1797

Middlesex   (1) Enfield Association for Prosecuting Offenders ...
                           (2) Hammersmith Association for Prosecuting Thieves, Felons apprehended within the Hamlet
                           (3) The Society for Prosecuting Felons, Forgers etc.

Associations for Prosecution of Felons   157

Norfolk	(1) Diss Association for Prosecuting Felonies and Misdemeanors
	(2) Harleston Association for Prosecution
	(3) North Elmham Association for the Prosecution of Felons
Northamptonshire	(1) Corby, Huxloe and Rowell Hundreds Society for Prosecuting Robbers, Thieves, etc.
Northumberland	(1) Blyth and Cowpen Association for Prosecuting Felons
	(2) Chirton Association for Prosecuting Felons
	(3) Earsdon and Horton Association for Prosecuting Felons
	(4) North Shields and Tynemouth Association for Prosecuting Felons
	(5) North Shields and Tynemouth Friendly Association for Prosecuting Felons
	(6) South Shields Association for Prosecuting Felons
	(7) United Association for Prosecuting Felons
	(8) Wall's End, Willington and Howden Association for Prosecuting Felons
Nottinghamshire	(1) Carlton-in-Lindrick Association for the Prosecution of Felons
	(2) Clumber Association for the Prosecution of Felons and other Offenders
	(3) Association of the Rt Hon Earl Manvers and his Tenants, for the Prosecution of Felons and other Offenders
	(4) Five United Parishes Association for the Prosecution of Felons
	(5) Gedling Association for the Prosecution of Felons
	(6) Newark-upon-Trent Association for the more speedy bringing to Justice and effectual Punishment of all Persons guilty of Felony
	(7) Nottinghamshire Association for the Prosecution of Felons (began as Nottinghamshire Association for the Prosecution of Horse Stealers)
	(8) Nottinghamshire New Friendly Association for the Prosecution of Felons
	(9) Rufford and Ollerton Association for the Prosecution of Felons etc
	(10) Rushton Association for Prosecuting Robbers
	(11) Southwell Association for the Prosecution of Felons
Oxfordshire	(1) Association for Defraying the Expenses of Apprehending and Prosecuting Thieves and Other

158 *David Philips*

Oxfordshire (*contd.*)	Offenders, in Banbury and its Neighbourhood.
	(2) Middleton Stoney Prosecuting Society
	(3) Neithrop Association for the Protection of Persons and Property
	(4) Oxford Farmers' Association for Prosecution
	(5) Oxford Gardeners' and Florists' Association for Prosecution
	(6) Oxfordshire Association for the Prosecution of Felons and Persons Guilty of Theft and Other Crimes, Offences and Misdemeanors
	(7) Wantage Association for the Prosecution of Felons
Shropshire	(1) Halesowen Association for the Prosecution of Felons
Staffordshire	(1) Bilston Association for the Prosecution of Felons
	(2) Bloxwich Association for the Prosecution of Felons
	(3) Brewood Association for the Prosecution of Felons
	(4) Chillington Association for the Prosecution of Felons
	(5) Great Barr and Perry Barr Association for the Prosecution of Felons
	(6) Handsworth and Perry Barr Association for the Prosecution of Felons
	(7) Wednesbury Association for the Prosecution of Felons
Surrey	(1) St Mary Rotherhithe Subscription for the Prosecution of Thieves and Robbers
Suffolk	(1) Bungay Tuns Association for Prosecuting Felons ...
	(2) Great Bealings Association for Prosecuting Persons Guilty of Felony
	(3) Great Bealings Association for Apprehending and Prosecuting Horse-Stealers (merged with (2) in 1802)
	(4) Loes and Wilford Hundreds Association for the Prosecution of Felons
	(5) Lowestoft Association for Prosecuting Horse-Stealers, Felons, and Receivers of Stolen Goods
	(6) Plomesgate Hundred Association for the Protection of Property, and the Detection and Punishment of Offenders
	(7) Southwold and Reydon Association for Prosecuting Felons
	Agreements to Prosecute
	(1) Parish of Melton 6 Feb. 1775
Warwickshire	(1) Birmingham Association for Prosecuting Felons
	(2) Coleshill Association for the Prosecution of Felons
	(3) Fillongley Association for the Prosecution of Felons

Associations for Prosecution of Felons 159

Warwickshire (*contd.*)	(4) Henley-in-Arden Association for the Prosecution of Felons
	(5) King's Norton and Moseley Association for the Prosecution of Felons
	(6) Kingsbury Association for the Prosecution of Felons
	(7) Leamington New Association for the Prosecution of Felons and for the Protection of Property
	(8) Meriden Association for the Prosecution of Felons
	(9) Tanworth Association for the Apprehension and Prosecution of Felons
Worcestershire	(1) Dudley Association for the Prosecution of Felons
	(2) Stourbridge Association for the Prosecution of Felons
Yorkshire	(1) Aston Association for the Prosecution of Felons
	(2) Bradfield Association for the Prosecution of Felons and Receivers of Stolen Goods and Cattle etc.
	(3) Bradford and District Association for the Prosecution of Felons
	(4) Bramley Society for the Prosecution of Persons on Charges of Felony, Misdemeanor ...
	(5) Doncaster Borough and Soke Association for the Prosecution of Felons
	(6) Ecclesfield Associations for the Prosecution of Felons
	(7) Halifax Society for the Prosecution of Felons
	(8) Heptonstall Society for Prosecuting Felons
	(9) Horbury Society for Prosecuting Felons
	(10) Kirkburton Society for Prosecuting Persons Guilty of Felonies and Misdemeanors
	(11) Laughton-en-le-Northern Association for the Prosecution of Felons
	(12) Leeds Borough Association for the Prosecution of Felons
	(13 Luddenden Society for Prosecuting Felons
	(14) Society for the Prosecution of Felons etc. in the Township and Neighbourhood of Midgley
	(15) Normanton and Featherstone Association for the Prosecution of Felons
	(16) Norton Association for the Detection, Prosecution and Conviction of Felons, Thieves, Robbers, Depredators, and Offenders
	(17) Romaldkirk Association for the Prosecution of Felons
	(18) Roystone Association for the Prosecution of Felons
	(19) Sandal Association for the Prosecution of Felons
	(20) Skircoat Society for the Prosecution of Persons

160   *David Philips*

Yorkshire (*contd.*)   concerned in Felonies, Burglaries, or Misdemeanors, etc.

(21) Snaith Association for the Prosecution of Felons
(22) Sowerby-Bridge Association for Prosecuting Felons
(23) Sowerby Bridge Society for the Prosecution of Felons
(24) Strafforth and Tickhill Association for Prosecuting Stealers of Horses
(25) Tickhill Association for the Prosecution of Felons
(26) Wakefield Society for Prosecuting Felons
(27) Wath-upon-Dearne Association for the Prosecution of Felons
(28) Yeadon Township Society for Prosecuting Felons ...

Agreements to prosecute:
(1) Township of Bradfield 1 Oct. 1737
(2) Township of Burton in Lonsdale 6 Jan. 1763
(3) Township of Warley 23 Nov. 1772
(4) Township of Hartshead-cum-Clifton 21 Oct. 1784
(5) People in Woollen Trade in Townships of Sowerby, Soyland & Skircoat 23 Aug. 1785
(6) Township of Austerfield 31 Dec. 1794
(7) Inhabitants of 'Constablery' of Alverthorpe with Thornes 23 Oct. 1802

Appendix 2

Known Dates of Establishment of Associations and Agreements

Estab. = Date of Establishment; Till = Date of Dissolution (if known)

Estab.	Association/Agreement	Till
1693	Stoke-on-Trent Agreement	
1699	Maghull (Lancs.) Agreement	
1737	Bradfield (Yorks.) Agreement	
1742	Dore and Tetley (Derbys.) Agreement	
1744	Bretherton (Lancs.) Agreement	(repeated 1777)
1752	Society of Gentlemen and Noblemen for the Preservation of Game	
1754	Freckleton (Lancs.) Agreement	
1758	Stourbridge Association (Worcs.)	
1761	Blackbourne Association against Horse-stealers (Suffolk)	
1763	Newton-cum-Scales (Lancs.) Agreement	
	Burton in Lonsdale (Yorks.) Agreement	
1764	Higham and West Close Booths (Lancs.) Agreement	
1765	Colchester Borough Association (Essex)	
1766	Potteries Manufacturers and Dealers Association (Staffs.)	
1767	Society for Prosecuting Felons (London)	(at least 1800)
	Walsall Association (Staffs.)	
1769	Ardleigh Association (Essex)	
1770	Nottingham Association	1890
	Lichfield Association	(at least 1817)
1771	St Mary Rotherhithe Subscription (Surrey)	
	Brereton/Rugeley Association (Staffs.)	
	Newborough Whiteners Association (Staffs.)	
1772	Warley (Yorks.) Agreement	
	Gloucestershire and Kingswood Agreement	

162   *David Philips*

1773	Harleston Association (Norfolk)	(at least 1815)
	Kingsbury Association (Warks.)	1920
	Wotton-under-Edge, Dursley etc. Agreement	
	Coventry Association (Warks.)	
	Colchester Association against Horse-stealers (Essex)	
1774	Newark-upon-Trent Association	
	Cirencester (Glos.) Agreement	
	Blockley Association (Glos.)	(at least 1801)
	Wethersfield Association (Essex)	
1775	Melton (Suffolk) Agreement	
	Essex Association	
1777	Witham Association (Essex)	
1779	Strafforth and Tickhill Association (Yorks.)	1782
	Barstable and Chafford Association (Essex)	(at least 1791)
	Essex Association for Preservation of Game	
1780	Southwell Association (Notts.)	(at least 1857)
1781	Gateshead Society	(at least 1869)
1782	Loes and Wilford Association (Suffolk)	1854
	Forthampton, Tirley, and Chaceley Association (Glos.)	(at least 1796)
1783	Salt Hill Society (Bucks.)	Still in existence
	Loughborough Association (Leics.)	(at least 1869)
	Corby, Huxloe, and Rowell Society (Northants.)	
	Bisley Area (Glos.) Agreement	
	Clothiers of Dursley etc. (Glos.) Agreement	
	Penkridge Association (Staffs.)	
1784	Horncastle Association (Lincs.)	
	Caistor Association (Lincs.)	*c.*1890
	Coleshill Association (Warks.)	1920
	Tanworth Association (Warks.)	Still in existence
	Meriden Association (Warks.)	
	Barnet etc. Association	1813
	Hartshead-cum-Clifton (Yorks.) Agreement	
1785	Association of Earl Manvers and Tenants (Notts.)	1912
	Birmingham Association	
	Wallington Association (Berks.)	
	Ely and Witchford Association (Cambs.)	(at least 1842)

Associations for Prosecution of Felons   163

1785	Sowerby, Soyland, and Skircoat (Yorks.) Agreement	
1786	Great Bealings Association (Suffolk)	1854
	Wakefield Society (Yorks.)	
	Stafford Association	
	Winstree Hundred Association (Essex)	
1787	North Elmham Association (Norfolk)	(at least 1889)
1789	Turton Society (Lancs.)	1856
	Great Bealings Horse-Stealers Association (Suffolk)	1802
	East Essex Game Association	
1790	Bedfordshire Association	(at least 1808)
	Halliwell (Lancs.) Agreement	
	Horwich (Lancs.) Agreement	
1791	North Shields and Tynemouth Association	1890
1792	Nottinghamshire New Friendly Association	(at least 1826)
	Bickerstaffe (Lancs.) Agreement	
	Thorney and North Level Association (Cambs.)	
1793	Blackwater Association (Essex)	
1794	Cranbrooke Society (Kent)	(at least 1800)
	Austerfield (Yorks.) Agreement	
1795	Padiham Association (Lancs.)	
	Dursley etc. Association (later Glos. General)	1850
1796	Olney, Turvey, and Harrold (Beds.)	1909
	Halifax Society	(at least 1821)
	Owston (Lincs.) Agreement	
1797	Great Bolton Special Constables' Society	1834
	Bramston (Lincs.) Agreement	
1798	Tenterden Society (Kent)	(at least 1862)
1799	Charing Society (Kent)	(at least 1827)
	Kirkburton Society (Yorks.)	
1800	Colchester Association (Essex)	1930
	Hockliffe etc. Association (Beds.)	(at least 1825)
	Aldermaston etc. Association (Berks.)	
1801	Tetbury Association (Glos.)	(at least 1814)
	Fenny Stratford Association (Bucks.)	
	Bolton Black Horse Society	(at least 1836)
	Bradley Association (Staffs.)	
	Penwortham and Howick (Lancs.) Agreement	
1802	Lincoln and Lincolnshire Association	Still in existence
	Barton (Lancs.) Agreement	

164   *David Philips*

Year	Association	
1802	Alverthorpe with Thornes (Yorks.) Agreement	
1805	South Shields Association	
	Sowerby Bridge Association (Yorks.)	
	Poulton-le-Fylde (Lancs.) Agreement	
1807	Bishop's Hatfield Association (Herts.)	(at least 1847)
	Stevenage Association (Herts.)	(at least 1816)
1808	Halsall and Downholland (Lancs.) Agreement	(Repeated 1829)
1809	Saffron Walden Association (Essex)	
	Preston (Lancs.) Agreement	
1810	Skircoat Society (Yorks.)	1891
	Hammersmith Association	1827
	Kingswood Association (Glos.)	
	Horbury Society (Yorks.)	
	Little Hilton Society (Lancs.)	
1812	Clothiers' Association (Glos.)	1826
	Eyam Association (Derbys.)	(at least 1848)
	Handsworth and Perry Barr Association (Staffs.)	(at least 1829)
1813	Barnet General Association	(at least 1839)
	Yeadon Township Society (Yorks.)	
1814	East Hendred Association (Berks.)	(at least 1844)
	Berkeley Association (Glos.)	
	Elvet Association (Durham)	
	Bloxwich Association (Staffs.)	
	Prescott (Lancs.) Agreement	
1815	East and West Mersea Association (Essex)	
	Henley-in-Arden Association (Warks.)	(at least 1856)
1816	Heptonstall Society (Yorks.)	
1817	Carlton-in-Lindrick Association (Notts.) (Re-founded 1848)	1894
	Caton Association (Lancs.)	
	Bradford Association (Yorks.)	(at least 1834)
	Wokingham Association (Berks.)	
	West Ham Society (Essex)	(at least 1840)
1818	Barkway and Reed Association (Herts.)	(at least 1838)
	Culcheth Association (Lancs.)	
	Epping Association (Essex)	
	Linton, Hildersham, Bartlow, and Hadstock Association (Cambs.)	1851
1819	Binbrook Association (Lincs.)	1853
	Neithrop Association (Oxon.)	1905
	Lartington Association (Durham)	
'1820	Clumber Association (Notts.)	(at least 1836)
	Luddenden Society (Yorks.)	

Associations for Prosecution of Felons   165

1820	Diss Association (Norfolk)	(at least 1829)
1821	Five United Parishes Association (Notts.)	1873
	Doncaster Borough and Soke Association	(at least 1838)
	Wath-upon-Dearne Association (Yorks.)	(at least 1842)
	Barnard Castle Game Laws Association (Durham)	(at least 1833)
	Wroot Parish Association (Lincs.)	
1822	North Shields and Tynemouth Friendly Association	
1824	Fillongley Association (Warks.)	1914
	Great Barr and Perry Barr Association (Staffs.)	
	Bristol General Association	
	Leamington Priors Association (Warks.)	Still in existence
1825	Shepshed Association (Leics.) (Re-founded 1883)	1975
1826	Market Rasen Association (Lincs.)	1894
	Southwold–Reydon Association (Suffolk)	1848
	Melton Mowbray Association (Leics.)	1875
1828	Oxfordshire Association	
	Chillington Association (Staffs.)	1857
1829	Sowerby Bridge Society (Yorks.) (Re-founded 1844)	1925
	Ecclesfield Association (Yorks.)	
1830	Sevenoaks Association for Detecting Incendiaries (Kent)	(at least 1839)
	Leeds Borough Association	
	Harrold and Sharnbrook Association (Beds.)	1836
1831	Radwinter Association (Essex)	
1832	Maghull, Lydiate, and Melling Association (Lancs.)	
	Snaith Association (Yorks.)	(at least 1856)
	Normanton and Featherstone Association (Yorks.)	(at least 1887)
	Bramley Association (Yorks.)	(at least 1844)
	Laughton-en-le-Northern Association (Yorks.)	
	Aston Association (Yorks.)	
1833	Hemel Hempstead Association (Herts.) (Re-founded 1853)	1881
	Bradfield Association (Yorks.)	1885
1834	Eastington Association (Glos.)	
	Stow-on-the-Wold Association (Glos.)	
1836	Banbury General Association (Oxon.)	
	Stourbridge Association (Worcs.)	

166   *David Philips*

1837	Hart Association (Durham)	(at least 1866)
	Sunderland Bridge Association (Durham)	
	Great Baddow Association (Essex)	
	Pembury Society (Kent)	
1838	Midgley Society (Yorks.)	
1840	Uttlesford and Clavering Association (Essex)	
	Dudley Association (Worcs.)	
1847	Gedling Association (Notts.)	(at least 1852)
1867	Leamington New Association (Warks.)	1930s

Appendix 3

Offences Reported and Cases Prosecuted by Selected Associations

(*Note:* These are all *minimum* figures, drawn from the Associations' records.)

Offs. = Offences reported; Av. = Average no. per year;
Pros. = Prosecutions brought.

Period	Offs.	Av.	Pros.	Av.	Comments
		Harleston Association (Norfolk)			
1773–1777	6	1.2	4	0.8	
1778–1782	10	2	5	1	
1783–1787	5	1	1	0.2	
1788–1792	19	3.8	3	0.6	
1793–1797	15	3	4	0.8	
1798–1802	14	2.8	5	1	
1803–1807	14	2.8	5	1	
1808–1812	37	7.4	6	1.2	
1813–1815	20	6.7	2	0.7	
		Nottinghamshire Association			
1786–1790	29	5.8	5	1	
1792–1795	44	8.8	5	1	
1796–1800	17	3.4	10	2	
1801–1805	14	2.8	11	2.2	
1806–1810	14	2.8	14	2.8	
1811–1815	3 + ?	0.6	2	0.4	
1816–1820	9	1.8	7	1.4	
1821–1825	13	2.6	5	1	
1826–1830	5	1	5	1	
1831–1835	8	1.6	3	0.6	
1836–1840	10	2	4	0.8	
1841–1845	6	1.2	1	0.2	
1846–1850	14	2.8	4	0.8	
1851–1855	4	0.8	1	0.2	
1856–1860	1	0.2	0	0	

168　　　　　　　　　　　　*David Philips*

Period	Offs.	Av.	Pros.	Av.	Comments
North Elmham Association (Norfolk)					
1788	6	6	2	2	
1797–1800	5	1.3	2	0.5	
1804–1808	9	1.8	1	0.2	
1809–1813	6	1.2	4	0.8	
1814–1818	11	2.2	2	0.4	
1819–1823	15	3	0	0	
1824–1828	12	2.4	6	1.2	
1829–1833	7	1.4	2	0.4	
1834–1838	5	1	2	0.4	
1839–1843	0	0	0	0	
1844–1848	2	0.4	0	0	
1849–1853	2	0.4	0	0	
1854–1859	5	0.8	5	0.8	
Society for Prosecuting Felons etc. (London)					
1795–1800	43	7.2	25	4.2	
Earl Manvers Association (Notts.)					
1786–1790	30	6	14	2.8	
1791–1795	21	4.2	3	0.6	
1796–1800	23	4.6	2	0.4	
1801–1805	28	5.6	2	0.4	
1805–1808	6	1.2	0	0	
Dursley etc. (from 1829, Gloucestershire General) Association					
1795–1796	13	6.5	8	4	
1809–1810	10	5	1	0.5	
1815–1819	31	6.2	6	1.2	
1820–1824	19	3.8	4	0.8	
1825–1829	28	5.6	5	1	
1830–1835	43	7.2	16	2.3	
Salt Hill Society (Bucks.)					
1796–1800	57	11.4	6	1.2	
1801–1805	34	6.8	6	1.2	
1806–1810	28	5.6	5	1	
1811–1815	42	8.4	5	1	
1816–1820	56	11.2	7	1.4	
1821–1825	47	9.4	5	1	
1826–1830	77	15.4	8	1.6	
1831–1835	65	13	8	1.6	
1836–1840	57	11.4	17	3.4	⎫ Increasing use of summary prosecutions
1841–1845	46	9.2	24	4.8	
1846–1850	83	16.6	35	7	
1851–1855	72	14.4	28	5.6	
1856–1860	79	15.8	42	8.4	⎭

Associations for Prosecution of Felons　　169

Period	Offs.	Av.	Pros.	Av.	Comments
North Shields and Tynemouth Association					
1811–1816	49	8.2	12	2	
1832–1836	42	8.4	10	2	
1837–1841	46	9.2	9	1.8	
1842–1844	36	12	6	2	
1846	5	5	3	3	
Goudhurst Society (Kent)					
1816–1820	18	3.6	12	2.4	
1821–1825	15	3	10	2	
1826–1830	13	2.6	7	1.4	
1831–1835	9	1.8	6	1.2	
1836–1840	15	3.0	12	2.4	
1841–1845	14	2.8	11	2.2	
1846–1850	8	1.6	6	1.2	
1851–1855	6	1.2	4	0.8	
West Ham Society					
1817–1821	26	5.2	8	1.6	
1822–1826	14	2.8	6	1.2	
1827–1831	10	2	5	1	
1832–1836	3	0.6	3	0.6	
Southwell Association (Notts.)					
1830–1834	13	2.6	2	0.4	
1835–1839	36	7.2	6	1.2	
1840–1844	27	5.4	2	0.4	
1845–1849	42	8.4	4	0.8	
Gateshead Society					
1833–1834	12	6	2	1	
1841–1845	25	5	10	2	
1846–1851	41	6.8	18	3	
Barnet General Association (Herts.)					
1813–1832	?	?	Over 200	10	Over 200 convictions
1833	?	?	26	26	20 convictions
Tickhill Association (Yorks.)					
1827–1836	64	6.4	13	1.3	12 convictions
Plomesgate Hundred Association (Suffolk)					
1832–1836	?	?	25	5	25 convictions

Appendix 4

Associations with Large Memberships

	Association	Period	Membership
Northumberland	North Shields and Tynemouth	1813–43	101–10
Notts.	Notts. Association	1778–1816	120–220
	Notts. New Friendly	1803–26	170–260
	Five United Parishes	1822–51	100–20
	Southwell	1854	177
Lincs.	Lincoln and Lincolnshire	1834–50	177–203
Leics.	Loughborough	1817–69	132–52
Yorks.	Wath-upon-Dearne	1833–41	115–60
Herts.	Barnet General	1832	246
London	Hammersmith	1811	188
Bucks.	Salt Hill	1854–61	106–30
Beds.	Olney, Turvey, and Harrold	1824–61	96–150
Warks.	Fillongley	1824	127
Suffolk	Plomesgate	1836	119

[16]

SIR JOHN FIELDING AND THE PROBLEM OF CRIMINAL INVESTIGATION IN EIGHTEENTH-CENTURY ENGLAND

By John Styles, M.A.

READ AT THE SOCIETY'S CONFERENCE 17 SEPTEMBER 1982*

EIGHTEENTH-CENTURY England witnessed an extraordinary transformation in the capacity to disseminate information. Improvements in communications, particularly the turnpike roads and the postal service, together with the multiplication of printing presses and newspapers, underpinned what has been described as an 'information explosion'.[1] The changes which these developments wrought in the political and commercial life of the nation are increasingly familiar to historians.[2] Their impact on eighteenth-century crime and policing is less so.

That impact was twofold. First, the new methods of disseminating information provided an important supplement to available techniques for the investigation of criminal offences. Advertisements of rewards for information concerning stolen property or offenders fled from justice became a familiar characteristic of almost all eighteenth-century newspapers. The newspaper offered an unrivalled vehicle for distributing such intelligence to a large public across a wide area. Handbills containing similar information, run off by most printers at an hour's notice, provided the same facility with less delay, but over a more restricted geographical span. Hardly surprisingly, these new techniques almost entirely superseded the principal pre-existing vehicle for the far-flung dissemination of criminal intelligence, the cumbersome hue and cry.[3]

Second, improvements in the capacity to disseminate information brought about a vast expansion in public access to news and interpretations of criminal activity. Criminal offenders, their offences, their

---

*I should like to thank John Brewer, Joanna Innes and John Langbein for their comments on earlier versions of this paper.

[1] J. Brewer, *Party, Ideology and Popular Politics at the accession of George III* (Cambridge, 1976), 158.

[2] See in particular N. McKendrick, J. Brewer and J. H. Plumb, *The Birth of a Consumer Society* (1982), *passim*.

[3] For an analysis of the impact of newspaper advertising, see my forthcoming article on crime advertising in the eighteenth-century provincial newspaper.

trials and their punishments had long been objects of fascination in
both polite and plebeian circles. Indeed they were the subject matter
of a great deal of sixteenth- and seventeenth-century pamphlet literature and printed ephemera. The eighteenth century, however, saw
not only an enormous expansion in the availability and dissemination
of literature concerning crimes and offenders, but also changes in its
character. Thus, at the same time as the volume of such literature
expanded, by means of the newspapers and the more extensive printing of broadsheets and chapbooks, information about crimes and
offenders of a more systematic character became available on an
unprecedented scale. The appearance in the press of reports and
advertisements about offences, the reporting there of assize and
quarter sessions trials, and the printing of calendars of prisoners provided both officialdom and a broad public with an accessible (though
not necessarily accurate) measure of fluctuations in the incidence and
character of offences. At the same time an expanded pamphlet literature, often reprinted in the newspapers alongside essays, correspondence and editorials on the subject of crime, provided a running com-
mentary on these burgeoning inventories of crimes, prisoners, and
executions. By such means those entrepreneurs of criminal prophylaxis
who so flourished in the later eighteenth century were supplied not
only with vehicles to distribute their remedies, but with much of their
empirical raw material and with an audience which, though still
obsessed with the particularities of offences and offenders, was learning
to envisage crime as an impersonal, statistical problem.

No-one during the eighteenth century exploited these developments
in communications more energetically than John (after 1761 Sir John)
Fielding. Throughout his twenty-six years as the government-financed
principal magistrate for Westminster, from 1754 to 1780, this blind
man managed a criminal investigation apparatus which centred on
the use of his office at Bow Street, Covent Garden, as a clearing house
for information about offences and offenders, in its early years mainly
from within the metropolis and its immediate vicinity.[4] At Bow Street,
information about unsolved crimes and offenders fled from justice was
recorded and then disseminated to the public in the form of advertisements in selected newspapers asking for further information. To encourage law officers and the public to make reports to Bow Street,
either in person or by post, Fielding publicised the facilities available
at his office in broadsheets and pamphlets, as well as in the newspapers.
He also encouraged the press to report his work as an examining
magistrate at Bow Street. Such reports were one element in a wider

---

[4] For general surveys of Fielding's activities see R. Leslie-Melville, *The Life and Work
of Sir John Fielding* (1934) and L. Radzinowicz, *A History of English Criminal Law* (4 vols.,
1948-68), iii (1956), 11-62.

educational effort that Fielding conducted by such methods to alert the public to the character and techniques of offenders and to promote his ideas for crime prevention.

The originator of this system of criminal information management was not John Fielding himself, but his half-brother and immediate (though short-serving) predecessor as principal magistrate for Westminster, Henry Fielding the novelist. John Fielding, however, considerably extended these techniques. He applied them most ambitiously in his General Preventative Plan of 1772, designed to collect, collate and circulate criminal information on a national scale for the first time. It is with the origins and significance of the General Preventative Plan that this paper is principally concerned.

In order to understand the form taken by Fielding's General Preventative Plan, its author's extremely sanguine expectations of it, and the highly favourable reception it enjoyed among those who administered the criminal law, it is necessary to consider the enormous obstacles which still existed in the mid-eighteenth century, despite improvements in communication facilities, to the apprehension of offenders who had secreted themselves in parts of the country distant from the scene of their crime. An examination of a particularly well-documented episode in 1756 will serve to illustrate those obstacles.

On Monday, 19 January 1756, a man calling himself William Wilkins appeared before Samuel Lister, an exceptionally active justice of the peace for the West Riding of Yorkshire.[5] Wilkins claimed to be a clothier from a place he called Lodgemoor, near Painswick, in the county of Somerset. He came before Justice Lister, at the latter's house near Bradford, as a consequence of his failure to pay his reckoning at various inns. Although he had virtually no cash, among the items found in his possession were a pocket book containing two bills of exchange (for £20 and £80 respectively), made payable to William Wilkins, and a promissory note for the enormous sum of £1100. These Lister suspected to be forged, because two letters, one postmarked Gloucester, found in Wilkins's pocket indicated that he and his wife had been associated with others in the forgery of bills of exchange and other commercial paper. They suggested that he had fled from his home to Yorkshire in order to escape prosecution.

In fact the so-called William Wilkins was one Edward Wilson, a woollen clothier from Painswick in Gloucestershire (there was no such

---

[5] The following discussion is based on Bradford City Library (henceforth B.C.L.), Deeds Collection, 16/11/10, Samuel Lister's letters and undated drafts on the case. For a fuller account of Lister's career as a magistrate and the contribution to it of this case, see J. Styles, 'An eighteenth-century magistrate as detective: Samuel Lister of Little Horton', *Bradford Antiquary*, New Ser., 47 (1982) 98–117.

place in Somerset), over 140 miles from Bradford. During 1754 and 1755 he had been involved in the forgery and circulation in the West Country of commercial paper to the value of £4000 or £5000. It appears that some time before August 1755 Wilson fled from Gloucestershire, for during that month he appeared in Leeds in Yorkshire. His choice of the town as a refuge was probably determined by his occupation, Leeds being the marketing centre for the West Riding woollen textile industry. On his arrival there he was able to make himself readily accepted by offering to instruct manufacturers in the production of thin cloth for the Turkey trade, a Gloucestershire speciality. He was shown considerable respect and was said to have behaved with 'modesty and decency'.[6] But his manufacturing scheme failed, leaving him destitute (apart from the forged note and bills in his possession). It was in these circumstances that he took off on a round of inns in various West Riding textile towns that culminated in his appearance before Justice Lister.

Lister was convinced that Wilson was guilty of forgery—a capital offence—and determined that he should not escape justice. Having committed his suspect to prison on the grounds of failure to find sureties for his good behaviour, the Yorkshire magistrate was faced with the problem of how to obtain more information about him. He was not without clues as to Wilson's origins. The fugitive's statement and the letters found in his possession suggested he came from either Somerset or Gloucestershire. Lister, however, had very little knowledge of or connection with the West Country. Despite the fact that Painswick was, like Bradford, a cloth-producing centre, neither he nor his friend the Recorder of Leeds, a prominent barrister whom Lister consulted, were sure whether the town was in Gloucestershire or Somerset. Nor were they acquainted with even the names of any magistrates in those two counties. Time was short. The letters suggested that Wilson's associates were to appear at the forthcoming Lent Assizes in one of the western counties. If they were acquitted in Wilson's absence, they could not be tried again on the same change.[7] Moreover, it was uncertain how long Wilson could be held in custody merely for want of sureties. He might secure a rapid release if friends came to stand bail for him.

Confronted with these difficulties, Lister was obliged to resort to speculative expedients to establish the validity of his suspicions. By securing the names and addresses of individuals of some standing in the western counties with whom people he knew in Yorkshire were acquainted, he attempted to send particulars of the affair by post into the vicinity of Wilson's crimes. His friend the Recorder of Leeds

[6] B.C.L., Deeds, 16/14/10, Richard Wilson to Lister, 19 Jan. 1756.
[7] They would have been able to plead 'autrefois acquit'.

provided the name and address of his former landlord at Bath, whom he believed (mistakenly) to be an *ex officio* magistrate for that borough. Some time later the Recorder recalled the name of a major Gloucestershire gentleman clothier of his acquaintance. At the same time Lister spread the word in the Bradford area that he required contacts in the West Country. His Bradford mercer and a Gloucestershire man travelling in Yorkshire were able to supply him with the names and addresses of two Gloucestershire gentlemen, both of whom were probably large-scale clothiers.

Lister wrote to all four with a description of the suspect, copies of the bills, note and letter, and a request that all these items be made public. He asked his correspondents to undertake inquiries themselves, or, if the 'places mentioned should be at too great a distance from you, you will please to transmit the papers to any magistrate or gentleman of your acquaintance that can make inquiry more conveniently'.[8]

There was no certainty that any of the people to whom the Yorkshire justice had written (none of whom were acting magistrates) would either be able or prepared to assist him. The same weakness applied to his other detective strategy—the newspaper advertisement. On the advice of the Recorder of Leeds, Lister drew up an advertisement describing Wilson and giving an outline of the case. This he arranged to have inserted in a London newspaper by a Gray's Inn barrister who regularly corresponded with a Bradford attorney. The London barrister chose *The General Evening Post*. This was one of a number of thrice-weekly London evening newspapers which circulated more widely in the provinces than other metropolitan papers. However, Lister could not be certain that anyone in the West Country acquainted with the affair would see it. After all he was advertising in a London, not a local paper.

In the event, the newspaper advertisement proved successful. The Yorkshire magistrate received four letters in reply to it from parties with an interest in the case. Some of them came to Yorkshire to identify Wilson, who was removed by habeas corpus to Gloucester, where he stood trial for forgery at the 1756 Lent Assizes. He was convicted and sentenced to death.

This did not mark the end of Lister's involvement. Wilson's execution was respited, which suggested that he was likely to receive a commuted sentence or a pardon. The forger proceeded to send Lister an extremely cheeky letter, demanding the return of the papers which the magistrate had taken from him in January. Lister received other requests for some of the same documents, in particular one on behalf of the man who had acted as prosecutor in Wilson's trial at Gloucester, but who was himself charged after the assizes with forgery by the other

[8] B.C.L., Deeds, 16/14/10, draft of Lister to anon., n.d. (about 1 Feb. 1756).

interested parties. Confronted with these various requests and not at all sure what was going on, Lister turned to another London barrister. The latter consulted a judge on his behalf about the propriety of returning the forgeries to the convicted man and arranged the final disposal of the various papers after the judge refused to assist. That was the end of the affair as far as Lister was concerned, but it was an ending that left him confused and exasperated. At the end of May 1756 he commented that 'there has been a great scene of villainy amongst these people, and ... I do not know which of them is the greatest'.[9]

The obstacles to the transmission of criminal intelligence over long distances which are revealed by the 1756 Gloucestershire forgery case were regularly met with by those attempting to bring serious offenders to justice under such circumstances in the mid-eighteenth century. The 1756 affair provides a particularly striking illustration of these obstacles because the problems associated with acquiring and disseminating information were especially acute in this instance. Those in Yorkshire who became involved were third parties in the affair, ignorant of the precise circumstances, and great urgency attached to their efforts. The particular problems of criminal intelligence which the case illustrates can be grouped under four headings.

First, the very ease with which an offender could escape discovery by flight to a part of the country remote from the scene of his offence. Edward Wilson was not advertised in the Gloucester newspaper by those he had defrauded, but considerable efforts were made in his native county to apprehend him. Yet even when he was taken up in Yorkshire it is doubtful whether his secret would have been discovered, had he not had the misfortune to appear before Lister, who was an exceptionally assiduous justice and considered himself unusual in his practice of searching those accused of trivial offences.[10] Admittedly Wilson's expertise in the woollen industry provided him with a plausible front in Yorkshire, but the experience of much more notorious fugitives suggests that an innocuous cover was not essential to escape detection in a distant locality.[11] Nevertheless, it helped. Offenders of a professional character, like the renowned John Poulter and his

---

[9] B.C.L., Deeds, 16/14/10, draft of Lister to Mr Rookes, 26 May 1756.

[10] B.C.L., Deeds, 16/14/10, draft of Lister to 'Dear Alan', n.d.

[11] Take, for example, Thomas Rowden, with Dick Turpin and Samuel Gregory one of a group of men who achieved extraordinary notoriety as a result of their robberies in the London area in 1734 and 1735. They were advertised in the official *London Gazette* and much reported in other London newspapers. Rowden, having fled to Gloucestershire and adopted an alias, was apprehended there in 1736 for putting off counterfeit coin and convicted. Neither at his trial nor during nine months he subsequently spent in Gloucester gaol was his true identity discovered. See D. Barlow, *Dick Turpin and the Gregory Gang* (Chichester, 1973), 123, 231-2, 241-4, 301-3.

associates in the early 1750s, or the Coventry gang in the early 1760s, used networks of safe houses, were possessed of a multiplicity of well-established aliases and were often adept at disguise. These offenders appear to have been able to move with considerable security to and fro across provincial England, between the provinces and London, and even across the Atlantic, often returning from transportation almost as soon as they arrived in America. The risk of apprehension for such people appears to have been largely confined to the period during and immediately after the commission of their offences. These included burglary, horse stealing and pickpocketing, as well as the infliction on the public of a variety of frauds at fairs, races and other gatherings.[12]

Second, the profound ignorance displayed by a leading county magistrate and a prominent provincial barrister of places and people, particularly justices of the peace, in a distant part of the country. It is important to bear in mind, however, that it was only after 1790, with the publication of national directories which carried (incomplete) information on the identity and addresses of acting magistrates in any particular locality, that information of this kind became readily available in print.[13]

Third, the expense and inconvenience which the dissemination of criminal intelligence could entail. Lister's advertisement in *The General Evening Post* cost him approximately seven shillings.[14] In addition he incurred considerable postal charges. The affair illustrates how unpredictable the cost and inconvenience of involvement in such a case might be. The complications that followed Wilson's conviction not only perplexed Lister, but put him to the expense of additional letters and of engaging a London barrister. He appears to have received no

---

[12] For Poulter see J. Poulter alias Baxter, *The Discoveries of John Poulter alias Baxter* (6th edn., Sherborne, 1753), 3-27. For the Coventry gang see J. Hewitt, *A Journal of the Proceedings of J. Hewitt, Senior Alderman of the City of Coventry and one of His Majesty's Justices of the Peace for the said City and County, in his Duty as a Magistrate* (2nd edn., 2 vols., Birmingham, 1790), i, 117-220.

[13] See P. Barfoot and J. Wilkes (compilers), *The Universal British Directory of Trade, Commerce and Manufacture* (2nd edn., 5 vols., 1793), *passim*. It is curious that Lister did not attempt to write to the mayors of Gloucester, Bath or Bristol, who were magistrates *ex officio* and could be located without knowledge of their names. However, it is also striking that the surviving documents suggest he wrote only to people to whom he had a formal introduction from someone in Yorkshire. Perhaps he considered such connections were more to be depended on in such a case than the sometimes questionable enthusiasm of anonymous magistrates for upholding the law.

[14] The editions of *The General Evening Post* that carried Lister's advertisement (which appeared twice) do not appear to have survived. It is possible to establish the approximate cost to Lister by comparing a draft of the advertisement among his papers with the run of *The General Evening Post* for 1736 held at the Guildhall Library, London, which carries the prices charged for different lengths of advertisement.

offer of reimbursement from the aggrieved parties. A single episode of this nature was hardly a difficult financial burden for a provincial gentleman to bear, but the inconvenience alone was enough to discourage many lesser magistrates from following Lister's example, let alone poorer victims of crime. If a number of offenders were involved, the cost, in both time and money, could become prohibitive for even the most zealous justice of the peace.[15]

Fourth, the absence of any official facility for distributing information about suspected offenders between counties and regions, other than the traditional hue and cry, which had (with certain exceptions) already fallen into desuetude. The 1756 affair demonstrates that the newspaper advertisement could serve as an effective substitute for such a facility, but it was a substitute that suffered from serious shortcomings. Resort to a newspaper advertisement was far from universal in such cases. As we have seen, those in Gloucestershire attempting to apprehend Edward Wilson did not choose to advertise him in *The Gloucester Journal*. Newspaper advertisements, and more particuarly, the rewards customarily offered for information in advertisements placed by victims of offences, could be expensive. Moreover, the pattern of mid-eighteenth century newspaper circulation did not lend itself to the dissemination of information over very long distances.

The thirty-five provincial newspapers in existence in the mid-1750s were geographically restricted in their circulations.[16] England was divided into a patchwork of newspaper territories, each based on a particular printing town. A potential advertiser who was ignorant of the precise destination or provenance of a fugitive, having advertised in his local paper or made local enquiries, had little to gain by advertising in other provincial papers, unless he went to the trouble of advertising in all of them. For most potential advertisers this was an entirely impractical undertaking, given the difficulty of locating the other papers, delivering the advertisement and paying for it. Crime advertisements originating well outside the established territory of a particular provincial newspaper were extremely rare during the 1750s.[17]

The thrice-weekly London evening papers were distributed much

[15] This was the predicament of which John Hewitt, the extraordinarily active Coventry magistrate, complained to the Treasury in 1766. See P.R.O., T 1/449, Treasury In-letters, 1766, Memorial of John Hewitt, 20 March 1766.

[16] G. A. Cranfield, *The Development of the Provincial Newspaper, 1700–1760* (Oxford, 1960), 21, 202–6.

[17] Take, for example, *The Gloucester Journal* in the years 1754 and 1755. Although crime advertisements came from quite distant parts of south and mid Wales, which evidently fell within the paper's territory, all those originating in England came either from Gloucestershire itself, or from immediately adjacent counties, with the sole exception of one from a place in Shropshire barely fifty miles from Gloucester.

more extensively and regularly carried crime advertisements originating in distant parts of the country.[18] Yet despite the evidence of the 1756 forgery affair, there are grounds for caution as to the effectiveness of the London press in this regard. The London evening papers enjoyed an extensive provincial circulation, but they were distributed relatively thinly. One of Samuel Lister's correspondents pointed out that 'the General Evening Post is not, you know, universally received', and urged him to place his advertisement in every London paper and in *The Gloucester Journal*.[19] Moreover, it was probably not easy for people in the provinces to place such advertisements in the London papers if they had no-one to act on their behalf in the capital.

The obstacles to long distance detection illustrated by the 1756 Gloucestershire forgery case were precisely those that Sir John Fielding addressed in his General Preventative Plan of 1772. The Plan has been described in several histories of eighteenth-century policing.[20] A brief outline is necessary here to demonstrate exactly how it was tailored to confront those obstacles and to point out a number of features that have gone unrecognised.

Between September 1772 and September 1773 Fielding sent out five printed circular letters to the clerks of the peace of all the English and Welsh counties for submission to the county magistrates in sessions and to the mayors and other chief magistrates of corporate towns. These outlined his Plan and solicited support.[21] The scheme he proposed had two elements. First, he asked the provincial magistrates, borough and county, to supply detailed descriptions to his office in Bow Street of felons or cheats escaped from justice and of people apprehended on suspicion of such offences. He requested that gaolers should be required to keep descriptions of those committed to their custody and to enter them in the assize calendars, which were already being sent to Bow Street. He also asked officials and the public to supply descriptions of horses stolen or stopped.[22]

[18] *The General Evening Post* in 1736 carried crime advertisements from as far away as Yorkshire, Bristol and Norfolk, and *The London Evening Post* in 1756 as far as Flintshire and Lancashire, although in both cases the vast majority of their crime advertisements originated in the metropolis or adjacent counties.

[19] B.C.L., Deeds, 16/14/10, A.B. to Lister, n.d. (about 3 Feb. 1756).

[20] For example, Radzinowicz, *History*, iii. 47-54; P. Pringle, *Hue and Cry: The Birth of the British Police* (1965), 183-194; T. A. Critchley, *A History of Police in England and Wales, 900-1966* (1967), 32-5.

[21] Radzinowicz, *History*, iii. Appendix i, 479-485, reprints four of the circulars, and some of the covering letters. For the fifth circular (that dated Bow Street, 11 Sept. 1773) and other covering letters, see Surrey Record Office, Kingston, Q5 2/6, Surrey Quarter Sessions bundles, Mich. 1772 to Mich. 1773. The following outline of the Plan is, unless otherwise stated, based on these circular letters.

[22] *Manchester Mercury*, 22 and 29 Dec. 1772.

This element of the Plan was hardly original. The Bow Street office had served as a central clearing house for criminal information within the metropolis and its immediate vicinity since Henry Fielding's day. Moreover, John Fielding had already enormously extended the very limited provincial connections of his half-brother and the latter's prededessor as principal magistrate for Westminster, Sir Thomas De Veil.[23] As early as 1756 John Fielding was inserting advertisements in the London papers about provincial fugitives on behalf of the victims of their crimes, although there is no evidence that Samuel Lister knew of or made any attempt to use his services in that year.[24] By the 1760s, Fielding regularly placed advertisements in the London evening and many provincial papers, some about specific offences and others asking magistrates to correspond with him about unsolved crimes, suspects taken into custody and offenders fled from justice.[25]

It was the integration of these procedures into a national system for collating and circulating the information thus obtained that was the second and truly innovatory element of the 1772 Plan. Fielding proposed to redistribute this information throughout the country in a printed format suitable for public display. He and his half-brother had both operated an equivalent system within the London area, after 1752 by arrangement with daily newspapers, initially *The Public Advertiser*, but later also *The Gazetteer*. Prior to 1772, however, Fielding had not attempted systematically to provide such a facility on a national scale.[26]

The pattern of newspaper circulation in the provinces made it impossible for advertisements in a couple of commercially-circulated newspapers (London or provincial) to offer the combination of national coverage and local penetration that Fielding required for his criminal intelligence. His solution was a twofold one. First, he had all the information he received from the provinces regarding offences, stolen property, fugitive offenders and those committed to prison, as

---

[23] For Henry Fielding see *Covent Garden Journal*, 30 June 1752; for De Veil see Pringle, *Hue and Cry*, 68-9. A clearing house for criminal information, operating mainly within the London area, but with provincial connections, had been the lynchpin of Jonathan Wild's activities in the 1710s and 1720s: see G. Howson, *Thief-Taker General* (1970), 66-9 and 125-6.

[24] *London Evening Post*, 5 Feb. 1756.

[25] See *York Courant*, 8 Nov. 1763; *London Evening Post*, 7 Aug. 1766; *Salisbury Journal*, 1 Sept. 1766; *Cambridge Chronicle*, 3 Aug. 1771. By the 1760s Fielding was already experienced in the use of such advertisements in provincial papers, having employed them to promote his Universal Register Office during the previous decade. See, for example, *Gloucester Journal*, 16 July 1754.

[26] His advertisements about offenders and offences in the London evening and provincial newspapers before 1772 were essentially sporadic. He continued after that year to place advertisements in the provincial press on the same basis. See *Manchester Mercury*, 14 Sept. 1773 and *Norwich Mercury*, 24 Dec. 1773.

well as information of the same kind from the metropolis, entered in a newspaper. This was sent *gratis* to mayors, acting county magistrates and gaolers throughout the country and was available on sale to the public at large. It also included advice about criminal matters, news of improvements in the General Preventative Plan and reminders to law officers to promote it.

During the first year of the Plan's operation (October 1772 to October 1773) this purpose was achieved by an arrangement with a London thrice-weekly newspaper, *The London Packet or New Lloyd's Evening Post*. Every Monday the paper transformed all or part of its front page into 'The General Hue and Cry', printed in large type with a distinctive border to facilitiate cutting out for public display. Fielding asked that the section be stuck up by mayors in the market places of their towns and by county magistrates at some conspicuous place on a public road. From the autumn of 1773, when the Plan secured long-term government finance to the tune of £400 per annum, Fielding dispensed with the arrangement with *The London Packet* and published his own newspaper entitled *The Hue and Cry*, which he circulated in the same way. Its contents were similar to its predecessor's. At first it was published on a weekly basis, though it soon became fortnightly and by the end of the 1770s appeared monthly.[27]

Second, Fielding supplemented *The Hue and Cry* by circulating cumulative, printed lists of those offenders who remained at large despite the appearance of their descriptions in his newspaper. The lists were originally intended to be produced quarterly, but from the start Fielding omitted printing a quarter's list if he felt sufficient names were not available. By the later 1770s they were appearing half yearly or yearly. Initially Fielding sent a copy to all mayors and clerks of the peace, with the request that enough should be reprinted at the expense of each corporation or county to be distributed to constables for stricking up on the church door or in another prominent place in every parish. After the Plan acquired government funding, he was able to have sufficient printed himself to send to every magistrate, high and petty constable, gaoler and house of correction keeper in the country, most of whom he supplied via the county clerks of the peace.

Yet however effective the machinery Fielding devised for circulating his criminal intelligence, the success of the Plan ultimately depended on the ability and willingness of those whom it reached to act

---

[27] Some, but not all, of the copies of *The London Packet or New Lloyd's Evening Post* for the period Fielding used it survive in the Bodleian Library. I have been unable to discover any copies earlier than 1786 of *The Hue and Cry* that Fielding and his successors published from Oct. 1773. However, a virtually continuous run of much of the information Fielding and his successors inserted in these publications is available from Dec. 1772 in *The Newcastle Courant*, which reprinted most of it on its front page.

appropriately. Fielding was, of course, supplying a public that was already responsive enough to information of this kind to make local crime advertising in newspapers and handbills a much-used detective technique. Nevertheless, all the literature associated with the Plan carried exhortations to greater responsiveness from the public and local officials alike. To stimulate the participation of the latter, Fielding also made more concrete proposals. He suggested that after each list was issued, magistrates should instruct all parish constables to make searches under the terms of the 1744 Vagrant Act (17 Geo. II, c. 5), in order to flush out the offenders named therein. He also requested that he should be supplied by the county clerks of the peace and gaolers with the names and addresses of all acting magistrates and high constables. These were important not simply for the purpose of his general correspondence. Fielding insisted that a warrant should accompany descriptions of fugitive offenders sent to Bow Street. Knowledge of the names and addresses of local officials enabled him, on a discovery being made, to send the warrant direct to the appropriate locality, thereby avoiding delay, inconvenience and the expense of moving the prisoner by habeas corpus.

Thus the General Preventative Plan provided specific remedies for each of those obstacles to the dissemination of criminal intelligence that were evidenced in the 1756 Gloucestershire forgery affair. It put regular, detailed descriptions of fugitives and unidentified suspects in custody, including their occupations, their customary aliases and disguises, and their *modus operandi*, into the hands of local officials throughout the country and made them widely accessible to the public. In addition, it provided both a central repository for criminal intelligence and a machinery for transferring information rapidly between officials in different parts of the country. This facility was provided at minimal expense, Fielding paying for correspondence, as well as for distributing *The Hue and Cry*.[28]

Fielding promoted his 1772 and 1773 proposals with enormous zeal—he was nothing if not an inspired self-publicist. His enthusiasm was reciprocated by county benches and corporation authorities throughout provincial England. It is impossible to provide a definitive list of their responses, but it is clear that Fielding did not greatly exaggerate when he claimed his proposals had received 'their unanimous approbation'.[29] Out of forty-six English counties or divisions of counties with their own quarter sessions for which sessions records survive and have been surveyed, evidence of a positive response from the magistrates in sessions to Fielding's proposals is found in twenty-

[28] Although it should be noted that the vast majority of entries in *The Hue and Cry* carried rewards.

[29] P.R.O., SP 37/10, Sir J. Fielding to Earl of Suffolk, n.d. (January 1773).

six. Newspaper reports reveal a positive response in another four of that forty-six. In only one county—Surrey—is there any evidence of opposition. This appears to have arisen from an unwillingness to pay for reprinting Fielding's lists.[30] By contrast, in twenty-five of the counties or divisions surveyed there is evidence of a decision to reprint the lists and have them circulated for display, the expenses to be met out of the county or divisional rate. Because county sessions documents and newspaper reports were not compiled in a uniform manner, it is probable that many of the counties for which no response is recorded did in fact support the plan, as Fielding claimed. Borough records for the period are, unfortunately, very uninformative about such matters. Nevertheless, the newspapers indicate positive responses in large corporate towns like Worcester and Newcastle, while no record of opposition has been discovered.[31] Subsequently Fielding was to assert that *The Hue and Cry* was 'stuck up in the market place of every corporation town from Cornwall to Edinburgh, by order of the Mayors and chief officers of such corporations'.[32]

In some places the authorities did much more than Fielding had requested in his circular letters. In 1772 the magistrates of Northumberland, Durham and Cumberland, in conjunction with those of the borough of Newcastle, paid for Fielding's 'General Hue and Cry' (later his *Hue and Cry*), together with a compilation of local crime information along the same lines, to be inserted weekly in *The Newcastle Courant*. This was to continue into the 1790s. At Manchester in the same year a meeting of the principal inhabitants, at the suggestion of T. B. Bayley, the active local magistrate, set up their own 'Bow Street' office for criminal intelligence. For almost a year, they too had Fielding's 'General Hue and Cry' reprinted in the two Manchester newspapers, in conjunction with local crime information. The proprietors of *Jackson's Oxford Journal* and *The Stamford Mercury* also reprinted "The General Hue and Cry' for approximately the same period.

The co-operation that Fielding received from the localities was not restricted to disseminating his criminal intelligence. An analysis of the provenance of the 187 entries in *The Hue and Cry* (as reprinted in *The Newcastle Courant*) for the year 1774 reveals that although there was a bias towards London, Middlesex and the home counties, which accounted for forty-three per cent of the 168 entries whose origin is known, only five English counties were not represented.[33] A similar

---

[30] Surrey Record Office, Kingston, Q5 2/6, Surrey quarter sessions bundles, Mich. 1772, Sir J. Fielding to T. Lawson, 17 Oct. 1772.

[31] Fifteen borough quarter sessions records were surveyed.

[32] *Newcastle Courant*, 20 July 1776.

[33] The counties of Northumberland, Cumberland and Durham are not included in this calculation because entries from those counties went in the local crime section.

pattern and diversity of origin characterises the entries in the lists that
survive. The numbers of cases that appeared in *The Hue and Cry* may
appear to be small, but the numbers of offenders moving between
regions was probably not very large. However, almost all the entries
concerned those serious offences—murder, aggravated theft and horse
theft—that were the occasion of disproportionate public and official
anxiety.

How successful was the General Preventative Plan? An example
from 1773 and 1774 will serve to illustrate the Plan in operation. In
July 1773 Richard alias John Myett, alias Early, alias Dart, alias
Mason, described by Fielding as 'a very extraordinary offender', broke
into a silversmith's shop at Wallingford in Berkshire and stole a large
quantity of silver. Particulars of the theft and a description were
promptly inserted in 'The General Hue and Cry'. Within a fortnight
Myett was apprehended at Lawton in Cheshire, 130 miles from Wallingford. There he succeeded in escaping, though without his booty.
He was advertised again in 'The General Hue and Cry', but evaded
capture. During the ensuing autumn and winter he undertook various
burglaries in the Salisbury area, where he had worked some two years
previously. When his former employer at Salisbury was burgled in
February 1774, Myett was suspected. He was therefore advertised
once again in Fielding's paper and two weeks later was apprehended
as a consequence at Darlington, 260 miles from Salisbury. He was
subsequently convicted and hanged.[34]

This and the other available examples of the Plan's successes derive
principally from reports in the provincial press.[35] It is impossible to
provide a systematic assessment of its success rate, because such reporting was sporadic and Fielding's own Bow Street records have not
survived. We do know that, by March 1773, at least ten of the
thirty-six offenders in Fielding's September 1772 list had been apprehended.[36] However, there is no certainty that they were apprehended
because they were in the list and the representativeness of these figures
is questionable given that the 1772 list had been compiled before the
Plan took effect. Even if a satisfactory clear-up rate could be established, its significance for an evaluation of the scheme's impact would

[34] *Newcastle Courant*, 31 July, 21 Aug. 1773; 5 and 12 Mar., 23 July 1774. *Salisbury
Journal*, 14 Feb. 1774.

[35] For other successful cases see *Chelmsford Chronicle*, 23 July 1773; *Leeds Intelligencer*, 19
Oct. 1784; *Manchester Mercury*, 9 Feb. 1773; *Newcastle Courant*, 11 Sept. 1773; *Nottingham
and Newark Journal*, 1 May 1773; *Norwich Mercury*, 9 Nov. 1776; *Reading Mercury*, 12 Sept.
1774.

[36] The Sept. 1772 and Mar. 1773 lists (the second included a list of those in the first
who had been apprehended) survive in several quarter sessions collections, for example
Essex Record Office, Q/SB b272/58 and 64, Essex quarter sessions bundles, Easter
1773.

be difficult to gauge, because there is no available data for equivalent cases before 1772. Moreover, it is important to bear in mind that Fielding's objectives were as much preventative as detective.

Perhaps the best judgment one can offer is that the Plan could hardly have failed to be an improvement on pre-existing long-distance detection techniques, given their inadequacies. That this was widely believed to be the case is indicated by the praise that the 1772 and 1773 innovations continued to receive after some years in operation. For example, in 1775 a Coventry correspondent to *The London Evening Post* referred to the Plan's 'multitude of admirers'. The next year the printer of *The Norwich Mercury*, a paper with no special links with Bow Street, described *The Hue and Cry* as a 'useful paper'. After 1776, successive editions of Burn's *Justice of the Peace* carried a paragraph commending the Plan as an established success.[37]

Although the General Preventative Plan was widely regarded as a success, it was also subject to limitations, which became increasingly obvious when Fielding attempted to intensify its operation in 1775. In order to understand these limitations it is first necessary to explain why his 1772 and 1773 proposals were, from the start, so favourably received. The shortcomings of the existing facilities for long-distance dissemination of criminal intelligence, Fielding's enormous national reputation and his established links with influential provincial magistrates all played a part here.[38] The visibility of the problem of inter-regional offenders during the 1760s, in particular the publicity given to the Coventry gang, combined with the increase in indictments for serious offences after the Seven Years War, may have predisposed local officials to favour the Plan.[39]

Another key element in the Plan's favourable reception was the particular form Fielding chose for it. The 1772 and 1773 proposals offered the benefits of a police apparatus that was integrated and centralised, without demanding a wholesale reconstitution along uniform lines of the administration of criminal justice. What Fielding described as his 'favourite preventative machine' was not a bureaucratic engine that necessitated new personnel performing a novel set

---

[37] *London Evening Post*, 14 Jan. 1775; *Norwich Mercury*, 9 Nov. 1776; R. Burn, *The Justice of the Peace and Parish Officer* (16th edn., 4 vols., 1788), ii. 655-6.

[38] Fielding's provincial reputation was such by 1762 that in that year a Penrith bailiff who operated a horse theft and retrieval operation along the lines of Jonathan Wild could refer to himself as 'Justice Fielding': P.R.O., ASSI 45/26/6/50 P: Assizes Northern Circuit Depositions, examination of J. Winter, 10 Aug. 1762.

[39] For public familiarity with the Coventry Gang, see *York Courant*, 30 Oct. 1764; for indictments see D. Hay, 'War, Dearth and Theft in the Eighteenth Century: The Record of the English Courts', *Past & Present*, no. 95 (1982), 123-6, 135-46.

of duties.[40] As he was at pains to emphasise, it was entirely consistent with the existing character of the English civil power. Indeed he cleverly argued that it constituted a form of police superior to that of foreigners for this very reason.

Such an argument was not, however, entirely consistent with the underlying thrust of Fielding's proposals. In part, the scheme represented an extension of the voluntary principle on which the established success of the newspaper crime advertisement was founded. Fielding's Plan provided a more extensive and systematic facility than any newspaper, but it exploited the same willingness among the general public and officials to respond to such a facility. From the start, however, it was distinguished from newspaper crime advertising by a disproportionate emphasis on the role of officials—especially magistrates—in channelling information and taking appropriate follow-up action. Fielding's subsequent efforts to intensify the operation of the scheme concentrated almost entirely on the activity of officials. This is hardly surprising, given that once the Plan was widely known the capacity of his promotion techniques further to increase public responsiveness was probably limited. But in order to secure the sort of action from local officials that he believed the Plan required, he was eventually obliged to propose far-reaching changes in the character of the existing local government apparatus.

Initially many county and borough magistrates proved eager to respond to Fielding's requests for intensified activity by local officials. As we have seen, a large number of counties and boroughs paid to reprint his lists. In those counties, orders were given to the high constables of the various hundreds to undertake the dispersal of the lists among the petty constables. The response to Fielding's other requests for official action in 1772 and 1773 is more difficult to establish. In making these requests, he did not ask for a specific reply from the magistrates in sessions. A note of their decision is, therefore, much less likely to have been entered in the sessions records than in the case of reprinting the lists, where a reply was requested. The sessions records surveyed do reveal six counties that in 1772 and 1773 ordered gaolers to compile descriptions of prisoners, five that provided the names and addresses of chief constables, and three that began to order searches under the Vagrant Act of 1744, but it is probable that there were many others.

These were not, however, forms of official action that were new in principle, or that implied a major transformation of the roles of the officials involved. Payments out of the county rates for advertising offenders, especially those escaped from houses of correction, were not uncommon. High constables had long been the principal intermedi-

[40] Fielding circular dated 19 Oct. 1772.

aries between the county quarter sessions and the petty constables, in particular superintending the enforcement of various types of warrant. In some counties (though not all) quarterly searches under the Vagrant Act were regularly enforced. Gaolers already kept records of their charges. The compilation by county officials of register books of offenders' descriptions was not unknown.[41]

The proposals Fielding circulated to the county benches in February 1775 were more radical. He had already expressed concern about the problem the lack of justices in many districts posed for a Plan that relied so heavily on the magistracy for its execution. In his 1775 circular he expressed doubts about the capacity of even the most enthusiastic magistrate to operate the Plan to best effect. 'Magistrates in the country, however public-spirited they may be, can only back our warrants, recommend peace officers to execute them, and examine offenders when taken, and such like; but ... in general, much more is required, in cases of these pursuits, than is proper to ask a magistrate, or possible for his superior station to admit of'.[42]

His recommended solution was to have the high constables pursue and apprehend fugitives. Indeed he proposed that for at least one hundred miles from London, high constables for those Hundreds through which ran the principal roads from the capital should be resident on those roads, that their expenses in pursuits should be paid by the county, or that they should be paid a salary to enable them to keep a horse for that purpose. This expenditure was to be financed out of a tax on places of public entertainment, in itself a preventative measure. He also suggested that the high constables' houses should display a board with the words 'HIGH CONSTABLE', so that travellers could give notice of robbers. In addition, he called for the number of petty constables in each parish to be increased.

The reaction of the county benches to these proposals was cool. Although Fielding asked for a reply, evidence of any kind of response is limited to eight counties or divisions out of forty-five surveyed, in marked contrast to the reception of his earlier proposals. Of that eight, five expressed hostility at least some of the proposals, or did no more than send Fielding the names of the existing high constables (which several counties had been doing since 1772). The only response of the

[41] The Clerk of the Peace for Cumberland was ordered early in 1772 thereafter to make out lists of the names and descriptions of vagrants passed; Cumbria Record Office, Carlisle, Q 7/3, Cumberland quarter sessions Public Order Book, 1767–78, Easter 1772.

[42] Undated printed circular from J. Fielding headed 'To the Acting Magistrates of the Counties at large throughout ENGLAND, in their Quarter Sessions assembled'. This circular and its covering letter, dated 28 Feb. 1775, survive in several quarter sessions collections, for example Kent Record Office, Q/SB 1775, Kent quarter sessions papers, 1775.

Westmorland magistrates was to order Fielding's circular to be filed. In Suffolk, the Beccles bench informed Fielding that the high constables were already resident in parishes on the great road to London, but they 'being persons of very considerable property would not approve of having such boards over their doors as Sir John desires'. The Lincolnshire Lindsey bench informed him that, although his proposal 'would very much contribute to the end proposed', their division was not on any of the great roads, was over one hundred miles from London and few of the offenders escaping from the capital came there. 'Therefore the justices do not think it necessary to appoint an additional number of petty constables within this division.' Their only practical measure was to send the names of the existing high constables. This course of action was also the sole recorded response of the Staffordshire and Devon benches, and one that, in the case of Devon, was associated with reservations about Fielding's 1775 proposals as a whole.[43]

For one of the three remaining counties—the East Riding of Yorkshire—there is no record of a specific quarter sessions response to Fielding's 1775 circular, but each high constable was provided in that and the next year with four pairs of handcuffs to be kept for the use of their Wapentake. This suggests a move to employ the high constables as thief-takers in the way Fielding had proposed. The other two counties—Derbyshire and Lincolnshire Holland—both recorded their approval for the scheme.[44] In Holland, which, unlike Derbyshire, was within one hundred miles of London, the high constables were ordered to put up boards on their houses. None of these three counties appears, however, to have taken any further practical steps to carry out Fielding's proposals. There is no record of a salary being paid to high constables after 1775, nor were extra petty constables appointed in each parish or township. This also appears to be true of those counties for which there is no direct evidence of any response to the 1775 circular, or at least of those among them for which it has been possible to make some assessment of the appointment

---

[43] Cumbria Record Office, Kendal, WQO/9, Westmorland quarter sessions Order Book, 1770-80, Easter 1775; Suffolk Record Office, Ipswich, B 105/2/44, Suffolk quarter sessions Order Book, 1770-1776, Beccles, Easter 1775; Lincolnshire Record Office, Lindsey quarter sessions Minute Book, 1774-7, Gainsborough, Easter 1775; Staffordshire Record Office, Q/SO 17, Staffordshire quarter sessions Order Book, 1775-81, Easter 1775; Devon Record Office, Exeter, Q/S 1/2, Devon quarter sessions Order Book, 1759-1776, Easter and Summer 1775.

[44] Humberside Record Office, Beverley, QSV 1/6, East Riding quarter sessions Order Book, Michaelmas 1775 and Easter 1776; Derbyshire Record Office, Derbyshire quarter sessions Order Book, 1774-80, Easter 1775; Lincolnshire Record Office, Holland quarter sessions Minute Book, 1771-84, Spalding and Boston, Easter 1775.

and payment of high and petty constables.[45] For example, even in the Liberty of St Albans, immediately adjacent to Middlesex, the bench did not see fit after 1775 to appoint high constables resident on either the Great North Road or the London–Manchester road.[46]

At first sight it is curious that Fielding's 1775 circular received such limited support. In themselves, many of its proposals were neither new in principle or in practice. High constables were, like petty constables, peace officers, with an obligation to make pursuit in cases of felonies reported to them. In many counties they were paid at least some of their expenses. In a number they received a salary—£12 per annum in Cumberland after 1772. Elsewhere they were allowed to deduct 'poundage' from the county rate which they collected.[47] Nor was it uncommon for a quarter sessions or a vestry to appoint an additional petty constable for a parish, or a beadle or watchman to assist the petty constable.[48]

Viewed as a package, however, Fielding's 1775 proposals implied remodelling the customary roles of the officials concerned. The most important task of the county high constables was to collect the county rate. In addition they had a wide range of administrative duties. Their activities as peace officers were almost entirely confined to superintending the petty constables. To transform them into active pursuers of fugitives from justice and of highway robbers was to add a new dimension to their office, and one that was in some respects at odds with their existing duties. It is hardly surprising that county benches were unenthusiastic, when Fielding's proposal would have restricted their choice of candidates for a vital revenue-raising office to those resident on the principal highways. Even if magistrates had wanted to put Fielding's scheme into operation, the fact that in perhaps half the counties high constables held office for life made any rapid shift towards roadside locations impossible. Moreover, high constables in many counties were men of some standing—wealthy yeomen or lesser gentry. Such status reinforced their authority in their superintending and revenue-raising duties, but it meant that for them to be put on

---

[45] Given the difficulty of proving a negative this cannot be a definite conclusion. It is based on a survey of quarter sessions collections and, in the case of the East Riding, Derbyshire and Holland, of parish (particularly contables') records.

[46] Hertfordshire Record Office, LSMB/1: St Albans Liberty quarter sessions, Draft Minute Book, 1776–86, Epiphany Sessions 1777.

[47] S. and B. Webb, *The Parish and the County* (1963), 501; Cumbria Record Office, Carlisle, Q/7/3: Cumberland quarter sessions Public Order Book, 1767–78, Easter Sessions, 1772.

[48] For example see Gloucestershire Record Office, Q/SO/5, Gloucestershire quarter sessions Order Book, 1724–34, Summer Session 1724.

public call as pursuers of criminals was probably no more acceptable socially than it was for magistrates.[49]

To interfere with the established mix of duties undertaken by the high constables must have appeared all the more unnecessary in view of the relatively small numbers of inter-regional fugitives or highway robberies in most provincial Hundreds. As the comments of the Lincolnshire Lindsey bench indicate, this was certainly a powerful argument against appointing extra petty constables in every parish. After all, in many places where the weight of business necessitated them, supplementary constables or ancillary officers were already provided. This was the case in a large number of non-incorporated urban areas, including Horncastle in Lindsey itself.[50]

Fielding's 1775 proposals are best understood as a further step in what amounted to a programme to extend to the nation as a whole the essentials of the Bow Street system as it operated within the metropolitan area. There, the collection and dissemination of criminal intelligence were combined with systematic follow-up action by officials under Fielding's direction. But such official action was possible precisely because this was an urban area with a distinctive institutional framework, where the pressure of criminal business was on a scale that was without parallel in provincial England. London, Westminster and urban Middlesex, though smaller in total area than many provincial Hundreds, contained perhaps a tenth of the nation's population and a disproportionate share of its serious criminal offences. To confront such offences throughout the metropolis, Fielding was in receipt of government finance, which enabled him to devote all his energies to crime fighting and to employ a small team of full-time thief-takers. He was also able to call upon the services of large forces of constables and watchmen, including some exceptionally diligent high constables, such as Saunders Welch, high constable of Holborn from 1747 to 1755. The latter were probably the inspiration for the new role he envisaged for their provincial counterparts.[51] In the provinces the pressure of criminal business and the numbers and character of the local peace

[49] For the character and duties of high constables see S. and B. Webb, *The Parish and the County*, 489–502 and Cumbria Record Office, Kendal, Browne of Troutbeck *Mss.*, vol. XV, Accounts of Benjamin Browne's disbursements as high constable of Kendal Ward, 1711–31.

[50] J. N. Clarke, *Watch and Ward in the Countryside* (Horncastle, 1982), 8.

[51] For Fielding's activities in London see the sources cited in note 4. From the 1750s Fielding used his London thief-takers on provincial pursuits and enquiries, sometimes at the request of magistrates or others in the provinces. However, their use in this way appears to have been limited and sporadic, partly because of the pressure of metropolitan business and partly because Fielding could afford to employ only a small number of thief-takers: see for examples P.R.O., T 1/449, Treasury in-letters, 1766, Fielding's account for 1765–6.

officers were very different. Indeed, the only places in provincial England that provided the density of local peace officers that Fielding felt his Plan required were the corporate towns. It is significant that, unlike his earlier circulars, that of 1775 was not directed to the mayors of those towns.

Yet the lack of enthusiasm in the counties for the 1775 proposals did not undermine the operation of the established components of the General Preventative Plan. It continued to flourish after Fielding's death in 1780 and under the 1792 reforms of the police of the metropolis. It was the object of much interest from later police reformers and eventually developed into the modern *Police Gazette*.

For most historians of police, the endeavours of Henry and John Fielding mark the beginning of that process of police reform which culminated, after 1856, in a national system of semi-autonomous, uniformed police forces. They have identified as the stimulus to reform the contradiction between a manifestly inefficient eighteenth-century criminal justice system and the growing problems of crime and control associated with the socio-economic changes of the era of the industrial revolution. The character of the eventual outcome and the time taken to reach it are explained as the consequences of tension between on the one hand a widely-recognised need for an efficient police system and on the other a combination of constitutional scruple, official parsimony and general inertia.[52]

This paper has focused on a single episode of police reform, but it serves, nevertheless, to draw attention to some objections to the broad thrust of this historiography. These objections centre on the notion of police 'efficiency'.[53] Insofar as the efficiency of eighteenth-century policing has been analysed by historians, it has been either by drawing on the works of eighteenth-century commentators on the subject, such as the Fieldings or Patrick Colquhoun, or by counting the numbers of law officers. The danger of over-reliance on the evidence of commentators who were in the main advocates of police reform, with an interest in blackening the reputation of the existing law enforcement apparatus, is clear enough. It is also important to emphasise the drawbacks of attempts to gauge efficiency by counting officials. More did not necessarily mean better, and, as this paper has indicated, changes in the performance by law officers of their responsibilities under the criminal law might owe as much to changes in the facilities available to them—in other words in the manner in which they were

[52] See, for example, Radzinowicz, *History*, iii, *passim*, iv (1968), p. v, and Critchley, *A History of Police*, 18–50.

[53] For the use of 'efficiency' see, for example, ibid., 69 and 71, and Radzinowicz, *History*, iii. 324.

able to discharge those responsibilities—as to changes in their numbers.[54]

Nevertheless, there were limits to the willingness and ability of those who manned the existing law enforcement apparatus to exploit opportunities that became available to them. This was Fielding's experience in 1775. But did the unwillingness of many county magistrates in that year to reconstitute the role of the high constables or to appoint extra petty constables as Fielding requested, perpetuate 'inefficiency'? It probably did in the narrow, technical sense that an opportunity to apprehend and perhaps deter some additional offenders was thereby lost. But the significance of that lost opportunity for policing in a wider sense depends on whether controlling such offenders was a policing priority important enough to outweigh any costs their apprehension would have imposed on the law enforcement apparatus as a whole. It was over precisely this issue that Fielding and the county magistrates were in disagreement, a state of affairs that itself reflected differences in their conceptions of policing.

Fielding, sitting in Bow Street at the controls of his preventative machine, viewed the problem of the inter-regional criminal in its totality. His experience of managing the Bow Street system in the London area and the success of his provincial criminal intelligence-gathering made him peculiarly aware of the problem of the serious offender. He was especially concerned at the ability of those offenders he frightened out of London to find refuge in the provinces. Effective prevention demanded that the machine operate throughout the nation on as uniform a plan as possible, irrespective of local need. He saw a vast pool of fugitives from justice waiting to be trawled. Only by denying them any haven could they be eliminated and, more particularly, others deterred from following in their footsteps.

The county magistracy had other priorities. This is not to suggest that they were hostile to the idea of a general, preventative police system, designed to increase the proportion of offenders apprehended. On the contrary, such systematisation had considerable attractions, especially to those exceptionally active magistrates who were key figures on the county benches and who increasingly conceived of their role in terms of a notion of disinterested public service.[55] The reaction

---

[54] See, for an example of the use of numbers of officials as a measure of their efficiency, J. M. Beattie, 'Towards a Study of Crime in Eighteenth-Century England: A Note on Indictments', in *The Triumph of Culture: Eighteenth-Century Perspectives*, ed. P. Fritz and D. Williams (Toronto, 1972), 309. For modern research which suggests that increases in police manpower do not necessarily lead to significant improvements in detection, see J. Burrows and R. Tarling, *Clearing up Crime* (1982).

[55] I think there is a danger in some recent studies of underestimating the concern of many provincial magistrates to see serious offenders apprehended; for example, D.

of the county benches to the 1772 and 1773 circulars demonstrates that they were willing to respond with enthusiasm, flexibility and some expenditure to proposals of this kind, if they were based on the existing law enforcement apparatus. The attractions of Fielding's preventative machine only began to pall when, for the sake of a national uniformity that bore no relation to local needs, it threatened to unbalance what was a multi-purpose local administrative apparatus. Thus what appears from one perspective as a characteristically eighteenth-century failure to adopt sensible reforms offering efficient policing, emerges from another as a concern to ensure what is best described as policing appropriate to local circumstances. As so often, to adopt a narrow criterion of technical efficiency is to embrace the standards and perceptions of the reformers.

Philips, '"A New Engine of Power and Authority": The Institutionalization of Law Enforcement in England, 1780-1830', in *Crime and the Law*, ed. V. A. C. Gatrell, B. Lenman and G. Parker (1980), 160-1.

[17]

"An Imperfect, Inadequate and Wretched System"? Policing London Before Peel

Ruth Paley
London

Introduction

"The continued increase of crime in London and its neighbourhood appears to me to call for some decisive measure." With these words, according to the conventional interpretation of police history, Robert Peel signalled the beginnings of the final triumph of the forces of reason and progress. After nearly a century and a half of blind adherence to an irrelevant and outdated set of constitutional principles, coupled with an equally blind fear of introducing despotic foreign practices, the English had at last recognized the virtues of an unarmed, preventive police. This new police would replace what Lord Shelburne, one of Peel's predecessors at the Home Office, had dismissed nearly fifty years earlier as "An imperfect, inadequate and wretched system." It would soon prove its worth by imposing a code of social discipline on an otherwise dissolute, disorderly, and degenerate populace. It would provide a model for free people everywhere of how demands for order could be reconciled with those of liberty. Pushed to its logical extreme, this argument would even bestow on the Metropolitan Police at least partial responsibility for saving the nation from the revolutionary upheavals that were soon to engulf Britain's continental neighbors.[1]

In the light of recent research, however, such an analysis begins to look suspiciously simplistic. Pioneering work by John Beattie, David Philips, and Robert Storch, amongst others, has already shown us that the conventional historiography of law enforcement institutions places too heavy a reliance on the supposed inadequacies of the "old" police whilst ignoring considerable continuities (both of practice and personnel) between the "old" and "new" forces.[2] This essay is an attempt to build on their work by re-examining some of the issues that lay behind the introduction of the Metropolitan Police in the light of the author's ongoing research into the administration of the criminal law in eighteenth-century London. It should be made clear from the outset that the purpose of this essay is not, as yet, to offer an alternative explanation of the origins of the Metropolitan Police Act of 1829; rather, the intention is to open up discussion on a topic that is neither as well-researched nor as easily understood as historians once believed it to be.

The Pressure for Reform of the Police

Part of the conventional schematization of the origins of the Metropolitan Police Act depends on the existence of a growing public demand for a major government intervention in the policing of London. Beginning with Henry Fielding, and progressing via a host of lesser writers such as Jonas Hanway and William Godschall, one arrives at Patrick Colquhoun, "the architect who designed our modern police."[3] Such an analysis depends on three basic premises, each of which will be examined in more detail below.

1. That the maintenance of public order posed a serious problem to the authorities in eighteenth-century London, and that standards were deteriorating rather than improving.
2. That the torrent of publications on crime and public order (most notably those by Henry Fielding and Patrick Colquhoun) played a crucial role in influencing public opinion and shaping the responses of the executive government.
3. That London's law enforcement agencies were ineffective because they were inappropriate to an urban setting.

The first point is perhaps the most difficult to argue, since it is bound to depend on a somewhat subjective evaluation of the available evidence. But it is all too easy for those accustomed to the conditions of twentieth-century urban society to assume that late-eighteenth-century London endured a high level of disorderliness without making sufficient allowance for the possibility that contemporaries, who had never experienced anything other than a vibrant street culture, almost certainly perceived order and disorder in very different terms. In examining the records of crime in the metropolitan area over a long period, one is struck by the relative orderliness of the late eighteenth century, and it becomes difficult to avoid the conclusion that (whatever may have been the situation elsewhere) problems of law and order and the stresses associated with rapid urbanization had been at their worst in London in the late seventeenth and early to mid eighteenth centuries. In particular, one is impressed by an apparent decline in violence, and by the ways in which casual street violence (once an integral feature of everyday life) seems to have become increasingly unacceptable.[4]

The corollary to this is that it may be necessary to stand the conventional historiography on its head. If, by 1829, the public had become predisposed toward an acceptance of new policing methods (and it is by no means clear that this was so), it may have been a rising tide of *order* rather than disorder that had brought about the transformation: in Allan Silver's words, "With rising standards of public order . . . come[s] an increasing intolerance of criminality, violence and riotous protest." Silver's perceptive essay also raises the interesting possibility that the character of modern police institutions may, in itself, lift public expectations.[5] Although these points are made in the context of modern democratic societies, they are nevertheless highly relevant to any discussion of the foundation of the Metropolitan Police. As will be demonstrated in the course of this essay, the Metropolitan Police Act did not come about as a simple knee-jerk response to public demand; rather it is highly likely that it is an example of the way in which a reform imposed from above and initially unpopular can yet bring about permanent and decisive changes in public attitudes and expectations.

Only when the mind has been freed from the assumption that a society without the benefit of a modern police force must of necessity have been a disorderly one, can one begin to understand contemporary attitudes. It then becomes clear that there was no single great reform debate in which public opinion moved inexorably toward an acceptance of police reform. Rather, there was a series of debates, both inside and outside government, which drew on a set of stock ideas and which broke out afresh every time fears about crime and disorder were renewed.[6]

These debates can be approached in two ways: either by a study of pamphlet and periodical literature, or by a study of the kind of reforms that were actually attempted, whether by parliament, by the executive government, by parochial authorities, or by any other interested body. The first approach is the easier. It can also be extremely misleading. The mechanisms by which "public opinion" (if such a term can be used) was formed and manipulated in the eighteenth century were very different from those that prevailed a hundred years later. In the eighteenth century (and especially in the second half of the eighteenth century), the printed word was all too often the instrument of the propagandist. Just because an idea went into print does not mean that it was either popular or influential. It was actually rather more likely that the opposite was the case: that those who sought to publicize their ideas in this way did so because of their very limited influence on those with real power.

Considerations of this kind need to be borne in mind in assessing any pamphleteer, but they are of particular relevance in relation to the works of Henry Fielding and Patrick Colquhoun, both of whom have been accorded an importance they do not deserve by later historians of police. Hugh Amory's account of the passing of the criminal reforms of 1751 has shown that (despite his fame and position) Fielding had no influence at all in shaping the legislation in question. It is likely too that Fielding's standing with the government (especially after his mishandling of the Bosavern Penlez affair) was very much lower than some of his admirers have been willing to admit.[7]

My own study of Patrick Colquhoun suggests that he, too, was a man of little or no influence in government circles. Indeed, the Home Office seems to have regarded him in much the same way as that interminable succession of cranks whose mission in life was to draw up fantastical schemes to eliminate the national debt. When the Home Office required advice on policing, it looked not to Colquhoun, but to trusted stipendiaries such as Richard Ford and Aaron Graham. The fact that Colquhoun published his treatise at all was symptomatic of his failure to gain attention in any other way. That it seems to have been received so well may indicate a receptive public, but in part at least it tells us no more than that Colquhoun was an astute self-publicist, prepared to go to considerable expense in order to present free copies to every influential individual he could think of (including an extra specially bound one for the King himself). Even the fact that the treatise ran into seven editions cannot be used as proof of its popularity, since each edition was produced with as much of an eye to opportunities for publicity as to sales.[8]

The second approach—that of studying a variety of reform initiatives— is potentially extremely rewarding, but it demands a mastery of an extensive range of sources and a very much more subtle and complex framework of discussion than has traditionally been allowed. In adopting this second approach, it is necessary to examine the following:

1. The various agencies of law enforcement that were available to Londoners and the extent to which they can or cannot be said to be "efficient." For the purposes of this essay, the focus will be on the magistracy and the watch, since they constitute the two principal law enforcement agencies of the period.
2. The nature of the reform initiatives that were attempted.

Only when this has been done does it become possible to explain why certain reforms were carried out and, even more important, whether the objectives that they achieved were those that were intended.

Agencies of Law Enforcement

The Magistracy

To those who believed that it was possible to order society in such a way as to render it crime-free (and this, in effect, is the message of almost all contemporary pamphleteers, including Fielding and Colquhoun), it was self-evident that existing law enforcement techniques and agencies were inadequate. No system that centered its efforts on coping with the results of crime, rather than on preventing it, could be justified. The magistracy, as the principal agency for law enforcement, naturally drew the brunt of such criticism.

Middlesex magistrates, who had jurisdiction over the largest and most populous sections of the metropolis, were said to connive at crime. They were, so it was said, men of low social status who were consequently unable to offer due reverence to the concept of justice. They did not enforce the laws properly, thus encouraging all the minor transgressions that were conventionally held to lead young men away from the paths of virtue onto the road to the gallows. Worst of all, they issued warrants and recognizances under circumstances in which they should have bent their efforts at mediation. That they did so could only be explained by reference to venality: "Send a dog to a Middlesex Justice with a shilling in its mouth," went the saying, "and he'll come back with a warrant."[9]

In reality, such criticisms were based on little more than unthinking prejudice. Whilst it seems unlikely that rural magistrates (even in the most closed of closed villages) were quite as powerful and as high-minded as critics of the Middlesex magistracy would have us believe, it remains clear that the role of the urban magistrate was very different from that of a rural one. To those accustomed to the view that magistrates were men of high social standing, able to use their social and economic status to back their legal authority in mediating disputes without formal recourse to the courts, it was difficult to appreciate the constraints under which metropolitan magistrates had to work.

Middlesex magistrates tended to be of lower social status than those elsewhere; and Middlesex residents were more litigious than those elsewhere. To outsiders, the existence of a causal link was self-evident: an active Middlesex magistrate was necessarily a "trading" one. Such an analysis took no account of the possibility that the more egalitarian social structure of the metropolis made people less willing to accept informal mediation by their social superiors and anxious for the apparent impartiality of a formal legal settlement. Indeed, a reluctance to accept the constraints of the kind of social structure that did encourage mediation may well have been one of the reasons that had driven them to the metropolis in the first place. It ignored the fact that a legal structure built around a system of private prosecution was inherently difficult to control,[10] especially in an urban area where the community was loosely knit, and where the complexity of the economic and social structure meant that the interests of the multiplicity of sections that made up the upper and middling classes were likely to diverge more frequently than in either a rural area or a major provincial town. It also left out of the equation the existence of large numbers of low attorneys and other unqualified advisers who were not only willing to counsel the poor on possible legal remedies, but who made those remedies readily available by their willingness to act on a contingency basis.[11] The problem of "trading justices," in the very limited sense of those who made a living from retailing warrants and recognizances, was almost entirely mythological.[12] The term was, as Norma Landau has remarked elsewhere, simply a convenient label "—and perhaps a libel."[13]

All this is not to suggest that Middlesex magistrates were men of integrity and honor: on the contrary, most, if not all, active justices were corrupt. The point to be made is that the kind of man likely to be recruited to the Middlesex commission was most probably a substantial tradesman of considerable importance in his own community. He was certainly not a gentleman (although he probably had aspirations to be regarded as one), but neither was he the "scum of the earth." Almost by definition, he was in a position to exploit the office of justice on a far larger scale than that involved in retailing a few warrants. A man might (if he were desperate enough) manage to scrape a living from criminal business; he could make himself both rich and powerful by using his judicial office to sustain and extend his leadership of the local community. The few who regularly transacted criminal business did so because they received a salary to do so or sought to reinforce their power-base. There may even have been a few who acted from a sense of duty. At least one (and probably more) were acting in collusion with criminal elements. But even here we are not talking of retailing justice to all comers—in the way usually alleged—but of corruption of a much higher order: a working partnership between magistrate and gangland leaders.[14]

The other major problem associated with the administration of justice in the London area was that of the fragmentation of authority. The City of London had long since spilled out of its boundaries into the county of Middlesex.[15] Worse still, authority in urban Middlesex was split between the county itself, the city of Westminster, and the liberty of the Tower Hamlets. Each jurisdiction had its own separate commission, although in practice there was a considerable overlap in the membership of the three Middlesex benches.

In theory, the major problem lay in the City boundary. The City was traditionally jealous of its privileges and ready to defend its rights against any encroachment. Any policing action close to or straddling the border thus required considerable cooperation. Perhaps the best examples of the need for joint action come from attempts to stage mass demonstrations, such as those that resulted in the Wilkite and Gordon Riots. In both cases people began to assemble, as was customary, in Moorfields. Moorfields was chosen, not just because it was a convenient open space, but because the City boundary ran right through it. When the magistrates of one jurisdiction tried to disperse the crowds, the mob simply moved across the boundary until the magistrates of the second jurisdiction could be found.[16] The need to produce two sets of justices naturally made dispersing crowds just that little bit more difficult. Perhaps it was something of a constructive difficulty, since it gave the crowd more time in which to register its protest.[17]

For the most part, however, the City boundary presented remarkably few difficulties—largely because the bulk of the metropolitan population was already living outside the City walls.[18] Paradoxically, the biggest problem of cooperation seems to have been not between Middlesex and the City, but between Middlesex and its subordinate jurisdiction of Westminster. Here the problem seems to have been very much one of leadership and personality. The Middlesex commission was by far the most important. It handled such a vast amount of criminal and administrative business that it had to sit eight times a year. The Westminster commission may once have rivalled it, but by the mid eighteenth century it was (despite the economic, social, and political primacy of the urban area it served) well on its way to becoming little more than a glorified divisional sessions.[19] Although it was competent to deal with serious criminal business, it rarely did so, since most Westminster residents chose to be tried in Middlesex. It met only four times a year and was poorly attended. The chairmanship of the Westminster sessions was thus an office of little significance compared to that of Middlesex.

The question of authority within the county, however, was not simply one of choosing between the two chairmen. The development of Bow Street as the center of policing in metropolitan Middlesex meant that the senior magistrate there was often the person best placed to advise the government on practical issues and strategic responses. The holders of all three offices thus had to cooperate and coordinate their activities for maximum effect. Such cooperation was not always forthcoming. Rivalries were at their worst between 1765 and 1780, when John Fielding was both senior magistrate at Bow Street and chairman of the Westminster bench, and when John Hawkins was chairman of the Middlesex one. Both men were arrogant, over-sensitive, and in possession of an inflated sense of their own importance. Each was jealous of the other and quick to take offense at any slight, however imaginary. The result was that strategic planning of the kind that was necessary, for example, during the Wilkite disturbances, suffered since Fielding was the man best placed to make decisions, while Hawkins was quick to take affront if he were expected to take orders from the chairman of a subordinate jurisdiction.[20] It would be wrong, however, to lay too much stress on such clashes. It was peculiarly unfortunate that the magistracy should contain two such domineering individuals in such important positions at the same time. Less abrasive personalities had less difficulty: we hear no more of such problems after 1780, when William Mainwaring was elected chairman of the Middlesex and Westminster benches, and when Sampson Wright succeeded as senior magistrate at Bow Street.

At a lower level, problems of jurisdiction presented few difficulties. The overlap in membership between the Middlesex, Westminster, and Tower Hamlets commissions meant that in practice many magistrates were able to act throughout the county. The result was that it became extremely difficult for the ordinary individual to distinguish between those who were and those who were not qualified to act in more than one jurisdiction. There are good grounds for suspecting that metropolitan magistrates habitually ignored their jurisdictional incompetence in minor cases.[21]

To modern observers (though not necessarily to contemporary ones), the most serious problem in terms of policing "efficiency" was the way in which the fragmentation of authority hampered the collection and collation of information. Yet this was scarcely a difficulty peculiar to London alone: the decentralized nature of government and the legal system made it a problem for the entire nation. Despite the obvious opportunities offered by London's wealth, what little we know about organized crime in the eighteenth century does not indicate that the problem was any greater there than elsewhere.[22] On the contrary, it might be argued that the very fact that historians have been more aware of the problem of organized crime in London than in other parts of the country is in itself evidence that London was exceptionally well served in terms of the collation of criminal intelligence, and that the emergence of Bow Street as a clearinghouse for criminal information provided the metropolis with a focus that was lacking elsewhere.[23] Nor should we ignore the importance of less reputable methods of gathering information: thieftakers ranged over the entire metropolitan area as a matter of course, and their intelligence networks were probably as good in their way as Henry or John Fielding could hope to achieve by more open means.

The Watch

Popular legend, fostered very largely by the proponents of Peel's police bill, would have us believe that the watch forces of London were fragmented, badly organized, and incompetent, being staffed largely by elderly and infirm individuals unable to earn a living in any other way. Fragmentation cannot be denied: the Metropolitan Police district replaced more than eighty local government units. Poor organization and incompetence are, however, another matter. By 1829, almost all urban parishes had reorganized their watch by means of local acts.[24] The provisions of such acts were not uniform, but the principles on which they were based were as follows: each abandoned the principles of voluntary service enjoined by the Statute of Winchester, and had substituted a force paid from the local rates.

Some parishes were regulated by more than one act. The classic and most often quoted example being that of St. Pancras, which is said to have had some eighteen different watch authorities in an area of little more than four square miles.[25] Once again, however, close inspection of the evidence suggests that fragmentation of this kind can be overstressed. Preliminary indications are that it was most characteristic of areas on the fringes of the metropolis. In other words, it was a product of the wave of speculative

Designed Etched & Published by George Cruikshank — Nov.r 1st 1829

Two policemen herald the beginning of the new regime by assaulting three ancient watchmen outside a tavern—but once the new police had taken to the streets, favorable representations of their conduct were rare. (British Museum, Dorothy George catalogue number 15982 no. 8 [1829]—*The New Police Act*)

building that hit London in the second half of the eighteenth century. As building developments reached into previously rural areas, they were provided with a watch force. Such forces were naturally confined to the new development, partly to make it more attractive to potential residents, and partly because it was neither feasible nor necessary to provide the same level of patrolling for remaining rural areas. Seen from such a perspective, one's attention is drawn less to the organizational weaknesses caused by fragmentation, and more toward a realization of just how highly watch forces must have been valued. Speculative builders or groups of residents would scarcely have gone to so much trouble (and expense) to provide an amenity that no one wanted.

The more one looks at the question of fragmentation, the more one begins to wonder just how much of a problem it was. To be sure, the existence of so many watch authorities in a large urban area ensured a certain lack of coordination. It also meant that the level and intensity of patrols varied from area to area, as did the quality of supervision and the extent to which parochial officials were willing to divert funding from other equally pressing aspects of local administration. But it would be a gross exaggeration to suggest that the necessary result of fragmentation was that each watch authority acted in isolation from the others. There may have been no formal coordinating machinery, but watch committees were nevertheless anxious to copy models of good practice, and they looked to each other for advice and information on the best ways to improve their service to the ratepayers.[26] It must also be recognized that fragmentation of control carried its own compensations in that it ensured that the watch was an extremely flexible instrument of policing—one that was highly responsive to local demands. Patrols could be increased, decreased, or completely redeployed virtually overnight in a way that would no longer be possible once the cumbersome bureaucracy of the Home Office and of the Metropolitan Police had intervened between people and police.

Nor is it clear that watchmen really were, as so often claimed, the "refuse of the workhouse."[27] It may have been true, at times when public concern was at a low level, that some parishes did recruit elderly or infirm men, but there is surprisingly little information to confirm it. Where there is evidence of the employment of individuals who would otherwise have become chargeable to the parish, the men concerned turn out to be surprisingly young: casualties of an economic system that could not eradicate seasonal unemployment and which, even at the best of times, left certain sections of the adult male population struggling with the effects of chronic underemployment.[28] A preliminary examination of the records suggests that watchmen were selected with considerable care. Applicants had to supply evidence of good character, and an upper age limit was invariably specified either by local regulation or in the Watching Act itself. Careful consideration was also given to the organization of beats, the positioning of watch boxes, and the best ways of maintaining an effective service.[29] Naturally, concern was at its height at times of crisis, but this is probably true of the administration of almost any policing agency either before or since.

Some parishes were certainly patrolled more intensively than others. In 1811, for example, Bethnal Green with a population of just over 33,000 had eighteen watchmen, two inspectors, and a beadle, whilst neighboring Shoreditch had seventy-five watchmen and six patrolmen to cope with a population of just under 44,000.[30] Put another way, Shoreditch provided more than three times as many watchmen per head of population as Bethnal Green. Yet in terms of the very limited job that watchmen were expected to do, variations of this kind presented few problems. The real difficulty came when an area that presented a single policing problem was policed by one or more parishes with differing priorities. Responsibility for patrolling the footpaths across Shepherd and Shepherdess Fields provided just such a problem in microcosm. These paths were used by people passing between Shoreditch and Islington, but although Islington was prepared to patrol its own section of the paths, Shoreditch refused to patrol the remainder, arguing that the paths were principally used by the parishioners of Islington and that it was no part of their duty to protect the residents of another parish.[31]

The same problem arose on a far grander scale in relation to the approach roads to London. Individual travellers, coaches, and post-boys provided rich and tempting targets for footpads and highwaymen, especially as almost all these roads ran through virtually deserted tracts of common or heath very soon after leaving the metropolis. Who was to protect these travellers? The roads in question did not simply run through more than one parish; they ran through one or more counties, and they were vital to the economic well-being of the entire region, if not of the nation. At times of crisis, the problem was solved by government financing. First in 1760–62, and again in the early 1780s, the magistrates of Bow Street organized mounted patrols. On both occasions they seem to have been successful; and on both occasions they lapsed on the government's refusal to take on a permanent commitment to what was perceived as essentially a local responsibility. Indeed, in 1764, George Grenville made his opposition (and incidentally his utter incomprehension of the problem) quite explicit when he complained that he simply could not see why anyone should expect the king of England to pay for a watch for the county of Middlesex.[32]

Reform Initiatives

The Magistracy

Throughout the second half of the eighteenth century, and possibly also earlier, there was a continuous though rarely publicized preoccupation with the shortage of active justices in the metropolitan area. In part, a periodic awareness of such a shortage was simply a product of the heightened anxieties generated by lengthening gaol calendars. But it was also true that the Middlesex commission suffered from a generational pattern of recruitment. When vigorous and active leadership was forthcoming—as for example in the persons of Thomas de Veil and Sir John Fielding—lesser men would come forward. As the leaders aged, so did their followers, with the result that a crisis of leadership was often accompanied by a crisis of numbers. This pattern can be traced very clearly in the period from the 1740s into the early 1750s, and again from the mid 1770s to the end of the 1780s. On both occasions, the fall in the numbers of active justices caused little anxiety until fears of a crime wave drew attention to the failings of the magistracy.[33]

The problems of recruiting active magistrates led to a variety of solutions. Those responsible for selecting magistrates took great care in vetting each and every applicant. They were heavily influenced by contemporary discussion of the problem of trading justices, and did their best to exclude persons of low social status. Critics continued to be scathing in their condemnation of recruitment procedures, but in reality they were so strict that it was probably more difficult to become a Middlesex magistrate than to join benches elsewhere: Henry Bate Dudley, for example, better known as the "Battling Parson," was not respectable enough for the Middlesex Commission, but he seems to have had little difficulty in becoming an Essex justice.[34]

Careful recruitment procedures were not necessarily the answer to the commission's problems. In some respects, they may actually have exacerbated the situation. A sense of public duty and an impartial interest in public affairs does not necessarily correspond to an index of social status. Amongst the applicants initially refused were John Harriott and Rice Davies, both of whom later became prominent and useful magistrates; others excluded may have been equally worthy.[35] By making it difficult to become a magistrate, successive lords lieutenant were concentrating power in a small number of hands, and thus increasing the opportunities available to those who, for whatever reason, did sell justice.

It might also be argued that a concentration on recruitment failed to address the important question of social legitimacy. Rural magistrates derived their legitimacy from their recognized social and economic position within the community. In almost all pre-industrial urban areas, the selection of magistrates was closely tied to the local government structure of the ruling corporation. Many of the criticisms that were regularly levelled at the Middlesex magistracy could also have been made of the City magistracy. That they were not was partly because the bulk of metropolitan criminal business arose from Middlesex, but also because of the office of City magistrate was coterminous with that of alderman. The process of becoming an alderman conferred upon an individual a social legitimacy that spilled over into his function as magistrate.

Arguably, the best way in which the Middlesex magistracy could cleanse itself of the reputation of the "trading justice" was either by the creation of a second metropolitan corporation (probably based on Westminster, which was traditionally known as a city but which was closer to a liberty in terms of its local government structure), or by the introduction of an elected magistracy. Neither were solutions that attracted widespread support. Central government already went in awe of the power of the City of London; the creation of a second great political fiefdom on the very doorstep of parliament was scarcely likely to command executive support. The one agency that might have formed the nucleus of a stronger local government structure in Westminster (the Court of Burgesses) had seen its powers steadily eroded. Similarly, proposals for an elected magistracy never became part of a serious political agenda, in part because they were increasingly associated with metropolitan radicalism.

Although concern about the quality of recruitment to the magistracy forms a continuous backdrop to the problem of magisterial shortages, it was by no means the only response. Whenever a sense of crisis about crime and criminality re-emerged, positive steps were taken to make serving as an active justice more attractive. In the early part of the century, the Middlesex commission benefited as much and probably more than other counties when political purges of the magistracy were abandoned.[36] Fear of litigation was also advanced as a major deterrent to service. Accordingly, in 1751, a year in which our attention is more usually drawn to attempts to reform the criminal law, the very substantial legal protection already enjoyed by justices was strengthened still further by the passage of "An Act for Rendering Justices of the Peace More Safe in the Execution of their Office." The preamble to this act makes great play with the need to afford proper protection to both justice and subject, but in practice its provisions made it extremely difficult to bring a successful civil action against a magistrate no matter how unjust his actions.[37]

But perhaps the most obvious of positive steps that could be taken was the provision of salaries to selected magistrates. Quite how far back this goes is difficult to determine. There had always been a "court justice," that is, one who could be relied upon to carry out government policy in the metropolitan area; and it seems unlikely that those who undertook this role went unrewarded. Thomas de Veil was in possession of a sinecure office, was able to reclaim his expenses and, toward the end of his life, also had a salary. John Poulson, who was active in the few years immediately before Henry Fielding's appointment, also received expenses. Fielding himself made no secret of his salary, and it is known that payments were also made to his successors at Bow Street as well as to Saunders Welch. Later in the century, it is possible to trace a single payment to the active East End magistrate David Wilmot, although whether this was a one-off payment or part of a regular arrangement remains unclear.[38]

One suspects that other justices were also in receipt of salaries, although it should be stressed that these were not necessarily paid by the government. In some areas (notably Shadwell), there was a continuity of judicial activity that leads one to suspect that some vulnerable local group (possibly shipowners and/or coal undertakers) were contributing toward a magisterial stipend.[39] Certainly the "generosity" of some sectional interests cannot be overlooked. In the 1790s, for example, Patrick Colquhoun made little secret of the valuable gifts of plate he had received. Who can tell how many others received such gifts, or how much greater Colquhoun's might have been if the bodies concerned had not known that he already received a government salary?[40]

Even if it were true that salaries were available on a wider basis than has usually been assumed, provision was nevertheless patchy and incoherent. All the same, it was extremely effective. By paying a few key figures, the government secured a high quality of leadership that in itself attracted more men to serve. It also ensured that those who were attracted knew that they would be serving alongside experienced men, and that they would not be overwhelmed by the pressure of business. Becoming an active magistrate did not mean taking on an open-ended commitment: the man who chose to act alongside the Fieldings or Saunders Welch knew that his service was valued even if he were only able to act for a few hours a month.

The success of the system of salaries was to have a decisive influence on all subsequent debates about the future of the metropolitan magistracy. Experience of the Middlesex Justices Act would demonstrate that in practice the creation of a stipendiary magistracy would simply encourage ordinary justices to desert criminal business altogether, but this eventuality went largely unforeseen. It seemed much more obvious that if a few salaries could have such a beneficial effect, the provision of even more could only improve things still further.

The problem was that establishing a network of stipendiary magistrates would need both executive sanction and legislative change. It was difficult enough to persuade successive and somewhat parsimonious governments that the necessary expense could be justified—although here at least the fabled profits of the trading justices must have helped foster a belief (subsequently proved to be erroneous) that income would offset expenditure. The real difficulty came with the necessity for legislative action. Domestic policy initiatives were not high on any eighteenth-century government's agenda. Domestic policy initiatives that would provoke major constitutional debates were even more unlikely than most to attract the necessary ministerial backing.

The office of Home Secretary, and before that of Secretary of State, was one that was traditionally filled by men of considerable political importance; it was, however, rarely occupied by astute or ambitious politicians. It should not go unmentioned that the Middlesex Justices Act of 1792 and the Metropolitan Police Act of 1829 (both of which represented major inroads on traditional constitutional principles) were put through by exceptionally determined and able politicians, and that even so they were forced to resort to a certain measure of stealth. The Middlesex Justices Act escaped close scrutiny by being dressed up as a temporary measure. The Metropolitan Police Act was given an innocuous title ("An Act for Improving the Police") and passed in the wake of recommendations by a packed committee; part of the fury that greeted it derived from the belief that parliament had been tricked into passing it. In addition, of course, opposition to both measures was weakened by excluding the City from their provisions.

An awareness of the possible depth of opposition is crucial to understanding just why it took so long for a fairly limited measure such as the 1792 Act to pass. It is clear that a stipendiary magistracy was under discussion in the early 1760s, and that the system of rotation offices that was established in 1763 resulted from those discussions. There are indications that the scheme was revived c.1774. On both occasions it was pushed aside because of changes in the political climate: in 1763 because of the fall of Lord Bute, and in 1774 because of the general election and the intensification of the long-running disputes that would shortly lead to the secession of the American colonies. But a major factor must also have been the nature of opposition itself. Given the constitutional difficulties, it was essential that support from metropolitan leaders should be strong, united, and unequivocal. It is unlikely that this was so. The major proponent of reform was John Fielding, but the very fact that he supported such a measure was probably enough to dilute any enthusiasm felt by Sir John Hawkins, the powerful chairman of the Middlesex bench. Nor was Fielding particularly popular with Middlesex's most famous member of parliament, and it seems unlikely that any government would have been willing to risk a renewal of the cry of "Wilkes and Liberty."[41]

A decade later many of these problems had been removed. In 1780, the arguments about London's policing were revived amidst the flames of the Gordon Riots. Three years later, the end of the American War of Independence signalled the outbreak of yet another period of rising crime rates and ensured the continuation of the debate. The initial reaction to the crisis was, somewhat predictably, a campaign to attract more justices which culminated in a major revision of the membership of the commission in 1783. It was the failure of this attempt to provide additional active justices that forced the issue of a stipendiary magistracy back on to the agenda. The uproar that greeted the Westminster Police Bill of 1785 should not be permitted to divert our attention from the fact that even the severest critics of the bill went out of their way to reiterate their support for a more limited measure.[42] There can be little doubt that John Reeves, who was commissioned by the Home Office to draw up the bill, went far beyond his brief.

One must also add that those who criticized the bill as impracticable were probably right—and that those who criticized it as draconian were probably overreacting. It was adopted almost clause for clause by the Irish Parliament on behalf of the City of Dublin, but the force was too small to carry out its extensive duties properly, and it suffered from the additional handicap of being both expensive and unpopular. Its ultimate failure had more to do with the political struggle between Dublin Castle and Dublin Corporation than to its intrinsic merits, or lack of them. In 1795, the castle handed control back to the corporation and the parishes.[43]

The Middlesex Justices Act of 1792

In retrospect, it is easy to see the introduction of a stipendiary magistracy as a major extension of state power, but it must be emphasized that this was not at all the way in which contemporaries perceived the matter. One thinks now of a stipendiary as a professional lawyer who is paid to deal with the criminal business generated by an area with which he may have little or no close ties. In 1792, the vision of a stipendiary was rather different. Then a stipendiary was simply an ordinary magistrate who received a payment to compensate for the unusually onerous nature of part of his duties. The salary was to encourage men to take on the burden of criminal business, not to create a separate class of professional magistrates. In short, the purpose of the act was to strengthen local rather than central institutions. In this way it provides a striking contrast to the Metropolitan Police Act, which was clearly designed from the beginning to strengthen central government at the expense of the parochial authorities.

In the long run, of course, the Middlesex Justices Act did have the effect of strengthening central government, and it is perhaps worth examining just how this came about. It was a process that began almost as soon as the act had passed. Dundas did his best to appoint active and respected Middlesex magistrates to the new posts, but the general shortage of justices made this difficult. Many of the men he appointed were new to the bench; few thought it necessary to take on a wider role in either parochial or county affairs. There was thus from the beginning an incipient gulf between the stipendiaries and the Middlesex magistracy in general.[44]

The policies of later Home Secretaries widened the gulf still further. It became less and less common for serving Middlesex magistrates to be appointed. Instead, stipendiaries were increasingly drawn from the ranks of the nation's barristers. This transition, which was crucial to the transformation of the role of the stipendiaries, seems to have taken place with virtually no discussion at all (at least not public discussion). The most obvious explanation—that it was to secure a level of professional expertise—is not wholly convincing. In the early stages, many of the barristers appointed had either never practiced or had practiced without success; one was stone deaf.[45] It seems likely that in these early stages the selection of barristers simply masked the real preference, which was as always for gentlemen. The belief that stipendiaries should have a professional legal training emerged at or about the time of Lord Sidmouth's appointment as Home Secretary, and may have been something of a reaction to criticisms of incompetence in the handling of the Ratcliffe Highway murders.

The gulf between the Middlesex magistracy in general and the stipendiaries also had important organizational implications. In the early years, the Home Office made no consistent attempt to impose its authority on the stipendiaries, and rarely tried to interfere in day-to-day matters. Its role was rather more active than before—it sent circulars and exhortations—but it was still a very low-key affair. At the same time, the very fact that so few stipendiaries took part in parochial or county affairs meant that it was extremely difficult for traditional local government agencies to exert any influence over them. Indeed, in many areas, relationships between the stipendiaries and the vestries were extremely strained.

The stipendiaries thus existed in a sort of power vacuum. Although in retrospect it is easy to see that the Home Office would eventually fill that vacuum, it actually took a remarkably long time for this to happen. The process was still far from complete by the time Sidmouth left office. Interventions were becoming more common, but there was still no coherent overall strategy or offer of leadership. What one sees is a series of minor bureaucratic and administrative interventions rather than a definite attempt to set (let alone enforce) policy objectives.

There seems to be no doubt that as far as contemporaries were concerned the Middlesex Justices Act was a resounding success. As soon as the act had been passed and the stipendiaries had taken office, the crime figures began to fall just as sharply as they had risen a decade earlier. Historians rightly doubt that there was any causal link between these events: crime fell in much the same way all over the country for reasons that probably have more to do with the outbreak of war with revolutionary France than changes in the organization of the magistracy.[46] What we have to appreciate is that contemporaries saw things very differently; they sincerely believed that the reduction in crime was due to the introduction of a stipendiary magistracy.

The Nightly Watch Regulation Bill

The birth of the new century brought with it a renewal of fears about rising metropolitan crime. But the apparent success of the Middlesex Justices Act meant that the framework of debate had altered. On the one hand, it was no longer possible to blame the magistracy for crime—though it was easy enough to accuse individual stipendiaries of incompetence. On the other hand, the very existence of the stipendiaries meant that the Home Office now had access to a pool of virtually professional police advisors, of whom the most important were Richard Ford and Aaron Graham. The result was that more and more criticisms of policing came to center on deficiencies in the watch. This was, of course, nothing new. Problems in the watch had attracted attention at every period of crisis and had regularly resulted in small-scale local initiatives, some of which were temporary (such as offering rewards and/or organizing extra patrols), and some of which were permanent (such as Watching Acts). What was different this time was the emergence of a consensus of opinion amongst those in power about the nature and scale of reforms that were required. Stipendiaries and the Home Office both believed that the way forward was by legislation that would force the parishes to provide a more uniform standard of watching and which would provide for a greater measure of cooperation between them, most probably by transferring at least part of the responsibility for supervising the watch from the vestries to the stipendiaries.[47]

Stipendiaries were advocating reform along these lines as early as 1802, but nothing was actually attempted for another decade. One factor in the delay was undoubtedly the reluctance of a relatively unstable ministry to become embroiled in what was bound to be a controversial initiative—one which would almost certainly provide a welcome platform for Sir Francis Burdett, whose views on policing were so far out of tune with reality that he quite seriously advocated a return to the provisions of the Statute of

Winchester.[48] The second, and perhaps equally important factor, was Treasury opposition to any proposal that would involve increased expenditure: Britain was, after all, engaged in a major war—one that was generating unprecedented expense. The government took over the Thames Police Office only when the Treasury was convinced beyond doubt that savings in revenue justified the cost of the establishment. In 1805, the Bow Street magistrates were at last allowed to introduce a horse patrol on a permanent basis. Even this modest proposal had to be accompanied by an explanation stressing the economies that were likely to ensue since "one of the necessary consequences of the measure will be to render a considerable part of the Foot Patrol . . . no longer requisite."[49]

In December 1811, attitudes concerning the need for further police reform were given a greater sense of urgency by the Ratcliffe Highway murders. It is difficult to envisage just what kind of police force could deter a mass murderer of questionable sanity; nevertheless, the panic that these events engendered was such that the Home Office was flooded with proposals for police reform. For its part, Parliament set up a select committee to examine the problems of the policing of London. The bill that emerged from the select committee's discussions deserves, it is argued, a rather more prominent position in the history of police reform than it has hitherto been given.

It has already been suggested that the Middlesex Justices Act was intended to strengthen rather than to weaken local institutions. The Nightly Watch Regulation Bill shows a similar determination to balance the needs of greater uniformity with demands for local rather than central control. In essence, the bill attempted to set minimum standards for every parish in metropolitan Middlesex. Each parish was to appoint patrols and watchmen whose numbers would be determined by the size of their population. The power of selection and appointment was to remain in local hands, that is, with the trustees of any existing local act, or with elected representatives in areas where there was no local act. Efficiency and uniformity were to be ensured by giving the supervision of the watch (including powers of dismissal on grounds of corruption or incompetence) to the stipendiaries.[50]

From the point of view of the central government, the solution was ideal. It avoided the appearance of an increase in executive power and patronage, and it was cheap, since the cost would be borne by the parishes. To the vestries, the benefits were less clear. Few wanted to relinquish control of the watch to the Home Office; on the other hand, they almost all wanted financial help. The increased expenditure required to implement the reforms would place a heavy burden on metropolitan ratepayers during a period of considerable economic hardship. Shoreditch estimated that its expenditure would have to be doubled at a time when it was already unable to collect rates from nearly half its residents. The vestries also resented the idea of giving up the supervision of the watch to the stipendiary magistrates. To give such wide powers to the stipendiaries was to risk, as one writer put it, producing "discontent in the minds of men who dedicate their time gratuitously to the service of the public." The strength of parochial opposition ensured that the bill was dropped.[51]

The Metropolitan Police Act

London: The Testing Ground of Reform

The failure of the Nightly Watch Regulation Bill did not of course mean that demands for the reform of the watch went away. Under Lord Sidmouth, the Home Office took an increasingly active role in supervising both Bow Street and the stipendiaries. The police magistrates themselves remained firmly convinced that the way forward lay in a new system of watching which would be under their control. Sidmouth went some way toward meeting their demands by banning the employment of watchmen over the age of forty and giving the stipendiaries powers to dismiss parochial officers.[52] The parishes themselves were also taking steps to improve the quality of their watch forces. Local government institutions in the metropolis were strong and active. In the early nineteenth century, they responded to fears of rising crime in exactly the same way as they had done in the eighteenth century: by increasing the strength of their watch forces, and by improving supervision and reorganizing shifts and beats. Others encouraged the formation of Associations for the Prosecution of Felons.[53]

It was perhaps only to be expected that the question of reform would be re-examined with the appointment of a new Home Secretary in 1822. This was in part because of a continuing sense of crisis about crime, but there was also a new factor: a growing concern about riot and disorder. If one focuses narrowly on the experience of London during this period, it becomes abundantly clear that such fears were, if not unfounded, certainly extremely exaggerated. In the wider context, however, they are easily explicable. For much of its history, London's precocious social and economic development had set it apart from the rest of the country. But by the early nineteenth century the nation was well on its way to becoming an urban rather than a rural society, and a new generation of commercial and manufacturing cities had emerged in Wales, the midlands, and the north. To men of rigid social outlook (such as Peel himself) such a development—with all its potential for overturning traditional patterns of order—was a fearsome one. They were not reassured by the mere absence of disorder in London. In their eyes the metropolis was little more than Blackburn or Burnley writ large; it was therefore self-evident that it might erupt into riot at any moment.[54] Indeed, one sometimes suspects that memories of the Gordon Riots were sharper in the 1820s than at any time in the preceding four decades.[55]

Nor should we ignore the possibility that the national context impinged in other ways. The creation of a metropolitan police force proved to be a somewhat isolated reform: professional police forces were not created in other areas until much later, and even then the importance of some form of local control remained paramount. But it is far from clear that this was the result Peel intended. On the contrary, an examination of the few pronouncements that he made on the subject would suggest that for him London was simply a testing ground for the creation of a national police force that would be firmly under the control of the central government. It was not just London but "the whole country" which had "entirely outgrown its Police Institutions."[56]

Personnel and Service

Furthermore, it is questionable whether the introduction of the new police really did bring about the marked improvements that traditional accounts of the reform process would have us believe. Before 1829, the typical London watchman was under forty (and even before Sidmouth insisted on this, most parishes operated an upper age limit of forty-five). His primary task was to patrol the streets at night and to cope with drunks, prostitutes, and brawlers. He was poorly paid and augmented his income by performing various services for local inhabitants such as providing early morning alarm calls. Depending on the opportunities presented by the economic and social structure of his neighborhood, he may or may not have been in a position to receive "gifts" from publicans, prostitutes, and others anxious to secure his goodwill. He would check that premises were properly locked, and he would stop and search unusual or suspicious characters, even though he had no legal authority to do so. His pay was so poor that he would almost certainly have a second job. Fatigue, bad weather, or sheer boredom would impel him from time to time to duck out of his duties unless carefully supervised. In the unlikely event that he came across a serious crime in progress, he would attempt to deal with it; but, in general, his was a job of order maintenance rather than of detection.[57]

There was little about the advent of the Metropolitan Police that altered any of this. Technology apart, there is after all very little about the work of patrolling the streets that has changed in the past century and a half. Constables in the new police were as badly paid as their predecessors in the watch—perhaps even more so since most parishes gave their watchmen clothing (usually a greatcoat but sometimes boots and other items too) in addition to their wages, whilst police constables were made to pay for their uniforms. Not surprisingly, the regulations prohibiting constables from taking other jobs were regularly broken, and moonlighting appears to have been a commonly accepted practice until comparatively recent times. Nor is it true that constables in the new police were any healthier than the watchmen they replaced. Living conditions for the poor in early nineteenth-century London were scarcely conducive to the promotion of a high standard of physical fitness, and early Metropolitan Police records make it abundantly clear that the poor health of recruits (and their consequent inability to cope with even moderate physical exercise, such as that involved in walking the beat) was a major problem for the commissioners.[58]

Conventional accounts of the formation of the Metropolitan Police emphasize the efficiency of the new organization and the way in which this led to higher standards of policing. In the short term, at least, this was simply not true. One of the main reasons for parochial opposition to the Metropolitan Police (apart, that is, from constitutional objections) was that the service offered was so poor. Traditionally, the watch was a night one. Most parishes employed a few streetkeepers to patrol by day to cope with obstructions and nuisances, but they reserved the major part of their resources for the provision of an intensive night patrol. As early as 1744, the parish of Christ Church, Spitalfields, had organized its watchmen so that "every inhabitant may have a watchman by their door every three-quarters of an hour."[59] Note that the word "inhabitant" was carefully chosen: this was not a watch on the principal thoroughfares (which was all that the Metropolitan Police would provide), but included every street, alleyway, and courtyard in the parish. Preliminary indications are that this kind of service was far from exceptional, and it should be noted that the number of watchmen employed by Spitalfields (relative to its population) was actually rather lower than in most metropolitan parishes. Furthermore, watchmen knew their beats intimately: few were longer than five or six hundred yards, and many were considerably shorter.

All this changed for the worse with the advent of the Metropolitan Police. The new police had beats that were measured in miles rather than yards, and each police division was patrolled, at all times, by a total of forty men. In most areas this was an increase in terms of daylight patrols, but it was a major cut in night patrols. Since the boundaries of a police division did not correlate to those of the parishes, it is difficult to make an exact comparison. But it is perhaps worth pointing out that in 1828, some 1,700 watchmen were employed in the City of Westminster and other urban parishes. Even if all the parishes employed a double shift system (which they did not), this meant that well over 800 men were on patrol at any hour of the night. In 1829, they were replaced by some 900 police constables—only a quarter of whom were on patrol at any one time. By 1830, when the organization covered the entire Metropolitan Police District—that is, an area bounded by a radius of twelve miles from Charing Cross—there were just over 3,000 police constables. Later in the same year, a reorganization of shifts to concentrate more men on night patrols meant that some 2,000 of them were available to police the whole of the Metropolitan Police District at night.[60]

Added to the decline in numbers of men patrolling the darkened streets was the apparent decline in the caliber of men recruited. Policemen were unpopular, badly paid, and subject to an onerous discipline that forced them to wear uniforms, even when off duty; to live in cramped and uncomfortable section houses even when married;[61] and which forbade them to enter into any conversation (especially with their colleagues) when on duty.[62] They were given little training and sent out on the streets to do a boring and tedious job that they did not fully understand. Not surprisingly, a large proportion of those recruited were unsuitable. "The men attached to the police," reported one parish in 1830, "have frequently been seen drunk upon duty and openly to associate and to frequent public houses with prostitutes and other suspicious characters." Such allegations were not founded on mere anti-police prejudice. One has only to look at the extraordinarily high turnover in police personnel to realize just how difficult it was for the commissioners to recruit and to keep good men. In the first two years, more than 3,000 constables left the force, of whom nearly two-thirds had been dismissed (eighty percent of them for offenses involving drunkenness). In addition, the decision to avoid recruiting former watchmen (coupled with the very low wages) meant that almost all the new policemen came to the job as strangers both to the tasks they were expected to perform and to the areas in which they were to serve. Many came from outside London, and a distressingly high proportion seem to have been Irishmen "in whom," as the vestry of St. Thomas, Southwark, delicately phrased it, "they cannot place that confidence nor feel that security they could in their own countrymen."[63]

The parishes were further incensed by their inability to control the costs of the new police. This is a question that deserves far more attention than it is possible to give here. There are three issues to be considered. The first is whether the cost per parish went up or not. The government's answer to criticisms of increased costs was to cite the example of Hackney, where the expense of the new police was just over £200 less in its first year than under the old watching system. This reply was almost certainly deliberately disingenuous, since Hackney had had the reputation of maintaining a higher level of watch service than any other London parish. St. Luke estimated that it was paying some £1200 extra under the new system, and that the service received was so poor that twenty of its former watchmen were being employed by means of a voluntary subscription. St. Thomas, Southwark, maintained that its rate had gone up from £50 (for the services of a full-time night watchman) to £156 13s. 1d (for an unpredictable once-a-day visit from a police constable). The second issue is whether the new police rate was paid in the same way as the old watch rate. Many of the early complaints seem to indicate that

But I tell you tis no use your coming here there is no property left on my land but the Old Scare Crow - no one will steal him I should think

The extension, in 1830, of the Metropolitan Police District to cover the whole of the area within a twelve-mile radius from Charing Cross, meant that it included substantial stretches of open countryside and farmland. Even in the center of London, ratepayers found the cost of the new service to be exorbitant; little wonder that their rural counterparts wondered why it cost so much to protect so little. (British Museum, Dorothy George catalogue number 16144 [1830]—*Extension of the New Police*)

more residents found themselves liable to pay the new rate than the old one; it may also have been more difficult to evade. The final consideration is the extent to which the creation of a universal rate for the new Metropolitan Police District shifted the burden of cost *between* parishes, and in particular the way in which it forced rural parishes to contribute toward the expense of policing the urban area. Thus the inhabitants of Ealing protested in 1830 that the average cost of depredations in the parish had not exceeded £100 per annum at any time in the previous twenty years, but that under the new system they would be paying £880 police rate annually.[64]

The Question of Central Control

The destruction of the parochial watch and the substitution of an inferior and allegedly vastly more expensive service—one that was deliberately constructed to make it difficult to complain about the conduct of individual officers—provide reasons enough for much of the opposition that greeted the Metropolitan Police. But there were other elements too—questions that related to constitutionality and the nature of English liberties. It has previously been suggested that the task of policing any community is inherently very similar, and that there was thus very little difference between the basic tasks of the Metropolitan Police constable and the parochial watchman. This should not be taken to mean that continuities outweighed discontinuities, for the Metropolitan Police Act introduced two major innovations that had profound constitutional implications.

The first was the way in which the new institution was deliberately divorced from the local community. The police were completely under the control of the central government: Londoners had no say whatsoever in either its organization or its deployment. It cannot be emphasized too strongly just how extraordinary was this extension of central government control. The great social reforms of the nineteenth century all led, to a greater or lesser extent, to an increase in the power of the central government; but in every other instance there was some attempt to preserve local power structures. Only in the creation of the Metropolitan Police does one see the deliberate and total destruction of local government powers. Local ties were weakened still further by ensuring that the boundaries of police divisions were established without reference to existing local government units, and the commissioners made their contempt for the parishes still more explicit by their overt prejudice against the employment of former watchmen. Policemen were expected to get to know their beats and to reside within their areas, but they were not permitted to live in the community in the normal way. Rather, they were forced to live in what their commissioners chose to call section houses, but which in fact were nothing more than barracks—and perhaps readers should be reminded that at this time barracks were something of a rarity on the British mainland, since contemporaries associated them with the threat of military despotism.

The second major innovation of the Metropolitan Police Act was the appearance of this highly visible quasi-military force on the streets of London during the hours of daylight. Although a small Bow Street Day Patrol had been formed in 1822, before 1828 no parish anywhere in London had considered it either necessary or desirable to provide the kind of intensive daylight patrols that were the hallmark of the new police. Even after the reorganization of shifts in October 1830 that put the majority of police constables on to night duty, the number of men patrolling the streets by day was greater than it had ever been under the old watching system.

Day Patrols and Standards of Social Discipline

The characteristic of daytime patrolling, as we know from studies of policing initiatives in provincial Britain a generation or so later, is the attempt to impose a new standard of social discipline.[65] Sure enough, in these early years a consideration of both the complaints against the police and of the commissioners' directives to their men reveals a pattern of conflict in which the police came to be seen, in Edwin Chadwick's own words, "as reformers of the rich [sent] to act against the labouring classes."[66] There are indications, however, that the conflict in London was far more serious than the battles that were yet to be fought in the provinces. In the early years there are no signs of the emergence of the legendary British "bobby"—those restrained, deferential individuals who came to be seen (by the respectable classes at least) as little more than "useful servants for coping with the various unpleasantries of urban life."[67] Rather, we see a widespread belief amongst respectable and dangerous classes alike that the introduction of the Metropolitan Police amounted (both in practice and in theory) to nothing less than a systematic and deliberate attack upon English liberties. This belief deserves greater and far more sympathetic consideration than has generally been allowed.

Confirmation of the repressive nature of the new institution comes from a consideration of its structure. Colonel Rowan, the man who was clearly regarded as the senior of the two commissioners and who was in effective operational control, was not only an ex-army officer but an Irish magistrate to boot, and therefore accustomed to a far more authoritarian social and legal structure than had hitherto existed anywhere on the mainland. The military nature of the new force was further emphasized by the recruitment of ex-NCOs to fill senior positions, by the use of uniform, and by the insistence on elementary drill. It was made still more explicit by the construction of section houses in which constables were to live more like an occupying army than a civilian force.

The metaphor of an occupying army is not one that is chosen at random, for Londoners in 1829 must have found it extremely difficult to distinguish between this new and supposedly civilian force and the military. True, the new police were not issued with firearms, but contemporary firearms were so inaccurate that they would have been of very little use in an urban situation anyway.[68] One is tempted to wonder, therefore, like the critic of the Irish County Police Act of 1787, whether the Metropolitan Police Force really was meant to be a new institution, or whether it was not perhaps an attempt "to disguise an army of soldiers under the name of constables."[69] The conventional historiography makes much of the virtues of a civilian police, suggesting, amongst other things, that a civilian police would be more effective in crowd control than the traditional resort to the army. But to assume that a new and untried institution would automatically have

THE POLICE FORCE ON DUTY.

Early policemen bore little resemblance to the legend of the restrained and deferential British "bobby"; allegations of police brutality were widely publicized—and believed. (British Museum, Dorothy George catalogue number 16981—*The Police Force on Duty*)

greater expertise in techniques of crowd control than the army—which had been doing the job (albeit reluctantly) for generations—is to underestimate the difficulties and complexities of the task. One also needs to remember that calling out the army to assist the civil power did not carry with it the connotations of ultimate armed confrontation in the eighteenth century in the way that it would do in modern Britain. Troops rarely fired on crowds; their presence was just one more step in a complex and almost ritualized process of confrontation and intimidation that was designed to defuse tension with as little bloodshed as possible.

Perhaps it is not too cynical to suggest that the one major and easily identifiable distinction to be made between the new police and the army was a very simple one: the new police were not counted in the army returns, and consequently the costs did not come out of general taxation but out of the pockets of London ratepayers. The return of peace had brought two major problems for the government's conduct in relation to the army. Traditional fears about the role of a standing army, and its possible misuse by an authoritarian executive government, had soon reappeared. Moreover, the legacy of war debt and economic dislocation made an army look like an expensive luxury. In 1829, there were some 22,000 troops in England and Wales, nearly 6,000 of whom were tied down by the disturbances in the Northern District;[70] the creation of the Metropolitan Police Force therefore represented a covert increase of some fifteen percent in the numbers of men available to deal with the government's domestic difficulties.

In short, despite Peel's assurances of moderation, and his low-key presentation of the measure as one designed to improve rather than radically to reform the police of the metropolis, it is highly likely that this *was* a deliberate attempt to create exactly the kind of semi-military system of surveillance that opponents of police reform had always feared. Peel's new police was designed to be a "preventive" one in the classic eighteenth-century sense of those words. It was not intended to discourage crime by guarding the streets, but to regulate and prevent social indiscipline (including, one suspects, manifestations of lower-class political discontent).

"The absence of crime," wrote the commissioners to their men, "will be considered the best proof of the complete efficiency of the police." And this great end was to be achieved by ensuring that all potential criminals realized "that they are known and strictly watched, and that certain detection will follow any attempt they may make to commit a crime." So great was the emphasis on the preventive effects of police surveillance in these early years that it was not uncommon for constables responsible for beats on which burglaries had occurred to be suspended or even dismissed altogether, since the commission of the crime was interpreted as conclusive evidence of some dereliction of duty. The climate of opinion that led *Blackwood's Magazine* to denounce the new police as "general spies," which led a coroner's inquest to return a verdict of justifiable homicide on the body of Police Constable Culley (stabbed to death by a political demonstrator), and which caused a respectable jury to acquit the man who killed him, was neither created nor sustained by radical agitation alone. Peel's "crushers" were feared and disliked by all.[71]

Seen from this perspective, the emergence of the Metropolitan Police as

JOHN BULL & HIS NEW POLICE.

John Bull, weighed down by a double burden of taxes and debt, stands between two savage dogs. The dogs—dressed in police uniform—make it abundantly clear that no protest will be tolerated. (British Museum, Dorothy George catalogue number 16201 [1830]—*John Bull and his New Police*)

a new and distinctive model for urban policing was a sign not of success but of failure. The image of the restrained, imperturbable British "bobby" was formed in the course of a wholesale retreat from the aggressively authoritarian stance initially adopted. In part, this was clearly a function of the complexities of metropolitan society and culture. Peel's knowledge and experience of policing were drawn from his experiences in Ireland, but the kind of semi-military policing that had been imposed on a rural peasant society was much more difficult to sustain in a cosmopolitan area renowned both for its political egalitarianism, and for a social and economic structure that encouraged extremely subtle gradations of rank and property. Again, one would point out that, despite contemporary fears, London was probably a far more orderly place in 1829 than at any time previously: repressive policing was both inappropriate and unnecessary.

The Question of Efficient Policing

But it is also necessary to return to the vexed question of what constitutes "efficient" policing. The formation of the new police has traditionally been discussed in purely organizational terms—a single policing authority being perceived as a more rational and therefore more efficient use of resources than several. To modern commentators, accustomed to criticisms that center more often on the complexity and impersonality of its vast bureaucracy, such a view seems hopelessly simplistic: if the task of administering and coordinating the activities of the Metropolitan Police Force seems formidable even in the age of the computer, we can reasonably suppose that it was not without difficulty in the age of the quill.

In the course of this essay, the writer has attempted to show that whether judged in terms of perceived need, of quality of personnel, or of cost, it is highly unlikely that the new police really were more efficient than the old. Quality of performance is a far more difficult measure to apply. Although it is believed that the new police had a considerable impact on minor street crimes—drunkenness, loitering and the like, surprisingly little is known about their role in the enforcement of the law in a broader context—especially in the prevention, detection, and prosecution of serious crimes such as burglary, theft, or murder. Moreover, it is highly unlikely that quality of performance is determined by organizational structure alone, as some of the older accounts of the formation of the Metropolitan Police would seem to assume.

In assessing the impact of the new police one must also bear in mind the almost symbiotic relationship between policing and the trial process. In purely functional terms, the object of policing is to generate convictions. The nature of policing is thus determined as much by the courts as by organizational structures. This can be seen even before 1829 in the way in which changes in the trial process, such as the increased use of defense counsel and the evolution of rules of evidence, had helped bring about a degree of professionalization amongst London's thieftakers. After 1829, the courts became extremely sensitive to the question of police abuses. This was fostered in part by institutional rivalries, since the vast expansion of summary jurisdiction meant that an increasing number of cases were tried by stipendiaries who were deeply resentful of the new police. But the stipendiaries' fears of police powers were also shared by the higher courts.[72]

The result, as Wilbur Miller has pointed out, was that the Metropolitan Police were forced to cultivate an image of impersonal authority, and in so doing greater restraints were imposed on the policeman's use of his personal power than was common in more democratically controlled urban police forces. By mid-century, London policemen employed their powers to arrest on suspicion, or use a charge of disorderly conduct to cover an otherwise arbitrary detention, far less frequently than their New York counterparts, although in theory the structure of the Metropolitan Police imposed a far more authoritarian concept of policing than did that of the New York police. Indeed, if the freedom to use stop and search techniques at will, to resort to physical violence, or to wield powers of arbitrary arrest are conducive to "efficient" policing, then arguably the Metropolitan Police constable was far worse off than his eighteenth-century counterpart.

Toward a Reassessment of the Metropolitan Police Act

It should by now be apparent that what we see in 1829 is by no means a long overdue reform, but rather a major innovation that is difficult to explain by reference to the problems of London alone. Metropolitan policing arrangements were certainly fragmented, but they were not outmoded or inefficient. Indeed, the one area in which it might have been possible to sustain serious criticisms of inadequacy—the absence of a coherent detective force—remained untouched. What is even more puzzling is that the reform that was introduced was so different from that which "expert" opinion had so long advocated in that it weakened instead of strengthened the executive role of the stipendiary magistracy, and thus began a process that would soon lead to the complete separation of the magistracy's executive and judicial functions.

What then was the motivation behind the Metropolitan Police Act? Much of the explanation must lie with Peel himself. Peel, as is so often pointed out, was no conventional Tory squire, but a representative of that new force in British political life: the aggressive and upwardly mobile industrial middle class. His commitment to police reform was clearly generated by a belief that higher standards of social discipline could and should be enforced. It was probably also part of his equally famed commitment to the reform of the criminal law; a commitment which grew out of his belief that the arbitrary and discretionary elements so characteristic of the contemporary legal system should be overturned in favor of a system of justice that could be enforced rationally and consistently.

In a way, therefore, the argument has almost travelled full circle, and one is back to explanations that invoke changes in the intellectual climate and in the distribution of power brought about by the industrialization of the economy. Yet one must be wary of generalizing from the motives of a single individual to those of an entire class or section of the ruling elite. Successive enquiries into the policing of London had certainly alerted parliamentarians and public alike to its deficiencies, but it is far from clear that such discussions had created a climate of opinion receptive to Peel's ideas. The very fact that he had to resort to so much deception to get his act through parliament suggests that Peel himself doubted that such a climate of opinion existed. One should not overlook the possibility that constant discussion of the subject was as likely to reinforce as to undermine traditional prejudices against despotic foreign practices. Nor should one forget that Edwin Chadwick, the man who was to become the most famous of advocates of police reform, believed that the Metropolitan Police Force was not a preventive one, in the modern sense of the words, at all.[73]

The major factor to be considered must surely be the effect on Peel's character and on his beliefs brought about by his long service in John Bull's other island. Londoners discussed the question of police reform in extraordinarily parochial terms. They were intensely aware that their city was, if not superior to all others, certainly very different. If they looked elsewhere for instruction or enlightenment, it was invariably no more than a passing glance at the somewhat exaggerated tyrannies of the police of Paris. Peel, however, had first-hand experience of policing and police reform through his long tenure of the office of Chief Secretary in Ireland, where the priorities for executive action and the constitutional assumptions that governed those actions were very different from those that prevailed on the mainland. In Ireland, we can see all too clearly how a government constantly preoccupied with problems of law and order could be dazzled by the powerful attractions of a centralized French style gendarmerie, and how easily such a preoccupation could lead to a contemptuous disdain for the constitutional liberties that were prized so highly on the mainland.

Peel's attempts to resolve the problems he found in Ireland—in particular his overt distrust of local power structures and his overwhelming urge toward centralization[74]—have much in common with his later proposals for police reform in England. It is not inconceivable that Peel (and perhaps others like him) saw very little difference between the policing needs of the two societies. What with agrarian disturbances in the south of England, machine breaking in the industrial north, and perhaps even banditti/cattle raiding persisting on the Scottish borders, it was possible to argue that lawlessness was as endemic to the lower classes of England as it was to the peasantry of Ireland. Indeed the conventional image of the orderly and law-abiding Englishman, and his disorderly, lawless Irish counterpart depends on a somewhat selective reading of the evidence. There were certainly a number of contemporary commentators who thought that standards of law and order were actually higher in Ireland than in England. Such evidence need not be accepted uncritically; but one does need to be aware of the very real possibility that high levels of policing (such as that endured by the Irish) were likely to produce more cases for the courts.[75] At the same time, the more we learn about the very low levels of activity of the vast majority of justices of the peace in England, the more we are forced to realize that there was nothing at all unusual about the fabled weaknesses of the Irish magistracy.

Perhaps we have been too ready to over-emphasize the differences in policing the two societies, and to ignore the common thread of experience that shaped responses on both sides of the Irish Sea. But the differences in the development of police in Ireland and on the mainland should also remind us that the question of police reform is not just about problems and responses: it is also about the nature of the state and government. It is about how governments define what is, and what is not, acceptable behavior; it is about how governments decide what interventions can and should be made. In short, it is about how easy (and how dangerous) it is for central government to become obsessed with threats of crime and disorder which local power structures may perceive in very different terms—if, indeed, they perceive them at all.

Notes

I should like to thank Donna Andrews, David Philips, participants in the Police History Workshop at the University of Warwick, and members of the Law and Society Seminar at the Institute of Historical Research, London, for commenting on an earlier version of this paper.

1. British Library, Peel Papers, Add. Ms. 40390, fols. 186–89; *Parliamentary History* 21, col. 680; W. L. Melville Lee, *A History of Police in England* (London, 1901); Charles Reith, *A New Study of Police History* (London, 1952); T. A. Critchley, *A History of Police in England and Wales* (London, 1967); David Ascoli, *The Queen's Peace, the Origins and Development of the Metropolitan Police, 1829–1979* (London, 1979).

2. J. M. Beattie, *Crime and the Courts in England 1660–1800* (Oxford, 1986), 59–72; David Philips, *Crime and Authority in Victorian England* (London, 1977), 53–87; and Robert D. Storch, "Policing Rural England before the Police: Opinion and Practice, 1830–56," in *Policing and Prosecution in Britain 1750–1850,* ed. Douglas Hay and Francis Snyder (Oxford, 1989), 211–66.

3. Lee, *History of Police,* 209.

4. For a much fuller discussion of the way in which the pattern of crime in London differed from that of the rest of the country, and also of changing attitudes toward violence, see Beattie, *Crime and the courts,* 4–15, 132–39. I find Beattie's account far more convincing than the problem-response model that underlies Stanley Palmer's otherwise valuable account of police reform during this period, and which leads him to lay undue stress on the "general condition of disorderliness" in the metropolis. Stanley H. Palmer, *Police and Protest in England & Ireland 1780–1850* (Cambridge, 1988).

5. Allan Silver, "The demand for order in civil society: a review of some themes in the history of urban crime, police and riot," in *The Police: Six Sociological Essays,* ed. David J. Bordua (New York, 1967), 20–24.

6. Naturally, fears about crime and disorder were at their height at times when crime seemed to have got out of control. Prosecutions for crime in metropolitan Middlesex followed, in broad general terms, the pattern that has already been established by John Beattie and Douglas Hay. That is, the figures rose (sometimes massively) in years of peace, and declined with the outbreak of war. For the purposes of this essay, it matters little whether such fluctuations did, or did not, reflect real changes in criminality; what matters is that they led men to believe that they were facing a crime wave, and to react accordingly. See Ruth Paley, "The Middlesex Justices Act of 1792: its origins and effects" (PhD diss., Reading University, 1983), 393–96; J. M. Beattie, "The Pattern of Crime in England 1660–1800," *Past and Present* 62 (1974): 47–95; and Douglas Hay, "War, Dearth and Theft in the Eighteenth Century: The Record of the English Courts," *Past and Present* 95 (1982): 117–60.

7. Hugh Amory, "Henry Fielding and the Criminal Legislation of 1751–2," *Philological Quarterly* 50 (April, 1971): 175–92; and Peter Linebaugh, "The Tyburn Riot against the Surgeons," in *Albion's Fatal Tree,* ed. Douglas Hay, Peter Linebaugh *et al* (London, 1977), 89–98.

8. Paley, "Middlesex Justices Act," 325–61.
9. For a thorough (albeit uncritical) overview of the contemporary denigration of Middlesex trading justices, see Sidney and Beatrice Webb, *English Local Government: The Parish and the County* (London, 1906), 326 *et seq.*
10. For a more wide-ranging discussion of some of the problems associated with the contemporary prosecutorial system, see Douglas Hay, "Prosecution and Power: Malicious Prosecutions in the English Courts, 1750–1850," in Hay and Snyder, *Policing and Prosecution*, 343–395.
11. For the existence of forms of contingency fees, I rely on my own unpublished research on metropolitan litigants in the KB (Crown Side).
12. I intend to explore this subject in greater detail elsewhere.
13. Norma Landau, *The Justices of the Peace, 1679–1760* (Berkeley, 1984), 184.
14. Ruth Paley, "Thieftakers in London in the age of the McDaniel gang c1745–1754," in Hay and Snyder, *Policing and Prosecution*, 301–41.
15. In accordance with common English usage, I use the term "City" (with an initial capital) to refer to the specific administrative area governed by the Corporation of the City of London—that is, an area of approximately one square mile at the heart of the metropolis.
16. In 1773, for example, the Middlesex justice, David Wilmot, was unable to deal with a group of riotous weavers because they refused to leave the shelter of the City boundary. Nothing could be done to quell the disturbance until the lord mayor arrived. Fortunately, his whereabouts were readily ascertained—he was presiding at the Old Bailey.—Public Record Office, London [PRO], State Papers [SP], 37/10, 96, 101.
17. We know just how spectacular the results of failure to cooperate could be. The events that were to become known as the Gordon riots began with violent demonstrations in Moorfields. The City authorities, who were in sympathy with the demonstrators, refused to act; the Middlesex magistrates (who *were* in attendance) were unable to act because of their jurisdictional incompetence. It seems fairly clear that it was this initial lack of cooperation that allowed the riots to get out of hand—PRO, Privy Council [PC], 1/3097, Information of Justices Hyde, Triquet, and of the Solicitor to the Treasury, 11 June 1780.
18. Recent research suggests that, as early as 1680, some three-quarters of the total population of London lived outside the City: Roger Finlay and Beatrice Shearer, "Population Growth and Suburban Expansion," in *London 1500–1700: the Making of the Metropolis*, ed. A. L. Beier and Roger Finlay (London, 1986), 40–48. My own work shows that by 1748 only 4% of metropolitan cases on the Crown Side of the KB originated from the City; the rest were from Middlesex.
19. The Westminster Sessions were abolished in 1844 (7 & 8 Victoria, c. 7).
20. See, in particular, correspondence on the weavers' disturbances of 1773 in SP 37/10, especially fols 89, 93.
21. See, for example, Greater London Record Office [GLRO], MJ/OC/10a, fols 192/3, 197–200.
22. For a preliminary discussion on the ways in which the nature of available sources has led historians (and contemporaries) to underestimate the importance of organized crime (especially outside London) see Paley, "Thieftakers."
23. For a discussion of some of the difficulties encountered by John Fielding when he tried to extend the Bow Street system outside London, see John Styles, "Sir John Fielding and the Problem of Criminal Investigation in 18th Century England," *Transactions of the Royal Historical Society*, 5th series, 33 (1983): 127–49.

24. See the very interesting table of "Night Police of the Metropolis and Surrounding Districts" which forms part of the report of the Select Committee of 1828, and which contains information very much at odds with its conclusions: *Parliamentary Papers*, 1828, *Report of the Select Committee on the Police of the Metropolis*, App. M, 374–97. The author's own somewhat cursory survey of watch acts suggests that in most urban parishes the transition to a paid watch had been accomplished well before 1800.
25. Lee, *History of Police*, 182.
26. GLRO, P83/MRY1, 652/2, 659, 660.
27. The phrase is Chadwick's: University College, London, Chadwick MS 2/2, fols. 75–76.
28. A list of watchmen in St. Mary, Islington, in 1826 shows the youngest was 19 and the oldest 40; most were in their 20s or early 30s. The employment of chargeable men was not a matter of *policy* but was clearly something of a bonus, for the report of the Watch Committee stresses the benefit of being able to provide employment for "a number of stout able men who are continually seeking relief from the parochial funds, particularly during the winter season." Even so, priority was given to those men willing to make a year round commitment.—GLRO, P83/MRY1, 661/2, 657/1.
29. *Parl. Papers*, 1828, *Report of the Select Committee on the Police of the Metropolis*, 124–33; GLRO, P83/MRY1, 653–661; J. J. Tobias, *Crime and the Police in England, 1700–1900* (London, 1979), 36–43.
30. PRO, Home Office [HO] 42/118, Police Office, Worship Street [Dec. 1811].
31. HO 42/147, James F. Blake to Sidmouth, 18 Dec. 1815 and enclosures.
32. George Grenville to Charles Jenkinson, 2 and 4 July 1764, in John R. G. Tomlinson, *Additional Grenville Papers, 1763–1765* (Manchester, 1962), letters 151 and 155.
33. Paley, "Middlesex Justices Act," 50, 207–19.
34. For recruitment to the Middlesex magistracy see Paley, "Middlesex Justices Act," 123–149; for Henry Bate Dudley see the *DNB*. He had been recommended to the Middlesex commission as early as 1774: Northumberland MS, Alnwick Castle, Northumberland, Y/IV/6a, D Garrick, 7 Oct. 1774.
35. Harriott (like Bate Dudley) had had little difficulty in getting into the Essex commission: Northumberland MS, Y/IV/6a, John Spiller to Butler, 13 April 1775; and Y/IV/6a, undated note.
36. Landau, *Justices of the Peace*, 127–28.
37. 24 George II (1751) c.44. I intend to write more fully elsewhere about the near-impossibility of bringing successful civil or criminal actions against errant justices.
38. PRO, Treas. [T] 38/741, fol. 20.
39. See the experience of the Birmingham magistrate, Joseph Carles, whose continued activity was ensured by means of a subscription to pay his debts.—John Money, *Experience and Identity: Birmingham and the West Midlands 1760– 1800* (Manchester, 1977), 12–14.
40. HO 42/66, Account of the Public Services of Patrick Colquhoun Esq, 1 Sept. 1802.
41. For a preliminary outline of events leading to the passing of the Middlesex Justices Act, see Paley, "Middlesex Justices Act."
42. GLRO, MJ/OC/11, fol. 147; HO 42/7, Reeves, 29 July 1785; and Richard Clarke to Lord Sydney, 3 July 1785.
43. Palmer, *Police and Protest*, 119–36. The struggle for control of the Dublin police provides an interesting parallel to the arguments about control of the

Metropolitan Police after 1829. Clearly the Dubliners had something of an advantage, in that they had the Corporation to voice their demands—and even so, their victory proved to be a temporary one. One of the problems for Londoners in 1829 was that the exclusion of the City from the new police meant that there was no single powerful voice to speak on their behalf.

44. Paley, "Middlesex Justices Act," 263–64, 266–70.

45. William Lorance Rogers, for example, specifically stated that the reason for his application was his lack of success at the bar. William Fielding had had a moderately successful career, but by the time of his appointment was unable to walk or even to get into a carriage without difficulty. Baker John Sellon had had to abandon a distinguished career at the bar (together with the near-certainty of promotion to the bench) because of his inability to hear evidence being given in open court (even when that evidence was relayed to him by an assistant speaking directly into his ear trumpet).—Sidmouth MS, Devon County Record Office, Exeter, 152M/C1813/OA, W. L. Rogers, 15 Sept. 1813; *Parl. Papers*, 1816, vol. 5: *Report from the Committee on the State of the Metropolis*, 136; and H. W. Woolrych, *Lives of Eminent Serjeants at Law* (London, 1869), 2:808.

46. See n. 6 above.

47. Pelham Papers, British Library, Add. MS 33110, fols 215–23; HO 42/118, Sir Daniel Williams, 28 Dec. 1811; and HO 42/118, A. Graham to J. Becket [Dec. 1811].

48. Sir Francis Burdett, 18 Jan. 1812, *Parl. Debates*, vol. 21, cols 212–13.

49. HO 42/80, Drafts to Treasury, 17 and 18 Jan. 1805.

50. *Parl. Papers*, 1812, vol 1, 1059–76.

51. Sidmouth MS, 152M/C1812/OH, J. Wilks to Sidmouth, 7 July 1812 (two letters); and enclosed statement headed "Nightly Watch Bill," and printed statement headed "Nightly Watch Bill."

52. 1 & 2 George IV (1821), c.118.

53. HO 59/1, John Longley, 12 Dec. 1820; D. Williams, 26 Dec. 1820; W. Ballantyne, "Suggestions on the subject of the metropolis police," 28 Aug. 1821; GLRO, P83/MRY1/657, 1, Report of the Watch Committee of St. Mary Islington. Between 1812 and 1818, there were at least 14 acts of parl. concerning metropolitan parishes which either amended existing watching acts or created new paid watch forces.

54. For a more broadly based discussion of the role of fear see David Philips, "'A New Engine of Power and Authority': the Institutionalization of Law Enforcement in England, 1780–1830," in *Crime and the Law, The Social History of Crime in Western Europe since 1500*, ed. V. A. C. Gattrell, Bruce Lenman, and Geoffrey Parker (London, 1980), 182–83.

55. So much so that in the wake of Catholic emancipation in April 1829, Peel was setting up a contingency plan to deal with a repetition of "what happened in 1780": Philips, "A New Engine," 183 n. 65.

56. Peel Papers, Add MS 40395, fol. 205.

57. Perhaps one should not underrate the expertise that came from long experience. On one occasion at least the vestry of St. Thomas, Southwark, thought that the new police were partially responsible for the escape of a murderer: "a murdered child was found in one of the public thoroughfares [but] no policeman could be found and all clue to the murderer is lost."—GLRO, P71/TMS/481.

58. Note, for example, the circular of 7 Oct. 1829 in which the commissioners were at pains to explain to their men that "a great part of the fatigue they now experience in doing their duty arises from their not being in the habit of walking

and from their having to come some distance to their duty. When once lodged in their several sections and accustomed to the walking they will not find the fatigue half so great."—PRO, Metropolitan Police [MEPO], 7/1, fols 7–8.

59. Tower Hamlets Local History Library, MS S86.

60. Ronald Charles Sopenhoff, "The Police of London: The Early History of the Metropolitan Police, 1829–56" (Ph.D. diss., Temple University, 1978), 68, 74, 172–73.

61. For which they should perhaps have been grateful. At one stage Peel seems to have been giving serious consideration to introducing a regulation that would have led to the instant dismissal of all married men.—MEPO 1/1, fols. 199–206.

62. In the very early days, this regulation applied whether the constables were on or off duty. It was relaxed on the introduction of armbands which could be worn to indicate to the public that the officer concerned was off duty.

63. GLRO, P71/TMS, 481.

64. GLRO, P83/MRY1, 424; GLRO, P71/TMS, 494; and GLRO, Accession 10/2.

65. R. D. Storch, "The Plague of Blue Locusts," *International Review of Social History* 20 (1975): 61–90, and "The Policeman as Domestic Missionary," *Journal of Social History* 9 (Summer, 1976): 482–509; and David Philips, *Crime and Authority in Victorian England* (London, 1977), 84–87, and "A New Engine," 188–89.

66. Chadwick MS, 2/2 fol. 82.

67. Wilbur Miller, "Police Authority in London and New York City 1830–70," *Journal of Social History* 8 (Winter, 1975): 91.

68. Cutlasses, however, were issued, as and when necessary. We do not, as yet, know how often this was. On the weaponry of the contemporary army, see Tony Hayter, *The Army and the Crowd in Mid-Georgian England* (London, 1978), 24–25.

69. James Stewart of County Tyrone, quoted in Palmer, *Police and Protest*, 113.

70. Palmer, *Police and Protest*, 280.

71. "New Police Instructions," printed in *The Times*, 25 Sept. 1829; MEPO 7/1, fols. 21, 25–26, 44; Leon Radzinowicz and R. Hood, *History of the English Criminal Law*, 5 vols (London, 1948–86), 4:163–64, 184–85, 181–82; Sopenhoff, "The Police of London," 138–56; and Gavin Thurston, *The Clerkenwell Riot, The Killing of Constable Culley* (London, 1967).

72. Paley, "Thieftakers"; and Miller, "Police authority," 87–90.

73. Chadwick MS, 2/2, fols 69–93.

74. For an extended discussion of policing Ireland during this period see Palmer, *Police and Protest*, which now largely supersedes Galen Broeker, *Rural Disorder and Police Reform in Ireland 1812–36* (London, 1970).

75. Note, for example, Palmer's comparison of the strengths of the London and Dublin police which shows that, even after 1829, Dublin was twice as heavily policed, relatively, as London: Palmer, *Police and Protest*, 102, 103, 156–57.

[18]

THE MILITARY AND POPULAR DISORDER IN ENGLAND
1790-1801

By Clive Emsley

The 1790s were a decade of crises for Britain. The war against Revolutionary France which began in February 1793 put enormous strains on the economy, on manpower and on finances. Plebeian radicalism mushroomed in 1792, and after 1795 elements of the radical movement, which had weathered the storm of the loyalist counter-attack, plunged into the twilight world of conspiracy. The food shortages of 1795-96 and 1799-1801 provoked widespread disorder and, especially during the second crisis, at times the language of popular disorder adopted the language of the French Revolution.

There was no organisation worthy of the name of police in eighteenth-century England. During the eighteenth-century it was common for troops to be used to suppress popular disorder when the civil power was unable, or believed itself unable to cope. The recent historian of the army and the crowd in mid-Georgian England has argued that these constant calls for help made the Secretary at War "a sort of police chief or minister of the interior."[1] The Home Office papers for the 1790s contain scores of letters from magistrates requesting a military presence to reinforce their authority. In peace time only regular troops were available for police action, but the war with France brought a greater variety: regular troops, county militia regiments embodied either during the scare of December 1792 or shortly afterwards, and Volunteers—citizen soldiers who organised themselves into corps for home defence against foreign invaders and internal disorder. The aim of this article is to look at the effectiveness of the military in fulfilling its public order role during the nineties and at some of the contemporary attitudes to this role. Accordingly it is divided into four sections. The first is a discussion of the soldiers' policing role, and how this role was authorised by the Law and perceived by individuals. The second section looks at the government's policy of barrack building, begun in 1792, and assesses to what extent this was a police measure. In sections three and four the political reliability of the military is probed, together with the threat to public order which the military sometimes constituted.

In coastal areas police duties assigned to the military could include assisting excise officers. Although most of the coastline of Europe fronting Britain was hostile from early on in the war, smuggling continued. Regulars, militiamen and Volunteers were all involved in affrays with smugglers. Captain John Tremenheere boasted to Dundas how part of his Penzance Volunteer Company carried a position with the bayonet against smugglers armed with cannon, surprisingly with no casualties.[2] In December 1801 a pitched battle was fought near Cawston in Norfolk between two excise officers with a party of regular dragoons, and "upwards of thirty desperadoes" engaged in smuggling Geneva and tobacco. An excise officer and a dragoon were wounded, two of the smugglers were killed and several wounded, but the smugglers succeeded in getting away with some of their Geneva.[3] The problem for the soldiers was that if they killed a smuggler in such an affray they were liable to be charged with murder, and the case might be heard before a local jury containing friends of the dead man and even his fellow smugglers. In the correspondence between the Customs House and the Home Office during the 1790s there are several requests for Royal Warrants respiting any sentence passed on men charged with killing or "assaulting" smugglers, "as it is doubtful what a Jury may do on such an occasion."[4] For the most part, however, police duties for the military meant dealing with riots.

Troops were used to protect property and disperse rioters throughout the eighteenth century. The army was not a popular institution; its employment as police probably exacerbated its unpopularity and a widespread conviction prevailed that the use of military power in suppressing riots was alien to the constitution. Nor was crowd control popular with the soldiers themselves; as Home Secretary in 1796 the Duke of Portland acknowledged that it was a "disagreeable service" for troops.[5] Yet they were given no training for it; there was no manual for the officers' guidance. The Law of Riot was misunderstood by both magistrates and soldiers, and many magistrates appear to have believed that the position at Common Law, whereby any individual might use force to suppress a riot, had been superceded by the Riot Act of 1715 and that force could only be used after the reading of the proclamation attached to that Act. Throughout the century the War Office and individual officers sought guidance from the central government and its law officers about the military's role in suppressing riots. The soldiers always received reassuring replies but the constant raising of the question suggests unease and a lack of confidence among the military. At least some of this lack of confidence stemmed from the fear of being tried for murder if a person was killed during a police action. After the "Massacre of St. George's Fields" in 1768 a magistrate, an army officer and two private soldiers were charged with murder. Not one of them was found guilty, but the incident made a profound impression and probably contributed to the failure of the magistracy and the army at the beginning of the Gordon Riots.[6]

[1.] Tony Hayter, *The Army and the Crowd in Mid-Georgian England* (1978) p.57.

[2.] H.O. 42.29, Tremenheere to Dundas, 4 March 1794. The Penzance Volunteer Company must have been one of the earliest corps; Tremenheere's commission was dated 11 April 1793, H.O.51.147.73.

[3.] J. R. Harvey *Records of the Norfolk Yeomanry Cavalry 1780-1908* (1908) p.110.

[4.] [Public Records Office] H.O.42.210, Commissioners of Excise to Grenville, 12 March 1794; James Hume to Thomas Broderick, 6 August 1794; H.O.42.212, Hume to King, 2 March 1797.

[5.] H.O.43.8.205, Portland to Col. Villiers, 6 December 1796; H.O.43.8.214, Portland to Earl of Northampton, 8 December 1796.

The doubts and problems continued during the 1790s. Soldiers would not act without a magistrate whatever the danger or the provocation. When the reformer Thomas Walker had his house attacked in December 1792 the dragoons billeted in Manchester paraded ready to suppress the riot, but they did not act because they received no authorisation from the magistracy.[7] When John Thelwall's radical lectures were broken up by a "Church and King mob" in Yarmouth in August 1796 Lord Spencer, in command of troops in the town, signified his willingness to suppress the riot; but the *Cambridge Intelligencer* reported the mayor, Sir Edmund Lacon, as saying: "Well, Lord Spencer may send the soldiers if he pleases." The paper went on to add

> But as it is well known that the military cannot act without the presence of a magistrate, Lord Spencer, who expressed his readiness to assist on a legal requisition, was obliged to decline making use of this verbal permission.

In Mansfield in August 1800 a lieutenant and several infantrymen were injured by stones thrown by food rioters. The crowd's "knowledge of no magistrate residing in Town" encouraged them. They even told [the soldiers] "They dare not Fire till the Proclamation was read!"[8] Army officers continued to write to the government requesting clarification of their role in aiding the civil power.

In 1796 Lieutenant Colonel Montague of the Wiltshire Militia was the principal figure in a long correspondence concerning the military's relationship with the civil power. Montague, as is clear from his letters, was unaware of the Common Law position in cases of riot; the advice which he received never delineated this clearly and concisely. The occasion of Montague's original questions were the events surrounding the imprisonment of seven rioters in Cornwall. The men had been apprehended in their beds on warrants issued by two Cornish magistrates, Lord de Dunsterville and his brother-in-law John Rogers of Penrose. The prisoners had to be conducted to Bodmin Gaol through a large mining district where the inhabitants were known to be in sympathy with them. The magistrates accordingly requested a Sergeant's guard (twelve men) to assist the constables escorting the prisoners. Lieutenant Wych, commanding the detachment of Wiltshire Militia at Redruth, agreed to the request, and the presence of the soldiers apparently overawed the crowd of 200 or 300 which threatened a rescue. But Montague believed that the magistrates had over-stepped their authority in, as he thought, asking soldiers to serve as constables. "If I understand right," he protested to de Dunsterville,

[6.] Hayter, *Army and the Crowd, passim.*
[7.] F. Knight, *The Strange Case of Thomas Walker*, (1957), p.97.
[8.] *Cambridge Intelligencer* 27 August 1796; H.O.42.50, W. Watson to Portland, 31 August 1800.
[9.] H.O.48.5, Montague to de Dunsterville, 5 June 1796.

the assistance we can give the Civill Power is in actual tumult or riot, or when there are sufficient and express reasons to apprehend they will be obstructed in their duty, but in this last case the Military ought only to be in the background waiting for the order and personal attendance of a Magistrate without whose presence they cannot act. If it were possible a Magistrate could order a Military party to march when and where he pleased, by the same rule he might order the whole Regiment, or all the troops within the County; an act the Commanding Officer of a Regt. himself has not the power of doing . . .[9]

Several letters passed between Montague and de Dunsterville, then on 8 June the latter forwarded the correspondence to Portland with the request that the power of the magistracy over the military be "clearly defined."[10] Later in the month Montague wrote to the Colonel of the Wiltshires, Lord Carnarvon, who forwarded the letter to Portland. Montague was now worried about the consequences of magistrates being able to delegate authority to constables.

Has a Constable any authority to disperse a mob by force of military arms . . . It would be a very unpleasant circumstance for a young officer to be sent under the command of a constable to escort a felon to gaol and a mob was to collect and attempt to force to rescue the prisoners, and his party was to kill a man, a coroner's inquest might bring it in murder and the officer be lodged in Gaol to take his trial at the next assizes, something similar to this happened once to my knowledge.

Cornwall being a favourite area for smuggling, Montague also wanted to know the extent of the responsibility of excise officers over military officers and how far they could proceed without a magistrate.[11]

Montague's and de Dunsterville's questions were forwarded to the Crown Law Officers, who replied to Portland at the end of July. They declared that

so far, as is consistent with obedience to Military discipline and command, we apprehend the Civil Magistrates have the same power to call for the assistance of the Military as they have to call for the assistance of others of his Majesty's subjects. But we apprehend the Magistrates have no power to call for the assistance of the Military in cases in which they cannot call for the assistance of others of His Majesty's subjects.

[10.] H.O.48.5, de Dunsterville to Portland, 8 June 1796, with four enclosures.

[11.] H.O.48.5, Carnarvon to Portland, 30 June 1796, enclosing undated letter from Montague.

14 ARMY HISTORICAL RESEARCH

They added that Magistrates

> cannot require from the military any assistance repugnant to the
> obligations of their military duty; such as to march from that part
> of the country in which they are stationed by their military orders,
> to another part of the country to which their military orders do not
> direct or authorise them to go. We also apprehend that the Magistrates
> have no right to order any person, of any description, to assist in
> conveying to gaol any person against whom they shall have issued
> a warrant of commitment, except the person or persons to whom
> such warrant shall be directed; and we apprehend that such warrant
> cannot be directed to any person, except high constables or petty
> constables, without the consent of such person to act in the execution
> of the warrant. But where a warrant . . . directed to a constable is
> made by a Magistrate, the constable may take such assistance as he
> shall think proper; and we apprehend His Majesty may give such
> orders to the Military, as will enable them to afford to constables
> executing such warrants such assistance as they could legally require
> or receive from other persons.

The Law Officers did not think that a Magistrate could legally "order the
Military or any other person to assist in the preservation of the public peace,
unless he is personally present." Portland communicated these opinions to
de Dunsterville at the end of August; he also considered it worthwhile to
forward them to Pitt,[12] but there was no general circulation to magistrates
and army officers.

Colonel Montague was not satisfied. He concluded from the Law Officers'
report that soldiers acting under a magistrate were no longer, technically,
soldiers. At Portland's request the Attorney and Solicitor Generals produced
another report at the end of the year. They explained that soldiers remained
responsible to their military duty even while acting under a magistrate, and
continued:

> Lieut. Coll. Montague mentions a case which he represents as highly
> inconvenient to the Military service; the case of a constable requiring
> soldiers to assist him in executing a warrant, without asking the
> permission of their commanding Officer. We feel no difficulty in
> saying that we think the soldiers who were thus absent from their
> military duty without leave, were guilty of military offence, for which
> the requisition of the constable afforded them no lawful excuse; altho'
> the circumstances may have been such as might induce their

[12.] H.O.48.5, Scott and Mitford to Portland, 30 July 1796; H.O.43.8.16-20, Portland to
de Dunsterville, 27 August 1796; P[ublic] Re[cord] O[ffice] (Chatham MSS) 30.8.168,
Portland to Pitt, 30 August 1796.

commanding officer to consider their fault as not meriting very severe reprehension.

This time they declared that a magistrate's presence was "absolutely necessary" to warrant military aid; however an officer could order troops to help a constable in the lawful execution of his duty supposing, for example, that the constable was conveying prisoners, that a rescue was threatened and the constable requested military aid which was on the spot. The Law Officers went on to explain that the military should aid excise officers in the same way that they aided magistrates.[13]

This at last may have satisfied Montague, but in the next five years at least one other officer sought a definition of magisterial power over the military, and of military responsibility in police actions. At the end of 1799 or the very beginning of 1800 Lieutenant-General Grinfield, the officer commanding military forces in the manufacturing areas of the midlands and the north-west, sent a list of questions to John King, permanent under-secretary at the Home Office. If troops received information of disorder should they march to the spot without the personal or written requisition of a magistrate? In the absence of a magistrate, could a constable be considered as such? Should troops withdraw from an assembly not yet breaking the peace, if, though requisitioned by a magistrate, no magistrate was actually present when they arrived? Could troops quell acts of violence without the presence of the civil power? Were troops entirely under magisterial guidance during action against rioters, or could the military commander use his own discretion? Should troops act alone if a magistrate refused to quell a disturbance? He also enquired:

> Whether Military Officers of certain ranks ought not to be entrusted with power of acting as Civil Magistrates where tumults actually do exist or where there is every probable reason to apprehend serious disturbances?

King referred Grinfield to some solicitors and some confidents in the area of his command, but went on to answer to the best of his ability. He urged that troops should march to the scene of a disturbance without a magisterial requisition; after all he pointed out, they could always apprise a magistrate of any trouble. Constables, he warned, could never be regarded as magistrates. Action taken in the absence of, or because of the reluctance of a justice, King said, was at the discretion of the military officer on the spot, and he proceeded to describe the situation in common law:

> when persons are in the act of destroying, or pulling down houses or other buildings, it is a Felony without benefit of Clergy, in such cases there can be no doubt of the authority of all Persons to act in quelling the same.

King trusted that magistrates would always authorize a military commander to use his discretion in suppressing a disturbance. As for Grinfield's query about entrusting army officers with magisterial powers, King thought "such a measure might be of great service, but it merits great consideration."[14] Nothing was done in this respect and indeed the suspicion surrounding the army's role in riot control would have militated against any government attempting to introduce such a proposal in parliament. However it is worth noting that the combination of military officer and magistrate was possible for gentlemen serving in the Volunteers. During the Norfolk Street riot in Sheffield in August 1795 R. A. Althorpe acted as both magistrate and colonel of the Sheffield Volunteers.

Besides having no special training, and often being unsure of their responsibility, troops were given the additional problem of handling police actions with their conventional weapons of war—musket and bayonet, horse-pistol and sabre. These weapons were designed for killing on a battlefield, not for subduing crowds. Often the need to use weapons never arose; the mere appearance of troops could be sufficient to disperse a crowd; an advance by cavalry, with their sabres still sheathed, or by infantry with fixed bayonets sufficed in other instances.[15] But on a few occasions the order was given to open fire. An eighteenth-century musket may not have been an accurate weapon, but fired into a crowd the musket ball would almost certainly hit one person and was quite likely to pass through the first victim and into a second. One military musket was fired into a crowd in Birmingham in June 1795; the ball killed one man and lodged in the chest of a second.[16] The prospects of a volley being fired into a crowd are too appalling to contemplate, and they were probably equally appalling for the officers and men on riot duty. When muskets were fired therefore, it seems that they were generally aimed over the heads of the crowd. But musket balls aimed in the air had to come down somewhere; in August 1795 sixteen Volunteers fired over the heads of a crowd in Rochdale, and killed two old men who were watching some distance away.[17] On occasions in the south-west artillery was deployed against rioters, most notably against the turbulent Cornish tinners. Here again it was only ever fired over the heads of a crowd, and this very rarely.[18] At Plymouth Dock in 1801 magistrates allowed cannon to be loaded in an attempt to overawe rioters; but this was their last resort for when the rioters defiantly refused to disperse no order to fire was given, and the magistrates agreed to the rioters principal demand for the release of some prisoners.[19]

[13.] H.O.48.5, Scott and Mitford to Portland, 19 December 1796.

[14.] H.O.42.49, King to Grinfield, 7 January 1800.

[15.] Hayter, *Army and the Crowd*, chapter 13 *passim*.

[16.] *London Chronicle* 27 June 1795.

[17.] *York Herald* 8 August 1795; *York Chronicle* 13 August 1795.

[18.] H.O.42.34, Tremeheere to Portland, 13 March 1795 (Tremenheere was eager to have field pieces for his company); H.O.42.38, draft to Lord Mount Edgecumbe, 11 April 1796; *London Chronicle* 12, 14 April 1796.

The Hammonds maintained that during the wars against Revolutionary and Napoleonic France, the north and midlands and the manufacturing areas of the south-west resembled "a country under military occupation." As evidence of this they particularly instanced Pitt's barrack-building programme.[20] Before 1792 there were only seventeen permanent infantry barracks in England, mainly on the coast (Carlisle, Chatham, Chester, Dover, Hull, Languard Fort, Pendennis, Plymouth, Portsmouth, St. Mawes, Scarborough, Seaton Sluice, Sheerness, Tilbury Fort, Tower of London and Tynemouth); there was also a temporary barrack at Hilsea. By the end of 1801 there were seventy-one "established" barracks, at least twenty-one "temporary" barracks and some other rented accommodation. Four years later, when the Commissioners of Military Enquiry began their investigations into the barrack system there were a total of 168 established, temporary and rented barracks, capable of holding nearly 133,000 men.[21]

Pitt began building barracks in 1792 following the system adopted earlier in the century by the British Army in North America: a barrackmaster general, acting directly under the commander-in-chief, provided barracks for troops on active service, the expenses were met out of the extraordinaries of the army, and the whole thing was undertaken under the direct authority of the Crown, without recourse to parliament. Pitt probably steered clear of parliament initially, fearing a repetition of the defeats, in 1785 and 1786, of his attempts to establish a regular police force and to build a system of military works, including some barracks, as a defence against invasion. However, when the question of barracks was brought up in parliament in February 1793 and in April 1796, Pitt carried the day with handsome majorities.[22]

In February 1793 Pitt freely admitted that the building of barracks was a police measure. "The circumstances of the country" he told the commons,

> coupled with the general state of affairs, rendered it advisable to provide barracks in other parts of the kingdom. A spirit had appeared in some of the manufacturing towns which made it necessary that troops should be kept near them.[23]

The first seven barracks built in 1793 under the new policy were to house from 170 to 320 cavalrymen. Significantly six of them were in industrial centres where plebeian radicals had been active during 1792: Birmingham

---

[19.] J. H. Bohstedt, "Riots in England 1790-1810: with special reference to Devonshire", unpublished Ph.D. Harvard, 1972, pp.329-30.

[20.] J. L. and B. Hammond, *The Town Labourer 1760-1832* (4th edn. 1966) pp.92-93.

[21.] These figures are taken from the *Fourth Report of the Commissioners of Military Enquiry* (1807) Appendix 1. The date at which "rented" accommodation was taken over by the army is not given in the returns.

[22.] *Parliamentary History* xxx, 473-96 (debate of 22 February 1793) and xxxii, 924-44 (debate of 8 April 1796).

[23.] Parlt. Hist. xxx, 495.

(170 men), Coventry (200 men), Manchester (320 men), Norwich (230 men), Nottingham (175 men) and Sheffield (170 men); the seventh barrack was that at Hounslow with room for about 300 men who could be brought rapidly into the metropolis. In 1794 cavalry barracks were erected to cover the west country. The largest were at Dorchester and Exeter, each with room for about 400 men. Barracks for single troops of about sixty men were constructed in Barnstaple, Bridport, Honiton, Modbury, Taunton, Totnes, Trowbridge and Wareham. The north and London were further covered in the same year with barracks at York (250 men) and in Hyde Park (360 men).[24] Three large infantry barracks were also built in 1794 at Blatchington (730 men), Chelmsford (4000 men) and Colchester (4000 men), and from 1795 onwards there was a significant shift to large infantry barracks in areas on or near the coasts menaced by French invasion. Indeed few of the barracks built after 1794 appear to have been sited for a potential police role.

Sir William Blackstone, the revered eighteenth-century exponent of the English Law, had criticised any idea of building barracks in his *Commentaries;* a permanent professional army separated from the people in barracks was, he argued, dangerous to liberty. M. A. Taylor who introduced the motion critical of barracks into the commons in February 1793 quoted Blackstone. Fox, Grey, Courtnay, and the other opposition M.P.s who participated in the two debates, all took a line based, more or less on Blackstone; though the motion of April 1796 was ostensibly about the money spent on barracks and not on their constitutional basis. Plebeian radicals protested on lines similar to Blackstone. A handbill circulated in Manchester began: "In England our governors think the SWINISH MULTITUDE cannot be kept in order without barracks in every great town, and a standing army of 18,000 men."[25] In January 1794 the London Corresponding Society (hereafter LCS) proclaimed:

> We are at issue. We must now choose at once either liberty or slavery for ourselves and our posterity. Will you wait till BARRACKS are created in every village, and till subsidized Hessians and Hanoverians are upon us?[26]

The poor in the industrial districts probably disliked the new barracks, though more perhaps from a traditional hostility to the military than because they were convinced by the constitutional fears of the radical societies. The

---

[24.] I have approximated number of men which these barracks were capable of holding from the returns of 1805 in the *Second Report of the Commissioners of Military Enquiry* (1806).

[25.] H.O.42.21.52a.

[26.] *First Report of the Committee of Secrecy* (1794) pp.19-20. The fear that the government would recruit foreign mercenaries for service in England ran parallel with the fear of barracks among the popular societies. But there does not appear to have been any occasion during the 1790s when foreign-born troops were used in a police action, and this was probably deliberate policy on the part of the government and War Office.

propertied classes in general appear to have supported the barracks. Lord Beauchamp told the commons that the inhabitants of Warwickshire were whole-heartedly behind the policy. Daniel Parker Coke "enquired in the town of Derby and [did not] find that the Inhabitants of the two disapprove of Barracks."[27] The only letter extant addressed to the Home Office complaining about the building of barracks during the nineties came from a Mr. Tudway of Wells, Somerset. He argued that Wells was "a mere village, free from seditious Societies, and turbulent manufacturers, and was never esteemed very good quarters for Horse or Foot." Furthermore, he explained, the site selected was very pleasant and barracks would spoil it.[28] John Hawtrey, the vicar of Ringwood, supported the policy of barrack building, but he protested vehemently when the local barrackmaster proposed to use a barn overlooking Hawtrey's garden to house troops. The vicar even threatened to leave the district; the barrackmaster eventually gave up the point.[29] Sir Leon Radzinowicz is probably right in concluding that "such a revolution [as the building of barracks] could hardly have been achieved in the teeth of really determined opposition from Parliament and the local leaders most affected."[30]

Innkeepers welcomed the building of barracks. Before they were built, and indeed afterwards in those districts which were not furnished with them, troops were billeted in inns—the billeting arrangements were handled by the local magistrates who decided how many men to allot to each inn. The innkeeper received a set rate for each soldier and each horse that he had to feed and house. In September 1792 the *Leeds Intelligencer* declared that the government was embarking on its barracks building programme simply "with the liberal view of relieving the publicans of large towns, upon whom a number of horse and other soldiers are oftentimes very inconveniently quartered". The newspaper re-emphasised the point the following month.[31] Wartime troop movements and the enormous increase in the military, increased the burdens of innkeepers. In July 1793 the *London Chronicle* reported that publicans in Winchester, and in several other towns had given up their licences and taken down their signs on hearing that troops were marching through their district.[32] The twenty innkeepers at Ringwood threatened to give up their licences unless something was done to ease the burden on them. The Rev. Mr. Hawtrey believed that if the principal inhabitants had not promised some relief there would have been a riot. Twenty miles due north the innkeepers of Salisbury were required periodically to provide billets for a thousand or more soldiers. Further north in the Wiltshire village of Everleigh, according to the *Salisbury and Winchester Journal,* the landlord of the Crown

---

[27] *Parl. Hist.* xxx, 483; H.O.42.32 Coke to Broderick 29 July 1794.

[28] H.O.42.30, Tudway to Dundas (?) 5 May 1794.

[29] Bucks R[ecord] O[ffice]. Hawtrey Family Papers D.65 2/1/3/8.

[30] Sir Leon Radzinowicz, *A History of English Criminal Law,* (4 vols. 1948-68) iv, 121.

[31] *Leeds Intelligencer* 3 September and 15 October 1792.

[32] *London Chronicle* 9 July 1793.

Inn had to find accommodation for "no less than *seven hundred and eighty seven* soldiers" on separate marches between 4 and 20 August 1794.[33] The situation became serious for the innkeepers in the neighbourhood of Newcastle-upon-Tyne at the end of 1794 and early in 1795, when cavalry moved into the area during a dispute between pitmen and their employers. According to the *Newcastle Chronicle* in March 1795, one Newcastle publican was losing between thirty and forty shillings a day because of the troops quartered on him. Innkeepers as far away as Morpeth and Hexham were also affected. The large demand for hay for the cavalry horses had raised its cost; at Hexham it reached a higher price than ever before and there were stories of men hoarding their hay until the price rose even higher. The publicans in Newcastle arranged a meeting with General Balfour, the military commander in the town, and convinced him of their plight. The general promised them that if those who wanted the cavalry in the area did not contribute to their support, he would take steps to have the troops removed. Several meetings were held by gentlemen in Newcastle to discuss the best way of relieving the innkeepers, and a subscription was opened out of which each innkeeper was to be paid sixpence a day for each horse quartered on him. Donations for the subscription, however, do not appear to have been particularly generous.[34]

In 1795 the set rate to innkeepers was increased by an act of Parliament (35.Geo.III,64). But this did not appease the general discontent among publicans; the Treasury was notoriously slow in paying bills. In 1797, after the Gloucestershire Supplementary Militia had finished their twenty days' training in Gloucester, the local innkeepers detained the Militia's arms, refusing to return them until they had received the money which they were due for each militiaman's beer—three-pence a day for each day that the man had been quartered.[35] In 1800, in spite of the barracks which had been built, and the increased financial rate, publicans still complained of the imposition and expense of quartering troops. The Mayor of Appleby transmitted to Portland copies of printed circular letters from innkeepers in Market Harborough and Hull to the innkeepers of Appleby; the letters complained about the heavy losses incurred by quartering troops and suggested a petition to parliament.[36] In this situation it is hardly surprising that, once barracks had begun to be built in the country, groups of innkeepers, often supported by other inhabitants of their locality, began requesting barracks for their neighbourhood.[37] The constitutional opponents of barracks might protest; the *Cambridge Intelligence* declared

---

[33] Bucks R. O. Hawtrey Family Papers D.65 2/1/3/9; *Salisbury and Winchester Journal,* 15 September 1794; 9 May 1796.

[34] *Newcastle Chronicle* 21 and 28 March, and 4 April 1795.

[35] E. Moir, Local Government in Gloucestershire, 1775-1800 (1969) p.149.

[36] H.O.42.49, Robert Whitehead to Portland, 20 March and 5 April 1800. Whitehead was particularly worried because "the most plausible Pretexts have not unfrequently been a cloak to unwarrantable Meetings, and there may be, it is to be feared, still in some neighbourhoods, individuals who would lose no opportunity to fan the Flame of Discontent, Anarchy and Disaffection."

No-one can deny but the publicans are sufferers by the present mode of quartering soldiers upon them: but they unhappily mistake the redress which is properly CONSTITUTIONAL. Instead of petitioning for the erection of barracks, *they ought to remonstrate against a standing army in time of peace, and pray for a full and adequate compensation in time of war.*[38]

Such advice fell mainly on deaf ears.

There were other reasons why barracks were preferable for quartering troops. The dispersal of raw recruits among different public houses, often spread over a wide area, could retard training.[39] The similar dispersal of seasoned veterans meant that they might arrive piecemeal on the scene of a riot. In October 1792, for example, during a provision riot in Yarmouth the town's mayor had to send ten miles south of Lowestoft and ten miles north to Winterton to collect all the cavalry quartered in the area; twelve dragoons were in the immediate vicinity of Yarmouth, four were in Lowestoft and two in Winterton.[40] Finally, in the eyes of many during the nineties, one of the greatest advantages of barracks was that they isolated troops from those who were thought to be eager to subvert them politically. In 1794 Pitt declared that barracks "would also operate as a preventative of the seduction of the army [which was] by certain persons considered as the chief obstacle to the execution of their designs." Windham made the same point more dramatically two years later quoting from a French comedy: "If I cannot make him dumb, I will make you deaf." Charles Abbot noted in his diary that during the 1796 debate

The chief argument for barracks, besides their conducing to good discipline, was that it cut off all improper intercourse of the soldiery with the people at evening hours, in public houses, where seditious or traitorous seduction might be practised; without preventing their general intercourse at other times sufficiently for them to have a common sentiment with the public.[41]

Thus, in the situation of the 1790s in England, many of the propertied classes in England were prepared to stand Blackstone's dire warning about barracks on its head: keeping regular soldiers separate from civilians became a positive virtue.

To be continued

[37.] Clive Emsley, *British Society and the French Wars, 1793-1815* (1979) p.39.

[38.] *Cambridge Intelligencer* 26 October 1793.

[39.] N[ational] A[rmy] M[useum] 6807. 328 Duke of Richmond to Capt. Twiss 8 February 1793.

[40.] H.O.42.22.186, Mayor of Yarmouth to Dundas, 28 October 1792.

[41.] *Parl. Hist.* xxx, 495, and xxxii, 935; Charles, Lord Colchester (ed.) *Diary Correspondence of Charles Abbot Lord Colchester* (3 vols. 1861) i, 52.

THE MILITARY AND POPULAR DISORDER IN ENGLAND
1790-1801

BY CLIVE EMSLEY

Continued from page 21

From at least as early as May 1792, when it was reported that handbills were being circulated among militiamen in London, there were fears of attempts to subvert the military politically.[42] Probably many of these fears were grossly exaggerated. In January 1793, at a general committee meeting of the LCS, a motion that soldiers should be allowed to join the society without paying the subscription was withdrawn, apparently without discussion.[43] But there were some who endeavoured to subvert soldiers, and probably some of these were members of the radical societies. Early in 1795 seditious papers were thrown into the barracks at Modbury in Devon.[44] In June that year two handwritten posters were pasted up in Lewes

> Soldiers to arms, arise and revenge your cause
> On those bloody numskulls [sic] Pitt and George . . .
> Haste Soldiers now, and with intrepid hand
> Grasp Sword and Gun to save thy native land
> For see your comrades murder'd, ye with Resentments swell
> And join the Rage, the Aristocrat to quell
> Let undaunted Ardor each Bosom warm
> To down with George and Pitt, and England call to Arms.[45]

The same year William Wilberforce informed Pitt of attempts to subvert soldiers and suggested that a man might be employed to investigate.[46] In May 1800 'a very confidential person' who, according to Sir Richard Ford at the Home Office, could be depended upon, recalled:

> Three or four years ago a number of the Society [LCS] enlisted with the army as it was then said with the professed intention to corrupt their fellow soldiers . . . I can immediately get into the confidence of a man who was always the most active in corrupting

---

[42.] C. Emsley, "Political Disaffection and the British Army in 1792", *Bulletin of the Institute of Historical Research* XLVIII (1975), pp.232-33.
[43.] B[ritish] L[ibrary] (Place MSS) Add. MSS. 27812 f.31.
[44.] H.O.43.6.198, John King to Abraham Hawkins, 10 February 1795.
[45.] H.O.42.35.170, Duke of Richmond to Portland, 22 July 1795.
[46.] P.R.O. (Chatham MSS). 30.8.189, several notes from Wilberforce dated simply 1795.

the soldiers. F. Place a tailor opposite the Admiralty, he in conjunction with Ashly, Hodgson and Bone was the man that distributed some time since all the seditious papers amongst the army. He alone scattered all those found in Hyde Park and was one morning as he himself told me, nearly taken being pursued by a troop of horse and only saved himself by laying flat on his belly in the grass.[47]

From the handwriting the informant was almost certainly James Powell, an acquaintance of Francis Place but, at the same time, a government spy. Though in later years Place and others played down extremist elements in radicalism, Powell's information generally appears correct in essentials.[48] The seditious papers to which he referred warrant further discussion here.

During May 1797, at the time of the mutinies in the home fleet, seditious papers were discovered in many barracks and towns where troops were billeted. It is impossible to state categorically that it was the same paper in every case. H. B. F. Wheeler and A. M. Broadley, in their history of the French invasion threat, believed that it was.[49] In Maidstone and Chatham the same paper did turn up, and a similar, if not identical paper was discovered in Lewes and Chichester. In the Sussex towns bundles of the seditious handbill passed into the hands of the authorities almost as soon as they arrived on the stage-coach; none appear to have been circulated among the troops. The Lewes bundle was addressed to a servant of the town constable who belonged to the local Volunteer Cavalry; he denied knowing from whom or from whence it came. The Chichester papers were addressed to Joseph Prichard, a soap boiler, described by the Duke of Richmond as a man "who [had] been for some years the most active leader of what was consider'd as a democratic Party amongst, the Lower sort of People" there. Prichard handed the papers over to the mayor, protesting that he did not know who had sent them and that although he hoped for a reform of Parliament, he did not approve of subverting the army to achieve it.[50]

The Chatham and Maidstone paper began with words very similar to those of a manifesto issued by naval mutineers at the Nore in early June: "Comrades, are we not men? Is it not high time we should prove that we know ourselves to be such?" It praised the sailors' example:

> Were not the sailors, like us mocked for want of thought, though not so much despised for poverty as we are? Have they not proved

---

[47.] [Public Record Office] P[rivy] C[ouncil] 1.3490, unsigned paper in handwriting f James Powell, 20 May 1800, annotated by Ford and John King. I am indebted to Dr John)inwiddy for this reference.

[48.] C. Emsley, "The Home Office and its sources of information and investigation 790-1801" *English Historical Review* XCIV (1979) pp.553-54.

[49.] H. F. B. Wheeler and A. M. Broadley, *Napoleon and the Invasion of England* (2 vols. 908) i, 203-04.

[50.] H.O.42.40. W. Shelley to Portland, 20 May 1797; Richmond to Portland, 21 May 797; H.O.43.9. 322-23 Portland to Richmond, 25 May 1797.

that they can think and act for themselves and preserve every useful point of discipline, full as well, or better than when under the tyranny of their officers?

It questioned the differences between privates, NCOs and officers.

Are they [officers] better men? You must laugh at the thought? Do they know discipline half so well as our Serjeants? Don't they owe their promotions to their connections with placemen and pensioners, and a mock parliament, which pretends to represent the people?

It went on to list soldiers grievances; insufficient pay, profiteering Colonels, poor clothing, and being locked up in barracks and making long marches to ensure that they remained strangers to the people. The soldiers were offered two choices "either to submit to the present impositions, or demand treatment proper for men."[51]

Henry Fellows, a carpenter, was found guilty of circulating the handbill in Maidstone and was sentenced to two years in gaol and, before his release, to find sureties for his good behaviour for seven years. John Bone, a Holborn bookseller who became secretary of the LCS for a short period after John Ashley's resignation early in 1797, protested (while imprisoned under the suspension of Habeas Corpus in 1800) that the Committee of Secrecy of 1799 had insinuated that he had supplied Fellows with the handbill; he maintained his innocence in a long letter to the Duke of Norfolk. Yet there is circumstantial evidence which suggests that Bone was involved. Bone helped to arrange Fellows' defence and he admitted supplying Fellows with other pamphlets and papers.[52] During recruiting riots in London during 1794, Bone, according to the spy William Metcalfe, wrote an address for the LCS denying that the society was in any way involved in the riots. This address, however, was couched in such inflammatory language that the LCS Committee of correspondence rejected it.[53] In 1797 Bone had the facility, as secretary of the LCS, for knowing the names and addresses of radicals and provincial booksellers who might consider circulating handbills among soldiers. He had the facility, as a bookseller, either for printing or knowing where he could get handbills printed. The evidence of Metcalfe in 1794, and of Powell in 1800, further suggests that he may have had the inclination to produce the handbills of 1797.

[51.] N.A.M. (R.U.S.I. MSS) MM 370 f.38; [Public Record Office] ASSI [ZES]. 35/238 Part 1. The manifesto of the Nore delegates can be found in R. W. Postgate (ed.) *Revolution from 1789 to 1906* (2nd edn. New York, 1962) pp.73-74.

[52.] H.O.42.55. 135-44, Bone to Norfolk, 19 December 1800. P.C. 1.41.A.138, contains correspondence between Bone and Fellows 6 October 1797 to 16 March 1798.

[53.] [Public Record Office] T[reasury] S[olicitor] 11.956. 3501(1), Metcalfe's report 27 August 1794.

[54.] H.O.42.45, Deposition of Samuel Paterson, 17 April 1798.

William Cheetham, one of the United Englishmen arrested in Manchester in 1798 was accused of saying that "if any more Volunteers were raised in Manchester he would urge all his friends, the Democrats, to join that they might get arms."[54] Whether any political extremists did join the Volunteers for this reason, or to proselytise it is impossible to say, but the fear was ever present. An anonymous informant urged Henry Dundas to enquire into the political principles of those volunteering for the Lincolnshire Yeomanry Cavalry in 1794.[55] The Duke of Northumberland forwarded an application to Portland on behalf of the gentlemen, merchants and tradesmen of Newcastle who wished to form a Volunteer corps in February 1795, but he refused to be answerable for the list of proposed officers since the

> Corps is to be solely under the Guidance and Direction of such orders, as they shall receive from their own Committee, and are on no account to be under Military Discipline, and the Oath of Allegiance is not directed to be taken, or any Test or proof of Loyalty given by those into whose hands Arms are thus indiscriminately to be placed. For Your Grace will see by the Proposals, that any Person willing to serve without pay has a right to enroll himself; to be armed; and trained.

Northumberland was no friend to Pitt's administration and was no alarmist, but he went on to refer to

> the supposed numbers and designs of disaffected Persons, who have been represented as particularly anxious at any rate to obtain Arms, and to be instructed in the use of them, for the very worst of purposes.[56]

The Marquis of Townshend advised Dundas not to accept offers to establish Volunteer infantry companies, made by Norwich parishes noted for their radicalism.[57] In April 1798 another anonymous correspondent warned Dundas against arming people in and around London as "most parishes and districts . . . swarm with rank Jacobins."[58] During the same month the *Manchester Mercury* cautioned

> The Gentlemen who wish to shew their loyalty to their country by forming Associations, cannot be too much on their guard in carefully inspecting and enquiring into the characters of those who offer to enlist. The Partizans of the French in this country depend a great deal on the success of this part of their plan which is to introduce

---

[55] H.O.42.30, "Rufus" to Dundas, 8 May 1794.

[56] H.O.42.34.42, Northumberland to Portland, 21 February 1795.

[57] C. B. Jewson, *Jacobin City: A Portrait of Norwich 1788-1802* (1975) pp.89-90.

[58] S[cottish] R[ecord] O[ffice] Melville MSS. G.D.51.1.921, Anon to Dundas, 22 April 1798.

dis-affected persons into different military corps. This was the trick which the Jacobins played off in breeding a mutiny among the navy.[59]

Some of the fears of political disaffection in the army seem to have been justified. A dozen or so men of the Royal Scots Greys quartered in Manchester at the end of 1792 met regularly on Saturday evenings to read and discuss Tom Paine and similar writers; the group appears to have originated in a committee established in the regiment earlier in the year to consider the best means of increasing soldiers' pay. There were other isolated and not very serious incidents at the end of 1792 and three army officers—Hugh, Lord Sempill, Lord Edward Fitzgerald and Captain John Bellenden Gawler—were cashiered for their political opinions and activities.[60] There was trouble in some corps at the time of the naval mutinies. About seventy men of the Midlothian Light Dragoons refused to embark for Ireland from Liverpool in May 1797. There had been some "untoward circumstances" during the regiment's march to Liverpool, but Lord Ancram the commanding officer, put the principal cause of the mutiny down to "the assiduity of many disaffected inhabitants" of Liverpool persuading the soldiers not to embark for Ireland. Two men were arrested for using seditious language to the soldiers.[61] At the same time unrest was reported among the Guards in London and the gunners in Woolwich; this trouble seems to have been principally over conditions and pay.[62] In July 1797 three marines were shot and a fourth was flogged for having attempted to excite a mutiny among their comrades, to fire the powder magazines in the barracks at Plymouth, and to free French prisoners of war. But if the marines had any civilian connections they appear to have been with the United Irishmen rather than with English Jacobins.[63] How far the United Englishmen's conspiracy in Manchester had spread among soldiers in the area it is impossible to assess. Robert Gray, the government's principal informant, testified that over 700 soldiers had been sworn in to the society but given his unreliability as a witness this needs to be treated with caution. John Floud, the London stipendiary magistrate sent to assist the local justice, Thomas Butterworth Bayley, did not think that he would be able to procure evidence of any more than two or three

---

[59.] *Manchester Mercury* 24 April 1798.

[60.] Emsley, "Political Dissaffection and the British Army . . .", *passim*.

[61.] H.O.42.34.202, Ancram to Portland, 15 May 1797 mistakenly filed among papers for 1795); H.O.42.40, George Dunbar to Portland, 16 May 1797; H.O.43.9.291-93, Portland to Dunbar and to Ancram, 17 May 1797; H.O.42.40, Messrs. George, Serle and March (Transport Office) to Portland, 18 May 1797.

[62.] Life of Wilberforce, ii, 217-18; *London Chronicle,* 27 May 1797; James Dugan, *The Great Mutiny* (1966) p.218 and p.225; Wheeler and Broadley, *Napoleon and the Invasion . . ., i, xix-xv.*

[63.] Ann[ual] Reg[ister] 1797 Chron[icle]. p.37; Dugan, *Great Mutiny,* pp.309-10 and 330.

soldiers having been sworn in.[64] The two magistrates succeeded in arresting only two soldiers for involvement with the United Englishmen; a third soldier, private Twiggs, an Irish recruit in the 36th Foot who Gray described as enlisting many soldiers into the society and "lecturing" near Manchester, eluded them. Of the two men arrested, James Murdoch, a trooper in the Galloway Fencibles, confessed to being sworn in by his cousin while he was "a little in liquor"; Murdoch was kept in custody for only a short period. William Simmons, on the other hand, an Irishman in the Lancashire Supplementary Militia, was held for some considerable time under the suspension of the Habeas Corpus Act. Simmons was said to be a delegate from soldiers at Preston; in his testimony he claimed that he had received papers from the spy Gray, but such evidence as there is suggests that Simmons was deeply involved with the United Englishmen.[65]

In 1802 300 of the third battalion of the Grenadier Guards and 30 to 40 men of the second battalion were said to have been involved in Colonel Despard's abortive conspiracy. In fact only about thirty men were arrested with Despard, and here again there was a strong Irish connection. Despard himself, and most of those arrested were Irishmen, and the 'plot' itself appears to have been only one small link in a chain involving the French government, the remnants of the United Irishmen, and a scattering of revolutionaries particularly in northern England.[66]

Generally speaking, however, the army remained loyal during the nineties. The handbill circulated by Fellows received a defiant reply from the N.C.O.s and marines at Chatham.

> You say, Are we not Men?
> We are men! we know it. And should the Enemies of our King, our Country, or Constitution (either Foreign or Domestic) ever oppose us, we will prove ourselves such . . .
> We are not only respected as Men, but by every good Man regarded as the Protectors of our Country. If there are any Class of Men who hold us not in proper respect we are well assured it is only those, who lost to every sense of Virtue, and blind to the real Interests of their Country endeavor to disseminate principles of Jacobinism and sedition . . . *but we are united and resolved to shed the last drops of our Blood in the opposition of such detestable Doctrines* . . .[67]

[64.] P.C.1.41.A139, Examination of Gray, 15 April 1798; Floud to Wickham, 13-14 April 1798. For Gray's unreliability see Emsley, "The Home Office . . ." p.557.

[65.] H.O.42.45, Examination of Murdoch, 14 April 1798; P.C.1.42.A140, Examination of Simmons, 18 June 1798. For Simmons see also P.C.1.41.A139, Bayley to Lord Stanley, 3 April 1798 and Simmons (while imprisoned in Lancaster Castle) to Mr. Shaw (King's Messenger) 12 May 1799.

[66.] Marianne Elliott, "The 'Despard Conspiracy' Reconsidered," *Past and Present*, No.75 (1977).

The Surrey Militia, quartered in Durham, sent a printed address to the Duke of York requesting that he inform the King of their loyalty and declaring that they would support King and constitution "against all innovations either foreign or domestic." They lamented that there were men "base enough to warp the affections of His Majesty's forces" and declared their readiness "to a man [to] resist such diabolical attempts."[68] Other units sent similar replies, and often offered a reward out of their own pockets for the apprehension of the authors, printers and distributors of the handbills. At least one contemporary believed that the circulation of these handbills had provoked the Inniskilling Dragoons into smashing up public houses in Norwich where Jacobins were known to meet.[69] A year later two government spies reported that a party of United Englishmen had travelled from London to Woolwich armed with test cards for their society; they were given a rough reception by the troops, and returned to London without making any converts.[70] During that same year many army units donated part of their pay to the voluntary contribution collected for the war effort.[71] The loyalty of the troops may have been strengthened by their pay increase awarded at the time of the naval mutinies. Of course it is quite possible that pressure was put on some soldiers to get them to contribute to both the rewards of 1797 and the Voluntary Contribution of 1798, but the evidence of such pressure is hard to find and the extent of the contributions throughout the army suggests a genuine support from the ranks, particularly when it is remembered that grievances over pay often caused trouble. Furthermore on at least one occasion it was the loyalty of militia privates in volunteering for service in Ireland which compelled a reluctant officer to go as a matter of honour.[72]

But if, with very few exceptions, the military remained politically loyal during the period, there were occasions when groups, and even whole regiments, could present a serious threat to order. The other ranks of both

[67] Beds. R.O. DD.X.52/86 ff.101-112. The reply was signed by thirty-nine sergeants, nine corporals and six lance-corporals on behalf of themselves and the men in their companies. The author, however, was no ordinary marine. Sergeant John Johnston had once held an ensign's commission but after an "imprudent matrimonial connection" he was disowned by his family and enlisted in the marines. His background led to his immediate promotion to sergeant. The reply earned him a £50 reward from the committee of merchants, shipowners, insurers and other inhabitants of London set up to counteract the Nore mutiny; it was also a key factor in his promotion to second lieutenant in May 1799 (after four years' service as a sergeant).

[68] N.A.M. (RUSI MSS) MM 370 f.38.

[69] Jewson, *Jacobin City*, pp.81-82.

[70] P.C.1.42.A.144, Reports of William Gent (6 August 1798) and John Tunbridge (7 August 1798).

[71] D. G. Vaisey, "The Pledge of Patriotism: Staffordshire and the Voluntary Contribution of 1798" in M. W. Greenslade (ed.) *Essays in Staffordshire History presented to S. A. H. Burne*, (1970) pp.212-13.

[72] Cambs. R.O. Huddleston of Sawston MSS 488/C2/H.D.204.

[73] John Prebble, *Mutiny* (1975).

regulars and militia were recruited from the lower orders of society and, like their civilian counterparts, soldiers—especially new recruits only recently drawn from their civilian background—were likely to take riotous action when they considered that word had been broken with them or when they were unable to purchase provisions at a "fair price".

John Prebble has chronicled some dozen mutinies in Highland regiments between 1743 and 1804. These were provoked by broken promises, by trickery or deception by clan chiefs or military commanders.[73] But such mutinies were not confined to Prebble's highlanders. At the beginning of the war with Revolutionary France fifty or more new regiments were raised from scratch. The centre of recruiting was often in populous urban localities where the economic dislocation of war hit hard; Coventry, Birmingham, Leeds, Manchester, Norwich, Sheffield, Wakefield all saw regiments raised in this way, and the towns' names were incorporated into the new regiments titles. But many of the officers were lax and absentees; consequently discipline was poor. The War Office decided that the best thing to do with these units was to disband them and distribute the men among existing, better-disciplined corps. The news that they were to be disbanded led to mutinies in the 104th (Manchester), 105th (Leeds), 111th and 113th (both raised in Birmingham). The men of the 105th and 113th jointly issued a printed handbill protesting that they had been tempted to enlist "by large Sums (badly paid)."

> We did so, on condition of returning to our homes at the approach of peace; but what now is the case? All faith is broken with us. We are led to be incorporated with Regiments that will never be reduced, except by a formidable enemy and the more formidable climate of the WEST INDIES.[74]

There were similar mutinies in Newcastle and Exeter in 1795 and 1796 when newly raised Irish regiments were informed that they were to be disbanded.[75]

Some ugly scenes developed when troops felt that they were being cheated over pay. The riot in Sheffield in August 1795 began with the refusal of Colonel D. J. Cameron's newly-raised Loyal Sheffield Regiment to disperse from a parade. The men protested that they had not received "bread money", apparently arrears in both bounty-money and pay.[76] In militia regiments there was trouble over failure to give the men prompt payment of the

---

[74.] N.A.M. (R.U.S.I. MS) M.M. 370 f.17; T. H. McGuffie, "The Short Life and Sudden Death of an English Regiment of Foot", *JSAHR*, xxxiii; *Ann. Reg.* chron.p.33. For the regiments raised in 1793-94 see Hon. J. W. Fortescue, *A History of the British Army* 13 vols. 1899-1930), iv part 2, appendix A.

[75.] *London Chronicle*, 21 August and 15 September 1795; E. A. Freeman, *Historic Towns: Exeter* (1887) pp.226-27.

[76.] *York Herald* 8 August 1795; *York Courant* 10 and 11 August 1795.

"marching guinea" which they were allowed on embodiment to be spent on extra items of equipment or clothing described as "necessaries". Furthermore militiamen seem often to have been unaware that this guinea was already pledged for such purposes. The decision to keep some corps on the coasts throughout the winter of 1793-94, rather than marching them to winter quarters, provoked anger. Commanding officers sought to reassure their men that they would all be comfortable in the "barns, stables and hog-sties" temporarily commandeered as barracks,[77] Captain Richard Huddleston received an anonymous complaint from his company of the Cambridgeshire Militia, combining dissatisfaction at broken promises over quarters, with concern over food shortages.

> Onred captin who are in hop that you wilt git us changed for whe have ben thiertin weaks and my Lord Hardick [Lord Hardwicke, Lord Lieutenant and Colonel of the regiment] promised before whe cam from Harwich that whe shold be changed every tew months and if whe ant changed in a short time thalne wilt bee a strang confusen among us . . . whe wold have you reply to Lord Hardick for we ant resolved to bee changed by that word of my Lord for whe have sumtimes . . . purvishen and sumtimes none.[78]

Regulars and militiamen were expected to buy their food. Consequently when prices rose they were as vulnerable as other members of the poorer classes. During the provision riots of 1795 troops—most notably recruits and militiamen who were less well-disciplined than regulars of long standing and, arguably, closer to their civilian roots—were found as allies, or even instigators of some crowds. The most serious incident was the two-day riot of the Oxford Militia around Seaford and Newhaven when sacks of flour were taken at bayonet point. In the same month, April 1795, there were at least five other such incidents, principally along the south coast or in its hinterland where large bodies of troops on invasion duty or en route for foreign parts put additional strains on local supplies. In response court martials and assizes treated the rioters from the Oxford Militia with severity, while the government increased the troops' bread allowance and diverted some emergency supplies to soldiers. These actions, together with a general tightening of discipline in the militia regiments, appear to have prevented any similar military participation in the riots at the turn of the century.[79]

The Volunteers could not be disciplined or isolated from the civil

---

[77.] *London Chronicle* 20 July 1793 and 28 and 30 October 1793. Early in 1793 there appears to have been an attempt by some civilians to encourage meeting in the Surrey Militia over the "marching guineas" which they were due. H.O.42.63-64, testimonies of six militiamen 28 February to 7 March 1793.

[78.] Cambs R. O. Huddleston MSS 488/C3/A1. No date, filed as c.1794, but the reference to Harwich suggests that it could be 1798 when the regiment spent some time in quarters there.

[79.] Emsley, . . . *French Wars*, pp.41-3.

population as regulars and embodied militiamen. Essentially the Volunteers remained civilians, still living in their own homes, prepared, if need arose, to oppose invasion or internal disorder. In the summer of 1795 the Newcastle Volunteers were used to over-awe gathering crowds of pitmen north of the Tyne. A few weeks later Thomas Purvis, a carver and gilder and a bandsman in the Newcastle Volunteers, was singled out by a group of pitmen in an argument which began in a beer tent on the Town Moor one Sunday afternoon. Purvis was wearing his uniform jacket which prompted the pitmen to cry "Damn your Volunteer soul!" That evening, on the way home, the pitmen were waiting for him, and again singled him out from the group accompanying him: "Here's the damned Newcastle Bugger of a Volunteer!" Purvis died as a result of the beating he received.[80] The murder was exceptional, but it illustrates how the Volunteer was that much more vulnerable than the regulars or militiamen who were likely to be quartered in a district only for the duration of any disorders. Moreover dealing with provision riots in times of economic hardship raised acute problems of loyalty for the poorer Volunteer who was probably in sympathy with the demands of his friends, relations and neighbours among the rioters. At least three Rochdale Volunteers appear to have been pressurized by their wives and neighbours to hand in their arms and equipment after their corps had fired on food rioters in August 1795. The Volunteers of Fishguard also turned out in August 1795 and again at the end of the year. On the second occasion they were accused of encouraging and assisting the rioters, and while the corps' officers strenuously denied this, they did admit to expelling one private who had used some "disorderly expressions".[81] At Honiton ten Volunteers who had not paraded to help suppress a disturbance were expelled from their corps; one entire Devon company was accused of sympathy with rioters, and similar fears were expressed about the Volunteers of Whitby.[82] Five years later such suspicions and accusations became more widespread as the economic crisis bit deep into the budgets of artisan Volunteers. At least one such deposited his uniform with a pawnbroker.[83] Several of the Huddersfield Volunteers refused to turn out against a crowd in November 1799 and were dismissed. One who had turned out was branded as "the scum of the country" by former

---

[80.] ASSI 45.38.3.81-92 despositions concerning the murder of Purvis; J. A. Huitson, "Defence and Public Order in Northumberland 1793-1815", unpublished M. Litt. Durham, 1966, p.239. Purvis's comrades in the Volunteers offered a reward for the apprehension of his murderers, three of whom were identified as pitmen and one as a blacksmith. Three men were tried for murder, one of whom Thomas Nicholson, was found guilty and executed. ASSI 44.110 Part 2; *Newcastle Courant,* 4, 11, 18, 25 July, 8 and 15 August 1795; *Newcastle Chronicle,* 8 and 15 August 1795.

[81.] A. V. Mitchell "Radicalism and Repression in the North of England 1791-97" unpublished M. A. Manchester 1958, p.290; H.O.42.35.213, John Philipps to Portland, 24 August 1795; H.O.42.38, Lady Milford to Portland, 2 January 1796 (two enclosures).

[82;] Bohstedt, "Riots in England . . ." pp.224-25; H.O.42.36.27, Henry Cholmley to Portland, 15 November 1795.

[83.] Humberside R.O. Grimston MSS. DDGR.43/21.

comrades. Sir George Armstrong, the corps commander, warned a local magistrate against any further proceedings which "would incur the resentment of the Volunteers" and after which "he could not . . . be answerable for [their] conduct." The following year a Sheffield Volunteer who had joined the colours during a provision riot was set upon by his workmates and ducked in a tub of water till he almost drowned. Earl Fitzwilliam concluded that the corps could no longer be relied upon to handle food riots.[84] Volunteers near Wolverhampton told a local magistrate that they had enrolled

> to protect their King and Constitution and that they hold such offers sacred; but that it was never intended by them to give security to the inhuman oppressor, whilst the Poor are starving in the midst of Plenty.

They believed that the high prices were caused by speculation.[85] Ten miles away in West Bromwich a handbill emphasised the social divisions between the well-to-do Volunteer officers—"big Devils as wear that damnation bloody bloody rag about [their] damnd paunch bellys"—and the "poor fellows" who were the privates.

> What they [the officers] want from you is to protect their lives and their liver, and their ill gained property and to dam you to death, and when you have done all you are able you may go to hell for all they care.

In Devon Volunteers sided openly with those who sought a "fair price", and refusal to aid the civil power became an epidemic climaxing, in March 1801, with officers of the Brixham Volunteers directing a food riot.[87]

Even among the Yeomanry Cavalry, the pinnacle of country society, there were some who took strong exception to acting against food rioters. In 1795 Major Ackland of the Castlemartin Yeomanry resigned at the prospect of having to fire on "our poor creatures", while John Dyke was dismissed from the Somerset Yeomanry for repeatedly refusing to turn out to aid the civil power.[88] But in general, where they existed Yeomanry Cavalry did not present the same problems as the poor urban infantry Volunteers. At the close of

---

[84.] Leeds C.L. (Archives) Radcliffe MSS I 578-79; Sheffield C.L. Wentworth Woodhouse Muniments. F.44/51 and F44/54 Fitzwilliam to Portland 3 and 8 September 1800 (I am indebted to Sheffield City Libraries, to Earl Fitzwilliam and his Estates Company for permission to read and cite these documents); R. A. E. Wells, *Dearth and Distress in Yorkshire 1793-1802*, (York, 1977) pp.33-4.

[85.] H.O.42.50. A. B. Haden to Portland, 10 May 1800; see also the Hammonds, *Skilled Labourer*, p.66 and *Town Labourer*, p.95.

[86.] H.O.42.49, Richard Jesson to Lord Gower, 11 April 1800, forwarded to Portland 21 April 1800.

[87.] Bohstedt, "Riots in England . . ." pp.124-28.

[88.] E. H. Stuart Jones, *The Last Invasion of Britain* (Cardiff, 1950) p.210; O. Teichman, "The Yeomanry as an aid to Civil Power 1795-1867", *JSAHR*, XIX pp.75-6.

1795 the Marquis of Townshend declared that it was the Yeomanry whose presence had suppressed disorder in Norfolk. Lord Hardwicke appears to have shared Townshend's faith in the value of Yeomanry, but he lamented that "the extraordinary listlessness and apathy" in Cambridgeshire 'has hitherto rendered every attempt to raise Volunteer Yeomanry Cavalry ineffectual.'[89] Gloucestershire had no Yeomanry Cavalry until the end of 1795. The riots of that year encouraged gentlemen to offer "to enroll themselves with obligation to march out of the Country on Invasion; and to act within the Country on Tumult." But initially there was some doubt in the country about whether such a corps could be formed

> as the Act on this Subject has not provided for the Existence of such corps beyond "the continuance of the present War," and as the apparent Danger of Invasion is (at least) removed.[90]

However gentlemen farmers in the Yeomanry were the very men that food rioters accused of hoarding and profiteering. It is probable that even before Peterloo the appearance of Yeomanry on the scene of a riot (and especially a food riot) led to an initial exacerbation of violence and deepened the anger and resentment of the crowds. It was for this reason that in subsequent years the Home Office began to show reluctance in authorising the use of Yeomanry; while Chartist orators insisted that the very existence of the Yeomanry demonstrated that one class had been armed against another.[91]

On occasions army officers ordered their men to participate in loyal demonstrations organised by local gentlemen or even by the officers themselves. At the end of 1792 Captain Cranford of the Queen's Dragoon Guards organised anti-Paine demonstrations in the various quarters of his regiment—Dorchester, Bridport, Poole, Weymouth, Bradford-on-Avon and Trowbridge. He boasted that:

> I did not admit the doctrine of equality for one moment (in these demonstrations), I adhered to our invariable rule, and made the non-commissioned officers, even to the Lance Corporals and Rough Riders assemble in a separate room from the Privates.[92]

Gentlemen and army officers surely recognised that in all probability the spectacle of a military band and military parade would increase the spectators at any loyal demonstration. There is also evidence that some army officers

---

[89] H.O.42.37.113-14, Townshend to Portland, 22 and 23 December 1795, H.O.42.36.226, Hardwicke to Portland, 18 September 1795.

[90] Nottingham University Library, Portland MSS PwF 7391 Sir George O. Paul to Portland, 4 September 1795.

[91] F. C. Mather, *Public Order in the Age of the Chartists* (Manchester, 1959) pp.93-5 and 147-48.

[92] H.O.42.25.56, Crauford to Dundas, 20 December 1792.

may have participated in, or encouraged their men to participate in, assaults on Jacobins. John Harrison, the radical Sheffield razor-maker, complained of dragoons attacking civilians in Sheffield, led by four of their officers.

> All this was done in the name of *"Church* and *King* for ever". Why did the soldiers tell me, and all the town, "that they acted by orders of Secretary of State, to create a riot if possible, and to put an end to the Constitutional Meetings held in Sheffield?" Why did Captain say, "d--n them, he wished he might have the killing of a thousand of the d----d Sheffield Blacks etc?"[93]

Harrison's account needs to be treated with scepticism, especially his assertion that the Home Secretary ordered the assaults; yet, as many believed, the Sheffield radicals had gone out of their way to subvert the soldiery these assaults may have been by way of retaliation. Thelwall claimed that there was a military presence in the attacks on him and his audience during his East Anglian lecture tour in 1796. He maintained that Militia officers "most of them *disguised* in coloured clothes" were among a party which attempted to disrupt his lectures in Yarmouth, though he also noted that army officers refused to join a press-gang sent by a naval officer to apprehend him. He asserted that the mob which attacked him in Lynn Regis was stirred up by a surgeon belonging to a Fencible corps. The "Church and King mob" which jeered at those who attended his lecture in Wisbech and which subsequently rampaged through the town, was led by a military band; furthermore, he stated, the officers "plied the riotous soldiers with drink".[94]

There were many accusations levelled against soldiers of disorderly behaviour. Probably, on occasion, soldiers were provoked. The general unpopularity of the army as an institution in eighteenth-century England could not have been unknown to the troops themselves. Pitt was informed of an incident in Bristol in May 1795 when two soldiers asked a butcher the cost of a piece of beef.

> With an erect Nose of visible contempt the butcher replied—"I don't deal in meat for soldiers!" The soldiers' reply was fierce and menacing, saying they would have meat for the poor and for themselves—at a fair price.[95]

Occasionally civil authorities refused to billet troops in their neighbourhood, or at least made life difficult for the actions which naturally provoked

---

[93.] Citizen John Harrison, *A Letter to the Right Honourable Henry Dundas M.P., or an appeal to the people of Great Britain* (1794) p.6.

[94.] John Thelwall, *An Appeal to Popular Opinion against Kidnapping and Murder* (1796) pp.19-20 and 22; John Thelwall, *A Particular Account of the late Outrages at Lynn and Wisbeach* (1796) pp.9 and 17-18.

[95.] P.R.O. Chatham MSS 30.8.140, G. Grenville to Pitt, 31 May 1795.

trouble.[96] But trouble, when it came, could be out of all proportion to any provocation. In October 1794 men of the 69th Foot paraded the streets of Winchester nightly beating up civilians or attacking them with bayonets.[97] This kind of violence was not confined to the other ranks. Drunken officers of the 84th Foot drew their swords on a crowd at Basingstoke wounding several, including an alderman; there was a similar occurrence at Southwell near Nottingham.[98] In May 1795, soldiers who fought with constables and townspeople of Cowes on the Isle of Wight, were led by two of their junior officers. Lieutenant Nicholas Forster was subsequently tried at the Quarter Sessions in Winchester, found guilty, fined, sentenced to six months imprisonment, and ordered to find sureties for his good behaviour for one year, himself in £200 and two others in £100 each.[99] In July 1795 in Northallerton, an ensign of the 115th Foot was accused of insulting a woman and her daughter. The woman called a constable, who was promptly knocked down by the ensign. Troops rushed to the officer's defence with fixed bayonets and townsmen rushed to assist the constable. Three officers subsequently stood trial for riot and assault at the North Riding Sessions; they entered a plea of guilty, and were each fined sixpence. The 13th Light Dragoons were condemned by the *Salisbury and Winchester Journal* for their "extremely licentious and wantonly brutal" behaviour towards the inhabitants of Salisbury. The trouble began when two dragoons were arrested for burglary—they were both acquitted at the subsequent assizes.[100] The sort of regimental loyalty which seems to have brought the 115th to the defence of one of its ensigns, also led to serious inter-regimental fights. Near Southampton a dispute between Irish cavalrymen and Highland Infantry was resolved with sabres and bayonets. At Norwich the victory of the Northumberland Militia's champion pugilist over the Warwickshire's led to a fierce bayonet fight with many casualties. The Westminster Militia and the Lowland Fencibles drew up opposite each other on the barrack ground in Sunderland for a pitched battle after one of the Westminsters had killed the Fencibles' goat mascot. Prince William of Gloucester persuaded the soldiers to disperse without serious trouble and the goat's killer was tried by court martial. These affrays could be dangerous for any civilians who found themselves in the way. Several inhabitants of Newcastle were among the injured in September 1797 when the Cheshire Militia and the West Lowland Fencibles fought each other—a fight finally suppressed when a third unit, the Dumfries Light Dragoons, was called in by the authorities.[101]

[96.] J. R. Western, "The Recruitment of the Land Forces in Great Britain 1793-1799", unpublished Ph.D. Edinburgh, 1953, pp.118-120.

[97.] H.O.42.33, Mayor and justices of Winchester to Portland, 12 October 1794.

[98.] H.O.42.33, Thomas Orde to Nepean 10 and 11 August 1794; Mr. Russell to Nepean 11 August 1794; H.O.42.44, Sir Richard Sutton to Portland (?) 28 July and 12 August 1798; Mjr. Gen. Morgan to Portland, 3 August 1798.

[99.] *London Chronicle,* 26 May and 22 July 1795; *Salisbury and Winchester Journal* 20 July 1795.

Soldiers robbed, poached and vandalised. Early in 1795 parties of the Cheshire Militia stationed at Eastbourne were reported to be stealing rabbits. The gentleman who informed the regiment's officers seized some of the nets used; for his pains the Cheshires beseiged his house and advised him to prepare his coffin.[102] Lord Petre gave troops in camp on Warley Common permission to cut timber on his land. The timber was carefully marked out, but the soldiers tore up several hundred young trees by the roots.[103] In November 1797 a private and a drummer of the 1st Foot Guards were fired on by a gentleman while robbing his garden which backed on to the barracks at Windsor; the drummer ended in hospital, the private in gaol.[104] Three years later the 7th Dragoon Guards were described as "the terror of the principal Inhabitants" of Gloucester because of their "repeated Robberies and attempts to Rob." Furthermore, Colonel Close reported, "the soldiers have been heard even to advise the People 'not to put up with the small bread'." Close believed that barracks were the only remedy. The following year, after they had been moved to Thanet, the 7th Dragoon Guards were again accused of robberies and violent behaviour. Senior officers did their best to prevent such depredations. During 1795 General Bruce, commanding one of the large cantonments on the south coast, received so many complaints of pilfering and of his men trampling cornfields and breaking fences and gates, that he resolved upon drastic action. He ordered severe punishments for any soldier caught without a pass, and authorised roll-calls to be taken "at uncertain hours during the night."[106] In the north-east General Nicholls took a rather more personal initiative to preserve the property of local farmers. In July 1797 Lord Delaval was informed by one of his agents:

> The soldiers so far behave better in respect of game and rabbits than any year since the camps came. I believe that General Nicholls does his best to prevent them and he frequently every day comes through the farm once or oftener and has several times sent a file of soldiers to take hold of some that he has seen digging for rabbits.[107]

Many of these depredations were probably the result of boredom as the soldiers

---

[100.] *Newcastle Chronicle* 11 and 25 July 1795; North Yorks R.O. Q.S.M. 3/2 (Summer and Michaelmas 1795); *Salisbury and Winchester Journal* 24 August 1795 and 14 March 1796.

[101.] *London Chronicle* 22 October 1794 and 2 June 1796; *Newcastle Courant* 3 December 1796; J. Sykes, *Local Records or, Historical Register or Remarkable Events . . . in Northumberland and Durham,* (2 vols. Newcastle 1866) i, 385.

[102.] *London Chronicle* 19 March 1795.

[103.] *Times* 23 October 1795.

[104.] *London Chronicle* 16 November 1797

[105.] S.R.O. Melville G.D.51.1.729, Col. Close to Dundas, 5 December 1800; [Public Record Office] W[ar] O[ffice] 40.17, Anon (Margate) to Charles Yorke, 8 October 1801.

[106.] N.A.M. 6807/246 General Bruce's Order Book, Orders 27 May, 1 July, 10 and 19 August 1795.

[107.] Northumberland R.O. Delaval (Waterford) MSS 2 D.E./4/23/26.

waited for the invasion which never came, but, of course, poaching could provide tasty additions to their diet.

The anonymous informant who criticised the 7th Dragoon Guards in Thanet emphasised that the men in the regiment were mostly Irish; the *Salisbury and Winchester Journal* noted the same point about the "brutal" 13th Light Dragoons. Irish soldiers figure prominently in other complaints about unruly behaviour during the 1790s. The fraudulent and corrupt practices of recruiting in Ireland, often it seems, far worse than in England,[108] were probably much to blame for the unrest among Irish troops. In Wolverhampton in July 1793 seventy Irish rioted declaring that, "as they were paid for fighting, they would as soon fight here as anywhere else, or even die, if it so happened".[109] The War Office was asked to remove the 114th Foot, "a young Irish regiment", from its quarters in Wantage and Faringdon in April 1795 after the regiment had disturbed the local fairs by fighting with countrymen and had threatened to pull down bakers' ovens and sell bread and meal at their own price. "We do not want them as a defence", protested one man, "for the people are quiet and well disposed (unless they are incensed)".[110] In August 1798, fifty Irish recruits for the 17th Light Dragoons ran amok in Somers Town injuring several inhabitants. They dispersed and took refuge in their barracks when a Volunteer Corps, the St. Pancras Association, was called out to oppose them. The Volunteers seized several of the ringleaders and at the Clerkenwell Sessions the following month a sergeant and two dragoons were sentenced to six months, three months and two months in solitary confinement respectively.[111] Similar trouble in Manchester prompted a magistrate to write to Portland in April 1795 requesting that no more Irish corps be quartered in the town.[112] After the rebellion of 1798 however, provocation appears to have played a significant part in trouble between Irish troops and English civilians. In May 1800 complaints were made about Irish soldiers attacking civilians in Wellington in Somerset, and in Sunderland. On investigation, though the soldiers' conduct was inexcusable, it appeared that on each occasion before the violence some townsmen had taunted the soldiers with shouts of "Croppies", "Irish Rebels", and "Irish Rascals".[113]

[108.] Co. H. De Watteville, *The British Soldier* (1954) p.99.

[109.] *London Chronicle* 20 July 1793.

[110.] W.O.40.17, Six letters dated 8-13 April 1795. It is worth noting that another party of the 114th Foot was quartered at Abingdon and although there was a complaint about its behaviour in February 1795 in April it was given a certificate of good behaviour by the Mayor and 29 publicans of the town. Furthermore, when a detachment was called from Abingdon to a riot near Farringdon, it was noted for behaving "in a proper and soldierly manner" (W.O.40.17, Lt. Henry Blanquieu to Mjr. Gen. Bruce, 20 April 1795).

[111.] *Ann. Reg. 1798* Chron. p.67; *London Chronicle*, 9 August and 18 September 1793.

[112.] H.O.42.34.125, Bayley to Portland, 25 April 1795.

[113.] W.O.40.17, Lt. Col. Grey to Mjr. Gen. Horneck, 18 May 1800; Lt.Col. Napier to Mjr. Gen. Murray, 17 May 1800.

[114.] Ibid.

The threat to public order from soldiers was hardly surprising. Many of the regulars had been crimped or tricked by recruiters; others, together with many militia substitutes, had enlisted because of economic hardship. Once in uniform the men found themselves subjected to a harsh discipline enforced by the lash; they also found themselves regarded by many civilians as social outcasts, which may have helped engender a cameraderie among them and may also have led some troops to take a reciprocal dislike of civilians. The brutalising effect of these factors, and the boredom of much of military life probably coalesced to make many soldiers so unruly when no longer under the eyes of officers and N.C.O.s. Yet the troops, with very few exceptions, remained politically reliable and in spite of the unpopularity of police action, regulars and militiamen never mutinied and refused to act against rioters. In May 1800 Lieutenant Colonel Napier admitted that some of the men under his command were turbulent and had fought with townspeople in Sunderland, but

> as to the idea of Soldiers joining the Pitmen, it is altogether erroneous, and I appeal to every person of Candour, if the Detachment order'd out on the 24th April under Captain Lucas to Houghton, did not march with the utmost alacrity, and on this occasion, I have the satisfaction to remark that the Detachment behaved with the Greatest Regularity during their stay there, until 29th.[114]

[19]

THE BANK OF ENGLAND AND THE POLICING OF FORGERY 1797–1821[*]

Randall McGowen

Recent scholarship has gone a long way towards overthrowing the conventional portrait of policing in the century before 1829. That image, composed in equal parts of anecdote and ignorance, cast the local forces of order as inept, lazy and corrupt. Police reformers appealed to such a caricature in arguing for radical measures to reshape the arrangements for preventing crime and detecting offenders. They suggested that the reliance upon the traditional forces was scarcely better than having no police at all. Over the past two decades, scholars of the eighteenth century have offered a more positive evaluation of the capacity of constables and the night watch to have an impact upon crime. Even while admitting that a large measure of the responsibility for the detection, capture and prosecution of offenders rested with the victims of crime, these historians argue that local officers played an important role in lending them assistance. In addition, these studies suggest that law enforcement underwent considerable transformation over the century, not only in London but in many less urban areas as well. From the rise of prosecution societies to the improvement of the watch in a number of towns, local authorities experimented with a range of strategies for fighting crime. John Beattie's work, in particular, has made us aware of the wide variety of initiatives in London, proposed at several points during the century, for coping with the problem.[1] By the early nineteenth century, rural areas were

[*] Research for this essay was carried out with support from the American Bar Foundation and a University of Oregon summer fellowship in 1999. An earlier draft was read at the Social Science History Society meeting in Luton in January 1994. Some of the archival material upon which the essay is based was, according to the Bank of England, 'heavily weeded in the 1980s', subsequent to my examination of it. I would like to thank John Beattie, Clive Emsley, Henry Gillett, Joanna Innes and Peter King for their assistance.

[1] J. M. Beattie, *Policing and Punishment in London, 1660–1750: Urban Crime and the Limits of Terror* (Oxford, 2001); J. M. Beattie, *Crime and the Courts in England, 1660–1800* (Princeton, 1986). See also Elaine A. Reynolds, *Before the Bobbies: The Night Watch and Police Reform in Metropolitan London, 1720–1830* (Stanford, 1998); Clive Emsley, *Crime and Society in England, 1750–1900* (London, 1996); Ruth Paley,

(cont. on p. 82)

adopting some of these expedients. The landed elite, too, came to look for new ways of organizing policing at both the parish and the county level. For the most part, these experiments followed lines laid down in the last decades of the preceding century.[2] In sum, recent work has disrupted the older picture of a homogeneous and unchanging early modern police, while also diminishing the claims to novelty of post-1829 developments.[3]

Still, many questions remain about the nature of policing in late eighteenth- and early nineteenth-century England. We know more about London than about police arrangements in the provinces. While we can occasionally glimpse the activities of individual magistrates or constables displaying considerable skill in the pursuit of a particular offender, it has been more difficult to assess the quality of policing over the entire country or for a number of years. Law enforcement was decentralized; no doubt its precise character and potential varied widely from one place to another. More challenging still, it has proved hard to determine what people expected of the legal authorities when it came to dealing with a range of criminal conduct. In the absence of such a standard, we tend to employ uncritically the perspective of the reformed police as our measure of the adequacy of eighteenth-century policing. Thus we accept at face value the familiar claim that a significant portion of the public was dissatisfied with existing police arrangements, but that they accepted the situation as a necessary cost of preserving English liberties. Even the revisionists, in looking for hints of later developments in early modern policing and in offering assessments of its capacity that diminish the gap between 'old' and

---

(n. 1 cont.)
' "An Imperfect, Inadequate and Wretched System"? Policing London before Peel', *Criminal Justice Hist.*, x (1989); John Styles, 'Sir John Fielding and the Problem of Criminal Investigation in Eighteenth-Century England', *Trans. Roy. Hist. Soc.*, 5th ser., xxxiii (1983); Douglas Hay and Francis Snyder, 'Using the Criminal Law, 1750–1850: Policing, Private Prosecution, and the State', in Douglas Hay and Francis Snyder (eds.), *Policing and Prosecution in Britain, 1750–1850* (Oxford, 1989); Peter King, *Crime, Justice, and Discretion in England, 1740–1820* (Oxford, 2000); Gwenda Morgan and Peter Rushton, *Rogues, Thieves, and the Rule of Law: The Problem of Law Enforcement in North-East England, 1718–1800* (London, 1998), esp. ch. 2.

[2] David Philips and Robert Storch, *Policing Provincial England, 1829–1856* (London, 1999); David Eastwood, *Governing Rural England: Tradition and Transformation in Local Government, 1780–1840* (Oxford, 1994).

[3] For a useful summary of the scholarship, see David Taylor, *The New Police in Nineteenth-Century England: Crime, Conflict and Control* (Manchester, 1997), ch. 2.

'new' police, run the risk of minimizing the distinctiveness of pre-1829 practices.[4]

In this essay I want to deal with an episode that promises to offer us some perspective on the quality of English policing in the decades before Peel undertook his reform of the Metropolitan police. Between 1797 and 1821, the Bank of England faced a serious and extensive criminal challenge. The crisis was brought on by the decision of the government to suspend cash payments, while encouraging the Bank to issue large numbers of £1 and £2 notes in order to sustain the financial circulation of the country. These notes soon attracted the attentions of skilled forgers and an elaborate network of dealers. In order to meet this challenge, the Bank mounted what, in 1822, G. B. Mainwaring called 'the most extensive criminal operation of the day'.[5] The campaign stretched across the entire nation and came to involve a wide range of law-enforcement personnel. The forgers and dealers put together sophisticated schemes that might have been expected to tax the ability of the Bank to cope with them. Although it never came close to defeating the epidemic, the corporation succeeded, at great cost, in keeping its chief opponents on the defensive. There was little novel about what the Bank did to achieve this level of success. While the corporation enjoyed the co-operation of both local and national government, it carried on its effort as a private entity, one often prickly in defence of its privileges. It operated, in other words, as a private prosecutor, though admittedly one with vast resources and unrivalled influence. In particular, it exploited to the full what Clive Emsley has called the 'entrepreneurial system of policing'.[6] While the victims of crime not only had to bear at least some of the cost of prosecution, they also faced the burden of investigating the crime and seizing the perpetrator. In order to secure the attention and assistance of a constable or police officer in these latter tasks, it often took an offer of money. The co-operation of these individuals usually required a promise of

---

[4] Robert Storch, 'Policing Rural Southern England before the Police', in Hay and Snyder (eds.), *Policing and Prosecution in Britain*, 213; John Styles, 'The Emergence of the Police: Explaining Police Reform in Eighteenth and Nineteenth Century England', *Brit. Jl Criminology*, xxvii (1987).

[5] G. B. Mainwaring, 'Observations on the Present State of the Police of the Metropolis', *Pamphleteer*, xix (1822), 544.

[6] Clive Emsley, *The English Police: A Political and Social History* (London, 1991), 20.

payment for lost time and effort, along with the inducement of a reward. This form of policing has had a bad press. Still, the Bank was content to operate within the well-understood constraints of this system. Admittedly, there was nothing typical about the character of the challenge it faced, nor about the resources the Bank could command. Nonetheless, it was the scale of its effort, not the constituent elements of its practice, which represented the novelty.

Thus the story of the Bank's efforts to contain an extensive outbreak of forgery in the early nineteenth century has a good deal to tell us about how policing worked in this period, and, perhaps, something about its effectiveness. In this sense it not only makes clearer the potential of the traditional system of law enforcement, but also may help to explain why so many were content with its continued operation. In other words, the lack of urgency about reform may have owed as much to a sense of the advantages of existing arrangements, as to the belief that reform would infringe on cherished liberties. Yet the Bank's extraordinary efforts, ironically, may also have contributed to doubts about those practices, at a time when policing was coming under greater scrutiny. Even as the corporation's activities highlight aspects of eighteenth-century law enforcement, some features of its practice, as well as the reaction to these tactics, suggest the increasingly fluid character of the institutional situation by the early nineteenth century.

I

This unexpected chapter in the history of policing had its roots in the fiscal challenges arising from the long war with revolutionary France. The conflict produced severe financial stress in the nation almost from the first. By 1796, the Bank found its reserves of specie falling to dangerous levels. The Governor complained to Pitt that the corporation could no longer continue to meet the demands placed upon it by the government. As a private corporation the Bank felt its first responsibility was to its own investors. Despite this warning, the situation deteriorated rapidly, as subsidies sent to allies and the funding of military preparations, combined with heavy importations of grain, further drained the Bank of gold. The crisis came to a head amidst rumours of a French invasion. Country banks sent in alarming reports of an inability to meet the demands of their clients. As panic threatened to spread, the Privy Council, on 27 February 1797, instructed the Bank to suspend cash payments. When parliament met to consider the situation, it also suspended the acts restricting the issue of bank notes in amounts under £5. The government's primary concern was to sustain the circulation of the country by supplying low-denomination notes to replace the rapidly disappearing specie. No one greeted these measures with enthusiasm, though the financial community rallied to patriotic calls to support the nation. The government turned to the measure out of desperation, and the Bank joined it as a reluctant accomplice. The *Morning Chronicle*, an opposition newspaper, spoke for many when it warned that the action inaugurated 'a new chapter in the history of England'. 'Every moderate man', it wrote, 'must approach the discussion of this awful measure with fear and trembling'. In an effort to allay anxiety, the government sought to assure the public that the measure would be temporary. To the consternation of many, suspension would remain in effect for over two decades.[7]

As the Bank faced the suspension crisis, the directors, casting a worried glance towards the City and at the foreign money markets, could scarcely have imagined that one of the most serious consequences of the measure would be the rise of a troubling criminal threat. The problem arose from the issuance of large numbers of £1 and £2 notes. The Bank, ever the advocate of fiscal prudence, mistrusted such instruments. Only in 1793 had it begun issuing notes for less than a value of £10. After 1797 it faced the unpleasant task of distributing smaller notes. These instruments were a simple affair, scarcely more than a printed form with a number, a date and a clerk's signature. They presented little challenge to the criminal entrepreneurs, many of them dealers in fraudulent coin, who now seized upon the new opportunity for easy profit. According to Patrick Colquhoun, there were 120 major distributors of false coin in the Metropolis in 1797. Many were old hands skilled in the tricks of their craft. The perpetrators had, he wrote, an 'accurate

---

[7] *Morning Chron.*, 27, 28 Feb. 1797; A. D. Harvey, *Britain in the Early Nineteenth Century* (New York, 1978), 320–1; John Clapham, *The Bank of England*, 2 vols. (Cambridge, 1944), i, 257–72; W. Marston Acres, *The Bank of England from Within*, 2 vols. (London, 1931), i, 275–8; Clive Emsley, *British Society and the French Wars, 1793–1815* (Totowa, 1979), 56–9.

knowledge of the deficiency of the laws, and where the point of danger lies', so that it was with 'extreme difficulty' that they were detected and convicted. The naive and inexperienced were easy to detect, but their conviction did little to curtail the trade.[8] Within weeks of suspension, coiners had become forgers, the latter enterprise modelled on the methods of the former. 'This paper commodity', Mainwaring wrote in 1822, 'is too tempting for human avidity to resist, and numbers seek it from the facility and rapidity with which it promises to realize a large profit'. He described how the business attracted 'capitalist and large manufacturers'. The *Morning Chronicle* complained, in March 1798, that 'the melancholy experience of every day proves, that the facility of imitating the clumsy note of the Bank holds forth such temptations to desperate men as no example of punishment is able to repress'.[9]

The Bank soon began to find a small but slowly increasing stream of forged notes being turned in to its cashiers. The problem would become more severe with each passing year. Small changes in the design of the bank note in 1798, and the introduction of the waved line watermark in 1800, each had a temporary impact on the incidence of the crime. But skilled forgers in Birmingham soon triumphed over the alterations. As the number of notes in circulation swelled, especially after 1810, the challenge mounted as well. Nothing in the country's experience of the crime in the eighteenth century prepared the Bank for the kind of contest it now faced. Forgery had been a much feared offence throughout the century. Instances of the crime attracted attention from the press to a degree scarcely warranted by its incidence. London, for instance, seldom saw more than four or five prosecutions for the offence in any given year. It was the nature of the crime, as well as the circumstances of the punishment, that drew public concern. The penalty for conviction of forgery was death, and an execution usually followed a guilty verdict. Still, the crime had presented few challenges for the Bank. Prosecutions were expensive, but detection of the offender was

---

[8] Patrick Colquhoun, *A Treatise on the Police of the Metropolis* (London, 1797), 17–18, 21–3, 103–15, 131.

[9] Mainwaring, 'Observations on the Present State of the Police of the Metropolis', 544; *Morning Chron.*, 29 Mar. 1798. For more on the coiners and their operations, see John Styles, '"Our Traitorous Money Makers": The Yorkshire Coiners and the Law, 1760–83', in John Brewer and John Styles (eds.), *An Ungovernable People: The English and their Law in the Seventeenth and Eighteenth Centuries* (New Brunswick, 1980).

TABLE

ACCOUNT OF BANK NOTES (UNDER £5) IN CIRCULATION,
THE NUMBER OF FORGED NOTES RETURNED TO THE BANK,
AND PROSECUTIONS FOR FORGERY 1797–1824[*]

	Total value of notes under £5 in circulation	Number of forged notes under £5	Total number of forged notes	Total Bank prosecutions for forgery
1797	867,585	24	901	2
1798	1,531,060	838	1,179	12
1799	1,341,700	1,893	2,058	15
1800	1,598,640	3,549	3,947	44
1801	2,412,650	6,820	7,674	54
1802	3,249,160	4,338	5,018	63
1803	3,765,940	2,844	3,217	9
1804	4,687,100	2,930	3,311	25
1805	4,525,660	3,096	3,543	28
1806	4,269,540	3,441	4,008	10
1807	4,245,370	4,435	4,866	45
1808	4,118,270	4,471	4,719	34
1809	5,181,070	6,025	6,281	68
1810	7,223,210	4,953	5,341	29
1811	7,594,360	7,810	8,492	33
1812	7,641,410	15,985	17,290	64
1813	8,037,140	13,819	14,565	65
1814	9,665,080	13,420	14,446	47
1815	9,482,530	15,317	16,079	63
1816	9,097,210	22,712	23,442	120
1817	7,993,150	28,648	29,521	142
1818	7,525,930	27,420	28,351	260
1819	7,235,240	23,066	23,906	228
1820	6,698,610	29,233	30,217	404
1821	2,548,230	18,252	18,955	239
1822	855,330	3,312	3,756	16
1823	548,480	1,418	1,667	7
1824	443,140	835	970	5

[*] Sources: Bank of England, Roehampton F1; *Appendix to Reports from the Select Committee on Commercial Distress*, Parliamentary Papers, 1847–8 (395, 584), viii, pt 2; and *Supplemental Appendix*.

Note: In a reply to an enquiry from Edwin Chadwick in 1838, the solicitors wrote that the official return of forged notes understated the scale of the problem, because many Lancashire bankers did not bother to return bad notes to the Bank. Since the corporation refused to pay such notes, no doubt many more forgeries were simply destroyed by those unlucky enough to have taken them. The Bank chose to prosecute only a small proportion of all those detected possessing or passing forged notes, either because the chance of conviction was small or because the person held was a minor offender.

often easy. The forger was typically a respectable person, someone with a connection to the person or institution that was the victim of the crime. Paper instruments circulated within a limited geographical and social sphere. Shopkeepers and cashiers were careful to study the identity of the person presenting them. A poorly dressed or illiterate individual who offered a note was likely to be closely questioned. A few precautions were adequate to discourage most potential offenders. For all these reasons, forgery in the eighteenth century represented a far less pressing policing problem for the authorities than was the case with coining.[10]

After 1797 the scale of the challenge changed dramatically, especially for the Bank of England. Its small notes circulated widely, and in ever-increasing numbers, throughout the country. The traditional safeguards that had surrounded the employment of paper instruments no longer operated. Suddenly they were being used by a class of people less familiar with their form. As the volume increased, shopkeepers found it more difficult to attend to the details of each transaction or keep track of the location of each note — considerations of vital importance to a successful prosecution of the crime. Several banks in Stowmarket wrote to the Bank in 1805 that respectable tradesmen had received forged notes at a fair from strangers 'whom they had not the opportunity at the time to pay much attention to as to enable them again to recollect them'.[11] To some extent country bankers, who also saw their circulation increase dramatically, faced the same challenges. Their notes, however, circulated within a restricted region and were taken with more caution. Bank of England notes enjoyed greater prestige and were accepted with more reliance on the integrity of the claim they represented. The corporation had long cultivated a belief in the unique status of its obligations, a confidence that now left its notes more vulnerable to the schemes employed by those who dealt in forged instruments.

Given its history of sensitivity to fraud, the Bank could not treat lightly the appearance of forged notes after 1797. Within months of suspension it began to receive letters expressing concern at an outbreak of the crime (see Table for statistics). In 1801, an urgent letter from Plymouth warned that forged notes had become so frequent that people were growing reluctant to accept any paper instrument. 'If some steps are not taken to

---

[10] Randall McGowen, 'Forgery Discovered, or the Perils of Circulation in Eighteenth-Century England', *Angelaki*, i (1993–4); Randall McGowen, 'Knowing the Hand: Forgery and the Proof of Writing in Eighteenth-Century England', *Historical Reflections / Réflexions historiques*, xiv (1998).

[11] Bank of England Archive, London, Roehampton F24.

counteract this alarming increase in the circulation of forged paper', this correspondent stressed, 'we are apprehensive that it may prevent the negotiating of your notes altogether'. Similarly, a magistrate in Huntingdonshire wrote of the anxiety that the appearance of several forgeries had created in his neighbourhood. People had become very cautious about taking bank paper. Still other reports spoke of shopkeepers refusing to take a suspected note.[12] What these letters revealed was the way in which fear could ripple through a community, spreading mistrust of all financial institutions. 'The fabrication and circulation of forged bank notes', the Bank solicitor wrote in 1809, 'has lately become so systematic a matter of business that the security of the circulating medium of the country is seriously menaced and unless prompt and active measures are taken to detect and punish the offenders, the most serious consequences may be the result'. Nothing less, he feared, than the credit of the nation was under attack. In many places people were so afraid of being defrauded in taking a bank note that they gave 'a preference to local notes issued in many instances by persons possessed of little property and totally unworthy of that credit which this species of depredation contributes to give to their paper circulation'.[13] For seventy years assize judges had solemnly lectured juries on the danger that forgery presented in a commercial nation. Now, at a critical moment in the country's history, these dire warnings threatened to become reality.

II

Throughout the eighteenth century, it was the Bank's solicitors who had taken the leading role in coping with the pursuit and prosecution of forgers. They took charge not only of the legal aspects of each case, but of the police function as well. Like others of their profession, the solicitors sometimes found themselves managing sophisticated operations. They arranged for advertisements to appear in newspapers. They sought the co-operation of local magistrates and constables. In the case of the Bank, this often meant employing Bow Street officers,

---

[12] Bank of England, Roehampton F15, F19. The Bank, by its refusal to reimburse anyone who accepted a bad note, increased the reluctance people felt about taking its notes, once a rumour of an outbreak of forgery began to circulate.

[13] Bank of England, Roehampton F30.

sometimes sending them to distant regions of the country and, occasionally, to the continent. They reviewed the day-to-day expenses of the officers and determined the rewards that followed a successful prosecution. Although on a more modest scale, at least before the suspension period, the responsibilities of the Bank solicitors paralleled those that fell to the Mint Solicitor in his conduct of the campaign against coining. The latter was expected to give 'a general attention to all circumstances leading to the discovery of offenders against the Mint laws', including providing 'directions' to magistrates 'for their conduct'.[14] Like their counterpart at the Mint, the Bank solicitors offered leadership and direction to the various agents of law enforcement, often prodding local authorities to act while providing a necessary co-ordination of their activities.

In 1797 the legal business of the Bank was in the hands of the partnership of John Winter and Joseph Kaye; in 1800 they were joined by James Freshfield.[15] While earlier Bank solicitors had handled the occasional forgery case, Winter and Kaye had not had much recent experience in dealing with the crime. The Bank had had only four cases in the fourteen years before 1797, and none in the six years immediately before that date. Nonetheless, they showed no hesitation as they hastened to deal with the earliest reports of forgeries. They quickly added this charge to the great variety of other legal business, an ever-swelling volume of bankruptcies, wills and contentious stock transfers, which they handled for the Bank. As if these demands were not pressing enough, the firm also managed the steadily expanding property holdings of the corporation. By the second decade of the century the Bank was involved in an average of about a hundred cases a year in Chancery, and nearly as many again in the Court of Exchequer. Winter and Kaye had other business as well, much of it drawn to them by their connection with the Bank. Joseph Kaye served as solicitor to the Royal Exchange Assurance Company. James Freshfield came to represent the Globe Insurance

---

[14] Styles, '"Our Traitorous Money Makers"', 183, and more generally 156–7, 166–9, 173, 181–4, 225; Hay and Snyder, 'Using the Criminal Law', 21–2; John Langbein, *The Origins of Adversary Criminal Trial* (Oxford, 2003), 111–27.

[15] Partners in the firm (with years of active partnership) were: John Winter (1779–1808); Joseph Kaye (1788–1824); Joseph Cam Maynard (1797–1800); James William Freshfield (1800–40); Francis Beckwith (1801–8); John Winter Jr (1805–8); Charles Kaye (1811–25). For a history of the firm, see Judy Slinn, *A History of Freshfields* (London, 1984), 178.

Company. The firm handled the legal affairs of the banking house of Smith, Payne, and Smith, as well as the private legal concerns of the Smith family. These connections led to the addition of other wealthy clients, both aristocratic and mercantile. At some point during this period the solicitors began working for the cotton manufacturer Robert Peel, and the link to the Peel family would prove enduring. By the early years of the century the firm was one of the most prominent in London, and its client list revealed the dense and interconnected worlds of finance and government. Partners in the firm were also leaders of philanthropic and professional organizations. Freshfield, in particular, was active in the Evangelical movement. The solicitors were hard-working, serious men with a vast experience of every phase of civil litigation. Little in their social background or legal training, however, can have prepared them for the place that the struggle against forgery came to occupy in their lives between 1797 and 1821.[16]

By early 1798, the solicitors discovered that they faced a rapidly developing criminal challenge. At first the corporation hoped that a few dramatic executions would produce a salutary fear among potential offenders. This expectation soon proved illusory. Within months of suspension the solicitors were expressing concern among themselves about the difficulties they faced. Freshfield, then a young clerk with the firm, wrote from Birmingham, in 1799, that 'there are now . . . upwards of twenty persons who deal in forged bank notes, but they act with so much caution that it is difficult to get hold of them and the notes at the same time'. One of the Bank's inspectors, Thomas Glover, sent word from Bristol, in 1800, that he had spent several months tracking forged notes that passed because of the inattention of shopkeepers. Despite his strenuous efforts, he had failed to capture any of the dealers.[17] Even in 1806, a year of relatively few prosecutions, one of the partners wrote in dismay that there seemed no relief from 'this reviving mischief'.[18] Such sentiments were frequently expressed as the solicitors watched the epidemic soar to new heights by the second decade of the century. In 1820, the directors of the Bank acknowledged the heavy burden shouldered by the solicitors. Over the previous

---

[16] *Ibid.*, 25–34, 38–47.
[17] Bank of England, Roehampton F12, F14.
[18] Bank of England, Roehampton F28.

two years, they noted in recommending a reward of £525 for the firm, the corporation had prosecuted 557 forgers, 269 of them in distant parts of the kingdom, and had secured 488 convictions. Even these numbers only hinted at the true scale of the problem. The solicitors investigated many times the number of cases actually selected for prosecution. In 1820 alone, over thirty thousand forged notes were detected, and many of these occurrences earned a remark in a Bank file.[19]

The solicitors bore the brunt of the challenge. The partners and their clerks were kept busy monitoring the many different schemes undertaken to bring leading offenders to justice. Much expense and effort went into the organization of the prosecution. The solicitors were charged with responsibility for employing barristers and ensuring that they were properly briefed. They had to arrange for transportation and accommodation for witnesses, guarantee that appropriate documents were on hand, and manage all expenses. These activities, however, represented only the final stage of an enterprise that began with operations to detect forgers. A note of frustration or fatigue occasionally crept into their communications. Largely preoccupied with civil litigation, busy with the demands of a distinguished clientele, unfamiliar with the elusive world inhabited by forgers, coiners and other professional criminals, the solicitors might have appeared overmatched. Yet they proceeded to act with scarcely a misstep or hesitation. In the first years after suspension they developed a strategy for grappling with the crime, one that they pursued with remarkable consistency to the end of the crisis. They mounted a sophisticated, far-reaching and time-consuming operation that might have sapped the resolve and patience of any governmental agency.

Much of the struggle against forgery, especially in the early years, took place in regions distant from London. The Bank ultimately came to employ a force of some ten or twelve of its own inspectors, who were constantly travelling around the country to deal with fresh outbreaks of the crime. It also 'borrowed' men from the police offices of the Metropolis. Still, these forces were too few to deal with the scale of the problem, and their usefulness was compromised when their identities became known to the most experienced offenders. The Bank required additional help. It had long employed local solicitors to handle

[19] Bank of England, Committee on Law Suits, B577–16(Q), 21 June 1820.

THE BANK OF ENGLAND AND FORGERY 93

the corporation's business in the major towns, and it turned to them again as the need arose. Solicitors such as William Spurrier in Birmingham, John Lloyd in Stockport and John Lewis in Bristol brought vital local knowledge to the effort, while their social status guaranteed that the Bank interests and wishes would be respected. The tasks they undertook were similar to those assumed by Winter, Kaye and Freshfield in London. They collected information, secured witnesses and briefed prosecution counsel; they also worked closely with the local police forces. The latter assignment was especially important. For no matter how much good intelligence the Bank acquired, it was of little help if the corporation could not find local agents who could carry out its instructions with skill and energy. What it needed was someone in the vicinity of a reported forgery with both knowledge of the identity of the likely suspects and the means necessary to secure and prosecute them. The great challenge lay in the fact that it was not always clear where this capacity might be found. The solicitors recognized that the ability of individual constables and magistrates varied widely. Some were lax or timid; a few were hostile. Enthusiasm could be as difficult as apathy to cope with. Without advice, it was seldom obvious to whom one should turn for assistance. In almost every instance, however, the Bank found energetic and clever men ready to serve it. The solicitors in London proved remarkably successful in knitting together a network of associates, some of the relationships being more or less permanent, others occasional as need dictated. One example, from 1802, shows how these connections were created. In that year, the Bank received a letter from a man who lived near Wells describing the detention of a suspected forger and asking what to do. This correspondent also suggested to the solicitors that they might want to employ a local attorney named Tucker to manage this affair. Winter and Kaye then wrote to Tucker with a recommendation that he consult the jailer about the names of the people passing notes, their characters and habits. In this way, they advised, he might discover 'who the people are that use the house — in short if they are likely to belong to any gang of note circulators'. The solicitors also mentioned one name in particular, asking Tucker to enquire about the details of his life, 'how he lives and what he does'.[20]

---

[20] Bank of England, Roehampton F15.

This decentralized and often ad hoc network was capable of great flexibility in dealing with highly mobile offenders and widely dispersed outbreaks of crime. Spurrier occupied a key position in the Bank's police operations, since Birmingham was the universally acknowledged centre for the manufacture of forged notes. He was almost constantly in communication with the London solicitors, exchanging intelligence on the major manufacturers, and discussing various schemes to secure forged notes.[21] In one typical episode, in 1805, Kaye wrote to him warning that known offenders were heading for the Chester fair, and proposing that he mount an operation to secure them. Kaye advised against using 'your constables', as the very sight of them would scare off the old dealers. The central figures in the business, he explained, were known to have people stationed 'everywhere' on the lookout for police officers. It might be better, Kaye suggested, to write to the Manchester Deputy Constable, Joseph Nadin, for his help.[22] These informal alliances were employed time and again. For instance, in 1811, the solicitors received a letter from a man in Staffordshire. He told of a great increase in forged notes in his neighbourhood, and recommended 'the Bank to send down immediately some active officer that measures might be concerted for detecting the said parties'. Kaye informed the Committee on Law Suits that he had written to Spurrier, requesting that he send someone to investigate the situation. In the letter the solicitors mentioned in particular the Birmingham police officer William Payne as a man who had often served the Bank well. Spurrier replied several days later, advising the solicitors that Payne had visited the town, but had found the circumstances there too unclear to justify the searching of the homes of the suspects. Before the officer left town, however, he developed a plan with a banker named Kinnersley that he hoped might lead to their detection while in possession of the forged notes. Payne warned, however, that he doubted that the suspects were major dealers. This exchange of letters and the movements they detailed all took place between 5 and 14 December.[23]

---

[21] *Ibid.* For more on Spurrier, see Peter Cook, 'William Spurrier and the Forgery Laws', *Holdsworth Law Rev.*, xvii (1995).

[22] Bank of England, Roehampton F269.

[23] Bank of England, Roehampton F5; Committee on Law Suits, B577–5(E), 11 Dec. 1811. These links were also helpful in meeting unusual requests for assistance.

(cont. on p. 95)

THE BANK OF ENGLAND AND FORGERY 95

The office of the solicitors in London became the nerve centre for managing the conduct of the quarter-century war against forgery. The chief instrument of this vast effort was the letter. Much of the practical task of dealing with the crime was conducted through correspondence. Letters flooded into the Bank. The solicitors received missives from well-wishers, offering information on suspicious local figures or reporting an instance of the crime. Constables and magistrates wrote with word of someone being detained after the utterance of a note, or with a plan to capture a major operator. Jailers enclosed confessions offered by prisoners who hoped to secure the intercession of the Bank on their behalf. Some letters came from a miscellaneous collection of individuals who sought employment by the corporation to detect forgers. They were full of descriptions of suspects, names and addresses, as well as their mode of operation. Some of the letters were well written; others were scrawled and half literate. Many were no more than a paragraph, while a number wandered on for pages, full of hints and rumours about neighbours. Still, no matter how obscure the information, the Bank never let more than a day pass without replying to an enquiry. This efficiency became one of the chief ways the corporation maintained tight control over its ever-expanding operations. In late 1814, for example, Edward Banford, the jailer at Lancaster, wrote to the solicitors with an account of persons concerned in forgery that he had received from a prisoner. They, in turn, immediately forwarded the information to Spurrier in Birmingham and Nadin in Manchester, with a request that they take what measures they could to detain the people mentioned.[24]

Far from being dismayed by this deluge, the solicitors did their best to encourage it. They insisted on the rapid communication of news; they demanded that every scrap of information associated with a case be forwarded to them. Their office became a clearing-house for reports of the crime and an archive for details on offenders and law enforcement. While the Bank

---

(n. 23 cont.)

In 1818, Spurrier wrote asking that some person be sent from Manchester to Birmingham who understood the Lancashire and Yorkshire dialects. He needed such co-operation if he was to have success in detecting the forgers named by James Jelly in his confession. Kaye applied to Nadin for help. Committee on Law Suits, B577–14(O), 29 Jan. 1818.

[24] Committee on Law Suits, B577–9(I), 22 Nov. 1814.

sought to encourage local co-operation and prompt action, offering not only to cover costs, but also to provide rewards, it feared spontaneous and uncoordinated measures. Such efforts were invariably expensive and counter-productive. So the solicitors demanded obedience even at the expense of local initiative or the risk of antagonizing local authorities. The centralization of decision-making, with a clear acknowledgement of where ultimate responsibility belonged, was at the heart of the Bank's strategy for coping with the crime.[25] The tone adopted by the solicitors in these exchanges was firm and businesslike. Letters addressed to someone who had detained a suspect were filled with detailed instructions on how to proceed, and laced with warnings not to depart from Bank guidelines. In most cases the solicitors did not need to press this argument. Local authorities were aware of their ignorance about how to act, and even more cautious about the risk of incurring expenses that the Bank would not reimburse. In 1802, the mayor of Bristol wrote enclosing a bill taken by a respectable shopkeeper. The woman offering it gave an unsatisfactory account of who she was and how she came by the note. He asked how to proceed. The same year the solicitors received a letter from an Exeter shopkeeper who had stopped a woman for passing a forged note. She told a confusing tale of how she came by it. The tradesman took her before the mayor and had her committed. He said he would prosecute if the Bank would bear the expense. He, too, asked what he should do.[26] The first thing the solicitors demanded in such instances was a complete set of depositions, along with any other supporting materials. They recognized that in dealing with forgery networks, news had to be evaluated quickly, and decisions made about what steps to take. Successful prosecutions

[25] Once it became clear that the challenge of forgery was not a temporary emergency, the corporation created, in 1802, a Committee on Law Suits (composed of the governor or deputy-governor, and five other directors) to oversee the solicitors' management of the Bank's legal affairs. In part the directors simply wanted to exercise some restraint on the rising legal costs. But the move was also intended to lend the full weight of the institution's authority to the police effort. The committee received weekly reports from the solicitors, one of whom attended its meetings. Its members listened to selected correspondence sent to the Bank, and heard proposals from the solicitors about whether to fund schemes to entrap the principal manufacturers and dealers. The committee was also required to approve each prosecution. In practice, it seldom rejected the advice offered by the solicitors. Committee on Law Suits, B577–1(A).

[26] Bank of England, Roehampton F15.

required a rapid response from local agents. Witnesses had to be interviewed, evidence secured. The solicitors knew from bitter experience that word of a detention spread instantly, and that the value of any information provided by the detained or their friends would be rendered useless within a matter of days.

Within weeks of suspension the solicitors were at the centre of a web they had constructed to regulate the flow of information and instruction. A case from Oxford, in 1802, reveals just how prompt and detailed their direction could be, as well as how quickly they could set things in motion. On 7 January the Bank received a letter from a magistrate reporting that Richard Parkes had been committed to jail for uttering two forged notes. His friends were active on his behalf and sought bail for him. The magistrate desired to know the Bank's wishes. The solicitors responded the next day, asking him to investigate more fully and report any results to them. They pointed out that 'if Parkes knew the notes to be forged the offence is capital and although positive evidence cannot be adduced of such knowledge, yet it may be collected from circumstances, his conduct at the time of uttering the notes, and when detected, by similar notes in his possession'. They advised the magistrate that the town clerk of Oxford had much knowledge of what to do in such cases and should be consulted without delay. He was also told that if the case presented any doubtful aspects, the Bank was not inclined to prosecute. On 20 January a letter arrived from the town clerk to say that while Parkes had a brother who was suspected of being active in the forged-note trade, there was little in this case to excite strong suspicion. Still, the clerk recommended detaining Parkes in custody, as he thought it might produce some new revelations. Several months were to pass before the solicitors, having decided not to prosecute, wrote proposing that Parkes be discharged.[27]

In due course, the solicitors became quite shrewd about the ways of the underworld and even about the identities of its leading members. When a Dumfries prosecutor wrote with obvious delight that he had learned the name of one of the Birmingham forgers, they responded with a condescending note that 'we know them perfectly'.[28] The solicitors followed closely the

---

[27] *Ibid.*
[28] Bank of England, Roehampton F26.

movements of the most notorious of their opponents. They often
knew where they carried on their production. Freshfield wrote
from Birmingham, in 1799, that he had succeeded in having the
post office there regularly stop the mail of seven or eight major
dealers, and the same was being done for six Manchester suspects.
Copies of their correspondence were regularly sent to London.[29]
Here was an elaborate game of cat and mouse. The solicitors
even developed something like a respect for the intelligence and
caution of the leading offenders. One agent wrote that a well-
known dealer was no longer in Yorkshire. 'How to be caught
with anything in possession is the question among us', he confided. 'We any of us could take him, but not so readily get evidence'.[30] By 1803, the solicitors had been pursuing Washington
Patrick, a known forger, for several years. A letter arrived with
word from Salisbury that he was in jail there for possession of
stolen cloth, but that he was likely to be acquitted. Engraving tools
and paper like that which the Bank used had been discovered in
his lodgings in Bath. The solicitors responded that Patrick was
a 'notorious fellow', but that they did not have sufficient evidence to prosecute. They would continue to bide their time.[31]

III

The campaign mounted by the solicitors exhibited many of
those features John Fielding had sought to realize during his
tenure at Bow Street. It recognized the importance of central
direction and of the constant flow of information. Yet it would
have failed if the Bank had been unable to find allies in dozens
of different localities and, more particularly, if it had not found
a way to enlist their help and inspire their enthusiasm. The
changed character and scale of forgery that followed upon suspension presented a complex and frustrating contest. While it
was easy to catch the poor, often illiterate and frequently female,
small-time utterer, it was much more difficult to capture the
large dealers and the actual fabricators of the notes. The major

---

[29] Bank of England, Roehampton F15, F12. In a later letter, Freshfield added
the information that he had heard that two men had left Liverpool with forty-five
notes. He provided their descriptions and suggested that word be sent to the Bank's
agent in that town.
[30] Bank of England, Roehampton F29.
[31] Bank of England, Roehampton F21.

figures, the 'old hands', were extremely cagey about how they conducted their business. They worked in gangs and were careful not to touch the notes in a context that would provide witnesses to their activity. The solicitors shared the opinion of a Birmingham agent that dealers often 'played so cunning a part as to preclude every hope of detection'. The forgers worked in fortress-like security. They employed people to watch every entrance, and they would destroy evidence at the first sign of trouble. The gangs monitored police offices; in Birmingham an operative kept close watch on who entered the premises.[32] It took a good deal of patient police work to bring such offenders to justice. The schemes developed by the Bank to crack these operations required time and skill, as well as money.

When it came to the daily tasks of police work — the searching of a house, the pursuit of a suspect, the collection of evidence, or the watching of a coach office — the Bank, more often than not, relied upon parish constables or town police officers. It turned, in particular, to men who had been recommended to it as agile and co-operative. The corporation drew upon detective ability wherever it could be found, and the solicitors assembled the names of likely allies. This information rapidly became the most important part of their archive. When the Bank's investigator, Thomas Bliss, reported the detection of a parcel of forged notes in Norwich in 1807, he added that the town had a good officer named Pennyman, who could be relied upon to carry out a thorough investigation.[33] The corporation undertook its campaign at a time when the character of law enforcement was in flux. While most rural areas retained the traditional parish constable, an increasing number of towns employed a different figure, 'a man determined to make a trade' of his office. These individuals held the post for a number of years, slowly building up experience that might be useful in dealing with the challenge of crime. They were often creative in cobbling together a living out of a variety of local tasks such as serving summonses, inspecting ale houses, maintaining militia or jury lists, and a dozen other chores associated with local government. They kept their eyes open for opportunities to secure rewards. Here was the essence of 'entrepreneurial policing': they treated 'their

---

[32] Bank of England, Roehampton F16.
[33] Bank of England, Roehampton F27.

duties as a kind of small enterprise; many parish and small town authorities accepted it as such, and thought themselves lucky to have an active man, whatever his faults might be'.[34] Some of the larger towns had even created forces, under local government acts, that operated along the lines of the London police offices. Though these forces were seldom large, the men often brought a considerable level of professional skill to the task of criminal investigation. These officers received a modest salary, but it was widely recognized that they would earn a substantial portion of their income from 'other sources'. Among the most important of these were the arrangements the men made with the victims of crime. Local government was thus in no position to complain when officers spent long hours working for individuals or institutions who promised something in return.[35]

During the suspension period, the Bank became a major employer of town constables and police. Before the end of the crisis, literally hundreds of them would be involved in the corporation's struggle with forgery. Some the Bank enlisted; others were enthusiastic volunteers. The corporation soon developed a reputation among such men for the generosity of its rewards. The reward was a familiar way of securing police activity in the eighteenth century. It had legislative sanction. It was also a way of overcoming the most serious obstacle to effective law enforcement: the passivity of part-time or amateur officers. As Mainwaring explained, much of the income of even the new forces came from 'legitimate emoluments', typically 'derivable from the public or from individuals requiring assistance'.[36] Though the charge of 'blood money' continued to haunt the practice,

---

[34] Philips and Storch, *Policing Provincial England*, 12, 16–17, 27–8, 31; King, *Crime, Justice, and Discretion in England*, 70–5. As Tim Wales has demonstrated, thief-taking was a trade that arose in the first half of the seventeenth century, if not earlier. What had changed by the early nineteenth century, if Bank practice is anything to go by, was the displacement of private entrepreneurs by men with some sort of official position. Tim Wales, 'Thief-Takers and their Clients in Later Stuart London', in Paul Griffiths and Mark S. R. Jenner (eds.), *Londinopolis: Essays in the Cultural and Social History of Early Modern London* (Manchester, 2000); see also Beattie, *Policing and Punishment in London*, 226–47.

[35] John Wade, *A Treatise on the Police and Crimes of the Metropolis* (1829; repr. Montclair, 1972), 70–1. Reynolds argues that town officers had achieved a kind of professionalism by the first decade of the century: Reynolds, *Before the Bobbies*, 132. For a judicious summary of the evidence, see Emsley, *English Police*, 32–7; Emsley, *Crime and Society in England*, 216–26.

[36] Mainwaring, 'Observations on the Present State of the Police of the Metropolis', 541.

sometimes imperilling a prosecution, it remained a far from discredited means of promoting initiative in the pursuit of criminals. Colquhoun, in his influential book on London policing, called for more regular rewards as a way of securing more energetic co-operation at all levels of law enforcement. 'In suppressing great evils', he explained, 'strong and adequate powers must be applied, and nothing can give force and activity to those powers but the ability to reward liberally all persons engaged in the public service, either as police officers or as temporary agents for the purpose of detecting atrocious offenders'. Colquhoun believed that one of the great impediments to better policing was the failure to apply the principle of reward with enough consistency. It was, he concluded, 'vain to expect either vigour or energy can enter into that part of the system, where a great deal of both is necessary, without funds'. Since public money was not always forthcoming, private funds would have to do.[37]

The Bank never departed from its conviction that rewards were pivotal to securing a maximum of effort against forgery. It used its vast resources in order to gain the attention and support of a wide range of individuals. While the size of its awards was not out of line with those offered by the state or the private prosecution societies, the corporation simply had more funds to devote to the endeavour. It made widely known, from the very start, that it would cover the expenses of anyone involved in aiding its efforts. The Bank also advertised that it would reward generously all successful prosecutions of the crime. The solicitors hastened to repeat the offer in any correspondence linked to the report of an outbreak in a particular locality. When several Halifax bankers wrote of the appearance of a few forged notes, Kaye responded with instructions about how to proceed. He added that 'you may assure the officers that they will be liberally rewarded'. In 1819, the mayor of King's Lynn sent a letter to the Bank with information on a major dealer, and asking for the corporation's help. The solicitors responded by sending Foy, a Marlborough Street police officer, to organize an effort to take the man. The mayor was grateful for the

---

[37] Colquhoun, *Treatise on the Police of the Metropolis*, 120–1, 212, 337. On the role of rewards in eighteenth-century justice, see Beattie, *Crime and the Courts in England*, 51–5; Leon Radzinowicz, *A History of Criminal Law*, 5 vols. (London, 1956), ii, chs. 3–5.

assistance, reporting that Foy had inspired the town's constables with his talk of the 'Bank's liberal remuneration'.[38]

The Bank showed a preference for using the existing forces of order in its campaign against forgery. To this end, it employed rewards in a calculated and self-conscious fashion in order to secure an energetic response from local officers. In 1807, Joseph Pym, a constable for Derby, wrote describing a gang active in passing near-perfect notes. He had apprehended a woman and searched her house, but found no notes hidden there. He asked the solicitors what to do and whom to contact. They replied immediately, saying that he should consult the town clerk. Pym sent in a bill for £1. 18s. The solicitors wrote to their agent that in addition to his costs, Pym should be given £2. 2s. for his troubles. The reward, they noted, would keep the constable's attention.[39] With the prospect of a reward before them, the Bank found many capable officers ready to do its bidding. Though it advertised its rewards generally, it targeted more particularly men involved in law enforcement, in the hope of inspiring a maximum of effort from them. Perhaps not surprisingly, one of the earliest claimants upon the Bank's bounty was Colquhoun. He wrote in 1797, in his capacity as a stipendiary magistrate, pressing the merits of his constables. He stressed how much care he had taken in expending funds, and pointed out that he was close to making a major purchase of forged notes.[40] The knowledge of the Bank's generosity earned the attention of constables all over England. Caleb Atkins was tried at the Worcester spring assizes in 1816. The solicitors recommended that John Haddock, the constable for Bewdley, receive £15 because he not only seized the prisoner, after hearing a report that he had been passing notes, but then went from house to house collecting the evidence required to prosecute him. Similarly rewarded was Thomas Evans, the chief constable for Bristol. He gathered information from a mother and son who

[38] Bank of England, Roehampton F5, F59. Foy was a favourite with the Bank. He was employed so often that the magistrates at Marlborough Street finally, in 1817, expressed their unhappiness at his frequent absences. The Bank agreed to take over responsibility for his pay. Committee on Law Suits, B577–13(N), 4 Dec. 1817.

[39] Bank of England, Roehampton F27. See Philips and Storch, *Policing Provincial England*, 27, for their estimate of a constable's income. Radzinowicz reports that Metropolitan police officers were paid £31 in 1800 and £52 in 1811: Radzinowicz, *History of Criminal Law*, ii, 162; and see pp. 238–9 for his estimate of their 'real earnings'.

[40] Bank of England, Roehampton F5.

had come to him after they had been approached by Jeremiah and Elizabeth Dunn with an offer to help pass forged notes. Evans laid a plan to take the Dunns that included employing six constables in a co-ordinated assault on the suspects' well-defended house.[41] Officers frequently devoted long hours to the Bank's service. One Birmingham constable sent in an account to the solicitors totalling £87. 11s. 6d. for work he had done at Spurrier's direction. He reported that he had attended to Bank business almost every day between 16 July and 20 October.[42] Bank accounts recorded hundreds of cases of constables and officers operating at a considerable distance from their parishes or towns. They undertook their trips either on their own initiative or at the direction of the Bank solicitors. There is little mention of their needing to secure the approval of local authorities before they set off, and no evidence of discontent with these men for devoting so much of their attention to Bank concerns. What these operations suggest is that even as the officers remained charged with public responsibilities, much of their activity was regulated by private deals which they arranged with interested parties, and that they possessed considerable freedom to apply themselves to such tasks as promised a financial return on their efforts.

The anticipation of a reward led to a steady stream of information to the Bank, along with numerous proposals for how to capture the chief perpetrators. In 1817, James Smith, a constable for Clatter, wrote to say that he had intelligence on persons concerned in vending notes. He asked what remuneration 'he should receive on apprehending them, or if his expenses would be paid in attempting to do so'.[43] In 1818, the solicitors received a letter from J. Johnston of the Stamp Office, saying that he was willing to go to Birmingham with two other persons in order to detect forgers. He thought his expenses would be between £50 and £60, and that, if he succeeded, he was willing to leave the amount of the reward to the corporation. The Committee on Law Suits voted that his plan was worth supporting.[44] In 1819, James Wood, a constable for Chatham,

---

[41] Bank of England, Roehampton F1.
[42] Bank of England, Roehampton F23.
[43] Committee on Law Suits, B577–12(M), 23 Jan. 1817.
[44] Committee on Law Suits, B577–15(P), 22 Dec. 1818.

offered his services in return for the Bank paying his expenses. The directors instructed Kaye to interview him in order to assess the value of his offer.[45] The Bank never wanted for assistance; rather the major challenge it faced was deciding among the hundreds of proposals it received which were likely to bring success for the considerable outlay they involved.

Although the Bank spread its rewards widely among constables across the country, a few men in the main towns provided the most sustained support and derived the greatest benefit from the connection. The solicitors turned to these men when they were called upon to send knowledgeable people to deal with a report of a forgery. Payne, the chief constable for Birmingham, Nadin, the deputy constable for Manchester, or John Miller, the chief constable for Liverpool, joined a select group of London officers whose names appeared on almost every list of rewards distributed by the Bank. These men stumbled over each other in their rush to secure favour. What they offered was a level of sophistication in detecting and capturing the most elusive offenders. Payne was a regular recipient of Bank money. In 1813, he and the constable of Birmingham received £50 for pursuing an offender to Oxford and seizing him. In 1817, he, along with his assistant George Redfern, received £100 as a reward for employing two men (each of whom was given a separate gift) to convict four known dealers. The operation, the solicitors noted, took three weeks and intense application to develop.[46]

By the second decade of the century, rewards had become a major expense for the Bank. The Committee on Law Suits approved a grant of £2,615 following the spring assizes in 1820. As was often the case, £2,070 went to law-enforcement personnel, while £545 was distributed among co-operative citizens. Although many different names appeared on the list, a few turned up repeatedly. Redfern received £10 for his assistance in a Staffordshire case. In addition, he was given £10 each for two other Warwickshire prosecutions, and he participated in dividing £450 with several other constables who helped with three other cases. For his part in six trials, Miller shared in rewards totalling £430. One of these cases involved seven suspects and resulted in four capital convictions. No doubt these

[45] Committee on Law Suits, B577–15(P), 25 Feb. 1819.
[46] Bank of England, Roehampton F2.

sums conceal money the officers spent to gather evidence and employ subordinates to assist their investigations. Some letters to the solicitors told pitiful tales of debts incurred by policemen in elaborate schemes to capture dealers. Still, such rewards must have represented a considerable profit, as the Bank usually covered the bills submitted by officers for such things as meals, travel and the expenses associated with attending the assizes.[47]

A closer examination of a reward list from the summer assizes in 1817 illustrates the scope and character of the Bank's policing operations. Forty-eight individuals were tried, sixteen of them on the capital charge. The corporation was, as usual, a remarkably successful prosecutor. Five of those charged were acquitted, one escaped from prison, while forty-two were convicted. This achievement reflects the care the Bank used in deciding which cases to prosecute, but it also suggests the thoroughness of the police work in each instance. The Bank distributed a total of £1,150 in rewards. At least forty-seven different policemen earned some share of this bounty. Three constables in Cumberland detected and apprehended Mary Young, a task that involved considerable trouble. Each was given £10. John Cattell, a constable for Brainston, earned £10 for his hard work in one case. John Carter, a constable for Middleton in Northamptonshire, was awarded £10 for the determination he displayed in tracing different notes and apprehending several offenders. William Ashton, a constable for Boston, received £15 because he was the sole means of detecting and securing Richard Clarke in Lincolnshire. Officers were rewarded for many different activities. In Lichfield, the constable, John Cornfield, took a forger into custody, while John Preckett, the jailer, was active in collecting evidence. The solicitors often received long accounts of the hours spent watching a house, travelling to a fair or tracking a suspect to a distant town. Officers would tell of interviewing other shopkeepers in a neighbourhood in an effort to uncover previous attempts to

---

[47] Committee on Law Suits, B577–18(S), 19 Apr. 1820. Entrepreneurial policing could represent a considerable gamble for officers. John Cam, confined for debt in York, wrote to remind the Bank that he had done the corporation great service in securing four offenders. He had received £20 for each conviction, but he claimed that his expenses came to £104. The Committee voted him an additional £20. Committee on Law Suits, B577–7(G), 21 July 1813.

pass bad notes. In their letters constables advertised their skills in the hope of securing further employment or increasing the size of the rewards. They emphasized the inconvenience they endured in acting far away from home. John Cousins, a constable in Cheltenham, earned his reward for pursuing a suspect to Birmingham where the dealer was captured. Two constables from Blackburn 'displayed great energy in tracing the routes of notes' in Yorkshire. Two constables in Leicester watched Thomas Walker for a considerable time before they were able to take him and to discover his stock of forged notes concealed in a dwelling house. At Chester, Betty Wild was convicted of possession of forged notes. John Barratt, a constable, employed Thomas Dunlap to buy notes from her, and he also attended the assizes for several days. He had previously detected two men in Lancashire dealing notes, but in that instance the Bank decided not to prosecute. Perhaps in recognition of his earlier exertions, the directors voted each man £25. James Broadbent was acquitted at the Lancaster assizes, but the solicitors felt that the conduct of Samuel Newton, a police officer at Ashton-under-Lyne, deserved acknowledgement, so he was given £10. This list demonstrates that the rumour of the Bank's bounty reached well beyond the principal towns and travelled deep into provincial England. Wherever it arrived, it produced a frenzy of activity. The results could be impressive.[48]

Rewards not only attracted the attention of local law enforcement; they also gave the Bank a powerful instrument for controlling the actions of those who chose to work on its behalf. Even as the solicitors doled out rewards in excess of £300 to Birmingham police officers, it delivered a sharp rebuke as well. The directors expected 'that their liberality upon this occasion will stimulate them to further exertion'. They suspected that the offenders could have been 'got at sooner' if proper measures had been taken more promptly. If the officers did not put forth greater effort in the future, the solicitors warned, 'the liberality now experienced cannot be expected upon any future occasion'.[49] Generous as it could be, the corporation did not throw its money around haphazardly. Usually the Bank reimbursed

---

[48] Bank of England, Roehampton F2; Committee on Law Suits, B577–13(N), 11 Sept. 1817.
[49] Bank of England, Roehampton F2.

only successful prosecutions, unless the scheme had been well conducted and, especially, if it had the sanction of the directors. Henry Newton, a constable for Derby, complained to the solicitors that he had gone to Birmingham with a bank agent in an effort to take a known forger. The plan did not succeed. In rejecting his claim, Kaye added 'that the act was entirely at his own discretion, to get the reward offered for the apprehension and not by any direction from the Bank'.[50] Such firmness was all the more necessary because the scale of Bank rewards sometimes set off an unseemly or even treacherous scramble for favour. Richard Fletcher, a Bow Street officer who had been stationed in Lancashire for two years, was bitter that while he had played a large role in several cases, he had been given no reward. The Lancashire officers had pocketed it all. 'This is just a specimen', he wrote, 'how the Lancashire constables manage their Bank prosecutions if they can get a Bank case for the assizes it is all they wish for'.[51] Such conduct could imperil even carefully concerted plans. Independent or precipitate action promised to be expensive as well as counterproductive. The Bank had a long relationship with John Miller of Liverpool. Still, the relationship was far from untroubled. He wrote to the solicitors in 1811 to say that he was busy with a proposal to detect a ring of forgers. He was working with a woman who said she was familiar with several of their number. He expected to go to Birmingham himself to direct the transaction. This plan earned Miller a stern rebuke when the solicitors responded two days later. As he had taken the initiative without first consulting them, they warned, he could expect to get nothing unless he produced results. They wished he had contacted Spurrier first, since he was a stranger to the town. He should proceed with care, lest his independent action interfere with the plans of others. 'We should', Kaye concluded, 'have been better pleased if you had consulted us before you determined upon the measure, and even could then have given you such instructions as we thought it advisable, but as you have acted otherwise, we can give you no instructions upon the subject but leave you to your own discretion'. The same day Kaye wrote to Spurrier to inform him that he could offer Miller

---

[50] Committee on Law Suits, B577–14(O), 21 May 1818.
[51] Bank of England, Roehampton F70.

advice, but that under no circumstances was he to advance him any money.[52]

By the 1810s the steady increase in the number of low-denomination notes in circulation produced an even more dramatic rise in the number of forged notes turned in to the Bank. The solicitors found themselves investigating many more cases with each passing year. The situation seemed in danger of spiralling out of control. Yet no expression of alarm emerged from the corporation. Rather the solicitors and the directors doggedly pursued the policies they had employed since 1797. They sought to project an image of calm resolve in the face of commercial disquiet and growing public criticism. Perhaps what sustained them was the knowledge that the circumstance that made possible the epidemic, the issue of £1 and £2 notes, would not continue for much longer. For reasons that had little to do with forgery, the political community, supported by the authority of a majority of economic writers and even the Bank itself, strongly desired the return to cash payments.[53] Once the appropriate legislation was in place, the corporation moved quickly to diminish its issue of small notes. The solicitors could scarcely contain their sense of relief. By 1821 the police campaign was winding down as well. In November, the Committee on Law Suits voted to discontinue the special pay arrangements with Marlborough Street. Once resumption began, and even though its small-denomination notes continued to circulate, the corporation declined to prosecute for forgery of these notes. The solicitors responded to a request from a Welsh magistrate in December by informing him that 'the Bank having so long ago as the beginning of May last ceased to issue one pound notes and done all in their power to call them in and supply their place with gold and silver coin, they have for some time declined prosecuting the utterance of forged one pound

---

[52] Bank of England, Roehampton F2, F5. The correct conduct was displayed by a magistrate from Bolton in 1818. He wrote to warn the Bank that many forged notes circulated in his area. He added that a deputy constable knew someone who had wormed his way into the confidence of the utterers and had actually purchased notes. He asked if the Bank wanted him to proceed with the scheme. The solicitors urged him to make the attempt. Committee on Law Suits, B577–14(O), 2 July 1818.

[53] Boyd Hilton, *Corn, Cash, Commerce: The Economic Policies of the Tory Governments, 1815–1830* (Oxford, 1977), ch. 2.

notes'.[54] The extensive police operation the Bank had set in motion vanished almost as quickly as it had been assembled. Little was left behind but the dismay of police officers who had grown accustomed to pursuing the corporation's bounty.

IV

At first glance, the Bank strategy for coping with forgery may look ad hoc and haphazard. The corporation introduced no significant innovation in the techniques it employed to fight the mounting problem. It relied almost entirely upon existing police arrangements; it made use of such law-enforcement personnel as it could find. These local agents varied widely in their ability and enthusiasm for police work. The success of a given effort to capture an offender depended on the quality of an individual officer, the skill or knowledge he possessed. Nonetheless, the important point is that the Bank found able people in many localities ready to devote themselves wholeheartedly to its cause. Its widespread employment of capable officers outside their normal jurisdictions helped to compensate for incompetent or lazy constables. A jailer or town clerk might prove an antidote to inertia. The solicitors proved adept at making use of such expedients as were available. The challenge lay in determining who was most suited to the task in any given locality. What was missing, in the early decades of the nineteenth century, was an institution with a monopoly on policing. There was no shortage of options and agents for taking on crime; indeed, it was the variety of both that marked the period. As the solicitors scrambled to discover local allies, they turned, not to an office, but to individuals. They sought out those men who had made law enforcement a means of securing a livelihood and who had demonstrated an ability to achieve results.

The essence of the entrepreneurial system of policing, especially as it had developed by 1800, lay in the use of monetary incentives to secure active engagement, rather than merely passive acquiescence, in the pursuit of criminals. As we now know, prosecution in eighteenth-century England depended upon the

---

[54] Bank of England, Roehampton F68. The Bank continued to prosecute for the forgery of notes of £5 and over. The brief return of £1 notes in 1825 produced a temporary rise in prosecutions. The number declined as soon as the notes were withdrawn again.

decisions of the victim of crime. Individuals were responsible
not only for the detection of offenders, but for their prosecution
as well. At least some of the time they would need help with the
task. This assistance often required the commitment of funds —
either the offer to cover expenses or the promise of a reward.
The more energetic the policing that one desired, the greater
assurance of both one had to supply. The agents of law
enforcement had a wide measure of control over their own
activity; they were free to pursue their own profit, and, indeed,
they had to do so in order to supplement their meagre incomes.
Though they were public officers, vested with significant legal
powers, nonetheless, they also acted as private contractors,
always on the lookout for their own advantage. They regarded
the victim of a crime as a potential employer of their talents,
and their conception of their responsibility was shaped by this
expectation. The arrangement seldom excited negative comment.
It was accepted as inevitable, as part of the nature of things.
Private individuals offered rewards in response to crime. Here
was the means to gain information about offenders, and to enlist
the co-operation of the public and the police. These practices
produced a number of scandals, accompanied by demands to
purify the operation of justice. But such episodes rarely led people
to question the nature of the system as a whole.[55]

The conduct of the Bank between 1797 and 1821 demonstrates how much could be achieved by existing police arrangements. Although it brought these measures to a pitch of efficiency
that no other institution could hope to imitate, the corporation
was still entirely conventional in the means it employed. There
were several keys to the Bank's success. Its solicitors, however
new to the task of fighting crime, proved adept at organizing
the effort, in part because they were able to call upon a reservoir of knowledge and experience about what measures to take.
And, of course, the corporation had access to the commodity
that inspired the best policing in the period — money. It was
able to provide ample reimbursement for costs, and hold out
the promise of substantial rewards for success. The Bank never
had reason to complain about a lack of enthusiasm on the part of
the many different agents who joined its campaign. The problem
was more often the reverse: how to moderate the exuberance of

[55] Reynolds, *Before the Bobbies*, 65–8, 75, 82, 106–7.

officers in pursuit of rewards. Thanks to the discipline it was able to enforce through its bounty, and to the central control the solicitors exercised through their office, the Bank welded a rich variety of police expedients into a sustained national effort against a formidable criminal challenge. In so doing, the Bank came close to realizing the ambitions of Henry and John Fielding to create a more efficient police. Its effort conformed closely to the proposals made by Colquhoun for the creation of 'a well-regulated and energetic Police'. Colquhoun emphasized the need for co-ordination and subordination, 'to reduce the general management to system and method, by the imposition of a superintending agency'. He thought it would be useful to collect 'a complete History of the connections, and pursuits of all or most of the criminal and fraudulent persons who resort to the Metropolis'. He wanted this agency 'to establish a Correspondence with the Magistrates in Town and Country, so as to be able more effectually to watch the motions of all suspected persons; with a view to quick and immediate detection; and to interpose those embarrassments which a vigilant and active Police may place in the way of every class of offenders'.[56] These goals were precisely those articulated by the Bank solicitors in their correspondence with their agents throughout the country. The Bank, however, did not need Colquhoun to tell it how to proceed. Its ability to mount this kind of operation against forgery lay well within the capacity of the entrepreneurial system, at least for an institution with the resources it possessed, by the early nineteenth century.

Given how much it accomplished, it is somewhat surprising that the Bank police effort did not attract more favourable comment as the public devoted greater attention to the question of law enforcement by the 1820s. Its achievements — a centralized police operation, considerable success in breaking up forgery networks, and a high conviction rate — all went unrecognized. There were parliamentary investigations of policing on four occasions during the years of the forgery threat, in 1816, 1817, 1818 and 1822, yet its campaign earned little mention. The inattention was scarcely the product of ignorance about what

---

[56] Colquhoun, *Treatise on the Police of the Metropolis*, 1, 27–8, 71, 74. See Paley, '"An Imperfect, Inadequate and Wretched System"?', 98, for a caution about exaggerating Colquhoun's influence.

the Bank was doing. On the contrary, the corporation's activities were remarkably visible, because of the controversy surrounding its frequent recourse to the gallows. In part the explanation for this silence is that commentators were not surprised by any of the measures the Bank employed. The corporation simply did on a wider scale what victims of crime were expected to do: initiate a police investigation by offering a financial inducement to a local officer.

What was more novel about this period, and better helps to explain the peculiar attitude taken towards the Bank's activities, was the slowly developing discontent with the principle at the heart of the entrepreneurial system, the role of reward as a condition for action. For several decades, the conviction had been gaining ground that profit had no place in the operation of justice. It inevitably led, critics claimed, to partiality in the application of the law, and sometimes to outright corruption.[57] The present system, Mainwaring observed, drew to it men who made it 'a business and profitable pursuit'. This situation did not necessarily produce poor law enforcement, but it had a decisive influence on how policing was performed. For instance, he argued, those responsible for detection had little interest in securing the actual manufacturers of forged notes, since they supplied the steady stream of utterers who were 'the sources of their own profit'.[58] Advocates of police reform never tired of pointing out that the reward system operated only after a crime was committed. It did little to prevent offences, to attack the roots of crime or to monitor the population likely to break the law. Indeed, it was fatally at odds with the idea that the real goal of a system of police was the prevention of crime. As this principle captured the public imagination, the older policy came to appear flawed in all its fundamentals.[59]

Among the variety of charges levelled against the entrepreneurial system of policing, one took on special prominence in the light of the publicity surrounding the Bank's activities. Critics

[57] Norma Landau, 'The Trading Justice's Trade', in Norma Landau (ed.), *Law, Crime and English Society, 1660–1830* (Cambridge, 2002).

[58] Mainwaring, 'Observations on the Present State of the Police of the Metropolis', 548, 544.

[59] Wade, *Treatise on the Police and Crimes of the Metropolis*, 70–1; Mainwaring, 'Observations on the Present State of the Police of the Metropolis', 555; Emsley, *Crime and Society in England*, ch. 9.

asserted that it provided assistance inequitably. A reward, Mainwaring complained, even if 'it were an adequate inducement, is in its consequences highly exceptionable'. The police, he wrote, are 'for the protection of the whole public, for the poor as well as for the rich; but has not the present system of reward an inevitable tendency to make the rich rather than the poor, the objects of an officer's attention?' The same point was made to the parliamentary committee investigating the police in 1822. R. Rainsford, a magistrate at Queen Square, was asked pointedly, during a discussion of whether officers should subsist on their pay, whether he thought that 'if they are to receive money from private persons, the rich man would get justice, and the poor man not?' 'I think', he responded, 'if they had such an allowance as enabled them to live without it, so as to have no temptation, it would be desirable. If it was put a stop to, it would be better'.[60] By the early nineteenth century, the liabilities of the reward system appeared more glaring and threatening. The problem was no longer the occasional instance of corruption; the error was systemic. The pursuit of profit came to seem in contradiction to the development of equitable and effective law enforcement. At least in some circles the belief was gaining ground that a police tied more closely to the state would be a guarantee of neutrality and fairness in the distribution of the law-enforcement effort, in contrast to the bias in favour of the wealthy that was inherent in the loose arrangements of the eighteenth century.

Ironically, it seems that the Bank, through its policy of relying so heavily upon rewards, and spreading word of them so widely, contributed to the increasing doubts about a system of policing that depended so much upon them. The Bank was a deeply unpopular institution during the early decades of the century, as its profits inspired envy and its monopolistic position resentment. These attitudes spilled over into reaction to the corporation's campaign against forgery. Few commentators defended

---

[60] Mainwaring, 'Observations on the Present State of the Police of the Metropolis', 543; *Report from the Select Committee on the Police of the Metropolis*, Parliamentary Papers, 1822 (440), iv, 48. King notes that only the well-off could afford the assistance of Bow Street officers: King, *Crime, Justice, and Discretion in England*, 79. *The Black Book: or, Corruption Unmasked! Being an Account of Places, Pensions, and Sinecures . . .*, ed. John Wade, 2 vols. (London, 1820), i, 95–108, offered an extensive indictment of a police geared entirely to 'emoluments' beyond their low weekly pay.

its conduct. Rather, the Bank's mobilization of the tried and true methods of eighteenth-century law enforcement served to highlight what reformers felt was wrong with existing police arrangements. Its very success in using rewards to motivate officers and to command their attention provoked a popular outcry against the operation of entrepreneurial principles. The Bank, a powerful and privileged institution, seemed to employ its wealth with an arrogance and freedom of expenditure that may have earned the enthusiastic co-operation of many police officers, but aroused the mistrust and dislike of a wider public. Its awards distorted the priorities of what were supposed to be public agents. Francis Hobler, principal clerk to the Lord Mayor of London, testified in 1817 to the general belief that officers were unduly influenced by the Bank's reputation for generosity. 'From their readiness and eagerness to do the bank business', he reported, 'I should think they were very well paid'. He denied the charge that this money tempted the police to entrap innocent men, but he conceded that even the best officers were swayed by it. 'An officer who has any spirit, always will wish to appear to do his duty with courage . . .', he concluded, 'but many no doubt always look to the reward as the great incentive'.[61] Here was the reason the Bank's successes earned so little credit; the achievement seemed bought at too high a price.

It is tempting to read the debates over reform of the police as a symptom of the inadequacy of existing arrangements and as propelled by some clearly formulated alternative. A close examination of the forgery crisis that overlapped these debates warns that caution about both conclusions is necessary. This episode reminds us that we should not confuse the institution of the police with the policing function more broadly conceived. That function was distributed differently and diffused more widely in eighteenth-century England. What is striking is the vast range of different kinds of policing that went on, and the variety of people who engaged in it. The fact that so much of law enforcement was carried on by private initiative meant that knowledge of what to do, as well as the willingness to undertake it, were shared by many more people than would be true after the

---

[61] *Second Report from the Committee on the State of the Police of the Metropolis*, Parliamentary Papers, 1817 (484), vii, 323, 497. See Eastwood, *Governing Rural England*, 217, for an instance of complaint about rewards.

introduction of a 'reformed' police.[62] It was a decentralized system, dependent to a considerable degree upon the entrepreneurial spirit. It was, however, far from being as ineffective as many critics complained. On the contrary, at least by the early nineteenth century, England possessed a number of police capable of the energetic and professional pursuit of crime. The experience of the Bank of England offers valuable support for this conclusion. The corporation faced a daunting task during the period of suspension. The mounting costs, the steadily rising number of offenders, the widespread criticism of its actions, and, above all, the sense that the nation's financial system was at risk, all might have led to a sense of desperation in the face of an epidemic of forgery. Yet neither the solicitors nor the directors ever expressed panic or issued a cry for help. They never resorted to the hyperbole employed by Colquhoun in his descriptions of a threatening criminal class who preyed upon the wealth of the nation. The directors occasionally voiced frustration at the seemingly unending nature of the challenge, but they responded with renewed determination. They also defended tenaciously the privileges and independence of the Bank to shape its own policies for handling the problem.

Entrepreneurial policing, then, secured a considerable measure of success, at least for those wealthy enough to benefit from it. The police relationship, by the late eighteenth century, consisted of that between a police entrepreneur and his customer, rather than that between an agent of the state and the private victim of crime. Law-enforcement initiative, to a considerable degree, rested in private hands; it did not depend on a government authority to spark action. The Bank not only accepted the necessity of this arrangement, it embraced the institution for the advantages it offered. The corporation could purchase law-enforcement talent when it suited its purpose. It gained the undivided attention of the police and secured a maximum of effort. There seems little doubt that a powerful institution like the Bank valued its ability to regulate its own police effort, gear it tightly to its perception of its needs, and oversee what it got for its money.[63]

---

[62] Some of these points have been made by Hay and Snyder, 'Using the Criminal Law'.

[63] Norma Landau, 'Indictment for Fun and Profit: A Prosecutor's Reward at Eighteenth-Century Quarter Sessions', *Law and History Rev.*, xvii (1999). In this sense, entrepreneurial policing offered some of the same benefits as prosecution associations — the preservation of control: see Eastwood, *Governing Rural England*, 233.

The Bank was largely content with the character of existing arrangements. It never lent its prestige to a call for reform. The arguments of the reformers had little to offer the corporation. Their critique of existing policing failed to address the kind of criminal challenge presented by forgers and the more skilled dealers in false notes. There seemed little reason to seek more radical and unproved solutions when existing forces produced results. Even John Wade, himself an advocate for further reform of law enforcement, conceded that the unwillingness to experiment arose from a 'reluctance to risk the uncertain results of new establishments, or excite alarm respecting them, so long as the present were tolerably adequate to their purposes, and public opinion had not been very generally expressed against them'.[64] In the Bank's quarter-century struggle with forgery, we can see hints of future developments, but far more significant were the continuities with past practices. Yet this study of the Bank's conduct casts fresh light on the rise of the 'new' police. The decisive break, when it came in 1829, concerned at least as much a notion of what was an appropriate motive for police activity as it did a question of the effectiveness of the institution. Policing, reformers argued, should not be a trade; it should be a service provided to the entire public. The state asserted for itself a more active role in the struggle with crime, one justified by its claim to an indispensable role in that conflict. In separating the 'private' pursuit of profit from the 'public' provision of law enforcement, the goal was to present a new image of the police — one at least as significant as their new uniforms, as well as more suited to their expanded sphere of activity.

University of Oregon   *Randall McGowen*

---

[64] Wade, *Treatise on the Police and Crimes of the Metropolis*, 66–7.

Name Index